"Fascinating, compelling . . . and altogether necessary to read. It is about mind and body; the inner and the outer . . . Read it!"
—*Chicago Daily News*

THE CENTURY'S MOST ACCLAIMED VOYAGE TO INNER SPACE

"Adam Smith is the perfect Virgil—witty, pragmatic, learned—to lead the doubting reader into the shady realms of consciousness expanding. He has tried it all himself, with a tough skepticism and an intelligent, open mind."
—*Washington Post Book World*

"A bestseller with a considerable educational function as well as high entertainment."
—*Time*

"Adam Smith is both an enterprising reporter and an entertaining one."
—*The New York Times*

OTHER BOOKS BY ADAM SMITH

The Money Game

Supermoney

Powers of Mind

Adam Smith

BALLANTINE BOOKS • NEW YORK

Grateful acknowledgment is made to the following for permission to reprint previously published song lyrics:
C'Est Music/Quakenbush Music Ltd.: For the lyrics from the second verse of "Haven't Got Time for the Pain" by Carly Simon and Jacob Brackman (pages 46–47). Copyright © 1974 by C'Est Music and Maya Productions Ltd. All Rights Reserved. Used by permission.

Bob Dylan and Warner Bros. Music: For the selected lyrics from "Mr. Tambourine Man," music and words by Bob Dylan (page 46). Copyright © 1964 M. Wittmark & Sons. All Rights Reserved. Used by permission.

Library of Congress Catalog Card Number: 75-10310

ISBN 0-345-25426-0-195

This edition published by arrangement with
Random House, Inc.

Manufactured in the United States of America

First Ballantine Books Edition: November 1976

Contents

III. MEDITATIONS

IV. "SPORT IS A WESTERN YOGA"

V. VIBES

VI. PACKAGERS

VII. THE FAR SIDE OF PARADIGM

I. This Side of Paradigm

Mystery: Time, Space, Infinity, Statistical Aberration

Three Stories in Which Something Is Going On Which Is Very Hard to Photograph

Stewart Alsop Doesn't Get Off the Train in Baltimore

Norman Cousins Laughs Himself Back

A Case of Stigmata

Placebos and Rumpelstiltskin

Paradigms

The Astronauts of Inner Space

A Very Short History of Some American Drugs Familiar to Everybody

The World's First Acid Trip, and Subsequent Happenings

And a Short Chronicle of the Madness

What Did We Learn?

Mystery: Time, Space, Infinity, Statistical Aberration

Nel mezzo del cammin di nostra vita
Mi ritrovai per una selva oscura . . .

On the first day of Christmas, my alleged true love gave to me a silver pillbox. Infuriating. It was true, of course, that gentlemen of finance consumed pain-easing pills, traveled with them, and even offered them to each other, but then, there was a lot of pain around. Fund managers chewed absently on antacids, wondering where the last hundred million went to so quickly. When you met them, they might offer you one, as if proffering a cigarette or a Life Saver. A high-risk, high-stress profession, wrote one psychologist in a paper. The University of San Francisco offered a course for clergymen, a Laboratory in Pastoral Ministries, Course #261, to "communicate with persons with unusual needs . . . such as the sick, the aging, broken families, alcoholics, ethnic minorities, homosexuals, stockbrokers." No wonder drug companies had such nice profit margins, and sold at such high premiums.

Two gallants of my acquaintance wrote one of the best short reports I have ever read. The university portfolio they managed was down by a little over two hundred million dollars. (Do you know how long it takes to *raise* two hundred million dollars?) They remained fully invested, they said, because things were so bad they thought they could get no worse. "The light we saw at the end of the tunnel," they said, "was a freight train coming the other way."

Some people disappeared from the money business, and some disappeared right off the planet, ahead of schedule. If somebody had a heart attack,

3

we said, oh, sorry, when will he be back in the office? It was certainly a statistical aberration when I lost my panel, the investment strategy panel I moderated at the annual convention. My panelists were in their thirties and forties and not fat and they liked their work, so statistically they should not have exited with one heart attack, one ulcer attack, and one something I forget. We recruited another panel without even a moment of silence for our fallen comrades. Very cool, very macho, the show must go on.

I think what I had in mind when I began my research was that I would do some research on health. I would leave my nine-foot teak desk, my phone with all its buttons lit up, and my totally filled in Month at a Glance calendar, go find some answers, and be welcomed back to the business community, like the first Arapaho that came back to his horseless tribe with a Pawnee pinto. Look, fellas, now we can go twice as fast. I thought this might take a couple of months but well worth it, very important. (I could return the silver pillbox with the appropriate insult.) There was something else, misty, unarticulated, in this program. One of my convention panelists had told me what his plans were, just as soon as he had enough time and enough money. He certainly had enough money, but he had had time back when he thought he didn't, and then he didn't.

The first physicians I consulted in this venture had all the same symptoms as my compatriots. We have to take it easier, they said wisely. Then they would answer the phone, rub their eyes, and say, yes, they would cover for their buddy till midnight. And then they would say, what's happening, my Gawd, my stocks are down 40 percent, we may have to sell our ski condominium unless we raise our fees.

I would not have believed, at the outset, that I would be spending any time with exotics like Tibetan lamas and witch doctors and gentlemen who had beards and wore funny clothes. I did not have a beard and I did not own any funny clothes. I would not have believed that I would ever sit in a room chanting a Sanskrit syllable, or drawing a lotus in the air with a $1.98 G. Schirmer recorder.

Minds. The trouble is minds, not organic medicine, not some germ that comes flying through the air looking for a home. This is Dr. Hans Selye, sixty-eight years old, the distinguished dean of stress medicine. Stress is "a physiologic response inappropriate to the situation." Misfired signals between mind and body. The physiologic response is the caveman's response when the shadow of a pterodactyl falls over him. Adrenal secretions increase and muscles tense and the coagulation chemistry gets ready to resist wounds. Fight or flight. But what pterodactyl is this? They tell you: the market is down twenty points, or, the vice-president wants to see you, or, this whole operation is going to be shut down and moved to Chicago. Blam, pterodactyl time. Gives you, says Dr. Selye, headaches, insomnia, high blood pressure, sinus, ulcers, rheumatism, cardiovascular and kidney disease. And more. One from Column A, one from Column B. Some people have a pterodactyl every day. Why? An imbalance, says Dr. Selye, an imbalance. In what? In living. Western medicine doesn't extend its authority there, except to say take it easy, take off some weight, watch your diet.

So: lots of explorers have headed west by going east, saying, there must be a better way, and that was how this venture in—what? It's hard to define, some sort of psychology or awareness, maybe. That was how it began. Nonexistent pterodactyls flapping their great wings over fallen security analysts.

Some of my opening questions were:

Could we really learn to control our internal processes with our heads instead of with pills? (If true, I made a note, sell drug companies.)

Could we learn to pop ourself into an alpha state? What is an alpha state? What happens if we succeed?

If someone can't hear and they have one session with a psychologist and fifteen minutes' worth of hyp-

notic induction, and suddenly they say, "I can hear!"
what just happened in their brains?

What about all these claims for meditation? What
do they mean by meditation? (I had just read an
article in a technical journal.)

Is it true that a Sanskrit sound has a different effect on your head than one in English? (I don't
know where I got that one.)

The field was not well marked. For example, in
the great pharmacology textbook *The Pharmacological Basis of Therapeutics,* Goodman and Gilman
—it has the same lock on its field that Samuelson
does in economics—three phrases begin to recur
when you get to the effects of mind, or the interaction of some substance and the mind. *The etiology
is unknown.* We don't know the cause. *The site is
unknown.* We don't know exactly where it happens.
The mechanism is unknown. We're not exactly sure
how it happens.

Unknown, unknown, pictures of elephants and
white space in the middle of the old maps of Africa.

At one juncture I sent a careful letter to an official in the National Institute of Mental Health in
suburban Washington. I wanted to know, in this instance, about placebos—sugar pills—and I detailed
all my references and the work done so far, and
asked: where can I go to find more? Who is doing
the work in this field?

"You are," the answer came. "The field is open.
Please let us hear from you when you finish."

In an unmarked field, it is easy to wander. Why
on earth would I ever have read six years' worth of
a British medical journal called *Brain?* Sheer inertia. I looked up one article on consciousness and
then—look, the editor of *Brain* is Lord Brain. If
you sent him a post card, addressed only "Brain,
Brain, London," would it get there? Was his name
Brain already, or did he take "Lord Brain" as a title
because he was the editor of *Brain?* Let's see what

goes on here in Brain's *Brain.* (You do not have to turn to the back for the answer. The distinguished neurophysiologist Lord Brain, now deceased, was born Russell Brain, and the post card "Brain, *Brain,* London" would have reached him, but faster if you added "Harley Street" and the zip code.)

It occurred to me that all the answers were not in *Brain* or even in medicine as we know it, fabulous as it is. There is a case in one of the journals about a Nigerian princeling in London who got sick and depressed, about two generations ago. He sent home for the witch doctor, since the Harley Street crowd couldn't do much for him. The witch doctor chanted whatever witch doctors chant, gave him a magic extract of a plant, and the Nigerian recovered. The magic extract came from a plant called *Rauwolfia serpentina,* named by a French botanist.

A generation went by, and Western medicine sought to control high blood pressure and to calm people with tranquilizers. The detail salesmen from the big drug companies, CIBA and Riker and Squibb, fanned out to doctors and hospitals with their great new drugs, and one of the great new drugs was reserpine, called Serpasil or Rauwiloid or Raudixin, depending on the drug company. And what did reserpine come from? Of course, *Rauwolfia serpentina.* The drug companies found it and wrote it up in learned journals and analyzed it; the witch doctor didn't have any journals, he got it from his daddy, who got it from *his* daddy, who was one hundred years ahead of CIBA and Riker and Squibb, and he was late because Ayurvedic medicine in India knew *Rauwolfia* when the ancestors of the Harley Street crowd were staining themselves blue.

I had to go back to school. I brought certain abilities as a student and the willingness to be an utter fool, to make up for a native skepticism. Some of the customs had changed. I knew the dorms were coed, but when did they make the bathrooms coed? One evening in a movie theater near the University of California campus in Berkeley, the following conversation took place in the seats behind me:

She: Say, I dig George.

He: Mmmmmmmm.

She: I mean, I really dig George's bod.

He: *(a grunt)*

She: Why don't we have a threesome or a fivesome sometime?

He: Okay.

Often I felt a stranger in a strange land, or an anthropologist with a new tribe. What happened to the *even* numbers?

Strange schools, sometimes. Some trips, you go to Abercrombie & Fitch to get your mountaineering boots or your fishing vest. I had to buy tie-dyed jeans, because my new classmates were staring at my suit and tie.

I followed where the trail led. I met more Nobel Prize winners than I knew there were. I met biofeedback technicians who said people could train control of their heartbeats. I met meditators who said meditation was more restorative than sleep.

And: an astronaut who had a mystic experience on the way back from the moon. A pro quarterback who could send signals to his wide receiver by telepathy, or something like telepathy. A blue-eyed British witch doctor, apprenticed in Lesotho or Botswana, who could track lions by scent; Manhattan traffic gave him a tic, I had to help him across the street.

And: masters of martial arts, aikido and kung fu, who said those arts repatterned brains. Bushels of psychiatrists and pecks of gurus. A gentleman who could push a knitting needle through his arm, command the blood to stop, and it would. Another gentleman who could smoke a cigar and send his mind to Jupiter and Mercury, simply by having it clear.

Some of it gets very far out. That was a phrase I learned from my new classmates. Far out.

There is a peculiar characteristic to this field. It is never easy to explain, and it is impossible to photograph.

Three Stories in Which Something Is Going On Which Is Very Hard to Photograph

Two of these stories have a personal element and one is from a journal. They are here to show an odd power—even mysterious—which is present but not articulated, in the relationship of mind and body.

Stewart Alsop Doesn't Get Off the Train in Baltimore

Stewart Alsop was a tough-minded, brilliant reporter, a well-known correspondent from the wars and from Washington. He wrote a weekly essay on the last text page of *Newsweek* that was as tightly constructed as a sonnet. We exchanged literary references and had lunch perhaps once a year. Then he got leukemia. He wrote about the experience in his weekly essay: most of us, he said, spend our lives behind a "thick carapace," where we live, from fear, emotions unexposed, defended, not totally alive. His essays under this "sentence of execution," as he called it, were the best pieces of writing he had ever done.

I met him for lunch at the Metropolitan Club in Washington. He looked surprisingly fit. I knew he had been in and out of the hospital; he had skipped a number of columns. He had this one with him that day.

I woke up suddenly, feeling very wide awake, pulled the light cord, and sat straight up in bed.

"We'll be stopping in Baltimore," I announced loudly, in an authoritative voice. I looked around me. A private car, evidently. Good of the railroad people to supply those fruits, and all those flowers. The furniture looked a bit shoddy, but what can one expect these days? I got up to explore.

The car was swaying heavily—the roadbed must be a disgrace. I supported myself on a table, and then a desk. Then there was a space of empty floor. I was halfway across it when the car gave a lurch, and I fell down. I sat on the floor for a bit, getting my bearings, then scrambled to my feet again, and opened a narrow green door. A locker, with my own clothes in it. I opened another door —a small bathroom.

Then I came to a much bigger door, and opened it, and leaned against the doorjamb. The swaying had ˙stopped—the train, apparently, had halted. Outside was what I assumed was the Baltimore station—wide platform, dim lights, green tile. A whimpering noise, then silence, and no one to be seen. There was something hellishly grim about the place. Suddenly I was quite sure I didn't want to stop in Baltimore.

"We won't stop here," I said, again in a firm, authoritative voice. "Start up the train, and carry on."

I turned back toward my bed, and the big door closed behind me. I fell down twice on the way back—the crew must be pouring on the power, I thought—and getting into bed was like mounting a bucking horse. Safe in bed, I turned off the light, and was asleep in an instant.

Alsop had not been, he wrote, in a railroad car; he had been in the solid tumor ward of the National Institutes of Health, but his bruises from falling down were real. He had had pneumonia, a lung clot, three operations, and the lethal "infiltrate" was spreading across his lungs; the prognosis was "grim."

The day after he had "not stopped in Baltimore," the x-rays of his lungs looked a bit better. The infiltrate was receding. Some days later, they were close to normal. He resumed his column.

And in the Metropolitan Club, sipping a martini, pink-cheeked, he looked very well indeed. Was he really recovered?

"Well, I can't really play tennis, and if you wake up early, it's hard to go back to sleep if you're afraid. But the protective mechanism takes over. God tempers the wind to the shorn lamb."

And why the reprieve from the illness? That was in the column:

Why? . . . the doctors say frankly they don't know, though they all have a favorite guess. I have a favorite guess, too. My guess is that my decision not to stop at Baltimore had something to do with it. In a kind of fuzzy, hallucinated way, I knew when I announced the decision that it was a decision not to die.

Perhaps my decision not to stop in Baltimore had nothing to do with my astonishing recovery. But there are mysteries, above all the mystery of the relationship of mind and body, that will never be explained, not by the most brilliant doctors, the wisest of scientists or philosophers.

But, some time later, his reprieve was over. The deadly infiltrate came back, and, three years or so after his cancer had first been diagnosed, he died. But I was not in touch with him closely then, so I never knew whether there was a chapter after the Baltimore station.

Norman Cousins Laughs Himself Back

The end of Norman Cousins' Russian trip was not particularly pleasant. Cousins was—and is—the editor of *Saturday Review*. He publishes a lot of people, and he sits on a lot of committees, and in addition the magazine business is never without problems. Now Cousins was in Moscow, on his way to an important intercultural dinner set for 7:30 P.M., and he was late. The dinner was somewhere on the outskirts of Moscow, and the driver assigned to him by the

Russians couldn't find it. While Cousins fumed in the car, the driver wandered endlessly around Moscow, looking for the site of the dinner. When they finally arrived, it was after nine. The hours from seven to nine were full of outrage: Cousins was an honored guest, and the dinner had been set up for a long time. After the embarrassment of being an hour and a half late to dinner, Cousins went back to his hotel, but he did not sleep well. The windows were open, he was on the second floor, and heavy diesel trucks roared by all night on the way to a construction site.

During his return trip to the U.S., Cousins had a headache on the plane, and noticed some heaviness in his legs and back. By the time he landed, he had a fever of 104°. After two days in bed, his doctor put him into the hospital. The heaviness in his legs and back was becoming paralysis. The least movement brought excruciating pain. Tests did not show what might have been the first guess—heavy metal poisoning, perhaps from breathing in the fumes from the trucks. But one of the tests was alarming. The sedimentation rate of his blood—the rate at which blood precipitates solids—was high. If normal is 12 to 20 mm per hour, 80 would represent danger. Cousins' rate was 85. Perhaps, said his physicians, it was a collagen disease, a disintegration of the connective tissue between the cells. But they weren't sure. They gave him two dozen aspirin a day, sleeping pills to sleep, and drugs for the pain. With the drugs, his disabilities intensified. "I wasn't hurting any more, but I wasn't moving, either," he says.

For more than two weeks, in the hospital, Cousins got quietly worse. He could not move his neck—then he could only move his jaws with difficulty.

"I was very scared," he says. "My doctors said something had happened. Maybe an allergy had lowered the normal protection. My physician was trying to get me to put my affairs in order." One of the doctors left a note for another doctor. When no one was in the room, Cousins read it. "I'm afraid," said the physician, "we may be losing Norman."

Cousins thought back over his trip and over the

previous six months. It had been a very stressful time. He sent his wife out for books on stress, Cannon and Selye. "If negative emotions produce negative chemical changes, then positive emotions could produce positive changes."

Cousins announced he was taking the responsibility for himself. He checked out of the hospital and into a hotel room. He went off all the drugs. The pain was intense. "To move your thumbs was like walking on your eyeballs," he said. "But what I needed was laughter."

He sent out for Marx Brothers movies. A projector was set up in the hotel room. "I watched *A Night at the Opera* twice. It's still funny. I watched *Animal Crackers*. I sent out for segments of old *Candid Camera* shows. You know, *Candid Camera?*"

When I was taping these accounts, Cousins was harried and behind schedule. He had to be two places simultaneously, fifteen minutes ago. But as he told this part, his face began to change. The lines went out of it.

"Do you remember," Cousins said, "the *Candid Camera* where they put a speaker in one of those big street mailboxes? The guy is walking by, and the mailbox says, excuse me, sir, do you have a minute? And the guy stares. And the mailbox says, could you open the lid, there? The guy opens the lid, and the mailbox says, ah, that air feels good. Finally the voice in the mailbox says that it's fallen into the mailbox, could the passer-by go get a cop? And the passer-by brings back this cop, explaining there's somebody in the mailbox, and as the passer-by and the cop peer into the mailbox, there's no sound at all."

Harried, and fifteen minutes behind schedule twice, Cousins was breaking up just telling the *Candid Camera* mailbox story. Then he looked at his watch and began dictating crisply.

"Ten minutes of belly laughter gave me an hour of pain-free sleep. My sedimentation rate dropped from 115 to 109 the first morning. I was caught up in something exciting. The body writes prescriptions for itself. I knew I needed adrenalin, or nor-adrenalin, and I knew Linus Pauling, who experimented with vitamin

C and I knew vitamin C was related to collagen problems, so I took massive doses of vitamin C intravenously, slowly, so the acid wouldn't burn my veins out. The sedimentation rate began to come down ten points at a time.

"And every day I watched the Marx Brothers and segments of *Candid Camera,* and the hours that were pain-free got longer and longer, and the more I laughed, the better I got."

"Under this treatment," wrote Cousins' physician, "his sedimentation gradually became normal. Since then he has never regained the slightest vestige of the syndrome. Was it a streptococcus contracted in Russia? There was also a diagnosis of severe, possibly irreversible, ankylosing spondylitis of the rheumatoid type."

Cousins' doctor went on: "The relationship of Mr. Cousins' treatment to his recovery was not clearly understood nor adequately explained, and was initiated at the specific insistence of Mr. Cousins. To date, I have not clearly established a rational cause, nor how Mr. Cousins cured himself via his own hand and mind."

A Case of Stigmata

A ten-year-old girl began bleeding, without any pain, from her left palm one day in school, several years ago. It was two weeks before Easter. A couple of days later she bled from her right palm, then later from the upper part of her left foot, upper right foot, right chest, and, by the fourteenth day, from the middle of her forehead. On Good Friday she bled from all six areas. Then the bleeding stopped, and never came back again.

About a week before the bleeding began, Miss X had read a religious book about the crucifixion, and a few days later she had watched a television movie on the same subject, and had had a vivid dream that night. She liked Bible stories, particularly the life of Christ, and could quote Bible verses. She said she also heard voices during her bedtime prayers a few days before the bleeding began, the voices being a few simple phrases such as "Your prayers will be answered."

Miss X continued to go to school while her two weeks of bleeding went on; she didn't want to miss playing the clarinet in the school band.

One can speculate on what might have happened had Miss X lived a while back in Spain or France or Italy.

But Miss X is black, a Baptist, and lives in Oakland, California.

She had never heard of stigmata, or of St. Francis of Assisi. The school nurse took the dressing off her right palm one day so she could play the clarinet in the school band. There were a couple of drops of blood on her palm, and no lesions. The pediatrician who examined her said there was no skin damage, even when the skin was looked at under a magnifying glass.

Miss X was cheerful and in no pain throughout. On Good Friday she said, "It's over now," and presumably took the dressing off so she could handle the clarinet better.

The pediatrician was joined by a psychiatrist who had written previously on psychogenic bleeding, and who was coordinator of psychiatry in various capacities at the University of California at Berkeley. They wrote it up in the *Archive of General Psychiatry,* Volume 30, February 1974, which is where I found it.

The possibility of fakery was almost nil, they said. They referred to other cases of strange spontaneous hemorrhages which did not result from physical injury "in people of strong hysterical dispositions." "One can no longer dispute the power of mental and emotional forces to control such [bleeding]," they wrote. "By analogy we need not doubt that profound, intense, religious and emotional forces, conscious and unconscious, could cause stigmatic bleeding."

I showed these cases—and some others—to the physicians who were kind enough to help me with research. This was their reaction:

Of Stewart Alsop, they said, "Well, in cancer there are many cases of unexplained remissions. Surgeons open up a patient, shake their heads, sew him back up, and write him off. Five years later the patient turns up on a visit, feeling very chipper." Did the unexplained remissions have anything in common? Nobody knew. Could mental states have an influence? The physicians passed on some reprints of an oncologist in Texas who was treating cancer with radiation and with certain mental exercises; the results so far were sketchy.

Of Norman Cousins they said, "He probably would have gotten better anyway." And, "He was aware of the stress he'd originally imposed on himself, and he found a way to un-stress himself."

Of Miss X, they said, "The case is interesting, but the article is right, intense emotional forces can cause bleeding, and curiously, even stigmatic bleeding."

All of these cases seem to suggest that our minds affect processes at the level of our cells. That isn't such a radical notion—psychosomatic medicine is defined on such cases. But could we get into the act, consciously, with our word-using, symbol-using consciousness?

Placebos and Rumpelstiltskin

Placebos also show us how our minds affect our bodies. Placebo is *I shall be pleasing* in Latin, and nothing at all in pharmacology. It's a fake. Sugar and water. It's there to fool the mind. Of course, you have to believe the placebo is real, and clever psychologists have even tested what is most real in this nothing pill. If you can taste it, it should taste slightly bitter. It works best when it's either large and purple or brown, or small and bright red or bright yellow.

The clever psychologists compared placebos and pain relievers, in a double blind, where neither the experimenter nor pill taker knew what was what, and the placebos were 50-something percent as effective as practically everything: 54 percent as aspirin, 54 percent as Darvon (a tranquilizer), 56 percent as effective as morphine. Two placebo pills work better than one. Placebo injections are more powerful than placebo pills. Placebos work better when they aren't given by doctors, because doctors like to give real medicine, not sugar pills, and the patient gets the unverbalized message from the doctor's face and tone: the vibes give it away.

When the actor in the white coat on the TV commercial holds up the bottle of pills and says, you'll be better by morning, the odds are with the company sponsoring him, because almost everything is better by morning.

When a drug company wants to test a new pill at a certain stage, it uses a double-blind procedure, new drug vs. placebo. Confusing, because sometimes the placebo group improves, too.

A team of researchers working on high blood pressure ran into this. They tested the medication and placebos with four groups of subjects; down went the blood pressure in all four groups. Placebos even work specifically. When asthma sufferers were given a new drug, their bronchial dilation—their ease of breathing—was twice as great when they were told that the pill would open them up as when they were told the opposite.

Another experimenter gave his subjects a stomach pill. There wasn't anything in it except something magnetic to help the measurement. The stomach activity of the subjects increased when they were told that's what it did, decreased when they were told that's what it did, and stayed the same when they were told it had no effect.

Not all symptoms are mental, and placebos don't work better than drugs, but how can a placebo work at all? This is a mind-body debate that goes back a long way. Franz Anton Mesmer—from whom comes our word "mesmerized"—was an eighteenth-century physician who used to cure with techniques we now call hypnotic induction. He named his technique "animal magnetism" because he used magnets in his first experiments. Louis XVI was so interested he appointed a Royal Commission to investigate, headed by the astronomer Bailly. It also included Lavoisier, the chemist, Dr. Guillotin and Benjamin Franklin. The Bailly Commission decided that mesmerism worked due not to magnetism but to imagination. "Imagination without magnetism can produce convulsions," said the Bailly Report. "Magnetism without imagination has no effect at all." (This is from *Rapport des Commissaires par le Roi de l'Examen du Magnétisme Animal,* J. A. Bailly, Imprimerie Royale, 1784.)

A young physician who is both psychiatrist and anthropologist, Fuller Torrey, wrote a comparison between witch doctors and psychiatrists. People who went to see each felt better immediately because of the certainty exuded by the authority figure, the diploma on the wall, or the proper headdress, bones and rattles, and, finally, because the authority in each case gave the condition a name. You have a curse from your dead mother-in-law, or you have a bug that's been going around. Torrey called it the Rumpelstiltskin effect. Rumpelstiltskin, you remember, was a dwarf who helped the miller's daughter weave the flax into gold and claimed her first-born child after she was queen. The miller's daughter wanted to renege, and the dwarf said, you don't even know my name. If she could learn his name by midnight of the third day, she could keep the kid. At midnight the third day there is a scene where the queen says archly, "Is your name Michael? John? Rumpelstiltskin?" And poor Rumpelstiltskin goes POP! Vaporizes. Disappears. If you can give it a name, it will disappear.

Harvard psychologists tested people at a clinic. The people felt much better after they'd been to the clinic. More tests—the people in the waiting room. They feel better, too. Finally, the people who hadn't even come to the clinic yet, but had made an appointment. They felt better already.

No one doubts the effect of mind on body to some extent, and the extent varies with the believer. George Bernard Shaw said he considered Lourdes a blasphemous place because they kept there all the crutches and wheelchairs of the people who walked away, but among these items was not one wooden leg, one glass eye, or one toupee.

Stewart Alsop said, "There are mysteries, above all the mystery of the relationship of mind and body, that will never be explained, not by the most brilliant doctors, the wisest of scientists or philosophers."

There is a reason we are so sketchy on minds, and that is that we perceive the world through whatever paradigm we live in, and our present paradigm is sketchy when it comes to "mind." The design of this book is to begin well within the paradigm, with the familiar, work up to the edges, and then go beyond, and since "paradigm" is so important we had better have a brief look at what it is.

Paradigms

The dictionary says a paradigm—pronounced *paradime*—is a model or a pattern. This usage of "paradigm" goes beyond that. A paradigm is a shared set of assumptions. The paradigm is the way we perceive the world, water to the fish. The paradigm explains the world to us and helps us to predict its behavior. When we are in the middle of the paradigm, it is hard to imagine any other paradigm.

For this use of the word I have to do some hat-tipping. Many years ago James Bryant Conant, the president of Harvard and a distinguished scientist and educator, taught a course in science for nonscientists.

Conant called the paradigm a "conceptual scheme." Science was not merely the careful and accurate observation of facts, biologists classifying worms and physicists reading instruments. A concept tied those observations together—then there were more observations and experiments—and new concepts rose from those, and the concepts led to still further observations and experiments. Conant wrote a little book on conceptual schemes, called *On Understanding Science*. (At the end of the year, when we got to ask sassy questions, I asked Dr. Conant why our busy president would take the time to teach us clunks, who could barely light a Bunsen burner, and he said it was important for citizens to understand the nature of science, and if we could grow up and keep the basic idea in later years, his efforts would have been worthwhile.)

An instructor in the course was Thomas Kuhn, a physicist who became a well-known professor of the history of science. Kuhn extended the "conceptual scheme" still further into "paradigm" in a seminal book, *The Structure of Scientific Revolutions*.

A famous historical paradigm is the Ptolemaic view of the world. Here's the earth in the middle of the universe, for as any fool can plainly see, the sun comes up in the east, moves overhead, and sets in the west and the stars move around in very predictable courses. Ptolemy's science won out in its day because it explained the world better than its competitors.

Astronomers using Ptolemy found discrepancies and tried to solve them. The discrepancies just moved to another place in the scheme. By the sixteenth century the advanced astronomers were saying that no system so cumbersome and complicated could be true to nature. The paradigm, said Copernicus, though he didn't call it that, was a monster, and he began to look for a new one. The earth, said Copernicus, moves around the sun.

Paradigms do not change easily. Copernicus was cautious. Galileo considered himself cautious; he was genuinely surprised when he was called to Rome before the cardinals. He had engineered new telescopes, unfolded new areas of the heavens, scientists everywhere made their way to see him, but he had written that perhaps the earth was not the center of the universe. In Rome, they took him downstairs and showed him the thumbscrews and the rack. Galileo was seventy and he recanted. The Establishment was so eager to silence him it introduced a forgery into his prosecution. Galileo spent the rest of his life under house arrest, and the official Church view continued: the sun moves around the earth.

The Establishment is always invested in the old paradigm. So the new paradigm does not get adopted just because it is neater and works better than the old one. The old crowd wins the first few battles, and in fact the paradigm doesn't change until the old crowd dies and the new young crowd grows up and rewrites the textbooks and becomes the Establishment itself.

"Paradigm" in this book is extended from *The Structure of Scientific Revolutions.* The grand paradigm in which we live is basically rational and scientific. Scientists measure a phenomenon, and try to set up an experiment that can be repeated by other scientists. What is measurable and repeatable becomes "true."

All of us, scientists or not, share the assumptions of the paradigm. If something comes along that doesn't fit the paradigm, it makes us feel uncomfortable, and it sounds bizarre and kooky. We assume, for example, that for an effect there must be a cause. What if the connection between cause and effect is just something we made up, a cumbersome system that sometimes works, just as Ptolemaic astronomy sometimes worked? What if there is no objective connection between cause and effect, but just something we supply from our perception? That gets to be very confusing. In our paradigm, we assume that causes produce effects.

Obviously, paradigms have great utility. They provide us a ground for communication, so we don't have to start over each time, and they make the world seem continuous and stable and somewhat predictable. But they also limit us, especially when we forget that we made up the paradigm in the first place.

Now let's say we want to explore the powers of

mind, from the safest part of the paradigm to the thin air outside the paradigm.

We could begin with brains. Surgeons, paradigmatic gentlemen always, will give us a Latin or Greek name for every last ratchet and gear in the brain. The surgeons can even tell us what parts do what: see, this is sight, and this is sound, and this little ratchet controls the little finger, and here we come to the Fissure of Rolan, and here we come to the Fissure of Sylvius. Memory's in here somewhere, but we haven't found it yet.

Then there are experimental psychologists. They can't work with human brains very well, so they use rats and cats, and leave us the hint that if that's the way a cat's brain is, maybe so is ours. They run rats through mazes, keep the cats up all night, and teach monkeys to communicate by hitting colored buttons hooked to a computer. The physiologically oriented psychologists peer into the brains of beautiful fluffy white New Zealand bunnies, big as cats, the bunny with his nose in a nozzle of anesthetic and his brains all hooked up—look, the bunny learns at the end of the sixth cranial nerve, implications for science and medicine.

Now we know the names of all the parts of the brain, and what they do, and we know about cats and monkeys, and we have a lot of very accurate measurements published in technical journals.

Along come the social scientists. They ask people: What's on your mind? Then they tabulate the results, using more and more complex statistics. The results may or may not be what's on people's minds. Sometimes the pollees lie, sometimes they can't quite articulate what's on their minds, sometimes they don't know, but the statistics have a kind of symmetry after a while, like a wasp's nest.

Then come the psychiatrists. They too are trying to find out why we behave as we do, so they say, tell me your dreams. Or, let's talk. Or, scream a little and see what happens. Up to this point, we have been very safely within the paradigm, because everything has been so accurately measured. But dreams are not so easily measured. We can tell when they occur, from the sleeper's rapid eye movements, but the meaning of the dream is an old human mystery. That makes psychiatry more art than science. Or, as defined by Eric Berne, the transactional analyst who wrote *Games People Play,* a science about the level of science in sixteenth-century Paris.

Could you get a message from your grandmother across the country, no telephone, straight ESP? Not in our paradigm. Of course, if you and your grandmother can repeat the experiment on command, and you can analyze the technique for us, and then other people can do it, we will adopt the paradigm to incorporate your achievement, and you can be just like Copernicus and Lavoisier and Newton. Or we will get a new paradigm. Sometimes the paradigm bends, and sometimes it falls apart and gets replaced.

Is there any way we can know the future? Not so far, in our paradigm. Crazy Horse, the Sioux chief, would get, so he said, symbolic messages that told him the future—even as to who would kill him—but Crazy Horse did not have very accurate measurements and the experiments were not repeatable.

Our scientific paradigm has produced the absolute and splendid technological achievements of Western man. But it leaves us with a problem, and that is that we have an unconscious tendency to consider as "real" that which can be easily measured, and less real, or unreal, that which can't. What cannot be mathematically or empirically manipulated is "irrational" or "subjective."

The danger is that we consider what can be measured easily as more important than what can't, or to ignore what can't.

With the advent of the computer, social scientists have joined the physical scientists in quantifying everything within reach, and even English scholars are quantifying the lines of seventeenth-century sonnets.

But quantification has not noticeably increased our understanding of dreams or feelings, and some observers think we exclude those of our perceptions that don't match the paradigm because that's what we're trained to do. To give an exaggerated example, the child says, oh look, Mommy, a purple cow, and the mother says, there is no such thing as a purple cow, sweetheart, and so the kid stops reporting purple cows, and gradually as he gets older the visual messages processed by his brain are modified and translated in terms of Mommy's world until he can't remember seeing a purple cow. (The purple cows then walk around with impunity, unseen by anyone.)

A team of Stanford psychologists raised batches of kittens, some of whom were brought up seeing only vertical stripes and some of whom were brought up in a horizontally striped world. Even after they grew up to be smart Stanford laboratory cats, with the ability to move anywhere, the vertical-stripers thought the world was vertical and the horizontal-stripers thought the world was horizontal, both groups behaved that way, and it wasn't just belief, their brains actually recorded the impressions that way. The horizontal-stripers could not see the vertical world, and vice versa. In their technical language the psychologists wrote: "Functional neural connections can be selectively and predictably modified by environmental stimulation." In other words, even physiologically *our experience shapes our perception.*

We know that our perception does not tell us the world the way it "really" is. Otherwise, the railroad tracks really would meet at a point on the horizon. When we look out the window as the plane banks to land, we can see little toy cars on the road, but we know that when we land, the little toy cars will have grown to full size. So we test our perception against what we know, and we have a model of reality that provides day-to-day continuity. We learn from our parents and our society and our language to construct categories that help us maintain that day-to-day continuity, Rumpelstiltskin Rumpelstiltskin, and we all agree on the categories. If somebody "sees" something that the rest of us do not see—seeing being a certain excitation of the central nervous system, to which the eyes contribute—we say he is dreaming or crazy or out of touch with reality, because reality is the model, the consensus, the paradigm. Our experiences are different. So what is it that's real out there?

Does the world have vertical stripes or horizontal stripes? It depends on the paradigm, and paradigms are not only belief systems, they can be innate.

All of this is to show that there are paradigms we are not aware of, because our daily assumptions aren't articulated. We have a hard time quantifying "mind," but our big rational and scientific paradigm insists that what is real is measurable and predictable, and sometimes all we know of "mind" is the size of its footprints in the snow the next morning. "Mind" becomes real as it is quantified, because that's the name of our particular game.

We can start with mind as a subject for quantification. Mind plus placebo equals new drug, and since placebo is nothing, we have a quantity for mind, in one context. We can keep thinking up contexts to give us a quantity, what can we do, what can we measure. But if we keep going long enough, the outlines of the paradigm in which we operate appear, and then the question becomes "What is it that is really real?"

The Astronauts of Inner Space

A tenet of psychiatry is that unconscious memories affect present behavior. The dead hand of the past is irrationally alive. But no one ever located these memories in a specific spot in the brain. There was a flurry of excitement two decades ago when a Canadian neurosurgeon, Wilder Penfield, seemed to have found physical locations for repressed feelings and repressed memories; the touch of an electrode would bring them out.

For medical reasons, Penfield had to perform more than a thousand brain operations with local anesthesia. The housewife who had grown up in Holland was on the operating table, conscious, her skull open, Penfield's electrode probing, and: "That song," she said, "it's Christmas Eve, in Amsterdam, in 1945 . . . the choir is so beautiful." "The stimulation," Penfield wrote, "activates a neuron sequence that constitutes the record of the stream of consciousness . . . a selected past is made available—selected by some event in the present."

The recall was so clear that the smallest details could be identified, though they had been out of present, conscious mind for years. "A strip of time seems to run forward again at time's own normal pace," Penfield wrote, "and the individual is aware of the things he selected for his attention then. All of the available sensory information that he had ignored is absent. If he was frightened by the experience, he is frightened again. If he thought the music was beautiful, he thinks so again."

That was exciting—a physical location to hidden feelings and forgotten experiences! If you could find them, maybe you could let them out, and be at least conscious of the hand of the past! But no one, to date, has been able to find memory in a specific spot in the brain; it seems to be all through it.

About fifteen years ago I was in a psychology experiment at UCLA which produced with pharmacology the same result Penfield had found with an electrode: detailed recall of something out of conscious mind.

The experiment did more than that: it also showed, firsthand, how strong are the unquantified feelings which guide so much of our behavior from subterranean locations, and the visual symbols these feelings sometimes wear. The experiment was billed as exploration.

"You are the astronauts of inner space," said the project director. "You are going deeper into the mind than anyone has gone so far, and you will come back to tell us what you found."

That made me a bit nervous, astronaut of inner space. So did one of the astronauts who had returned. "You get to know your own mind," she said. "You will be amazed at what's in there." I wasn't sure I wanted to know. "All the pill does is to make the unconscious conscious. Like a dream, only in a dream, you're dreaming, but with this, you're right there."

Mission Control, in the form of a graduate student, could sometimes provoke suggestions and feelings that weren't always pleasant. "For example, I saw this giant spider, maybe thirty feet tall. You just don't know how terrifying that is. I was terrified the spider was going to eat me, and my guide said, tell me about the spider, and describe it, and when it got closer, the spider was my mother, it had her face and it was just about to eat me—let it, said my guide —and zoop, it disappeared, and I had this incredible flow of feelings, I guess they had been locked in there for years, and I wept, and now I can talk to her all the time, where before I never even returned her phone calls."

I was uneasy. What were we astronauts to do if we met *two* thirty-foot spiders? Or a hundred-foot gnat?

There was a magazine lying around with a story by James Thurber. I began to read it, casually.

I swallowed my blue pill with a glass of water and sat down to read the magazine. Nothing happened. My guide from Mission Control was checking one-two-three-four into the tape recorder. Something in the Thurber made me giggle. It was hard to read further. I was getting gangrene in my left hand from this iron vise around the wrist. I took off my watch. That made my arm feel wonderful. A hot, leaden weight in the back of my pants threatened to drag me through the floor. I took my wallet out and hurled it across the room. That made me about six thousand pounds lighter.

The guide—they called them "baby-sitters" in that

lab—made some notes on the pad. Probably time and money.

"What's so funny?" she said.

I was not about to answer. First of all, I didn't want any intrusions. And second, everything was moving much faster than the words we invent to describe them. There weren't, in fact, any words.

There still aren't. Compared to the gradations of experience, words are leaden, clumsy, two-left-footed things. The blanket won't cover the bed. Mystics shrug and say the experience is ineffable, and the venerable *Tao* from China said, first line, "The way that can be described is not the Way." Physicists are glad they can talk to each other in mathematics because the concepts beyond everyday reality can't quite be expressed in language. But until you get one foot out of everyday reality, you don't know there's another kind.

Part of me was scampering like a puppy that feels green grass instead of floor under its feet, and has wriggled from its leash, and part of me was following with the leash, saying, here boy, here boy. What's so funny, the baby-sitter had said. There did indeed seem to be somebody laughing—no, that's not it, the laughter was laughing somebody. The part of me panting along with the leash thought, it's not *that* funny, thinking that it was some line of James Thurber causing the disturbance. The part with the leash tried to tell the baby-sitter why this serious job was not going to be accomplished on schedule—"No . . . words . . ." it gasped, already feeling guilty—we would have to get a sound movie camera inside the head somehow—and then it was swept away and was not heard from for several hours, the first time it had been silent since the age of probably one and a half.

Now then, on the other side of this breath-taking display of kaleidoscopic colors was a purple universe, a very profound discovery, which was the true universe, and if you just let go you would fall in; it was always there, but we held ourselves away from it; it vibrated at a certain frequency, and so did you, and that frequency was the frequency of laughter. The frequency of laughter extends from the limits of the galaxy to the other limits, and there's nothing to do, you don't even have to go ha-ha, you just float.

And there was this clock on the wall with Roman numerals and some spots of sunlight on it, the details very clear, the hands snapping with a loud click from 3:28 to 3:30 and then to 3:31, a soaring free feeling simultaneously.

I could see the basic molecules of the universe, too bad there weren't any words because there they were, all the component parts, little building blocks of DNA.

Out of control, I wrote in my report later. That feeling is quite frightening, but there was the baby-sitter, and all the other astronauts had come back, and the purple universe vibrating at the frequency of laughter seemed more wonderful and more human than the dreary ordinary one.

Other people's trips can be very boring—somewhat like other people's dreams—so I hesitate to extend the description. When I listened to the tape later, I realized I had never heard such gut-laughter coming from myself, or at least very rarely.

The molecule of DNA I drew was not DNA, alas. It was du Pont plastic, patented, called Delrin. That was just as mysterious as DNA; I am no chemist, and do not really know one chemical from another, especially at the molecular level, how come I could draw a du Pont plastic monomer? The clock with the Roman numerals indeed did face the western sun, it was on the wall facing the west windows of Miss Pannell's fourth grade, somebody had watched the hands of that clock a lot as they clicked ever so slowly toward 3:30 and the end of school. Who would have thought that old clock would still be there in the memory bank after so many years? And the feelings, the impatience and boredom and restlessness at 3:28, and the exhilaration at 3:30, those feelings were so clear, was it like that at first? And was it now 3:28 too much of the time, and 3:31 too seldom?

"That's some pill," I said the next day. I felt very good.

"There's nothing in the pill per se," said Mission Control. "It's a trigger. You provide all the comedy and all the drama. The first session is usually good."

I signed up to do more guinea-pigging. No more than once a month; this really was no search for highs. There was great excitement about the explorations, and that excitement was contagious. Frontiers of mind, astronauts of inner space.

The report of this astronaut sometimes sounded a bit bizarre. Second session, listening to Bach, I announced, "Bach wrote his music in the shape of a three-dimensional cross, the same architecture as a cathedral." You could walk inside the music. Stone columns of music, arches and naves and flying buttresses. Another session: real estate. Real estate? Sure, looking up from the middle of the earth, real estate becomes very comic if you see some tiny figure the size of a mayfly going into City Hall with a tiny paper clutched in his hand, saying he owns some bit of the earth's surface and everything under it all the way down to the middle. The earth is ignorant of the piece of paper. How can anybody own the earth?

As a guinea pig with credentials, when on the East Coast I reported in to an experiment there. Different chemical. Primordial big cobra, sun symbol, you could sit in front of it and get a sunburn. Did I really get a sunburn? It certainly looked like a sunburn, and felt like a sunburn. Package that snake and we can really cut into the sunlamp market.

The experiments opened an interest for me in altered states, as it did for many people who went through some similar experience. I began to read the technical literature.

"Did you see the weird things the yogis can do?" said somebody. "It's in *The Journal of Electroencephalography and Clinical Neurophysiology.*" I read the article. Only the first three sentences and the last three were in English, the rest was in some tortured form of noncommunication designed to show the methods, but after a while I got the hang of it. As an astronaut I was only a weekend warrior, a part-time guinea pig, since I was running a mutual fund portfolio the rest of the time. Reading the journals was a bit like reading *Motor Trend* and *Hot Rod* without owning a car, but among other things I was looking for the experiments in which I was a subject. If you come in second in the potato-sack race at the school picnic, you might very well look in the weekly paper for the results of the potato-sack races, to see if they spelled your name right.

Alas, the closest we came to publication was in a footnote on page 282 of a book called *Altered States of Consciousness,* and the group in the footnote wasn't even mine.

It is nineteenth-century psychology, this business of exploring the mind with chemicals and reporting back. (Chemicals are chemicals and minds are chemicals and they react on each other.) At the beginning of the twentieth century, a psychologist called John Watson turned the whole field away from this sort of thing, toward behaviorism and harder science and the more accurate measurement of rats.

One curious sidelight is that so many subjects made profound discoveries which were comically trivial later. Dr. Oliver Wendell Holmes sniffed ether and reported of the universe: "The whole is pervaded with the smell of turpentine." William James tried nitrous oxide, wrote down his cosmic discovery, and found the next day that the cosmic discovery was "higamous, hogamus, woman's monogamous, hogamus, higamus, man is polygamous." A contemporary psychologist perceived the absolute secret of the universe: "Please flush after using."

Naturally, physicians checked out the chemical effects. If you were in medical school, this is what you would find in your pharmacology course, in Goodman and Gilman, *The Pharmacological Basis of Therapeutics*: "The agents act upon the central nervous system, causing the pupil of the eye to dilate, though not by direct application to the eye. Muscular weakness also results." But what distinguishes these agents, says the text, "is their capacity to induce or compel states of altered perception, thought and feeling that are not (or cannot be) experienced except in dreams or at times of religious exaltation." Interesting language for a cautious medical school text. It goes on: "Frequently there is a feeling that one part of the self seems to be a passive observer (a 'spectator ego') rather than an active organizing and directing force, while another part of the self participates and receives the vivid and unusual experiences. The environment may be perceived as novel, often beautiful, and harmonious. The attention of the user is turned inward, pre-empted by the seeming clarity and portentous quality of his own thinking processes. In this state the slightest sensation may take on profound meaning. Indeed, 'meaningfulness' seems more important than what is meant, and the 'sense of truth' more magnificent than what is true. Commonly, there is a diminished capacity to differentiate the boundaries of one object from another and of the self from the environment. Associated with the loss to boundaries there may be a sense of union with 'mankind' or with the 'cosmos.' To the extent that these drugs reveal this innate capacity of the mind to see more than it can tell and to experience and believe more than it can explain, the term *mind expanding* is not entirely inappropriate."

An "innate capacity of the mind to see more than it can tell" is like the first line of the *Tao,* the way that can be described is not the Way. That's nice stuff for the medical students. And loss of boundaries, union with the cosmos—that's a description of a mystical experience. A chemical mystical experience. Eventually there grew up an argument as to whether chemical mystical experiences counted as mystical experiences, but then, in those days, serious intellectual theologians like Father John Courtenay Murray were participating. A Harvard divinity school student did a Ph.D. thesis: as an experiment, he recruited twenty divinity school students and, in a double-blind procedure, gave placebos to some and psychedelics to others. Deliberately he chose Good Friday.

He sent the future theologians off to church. The placebo-taking students said, "I think I'm dizzy," or, "I feel funny." The other students wandered out, crying, "I see God! I see God!" The divinity school student wrote up his results very soberly.

The chemical that produced the snake that produced a sunburn was mescaline, and the blue pill taken by the astronauts of inner space was lysergic acid diethylamide. It is hard to believe now that lysergic acid, or LSD, was around for twenty years as a neutral and interesting chemical agent, because in the Sixties it became a symbol of sensuality and witchcraft and decadence and terror. Our attitudes and assumptions are part of our paradigm, so it is useful to have a brief excursion into some of these attitudes, to see what happened to the tools.

A Very Short History of Some American Drugs Familiar to Everybody

Our attitude toward the word "drug" depends on whether we are talking about penicillin or heroin or something in-between. The unabridged three-volume Webster's says a drug is "a chemical substance administered to prevent or cure disease or enhance physical and mental welfare" or "a substance affecting the structure or function of the body." Webster's should have added "mind," but they probably thought that was part of the body. Some substances that aren't drugs, like placebos, affect "the structure or function of the body," but they work because we *think* they're drugs.

We are a drug-using society. We take, for example, twenty thousand tons of aspirin a day, almost one aspirin per person in the whole country. Aspirin is a familiar drug from a family called salicylates, specifically, acetylsalicylic acid. It lowers body temperature, alleviates some types of pain, and stimulates respiration.

Nicotine is a familiar and widely recognized drug, a stimulant to the central nervous system. It is addictive. The toxic effects of nicotine have been detailed at great length by the Surgeon General. Americans smoke 600 billion cigarettes a year.

Alcohol is also a widely recognized drug. In the United States 70 million users spend $10 billion a year. Five million of the 70 million alcohol users are said to be addicts, that is, they have a physical dependence on the drug. Alcohol is unique, says the pharmacology textbook, because it is "the only potent pharmacological agent with which self-induced intoxication is socially acceptable." Alcohol is so much a part of everyday life we do not think of it, on the rocks or straight up, as a drug or a potent pharmacological agent.

Then there is the family of drugs called the xanthines. Americans take xanthines at the rate of 100 *billion* doses per year. Xanthines are alkaloids which stimulate portions of the cerebral cortex. They give you "a more rapid and clearer flow of thought, allay drowsiness. . . . motor activity is increased. There is a keener appreciation of sensory stimuli, and reaction time to them is diminished." This description, again from the pharmacology textbook, is similar to descriptions of cocaine and amphetamine. Of course, the xanthine addict pays a price. He is, says Sir Clifford Allbutt, Regius Professor of Medicine at Cambridge, "subject to fits of agitation and depression; he loses color and has a haggard appearance. The appetite falls off; the heart suffers; it palpitates, or it intermits. As with other such agents, a renewed dose of the poison gives temporary relief, but at the cost of the misery."

Xanthines are generally taken orally through "aqueous extracts" of the plants that produce these alkaloids, either in seeds or leaves. In the United States the three most common methylated xanthines taken are called caffeine, theophylline and theobromine. The seeds of *Coffea arabica* contain caffeine, the leaves of *Thea sinensis* contain caffeine and theophylline, and the seeds of *Theobroma cacao* contain caffeine and theobromine. In America the three are known as "coffee," "tea" and "cocoa," and they are consumed daily, at the rate of billions of pounds a year. They are generally drunk as hot drinks, but Americans also drink cold drinks containing caffeine from the nuts of the tree *Cola acuminata*. The original drinks ended in the word "cola," but now there are many "colas" which do not bear that name in the title. The early ads for Coca-Cola said it gave you a lift.

Coffee, tea, cocoa and cola drinks are all drugs. Caffeine is a central nervous system stimulant, theophylline less so, and theobromine hardly at all. All xanthines increase the production of urine. Xanthines act on smooth muscles—relaxing, for example, especially in the case of theophylline, bronchi that may have been constricted. Like the salicylates—aspirin—xanthines can cause stomach irritation. Caffeine can cause sleeplessness, and researchers have found that it causes chromosome breaks.

Maxwell House, meet the Regius Professor of Medicine. Is the stuff good to the last drop, or another dose of the poison? Is it a food, to be sold in supermarkets, or a stimulant to the central nervous system like the amphetamines? "The popularity of the xanthine beverages depends on their stimulant action, although most people are unaware of any stimulation," says the giant pharmacology text.

It is surprising to find substances we think of so cheerfully, perkin' in the pot, listed as drugs. That's the point. In our society, there are some drugs we think of as okay drugs, and other drugs make us gasp. A coffee drinker who drinks coffee all day and cannot function without it is just a heavy coffee drinker, but someone using a non-okay drug is a "drug user" or an "addict."

Consumer Reports asked: how did drugs with such potential hazard spread without arousing the legal repression and social condemnation aroused by other drugs? They were domesticated, it said. There was no illegal black market, the dosages were relatively small, and some people buffered the drug effect with cream and sugar.

The worst of what our society thinks of as "hard drugs" comes from the unripe capsule of the opium poppy. In the nineteenth-century United States, you could buy opiates at grocery stores and drugstores, and by mail. Godfrey's Cordial—a molasses, sassafras and opium combination—was especially popular. Genteel Southern ladies in lace and ruffles, smelling of verbena and other sweet things, sounding like Scarlett O'Hara, were slugging down daily a combination of opium and alcohol called laudanum. The first surveys of narcotics showed that women outnumbered men three to one, because "the husbands drank alcohol at the saloon, and the wives took opium at home."

The point of this capsule history is not to warn people from the perilous xanthines. (I drink them all, *Coffea arabica and Thea sinensis,* sweetened, no cream, please, and *Theobroma cacoa* on cold winter days, and *Cola acuminata* on warm summer ones, and I have to be paying attention to be aware of the stimulant action.)

Nor is it to diminish the danger of illegal narcotics. (Legal narcotics are part of legitimate medicine). There is no comparison between legal, domesticated, mild, buffered drugs and illegal and undomesticated ones, but it is society that has produced the legalities and the domestication. Illegal narcotics, producing huge profits and employing the worst criminal elements, are merchandised to the least stable elements of society, producing tremendous social problems.

A Coke at snack time, a drink before dinner, a cup of coffee after dinner, a cigarette with the coffee —very relaxing. Four shots of drugs. Domesticated ones. It would be rather comic to have addicts sneaking down dark alleys for a shot of coffee, but nicotine is so strong that when currencies fail— Germany right after World War II, for example— cigarettes become currency.

In some Muslim countries, you can sit and smoke

hashish all day at a café, but possession of alcohol will land you in jail; in the United States you can sit in a saloon ingesting alcohol all day, but possession of hashish will land you in jail.

The drug taken by the astonauts of inner space was, at that time, legal. It was also nonnarcotic and nonaddictive. It crops up in the story not only because it was used in the exploration of the mind, but because so many explorers in meditation, biofeedback and other disciplines went through a stage with it.

Lysergic acid diethylamide was invented by the Swiss. Curious to think of the Swiss, the symbol of sobriety and industry, watchmaking and cuckoo clocks, as having invented LSD, Librium and Valium, psychedelics and tranquilizers, the turn-ons and the turn-offs, but then the Swiss have been in the drug business since Paracelsus of Basle, roughly a contemporary of Columbus.

The World's First Acid Trip, and Subsequent Happenings

On April 16, 1943, Dr. Albert Hofmann, a chemist, was working in his lab at Sandoz, a pharmaceutical firm in Basel, Switzerland. He was working with the derivatives of ergot, a fungus that grows on grains. Sandoz had successfully marketed ergot derivative for use in obstetrics and in treating migraine headaches. Midway through Friday afternoon Hofmann decided to go home. He felt restless and dizzy. At home, "I lay down and immediately fell into a peculiar state similar to a drunkenness, characterized by an exaggerated imagination. With my eyes closed, fantastic pictures of extraordinary plasticity and intensive color seemed to surge towards me. After about two hours this condition disappeared." Hofmann had just taken the first acid trip.

He had been working with three chemicals. The effects of the first two were well known, so he must have unwittingly ingested the third. He and an associate had discovered it five years before, but when preliminary tests on animals revealed nothing of interest they put it aside. Since it was the twenty-fifth compound in the lysergic acid series, it had been named d-lysergic acid diethylamide, or LSD-25.

Hofmann went back to the lab the next week and took what he thought was a very small amount of his new chemical. He began taking notes: "mild dizziness . . . inability to concentrate . . . uncontrollable laughter." Because of the war there were no cars, so Hofmann got on his bicycle to ride the four miles home, probably the last time anybody has tried to ride a bicycle four miles on LSD. "My field vision swayed before me and was distorted like the reflections in an amusement park mirror. The faces of those around me appeared as grotesque, colored masks; marked motoric unrest." He also had "a clear recognition of my condition, in which state I sometimes observed, in the manner of an independent, neutral observer, that I shouted half insanely or babbled incoherent words. Occasionally I felt as if I were out of my body. Sounds were transposed into visual sensations so that from each tone or noise a comparable colored picture was evoked, changing in form and color kaleidoscopically." That was the second acid trip. Sandoz sent the new drug off to the University of Zurich, and Hofmann's associate, W. A. Stoll, wrote up the results of the testing. LSD was not toxic and was not addicting, but an extremely small dosage had profound results. Most drugs are measured in milligrams, or thousandths of a gram; LSD was measured in micrograms, or millionths of a gram. Five grains, an aspirin-sized tablet, could produce effects in 3,000 people.

The United States Army began to stockpile LSD. Therapists around the world began to use it with patients. It allowed, they said, repressed memories to come forth, and the material that came up could be better understood because it took the form of visual symbols. Yet, with all the imagery, the patient kept a state of awareness, and retained his insights after the experience. Originally, LSD, was called a hallucinogen, that is, an agent that causes hallucination. But the LSD ingester was not quite like, for example, an alcoholic with delirium tremens, who sees snakes and green elephants. The alcoholic thinks the snakes and green elephants are real; the LSD subject "does not ordinarily accept them as real. He remains aware that what he is experiencing is a drug-induced phenomenon." So LSD was not a hallucinogen. Dr. Humphrey Osmond, one of the first psychiatrists to use the drug, called it psychedelic, mind-manifesting or mind-expanding. Osmond is an Englishman of diverse enthusiasms whose speech comes in a torrent; he had sat up all night with Indians in peyote ceremonies, and he hoped LSD would be an aid to curing schizophrenia in his Saskatchewan hospital.

An American authority on LSD amassed some statistics: after the first seventeen years of LSD usage, it had been tried thousands of times, with medical supervision. Fifteen hundred papers had been written on it, and it was a promising research drug, suitable for the volunteers, the astronauts of inner space.

The Maryland Psychiatric Research Center reported great success in curing alcoholics. Researchers there and at the Cook County Hospital in Chicago and the Sinai Hospital in Baltimore tried LSD on terminal cancer patients in great pain. They reported that the pain diminished more than with opiates, that the pain no longer seemed important, and that the outlook under these grim sentences of death became more serene. They did caution that the results did not come from the psychedelics only; an experienced researcher or therapist came along with it.

No one ever said that the agents were not powerful, or that they were to be treated lightly, or that the experiences were all pleasant, or for entertainment. There were adverse psychological reactions possible in unstable people, but a review of the literature said "no instance of serious, prolonged physical side effects was found" in the use of psychedelics. One hospital team reported four such instances in 6,522 supervised sessions. The long-range effects had not been tested.

Then it all changed.

The Sixties took over, the psychedelics became a subcult, the partisans said it brought Utopia, the antagonists said it brought the plague; LSD became a terror symbol, which made it attractive to children whose bones had not fused and whose minds had not matured but who knew that the Establishment and the law and their parents were all lying. "The anti-LSD publicity, the scare campaigns, and the laws," said *Consumer Reports,* "helped to convert what had been [for twenty years] a relatively unknown and innocuous drug into a quite damaging one."

Sandoz Pharmaceutical stopped making LSD. It had been only an experimental drug, not the source of any real revenues, and Sandoz did not want to jeopardize its legitimate drugs. Restrictive laws were passed. The legitimate researchers turned in their drugs, sorrowfully. They were worried about black market LSD. One noted that all the statistics showing safety had come from clinicians and supervised surroundings. Another used the analogy of x-rays: they were an incredible boon to medicine, but if untrained people shot x-rays in all directions, there might be some damage. All the researchers worried that historic opportunity for exploration would be lost in all the sensationalism; it had taken hypnotism a hundred years to recover from "animal magnetism."

The laws were passed, the police were alerted, raids began, the generation gap widened, and the epidemic spread.

And a Short Chronicle of the Madness

The research in psychedelics now stands as a discrete unit in time, with finite boundaries, twenty years or so and a few thousand papers. We will come back to what was learned in a moment.

It would take an acute social historian to chronicle the epidemic, the children, the hippies, the parents, the law, the police, the media. LSD was colorless, odorless, not too expensive to produce, and a very small amount went a very long way. The markup from LSD to "street acid" was 1,000 percent to 3,000 percent. Two million people took what they thought was LSD, but except for brief periods (1965-66) almost all of it was bulked out with other active chemicals. A team of researchers reported in *Science* from nationwide samples that the "so-called LSD" was in many cases not LSD at all, but anything ranging from arsenic to rat poison. They said, uniformly, the drugs were not advertised, and "very frequently they contain only inert substances and/or dangerous drugs." Professor Charles Tart reported that many people who believe they had the experience never had any LSD."

Alas, the efforts of the entrepreneurs extended even to the organic items from woodland and forest, the psilocybin mushroom. Wide profit margins invite such activity. The mushrooms sold, reported another authority, were not directly from woodland and forest. They were from cans in the grocery store. Then they would be soaked in phencyclidine (PCP), a veterinary anesthetic that causes an alcohol-like intoxication and makes muscles feel rubbery. Frozen and packaged in plastic bags, the mushrooms were sold up and down the West Coast, "very trippy."

The consumers were not suspicious enough. They said: my LSD is pure, it's made by the graduate student in chemistry who wants to earn a little extra money, he just turns out enough for his friends. Or: "This is the real Owsley." For a while, it looked as though Owsley was going to have his name become part of the language, like Captain Boycott and Samuel Maverick and Mr. Booze of Glassboro, who stamped his names on the glass bottles used for spirits.

The acute social historian could chronicle Owsley, August Owsley Stanley III, grandson of a governor of Kentucky, sound man for the Grateful Dead, acid entrepreneur. Owsley's chemists in their hideaway lab in northern California took lysergic acid and ergotamine tartrate and produced a million tabs of Orange Sunshine, but Owsley was no Sandoz: like a crazed Julia Childs, he salted and peppered the Orange Sunshine with strychnine and amphetamines, trying recipes; he wanted to see what would sell best. A million tabs—that was just Orange Sunshine, the statistics on Clear-Lite and Window Pane and Purple Pie and Yellow Smash are uncertain, but all of them outsold Sandoz' all-time output.

When the children took the strychnine, or the arsenic, or the atropine, or the Methedrine, or even LSD—sometimes there really was a college chemist just cooking for his friends—they sometimes had adverse reactions, whereupon their friends dumped them into the emergency room of a hospital, an environment that can produce a bad trip in people who are stone cold sober and just passing through. Imagine being in the waiting room stoned and watching the bloody accident victims come in. It took years for the word to filter down: do not take the people on bummers to the hospital, or the doctor, doctors don't know. (Indeed, they did not know; harried interns and busy doctors do not read technical papers in experimental psychology, which would have been useful.)

The acute social historian would have to spend some time on Timothy Leary, handsome, charming, charismatic, the guru of the Brotherhood of Eternal

Love, a non-profit California corporation, itself merged into the League for Spiritual Discovery, patron saint of Orange Sunshine. Leary was a military child, the son of Eisenhower's dentist. He went to Holy Cross. Is he remembered in the alumni bulletin? He went to West Point for a year and a half. Are there generals at the outskirts of empire who recall him? He went to the University of Alabama. Did he watch the Crimson Tide roll?

As a young psychology instructor, Leary was thrown out of Harvard for his LSD experiments, together with his sidekick, Richard Alpert. Post expulsion, they landed in a fifty-five-room mansion in Millbrook, New York, owned by a Mellon heir, Billy Hitchcock, with the local cops peering through the bushes. The local cops were led by G. Gordon Liddy, later known as a Watergate burglar. Small world.

"Turn on, tune in, drop out," said the Pied Piper of psychedelics, and a lot of children did. The story is not over, but the social historian will be able to chronicle a fascinating tale: G. Gordon Liddy went to prison for burglarizing the Watergate, and Leary went to prison for possessing a fingernail's worth of marijuana, and Owsley went to prison and paid $142,276 in taxes, plus penalties, taxes due on unreported income from Orange Sunshine, and Richard Alpert went to India and became Baba Ram Dass, the very symbol of the seeker.

Aldous Huxley, the novelist, had written of psychedelics in *Heaven and Hell* and in *The Doors of Perception,* which described his own experience in the early 1950's with mescaline. Huxley brought great cultural depth to the experience, and Leary went to see him, since Huxley was the Respectable Intellectual of the Further Reaches. Leary's visit in 1962 brought forebodings to Huxley. "He talked such nonsense," Huxley wrote to Humphrey Osmond. " . . . this nonsense-talking is just another device for annoying people in authority, the reaction of a mischievous Irish boy to the headmaster of the school. One of these days the headmaster will lose patience—and then good-bye to the research. I am fond of [him], but why, oh why, does he *have* to be such an ass? I have told him repeatedly that the only attitude for a researcher in this ticklish field is that of an anthropologist living in the midst of a tribe of potentially dangerous savages. Go about your business quietly, don't break the taboos or criticize the locally accepted dogmas. Be polite and friendly—and get on with the job. If you leave them alone, they will probably leave you alone."

But Leary thought he was on the edge of a revolution, and did not heed the advice. "You are never the same after you've had that one flash glimpse down the cellular time tunnel," he said. "Turn on." The savages did not like having their customs taunted, and they put the anthropologist into a big iron pot and boiled him for supper.

An Evelyn Waugh guerrilla warfare broke out. One Briton traveled the fruit stalls of London, injecting the apples and oranges with LSD; another spiked the punch at a party given by Queen Juliana of the Netherlands, and made his escape in a stolen limousine. The savages stoked the fires higher.

Poor Dr. Hofmann of Basel, his name was not to be one with Pasteur and Salk and Fleming. Fifteen years after his LSD bicycle ride, in another burst of brilliance, he synthesized psilocybin, the element in the "magic mushrooms" used by Indian cultures for the ceremonial altering of consciousness. The Nobel prize committee looked the other way. He was not even getting royalties on LSD. The U.S. Patent Office supplied the formula for LSD for fifty cents.

For twenty years, from 1943 to 1963, the dissolving boundaries and unleashed memories and flowing feelings produced by the interaction of Dr. Hofmann's chemicals and minds brought no talk of revolution. The subjects and the therapists both had short hair, and society paid them no attention. Of the loves and fears that burbled beneath the surface with such intensity the researchers said, ve-r-y interesting. The Freudians found Freudian symbols. The Jungians found Jungian archetypes and the collective unconscious, the Rankians found separation anxiety, the Sullivanians found oral dynamism. In short, everybody found something, and they used their own language to describe it.

Much of the early work involved patients in therapy, but anthropologists and artists and social scientists were also beginning to show interest.

Then came: Free Speech, birth control pills, long hair, brotherly love, Flower Children, predators on the Flower Children, cops, narcotics, speed, laws, judges, politicians campaigning, busts, riots, Vietnam, war resisters, the Mafia, Richard Nixon, Woodstock. Confrontation.

Psychedelics were no longer experimental substances used by researchers to peel back the layers of the mind, they were a social issue—and a divisive one at that. LSD ADDICTS STARE AT SUN, the newspapers reported; no point in detailing the hoax, newspapers print what they believe sells. Someone at *The Saturday Evening Post* must have known that picture was thalidomide babies, not "LSD babies," but they gave it the LSD caption; more proof that the Establishment lies, said the counter-culture. Were there some chromosome breaks in the lab experiments? Why was that front-page, said the counter-culture, when the same breaks for caffeine and aspirin go unreported? Could it be because coffee and tea and aspirin are major advertisers?

The research was over. Just before it ended, the researchers were detailing several stages of the psychedelic trip. On the surface, there were all those distorted images, the fireworks, the color displays. That was not from "seeing"; it by-passed the optic system; blind people had the same displays. And then there were the images, winged beasts, mythic animals, everything eating everything; the perspectives and the colors and the images went into the art and the music. College bookstores sold posters by Magritte and Dali and Man Ray—and M. C. Escher; the perspectives suddenly looked familiar. The underwater figures in *The Yellow Submarine* swallowed everything; Sergeant Pepper's Lonely Hearts Club

Band played psychedelic imagery—if you missed it, the initials of "Lucy in the Sky with Diamonds" spelled it out.

The imagery appeared long before the research died out. "I want to play you something," said our friend in the record business, in a house over the Pacific surf. At that moment, the rumblings of confrontation were still in the future. The record producer was one of the explorers. A nasal, reedy voice came on, with this crazy harmonica—*he-y-y, Mis-ter Tambourine Man, play a song for me, take me on a trip upon your magic swirling ship, my senses have been stripped, my hands can't feel to grip—take me disappearing through the smoke rings of my mind, down the foggy ruins of time, far past the frozen leaves, the haunted, frightened trees, out to the windy beach, far from the twisted reach of crazy sorrow, to dance beneath the diamond sky with one hand waving free, let me forget about today until tomorrow . . .*

"Who is that guy?" I said.

The Tibetan *Book of the Dead* no longer seemed quite so exotic; in fact, it seemed quite familiar. Same old winged beasts, same old time tunnel. The Egyptian *Book of the Dead,* too. A new burst of interest in anthropology, a new burst of interest in Oriental religions. Richard Alpert's guru, in India, said of the psychedelics, "Well, America is a materialistic country, it is natural that it should find consciousness through a material."

A decade later, the tambourine man leading through the smoke rings of the mind was a golden oldie, and a Carly Simon song went:

You showed me how, how to leave myself behind
How to turn down the noise in my mind

Now I haven't got time for the pain

I haven't got room for the pain
I haven't the need for the pain

Not since I've known you . . .

a love song, one would think, but, as it turns out, about meditation, and a meditation teacher.

The children's epidemic that shut down the research seemed very remote to me at the time. I was at work on other things, and the confrontations came through like the dull thump of unseen artillery over the horizon. My guinea-pigging was long over, and the journals did not seem as interesting once the high excitement of being on the frontiers of mind faded. It was easy to let subscriptions lapse, because the next issue was unlikely to bring a paradigm-busting discovery.

What Did We Learn?

The research in psychedelics, seen from here, is just sitting there in midair, suspended and frozen, overtaken by events like a potter working at his wheel in Pompeii when the lava flowed past and preserved him.

It is interesting to know that psychedelics expand the pupil of the eye, letting in more light, disorganizing the perception. But not very, unless you are working with schizophrenics and noticing some similarities in eye muscles. It is interesting to note the visual displays that by-pass the optic system so that even blind people see wild dancing colors. But most of the research was either sponsored by the government for somewhat ill-defined purposes, or concerned with abnormal people. Out of thousands of papers, surprisingly few were for sheer exploration. But some of those had some fascinating observations.

The depths of the memory bank were stunning. Never mind the molecular diagram of the du Pont plastic; there were subjects who knew no physics and came up with physics, and subjects who knew no foreign languages and yet could speak them.

Dr. Jean Houston is a tall, attractive woman of enormous energy and exotic vocabulary who did a lot of research not only with psychedelics but with other consciousness-altering devices. (She constructed, for example, a "witches' cradle" that would swing the subject around, disorienting him and producing parallel effects to some psychedelics, much as the medieval "witches' cradles" would do.)

Jean Houston had a subject in an LSD experiment who was walking on the waterfront in ancient Athens with Socrates. That is, he was lying on a sofa with a mask on and a calibrated amount of blue Sandoz, and he said he was in Greece, walking around with Socrates.

"What does Socrates have to say?" asked Jean Houston.

"I don't know," said the subject, "he's talking in Greek, and I don't understand Greek."

"Well, I do," said Ms. Houston. "I took six years of Greek in school. Just repeat the words."

The time traveler reported the conversation, which was indeed *in classic Greek, which he did not understand!*

Remember the Denver housewife who, under hypnosis, could come up with the details of "a previous life" in Ireland, where she had lived as "Bridie Murphy"? She knew all the details of Bridie Murphy's neighborhood, in a country she had never visited.

There are other examples—the uneducated cleaning lady who could speak cultured German under hypnosis, and so on.

Surprising, but all this is well within the paradigm. The rational hypothesis runs: *we perceive more than we are aware of, and on some level we remember what we perceive.*

The brain is more complex than a computer; it is as if somebody pressed a button—RECORD—when we start life, and it is never turned off, though sometimes the amplification varies. All the sights and sounds and feelings are recorded.

The Denver housewife had a maid, or a nurse, as a little girl, who told her about Ireland, though she did not consciously remember the details. (That explanation isn't totally accepted by Bridie Murphy enthusiasts.) The cleaning lady cleaned for a German professor and overheard him talking. One day I was reading a magazine and I read the caption under the molecular model of Delrin, and hurriedly turned the page.

The recall mechanism doesn't necessarily do the job right. For example, I really do not care about Delrin, I wanted to express some feeling about the building blocks of existence. There was no DNA model filed in the memory bank, so the memory bank coughed up Delrin instead.

Jean Houston had other subjects who reported back from ancient Egypt and medieval Europe. Previous lives? "The details," she says, "are a tribute to television and the news magazines and schools. So much information pours into us—and goes right through us—but some of it sticks, and we carry it around."

Ordinarily, of course, we get no exposure to the depths of the memory bank. It takes a jolt that disorganizes our everyday perception, extreme stress ("My life flashed before me") or a drug that scrambles the familiar neuronal pathways in the brain. Consciously, we find it easier to remember words that we can associate with images, that are meaningful, than words that don't have meaning. Scrambling or stressing can bring up feelings tied to old images, or images not there but assembled for the purpose of illustrating a feeling, or images recorded but not comprehended.

Think of all the books in school, and all the voices of different teachers, and all the movies, and the clock on the wall of your own schoolroom, and thousands of TV programs—and then think of that REC-ORD button being on all the time. Could you sing a Czech drinking song? No? Are you sure that in all the choral music you've heard, and in all the segments of *Foreign Intrigue* on TV and in all the movies, there was no Czech song?

If there wasn't, the retrieval system will come up with something it considers close enough. Maybe it will play back a bit of Swedish from some Ingmar Bergman movie.

Out of conscious mind and willful memory things pass very quickly; we have statistics by experimental psychologists on how rapidly we forget. And yet there is all that stuff sitting sullen in the memory bank. Wilder Penfield, the neurosurgeon, reported that what came up with the touch of the electrode was, for the most part, trivia. Why on earth was that time traveler carrying ten sentences of classic Greek, and why on earth would I squirrel away a molecular diagram?

I began to see the retrieval system as a surly messenger boy with untied gym shoes and a scruffy jacket that says *Roosevelt High* across the back. You need to know somebody's name—his face is right there before you, saying hello—or your sister's phone number, and you hit RETRIEVE, and the kid ties his gym shoes, goes back to the stacks, gets a Pepsi-Cola from the vending machine, smokes a cigarette, and comes back with the line-up of the 1956 New York Giants or the lyrics to "Blue Suede Shoes."

Feelings came up as symbols. That was something else the researchers found; words being a bit leaden, people came up with symbols, clocks and beasts and dark woods. And then: there was a commonality to the symbols.

I went by a dark woods in one session. It was really rather frightening, and it took some urging from Mission Control to get me to go in. My voice on the tape says: "Well, okay, but I'm going to hang this tape recorder on this tree, and if I don't come back, first person to see this tape recorder, come in and get me." (There was no tree, and there was a tape recorder, but they seemed equally real at the time, as real as the fear of not finding the way back.)

But it wasn't just me. Everybody had a dark woods in the middle of their head, and sooner or later they got around to it. So when Bob Dylan sang about the foggy ruins of time, past the frozen leaves, the haunted, frightened trees, he touched a universal of sorts.

Why did so many normal, integrated psychedelic subjects come up with the symbol of the dark woods? (There were a number of papers by psychologists on The Meaning of the Forest.) One answer could come from the extent of the retrieval system. You are in a disorienting situation, sensitive to the least suggestion, open to a flow of emotions greater than usual, and this recalls a childhood situation when emotions flow stronger, a Disney movie with dark woods, the illustration in a Grimms' fairy tale. The dark woods is a pervasive symbol in all of Western civilization. The prescript for the first chapter of this book is from the *Divine Comedy*: "In the middle of the journey of our life, I found myself in a dark wood." (What about other civilizations? The research never got intercultural enough before it stopped.) But the retrieval system answer didn't seem complete enough.

Symbols, of course, are old stuff to psychiatric theory. Some people don't like elevators, and some people have dreams about taking exams, and some people are afraid of flying. They know the elevator is okay and the plane isn't going to crash and the exam was years ago, but still wake up in a sweat because the exam in French 203 is tomorrow and they haven't done the work, or they drive a thousand miles rather than fly because they can't help it, the symbol is attached to a feeling and the feeling is still there.

That people are walking around with a woods in their head is taken for granted by some psychologists, but they have their own favorite symbols. One friend of mine leads transactional marathons. That's where everybody arrives Friday night and stays up, slogging, and by about four o'clock Sunday morning people say some interesting things. My friend's symbol was the Judge. Everybody had the Judge in their heads, and their actions and behavior would be shaped to what the Judge said. My psychologist would tape these encounters, and he would keep spinning the tape recorder like some electronic surveillance expert, and sure enough there would be sentences in there that belonged to the Judge and not to the people who said them. The eerie part was that between FORWARD and REWIND, as the recorder closed in on the phrases, the voices would actually change; the Judge had a different voice from the speaker's, like the demon in *The Exorcist*. My psychologist, index fingers on FORWARD and REWIND like a true virtuoso, would say, "Whose voice is that?" The voice would be something out of the past, a parent or teacher, or perhaps not even a real parent or teacher but a child's idea of those people, still alive in mid-age and mid-voice.

The psychedelic researchers were well enough versed. Jean Houston and her husband, R. E. L. Masters (no relation to Masters and Johnson), declared four stages in *The Varieties of Psychedelic Experience*. First there was the sensory stage, the geometry of the room changing, the light displays, the crossing of sound and vision, called synesthesia. That was almost universal. Then some subjects went on to a second stage, called recollective-analytical by Houston and Masters. This is the extended memory bank. Still fewer subjects went on to a third stage, the symbolic or mythic. And a very few went on to a fourth stage, integral, or mystic.

In the third stage—the Meaning of the Forest and all that—the subject in the experiment would go through, present tense, something that we would recognize as a myth: a sacred quest, a child hero, paradise and fall, eternal return, polarity (light and darkness, order and chaos). The subject, lying there with the mask and the blue Sandoz, would be the character in the myth. The thesis of Houston and Masters was that these turned up because "our society offers so little in the way of the important rites of passage and initiation provided by other civilizations."

If we never saw a Disney movie or read a Grimms' fairy tale, how do we get a dark woods in the middle of the head?

We inherit it, some people speculate. We know, for example, that if you pass a V-shaped shadow sideways or backwards over a baby chick in a lab, nothing happens. But if you move the same shadow forward, the baby chick goes into a panic. He has inherited the genetic message—*hawk, danger*—for a certain-shaped shadow, even though he is only a couple of days old and has not talked to his mother and may never see a hawk. Children from five to ten are afraid of the dark, and the animals they see in the dark—animals we know aren't there—are the same across the lines of cultural childhood. There was a time when humanity slept by the fire and the predators really were there in the dark. One cell carries the instructions on how to make a whole new person: let's see, make the eyes brown, make the ears thus, make the nose thus, let's set the trigger for adolescent growth at 12.2 years, and oh, yes, let's throw in the message about the bears, predators by the fire, for ages five to nine.

Stanislas Grof led a research team in Czechoslovakia. (Later, he came to the United States.) Grof ran more than 2,600 LSD sessions. Behind the thick carapace of daily life were violent emotions, devils and angels, love, hate, murder, jealousy. The dominant myth in Grof's accounts was death and rebirth. When the subjects were reborn, they went down the birth canal, twisting and grimacing, and exploded into the world again. On the mythic level, they identified with the death and resurrection of Christ. Alcoholics were not just drinking; they were trying hard to get to a space called DIE.

Grof is a Freudian psychoanalyst. But no existing theoretical system covered, for him, the phenomena that were coming up: "Freudian analysis barely scratches the surface," he said. "The model of personality and image of man emerging from LSD research is much closer to Hindu philosophy than to the Freudian concepts widely accepted by Western science and philosophy . . . [that is,] the human mind as a multilayered dynamic structure with elements of the individual and collective unconscious, as well as karmic and evolutionary memories buried in its depths."

Really? Could the disorganized Hindus have even a vague concept more complete at some level than ours?

R. Gordon Wasson is a businessman turned world's greatest mushroom expert. He has chewed with shamans from Siberia to Guatemala. The Hindu Vedas had referred to a godly substance, soma. In 1972 Wasson identified soma as a hallucinogenic mushroom, *Amanita muscaria*. The layers of the mind, as spun by *Amanita muscaria*, had already been catalogued for thousands of years, but not in the nice, neat way we like it—all analyzed with cause and effect. Much of it, in fact, was incomprehensible, all wound up with legends and myths. Did the legends and myths produce the layers of the mind, or the layers of the mind produce the legends and myths?

And what of the fourth stage, the integral or mystic experience? This is the most lightly researched of all, for no one knows exactly how to define a mystic experience.*

Trying to chart the mystic aspects, or perhaps playing turn on the clergy, Timothy Leary gave LSD to seventy certified pastors and priests. The religious myths and symbols were rampant in their minds, much as they had been for the divinity school student doing his Good Friday experiment. A Hasidic rabbi went outside into the garden about four o'clock in the morning. The trees, he said, had faces and arms which were threatening but which became friendly if you said, "Nice trees." "Sha, sha, trees," said the rabbi,

---

* Two sociologists, Andrew Greeley and William McCready, gave it the following attempt: "They are episodes of intense and immediate cognition in which the total personality of a person is absorbed in an intimate though transient relationship with the basic forces, cycles and mechanisms at work in the universe and in his own psychosomatic composite—gravity, cosmic rays, light, heat, electromagnetism, cycles of breathing, circulation, digestion, day, year, life, death."

"next time I will be a tree and you will be a human being."

Later the rabbi wrestled with the experience: was it a genuine *aliyath han'shamah,* an ascent of the soul as described by the founding rabbi of the Hasidic sect, the great Baal Shem-Tov? It certainly was something extraordinary. Did it turn plain folks into saints? He didn't think so. It upset him a bit, and left him with more questions than answers.

Aldous Huxley had suggested, in *The Doors of Perception,* that certain experiences, usually considered religious, which came from severe fasting and chanting, might also be available from vegetables, such as mushrooms. Were the experiences the same? A genteel and scholarly debate went on, intellectual Jesuits, theology professors, Oxford dons—were the experiences a "gratuitous grace"?

These shadings were lost in the roar of the Sixties. Jean Houston wrote, "It is frequent and funny, if also unfortunate, to encounter young members of the Drug Movement who claim to have achieved a personal apotheosis when, in fact, their experience appears to have consisted mainly of depersonalization, disassociation, and similar phenomena." But when the psychedelics were merchandised, IT—the Experience —became part of the commercial, along with peer pressure and curiosity.

It should be noted for the record that Albert Hofmann did not have a mystic experience in the lab at Sandoz. He felt dizzy and saw all those crazy colors, and the geometry of the room changed, and he went home and called a doctor. And for many years afterward, the experiences produced by the psychedelics were, for some reason, not thought of as "mystic."

We have been folding and unfolding some of the old maps, the stories of old expeditions. The stories are fascinating, but we cannot linger too long.

William James, resplendent in Victorian beard, Professor of Psychology at Harvard when there was almost no psychology, himself went on just such map-making expeditions. In contemporary psychology, James is barely looked on as a psychologist. He did not put knife to brain of rat. He did not set up experiments with controls, plain cats vs. dizzy cats. He did not take any polls. He never gave children funny-shaped blocks and clocked them. How could he be a psychologist? Maybe he belongs to philosophy; in psychology now we find him archaic and a bit speculative.

There were no synthetic chemicals for William James. He tried mushrooms. They made him violently ill, and gave him a monumental hangover, and once was enough. "I will take the visions on trust," said William James to Henry James. But after his experiment with nitrous oxide James wrote a paper, and then later he wrote an essay on the dimensions in life. In the essay was a paragraph which gets quoted over and over and over in the more speculative, non-rat parts of mind exploration. And this is it:

"One conclusion was forced upon my mind at that time, and my impression of its truth has ever since remained unshaken. It is that our normal waking consciousness, rational consciousness as we call it, is but one special type of consciousness, whilst all about it, parted from it by the filmiest of screens, there lie potential forms of consciousness entirely different. We may go through life without suspecting their existence; but apply the requisite stimulus, and at a touch they are there in all their completeness, definite types of mentality which probably somewhere have their field of application and adaptation. No account of the universe in its totality can be final which leaves these other forms of consciousness quite disregarded. How to regard them is the question—for they are discontinuous with ordinary consciousness. Yet they may determine attitudes though they cannot furnish formulas, and open a region though they fail to give a map. At any rate, they forbid a premature closing of our accounts with reality."

". . . they may determine attitudes though they cannot furnish formulas," said James, seeming to anticipate Freud, "and open a region though they fail to give a map."

And that is still where we are.

II. Hemispheres

Left Side, Right Side,
Why Ralph Nader Can't Dance

It is amusing to think that we could all have buried, in the depths of memory, some damn Czech drinking song. It is amusing, because we are not children any more, to think that the little beggars are afraid of bears in the dark when we know there aren't any bears. It is not so amusing to think that we have these symbols influencing our behavior, exams from long ago still there, and cops finding us naked on the streets at midnight. And for everybody to have some symbol in common, the dark woods in the middle of the head, gets a bit discomforting.

But neurophysiology and the skills of surgery have not found, in the brain, at any given location, a Czech drinking song, or a bear, or an exam, or a dark woods. Yet there is, in the structure of the brain, a division of function which affects our individual and social behavior. Not only that, it gives us a metaphor for a whole area of psychology that is not traditionally even in psychology.

The research in this area is called split-brain research, or lateral specialization, getting more attention now. It says that we have a mute self, and we don't usually know it's there because it can't talk, and the only way we know something is there is if it makes more noise than we do when we talk to ourselves. The mute self is at least potentially a dancer, an athlete, a sculptor—maybe screaming to get out, but not knowing the words.

Brains are divided into left and right. More specifically, a part of the brain most important for thought, called the cerebral cortex, is divided into left and right. A hundred years or so ago, the surgeons would notice that a damaged left half stopped speech, and a damaged right half stopped spatial recognition. Expression on the left side, recognition on the right, said the neurologist Hughlings Jackson, 1864. In the last few years, the research has accelerated.

The left brain controls the right side of the body, the right hand. And, cross-court again, the right brain controls the left side of the body. The left side is verbal, rational, functioning and practical. Left hemisphere, right-handed. The right side of the brain, intuitive, spatial, is the artist and dreamer.

Every culture in the world, with or without physiology, has picked this up, usually in terms of left-handed and right-handed. *The Left Hand Is the Dreamer,* novel title. Law and order in French is *le droit,* the right; an illegitimate descendant is *à main gauche,* on the left hand. The Australian aborigines hold a "male" stick in the right hand, and a "female" stick in the left hand. The Mohave, the Bedouin and the Bantu all have the concept that the right side is the father, the left, maternal and passive. "We listen for the heart on the left," wrote psychologist Jerome Bruner, in *On Knowing; Essays for the Left Hand,* "though it is virtually in the center of the thoracic cavity. Sentiment, intuition, bastardy."

Up to the ages of six to ten or so, both halves of the brain operate. After that, speech becomes specialized in the left side of the brain. If a small child suffers brain damage on the left side, the right side will take over language functions. But the same damage in adults leaves them mute. Damage to the right side, in an adult, interferes with musical ability, spatial ability, recognition of people, body awareness. (This is necessarily over-simplified, and is based on right-handers. Left-handers also speak with the left side of the cortex, but some are bilateral and a few are reversed.)

The captain of left-right research is a graying

Cal Tech professor, Roger Sperry. It was his contribution to show that both halves of the brain operate independently. In fact, sometimes the left half doesn't know what the right half is doing.

Sperry's team worked on epileptics whose left and right halves had been disconnected from each other in order to stop their seizures. "What is experienced in the right hemisphere seems to be entirely outside the realm of awareness in the left hemisphere," Sperry wrote.

For example: a subject would be blindfolded, and a familiar object—a comb, let's say—would be placed in the subject's left hand. Left hand, right brain. And the subject wouldn't be able to say, "That's a comb." The subject could *demonstrate* using a comb, and he could pick a comb from a whole pile of objects, so the right hemisphere indeed *knew* what a comb was, it just couldn't get out the word "comb."

The patient is still blindfolded. Now they let the left brain work—the right hand creeps over, feels the comb, and immediately, the subject says, "Comb."

Did the two halves of the brain get in each other's way? Wouldn't they get into conflict? Something like that, Sperry reported. "The left hand, after just helping to tie the belt of the patient's robe, might go ahead on its own to untie the completed knot, whereupon the right hand would have to supervene again to retie it. The patient and his wife used to refer to the 'sinister left hand' that sometimes tried to push the wife away aggressively at the same time that the hemisphere of the right hand was trying to get her to come and help."

As good as it was at knot-trying, the right hemisphere was hopeless at math. It couldn't even double the number four.

Furthermore, the left brain wouldn't trust its twin. It knew the left hand belonged to the right brain. So, in the split-brain patients, the left brain wouldn't believe that the left hand could retrieve the comb out of the bag, as if to say, that dummy can't do anything without me. When they were asked to reach with the left hand, patients would say the left hand was numb, or just didn't work. If the left hand did the job, the patient would say, "I was just guessing."

Sperry felt the right half was badly underrated in our society. Some of his papers read as if he is about to call the Civil Liberties Union and demand a better break for the Right Brains. "Excellence in one hemisphere tends to interfere with top-level performance in the other," Sperry said. If that's true, then Ralph Nader and the superrational lawyers and great mathematicians should make lousy dancers. (If any of them show up in a corps de ballet, their courtroom skills or their calculations should suffer. On the other hand—a figure of speech well ingrained—right-sided activities should be a nice vacation for verbal, rational people. Smart old Winston Churchill. Between volumes, writing the life of his ancestor, the Duke of Marlborough, or between speeches, he would daub away in the meadow, or build a brick wall.)

So: we experience outside of language—right-brained—but we can't communicate that experience in words without running it through the left brain. To be "knowledge," to live beyond the moment, it has to be communicated or articulated. "A thought comes," said Einstein, "and I may try to express it in words later."

The experimenters got to work. If you balanced something on each index finger, and timed it, and then repeated the balancing, this time talking while you balanced, would the time be the same? No: talking cut the balancing time. One activity inhibits the other.

If you were looking at a friend, and you asked which way George Washington faces on a quarter, would his eyes go left or right while he thought? Which way would they go if you asked, what is one hundred minus seven times two?

(Some of my friends, curve-busters to the end, shut their eyes, or rolled them straight up.)

"We added emotion to the lateral eye movements,"

said Harvard's Gary Schwartz. "Emotion is nonverbal, so it's right-brained. We would ask, what's the difference between 'thought' and 'rational' and track the eyes. Then we would ask, which do you feel more often, tearful or angry? The abstract questions led the eyes right, the emotional ones left."

Two researchers at the University of California Medical Center, David Galin and Robert Ornstein, asked: do the hemispheres work continuously in parallel and alternate body control, or do they share? In most activities, they concluded, we pick one and inhibit the other. Who could learn to ride a bicycle from purely verbal instruction?

Ornstein went further in his books *On the Psychology of Meditation* and *The Psychology of Consciousness.* The opposites had long been known: rational and emotional, Dionysius and Apollo, intellectual and intuitive. "Argument and experience are the two modes of knowing," said Roger Bacon. The complementarity had been known, and the left-right distinction in physiology had been known. The Italian psychiatrist Roberto Assagioli had noted how gingerly intellectuals treated intuition. Roger Sperry pointed out how our whole society was built on the left-sided presumptions of the verbal and rational. Robert Ornstein made a kind of metaphor of the right brain. To the unexplored right side, he said, belonged the "esoteric psychologies" of Sufism and yoga, dervish dancing and chanting, mantra and "magic words," meditation—all unexplored territory, from the left-sided, Western point of view.

To think of Oriental religions as Eastern psychologies, right-brained and left-handed, gave a new perspective. They would seem strange to us because we are left-brained, verbal and rational: they wouldn't make any "sense."

The *I Ching,* that venerable Chinese document, expressed the left-right complementarity by dividing the world into light and dark, creative and receptive. The *I Ching* itself is a right-brained document.

There was a time, in this research, when the *I*

Ching appeared simultaneously in the worlds I was shuttling between: psychology and finance. Psychology, well, yes, right-brained Eastern esoterica, but the *I Ching* and the stock market?

The I Ching Comes to Wall Street

There are no coincidences, said Carl Gustav Jung, the great Swiss psychiatrist. We think they're coincidences because our model of the world doesn't account for them. We're tied up in cause and effect.

The adventure of the *I Ching* on Wall Street began with one day's mail. At the time, I was out in "experiential" courses of some sort, right-brained, left-handed stuff, and the journals would pile up on my desk. Psychology journals and financial journals. The psychology journals I thought of as The Adventures of Freddie the Rat, In Which Our Investigators Reveal Some New and Dramatic Clockings.

And amidst The Adventures of Freddie the Rat, mixed in, were the economic journals, in this case a whole batch from the Wharton School of the University of Pennsylvania. Nice white plastic covers. Somebody had written, "The Association Between a Market Determined Measure of Risk and Alternative Measures of Risk." Somebody else had written, "The Error Learning Hypothesis and the Term Structure of Interest Rates in Eurodollars."

I know about the term structure of interest rates. It is full of equations that will bite you, and little Greek letters lying on their sides.

Someone at the Wharton School had added a title in ink at the bottom of the mimeographed list of published titles, maybe just for me. This paper was in the series but it hadn't been published. It was: "Can the *I Ching* predict the stock market?"

The *I Ching* and the stock market! Far out!

The *I Ching*, pronounced "E Jhing," not "eye Ching," is an ancient Chinese book of wisdom used to tell you what course of action to take and what the future may bring. It has sold one million copies in the last five years. You toss three coins or forty-nine yarrow stalks—most Americans throw three coins—and from the results of the tosses you create a hexagram, and then you look up the hexagram in the *I Ching*. I was learning not to scoff at such right-brained activities, since the left brain is the scoffer, but even not scoffing the *I Ching* sometimes seemed like a bag of fortune cookie slips from a Chinese bakery. "Youthful folly has success," said the *I Ching*. "The maiden is powerful. One should not marry such a maiden. It furthers one to undertake something."

Still, this was not some lunatic fringe, this was the Wharton School of Business and Finance, and there was the *I Ching*, right under the term structure of interest rates in Eurodollars.

I bought a $7.50 Bollingen edition of the *I Ching* and hastened to Philadelphia. On the train I noticed that the title of a best seller on the Vietnam war was taken from Hexagram #49: "FIRE IN THE LAKE. The image of REVOLUTION . . . starting brings misfortune. Perseverance brings danger. Changing the form of government brings good fortune."

The *I Ching* paper, it turned out, had been done by a student of a young, mustachioed professor, Dan Rie. Rie is a mathematical economist, into random walks and such, teaching security analysis. What do I spy on his shelves? *The Power of Witchcraft, The Magic Power of Your Mind* and a button that says REALITY IS A CRUTCH. I am on the right track.

"I had a student," said Rie, "who was into the Guru Maharaj Ji. He was a good student, but he said he wasn't interested in writing a thesis on capital asset pricing or income velocity, the only thing that interested him was the *I Ching*. Every day when he got up he would throw the *I Ching,* and he would follow its dictates. Other than the *I Ching,* he was into the stock market. So I said he could do his thesis on the *I Ching* and the stock market."

Wharton is a business school, and finance deals in precision, however artificial. Onto the computer went the *I Ching.* The heads-tails construction is a binary form anyway, and then the student assigned a range of numerical values for the hexagrams, started with A on the stock market page, and asked the *I Ching* about the first eighty stocks. "Whereas Aristotelian logic attempts to find causes, and on that basis make projections, the *I Ching* prefers to find patterns," said the thesis. "The potential of the moment is the future. The future however is to an extent dependent on the past. The basic circular nature of the *I Ching* patterns is now seen. Circles seldom have reasons."

"In his first sample," Rie said, "the *I Ching* significantly outperformed all the random portfolios. The department got quite interested."

I bet they did. I could see them, teacups trembling in the faculty common room—maybe they've tapped an ancient power, like atomic energy, Keynes after all endowed his Cambridge college by stock market speculations, what if the thing works? It's academically unrespectable, they would have to do it quietly, maybe hit the computer at night when nobody was around—

"So we ran the *I Ching* on two hundred and forty stocks. This time it did significantly less well."

I asked what time period the *I Ching* was being asked to predict. Eighty days, Rie said. That seemed like a short time for so venerable an instrument.

"When the *I Ching* didn't do as well the second time, the department cooled off," Rie said. "We're still working on it. Now we have the Fu Shi Circle on the computer, as well as the binary values and the subjective assignments." The Fu Shi Circle is a further refinement of the *I Ching.*

"So you really believe it works?" I asked.

Rie was cautious. "There is a mode of causality outside what we perceive," he said. "I collect these things but I don't have great faith in any one of them.

The *I Ching,* you see, gives you the answer you *need* rather than the one that is 'correct.' It works in your long-run best interest, maybe longer than a single life-time. To the *I Ching,* this lifetime is a minor mani-festation of something bigger."

I said I would like to concentrate on stocks for this lifetime—in fact, for the immediate future.

"Even if it works, I doubt if the *I Ching* will be used in security analysis," Rie said. "If the AT&T pension fund was run according to the *I Ching,* the managers just wouldn't be able to conform to it. They wouldn't be able to keep their hands off."

We got out the coins and the *I Ching* and the handy computer reference, and tried on a couple of stocks for size.

"Okay, *I Ching.*" I said. "IBM."

IBM came up *Shih.* Hexagram #7. K'un, the Re-ceptive, over K'an, the Abysmal.

"The superior man increases his masses," Rie said.

"I guess they'll throw out the antitrust suit," I said. "IBM will increase its share of the market."

We gave IBM a bullish reading.

I tried American Can.

"Enthusiasm," said the *I Ching.* "It furthers one to install helpers and to set armies marching."

"Gee, that's good," I said. "I wonder if they know how good business is going to be. I hope they're ready to put on the second and third shifts. Maybe they should build a new plant. Looks real good for Ameri-can Can," I said. "Let's try Leasco."

"If someone is not as he should be, he has mis-fortune," the *I Ching* said.

"Well, they shouldn't have tried to raid the Chemi-cal Bank, that was hubris, they're still trying to shake off that reputation," I said. Leasco had an unstable line in its hexagram: If you really get into the *I Ching,* you learn about unstable lines. The unstable line converts to another hexagram, which we looked up, for Leasco. It came out Work On What Has Been Spoiled.

"They'll be okay," I interpreted, "if they clean up

their accounting procedures and keep their nose clean."

When asked about the market, the *I Ching* hedged. At first it said, "Strength with elegance . . . leads to great wealth," and then it converted sourly, a black cloud over the sun, "Undertakings bring misfortune."

"I think one uses the *I Ching* to support what he already thinks," I said. "I've seen this with the people that consult the computer about the stock market."

"It works better when you're really sincere," Rie said. "When the second batch of stocks didn't come through, we asked the *I Ching* why our method wasn't working. The *I Ching* said, 'Even the best of hunters finds no game in an empty field.' "

To Jung, the *I Ching* was no bag of fortune cookie slips. He studied it for thirty years and wrote the preface to the Bollingen *I Ching*. He warned that the *I Ching* was not for "the frivolous minded and immature, nor is it for intellectualists and rationalists." He was impatient with "the heavy-handed pedagogic approach that attempts to fit irrational phenomena into a preconceived rational pattern."

The great attraction to Jung was that the *I Ching* presented a way to explore the unconscious. "If the *I Ching* is not accepted by the conscious, at least the unconscious meets it halfway, and the *I Ching* is more closely connected with the unconscious than with the rational attitude of consciousness."

In the West, cause and effect are assumed in the paradigm. The *I Ching* blithely ignores cause and effect; it is concerned with the quality of the exact moment the coins are thrown. Our Western axioms of causality are "merely statistical truths and thus must allow for exceptions," Jung wrote, "every process is partially or totally interfered with by *chance*," and it was this chance which the Chinese mind was concerned with. The yarrow stalks thrown to the floor formed the pattern characteristic of the moment, but that only meant something when you added the observer's knowledge. The Chinese, in other words, had skipped Aristotle and Newton and gone right to the probabilities of quantum mechanics, in which the observer had to be part of the process.

If you know any of Jung, you can see why he was attracted to the *I Ching*. Here is his theory of the collective unconscious, and here are the archetypes that are the same for everybody in the unconscious, the Wise Old Man and the Dark Woods and the Earth Mother and so on. And then here is this ancient Chinese document, which operates with archetypes, heaven and lake, prince and maiden, fire and earth. Further, Jung coined the term "synchronicity," which he opposed to causality. Causality was just a working hypothesis of how events evolve out of each other; synchronicity took the coincidence of events in space and time as more than chance, an interdependence of the event and the psychic state of the observer.

I got myself an *I Ching* teacher. My *I Ching* teacher did not have a long white goatee and speak in the fortune cookie talk of *Kung Fu*. He had two Ph.D.'s, one in economics, one in psychology, and he had read every word Jung had ever written, which is why my reading of the *I Ching* has such a Swiss accent. "Think of the *I Ching* as decision theory," said my teacher the economist. "What is your decision—consult the *I Ching*—see if you change the decision—the *I Ching* is information input, how beneficial is the additional information—utility maximization, cost benefit analysis." "The *I Ching* can free your intuition," said my teacher the psychologist. "You project your own unrealized thoughts onto its symbolism, just like Jung said in the foreword."

I asked the *I Ching* whether the study of it was a proper use of my energy. "The Clinging, Fire," said my teacher. "Your own idea implies that time and energy are finite. You are going to cram in as much as you can as fast as you can, or bewail and discard it. Time brings illumination, without the polarity you project."

That made me a bit dizzy, but I kept on practicing. One realization grew on me: the Wharton School had the *I Ching* pointed in the wrong direction, like using a microscope to view the stars, or a telescope to look at cells. The *I Ching*, Jung had said, was like having an old and courteous friend—I supposed a Ben Franklin, who would talk to you in axioms. Asked about the stock market, the old and courteous friend got vague and could not find his glasses. The *I Ching* should not be pointed at an *object,* such as a list of stocks, but at the *mind* of the questioner. That is the only Western use of the *I Ching*: to tell you what you already know in your own mind, but may not be listening to because of old habit patterns, or other voices in your head.

I wrote a respectful letter to the Wharton School on the subject of the *I Ching,* recommending that they unhook it from the computer and turn it around. If random-walk theoreticians asked the *I Ching* about the stock market, what they were going to get back would be a random walk.

I suspect the Wharton School was turning back to income velocity. In the next list of papers, there was no *I Ching;* in fact, Dan Rie was there with "Security Analysis in Efficiency Markets."

Then I went to Wall Street with the *I Ching* under my arm.

I would sit in the conference room of the firms I called on, and one by one the partners would come in and ask the *I Ching* a question.

Why did they put up with this? The moment is important, as the *I Ching* says. They were confused. Five years previous, they would not have taken the time, and their assumptions were that since they were smart, they put information together and evaluated it in such a way that they made a lot of money. But now everybody who was in the market at all was losing money—indeed, all this professional management was doing worse than the random averages. (In one investment partnership, my partners put out a monthly memo in which, month after month, they explained this performance with carefully rational reasons, saying they were right and the market was wrong. The next month again they would say they were right and the market was wrong because their reasons were right. If you're stubborn, you can lose a fortune with causality and plain logic.)

I explained that the *I Ching* was not about to predict the market, but maybe it would bring something up out of their minds, and they should pay attention to that something. They would throw the coins and I would simply read the hexagram and its interpretation and ask them what it meant.

Dick threw Work On What Has Been Spoiled, Keeping Still, Mountain, over The Gentle, Wind. He had asked about his view of the market. "That's very good," he said. "Very good. It means pay attention, and don't get sucked into the rallies. See, it says, 'Setting right what has been spoiled by the father.' Well, that means that the last guy to run this portfolio missed the market completely. We need a new tack. Intellectually is not the way to make money."

The hexagram had an unstable line, which converted to #46, Pushing Upward.

"You see that? You see that?" Dick said. "Encounters no obstruction! That confirms my technical position! When there are spikes off the bottom on the chart, we hit the supply!"

Dick was so turned on by the *I Ching's* confirmation of his technical position that he wanted another turn, but Chuck was waiting at the door to the conference room.

"I only have a couple of minutes," Chuck said. "I got a big European bank coming in here. I want to know: should I play my logic against other people's emotions, which is the way that's always worked for me?"

"*Shih Ho*, Biting Through," I read. I handed him the interpretation.

He nodded as he read. "Okay, this means Do you have the guts to do it? Go ahead. See—'Traitor': 'Traitor' is those who act emotionally. I've been feeling wishy-washy and giving decisions to Jack. I should make the decisions because I'm gentler. And when the lightning comes, there's a storm ahead, lightning clears the air. Once people see that the storm has cleared the air, rationality will prevail. So you buy at sensible prices and forget the storm. Thanks, my big bank is here."

"Splitting Apart," the *I Ching* said to Al. "It does not further one to go anywhere."

"That's easy," Al said. "You remain quiet. Nothing to do about the accounts, they will go through their steps. Wait till things get right. Let's see, 'Steep and narrow must topple over.' That means the growth stocks are going to get killed. 'Favor comes through the court ladies'—what the hell does that mean, date the secretaries? 'A large fruit still uneaten' means money in undervalued situations."

Does the *I Ching* really work?

There are all those people who swear by it, skiers who leave home on a warm ground-bare day, and when they get to the mountains there's the snow. If the *I Ching* says, "It does not further one to go anywhere," and you leave your home and get into a big traffic jam, you say, 'Well, the *I Ching* said so," and if you don't know the *I Ching* that morning, it's just another traffic jam. In order to have predictive power, the *I Ching* would have to be operating in some system of time other than the one we have in our paradigm.

But as a symbol around which unconscious thoughts can be projected—well, that is the area Jung thought so promising, and one which we use so little that anything we do seems like progress.

I did not keep up with my *I Ching* lessons, nor did I check to see how the *I Ching* had done in the stock market. It could not possibly have done worse than most of the professionals I knew. Using it for the market seemed almost a little profane for one of the world's great documents. Something must have worked, though, because a couple of months later I got a phone call from a busy trading room, with shouts of numbers in the background.

"Hey, where you been?" said the voice. "What the hell are you doing these days? Nobody ever sees you."

There was something in the caller's voice that made me ask what was on his mind.

"You know that Chinese book you had? I got a question for it. I already threw the coins, to save time. First line, two heads and a tail. Second line, one head, two tails."

I interrupted to ask: what was the question?

"Ask that book if my wife knows about my girl friend."

"The *I Ching* does not take calls over the phone," I said. "The best of hunters finds no game in an empty field," I added.

There is one more point. To pay profound attention, really profound attention, to the exact pattern made by forty-nine yarrow stalks in a moment requires a meditative state, almost a trance, and the serious users of the *I Ching* in the era of King W'en, like the oracles at Delphi, were most likely in some altered state of consciousness. I doubt that the subliminal and ethereal powers of mind have much chance to work in the five minutes before the man from the big bank arrives, or in a quick toss of the coins before breakfast. If we pull the *I Ching* into the rational, analytic, left-brained world we live in, we get fortune cookie stories and reruns of *Kung Fu* from this old and revered gentleman. Maybe the people who swear it works take the time, maybe they trance easily, and maybe the old gentleman is laughing up his flowered sleeve.

On the Left Hand (Right Brain), America's Leading Ashram

The *I Ching* is one monument to the right cerebral hemisphere. A couple hundred yards over the Pacific surf, in the timeless misty Big Sur range of the California coast, is another: Esalen, not as old as the *I Ching,* but certainly as well publicized. It was not the publicized group encounter techniques of the Sixties that made Esalen important as a right-brained citadel. Esalen was the counter-culture's university, where the right-brained techniques could surface, and the right-brained ideas could find articulation.

"Our primary concern," wrote Mike Murphy, its

founder, "is the affective domain—the senses and feelings, though we're interested in the cognitive, too." So, on the Esalen grounds, you might see a blindfolded person being led, to "restore the sense of touch and the experience of dependency." Or you could see people "conversing" with their eyes alone, or their hands alone, "cutting through society's excessive verbalism to authentic feelings."

Ah, those authentic feelings. What an effort to get to them, encountering and gestalting and confronting—the authentic feeling made king. There were the far-out therapists paying attention to the sound of the participants' voices, their breathing and posture.

You could take belly dancing at Esalen, and movement, and sensory awareness, or you could sit on the lawn and eat a single grape very slowly. Or you could find six or eight people rolling over and over each other in a sandwich, like kids do: it's all right to do that as a kid in our society, but not as an adult. It's all right to touch, said Esalen. It does your head good.

So you could go from the baths to your massage class and get sort of stoned amidst the sheer tactility of sunlight and oils and touch, and all the bodies would begin to look good, not only the light and tanned ones, but the flabby ones as well: all human, all together. A cheering experience.

"We shape our houses and then they shape us," Churchill said. Esalen was a small place, ninety acres or so, a hundred people at most there, more now, but it became a symbol. Let the mute right side speak!

Had Esalen not been so beautiful, it might have folded when the Sixties ran out, like all the other growth centers. Dr. Patrick Murphy had bought it for its beauty and its natural sulfur springs in 1910, when there was no road. The Esalen Indians had used the springs. Dr. Murphy intended to make it a spa for patients, but never did. It slumbered in the Pacific fogs. The state roads pushed through. The Pentecostal Church rented it.

Dr. Murphy practiced in Salinas, John Steinbeck's hometown. The Cain and Abel of *East of Eden,* it

was said, were Dr. Murphy's grandsons, Dennis and
Michael. Dennis would get stabbed in the chest in a
barroom brawl and blow cigarette smoke through the
stab wounds: Michael was high school class president
and gave speeches to the local Rotary Club—Why I
Am Proud to Be an American. Michael got turned
on by a course in Oriental religions at Stanford and
went off to the Sri Aurobindo ashram in India.
When he got back, he was a bellboy at the Del
Monte Golf Club. His Stanford classmates, clamber-
ing up the financial ladder, in white oxford button-
downs and narrow ties, would do a double take on
their way to the golf course.

To restore dance and touch and the other right-
brained activities, Murphy had to retrieve the place
from his grandmother and her tenants, the Pentecostal Church. (Murphy was not thinking in terms of
brain hemispheres, only in terms of an institute of
human potential, of nonverbal humanities.) The site
had become—unbeknownst to the church—a homo-
sexual hangout. Hunter Thompson, later of *Fear
and Loathing* books, was hired as caretaker. "Hunter
brought a lot of guns," said Murphy, "and he almost
got himself killed because he would sit in the caretaker's shack firing away at the homosexuals who
climbed the fence, and one night the window was
blasted away." Thompson escaped. The church left.
The institute was founded.

No television, no newspapers, only one phone, outdoors. The noise of the outside world quickly
dropped away in the mists of the mountains. For
the education of the nonverbal mode, it was a particularly sensual place. To sit in the hot sulfur baths
was an agreeable communal experience. The nudity
became natural. Esalen evolved its own massage
techniques and eventually published them. It was
said that if everybody gave a massage every day
and received one there would be less violence and
fewer wars.

And along came a neuropsychologist to say the
same thing. If you don't touch enough, your brain
dries up; societies that don't touch become aggressive. Witness, said Dr. James Prescott of the

National Institutes of Health, infants separated from their parents can develop mental retardation, they sit and rock for hours, like monkeys reared in isolation. "If the deprivation is extreme," said Dr. Prescott, "you get actual structural damage to the brain—the brain cells don't have as many dendritic branches, so the cells don't make contact with as many other cells." We're missing body pleasure, so we have visual substitutes like pornography; the Judeo-Christian belief had set up that body pleasure is evil. "Somatosensory deprivation" creates an environment that produces an aggressive species. The stakes were high: "If violence becomes fixed genetically, the species will no longer be capable of expressing affectionate, peaceful behavior. Mankind will be able to express only physically violent behavior. Mankind will self-destruct."

Make love, not war. If we could only get the Russians and the Chinese and the Arabs and everybody all together, and break out the massage oils —see, it sounds funny already, the way things sound from beyond the paradigm, like surrealist art can seem funny. But figure: the cost of one guided-missile submarine would keep the world in massage oil for years. A trillion and a half for arms, back and forth across the world: in massage oils, that would last forever.

Everything that surfaced in humanistic psychology checked in at Murphy's ashram. But the seekers perhaps no longer believe that the world is about to change so quickly. Alas.

Now you can stay at Esalen on an American Express card. It has become its own monument. College students take courses there for credit. Corporations send management teams for short sessions.

At the great outpost of nonverbal learning, you cannot buy an Esalen sweat shirt, or a candy bar, or a pencil, or in fact anything at all. Except books. You can buy books. Books written by the people who lecture or lead groups at Esalen. Every man jack of *them* has written a book or is writing one and has contracts for three more. The courses people sign up for are by the people they've read. Those are the "stars." Everything else is just the daily operation.

So: nice, linear, book-reading people come to Esalen, and they do their nonlinear, nonreading, touching, feeling workshop, and then they go to the bookstore and buy a linear, verbal book about the nonlinear, feeling experience they just had, and they take it home and read it. And the book said: get out of your head, you stupid, the head is not where it's at. The body is where it's at.

The body never lies.

The Grandma and Grandpa of Gravity

It was at Esalen that the right-brained body activities surfaced, and it was Esalen, or Esalaneers, who found Ida Rolf and Moshe Feldenkrais, or at least brought them to the attention of those interested in releasing their inhibitions and developing their personalities through new bodies and thence new minds.

The body never lies. So say the people who say the body never lies. I am not quite sure what it means, even after all this time. I understand part of the message: you have a lot of irrelevant stuff in your head and your head is not your friend, you are watching television and your body is reasonably happy, purring away, and the TV commercial says, we've come to a break in the action, folks, why don't you go get another beer. And you do it. Your body doesn't want the beer, in fact you had to wake it up with associations and images, and you sell it to yourself. You also sell yourself another ten pounds.

Or: you are playing something, something physical, and you want to win. Your body doesn't give a damn, it's right-brained, it can't even count beyond four so it certainly doesn't care who gets the highest number of whatever. But you do, so you give a little extra lunge, and there goes your back or your knee or your shoulder or your neck. If you and your body were grooving together, say the body people, you wouldn't have a bad back and a tennis elbow and a bursitic shoulder, and you wouldn't put on weight when you don't want to.

Well, okay. I have trouble squaring body-never-lies with my textbooks in physiological psychology, and in perception, which say the body lies all the time, or if it doesn't lie, at least it doesn't tell the truth because it doesn't know. It will tell you things are out there that aren't there, optical illusions, and it will give you false signals on how hot is hot and how full is full, and which is red and which is black in certain trick patterns. That may not be lying, but you wouldn't trust it, either.

The body-never-lies people say body and mind are all the same, in spite of the division made in Platonic and Christian and Cartesian theory, and if you get the body integrated and aligned, you get the mind integrated and aligned, too.

Ida Rolf's theory is based on your relationship to gravity. There is a right way for you to be in relation to gravity, to sit, stand, walk, and if you're out of line, so is your mind. Ida called her technique Structural Integration. Therapy by body manipulation, get yourself back in line with gravity and you will see life steadily and see it whole.

Practically nobody is in line correctly with gravity. When you were a kid, you fell off your bike, and some muscles went into trauma and they released only partially, and ever since, your right shoulder is a little higher than your left. Or you fell on the ice, or you were in a car accident, and you don't even remember these things but your body does, it's holding a little knot there in trauma and you don't even know it. Some of the knots aren't in trauma, and Rolfing is not only for the accident-stricken.

If this were only an extension of Swedish massage, or chiropracting, it would hardly belong among the powers of mind, but the mind-traumas are there, too; the insult that made you tense your shoulder, fight-or-flight, or the feeling that you had about your father is translated into stomach tension and is still there. (Followers of the character-armor theories of Wilhelm Reich like this part, since it was influenced by Reich.)

Nor does the insult or injury stay just where it was; in order to compensate, the body shifts, changing the pattern of carrying weight. Sometimes the temporary solution becomes permanent. The muscles thicken, and then the droopy shoulders or the sunken chest become familiar and comfortable. And, in this body-mind continuum, emotions thicken and grow inelastic as well.

Ida Rolf got a doctorate in biochemistry and physiology in 1920, worked as a biochemist for a dozen years, and spent the next forty on this physiological technique. Around the muscle groups are myofasciae—tissues that envelop and support them. The fasciae have a certain plasticity—they can be molded and moved, to a degree. Rolfing involves manipulating the fasciae, and detaching fibrils between muscles, and repositioning muscles, and ligaments. To this end the Rolfer uses his fingers, his elbow, his fist, his hand, and pretty nearly all of his weight.

The result is a massage given by Thomas Torquemada. (Torquemada was the bishop in Spain, during the Inquisition, who loved your soul so dearly that to save it he would tear your tongue out by the roots.)

But how much can it hurt? I met a psychologist who had a peak experience with his first Rolfing. His chest released and he breathed for the first time in his life and his shoulders undrooped and his works, his written work, started to flow. Sam Keen, a writer for *Psychology Today,* sang the Body Electric and said the memory of an old conflict had been encysted, and came out with pressure on the shoulder, and he warmed to new people and new events.

I signed up for Rolfing.

That buried feelings influence current action is, of course, an axiom in Freudian analysis. Bring it up and it isn't buried, and then you can at least have the option of whether you want it to be of influence or not. If the distorting influence could be brought up by an elbow into the belly, that might be quite interesting, except that most Rolfers aren't analysts.

A trauma-free body-mind! I lay down upon the Rolfing table with some apprehension. Who knew what knots were in there?

"Standard fucked-up American male body," said the Rolfer.

"I can do seventy-five push-ups," I said, defensively.

"That's just the trouble," said the Rolfer. "All that armor. No movement. No feeling. Thick muscles. No fluidity. American games are terrible for you. You need to dance."

"The games I play are all inside rectangles," I volunteered, "and come to think of it, so are the ones I watch. The playing fields are rectangles, never circles or ovals. Maybe those geometric shapes have a psychic dimension."

The Rolfer wasn't interested in my quite profound comparison between geometry and psychic space, he had his elbow in my chest and was pressing with all his weight.

"Hey," I said. "That hurts."

He continued to press, outlining some muscles all the way into the armpit.

"That hurts even more," I said.

Have you ever had the Novocaine wear off in the dentist's office, or had a tooth filled without it, and there's pain, and the dentist says just a minute, he doesn't want to stop right then, and you think it can't get more painful but it does?

"I am not making the pain, you are making the pain," said the Rolfer.

"I felt fine when I came in here," I said.

"Stop resisting. Relax. Breathe."

"How can I relax with your elbow in my armpit? I never knew armpits were so sensitive."

The Rolfer continued to press, push, twist.

"You enjoy this work?" I grunted.

A hot red sear of pain went around the left side of my chest. I decided to let my mind go elsewhere. Where did my mind want to go?

"Ve haff vays to make you talk. Schwein! Vere vill de invasion come?"

"Name, rank and serial number is all you get from me."

"So far ve haff been chentle. Vun more time— vich place do de shtupid Amerikaners land?"

"Name, rank and serial number . . ."

"You're not participating," the Rolfer said. "Stay with it. Stay here."

"I don't like it here," I said.

After the session, the Rolfer said: some people after they are Rolfed grow an inch or two. Their shoe sizes increase. It's a trip. At some point you have a *gestalt,* a breakthrough, and you're changed. "When I was Rolfed," he said, "I felt like I was sixteen again."

I did feel better after the session, but I wrote in my notes that I thought I felt better because it was over.

"Americans, Westerners, in general, have lost the balance in their bodies," said the Rolfer, warming up his knuckles for the next session. "They develop the big muscles, the ego-controlled muscles, and the smaller muscles behind those atrophy. Calisthenics only stretch the muscles temporarily, games traumatize them, even jogging isn't good."

It was very difficult, upon feeling a painful pressure, not to want the painful pressure to go away, not to resist. Resistance makes tension, tension makes pain, how come I couldn't get the message? Some sessions were easier than others. I thought I was improving when all the pressure on the backs of the legs didn't make me try to wriggle off the table. But then we hit the insides of the thighs. Who would think that moving all the muscles a couple of inches would cause such objections in the head?

The Rolfer had his elbow on the inside of my thigh, and he had so much weight on it he was perspiring. I looked at the ceiling: *Name, rank and serial number . . .*

"All men are sensitive here," he said, slightly out of breath. "Their mind fears the mutilation of the genitals. That's why African tribes have the mutilation of the genitals as an initiation ceremony—you have to go through the fear to the other side, to gain the use of your legs. Otherwise you don't have the full use of them. The tribe is interdependent, if you're an integral part of it they must have confidence in you, in your legs. Zulus can run fifty miles a day. If your survival depended on running down an antelope—"

"Absolutely—no—call—for—antelope—meat—in— my—family," I gasped.

The Rolfer pulled my feet together, halfway through the sessions. "There," he said, with some satisfaction. "See, one of your legs is an inch longer than the other."

"Match them up again, for God's sake," I said.

And so we proceeded. Did I stand a bit straighter? Was there more bounce in my step? Did I feel lighter? Maybe—but I was probably not a good Rolfee. (In every culture, the patient's failure is the patient's fault. You didn't work hard enough with the psychiatrist, or you quit, or you didn't bring the right chicken bones to the witch doctor and the old curse is still on.) About a month later, three of us Rolfees were comparing notes at dinner, and when we went out onto the street, there was our Rolfer walking along. Spontaneously the cry arose, *git im*. The Rolfer ducked into a doorway, went into a crouch, covered his head with his hands. I thought I saw terror in his eyes and a lack of confidence in his craft. (In fairness, the middle one of the three of us bearing down the street shouting *git im* was a former pro basketball player who was a shade over seven feet tall.)

A goodly year after the Rolfing, I talked to Ida Rolf, the inventor. She is said to be a very scary old lady. I found her snappish and curt. Yes, to be under elbow there would be scary.

"Your joints," she said, "are lifeless."

"But I've been Rolfed!" I protested.

"Who did it?" she asked.

I told her.

"Oh, well, him," she said, with a wave of her hand. "There are hacks everywhere. He shouldn't be Rolfing. Most Rolfers shouldn't be Rolfing."

"They come here and train," said Ida's son, who was also present, "and then we don't have their allegiance once they leave, and they start to do other things as well."

"There's no other profession," Ida said darkly, "where you can take six months' training and make twenty-five dollars an hour. I know why they come, most of them."

I asked how many hours of Rolfing one needed. Maybe I hadn't, with my lifeless joints, had enough; Dick Price, the co-chairman of Esalen, had had three hundred hours. "Ten hours is the course," Ida said. "Dick Price," she snorted. "Who Rolfed Dick Price?"

"Who are the good Rolfers?" I asked.

"There's me, and there's my son here," Ida said.

Then there was a silence.

"That's a very tight guild," I said.

"He was the only Rolfer for ten years other than me," Ida said. "Why should I train others? It's a damn hard job and there's no money in it."

"But there are others."

"A few. There are a few."

"Who would you like to have as trainees? Doctors? Psychologists?"

"Psychologists don't know bodies," Ida said.

"Doctors' minds are already set," her son said.

"Maybe if it were taught in medical school—"

"Not while I'm alive," Ida said. "I know them. They'll put it in a corner."

I began to have the feeling that Rolfing was not going to sweep the country.

"I don't like osteopaths and chiropractors, either," Ida said.

Who would they like to have as subjects? There must be, for example, athletes who have gotten themselves out of line—

"Athletes are too hard," Ida said. "I don't want to take on those oversized hard bodies."

"They take too much time, too," her son said.

I got the glimmer of a *gestalt*, a whole new thing. I had arrived at Madame Rolf's feeling slightly guilty about my Rolfing—was I a bad Rolfee? How come people swore by it? How come Sam Keen could sing the Body Electric and get a whole new self and lose his childhood body-traumas and I was still walking around scrunched up from when my bicycle ran into the guardrail? When I left Madame Rolf's, I felt freer and better, just for talking to her, without having had an elbow laid on me. The glimmer that hit me was from W. C. Fields or somebody like that: if at first you don't succeed, quit.

Ida Rolf is the grandma of the gravity and structure cult; Moshe Feldenkrais is the grandpa, but that is figurative, since they scarcely know each other. In person, Ida makes you feel like you have just farted in church; Feldenkrais is Grandpa-come-to-Sunday-dinner, making rabbit ears out of the handkerchief corners for you, telling terrible jokes and dramatic long stories. Feldenkrais is an Israeli, round, short, with twin crests of white hair like David Ben-Gurion used to have—and that accent! Lovable, but what is it? Feldenkrais surveys the American scene, *tranzen trichten meshugas blichten,* he says; those are nonsense words designed for flavor, since I couldn't catch the ones he did say, though I asked him twice; the only real word, as far as I know, is meshuga, crazy. "I said, Americans pay people to make them crazy."

No wrenching of myofasciae with Feldenkrais. They are all slow, deliberate, mild exercises, based on the "reversibility relationship" of the muscular and nervous system. Our patterns, and muscle movements of which we are all unaware, are brought into awareness by a reversed pattern. Most of the lessons are lying down, to help break the habitual motion of the muscle in gravity. Lying flat on the floor, wanting to get up, do we jerk ourselves up using our stomach muscles? What if we rolled over and pressed ourselves up, and put our feet slowly under our bodies? The Feldenkrais exercises are exercises in sensing. What does the motion feel like? Slowly, no strain, no push, stop whenever you feel a strain—"In the end one should improve to the point," says a Feldenkrais paper, "where one feels that one's body is hanging lightly from the head, so that the body glides when moving."

So we are all on the floor, a whole class worth of psychologists and dance people and so on— Feldenkrais has lectured to the company of director Peter Brook on movement—and Feldenkrais himself is sitting in a director's chair facing us, a lavaliere microphone around his neck, telling us motion by motion, watching—

"—now, slowly, move your hands away—fust row, second man, move your hands away, you're afraid somebody would steal them? hands away, and now, slowly, no strain, find the right knee and move back —back—where is back, dollink? redhead, in third row, where is back? good, back, and now, slowly sit back, sit back, left knee behind right—

"OY! Who said to take the hands from the floor! OY! Clumsy oxes! You need a discipline!"

The voice becomes soothing again—

"—nicely, nicely, slowly, roll to center position, good, with the right hand take the laft foot, LAFT FOOT which is laft you in first row, good, notice breathing, notice which way the knee turns, notice which way the shoulders go—the right path is the one the skeleton would move in as if it had no muscles, body must be organized so it will follow the shortest path, no strain, no effort, the bones will follow a path of the skeleton pulled by its head—"

Sometimes we do exercises on one side and then visualize them on the other side before doing them, and the other side has learned more quickly through the visualization. One Feldenkrais warmer-upper is to lie with the back on the floor, arms over the head in line with the legs, and scan the body for the contact points with the floor. Are all the vertebrae on the floor? If they aren't, what muscles are working to hold them off? It probably takes a conscious effort to press the spine to the floor, and as soon as that stops, the original pattern comes back. With a shoulder movement, raise the right upper arm until there is an infinitely small space between the back of the hand, and the floor, then let the arm drop back again. Rest, and repeat, twenty times. Is the back of the hand beginning to creep along the floor as the arm stretches before it's raised? Is the breathing beginning to match the exercise, with the exhale as the arm stretches? Slowly, slowly bring the arms back to the sides, draw up the knees, and rest. Scan the body. Is there a difference between right and left sides?

Something is going on: we come into the class and hold up our arm and turn in an arc and it goes to *there,* and then, after the reversal exercise, we try it again and it will go all the way to *there,* thirty degrees further—

It's easy to do this in a class, with a voice telling you, but it would be harder alone, because we are so used to gross, major movements, and these movements are so quiet, so small, so subtle—

And this is going to help our heads too?

"Certainly," says Feldenkrais. "We have a self-image in the motor cortex of the brain. We learn just enough to get by with that self-image. It limits our capacity. We maybe use five percent of ourselves, maybe ten percent. A man who has mastered several languages makes use of more combinations of cells than someone with one language, more neuronal pathways. If we say, 'I will never understand mathematics,' or 'I cannot dance well,' that limits us."

But we get to this expanded potential through movement?

"Certainly," says Feldenkrais. "We only know what is happening through muscle movement. We know it is laughter or fear or anxiety through the heart or the eye muscles or the lungs. Sometimes something happens within us and we don't know what it is until we interpret the new pattern of organization. These exercises attack at the hinge of habit. A change in the motor integration leaves thought and feeling without the usual anchorage, and open to change. If somebody can do something in half an hour that he thought he could never do, that changes his image of himself."

Feldenkrais is Dr. Feldenkrais, just as Ida Rolf is Dr. Rolf, but neither is a doctor of medicine. Feldenkrais' doctorate is in physics. He also taught judo for thirty years. An Israeli black-belt judo-expert physicist with a muscle-pattern system to change body-minds.

"I warn you, my life is complicated," Feldenkrais says. "I got interested in movement because of my own knees. I was a football player for years—soccer football, you call it. I was a left back. And when I began to have a lot of trouble, the surgeons wanted to operate—"

"This was in Israel?"

"No, in Scotland, the surgeons wanted to operate, and I didn't like the sound of the chances, so I started studying anatomy and physiology and biochemistry, and I didn't have the operation. Without knowing it, the judo had matured some ideas in my mind—"

"Judo in Scotland?"

"No, in Paris, the judo had matured some ideas in my mind, and after the war I put them down, in the evening—"

"In Paris?"

"No, in London, you know, you're still hung up in cause and effect. When will you learn cause and effect are not what you think?"

Feldenkrais' soccer days were in Israel, or rather, in British Palestine, and as a member of a touring club. He was also a member of the Haganah, the Jewish self-defense force under the British mandate in Palestine, and he wrote a booklet on jujitsu. "We had some Jews who had been on the Berlin police force, who taught jujitsu." When he went to Paris to study physics, he joined a judo club, and in fact became the chief disciple of an expert he calls Professor Kano, who had been impressed with his exposition in the jujitsu booklet, and felt that Feldenkrais could be a good teacher of judo. "It was not just judo Professor Kano taught, it was the way of teaching. He was a great man, more than a great man. The Japanese ambassador in Paris called him his father. When he died, six million people in Japan practiced judo in his honor on one day." Feldenkrais did his physics work with Joliot-Curie, the Nobel prizewinning physicist, in Paris, on ultra-high tension, and went, in World War II, to Fairlie, Scotland, to work as a scientist on submarine detection and anti-submarine warfare. He organized a judo club in Fairlie, and had trouble with his soccer injuries.

"I was thinking, I told you, how does a person ruin his knees? I mean, exactly what is it that happens when he ruins the knees? And then, from the judo, I was thinking, why is it some people can't learn to fall? Why can an intelligent man who understands the concept perfectly not perform a clean fall for years? Some people can do it in one day. What is anxiety in falling? Why do neurotic people have poor balance? What is the connection of structure and function in the body? I had in my own experience elements I didn't understand myself. My own accident with the knees became clear, a joke. I was a highly neurotic type and fought like an idiot during a game. So I had matured in my head without knowing it."

Feldenkrais presented his ideas in papers before his fellow scientific workers in Fairlie. After World War II, he went to work in an acoustical laboratory in London as a research scientist, and spent a lot of time, it seems, with the Japanese and the Indians.

"I did Zen, I did yoga, I met Kazuma and Suzuki, I spent six weeks with Suzuki, sometimes I would be up till three in the morning." Feldenkrais' papers on his body work were reworked and published in 1949 as *Body and Mature Behavior*. It is heavy in physiology, and has formulas from physics to demonstrate the body's movement in space. It was soberly reviewed in *The New England Journal of Medicine* and the *Quarterly Review of Biology*. It brought a trickle of interested people to see him—but Feldenkrais considered himself an amateur. "I was not confident," he said, "because it contradicted other books I had read, and I said to myself, you're an amateur, you said what you said, now go back to work."

Feldenkrais became a chief scientist with the Israeli Army, and on the side he began to treat people with his body theories.

"For the first three years, I wouldn't take any money, if you give me a ride in your car should I pay you like a taxi? And then after that I thought, I spent seven years in the British Admiralty on top-secret work, and three years in the Israeli Army on secret work, and no one knows what I have done, not even scientists. I am not even a scientist, I am more like a government official. And scientists made very little in the Israeli Army; it was not long before the body work promised to pay more."

"So we have a compendium of exercises," I said, "some of them never repeated even once in a course, from an Israeli physicist. But it looks to me like the grandfather of your thought is Japanese."

"No."

"No?"

"Japanese in Japan are like Englishmen in London now, or New Yorkers in New York. Not Japanese that way. But Japanese like Professor Kano, you could say that."

"Is this like a martial art, then, like judo and aikido and kung fu?"

"Like some maybe in a little technique, but martial arts are learned by doing, not understanding. My exercises the person understands and feels the first day."

"And doing the exercises makes a change in mental attitude, or habit patterns?"

"It's *how* you do the exercises," Feldenkrais said. "It's the learning that changes your attitude. It's not what, it's how, everybody painted apples, but Cézanne painted Cézanne apples. You only need to understand one exercise. What is awareness? What is consciousness? That's all. Waghhhhh."

Feldenkrais heaved a sigh, I suppose with the effort of getting through to so dense a pupil.

"America," he sighed. "Such a poverty of spirit. Books—how to fight with your wife, how to fuck, how not to kick yourself in the morning. Ask: What is awareness? You enlarge your ability to perceive in your own way, not what somebody said, it's a change in the mobilization of yourself, what do you need, what is the best way? Who is holding the body in such a way?"

"You've worked out thousands of these exercises. Do you do them yourself?"

Feldenkrais looked out with some amusement.

"Wagghhh, eh, I did them enough."

"You started to become known in your middle sixties, or late sixties—where do you want to go with this system? What do you want?"

"What do I want? I would like to have a clinic, if somebody would give me the money, and what do I want right now is maybe a sandwich and a cream soda, let's go." And he began to tell a story, about a man who had come to see him, who had been a footballer, who had a bad shoulder, who was a pilot, who was having trouble piloting, who was not helped by orthopedics, and who then, one day—and off we went, to get a cream soda.

The surgeon's probing electrode in a brain brings up a choir in Amsterdam on Christmas Eve. Chemical agents that disorient the perception also reveal engrams of memory beyond normal recall, and elements of symbolic language. The engrams, or bits, of memory have an influence over present-day behavior, and even over physiology and posture.

To run through that sequence you don't have to push the paradigm very hard. We are still within it. (That doesn't mean all the sentences are "true"; to be "true," you need a predictive hypothesis, repeatable experiments and independent verification.)

The psychologist whose chest muscles released, and whose breathing and work then flowed, was a sophisticated fellow, but he did not think this technique so extraordinary that he began to proselytize for it. If aerobics, or oxygenation, can affect one's daily outlook, why not an elbow in the myofasciae? But maybe I am a bit biased. It seemed like science from sixteenth-century Paris, pressing an elbow into the armpit to line up the body and clear the mind. Besides, the accustomed posture of the Rolfees would soon bring their frames out of line, and they would have to be "done" again. Whether their heads, or minds, also slipped a bit is not quite clear.

The Chinese of the *I Ching* certainly lived with kinds of attention which we do not grant ourselves, bizarre old right-brained stuff. They also developed patterns of ritualized body motion, some of which was called *t'ai chi,* variously described as a moving meditation or shadowboxing, which had its influence when the Japanese imbibed Chinese culture. Then the Jews on the Berlin police force learned one descendant, jujitsu, and took it to British Palestine, and foxy Grandpa wrote his pamphlet and became the student of Professor Kano in judo, and applied his understanding of physics to physiology, so these right-brained movements have a long lineage.

I met one other practitioner of this study of bodies, who made no claims for its influence upon the mind. He was a trainer, an athletic trainer on a university medical staff, working under a physician. It was said he could pick a broken quarterback up from the field in the second quarter and have him back in the third without any drugs or injections. I watched him with the most violent wrenches intercollegiate competition supplies to young male bodies—football, wrestling and hockey. Some required traditional athletic medicine. But he had also improvised his own exercises, somewhat like the reversibility relationship in Feldenkrais, and they were so small, the movements were so small, to perform them would drive you crazy. Until you changed your set of mind, and then the traumatized muscles began to release, with so little damage it was astonishing.

But these are all individual artisans, working pragmatically, like the metallurgists who used oxygen before oxygen was discovered. Only after Priestley discovered oxygen and Lavoisier quantified the results did the metallurgists have some glimmer of the conceptual scheme in which their craft functioned.

These unarticulated impulses of mind do get quantified in the next section, and because they are quantified and repeated, the paradigm bends to accommodate them.

Biofeedback: Who's at Home Here?

Biofeedback *sounds* so respectable. That Greek root "bio," as in biochemistry or biology, and "feedback" from the crisp, quantified world of engineering, from servomechanisms: "A method of controlling a system by reinserting into it the results of its past performance." Definition by Norbert Wiener. Your room thermostat turns the heat on when it senses that the room has gotten too cold. Biofeedback gives you a reading on something going on within your body, just as a thermometer does. But just knowing your temperature doesn't let you affect your temperature. Or does it?

Biofeedback machines monitor some function of the body and give you a continuous visual or aural report. And then—this is the part that got everybody so excited—you learn to change the signal, to alter the dynamics of that part of the body. But nobody knows how it's done. It seems to happen outside of the rational, language-using part of the mind. You can raise your arm if somebody tells you to raise your arm. But could you raise or lower your blood pressure, or your heartbeat, just by *thinking* about it? (Not *thinking,* precisely, because thinking implies the verbal and rational. Better say, putting your mind to it.) No Westerner believed it until recently; those functions belonged to the autonomic nervous system, over which we have no control. Or thought we had no control. The big outlines of the paradigm don't have to change, but they have to give in one sector.

The implications were terrific. If people could really control their own autonomic functions, they could bring down their blood pressure, relax, get to sleep, unlearn bad habits such as smoking and drinking, and do away with some of their daily drugs.

Unfortunately, biofeedback went through a fad stage where it was advertised as Electric Zen, where gushy reporters described it as the greatest advance since Copernicus. (The popular press was no more accurate on biofeedback than on drugs.) The Magic of Alpha.

I signed up for a biofeedback course.

"Put your fingers in these little loops here," Josh said. I was sitting in an easy chair in a darkened room at Josh's Institute.

"Okay, make that tone go down." The machine was giving an annoying whine.

"We are measuring GSR, galvanic skin response," Josh said. "Tension shows up as increased moisture on your fingers, and this picks up even a minute amount."

The whine on the machine rose. "I am not tense, you sonofabitch," I said to the machine. I glared at it.

Josh said, "Don't try," and then left us alone. Don't try?

The machine began to descend in tone. "That's better," I said. It whined up again. "You do that again, I'll kick you," I warned it. It whined higher. I decided to ignore it. It stayed on its high whine, just to let me know, and then grudgingly began to drop.

Finally it dropped to a low growl, and I began to get a bit bored. The growl went lower. Josh opened the door. The whine went up a bit.

"How you doin'," he said.

"Just keep it chained up, it bites," I said. The machine growled higher in response. I took my fingers out of the loops.

We moved on to the big stuff, the electrodes pasted on the head, EEG, electroencephalogram wired for sound. I was sitting in a big easy chair, with the machines on a table at one side. Josh fiddled the dials like a hi-fi mechanic, and plugged it in. The machine went beep boop beep boop.

"The beep is alpha and the boop is beta," Josh said.

"Hot dog, alpha already," I said.

"Most people have some alpha all the time," Josh said, "and some beta too."

Josh turned one of the dials. The boop went away and the machine went beep beep beep, pause, beep, pause pause beep.

"That's alpha," Josh said.

"So what's all the fuss about getting into alpha?"

"You want a nice, consistent alpha. See if you can lose the beta and make the alpha tone nice and steady, get some nice smooth waves going."

"How do I do that?"

"Don't figure it out, just let yourself respond. I'll leave you alone with the machines and you play around."

The alpha-beta terminology came from a German psychiatrist and researcher, Hans Berger, who first put electrodes to scalp in the 1920's. Berger found two distinct patterns; one he called alpha, at roughly eight to thirteen cycles per second, and the other beta, at fourteen and up. The beta state seemed to be associated with mental activity, and the alpha with drowsiness and relaxation. Years later, the machines got much more sensitive with transistorization, and filters for extraneous noise made the signals clearer. Theta, four

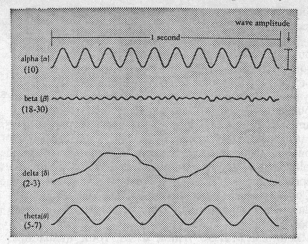

to seven cycles, and delta, four down to a half cycle, got added to the list.

In 1958, a husky, pleasant Nisei psychologist, Joe Kamiya, was looking at EEG patterns as part of a sleep project, and wondered whether there was a connection between what a person's brain was doing—as reported by the EEG machine—and what he reported verbally himself. He had his subjects sit in a darkened room wired up to the EEG, and asked them to guess what state they were in: A or B, alpha or not alpha. By the third hour, many of the subjects were guessing right three times out of four. Given a soft beep tone for alpha waves, the subjects learned to sustain the alpha, to turn it off and on, and—some of them—to control the wave amplitude. Yet none of them could describe, in English, what was going on. The internal cues were far more subtle than the vocabulary available to describe them. "The ineffability of the meditative state," wrote Kamiya, "so often stressed in mystical writings is similar to statements many of my subjects make, for example, '. . . I can't describe . . . this state . . . it has a certain feel about it.'" Kamiya found that people who were at home with images and feelings, and those who did, however loosely, some sort of meditation, made the best subjects.

The vocabulary never did get a whole lot better, but the enthusiasm increased. "I feel calm." "I feel sort of stoned." "I feel like I'm floating off the chair." Stoned! Floating off the chair! The biofeedback boom was off and running. Engineers working on hi-fi amplifiers switched to making biofeedback equipment, and ads began to appear in all sorts of papers and magazines: TURN ON WITH ALPHA. I clipped an ad out of the paper announcing A SPECIAL SEMINAR ON ALPHA WAVES AND ESP and I went to the special seminar. It was a come-on for Silva Mind Control, which does not use biofeedback equipment, and which is largely autohypnosis. Alpha, like energy, became a hot word in the counter-culture. ALPHA MACHINES, $199.50. THINK AWAY YOUR HEADACHES. ACHIEVE SELF-CONTROL. Tune into your own special genius. Electric Zen! Drugless high!

For a young profession insecure about its place in science, the biofeedback boom was a great embarrassment. "It was awful," said Joe Kamiya. "The hucksters got it, and the acid-heads, and all those cats who believe in magic. It didn't help me at all. And grants aren't easy to get anyway. I'd like to try it in education, let the kids play with it, no grades, no competition, just see what they can control with it." I told Kamiya about a short biofeedback course I'd just been to, where the wife came back from the machines and said to her husband, whadja get, and upon hearing his score, said, I did better. "That's it," Kamiya said. "Even the yogis are competitive, first they wouldn't do it, and then they all wanted to show they could do the best yoga. Competition doesn't do it."

Some of the biofeedback machines during the boom were so crude they would register all kinds of twitches. And, in fact, at one time my instructor, Josh, had gotten a tic in his eye because the out-of-kilter machine was giving him feedback for a twitch. It kept rewarding him with beeps for the eye twitch, like an FM tuner on the wrong station, and then he couldn't stop.

Going through journal literature and transcripts for

TV shows and meetings on biofeedback, I found some weird ideas amongst the public questioners. There were those who thought—machine-worshiping culture—that the machine put the alpha waves into people's heads, like radiation. There were those who thought if they could just borrow a machine—same principle—they could go zap somebody's brains with it.

Back in my darkened room at the Institute, in the easy chair, my machines were going beep boop beep boop. I could get many more beta boops simply by thinking of telephone calls I had to make, and I could get the machine to go beeeeeep pause beeeeeep by doing as little as possible and watching my breath go in and out and not even having a flicker of telephone calls.

Josh came in.

"Listen to this," I said. I wanted him to hear the alpha tone.

The minute I said, listen to this, the capricious little bastard started to go boop.

"Go out and come in again," I said. It took a while to get back to beep pause beep, and there were always boops cropping up, like crab grass in the lawn.

"Okay," Josh said, once I had the beep going, "what's a hundred minus seven minus eight minus seven?"

Boop boop boop boop went the machine, even before I could begin to think.

"Now, wait a minute," I said. "I hadn't even started when it started its damn booping."

"Who's I?" Josh said. "The machine's just a machine."

"Well, it's ahead of me," I said, "and that's a little eerie. I don't like its knowing what I'm thinking before I know myself."

A psychologist who was very good at amplifying the twitches from the base of people's thumbs once wired some up and then played soothing music. Into the soothing music, periodically, would come a loud, jarring, grating sound, and then it would cease, and the music would come back on. The subjects were wired up at a number of places, and they weren't told that a twitch at the base of the thumb would cut off the grating sound. Wouldn't you know it, the thumb twitch soon learned it could cut off the grating sound and get back to the pretty music. Now, obviously it took ears to register both the music and the harsh sound, and the interpretative cortex in the brain to distinguish them, but the people didn't know they were cutting the time of the grating sound down, and they wouldn't believe it when they were told it after the experiment. Who did that? Your thumb twitch, and it got better and better, you have a smart thumb twitch. How come I didn't know about it then? Why doesn't anybody tell me anything? they would, in effect say.

And here I am at the Institute, in this semi-darkened room, alone with this machine that has switched from beep pause beep to boop boop before I have switched myself. Who's at home here, anyhow?

My biofeedback course was in the summer, and I turned from a star performer into a very middling one because of the outside environment. The machines were in an air-conditioned room, and I would come up from the hot sidewalks into this nice easy chair in this darkened room and go: telephone calls to make, beta, boop boop, no telephone calls, white space, watch breath go in and out, don't try, alpha, beeeep pause beeeep, and then I would go boop beep zonk, right down through theta to delta and a wonderful nap.

"I can go from beta to delta in one minute flat," I said, when I woke up. "Express. No stops, not even alpha and theta."

"So can every exhausted commuter," Josh said. "Let's see you go from beta to delta and come back again."

Given those instructions, I couldn't even get out of beta.

At another session, my machine was going beeeeep pause beeeeep in a nice alpha and Josh did the number bit, what's fifty-six times seven hundred forty-eight. Have you ever had somebody try to wake you when the sleep you were sleeping was just going to keep right on going? The alpha beeeep kept right on, even though I heard the question, and "I" was quite willing to try for the answer, but the relaxation had cast molasses over everything. "In a minute," I said.

"Right now," Josh said, "fifty-six times seven hundred forty-eight."

The alpha tone went beeeep pause beeeep and the molasses felt very comfortable indeed.

"Go away," I said to Josh.

"You come up here every afternoon and go from beta straight down to delta and then you can't get back again until you've had your nap, and now you can't get out of alpha when you want to, that's not control," Josh said.

"I don't want to, I like it here," I said.

"Okay, stay there," Josh said. "Say, what happened in the stock market today? I heard on the radio it was down thirty-five points at noon."

Boop boop boop boop boop boop boop.

"Was it really?" I said.

"No," Josh said, "but now you're in beta and you didn't put yourself there. You have a way to go. A Zen monk in alpha wouldn't have been bothered."

"A Zen monk wouldn't be in the stock market," I said.

As far as alpha is concerned, you can see that alpha describes a brain state more relaxed than beta, and that you need beta to solve problems. Sometimes creativity is associated with alpha, for people who are creative while relaxed, but getting your head to fire at eight to thirteen cycles per second isn't going to make you Picasso unless you're already Picasso. And while some researchers associate alpha with creativity, some, like Barbara Brown, believe that "people who have a lot of Alpha in their EEGs are dull, uninteresting, unimaginative, hard-working, plugging-along, ordinary people." Alpha is easier to produce with your eyes closed, because focusing your eyes is a beta activity. Beta would seem to be a more left-brained rhythm, but all the rhythms occur in both hemispheres of the brain. So: eyes open, it is easier to produce alpha at the beach or in the mountains, because your eyes can be on the horizon, unfixated.

Alpha training does sensitize people to internal cues. No one yet knows the connection between various brain wave patterns and behavior traits, but there are lots of interesting theories.

The breakthrough was to show that some control of the autonomic nervous system was possible.

Respectability, Confirmation and The Mystery of the Rebelling Rats

Somehow, the dancers and psychologists who learned the quiet exercises of Feldenkrais used their minds to release their muscles. Or vice versa. And the biofeedback subjects used some unfamiliar part of their minds, or neurophysiological systems, to control autonomic functions, when nobody had been able to do that before. "Biofeedback" refers to the mechanical system; what the subjects were doing has been called "visceral learning." That is, crudely, learning from the gut, without the head. Controlling the involuntary with the assist of instruments.

They said it couldn't be done, and Neal Miller took his fellow behavioral scientists to task. Miller is an absolute duke of rat psychology, past president of the American Psychological Association. He has been teaching animals to learn for more than forty years, first at Yale, then at Rockefeller University—a hatchery for Nobel prizewinners along the East River in New York. Rockefeller University is a research place, no undergraduates. Miller is a burly, square-jawed man, bald except for a white fringe, who would look at home in a lumberjack plaid. There are, said Miller, general laws governing all learning, and visceral learning is similar to ordinary learning. "It's a common assumption," Miller said, "that the visceral system is stupider than the consciously-controlled system, but the evidence doesn't show that."

To have Miller and the Rockefeller University crew publishing in this area gave it respectability. What Miller and his collaborators did—we need repeatable experiments and common denominators, remember— was to teach rats visceral control. These rats were not just finding their way through mazes and pressing little levers, no sir. They were speeding up and slowing down their heartbeats, raising and lowering their blood pressure, and controlling their intestinal contractions.

That took the whole biofeedback and visceral learning business away from the kooks, and created a stir in the scientific community. At first Miller and one graduate student rewarded thirsty dogs for salivating. But they weren't sure that the dogs didn't produce some skeletal response, unobserved, that affected the result.

It was important for Miller to account for all the variables. To see if the heart was genuinely learning, for example, you would have to blank out all the other possibilities, immobilize the conscious, skeletal control, and yet leave the heart free to function. Could you paralyze an animal, and then teach his heart to control itself?

The Miller team used a drug, d-tubocurarine, derived from curare, the nerve poison that South American Indians boil up from jungle plants to dip their darts in. Curare paralyzes the end plates of those motor nerves connected to skeletal muscles, including those used in breathing, so if you got hit with a curare dart you would stop breathing very soon. Miller's rats, however, could be kept alive by a mechanical breathing machine, and though they couldn't move a muscle, everything else would be intact.

There isn't much you can do by way of rewarding a paralyzed rat, but the Miller people thought of hitting the pleasure center in the rat's brain with an electric jolt. (In the original pleasure-center experiments done by James Olds and Peter Milner at McGill, the rats would ignore food and water and go on hitting the bar that delivered the pleasure jolt to their brain until they were exhausted.) And that worked. The rats not only learned to control their heartbeats and their intestinal contractions on demand, but some of them learned to blush in one ear and not the other, and a couple of smart little fellows learned to control the rate of urine formation in their kidneys. To show that the visceral learning could be done without the electric jolt to the pleasure center, the Miller people fixed up a more standard experimental technique of escaping a painful stimulus, and that worked too.

If people could do what rats could do, then they could learn to control high blood pressure, spastic colon, irregular heartbeats, and other ailments without drugs or therapy or surgery. Out from the Miller group went a spate of papers, the results were duplicated in other labs, and worldwide attention in this particular branch of science focused on Miller.

People, of course, are more complex than rats, so there would be much greater flexibility. The response could be modified before it actually occurred—we do that through social attitudes and symbols anyway. Urination and defecation are visceral functions brought under voluntary and conscious control quite routinely; maybe we just hadn't gotten around to anything else. It's a tough job to teach a two-year old the concept of blowing his nose, and maybe we are pre-two in some other areas. "This may be oversimplified," said Miller, "but perhaps we can say that the average person does not have any specificity of feelings from the viscera because he hasn't learned the right labels for them, and perhaps he doesn't have the right labels because most visceral functions aren't normally observed by other people, and so are not normally brought under social control. It may be that we are not conscious of these sensations only because we have not been trained to label them."

If visceral learning was possible without the usual ego-controlled muscles getting into the act, then a specific learning situation can produce a specific response. "This means," Miller wrote in his contribution to a textbook on psychiatry, "that psychosomatic symptoms can be reinforced by the full range of rewards, including escape from aversive stimulation." If a kid finds that he can escape going to school by having some stomach distress, he may learn the stomach symptoms as a response to stress. The stomach symptom has been learned by reinforcement, a direct relationship between mama and the kid's stomach, while the kid walks around inventorying his bubble gum cards. The kid doesn't even know it; the contract is between his stomach and his mother. Presumably you could design a program to get the kid's stomach to unlearn its successful symptoms.

Some interesting hypotheses came up in the wake of the Miller work. One of Miller's associates, Barry Dworkin, speculated that some individuals learn high blood pressure because they have both the physiology and the unconscious tendency to regulate their cardiovascular reflexes. A sudden rise in blood pressure produces a decrease in general alertness, just as barbiturates do. Maybe these people learned early in life, unconsciously, that they could tune out a disturbing stimulus by raising their blood pressure; the stimulus could be noise or light or internal in origin, some sort of tension or conflict, and the awareness of it wouldn't come through to the cerebral cortex, or brain center, quite as strongly while the blood pressure was rising. Even a brief reduction in the unpleasantness would act as a reward that would keep the habit going, so, ironically, the person with this attribute would calm himself down unknowingly by boosting his blood pressure.

I asked Miller whether he thought too much conscious control of visceral areas could cross all the signals.

"Oh, I doubt it," he said. "When you're learning, you can't talk and ride a bike at the same time. You have to give all your attention to it. After you've learned, you can talk and ride a bike with ease."

The advancement of biofeedback and learning theory seemed well off the ground when it hit an air pocket, one of those most curious events that happen in science but are largely unreported because, as both

George Orwell and Thomas Kuhn said, history is written by the winners.

Miller's rats stopped learning. And then the rats in the other laboratories stopped learning. Check the machines, check the rats, check the curare, the beasts would not perform, a rat conspiracy. The rat learning curve continued to decline. "The unexplained difference between earlier repeated success and present repeated failure is an extraordinarily perplexing dilemma," Miller wrote. It could have been that the companies breeding the white rats were changing their product slightly, in an effort to improve it; or that the respirator wasn't as accurate; or that the curare wasn't consistent (curare is a natural product, and d-tubocurare batches can vary in make-up); or maybe, says Miller, it was mass hallucination, except that other labs did duplicate the results. The rat problems were ironic, because Miller's successes had inspired some of the successful clinical work with people.

I am less encouraged than I was at the start," Miller said of biofeedback in general. Miller's group went back to work, doing the experiments from scratch, concentrating on the breathing apparatus for the paralyzed rats.

The original reports of changes in autonomic functions were greeted with a lot of skepticism. The changes were quite small, and the critics said these changes could have been produced by something extraneous that didn't have any lasting medical significance. But when Miller's rat studies made biofeedback research with people a bit more respectable, some clinicians tried experimenting. Barnard Engel and Theodore Weiss in Baltimore were rigging devices even before the Miller work gained circulation. One device had red, yellow and green lights for people with irregular heart rhythms—premature ventricular contraction. The light cues indicated when a premature ventricular contraction occurred, and sensitized the patients to the sensation of the irregular beat, since most people with these PVC's don't even know they have them. The training sessions were long—eighty minutes a shot, three times a day—but a couple of patients not only learned to speed up and slow down their hearts, but got weaned eventually from the machine with a regular heartbeat and took the ability away with them.

"How do you do it?" Engel asked his patients. "None of them could tell me," he said, "and after years I realized it was a silly question. I can't tell you how I hit a golf ball."

There were other scattered successes. Some people get headaches because they have tensed the forehead muscle, the frontalis, and they get so used to the sensation they don't even realize they've tensed it. Using the EMG—the machine that picks up the electrical activity from skeletal muscles—two of the biofeedback pioneers devised a chattering of clicks that corresponded to the tension in the muscle. By slowing down the clicks, the patients were able to relax the muscle, and cut down their headache medication. Still another psychologist was able to use the EEG with lights, bells and pictures to cut down epileptic seizures.

There were also flops. Neal Miller tried getting a group to control its blood pressure and labeled the results disappointing, and undoubtedly there were others; people are slower to write up their marginal failures than their marginal successes. Miller's associate, Dworkin, said: "In biofeedback, success seems to be inversely proportional to the competence of the investigator, and directly proportional to the subjectivity of the symptom. It works best on capricious psychosomatic disorders, and is going to be more promising for research than for physicians."

So far we have looked at two types of biofeedback. In one, people responded to a signal; in the other, animals responded to rewards. In the first, nobody much asked the subjects themselves what they were doing to make the light go on, and anyway the subjects didn't have a great vocabulary to describe the process, since it went on outside the language department in their heads. In the second, no rat, of course, fills out a questionnaire, and the experimenters saw themselves as extending existing principles of conditioning.

Now let us introduce another element: what the subject, all wired up, is doing with his own head. One more step. For example, in the "straight" biofeedback, if the clicks were showing you that your forehead muscle was tense, you would not consciously do anything except to try to make the clicks slow down. Some part of you would learn that something—ineffable—made the clicks slow down and something else made them speed up, and that the learning process could go on without running through language in your head. In the next biofeedback step, you can help to trigger this by thinking with your conscious, language-using mind.

The use of a formula by the language-using mind is hardly a new technique. It was blended with biofeedback by Menninger Clinic researchers Elmer and Alyce Green and Dale Walters. The technique used by the Menninger researchers was called autogenic, or self-generated, training. It has its roots in both hypnosis and yoga, and has been more widely used in Europe than here. Dr. Johannes Schultz published his first paper on autogenic training in 1905. One should not, says the Autogenic Training text, combat stress with stress—"master distressful situations by will power." So autogenic training uses muscular relaxation, increase (warmth) or decrease (coolness) in circulation, and "the trainee's passive and casual attitude."

Schultz advised his German readers: "The system works automatically, you do not do it. Become more negligent. Do not please the therapist with notes." Tough stuff for energetic Germans, become negligent, stop taking notes!

And then you lie down, relax, mouth slightly open, and think, "My forehead is cool," and then, "Heartbeat calm and regular," and then, "My breathing is calm," or "It breathes me." ("It breathes me" sounds less awkward in German.) The phrases go on: "I feel quite quiet, my neck and shoulders are warm and heavy, warm and heavy," and so on, like hypnotic induction.

Autogenic training, said its author and his followers, produced relaxation, and cured insomnia, tension, and drug addiction. To get to sleep: "Waking does not matter, it sleeps me, warmth makes me sleepy." The abstinence formula, for cutting something out: "I know that I avoid." "I know that I avoid a single cigarette, at any time under any circumstances, in any mood; others smoke, but for me cigarettes do not matter."

At the Menninger Clinic, the Greens had combined the autogenic my-hands-are-warm with biofeedback, and were testing a group of volunteers. The slightest increase in hand-warming would give the volunteers a signal. By chance, one of the volunteers was a Kansas housewife who had migraine headaches, and she began to have one during her training session. She was allowed to sit quietly in a darkened room, still hooked up to the equipment, and the Greens were surprised to see the hand-temperature indicators pop ten degrees. The housewife said that when her hands warmed with a surge of blood, the headache vanished. The Greens leapt upon this and launched an experiment with migraine sufferers, more than two-thirds of whom ended up with warmer hands and fewer headaches.

During a migraine attack, the blood vessels in the head dilate, and while no one has matched this up or knows exactly why, the blood vessels in the hand contract. The migraine sufferers were given portable temperature meters to practice with at home. Normal hand temperature is about 90°; migraine sufferers may have hand temperatures as low as 70°. Those who could send their hand temperatures up—and some could by fifteen to twenty degrees—had fewer and less intense headaches.

Why not just plant your hands on the stove, then? Well, that doesn't help much, because this isn't really a hand exercise, it's a head exercise. The Greens and their colleagues postulated that a part of the brain —we'll call it the emotional brain, for the moment —responds to stress by triggering the sympathetic nervous system, the one that increases the heart rate and blood flow and screams fight or flight. In the case of the successful migraine feedback, the migraine subjects learned not to redistribute the blood through various parts of the body, but to turn off excess juice in the sympathetic system.

The Greens expanded the migraine workshops, and found that some people had no success at all—these were "skeptical of the training, or suspicious that hypnosis was being used, or very self-determined." People who *tried,* like the conscientious Germans, also flopped; in fact, the physiological changes were the opposite, the stress on stress made the hands get colder and the headaches worse. Passive volition and a casual attitude, like the good German doctors said, were necessary. Another researcher reported that people who picked up the internal cues could head off the headache; one woman would "focus on serenity and say to the blood in her head, go back down, blood, and continue her activities without concern." The Greens released some of their volunteers from the exact autogenic formula, my-hands-are-warm, and let them visualize whatever they wanted that would get them warm, lying on the beach and so on, and that individual tailoring improved the results.

The number of people who have actually learned a visceral response with biofeedback is still very small, and the results are not consistent. (Still, it took only two of James Lind's sailors, sucking on limes, to produce the breakthrough with what turned out to be vitamin C in curing scurvy.) Volunteers may well get hyped up for an experiment, and perform in a lab, which is a kind of theater, with an audience. It is harder without the theater and the audience. Taking a pill is a lot easier than learning a new skill, and even so, more than 20 percent of patients on medication don't take their medication. If Neal Miller is right, of course, the skill, once learned, would be like swimming or riding a bicycle: you would know it, safely, and wouldn't have to learn it again each time.

The relief from headache pains is so obvious that headache sufferers will pay for biofeedback sessions, but the results from controlling blood pressure take years to show up, so that the researchers in controlling blood pressure have to pay their subject. One such subject in a Harvard experiment would lower his blood pressure each week, get paid, and arrive the following Monday with the blood pressure back up again, because he took his biofeedback pay to the track and blew not only the money but his blood pressure.

In general, the patterns of reaction that people have to their environments are not easy to unlearn. People will change their bodies before they will change their environments. It's one thing to sit in a lab and be rewarded with pleasant slides for lowering your blood pressure. It's another to go back to the plant or the office or the house and *still* keep your head relaxed or your blood pressure down. The biofeedback devices have gotten more sophisticated, but they are still not totally portable, continuous and dynamic; if and when they are, somebody with high blood pressure, for example, might walk around wearing one, and when the device started to go boop boop boop he could add years to his life by walking out of that place, shutting his eyes, and saying, I am lying on a bowl of lime jello, I am lying in a bowl of lime jello, or whatever else works.

We have been looking at the first tottering steps taken in the area of visceral learning, which nobody believed possible only a few years ago. We are not used to producing change by "a passive and casual attitude." We think we have to control with our language-using, ego mind. (It should be noted that the passive and casual attitude was for states of relaxation, lowering metabolism. To increase the heartbeat required a more active, if still unarticulated, effort.)

There are, of course, people from outside our paradigm of Western science who never knew it wasn't possible, so they amazed us with their feats, because the feats just weren't part of the logic of our system. Those were the practitioners from the East. If Kansas housewives could calm their heads by warming their hands on the first try, what could someone do who had real experience in tuning internal controls?

Wiring Up the Yogis

For two hundred years the British in India had been reporting that yogis could do odd things; in fact, there is a classic, recognizable scene in Victorian adventure literature. Everybody else is off pig-sticking on Saturday afternoon, and the curious, pipe-smoking Regimental Surgeon is wandering around the countryside, and there is this yogi being buried alive, or stopping his heart, or walking on coals. The regimental Surgeon comes back to the mess, mm-mmm, most curious thing I saw this afternoon, mmmm, and between sounds of their smashing glasses in the fireplace the pig-stickers say, sure, sure, Reggie. You really believe that? No, I don't believe it, says Reggie, but I saw it. And then, later, Reggie gets an invitation: the old yogi announces that on Thursday at noon he is going to leave his body, and he invites all his friends, Reggie too, and everybody gathers and there is a nice ceremony and the yogi sits and crosses his legs and precisely at noon he isn't there any more, that is, his body is, but there's nobody in it any more. The CO says later, damn good surgeon, Reggie, but he was getting a bit too thick with the natives. Began staying out to all hours at strange ceremonies, staying in his room alone humming some damn wog tune, well, it doesn't do, you know. He'll be all right once he's been back in England six months.

Turns out Reggie was really on to something. For even before Miller's rats were developing their subtle shades of kidney functioning, the physiologists were fanning out across India with their portable EEG equipment, hunting for yogis. The yogi is sitting in his cave and suddenly a shadow falls outside the cave, and a voice calls in, "Excuse me, but we're conducting a little experiment . . ."

The yogis, of course, were not doing biofeedback, they were doing their meditating and ignoring the plates on their skulls and the wires leading to the machines. It wasn't that easy to get the yogis to cooperate at first, since the inward, meditative experience of yoga didn't have much to do with keeping score. The yogis sat in lotus position, eyes closed, for up to two and a half hours, and the GSR, the skin test, showed high resistance, meaning they were very relaxed. The EEG, brain waves, showed a strong alpha rhythm, and no evidence of drowsiness or sleep. Most people go through alpha on the way to sleep, but the yogis went to alpha and stayed there; that is, they were in a state of deep relaxation physiologically and they were wide awake. Normally, the alpha pattern is broken up, or blocked, when the brain has to process some information—visual, aural, or simply a hundred minus seven minus seven. In some yogis, outside stimuli—noises, lights—didn't show up on the machines; the alpha continued.

Most of the four hundred-odd yogis who were tested by the Physiology Department of the All-India Institute of Medical Sciences didn't show unusual abilities. The stopping-the-heart exercise, as it turned out, wasn't actually a heart-stopper, it was a combination of breathing and skeletal muscle contractions that shut off the veins bringing blood to the heart. With no blood to pump, the usual heart sounds— budd bump, budd bump—couldn't be heard even with a stethoscope, yet the EKG showed that the hearts went right on pumping. But if you didn't have an EKG machine, you'd certainly have thought there was no heartbeat.

One yogi could drop his heartbeat to half the normal rate by increasing the firing rate of the vagus nerve, the one that conducts impulses from the abdominal and chest cavities to the brain. The vagus nerve can inhibit the heart rhythm, and that, speculated the Chairman of the Physiology Department, is what would happen when the old yogi would have his going-away ceremony and leave his body. He would have such interior control that he could inhibit his heart rhythm.

I called up my consulting team of physicians. Could somebody sit down, cross his legs, and die, on command? No, absolutely not.

I gave them a little Rumpelstiltskin, names for the process. What if the subject could sit down, increase the firing rate in his vagus nerve, and block the action of the sinoatrial node?

Well, if somebody could increase the firing rate in his vagus nerve—and almost nobody can do that consciously—and could block the action of the sinoatrial node, and that led to something else, then sometimes, sometimes but probably not every time, it would work.

So there you are. Increase the vagus nerve firing, block the action of the cardiac pacemaker, the sinoatrial node, and you have a religious suicide and one hell of an example of internal control.

And buried alive? Well, consider "Studies on Shri Ramanand Yogi During His Stay in an Air Tight Box," which the good Chairman of Physiology, Dr. B. K. Anand, and his colleagues wrote up in the *Indian Journal of Medical Research*. Into the box, metal and glass, with electric leads for the information, went the yogi, and he stayed there until the oxygen got dangerously low. And what the experienced yogi did was to drop his body metabolism down to half its normal rate. In a normal person, body metabolism even in deep sleep never drops more than 10 to 12 percent. So a yogi in an Indian village could spend a good long time in a freshly dug grave, since fresh earth wouldn't be as airtight as a metal and glass box.

In Japan, the physiologists went knocking on the doors of the Zen monasteries. Sure enough, the Zen monks could go right to alpha, relaxed but alert, and the alpha amplitudes got bigger and slower as the meditation went on. A control sitting in the same position but not meditating stayed in beta. One difference between the yogis and the Zen monks was in the reaction to an outside disturbance. The yogis simply shut it out, and after the experiment they weren't aware that there had been any noises or lights. The outside world is phenomena, illusion, anyway, and they were transcending it according to their philosophy. The Zen monks, present here and now, registered each of a series of clicks, and the alpha went right on. Normal people—the control group—register the first click the most, and then—ah, that's a click, that's another click—each click is registered *less* as they get used to it. After the fourth click they aren't startled. But the Zen monks perceived each click afresh. Said Drs. Kasamatsu and Hirai: "The Zen masters reported to us that they had more clearly perceived each stimulus than in their ordinary waking state. In this state of mind, one cannot be affected by either external or internal stimulus, nevertheless he is able to respond to it. He perceives the object, responds to it, and yet is never disturbed by it. Each stimulus is accepted as stimulus itself and treated as such." One Zen master described such a state of mind as that of noticing every person one sees on the street but of not looking back with emotional curiosity. Not only did the Zen masters stay in alpha, some of them produced the long theta waves that most people generate only when falling asleep. This, said the authors, reflected concentration without tension. Zen meditation, they concluded, "influences not only the mind but the body as a whole organism," and "is the method through which we can communicate with the unconscious." Not Freud's unconscious, they added quickly, but more closely "that of Jung, C. G., or Fromm, E., what Dr. Suzuki called 'the Cosmic unconscious.' "

By the early 70's, the Menninger Clinic had gotten some big hitters wired up to its machines. There was, for example, Swami Rama, who looked, said one observer, more like an Italian nobleman than a swami, dressed in his turtleneck and Nehru jacket.

The swami, in his mid-forties and trained in yoga since four, had been told by his own teacher to go to the West and show the lesser folk without the law what could be done. On the first try, the swami made two spots on his right palm differ by ten degrees: the left side turned red as if it had been spanked and the right side turned gray. "He did this," wrote the Greens, "by apparently controlling the flow of blood in the large radial and ulnar arteries of the wrist. Without moving or using muscle tension, he 'turned on' one of them and 'turned off' the other." But how did he learn that control?

Well, the swami had put in his time meditating in a cave. He called the first step "even breathing"; he had practiced breathing slower and slower until he was able to take as few as one or two breaths per minute, which is below the threshold where an involuntary breathing reflex is triggered, forcing air into the lungs. The swami had approached the border between voluntary and involuntary very cautiously, sort of tiptoeing across, and once he could do that he could go on to other things.

How long could he stop his heart? Oh, three or four minutes, said the swami. The Greens got a bit nervous; this would give him indigestion, at least, since he hadn't fasted properly, so they settled for a ten-second heart stop. Elmer Green stood with him and a group of technicians sat in the control room. The swami took a couple of dry runs and then freaked out the machines. From a steady seventy beats per minute, he jumped, in the space of one beat, to three hundred beats a minute. "When you stop the heart like this, it trembles," he said, fluttering his hands. What the swami had produced was an atrial flutter, a condition in which the heart vibrates so fast the blood doesn't fill the chambers, the valves don't work, and no blood is pumped. The swami had no pulse for seventeen seconds; an atrial flutter can produce unconsciousness; the swami went off to give a lecture.

The second big hitter at Menninger was Jack Schwarz, a Dutchman now in his fifties who emigrated to the United States in 1957. Schwarz's thing is to show he feels no pain: he can push a knitting needle all the way through his arm. Which is what, all wired up, he did. "Will it bleed?" asked Elmer Green, and it bled for about fifteen seconds. "Now it stops," said Schwarz, and it stopped. The holes that were visible during the bleeding closed up. On the second try there was no bleeding at all. The skin monitors showed no stress, and the EEG showed that before Schwarz began, he was emitting the usual beta waves of activity, but when the needle entered his arm, he slowed right into alpha.

There is, of course, a condition called hypalgesia, in which the person is impervious to pain. Usually he doesn't survive, because nothing tells him to take his hand from the stove. And the perception of pain varies from culture to culture: witness the reports of cheerful Gurkha recruits bringing chopped-off thumbs to the sergeant to be sewn back on. Schwarz has done his demonstration now for innumerable medical groups, and apparently doesn't come off as hypalgesic. Not only does Schwarz pierce his arms and cheeks with needles, he presses cigarettes to his skin, and nothing burns. "Pain," he says, "is an alarm clock that wakes you when something goes wrong, but if you're doing something of your own free will, something that you know is not going to hurt you, then there's no reason for the alarm, right?"

Schwarz has been into metaphysics and Oriental religions since he was twelve, and he says that he noticed the pain-blocking when he was sixteen and working in a clothing store, with needles in the lapel of his suit. One of the shopgirls slapped him playfully and, when the needles went into his skin, he noticed he could turn off the pain. He pulled the needles out, stuck them back in again, and went out to show everybody in the store. Then he went home and had a carpenter friend build a bed of nails.

A McGill psychologist, Ronald Melzack, posited that there were gates all along the axis of the central nervous system which either let the pain through or turned it back. Some people can learn to work the volume controls and the on-off switches.

Schwarz, of course, did not know from internuncial neurons or the reticular activating system. "I do it by changing a single word," he said. "I don't stick a needle through my arm, I stick it through *an* arm, I move outside my body and look at the arm from a distance; with that detachment it becomes an object, like the arm of a chair. My friend Swami Rama says, 'All of the body is in the mind, but not all of the mind is in the body.' "

Schwarz was careful, says Elmer Green, to get "cooperation from his subconscious. He does not force the phenomena to take place, but asks his subconscious if it is willing." When he was asked to repeat his demonstration, there was a pause before Schwarz agreed. "When we asked why he had paused, he said, 'I had to ask the subconscious if it was willing to do it again. When it said yes, I said okay.' "

Green was impressed by the possibilities for education: "If every young student knew, by the time he finished his first biology class, that the body . . . responds to self-generated inputs . . . it would change prevailing ideas about both physical and mental health. We are individually responsible to a large extent for our state of health or disease. Perhaps then people would begin to realize it is not life that kills us but rather it is our reaction to it, and this reaction can be to a significant extent self-chosen."

Pragmatic experimental psychologists were eager to demystify the yogic tricks and the needle performance of Jack Schwarz. Non-yogis, too, could vary their skin temperatures, they reported, by imaging warmth or cold, and they hypothesized it might work this way: If you imagine your arm or hand is cold, you may tense the muscles, and that cuts off the flow of blood, and that drops the temperature. Or, if you imagine it warm, that produces a relaxation which increases the flow of blood, which actually does warm the limb. As for the needles, we overestimate how much of our body is susceptible to pain. While the skin certainly signals pain, much of the interior of the body is relatively insensitive, which accounts for surgical incisions in which hypnotism or acupuncture is used, the first creating a state of relaxation, and the second, a state of distraction.

I have little interest in sticking needles through my arm, although certainly the state of mind that permits that degree of control is fascinating. And if I were to give a goodbye party Thursday at noon, and leave my body, I would probably give a big grunt, botch up the vagus nerve firing rate, and tell everybody to have another drink.

The researchers with the monitoring equipment noticed that subjects who practiced meditation had easier control of the involuntary systems. The yogis and Jack Schwarz were all heavily into meditation. (Jack Schwarz said the meditation so rested him that he slept only two or three hours a night.) But the meditation they used is not our usually defined meditation. Here again we have a problem with our language, which is primitive for feelings and extensive for things. The dictionary definition says, of *meditate*: "to consider as something to be done or effected. . . purpose." That's almost the opposite of Eastern meditation. As, "to meditate revenge." Certainly not. Of *meditation*: . . . "thought or contemplation"—certainly not thought. too linear and left-brained, maybe more like contemplation, but the verbs go: contemplate, plan, devise, contrive, ponder, muse, ruminate, cogitate, study, think.

You can see what the problem is. The activity described by our noun "meditation" is an activity which has to be controlled by the ego-mind. Even the Bible suggests this—happy is the man who meditates in the law of the Lord.

So we need another word for "meditation." The performer of this "meditation" is the self within you that can turn off the jarring sound when your thumb is wired up without your participation. Or it can talk to the biofeedback machine before you know there is any conversation going on. The proponents of meditation say that if you turn the job of meditating over to this person, who lives in there with you, a lot of the *have* to's in your make-up drop away like yellow leaves, and then you're more there than you were.

"Meditation"—we will drop the quotes now, but we mean Meditation II, the new definition—is not easy to read about because it is too easy. We read left-sided and cognitively, and the words have to have a rhythm, boomalaka boomalaka boom boom boom. To be really important, it has to be hard. It isn't the cognitive part that's hard, it's the understanding, from the old German doctors, of "It sleeps me," or, in this case, "It meditates me."

How do we get into this? Many of the Indian techniques use a sound, such as *hum* or *buz*—

And now we're suspicious. This suspicion is at least a thousand years old and certainly not indigenous to the United States. Here is a play first performed at the Globe in London in 1610, Ben Jonson's satire, *The Alchemist*. The master of the house goes away, and various dupes come to see the Alchemist, who is a servant with a hustle going. Some of the dupes want gold, and some want success, and power, and knowledge, and how to win friends and influence people, and how to find a nice mate, and how to achieve poise and fight moral decay. Same old stuff, things don't change that quickly. Everybody gets gulled by what they want most. Here, the Alchemist announces a prescription:

> *Sir, against one o'clock, prepare yourself.*
> *Til when you must be fasting; only, take*
> *Three drops of vinegar, in, at your nose;*
> *Two at your mouth; and one, at either ear;*
> *Then, bathe your fingers' ends; and wash*
>   *your eyes;*
> *To sharpen your five senses; and, cry* hum
> *Thrice; and then* buz, *as often . . .*

Too easy, three drops of vinegar and cry *hum,* look at the dupes go for it.

So we are prepared when a guy wearing a wrinkled bed sheet gets off an Air India flight and starts telling us what we need to know. How can anything good come out of a country as screwed up as India? Sixty-two different languages and cows in the streets and starving since anybody can remember—how can they really know something if they're starving? So assume we want all this interior control, and serenity, and how to find a nice mate—we're already slipping into the roles in *The Alchemist*—what do we do?

Well, says the guy in the wrinkled bed sheet, you fast, or you stop eating meat, or you watch the tip of your nose, and you say Om. Or Hum.

Hum? What about the three drops of vinegar, Jack? And which way to the Egress? We've seen this play, rewritten for each generation. That's the majority reaction.

There is a minority that thinks nothing good can come from the United States—rampantly materialistic, insensitive—and all good things come from where incense is burned and customs are more exotic. But the minority are setups. Witness:

Two friends of mine promoted the visit of a swami. I will give the friends the fictitious names of Michael Murphy and Robert Ornstein. The swami was the Swami Suchabanana, that's right, Suchabanana, and was said by some to look very much like Ornstein, who has a beard anyway.

The faithful of Los Angeles filed in, and "Murphy" introduced the swami. "Murphy," the audience knew, was very well qualified to introduce swamis, being an alumnus of the Sri Aurobindo ashram, and able to give long raps on the Atman and the Brahman and Consciousness. The swami was in his swami robes and his swami turban, and he had that singsong Indian accent—

"Now the mantram that I use is bah, nah, nah, say it, please, bah—"

"Bah" said the audience.

"Nah," chanted the swami.

"Nah," chanted the audience.

"Nah," chanted the swami.

"Nah," chanted the audience.

"Very good, bah-nah-nah," said the swami. "Very holy word, bah-nah-nah."

Bah-nah-hah? Bah-nah-nah? A couple of skeptics in the audience are beginning to eye each other. Bah-nah-nah? You know what that sounds like?

Murphy and Ornstein are still alive today, so it could not have been they. The two hoaxers were stoned to death.

But there's nothing wrong with bah-nah-nah, as we will see.

III. Meditations

Redefining meditation is a beginning. Meditation—that is, Meditation II—is not part of the fabric of our culture. It has been introduced, or reintroduced, in a very American way, not as part of religion, but as a process that will do you some good. The aspect of it that will do you some good is relaxation, but curiously, where Meditation II comes from, that aspect is almost trivial.

It may be that the importers know this, that they are selling what is easiest to sell, and they figure the other benefits will just creep up on their clients.

You Deserve a Break Today

Transcendental Meditation is the McDonald's of the meditation business. Or maybe the Howard Johnson's. Whatever suggests: a relatively low fixed price, a standard item, and increasing numbers of franchises, or outlets. Like McDonald's, TM suggests, "You deserve a break today," in fact, you deserve two, twenty minutes in the morning and twenty minutes in the evening. TM has processed somewhere between 400,000 and 500,000 Americans, most of them in the last four or five years, and that gives it respectable size among service organizations.

In one sense, TM is a pioneer. Indians have been bringing the vedanta, or Hindu scriptures, here for almost a hundred years, but TM made a meditation technique work with an audience that didn't want to hear any Hindi. And for de-Hindizing the technique, TM deserves its success, which has been spectacular. It took the strangeness—and the threat—from the second definition of meditation, and once the threat was gone, even the Rotary Club and the Illinois State Legislature took to it.

Transcendental Meditation comes from a gentleman called Maharishi Mahesh Yogi—born Mahesh Prasad Varma in 1918 in the Central Provinces, father forest ranger, degree in physics from Allahabad University in 1942, says the official biography. (Maharishi, or Maharaj Ji, appears as a title before a number of figures from the East, since it means Sage, or Wise One, and if you mix among the followers of several of them it can get confusing. There is Maharishi the TM leader, and Maharaj Ji the sixteen-year-old guru, and Maharishi the late guru of Baba Ram Dass. I once had file folders organized by my favorite technique among all the Maharishis, e.g., Maharishi—Sound, Maharishi—Light, Maharishi—Reads Minds.) Maharishi was on his way to become, like the members of his caste, a merchant or a clerk, and to have a marriage arranged for him when he met one of the major religious leaders of India: Swami Brahmanada Saraswati, the Jadgadguru Bhagwan Shankaracharya, and he became a disciple and spent thirteen and a half years with him. His assignment, given when it became time for the master to leave his body, was to find a simple form of meditation for everyone to practice. Maharishi spent two years in a cave in the Himalayas and emerged with TM. (Two years in a cave, for a religious Indian, is like two years at the Harvard Business School for a commercial banker.)

Maharishi seems to have started his efforts quite innocently, without any great world plan, talking to Indian businessmen. His instincts steered him in the direction of acceleration; things moved faster in the West, so by 1960 he was setting up the International Meditation Society in London. Being pragmatic in nature, he was not afraid to use radio, television and public relations—an approach that, needless to say, did not go down well with the gurus left in India. By the late 1960's he had, as followers, the Beatles and Mia Farrow; John Lennon, a former Beatle, once spent eight hours a day meditating with the Maharishi in the Himalayas. The bearded, giggly presence of the Maharishi became familiar on the talk shows: there was Maharishi on Johnny Carson.

And that crested and passed. John Lennon said that the gurus of India were like rock stars in the West, if you couldn't be Mick Jagger you could be a maharishi. The Maharishi went on a nationwide tour with the Beach Boys, another rock group, and nobody came. The tour had to be canceled, and it looked like TM was another one of those Sixties Things, fading with the natural rhythms of time. Within a couple of years, the Maharishi was to say he had failed in his mission, and yet even as he spoke another wave was beginning to curl.

Before we complete that story, it might be useful to see what this is all about. When I signed up for TM, I had already been through a year of other trips that involved meditations, and my attitude was more that of an engineer taking apart somebody else's widget—well, let's see how *they* do it. Unlike most of my TM classmates, I did not have a friend who had just done it, and also unlike my TM classmates, I had been through much of the literature of meditation.

I happened to do this at a university, so our first lecture was in a university building. On the table in our room were glossy reprints of articles telling us how TM would fix us up, color charts in them of stress relief. Not only was there TM's own literature, but also reprints from *Scientific American* and *The Wall Street Journal*. Our instructor was a clean-cut junior called Buzz, who wore a sport jacket and loafers, and who smiled a lot. The audience was naturally mostly students, but with a sprinkling of older people, for the TM lectures were advertised—mostly in diners and on tree trunks, it seemed to me—over a wide area.

"Anybody can do this," Buzz said, "no matter how old or how smart. As we meditate we become clearer, you can do more, students get better grades, the mind doesn't wander. TM rest is deeper than sleep. It gets rid of really deep stresses. It helps your relationship with other people. You will get along better with your roommates."

What we would do, if we wanted to sign up, was to come to two lectures, and then be initiated on the weekend, and then one more lecture and one more weekend—that's all there was.

"Previously, we had three states of consciousness," Buzz said. "Waking, sleeping and dreaming. This is the fourth state, cosmic and all-inclusive. The mind is evolutionary, a blessing of the Creator, approaching the Infinite One"—Buzz giggled a bit, and the audience got restless—"but there's nothing to believe in TM. You don't have to believe in anything. And nothing to give up."

"Is this the same as yoga?" somebody wanted to know.

"No, all you do in TM is sit still," Buzz said. "Yoga will give you a charley horse. Zen monks meditate for twenty-five years to get the same result TM will give you in two weeks. It's different from concentration, and from contemplation."

TM, said Buzz, used a sound. Different sounds match different people—you and your roommate might not like the same music. A sound in the Vedic tradition is a mantram. Each of us would get his own mantram. Were all the mantrams really individual? They were, though there were far more people than mantrams, since 20,000 people a month were signing up for TM. How do the instructors match the mantram to the individual? I wanted to know. Buzz said you went to a teacher training course—ten or twelve weeks—and learned how to do this, but it was privileged information how it was done. We would fill out a questionnaire, have an interview, and get our mantram.

"Never," Buzz said, "tell anybody your mantram. That will ruin the whole effect." How come? "We have found that through experience. Your mantram is secret. Every once in a while somebody goes through TM, and then a friend gets interested, and they tell the friend the mantram, just to save the initiation fee. It doesn't work. There was a guy in Rhode Island who used somebody else's mantram and he got edgy and irritable and lost energy. It's worth the fee." The fee was $45 for students and $75 for adults. The fee for adults is now up to $125.

All kinds of medical tests had showed that TM relieved stress, Buzz said. The body was carrying stress, the imprint of the daily activities, but sleep didn't relieve all the stress. Every mental condition has a corresponding physical one: the release of stress—Buzz drew bubbles rising on the blackboard—is an activity, maybe a chemical change, and that activity creates a mental activity, a thought.

If we got so relaxed, how would we ever get around to do anything?

The mind is spontaneously capable, said Buzz.

When anxiety is down, capabilities develop. It doesn't lead to inertia. Just twenty minutes, twice a day, would leave us refreshed.

If meditation was so good, why only twenty minutes?

So you can adjust to the change, Buzz said. You have to have a balance of meditation and activity.

We filled out questionnaires, rather brief questionnaires, age, occupation, and so on. The only unusual question was: had we used any drugs?

We made appointments for Saturday.

"Bring six to twelve fresh flowers, two to three sweet fresh whole fruit, and a clean white handkerchief. And the fee for the course," Buzz said. "Don't eat a lot. And we ask that you not use any recreational chemicals while you are learning TM. Give it a chance to work. We find that many people cut down on their recreational chemicals after learning meditation."

Hands went up in the audience. What kind of fruit? What kind of flowers? They wanted to be told exactly. *All* recreational chemicals?

On Saturday I reported with one apple, one orange, one white handkerchief, and a bouquet from the florist. We were in the basement of a university building. No English 212 today. One at a time, we went into the initiation room (English 212). Candles, incense, bowls of fruit, lots of flowers, very pretty.

It was so dark in the room I could barely see the pictures scotch-taped on the wall: Maharishi, I supposed, and Guru Dev, his teacher. The offerings, said Buzz, were symbolic, flower of life, fruit the seed of life, and the handkerchief, the cleansing of the spirit. We were both in our socks. Buzz went through a ten-minute ceremony, all by himself and all in Sanskrit, with rice, salt and sandalwood.

"What was that?" I said when he stopped.

"That's the ceremony, initiation," Buzz said. "Some of it is the names of the masters who preserved the technique. We're grateful to the Vedic tradition for having preserved it, it's as applicable today as thousands of years ago. Okay, I'm going to give you your mantram. The mantram is meaningless, a sound whose effect is known. Your mantram is *Shiam*."

"*Shiam?*" I said. "*Shiam?* You sure *Shiam* is mine?"

Buzz looked stunned. What's the matter with Shiam? And I was thinking: You sure it's Shiam and not Shiom? And I had been looking for some basic Sanskrit sound, Hum or Aum or Hrim or Bam, I didn't exactly remember Shiam. And I was also remembering an unpublished article on the "rise times" of sounds in physiological psychology, how mantra were always soft and mellifluous, never any k's, nothing sharp, lots of soft mmm's and o's, see, Campbell's Soup is secretly conditioning you, they have you going mmm-mmm good.

"Shiam," Buzz said. "Let's say it." We said it. "Okay, just keep it going, to yourself, and if thoughts come let them come, and don't try." We closed our eyes. I could see the letters: SHIAM. Then I thought, I bet these guys screwed up my mantram, that one doesn't sound quite right, there's no quality these days, car mechanics fake repairs; plumbers, no craftsmen left; but at the same time I knew just as many mantrams as Buzz, so I thought, well, what the hell, they all work, and I kept it going. It was very quiet. Toward the end of the twenty-minute period I peeked a couple of times. Buzz had his eyes shut and was breathing evenly. I tried it a couple of different speeds. S h i a m, slow, and Shiam Shiam Shiam, fast. It doesn't have to stay consistent. "Very slowly, open your eyes," Buzz said. "Take a couple of minutes to come out." Was it easy? Yes, Was it pleasant? Yes. Did the mantram change, get faster or slower or disappear? Yes. Did thoughts come? Yes. "Good," said Buzz.

Some people have reported dizziness and nausea and all sorts of wild things. I guess all that is possible, magnetism without imagination is nothing, imagination without magnetism can produce convulsions, as they told Louis XVI, but it's not my experience.

Buzz said I could have my handkerchief and flowers and fruit back. I took the handkerchief, I ate the apple, and I left the orange and the flowers.

In our midweek sessions, we discussed our experiences and asked questions. Did anybody forget their mantram? Some people had. Okay, don't worry about it, if it doesn't come back in a couple of days, call your instructor. Did the mantram show up sometimes when it wasn't TM time? Tell it cheerfully to go away, like a friend who has dropped in when you're working. Did people fall asleep while meditating? That's okay, that's a good meditation, wake up and finish. Did a lot of thoughts come? That's okay, just notice the thoughts and go back to the mantram. Why weren't we getting progressively better? Because there's always the release of stress, until the very last stress is relieved, and that's pure conciousness. When you're in pure consciousness, do you know it? No, you know it later. Does the appearance of the thought correspond in intensity to the stress released? No. A lot of people hadn't noticed any change in themselves. You won't notice the change, it's like staring at a rosebud all night, by morning it's bloomed, but it's hard to notice the changes.

I asked Buzz, after class, "Is this a good job? Part-time?"

"For me, you mean?" Buzz said. "Well, you make a little, but you could certainly make more doing something else in the same time."

There seemed to be a fair dropout rate between the first and second weekends. We went to get our meditations checked. Close your eyes, open your eyes, close them again. Do your meditation. Take a couple of minutes to come out when you're through. Was it easy? Was it pleasant? Good.

The girl who was doing my checking sounded like a recording. Did thoughts come? Yes. Good, the mantram should come as easily and effortlessly as the thoughts. We do not concentrate, we do not try. Any questions? Yes, do a lot of people think this is a waste of time? Yes, but the effects are going on whether you think they are or not, just keep going. Did a lot of people think they were doing it wrong? Yes, just keep going, there is no wrong way if you know there is no wrong way, we do not concentrate, we do not try. ("Be relaxed," said the German doctors, "und stop taking notes!") Well, I get the meditation part, but where is the transcendental? We are transcending thought when the mantram becomes so refined that it disappears, then the mind transcends everyday awareness and experiences pure awareness, or cosmic consciousness.

"That name puts people off," said one of the TM hierarchy. "We shouldn't say transcendental, we should say approaching transcendental, I wish Maharishi had called it creative intelligence. (The Science of Creative Intelligence is the name of a course within TM.)

But is it really different from sitting with your eyes shut, or taking a nap?

The Maharishi may have thought he had failed, at one point, but events were running independent of him. Actually, while TM faded from the newspapers, and the Maharishi faded from the talk shows, the word-of-mouth on TM continued, so that the numbers of people who signed up for the course didn't diminish. But the candidates were to change character; TM was to shift slowly from the exotic, Beatles-gone-to-Himalayas Sixties thing to the more traditional Ben Franklin, early-to-bed, Dale Carnegie self-help American procedure. At the pivot point of this turn was a slight, blond student in Los Angeles, Robert Keith Wallace. Wallace had begun TM as an undergraduate at UCLA, and he was a friend of Jerry Jarvis, who had been one of the protagonists in starting the Students' International Meditation Society. Wallace proposed a Ph.D. thesis in physiology at UCLA.

"Maharishi had been free to go out with a simple technique, because he wasn't part of a religious hierarchy, and I was free to try something in physiology that nobody with an established reputation would want to risk," Wallace said. Maharishi liked the idea. Nobody had done anything objective, the West was objective, Maharishi said. In India, people went uncritically from master to master, without distinguishing techniques.

For his thesis experiment, Wallace wired up twenty-seven meditators. Each subject would sit connected to instruments that would record continuously. Each subject had a catheter in one artery in the arm; the arm would be poked through a hole in a curtain so the subject wouldn't see the instruments and the blood, should they peek during meditation, because most people do not find the sight of their blood gurgling into instruments conducive to serenity. The wires were on for blood pressure, heart rate, rectal temperature, skin resistance and EEG. The subjects sat quietly for thirty minutes, then did twenty to thirty minutes of meditation, and then sat again quietly for another thirty minutes.

That must have been some group of meditators. I gave them points just for sitting still with all those wires and with a catheter in the arm.

In the middle period, the meditation period, the oxygen consumption on inhaling, and the carbon dioxide on exhaling, went way down. A 20 percent drop like that really should indicate a lower metabolism. The EEG showed nice alpha patterns. The heart rates slowed by an average of three beats per minute. Resistance of the skin to an electrical current went up fourfold—this is the GSR from biofeedback vocabulary, the higher the skin resistance, the greater the degree of relaxation. Blood pressure went down before meditation, and stayed low. The lactate concentrations in the blood took a steep dive. At the end of the meditation period, the lactate concentration rose a bit but stayed well under their premeditation period.

Lactate comes from the skeletal muscle tissue, and increases during any kind of stress. Exercise will bring it up, and so will the telephone call about losing all your money and your house burning down. Not only do you find lactate concentrations in people who are anxious, you can *make* people anxious, perfectly happy people, by giving them a shot of lactate. (You would only do that if you were researching lactate, naturally. The correlation between lactate and anxiety is controversial.)

And how did this differ from a good nap? Well, it does. Oxygen consumption starts to drop right away with meditation, and it takes a couple of hours to start tapering off during sleep. Skin resistance increases during sleep, but not as much as while meditating. (The carbon dioxide in the blood increases during sleep. There are, of course, different stages of sleep and different patterns within those stages.)

And how did TM compare to subjects who were hypnotized? Interesting: hypnosis has no particular physiology. The brain-wave and visceral readings for a hypnotic subject will be those of the state he is in; if he is super-relaxed, they may come up like meditation; otherwise they will be normal.

In short, the relaxation Wallace reported was, indeed, deeper than sleep, or than some stages of sleep. In fact, he said, the state produced by transcendental meditation was different from waking, dreaming and sleeping. It was a fourth state of consciousness.

Wallace's thesis, "The Physiological Effects of Transcendental Meditation," was not in the nature of the paradigm-busting papers of the *Annalen der Physik*, when Einstein and the other fellas used to publish in that journal; it was a descriptive proof of one technique where none had been done. But it was for Wallace the hat trick in this whole field.

Wallace's thesis went off to the prestigious journal *Science*. And with Herbert Benson, a cardiologist and assistant professor of medicine at the Harvard Medical School, the physiological changes of transcendental meditation appeared not only there, but in the *American Journal of Physiology, Scientific American* and *New England Journal of Medicine,* all very heavy, *Scientific American* as usual with nice graphs. Hat trick. That's not even counting *Connecticut Medicine, Science Digest* and the Proceedings of the American Societies for Experimental Biology.

Benson had been in public health service in Puerto Rico, working on blood pressure. Why did the Puerto

Ricans have fewer cardiac ailments than the main-landers?

"I give up, why," I said.

"Because of their attitude," Benson said. *"Mañana.* We need some of that if everybody doesn't want to keep dying so young, a different attitude."

Benson was working on primates at the Harvard Medical School, training them to control their blood pressure, when the meditators presented themselves. Wallace and Benson combined on a couple of experiments, and now the results went out with the prestige of a Harvard Medical School by-line. "Mental states can markedly alter physiologic function," wrote Benson and Wallace, as if nobody had ever reported to Louis XVI. They called the meditation state "a wakeful hypometabolic physiologic state," a phrase that went ringing through the journals. "Wakeful," because the subjects were awake and you would think they would have to be asleep to get those numbers; "hypometabolic," well, remember *hypo* is "under," Greek, and *hyper* is "over," excess. A hypermetabolic state —excess, over—accompanies "anticipated stressful situations"; a hypometabolic state may accompany meditational states." What an anomaly, a waking state with such low metabolism!

Benson was enthused. One-third of all the adults in this country suffered from definite or borderline hypertension, high blood pressure. By meditating, he said, "we may be able to prevent and even treat it." And, at the same time, Benson said of TM: "It appears that . . . TM is the fastest and easiest way of doing so at this time."

The partnership of Benson and Wallace was not to last. Wallace was quiet, sincere, soft-spoken, but you sense somehow the steel spring of the divinity student, the true believer. Wallace was, first and foremost, a meditator, a disciple of the Maharishi; Benson was a physician, a cautious medical researcher who had never meditated and didn't intend to. Benson winced when his enthusiasm turned up in sleek reprints at all the TM lectures, Herbert Benson, M.D., Harvard Medical School.

By the time I got to Benson and Wallace they were polite but not really speaking to each other. Wallace became the charter president of Maharishi International University near Santa Barbara (now in Fairfield, Iowa); when you call, the switchboard says, "M-I-U." Every course includes "the Science of Creative Intelligence" in its title, from astronomy on. Benson was back in the lab, so cautious it took him six months to send me his first paper, so cautious he wouldn't even let his students know what he was about to publish in some journal, lest somebody leak it to TM and have it turn up in the press or in a glossy reprint at the TM introductory lecture. For ten months, tracking research, I would be calling them alternately, trying to pin down points: "But Benson says . . ." "But Wallace says . . ." Benson said he had a new blood pressure study, it was going to come out in *The Lancet*, the distinguished British medical journal, *and it didn't use TM*. Could I see it? No, not now. "Herb," I said, "it takes three years to do a book like mine, *The Lancet* will have hit the stands and have been gobbled up long before." Nope. Three weeks after *The Lancet* hit the stands I had my copy from Herb, for which I thanked him, except that my interest had been so whetted that by that time I already had my copy from *The Lancet*.

The research rolled on. My favorite head-bump phrenology journal, *The Journal of Electroencephalography and Clinical Neurophysiology,* reported that not only did meditators have those dollops of alpha, and different thetas than sleep has, but the brain-wave rhythms were synchronized, and beta spikes were appearing from deep meditation. "That's when you're touching consciousness, the beta spike," said the TM physiology people. A California researcher reported that TM reduced the symptoms of asthma. Poor damn asthmatics, first they got cured by placebo pills and then by TM, absolutely nobody will believe the trouble is in their chests.

By now, researching TM was replacing the sit-in in the dean's office of a few years back. In my own TM class, two students handed out questionnaires. (What they were researching had already been done—they didn't seem to know it, but what the hell.) And the TM people were hitting research like a fixed slot machine, and printing it with pretty charts on sleek paper. FASTER REACTION TIME, said the poster, showing a quarterback with his arm cocked, linemen descending upon him.

The State Legislature of Illinois endorsed TM. So did General Davis of the Army War College. Joe Namath was into it, and Bill Walson the basketball pro, and "there are a couple of strong contenders for the Presidency—very strong—who practice TM," said the Research Coordinator.

TM put out a booklet for businessmen, *Creative Intelligence in Business,* which said that research showed that TM improved behavioral stability, lessened susceptibility to psychosomatic disease, reduced nervousness, aggression, depression and irritability, increased the clarity of perception, improved learning ability, speeded comprehension, produced better memory and faster absorption of difficult material—and that's only part of it.

Plainly, TM was the greatest thing since peach ice cream.

And all this from sitting still twice a day, closing the eyes, and going "Hrim, hrim," or "Shiam, shiam"?

Well, yes. "Sometimes," said Wallace, "people make things more difficult than they are."

There are critics. Some of the critics called up the local TM chapter and said send over some meditators, we want to test them. The local TM chapter seemingly always obliges. And then the critics found, well, in one instance the skin temperature didn't go up sharply at all, and in several others there was a lot of flak about TM promoting "creativity and intelligence." What's creativity and intelligence, anyway? The testers rolled out the Barron-Welsh Art Scale and the Wallace-Kogan Test and the TM people didn't do any better than anybody else, some things better, some things worse. Then Gary Schwartz, Harvard, noticed: the TM testees did better on right-sided activities, associations, twilight visions, and worse on the left-sided, cognitive, problem-solving activities. That would be consistent with left-side, right-side, but you need both sides, perspiration as well as inspiration. If you need a little less tension to be intelligent, okay; some people need a little more.

(I always get suspicious of the promises to help creativity and intelligence, because they make it sound like a twist of the key makes you a genius. Silva Mind Control says, "The difference between genius mentality and lay mentality is that the genius uses more of his mind and uses it in a different way." Other than being very close to meaningless—and Silva is full of meaningless phrases—that seems to promise if you can learn the different way in some two-weekend course you can be a genius. It's like: ah, tap that right side, the old subconscious, and there is genius. Well, maybe, if you've been working at something eighteen hours a day. Why don't people remember that James Joyce learned Norwegian just so he could read Ibsen, and Edmund Wilson just learned Hungarian just so he could read Molnar, and there were lots of translations in both cases, and for all his exquisite right-sidedness, Einstein carefully figured out he could wear the same jacket all week and not have to spend thirty seconds thinking on clothes, so he could spend eighteen hours thinking about geometrodynamics, space and time. Not much time goofing off for those fellas.)

And some critics said that the TM research was all a series of one-shots, though TM was starting longer-range longitudinal studies.

And other critics said, what is all that mumbo jumbo with the handkerchief and the flowers, what is this secret mantram business, some sort of gnosticism? And some critics said that TM sets up experiments, pops the results, and has them out in a sleek, glossy booklet before they can be critiqued. FASTER REACTION TIME, they said, was based on an unpublished experiment with eight undergraduates and uncritiqued statistics. And some critics said that people who had previously reported psychosomatic ailments such as ulcers and headaches, but had them under control now, didn't have them under control.

And some critics said TM was getting as metallic as the phone company, the checkers sound like telephone company recordings, nyeyun, fiyuv, threeyuh, that is not a working number. Of course they sound that way, they have memorized a thirty-point program, just like a computer:

It is better to refrain from using "you," "your," or "I." Whenever possible, use "we" or "our."

Say: (1) "Let's close our eyes." (Ten seconds).

There are choices along the way, just like a computer program:

(14) "Did you have any thoughts?"' If the answer is yes, go to (15); if no, go to (12).

Not much room for heresy in that program. With a university and a bureaucracy and secretaries who don't meditate, and gaining all the time on McDonald's, naturally TM is a target. But in one instance they have been discreet: they do not promote it as an alternative religion. You do not have to go to the Vedanta Society on Sunday morning instead of to church. The emphasis is on the technique, and not on the antecedents. If the technique is all you want, you take it and go away. Otherwise, you stick around and do Advanced Meditation, still twenty minutes a time, and learn more of the Vedas and Upanishads and Bhagavad-Gita as taught by the Maharishi. General Davis is probably not in it for the Bliss Consciousness; publicly, he says his blood pressure went down ten points.

This is not the first time Transcendental has come wafting across our shores, if you remember your American literary history, for there was good old Emerson telling his fellow Americans that there was something more than hard work and prosperity, there was the Oversoul, a good, natural, optimistic philosophy, a little short of Bliss Consciousness, but Emerson had been into "translations from the Hindoo" and German metaphysicians and he must have known his audience. Meditation: you can do it twice a day like brushing your teeth, and you can be sitting in a car or a plane or a train. It's almost—not quite

—American and respectable, but here's *The New Yorker* with a cartoon in which the imperious chicken-chested four-star general is saying to his orderly, I missed the prayer breakfast, Smedley, book me into the Meditation Room just before lunch.

As for me, I practiced my TM faithfully, well, almost faithfully, once a day if not twice a day, and I went to my checking sessions—was it easy? was it pleasant? did thoughts come? we do not try, remember, we do not try. Some of the time I was so nudgy I couldn't wait for the twenty minutes to be up, and spent them thinking of things to do, simultaneously mantraming away. But some of the time, once you get used to it, it is like a combination lock. You go nine right, twenty-five left, twelve right, and as you turn it close to twelve it just falls open. You don't even have to pull. Sometimes, planes, trains, kazonk, just like an awake nap, though sometimes at minute #14 you want to read the paper.

(Charlie Tart, of *Altered States,* wrote a journal article in response to TM. He said what he seemed to do was to churn through the undigested stuff of the day, images, thoughts, much as the dream mechanism is said to do. The dream mechanism, it is said, runs all that stuff through the brain that has been run through during the day, trying to get it organized on all levels, emotional as well as rational. The longer Tart did it, he wrote, the more all that churning calmed down, leaving him finally calmer, short of bliss, and with an aversion to alcohol. He went on to more complex disciplines, where alcohol is considered pretty gross anyway.)

My instructor Buzz was wrong literally but answered the question correctly when he was asked is this like yoga. The questioner meant hatha yoga, the quest for unified consciousness through physical means, breathing and postures; that is what yoga is to most people. But of course there are a lot of other yogas, of which TM is but part of one. The TM enthusiasts sometimes put down the other techniques, but then so do many religions and religious techniques.

I don't know when Joe Namath and Bill Walton

do their meditating, but I found it hard to do anything competitive afterward, for an hour or two. You just watch whatever ball it is go by and say, oh, nice shot. It's okay with you, like you've had two beers.

For some of the people, some of the time, TM works.

There, I said it. That is, it teaches a technique of meditation that produces relaxation, and relaxation has some beneficial effects. It may produce even more than relaxation. *Meditation works.* Funny phrase. Yet there it is. But before you put me in the newest TM booklet as an endorser saying "TM works"—which it does—you have to finish the story.

Benson, half of the great research team, was back in the lab at the Harvard Medical School, without Wallace. Now he emerged from the laboratory firing salvos into the medical journals. (The mysterious *Lancet* article was one.) Benson had analyzed, dissected and reassembled the whole mantram business, and TM had no monopoly.

No? What else works?

Some secular techniques, autogenic training, progressive relaxation—and some religious techniques—

Well, some forms of Christianity, some forms of Judaism, some forms of Islam, just possibly Subud (that's Indonesian), Hichiren Sho Shu, Hare Krishna, Meher Baba—

Everything works?

No, not at all, it's just that certain techniques can produce an altered state of consciousness, and some altered states of consciousness produce a response of relaxation. In fact, that's what we're calling it, "the Relaxation Response."

The *Lancet* article said Benson and his team had reduced the blood pressure in the experimental subjects without TM and without anything fancy and, in fact, just by a very ordinary English mantram. But he didn't call it a mantram. The magic English mantram, in a moment. First, let's see how, in this case, our Western scientific paradigm actually took us away from something that worked and substituted something much more complex.

To solve the mysteries of the brain, Western man has been pulling and pushing and analyzing and dissecting. Descartes had brain drawings, the eye sees here and the perception comes here. Camillo Golgi in the 1890's devised a stain and now you can see a neuron, a nerve cell. Golgi said these neurons were continuous through the brain, and the great Spanish microscopist, Santiago Ramón y Cajal, disagreed and said each cell was separate, and when they gave them a Nobel prize jointly in 1906 the fellas wouldn't speak to each other in Stockholm, threw pillows and sulked. Golgi stains are very pretty. A lady in physiology in Berkeley was making shirts with Golgi stains, very pretty, must be real conversation stoppers, what is that interesting pattern on your shirt, oh, those are neurons from the cerebral cortex. Oh. Must be one of the world's great in-groups when you're wearing a Golgi-stain shirt and you see another one in the airport.

So here is the neuron looking like, printed in black and white, a star or a rhombus, some say, but to me like a fried egg, a little too much pepper in one part of the yolk, and the white splatted out into fingers, as if the pan were really hot and the egg was dropped from a couple of feet. Between the end of one finger and the beginning of the next, on the next fried egg, is a gap, called a synapse by the British neurophysiologist Sir Charles Sherrington, 1897. Sherrington is a semi-poet of neurophysiology, as well as a great teacher who keeps asking his students at Cambridge to bring him something new to learn, and to whom the brain is an "enchanted loom." Nice. The synapses, the gaps, are devices for processing information, lots of neurons in the cortex, 10^{10}, and even more synaptic contacts, 10^{14}.

So an Impulse comes chugging down the axon, the long finger coming away from the cell body. Tra la la la la la la, and now it gets to the edge, and how is it going to get across the gap, the synaptic cleft, to the other side? A cliff-hanger. Just as the Impulse is about to give up, a Chemical Transmitter appears, naturally secreted by a vesicle, and gives the Impulse a ride. (That's if it's an Excitatory Transmitter; an

Inhibitory Transmitter backs up and lets the Impulse just sit there.)

Otto Loewi in Germany and Sir Henry Dale in England in the 1920's tell about the chemical transmitters, and so does Sherrington's pupil Adrian in Cambridge, and neuron/neuron is too hard to do at first so they study a neuromuscular junction where the Impulse is going to tell the muscle to do something, and later Bernhard Katz in London is going to say the transmitters get released in little packets, or quanta, and the technical equipment gets more sophisticated, electron microscopes, and the synapse gets measured and the impulse clocked, and John Eccles becomes Sir John and E. D. Adrian becomes Lord Adrian, and the work goes on and Nobel prizes come fluttering out of Stockholm.

And in the biochemistry lab they have found some of the transmitters, norepinephrine and serotonin and dopamine. Reserpine, from the *Rauwolfia* root in the story of the dumb Nigerian, cuts down the norepinephrine, and the chlorpromazines that the Swiss made so much money on blocks its release. No Chemical Transmitter, no ride for the Impulse. No ride for the Impulse, fewer messages, c-a-l-m, that's the idea. But that's a little heavy-handed, so the fellas keep working on MAO inhibitors, which is not political because MAO is not Tse-tung but monoamine oxidase, monoamine being the transmitter and oxidase being the enzyme that breaks it down, and the MAO inhibitors are more specific, mood elevators as they say, because you can pick what you're transmitting and what not, and you get into alpha blockers and beta blockers, very clever indeed, if still controversial.

But somebody in the lab spots a flaw in the MAO's. Oops, doctors are going to prescribe this and warn the people not to eat cheese, and you know some of those jerks are going to eat cheese, and then what do we do? Because there's an amino in the cheese, tyramine, and the MAO inhibitor is going to block the enzyme degradation—never mind what all this means, keep going—and the tyramine won't get deaminized and everybody's blood pressure is going to go up. Back to the test tubes, Harry. Let's see what we can do with that molecule, what did we have last time, carbon hydrogen carbon carbon nitrogen nitrogen, let's give it a pop of fluoride and see if we can change the benzine ring, nitrogen nitrogen *nitrogen,* because sure as hell those tensed-up anxious jerks are going to forget, they're going to feel very virtuous about turning down the Camembert and then they're going to have a cheeseburger with their kids, let's see, increase the budget, turn up the Bunsen burner— we're really huffing and puffing in the paradigm now—

—and along comes a character in a bed sheet stepping off the Air India flight and he says, "Why don't you say gazoom gazoom gazoom, twenty minutes twice a day but not before bedtime, shut your eyes, don't try, gazoom gazoom gazoom"—

—and *it works! Rauwolfia* time.

Noise

Why? Why does it work?

Start with noise. Even animals, say the ethologists, spend a couple of quiet hours a day, grooming and picking among themselves.

In our culture, the noise level is incredible. I don't mean just the jackhammer in the street outside your hotel room, or banging the garbage cans early in the morning. Look at it from the point of view of one of your neurons. There's something to do all the time.

A lot of people get up to an alarm radio, or even TV. Then maybe they read the paper with a cup of coffee. Then they get into their cars and turn on the radio, and they're so habituated to the noise they don't even listen. News: there is a tornado somewhere and traffic deaths somewhere and a house burned down somewhere. Every once in a while some paper runs the same story every day for a month to see if anybody notices, a hill in Korea or Vietnam or wherever the war is that month, or a running fight on Capitol Hill, every day for a month exactly the same story, nobody notices. All that noise goes pouring through the neurons like syrup through pancakes. And it starts very early. The average kid, say the child experts testifying about TV advertising, watches twenty-five thousand commercials a year, *twenty-five thousand* reinforcements for sugar-coated Popsy Flakes, Captain Goo, it's a tribute to the plasticity of the human brain that the kid can still talk and read— maybe he can't, but you can see why he will have his transistor radio clamped to his ear in Yellowstone Park. The pines and the sky are only partly real: real reality is a Popsy Flake commercial. Our experience shapes our perception.

So we have a lot of practice, a lot of conditioning, in what Huxley called "inquietude for the sake of inquietude." St. John of the Cross wrote about that, you get junked up just on the inquietude.

My favorite biology watcher tells how animals and insects use noise. Termites make percussive sounds by beating their heads against the floor; the sound is said to resemble sand falling on paper, but an analysis of the sound reveals a high degree of organization in the drumming; the beats occur in regular rhythmic phrases. Rabbits, mice and prairie hens drum with their feet, the deathwatch beetle makes a ticking sound with a bump on his abdomen, fish click their teeth, blow air, and drum muscles against special air sacs.

And all this registers with the respective termites, beetles and fish. Leeches tap on leaves and other leeches tap back. Animals with loose skeletons rattle them, and even earthworms emit faint, staccato notes.

Lots of music going on. Maybe some of it is just for practice, but most of it carries information; a certain click of the pointman termite turns the column, the dancer bee indicates the clover.

And what of us? Well, we are gifted with speech,

and we have supercommunication, in fact we have so much of it we come close to losing the meanings in the cacophony. I suppose we need the information about which streets are torn up, and how to take tax deductions, or what foods are cheaper this season. But so much of our noise is distorted, and designed to keep us off balance, the noise about office politics and school politics, the noise, well, the television commercials are a cliché but there they are, five hours per family per night saying you are not okay, your floors do not shine, your coffee tastes lousy, you are exuding odors from fourteen parts of your body and further: health is something you as a consumer have to buy, from the dispensers of health, otherwise you're going to be up all night and your stomach's going to churn, never mind the natural self-corrections in the body, you better get in there and do the job. You do not have health, you have to buy it. That one alone costs hundreds of millions, not only over the counter, but as a matter of public policy.

And so—almost instinctively—we don't believe it, or don't believe much of it, and the tension of sorting out, amidst all the noise, what is true and what is not true takes extra energy—we are not even aware of the tension. If the dancer bee said, clover, three hundred yards, north by northwest, but none of you jerks can fly by any means known to aeronautical science and furthermore you're too fat and your mother-in-law doesn't like your face and this whole hive is being transferred to Arkansas, the rest of the bunch could try, at some expenditure of bee energy, to extract the information from the dancer bee's neurotic goings-on, or they could, one day, commit him to the attention of a large bee-eating bird and try another dancer.

And that's just the exterior noise; the confusing messages in the exterior noise are quite enough to produce a need for a quiet interior place. But we also have the *interior* noise, being language-using, conscious, conceptualizing animals, and the interior noise is even louder.

Ratcheta ratcheta ratcheta, Molly Bloom's soliloquy, me my mine, that guy in the office is and I shouldn't have said that yesterday and the prices keep going up and when the phone rang I thought and so on. Even if you turn off the TV, thereby missing the possibility of a baseball game, a football game, a hockey game, a tennis playoff—no matter *what* time of year, lots of noise there—the interior noise will get you, you've had so much practice at it. Say Mommy, baby. Say Mommy. Say Grammaw. See Grammaw? Smile. Say Grammaw to Grammaw. The neurons have been twitching so long they think not twitching is abnormal. Once in mid-Arizona a friend of mine got up in the morning bleary-eyed and said he had had no sleep. Why no sleep?

There was a beagle outside my window.

I thought it was a great phrase, something worthy of Joyce, *Finnegans Wake* maybe, God is a shout in the street. There is a beagle outside my window. What kind of beagle? Friendly, tri-colored, tail-wagging, did it sit on the roof of its doghouse flying a Sopwith Camel and dodging the Red Baron?

This damn beagle, said the friend, must have been after a jack rabbit, yawp yawp yawp yawp. All night, yawp yawp yawp yawp. Ah. Well, we all have beagles outside our windows, yawp yawp yawp, and the sound echoes in the neuronal pathways even when we're asleep, even when there is no beagle there and even when we are asleep *we will talk to ourselves constantly.* Not only does that talk limit the perceptions of reality, it gives the neurons busy-work. So: the mantram gives you a bone for the beagle, you can throw it right out there, and once you've thrown it there's nothing much else to do. You may hear some growling and clicking, but if it works you won't hear yawp yawp yawp. Of course, the beagle may not pick up the bone.

But maybe it will.

Rest deeper than sleep? Some of the neurons are quieter when you're alseep, and others work even harder, trying to get things organized for tomorrow, all lined up and consistent. If you can wind up this phrase and send it through on its own momentum, balam balam balam, waking does not matter, it becomes a lullaby for twitchy neurons, they turn up their little toes and snooze.

Why does it work? "A good vibe," said a counter-cultural voice. "A mantram is a sound whose effect is known," said the telephone company.

Wallace had a guess. Wallace and I spoke in Physiology, in which he was fluent and in which I knew just enough to say, I wish please to cash a traveler's check, where is the bathroom, I wish to speak to the manager.

"Some structure in the brain creates order," said Wallace. "We know the reticular system gates out inputs."

"So far, so good."

"As you decrease the activity in the sympathetic nervous system, the system gets more orderly."

"Is that true?"

"Sure, not only do you have synchronization between the brain hemispheres, which you don't normally see, but you get *harmonics* of alpha as well as alpha, ten twenty forty eighty."

I said I must have missed an issue of my favorite head-bump magazine.

"The inward focus and the passive direction allow the thalamus to fire at its natural rhythm."

Firing in natural rhythm! Lovely.

"And that affects the hypothalamus."

Thalamus, the seat of all that sensorimotor activity in the midbrain, the word comes from *thálamos,* nuptial couch in Greek. Imagine that. And hypothalamus then is under the nuptial couch, and the instructions to fight or flee thus come from under the nuptial couch. Very insightful, Dr. Freud.

"I think in meditation," said Wallace, "there will be an analogy like superconductivity in physics, a place where there is no resistance at all." The rishis who invented the mantrams did not have in mind that you could go to the office and see the boss differently, or move the new warehouse to South Carolina without raising your blood pressure, or watch the portfolio go down another 15 percent with equanimity. They had in mind merging consciousness with Consciousness, they said. "Well, they study infinity in physics," Wallace said. "The purpose of the machinery is higher consciousness."

The beagles of the mind are well known to all philosophies, though they are called by many names. TM gives you an immediate device for beagle-soothing, but other schools want you to be aware first of how your mind works. It is always a different matter to recognize something conceptually and to *experience* it.

The year before I got to TM, I was in a course called Arica, which was a full-time esoteric school. One of the exercises—you could call it a meditation —went like this. You get a rock. (Some people got very pretty rocks, since they were going to be doing this exercise six days a week, four hours a day.) Class exercise. You put your rock on the floor in front of you; you can sit on a pillow. You put your consciousness in the rock. I was confused. How do you do that? Now you take a breath, pick up the rock, hold your breath, and move the rock in a circle in front of you. Your eyes are shut. And while you move the rock, you think, Om namo naraya naya, which you can spot immediately as a Sanskrit mantram. Then you exhale and put the rock down, take another breath, and do the same thing left-handed, two repetitions of the mantram per circle of the rock per breath. That's the beginning; it goes on. The last motion—same mantram going—is to circle your head with the rock, and visualize a white light making the same circle inside your head.

Then you start over. Four hours. Nobody ever said that was a relaxation exercise, though you would think with all those circles and mantrams and breathing the beagles would all be occupied. And you weren't supposed to think anything else; just Om namo naraya naya.

My first reactions were: my knee hurts, this is silly, this is very boring. Om namo naraya naya, I lost the count there, what time is it, now my other knee hurts, Om namo naraya naya, this is the dumbest thing I've ever seen, Om namo naraya naya, my nose itches, Om namo naraya naya, what shall we have for dinner, look, that guy is already circling his head with his rock, Om namo naraya naya, I think I'll quit this whole business, this is the most *boring* invention since *piano* lessons, these are the piano scales of the mind, dum da da da da da dum.

I went to lunch with two classmates on a third day, a physician and a psychologist. Physician, B.S., M.D., and psychologist, B.A., M.A., Ph.D. And you know what we talked about? How big do you make *your* circle? Is it better to have a big rock or a little rock? Is it better to have a pretty rock or a plain rock? Isn't this the most boring thing, I wonder what it leads to? Can you make a white light go on at the same time the rock is going around your head? Can I see your rock when we get back to class?

Along about the second week, I got very Prussian and conscientious. I was only going to think Om namo naraya naya, and nothing else! Just like the good Germans in Autogenic Training. Enough of the chitter-chatter! No more: what time is it, my knee hurts, it's so pretty outside why am I in here. No more!

And I couldn't do it. It was like reading the sentence: don't think of an elephant, by the time you've read "elephant" it's too late. Something always popped up; it wasn't a verbal thought, it was an image, and not a white light image, either.

So I decided to do the opposite: I would *not* say Om namo naraya naya, I was just going to go over a list of stocks and review what each company had earned the previous year and what it was expected to earn this year. That was more successful, except for the occasional Om namo naraya naya that crept in uninvited.

I went home that night and I looked up all the stocks and their estimated earnings and their prices, and I was rarely more than a nickel off. Reaction: first, a little flutter of pride; second, an absolute wave of horror. All those numbers are already in the books, and that's what I'm carrying around in my head! It was like opening the attic door and this foul air comes out and there's all this *junk* lying around, bits of pictures, pieces of papers with old phone numbers, legs of old toys, bicycle tires for vanished bicycles, wishes, inhibitions, dreams, old conversations, conversations the way they should have come out, junk! Who is that who has all that junk in his head?

By chance, a friend came by and we went off to meet an ex-psychologist called Richard Alpert in his old incarnation—the ex-sidekick of Leary—and Baba Ram Dass in his present, and he said what is it you're doing, and I said, well, we have an hour of sort of hatha yoga and an hour of Tibetan chanting and then we turn this rock in a circle for four hours —"Ah," he said—and I said, I am very depressed because my mind is a pile of junk.

"That's nice, that's nice," said Baba Ram Dass. "You're doing well. The Indians say the mind is a drunken monkey, you know. When I went to India, I went to this monastery, and they showed me into this little cell, and they said, count your breath, and we'll bring the food right here. And I said, well, I don't think I want to do that right now, and they said, okay, that's what we do here, so if you're not ready, let us know whenever you're ready. So I said okay, breathe in, breathe out, one, breathe in, breathe out, two. And I thought of all the ice-cream sundaes I had ever eaten, and old movies I had seen, and old conversations, and future conversations, and in the afternoons I would think, there's an afternoon flight from Delhi to New York at three-thirty, I could walk out of here, I could be in Delhi tonight, I could be on that flight tomorrow."

"But you didn't."

"No, I didn't."

"So your mind is a drunken monkey, too."

"Everybody's mind is a drunken monkey, but they aren't aware of it. Now you're aware of it."

"I may have been just as happy not being aware of it."

But too late; don't think of an elephant. I went back to Om namo naraya naya, only now there was a little distance between me and the drunken monkey, enough so I could say, what is the drunken monkey going to come up with now? Let's get back to work? What's for dinner? This whole exercise is dumb? What?

If you could see into the minds of the president of U.S. Steel and the president of the AFL-CIO, if those gentlemen were sitting turning a rock and going Om namo naraya naya, their minds would be next year's budget and last year's budget and old golf scores and children's marks, images of faces, images of secretaries, obsolete airline schedules, disjointed columns of numbers already in the books—the whole array. Czech poetry. Scandinavian drinking songs.

The lesson that seeps through can be a little chilling: *your head is not your friend.* Not automatically. "The mind," said St. Theresa, the fifteenth-century Spanish mystic, "is an unbroken horse." That gives us beagles, monkeys and horses, but you get the idea.

Not all religious disciplines want to teach you to still the mind, especially not in two weekends; some want you first to see its nature, or their version of its nature.

But perhaps religion to altered states to relaxation to lowered blood pressure is a bit cumbersome. TM had taken much of the doctrine out of its technique; now Benson, the Harvard Medical School half of the old research team, was to take out the rest. But first he had to review the physiological benefits religion had had when it and not science was the paradigm:

"In the Western world today," wrote Benson and his associates, in *Psychiatry,* "there is a growing interest in nonpharmacological, self-induced, altered states of consciousness because of their alleged benefits of better mental and physical health and improved ability to deal with tension and stress. During the experience of one of these states, individuals claim to have feelings of increased creativity, of infinity, and of immortality; they have an evangelistic sense of mission, and report that mental and physical suffering vanish. Subjective and objective data exist which support the hypothesis that an integrated central nervous system reaction, the '*relaxation re-*

sponse,' underlies this altered state of consciousness. Physicians should be knowledgeable of the physiologic changes and possible health benefits of the relaxation response."

A Nobel-winning Swiss physiologist, Walter Hess, had delineated the location of the fight-or-flight or "ergotropic" response, and its opposite, called the "trophotropic," in the brain of the cat. A relaxation spot in the brain! " . . . the anterior hypothalamus," wrote Benson, "extending into the supra- and pre-optic areas, septum and inferior lateral thalamus."

As Hess had said, there were no specific foci for isolated responses "but a collective representation of a group of responses."

And how do you get to the anterior hypothalamus to get the message to relax?

Benson delineated four elements:

(1) *Mental Device*. "There should be a constant stimulus, e.g. a sound, word, or phrase repeated silently or audibly, or fixed gazing at an object. The purpose of these procedures is to shift from logical, externally-oriented thought."

Benson did not mention "mantram."

(2) *Passive Attitude*. Don't worry about how you're doing, and if thoughts come, go back to the technique.

(3) *Decreased Muscle Tonus*. Sit in a comfortable posture and take it easy.

(4) *Quiet Environment*. Shut your eyes (except for meditations in gazing at an object).

Benson was eager to show that many religions contained techniques leading to "the relaxation response," but in fact the techniques might have been associated with mysticism, and mysticism has been greeted by repugnance. The Trappist author Thomas Merton wrote, "The tendency of Christians has been to regard all non-Christian religious experience as so obviously suspect as to be either too dangerous to study or else not worth the trouble . . . Sufism is shrugged off as 'sensuality' and 'self-hypnosis,' Hinduism is pagan pantheism, Yoga is considered a technique for inducing contemplative trances . . . even professedly Christian mysticism is tainted with the pagan eros."

It should be noted, too, that the Eastern religions distinguished between the mantram and prayer. The mantram was Benson's "mental device, a constant stimulus to shift from logical, externally-oriented thought." Prayer is prayer in any religion, and some of the prayers are quite elaborate, in the East as well as the West. In his enthusiasm, Benson blurred the differences.

Ecumenical Relaxation Techniques

"Perhaps one reason for today's decline of interest in these more organized religions is that the stress on altering awareness has been largely muted," it says in *On the Psychology of Meditation,* Naranjo and Ornstein. "And, although the techniques for altering awareness still persist, the practices have become 'automatic,' part of a set of ritual, lacking their original purpose."

You want to know what's gone from everyday life?

How to attain an altered state of consciousness, by an unknown fourteenth-century Christian author, in *The Cloud of Unknowing*: eliminate distractions, pick a single-syllable word, such as "god" or "love":

> Choose whichever one you prefer, or, if you like choose another that suits your taste, provided that it is of one syllable. And clasp this word tightly in your heart so that it never leaves it no matter what may happen. . . . with this word you shall

strike down thoughts of every kind and drive them beneath the cloud of forgetting. . . .

Here is the "Prayer of the Heart," or the "Prayer of Jesus," from Gregory of Sinai at the monastery in Mount Athos in Greece, also fourteenth century:

Sit down alone and in silence. Lower your head, shut your eyes, breathe out gently, and imagine yourself looking into your own heart. Carry your mind, i.e. your thoughts, from your head to your heart. As you breathe out, say "lord Jesus Christ, have mercy on me." Say it moving your lips gently, or simply say it in your mind. Try to put all other thoughts aside. Be calm, be patient and repeat the process very frequently.

Gershom Scholem, the Hebrew scholar, writes that practices leading to altered states extend as far back as the second century B.C., in the days of the second temple. In these practices the subject sat with his head between his knees, whispered hymns and songs, and repeated the name of a magic seal. Rabbi Abulafia, thirteenth century, developed a mystical system of contemplating the Hebrew letters of God's name, in the cabala.

Scholem:

. . . an important part in Abulafia's system is played by the technique of breathing; now this technique has found its highest development in the Indian *Yoga*, where it is commonly regarded as the most important instrument of mental discipline. Again, Abulafia lays down certain forms of recitation, and in particular some passages of his book, "The Light of the Intellect" give the impression of a Judaized treatise on *Yoga*. The similarity even extends to some aspects of the doctrine of ecstatic vision, as preceded and brought about by these practices.

Then there is Sufism, a part of Islam, which made use of rhythmic breathing, music, gestures and dances, and the constant repetition of God's name. Yoga has many variations, some of which involve staring at a geometric design called a mandala, and some of which involve breathing, positions or repeated movements.

Here is an example not cited by Benson, a Zen breathing exercise from *What the Buddha Taught:*

Bring your mind to concentrate on your breathing-in and breathing-out, let your mind watch and observe your breathing-in and breathing-out; let your mind be aware and vigilant of your breathing in and out. When you breathe, you sometimes take deep breaths, sometimes not. This does not matter at all. Breathe normally and naturally. The only thing is that when you take deep breaths you should be aware that they are deep breaths, and so on. In other words, your mind should be so fully concentrated on your breathing that you are aware of its movements and changes. Forget all other things, your surroundings, your environment; do not raise your eyes and look at anything. Try to do this for five or ten minutes.

At the beginning you will find it extremely difficult to bring your mind to concentrate on your breathing. You will be astonished how your mind runs away. It does not stay. You begin to think of various things. You hear sounds outside. You may be dismayed and disappointed. But if you continue to practice this exercise twice a day, morning and evening, you will gradually, by and by, begin to concentrate your mind on your breathing. After a certain period you will experience just that split second when your mind is fully concentrated on your breathing, when you will not hear even sounds nearby, when no external world exists for you . . . that is the moment when you lose yourself completely in the mindfulness of breathing.

The Eastern world, said Benson and his colleagues, had made these techniques a way of life; in the West, they had belonged to the mystics. The necessity of a trained teacher was always emphasized, but Benson's "relaxation response" was "a simple, non-cultic technique."

If the effects of the relaxation response held up long-term, Benson and his associates wrote, the effect on the economics of therapy would be profound, "since it is practiced at no other cost than time."

"You're talking about the $125 mantram at TM," I suggested.

"I think TM is fine if that's what you want," Benson said. "But other things work, too."

"Prayer?"

"Well, not prayer quite in the conventional sense. But if a Catholic comes in, say, and wants to use some childhood prayer, that's fine, although most of those prayers have a lot of syllables. We don't propose it voluntarily, because a lot of prayers aren't neutral, the way they were taught has left some emotional residue, guilt or tension."

"Do you have an alternate mantram, neutral and free of meaning?"

"Yes. You sit quietly, close your eyes, relax all your muscles, beginning at your feet and moving up to your face—"

"—like progressive relaxation—"

"—like progressive relaxation, and you become aware of your breathing. You breathe through your nose, and as you breathe out, you think to yourself, One—in, out—One—in, out—One."

"Your mantram is One? How did you pick that?"

"Well, we were looking around the lab, you can't use pen or pencil, some people might have hang-ups about pens or pencils, you can't have people count very high, if they're really relaxed, they'll lose the count, and if they start to worry they lose the passive attitude, and the Zen breathing exercises had people counting to some low number like three."

"So you picked One. No other numbers?"

"Well, the next one up that's euphonious, that doesn't have sharp sounds, doesn't require effort, is Nine."

"What about the religious significance of One?"

"What religious significance?"

"Well, there's the One in Oriental philosophy, as

opposed to the Nothing, there's the One in Meister Eckhardt, the mystic, and there's the One in Indian religion of the Being, the All, the Unity, there's the Hebrew. 'The Lord Our God, The Lord Is One—' "

"Oh, Lord, we didn't think of that," Benson said. There was some silence on the phone for a minute. "But I don't think that's going to hang up too many people. If they're hung up on One, we'll find another sound, but One is neutral to most people."

I called up Wallace. Wallace had been away, and hadn't seen the latest *Lancet,* or *Psychosomatic Medicine.*

"One?" he said. "One?"

"One," I said. "Maybe, in extreme emergencies, Nine."

"What was the drop in blood pressure?"

"It looks like about eleven millimeters of mercury in the mean systolic, and about five diastolic."

"What was the drop in oxygen consumption?"

"From 258.9 to 225.4, and carbon dioxide down about 12 percent."

Nobody said anything.

"That's nice," Wallace said. "That's very nice."

"I have this slightly used mantram—" I said.

"It may be that a lot of things will work," Wallace said, "though we were the first to test this technique, and we'll have the first long-range studies. Other techniques may produce relaxation, but there is a difference between a mantram and other sounds, a subtle but real difference. And we have classes and free checking, and the support of other meditators, people need that, people like that."

(In fairness, the TM fee is the initiation fee, and subsequent classes and checking are indeed free. In addition, TM runs retreat weekends in the countryside at nominal cost.)

In most (but not all) of the experiments, there were also "control groups"—a similar group of people who didn't meditate, measured for comparison. Sitting still in a quiet room with eyes closed obviously cut down their exterior noise, but there was nothing to dampen the interior noise. There was, then, a big gap between the control group and the meditators, even though obviously the control group sitting still was quieter than the control group before it sat still.

I did a little informal polling. Both Benson and Wallace were right. Benson's mantram—One—was cheaper, but Wallace did indeed have teaching and checking and group support. In the poll, I told people I had a meditation technique. The technique was the same, but one version of it came from the Harvard Medical School and the other version came from India. The Harvard Medical School version was free and the Indian one cost $75, a white handkerchief, some fruit, and two weekends. Which one works?

Nobody wanted the Harvard Medical School technique. What does the Harvard Medical School know about meditation? And free? Why free? How can it be any good if it's free? No, let's have the Indian technique. But what impressed the pollees about the Indian technique was not the fruit, the white handkerchief, the incense and so on, but the reprints from the Harvard Medical School! They wanted the mantram validated by the doctors!

Some further research showed that: Benson was right, TM had no monopoly as a relaxation technique, and Wallace was right, a *system* of meditation had many subtle gradations. It was true that meditation was a relaxation response as Benson said; many people fell asleep during their meditations. But it was more than just relaxation. Benson had stopped too soon, or had been too general. A Harvard psychologist, Daniel Goleman, got the wires out for a group of meditators and a control group, and showed them both an extremely stressful safety movie, in which fingers were lost in machinery, circular saws bit into workers' stomachs, and so on. The meditators perceived more quickly, and recovered their equilibrium more quickly. "Meditation practice is not simply a relaxed state, but the capacity for focused attention," said the report. It speculated that what this capacity for focused attention did was to unlink the cortical and limbic systems, that is, the thinking and perceiving system and the automatic and emotional system. Thus the meditators were not only quicker to return to equilibrium and more at home in that state, but more alert. "A wakeful, hypometabolic state," Benson and Wallace had written, but the emphasis seemed to be on the relaxation, on the word "hypometabolic." The meditators were also "wakeful," though there was not as much attention on that.

Of course, for busy people, there was the problem of when and where to meditate. For commuters in buses and trains, the commuting time was ideal. It looks like you're just catching a little nap. But for commuters who drive to work, there's a problem: you have to keep your eyes open while driving. (Advanced meditators in other techniques might be able to do it.)

What about non-commuters? What about busy people in mid-city?

"We have the solution," said some friends. "Churches."

"Churches?"

"Sure, churches are the one place in the middle of a city that are quiet and respect silence. Some of them even say, enter, rest, and pray. So you go in, you slip into the last pew, and you do your mantram for twenty minutes. It's terrific. You can do it on the way to lunch, or after work."

I tried it myself. Churches were indeed the solution—the only place open in mid-city that respected silence other than the public library. Fabulous! Sometimes the organist would be practicing— that didn't hurt the meditation at all. Sometimes I looked at the very few other people in the church— what was in their minds? Mantrams in what language? Were they asking for something or were they meditating?

We meditators were so grateful for the churches that we began dropping dollar bills in the collection box. It seemed proper and felt good.

Benson published his article—same article—in the *Harvard Business Review*. He added one point: a coffee break, he said, was better spent as a meditation break. Corporations should encourage meditation, instead of coffee, he said. He didn't say where you should meditate in your coffee break, but when you get good enough, it doesn't matter where.

Were there, then, no problems created by these techniques? None so far, when done for limited amounts of time, said Benson. If the meditation was increased in time to several hours a day over a longer period, "some individuals have experienced feelings of withdrawal from life and symptoms which range in severity from insomnia and uncontrolled movements of the limbs to hallucinatory experiences." (Interesting: the uncontrolled movements are shaktipat in the Indian religions, welcomed as an advanced state in the presence of the guru.) But these effects were difficult to evaluate "because individuals with emotional problems might be drawn to any technique . . . which evangelically promises relief from tension and stress."

I started musing about those symptoms from too much meditating.

Why Franny Fainted

Remember Franny in J. D. Salinger's *Franny and Zooey?*

The artists and writers, the real artists, generate some special harmonic that is a generation ahead of consensus logic. Franny came out in *The New Yorker* in 1955, and everybody talked about her. Franny went to see her rather stuffy boyfriend Lane on the Yale weekend at his unspecified but presumably Ivy League university. And they went off to the restaurant that served snails and frog's legs and they ordered martinis.

Franny is in a state of real upset. She hates the section men who *ruin* Turgenev and all the small-time people who are knocking everything in their casual, small-time ways, and she has dropped out of the play she was in.

"All I know is I'm losing my mind," Franny says. "I'm just sick of ego, ego, ego. My own and everybody else's. I'm sick of everybody that wants to *get* somewhere, do something distinguished and all, be somebody interesting. It's disgusting—it is, it *is*. I don't care what anybody says."

Lane says, isn't Franny just afraid of competing? And Franny says she's afraid she *will* compete, she's been "horribly conditioned to accept everybody else's values," and she's sick of it. "I'm sick of not having the courage to be an absolute nobody. I'm sick of myself and everybody that wants to make some kind of a splash . . . my teeth go funny. They're chattering. I nearly bit through a glass day before yesterday."

What's the little green book Franny is carrying? It's *The Way of a Pilgrim*. ". . . it starts out with this peasant—the pilgrim—wanting to find out what it means in the Bible when it says you should pray incessantly. You know. Without stopping . . . so he starts walking all over Russia, looking for somebody who can tell him *how* . . . he meets this person called a starets—some sort of terribly advanced religious person—and the starets tells him about a book called the 'Philokalia' . . . written by a group of terribly advanced monks who sort of advocated this really incredible method of praying."

And the starets tells the pilgrim that if you keep saying "Lord Jesus Christ, have mercy on me" over and over—"you only have to just do it with your *lips* at first—then eventually what happens, the prayer becomes self-active. Something *happens* after a while. I don't know what, but something happens, and the words get synchronized with the person's heartbeats, and then you're actually praying without ceasing. Which has a really tremendous, mystical effect on your whole outlook . . . you do it to purify your whole outlook and get an absolutely new conception of what everything's about . . . but the marvelous thing is, when you first start doing it, you don't even have to have *faith* in what you're doing. I mean even if you're terribly embarrassed about the whole thing, it's perfectly all right. I mean you're not *insulting* anybody or anything. In other words, nobody asks you to believe a single thing when you first start out. You don't even have to think about what you're saying, the starets said. All you have to have in the beginning is quantity. Then, later on, it becomes quality by itself. On its own power of something. He says that any name of God—any name at all—has this peculiar, self-active power of its own, and it starts working after you've started it up . . . in the Nembutsu sects of Buddhism, people say 'Praise to the Buddha' over and over . . . and in 'The Cloud of Unknowing' . . . you just keep saying 'God' . . . did you ever hear of anything so fascinating in your *life,* in a way? I mean it's so hard to say it's absolutely coincidence . . ."

But boyfriend Lane is a real 50's clot.

"You actually believe that stuff or what?"

Franny says she doesn't say she believes or not, but isn't it a peculiar coincidence that "all these really advanced and absolutely unbogus religious persons keep telling you . . . even in India, they tell you to meditate on the 'Om,' and the same result is supposed to happen . . ."

Lane says, what is the result? "All this synchronization business and mumbo jumbo. You get heart trouble? I don't know if you know it, but you could do yourself, somebody could do himself a great deal of real—"

"You get to see God. Something happens in the non-physical part of the heart," Franny says.

Poor Franny, a generation ahead of her time. Franny had spent five minutes in the ladies' room crying, and come back to Lane and the martinis and the frog's legs, and then she fainted.

I can remember very well the reaction to Franny and her fainting. Why did Franny faint? That was the mystery. The cadences of Franny's speech were so perfect we thought we knew her, the pretty girl going through a kooky phase, okay, but why did she faint? Franny fainted, said the consensus at the time, because she was pregnant. That shows that we didn't listen to what Franny was saying, and even if we had listened we wouldn't have known what to make of it.

And now we know. End of literary mystery. Franny put herself into a heavy meditation and very successfully, with the Jesus Prayer. (Also, she hadn't eaten and was a bit of a hysteric.) That synchronization she talked about would have made a nice EEG and EKG, head and heart, lots of alpha. The teeth chattering and crying show she couldn't quite handle the altered state; she was probably ahead of schedule, and she didn't have anybody to talk to about it, so she thought she was going crazy. Poor baby, she wasn't going crazy at all, she just didn't know about altered states of consciousness, they hadn't invented the phrase, if she had reported back to her meditation class they would have been envious at her progress, some of them would have thought, gee, I haven't cried yet and my teeth haven't chattered. Of course, a true meditation would have left Franny serene even with a clot of a boyfriend and stupid instructors, she could have separated her emotional, limbic response from her acute, cortical perceptions. The Prayer of the Heart was working for Franny, but she was certainly in some sort of transitional state. A generation later, Franny seems to have seen things the way they were, and she was so sweet, and vulnerable.

There is an obvious difference in a way of life that supports meditation, and the workaday world that doesn't. It's one thing to do a lot of meditation in a retreat where the very rhythms of life are set up to include the meditation, and another in a busy household or a crowded schedule that doesn't. If you are going to participate in the busy household or the crowded schedule, you need a little bit of fight or flight just to get going. A lot of meditation can wipe out the fight or flight so that the effort seems silly. It may or may not be: that is another topic entirely. But too little fight or flight is not, these days, most people's problem.

The repetition of a prayer or a phrase has its effect physiologically, but not everybody, it should be pointed out, agrees that this is the way to meditate. The Indian sage Krishnamurti is scornful of the techniques of TM and the Prayer of the Heart. "By repeating Amen or Om or Coca-Cola indefinitely you obviously have a certain experience because by repetition the mind becomes quiet . . . it is one of the favorite gambits of some teachers of meditation to insist on their pupils learning concentration, that is, fixing the mind on one thought and driving out all other thoughts. This is a most stupid, ugly thing, which any schoolboy can do because he is forced to."

Krishnamurti didn't say it didn't work, he just didn't think it was a high-class meditation. His own meditation was nothing: a blank mind, "empty, not filled with things of the mind. Then there is only meditation, and not a meditator who is meditating . . . the mind must be clear, without movement, and in the light of that clarity the timeless is revealed."

I don't think anybody argues with that, but a really blank mind is even harder than keeping only Amen or Om or Coca-Cola in the mind. Coca-Cola is Krishnamurti being snotty. It wouldn't work. Psychophysiologically, the hard c's would stub the mind as it settled down, not mellifluous enough, and psychologically in order for the process to work you have to, if not believe, at least suspend disbelief long enough for the images to clear, and while Coca-Cola has claimed many things in its history, quieting the mind has not been one of them.

It's so hard to say it's absolutely coincidence, said Franny, that here all these different people, the Indians doing Om, and the Russian pilgrims saying "Lord Jesus Christ, have mercy on me," and the Nembutsu Buddhists going Namu amida butsu over and over, and the *same thing* happens.

The same thing happens, leaving aside for a moment the question of where the vibe comes from, because a lot of different groups empirically found their way to the anterior hypothalamus extending into the supra- and pre-optic areas, septum and inferior lateral thalamus, according to Benson. And everybody has an anterior hypothalamus. Naturally the differing groups did not have the cold Western physiological language so important to our own ability to believe. Belief is important. Some people believe better if they use a word designated as holy, and some people believe better if they know this is a scientific process checked out by the Harvard Medical School with lots of fancy equipment. Remember, the placebo believers were rewarded by having their stomachs cured and their asthma clear up, and the scoffers are still taking Alka-Seltzer and wheezing. Nobody has checked out whether Ba-na-na Ba-na-na works, with catheters and EEG's and so on, and by the time you've read this it's too late to try, but if you could find somebody who didn't think bananas were funny or that the word banana meant something profound or holy, the odds would seem to favor it and the Swami Suchabanana could be right after all.

Whether we use the language of religion or the language of physiology, the end is the same: to quiet the mind.

The object of quieting the mind may be, in the West, to go back to work with your blood pressure down and your stomach calmer, but that was not the object in the religious techniques, it was simply a by-product, or a stepping stone, a preparatory phase. The instructions were to lose yourself in the contemplation of the object, whether the object was a prayer, a symbol, or a set of movements. One branch of yoga makes use of ritualized movements; the Orthodox Jew uses a rhythmic nodding called *dovining*. The Moslem equivalent of the Jesus Prayer is *La ilaha illa'llah,* there is no God but God. The devotee, in one set of instructions, repeats the prayer frequently: "banishing every distraction . . . with *La ilaha* he denies and excludes all competing objects." The object of contemplation in a visual meditation can be a cross in Christianity, a geometric symbol in Islam, the portrait of a guru or saint; the six-pointed star is not only the Star of David but a symbol in Tantric yoga.

Such are the intolerances of humanity that through most of history people have only been able to use the socially approved method of damping down and turning off. If you went whirling like the Mevlevi Sufis in Yankee America, they would have thought you were a witch or a warlock and taken appropriate action. The Shakers, who did whirl, were persecuted. If you wandered through old Russia saying the Jesus Prayer, they admired your piousness and welcomed you to table, but if you uttered a parallel Hebrew prayer you could have been in a lot of trouble. This is a more tolerant age, but if you say banana banana for twenty minutes a day, you better let your friends know it's all right.

Continued meditation leads to a state called, in Zen, one-pointedness, and in Indian terminology, the Void, or "emptiness." St. John of the Cross, a Spanish mystic, called it "the annihilation of memory." The *object* of the meditation—the syllable or the figure—has disappeared, leaving a state of blank, the blanking-out being a much desired end. This state can also be expressed in physiological psychology. Normally, we hardly ever look at anything steadily, as a meditator would gaze at a mandala or a cross or what have you. We have larger eye movements, saccades, and also very small involuntary ones, nystagmus, and both movements keep the image on the retina in constant motion.

A group of psychologists were testing the theory that the brain needs continuous change. They fixed tiny projectors on contact lenses, and tried out the apparatus on some volunteers. No matter how the eyes of the volunteers moved, the same stable image fell on the retina. The images disappeared! The volunteers did not "see." "Stabilizing" the input eliminated the continuous changes.

The same sort of thing happened in another group when the observers looked at a totally patternless visual field, a "ganzfeld" in psychologic jargon. Like a totally whitewashed surface, or the halves of a split ping-pong ball placed over the eyes. Here the experimenters reported that after about twenty minutes there was no visual experience, which they called "blank out." "Blank out" wasn't merely seeing white, or seeing nothing, it was a complete disappearance of the sense of vision; the volunteers didn't know whether their eyes were open or not.

So there is a similarity between "blank out" and the state of losing the object of meditation and arriving at one-pointedness or emptiness or Void. Franny said: all you have to have in the beginning is quantity, and it becomes quality by itself, on its own power. Blank out. If you're going to do the Jesus Prayer in the ladies' john, you can blank out on the Yale weekend.

And here we get to one of those gaps in communication. Obviously there is a big difference in set and setting for (a) a meditator involved in a belief system, and (b) a volunteer in a psych lab with a split ping-pong ball taped over his eyes. The vocabulary of the first says that if you meditate well and really cut off the outside, you can merge with Infinity. The vocabulary of the second says you are in blank out. The first seems vague and spooky, and the second seems like, if not a put-down, an outside description of an inside experience. It repeats in physiologic terms—he's showing lots of alpha, look, he's not registering any stimuli—what the meditator has been trying to do.

Meditators report that colors seem brighter and the world fresher. The world is the same as it was, whatever that is—the redness of the rose is in the eye of the meditator. We become habituated to things so well that we do not see them. Manufacturers know this, so they put New! New! on the giant-size box of detergent, and they change the clothing styles, and so on, otherwise nobody would really *see*. The first time we go into a room we can hear a clock ticking, or the traffic outside, or whatever, then after a while we don't notice. Another psychologist measured people's eyes—these guys are tireless—looking at the same picture every day. Sure enough, after a while, the people's eyes didn't really look at the picture. When they first looked at it, their eyes went tracketa tracketa tracketa all over it, and on succeeding days the eye movements became stereotyped. They hit a few spots, enough to match the model of the picture already held in the brain, and quit. That's why Jerome Bruner—still another experiment—got the answers he did with his crazy deck of cards. It had a red six of spades, among other things, and everybody called it a six of hearts. The little brain model said, spades are black, hearts are red. and the eyes didn't look closely—tracketa pop!—because what the hell, everybody's already seen a deck of cards, why look again? Why are there proofing errors in every book, when presumably a professional proofreader has gone over the copy word by word? The proofreader has to fight his optic system which "corrects" and adjusts as it goes along.

The turnoff from the meditation provides a little mini-vacation from the continuous input, and you know that when you get back from vacation, you look things over with more interest on the first day.

One of the concomitants of meditation is to open the doors of perception. "We must become like little children." Not just that the rose is redder, but that you thought the six of spades was black, and we put this red six of spades right before your very eyes and you didn't say, hey, that card is the wrong color, you said, that's a six of hearts.

Maybe your whole world is made up of these models, and every day you're betting that today is the same as the past, and that the symbol represents the same reality. But what is really real? Where are you living? The symbols are all there to help us get a grip, but maybe they're not reality.

If you can get used to this concept of symbols and reality, it can make a big difference. Of course, habituation does protect you from registering freshly the same commercial for the thousandth time.

Language and symbol divide up the world so we can grab it. Language goes with the action mode, getting ourselves fed and clothed, the eyes scanning, focusing, and establishing boundaries. The sympathetic system is dominant. (Sympathetic is a lousy word for the system, because sympathetic in another context means warm and comforting, but the medical vocabulary has stuck us with it. It is the sympathetic system that gears up to fight or flee. Sympathetic is arise! and shine! Parasympathetic is now, now, there, there, cool it.) In the dominant sympathetic system, the future and the past are important, and the mode—language, construct—is one for control, hanging on to time, hanging on to the symbol. Rather than let go of old constructs and old images, this mode will hang them on to the current scene, the current relationships. You're just like my first wife, Zelda, you're a red six of spades.

The other mode is nonverbal and parasympathetic:

letting, passive, feminine so-called, now as opposed to past or future. The other mode is what the good Germans meant by it breathes me, what Benson meant by a passive attitude, and what the Maharishi meant by we do not try, and so on.

It's not an easy concept to get across—even oversimplified like this—because it comes in words which are themselves symbols. You are reading in an active, past-and-future, sympathetic mode. What are you when you are not doing? they ask, in some meditation instruction. If you spend all your time there, anything else is as hard to imagine as antimatter.

Sympathetic/parasympathetic, active/passive, X chromosome and Y chromosome, the symmetry of twos, Yin and Yang you could say, if you were into the *I Ching*. The old gentleman with the flowered sleeves wasn't laughing at *everybody*.

The Ballad of the Zen Cowboy

While I admired Benson's ecumenical approach in his historical roundup of altered states, I suspect it may be hard for Westerners to utilize a prayer and be in the receptive, parasympathetic mode. In many prayers you *ask for something*. "Lord, grant us victory," says the pro football coach. Victory is something. Learning the prayer was something you had to do, therefore it has associations of rewards and punishment, as in school. Meditation, then, is something you attack to achieve. In that case, "one" would certainly be better, or a Sanskrit sound with no meaning to the user. "Lord, grant us victory, let us beat those bastids" is no mantram. If there is something you lack, such as victory, that's not equilibrium.

The meditative techniques we have so far looked at are the beginning ones. In Zen, this is *bompo* Zen, ordinary Zen, you can do it just for your health and well-being and stop there if you want to. The word *zen* itself is a Japanese word meaning meditation. It began as *dhyana* in Sanskrit, went to China and became *ch'an,* went to Japan and became *zen.*

All right, meditation, blank out in ganzfeld, it sounds like a German motorcycle movie. What happens after the first step of meditation, turning off, kazonk, but staying awake?

That depends. Naranjo and Ornstein, psychiatrist and psychologist one each, say there are two kinds of meditation: concentrative, or damping down, and opening up. The Zen scholars have five stages, the Maharishi has seven, yogas are even more numerous. Let's try Zen for just a moment, since D. T. Suzuki, one leading authority, says Zen is not mysticism and Zen is a way, not a religion. This is from Philip Kapleau's *The Three Pillars of Zen:*

First step, for *bompo* people, count breaths. That's all. Very good for the blood pressure, ulcers, asthma, and dying twenty years too soon.

Second step, follow the breath. Don't count any more. Just follow it.

Third step, shikan-taza. Which means just sitting.

I know, it sounds crazy. Forget anything you may have remembered about Zen from the days of "Beat Zen." Just sitting is very hard, you can only do it a half-hour at a time. It's really hard because you don't have the support of counting breaths or even following breaths. Here is Zen Master Yasutani Roshi, giving instructions that sound like one of the flashbacks in *Kung Fu:*

In this type of Za-Zen [just sitting] it is all too easy for the mind . . . to become distracted . . . the mind must be unhurried yet firmly planted or massively composed, like Mount Fuji, let us say. But it also must be alert, stretched, like a taut bowstring. So shikan-taza is a heightened state of concentrated awareness wherein one is neither tense nor hurried, and certainly never slack. It is the mind of somebody facing death. Let us imagine that you are engaged in a duel of swordsmanship of the kind that used to take place in ancient Japan. As you face your opponent, you are unceasingly watchful, set, ready. Were you to relax your vigilance even momentarily, you would be cut down instantly. A crowd gathers to see the fight. Since you are not blind you see them from the corner of your eye, and since you are not deaf you hear them. But not for an instant is your mind captured by these sense impressions.

That's the state of mind behind the martial arts, judo and jujitsu, aikido and kung fu. Alert, relaxed, and no-mind. Stage three, just sitting, gets you to unified mind, one-pointed concentration, dynamic power, even, says the roshi, certain supranormal powers. He doesn't say what. "One who has developed *joriki* is no longer a slave to his passions, neither is he at the mercy of his environment. Always in command of both himself and the circumstances of his life, he is able to move with perfect freedom and equanimity."

Now your knees hurt from all that sitting, but you do not fight pain, you say hello, pain, how are you, and you go into the pain and it disappears. Next stage, Enlightenment. Now in the monastery there they are really chasing your shredded ego, physically and mentally, you are sitting facing the wall, no-mind, and the guy creeps up behind you and wap! wap! with the *kyosaku* stick, and now your mind has a koan, or impossible question: what was your face before your parents' birth? The koan is not a riddle that can be solved by any sort of linear thinking whatsoever. So the scene of the student and the roshi can be sheer Marx Brothers.

The Master says, "What does one's Buddha-mind look like?" and the student says, "The fish play in the trees and birds fly in the sea." The Master says, move that boat on the lake with your mind, and the student turns a somersault and bumps his head. The Master is experienced enough to know how the student is coming along in this nonverbal, irrational procedure. What is the sound of one hand clapping?

The student is to keep the koan in his mind, turning and turning and turning. A contemporary American master asks: how can driving on the freeways lead to enlightenment?

There is a somewhat shocking axiom for those not familiar with this: "If you meet the Buddha on the road, kill him!" If you think you and the Buddha on the road are separate objects, then you still have shadows in your mind.

Sometimes the whole process takes years. Do not let go of your koan, says the roshi, even though you feel "like a mosquito attacking an iron bowl."

All right, you keep turning and turning this koan, what was my face before my parents' birth, and you run through every possible permutation and finally, the rap goes, your ego-mind, your conceptual, language-using mind, just throws up its hands, gives up, which is very tough because the ego-mind thinks everything will stop if *it* stops, death. But, the rap goes, you have to die in order to be born again. When the ego-mind has busted itself on the koan, not to mention having been set up with all that breathing and counting and not counting and just sitting, then you have ken-sho, enlightenment, in psychologic terms a direct perception, or perception without the model you were carrying.

That is why, if you think you got it, you didn't get it. If you think you got it, that implies not only that there was something out there to get, but that you could know you got it, which gives you away instantly because how would you know unless you were checking the old model, six of spades, there's something there to get.

If you don't get *that,* forget it, it will flash on you some morning when you're brushing your teeth and give you a little giggle.

When written up, the experiences of the Zen students sound just as far out as the koans. "I have it!" says one, overjoyed, as he bounces into the roshi. "Everything is nothing! I am everything! The Universe is One!"

The Zen master may not be impressed. "Everything is Buddha-nature?" he might say.

"Right, right."

"Your mind is liberated from everything that fits over it like a strait jacket?"

"Right, Master."

"Show me Buddha-nature. Divide it into two parts, sprinkle one part over your food and fly the other part like a kite."

Here's an interesting example, an American psychotherapist in Japan. First they have him counting ugggghhh, so boring he can hardly stand it. "I had perhaps never been so frustrated in my life." It goes on, one, two, three, hi-tot-su hu-tot-su, mi-it-su. His knees hurt, he counts, he listens, he falls asleep, his knees hurt some more. A couple of days later they give him another sound, "mu," nothing. And very exact, very exact ways to do it. Pretty soon he has stopped noticing the trains that come by this place periodically, and the other outside sounds, and late one morning:

—a white, clear screen came before my eyes. In front of the screen passed, or rather floated, simple images—faces, objects. I have no clear recollection of the images. A rush of feeling came over me.

I burst into tears; the tears became quiet sobbing.

I do not remember at what point I had stopped the exercise.

I can state my feeling but I am not sure I can communicate it with any real meaning. I would like not to be mysterious; I would like to communicate it clearly, at the same time knowing that it may be possible.

My feeling was that I was seeing something of great importance, as if everything fitted together for the first time. What had all my life struggles been about? Things were very clear and very simple.

They walk our psychotherapist up to see the roshi, and the roshi gets very close to him and goes "Ah!" so sharply the psychotherapist almost jumps out of his skin.

"What did you feel?" he asked.

"Surprise."

"And after that?"

"Nothing."

The roshi has him walk around, and he looks at the place where the psychotherapist walked.

"Are you able to see the footsteps?" the Roshi asked.

"No."

"They were not there before and are not there now. There was nothing in your life before and nothing in the furture, only AH!"

The next day the roshi gives him a little scroll that says, congratulations, J. T. Huber has seen unconditional nature. The roshi has two seals which he presses into red ink and then onto the card. One seal is his signature. The other says, "No moving mind." What did all this do for J. T. Huber?

I seemed almost to have a new pair of eyes, new ears, new abilities to taste and smell and feel. I had learned to give my full attention to whatever I was doing at any one moment and I wondered if I had ever really done this before.

Gradually I began to see I was eating when I was hungry, not when it was "time to eat." I began to eat when I wanted to eat, not because it was placed before me, because others were eating, because we must have three good meals a day . . . I was seeing and choosing what I wanted to do.

Mr. Huber's peak experience seems to have been something like that of Larry in Somerset Maugham's *The Razor's Edge.* Surprising more counter-culturalists didn't read *The Razor's Edge,* but then Maugham is out of favor. Larry had his peak experience in India and went home to drive a cab happily in New York.

The experience seemed to have a permanent effect on Larry. There's no indication as to whether the effect on J. T. Huber was permanent. Sometimes such experiences produce a change, and sometimes they don't. "Though there is an afterglow from this state," writes one authority, "on emerging from meditation one is still susceptible to the patterns of old mental habits. For this reason, in Abhidhamma [a Buddhist manual], this experience is seen as relatively trivial."

Back at the beginning I promised a meditation that would shed pounds. That was gimmicky but true. Spiritual materialism, says Chogyam Trungpa, the Tibetan lama. He's right, absolutely right. But I think it provides a good ordinary example for attention, so here goes.

"I had learned to give my full attention to whatever I was doing at any one moment," said the Huber account. That attention is the key to the whole process of continuous meditative action. You can see that kind of attention in the furniture made by the Shakers of nineteenth-century America, each simple box or stool now prized because the essence of attention shows up as the quality of the object, "concentrated labor" being part of their devotion. It is the opposite of schlock and shoddy.

Be mindful of everything you do, physically or verbally, it says in *What the Buddha Taught*. People do not live in the moment, they live in the past or future, "though they seem to be doing something now here, they live somewhere else in their thoughts . . . therefore, they do not live in nor do they enjoy what they do at the moment, so they are unhappy and discontented with the present moment, with the work at hand. Naturally they cannot give themselves fully to what they appear to be doing."

In a much repeated Zen story, the fella asks the Zen master for a maxim, and the Zen master writes, "Attention." "Is that all?" says the fella, and the Zen master writes, "Attention attention." Doesn't seem to be much to it, what's it mean? says the fella, and the Zen master says, "Attention means attention."

Okay, a little spiritual materialism here, to good end. Dr. Smith's guaranteed weight loss.

(1) Pay attention. If you're alone at the lunch counter, don't read while you eat, don't review the morning, don't preview the afternoon, just eat.

(2) Slow it down this way. With each bite, you go:

Reaching; reaching. Lifting; lifting. Taking; taking. Chewing; chewing. Tasting; tasting. Savoring; savoring. Swallowing; swallowing. Digesting; digesting. Pause. Reaching; reaching. Lifting; lifting. Taking; taking. Chewing; chewing. Tasting; tasting. Swallowing; swallowing. Don't eat it all just because it's there on your plate, because somebody once planted in your brain eat everything on your plate, or because somebody once said food costs a lot, don't waste it. If you're with somebody, don't keep eating because you want to keep talking, in fact, don't eat and talk at the same time because that isn't paying attention. Eating will come in second. The food will disappear without passing through awareness. You always get a signal at each meal that says, that's almost enough, that's enough. You can move the signal forward in time by paying attention. It's that simple. I think I'll skip the medical and physiological references. The medical references say fat people eat faster, their appestats are out of whack. The physiological references say taste habituates, that is, the seventeenth bite doesn't taste as good as the first. (Smokers say the last drag doesn't taste as good as the first, but smoking is usually an unconscious activity.)

People who eat too much have fouled up the signal-to-noise ratio, the noise being what else is going on, or lack of attention. If you've cleared some of the noise, you can start listening to the signal on *what* you eat; you don't crave a big slab of roast beef and a pile of mashed potatoes on a hot summer day.

I used to see executives in lunch clubs all the time, which is nothing striking since I was one. The reason you were having lunch with somebody was to talk to him and listen to him. A certain information exchange, and with it a certain tension. All morning had been spent sitting still, no movement except for opening a desk drawer or lifting a telephone, and now some motion and breathing are craved but nothing's available to move except mouth and stomach. The waiter plunks down a plate of bread and pats of butter. Not one man would voluntarily buy those mass-produced chemical rolls, but unless everybody says for the waiter to take the bread basket away, everybody will sit there buttering the rolls they don't want, and talking. They are eating not because they want the rolls but because they're a little excited with the vibrations of learning and self-expression. They are giving attention to the talk; somebody else is doing the eating. I ate a roll? What roll? I don't remember eating any roll. Who ate all the rolls? Waiter, I'll have a martini and the low-cal special.

If you go on a diet you have this terrific battle, you and you, and you feel good when you stick to it and bad when you don't, and at the end of the diet the weight comes back. Zen doesn't have renunciation, said the Zen master, so you don't have to give things up, *you have to accept that they go away.* Reaching, reaching; lifting, lifting; just accept that they go away, don't get into a fight. It's because we want to be on one side or the other. Psychologists would say, that's behavior modification, you see, you broke the stimulus/response pattern there, maybe you have gone and changed all the road signs so that when the impulses come roaring down the neuronal pathway all of a sudden it says detour, and then it says no left turn, no U-turn, right lane must turn right, and by the time the impulses get all this they want to stop at a gas station and get a map.

If the impulses are all back at the gas station poring over the map and squabbling with each other, the traffic patterns get changed. The eater is different. His only problem is to discard the model of what he always has for lunch, and how much is enough.

The Zen master told us a story. I had already read the story, there are only so many stories in English and this one is right at the top. Disciples of two famous masters meet. The first one says, the miracle of my master is, I stand on one side of the river, he stands on the other, and he can write on a scroll I hold up. The second disciple says, the miracle of my master is, he eats when he is hungry and drinks when he is thirsty.

I heard a tune. Words came with the tune. I was filled with ecumenical spirit: why, this very same philosophy is in an old cowboy ballad. I have even heard a real cowboy sing it in a saloon in Nogales, Arizona. So I went up to tell the Zen master of this American example.

> I eat when I'm hungry
> I drink when I'm dry
> If the sky don't fall on me
> I'll live till I die.

There are other people who have come up after the lecture and they are looking at me quite strangely. They want to know more important things, how long will it take them to get to satori, what should they be eating, why is Philip Kapleau, *Three Pillars of Zen,* so down on Alan Watts, *The Way of Zen,* and this crazy is standing here singing a cowboy ballad to the Zen master, we get all the crazies in here.

The Zen master frowned a little, as if he didn't get it. And I had to stop, because I remembered suddenly the verse that went

> Whiskey, rye whiskey
> I know you of old
> You rob my poor pockets
> Of silver and gold

and that didn't sound very Zen. I didn't sing that. So I repeated,

> I eat when I'm hungry
> I drink when I'm dry
> If the sky don't fall on me
> I'll live till I die.

I concentrated on the two yellowing beaver front teeth of the Zen master, to avoid the stares, and then up:

a little stubble in the mustache from a not quite clean shave, and the brown eyes with the frown between them and the bald head, he is concentrating on the crazy American, I watch *sssss* an intake go under the beaver teeth as the song ends and he does "Ah!" —a bark, a grunt, out goes the intake, I jump, they must teach them that at Zen school.

"People believe?" he said. "Believe this song?"

I thought about it. Do people really eat when they are hungry, or believe that they will live till they die, of course they do, but do they have that *attitude?*

"Not really," I said. "They eat when it's breakfast, and again when it's lunch, and a little bell rings for the coffee wagon and—"

"Ah," he said. "So. So."

Then he didn't say anything, I didn't say anything, he nodded vigorously a couple of times, and somebody who didn't have the attitude and was in one hell of a big hurry to get to satori plucked at his elbow, and the ballad of the Zen cowboy died right there.

The sleeve-plucker should have known you don't get anything for getting to satori, or enlightenment. I know, they gave the visiting American a seal that said "no moving mind," but they were being nice. The axioms run: before satori, chop wood and draw water; after satori, chop wood and draw water. Or: before satori, a river is a river and a mountain is a mountain; during satori, a river is not a river and a mountain is not a mountain; after satori, a river is a river and a mountain is a mountain.

Or how about: "It takes seven years to get over the stink of enlightenment." You thought you had tenure, did you. There can't be any tenure if it's always now.

Well, not to dwell on Zen, for all its intellectual and physiologic attributes, this is just a handy example, not even a thumbnail sketch. The handy example does not have "just-sitting" because they have always done it that way, no other reason, or corrupt monks selling the answers to koans, and it doesn't have even the basic elements of centering, move that center from your shoulder blades down to just below your navel.

All disciplines, they say, have a place for attention: karma yoga makes of each daily activity a sacrament; Western religions used the occasion of a meal.

But not many busy Americans are going to sit for hours facing a wall, or pursue a koan. (I wonder if "How do I pay the mortgage when the taxes are going up so fast" would count as an insoluble question. Too linear.)

We could move logically from here to the existentialist philosophy of Martin Heidegger, who indicated that man's freedom is in *Gelassenheit,* or letting go, letting be, which parallels the non-Aristotelian qualities of Zen and all the other—

—or we could retire to the playing fields, to see into what spaces the powers of attention can lead us.

IV. "Sport Is a Western Yoga"

Quarterbacking in an Altered State

Zen and the Cross-court Backhand

The Sweet Music of the Strings

Quarterbacking in an Altered State

Murphy, the great mystic, alumnus of Stanford and the Sri Aurobindo ashram, founder of Esalen, Murphy has been Rolfed and Alexandered and grouped and Zenned and yogaed and *gestalt*ed and God knows what, there is no trip he hasn't been on, every one that wants to surface has to check in with him, and serious, too, shelves of books on mystics and philosophers, lots of meditation every day, marvelous enthusiam, and what is Murphy into? Jogging. No, not jogging, *running,* jogging is only eight minutes to the mile, Murphy wants to run a mile in five minutes, five miles in thirty-five minutes, the mystical long-distance runner. The aikido black belt has checked his centering and Murphy is out there on the running track, what's-his-name the middle-distance runner who almost made the Olympics is running alongside of him, three miles, four miles, here comes the pain, pain is a cultural attitude it says in *Principles of Psychophysiology,* it is only as real as we make it, the Italians and Jews make it more than the Yankees it says, hello pain—Murphy is in his mid-forties, bound to be pain, hello pain, go into the pain, don't fight, see if you can come out the other side and—

"Five minutes and seventeen seconds!" Down the coast in Murphy's own famous ashram, Esalen, the gurus are guruing and the *gestalters* are *gestalting* and Bob and Carol and Ted and Alice are sorting out their hang-ups, people are screaming screams, letting it all hang out, getting out of all that linear crap, sitting on cushions listening to the residents with M.A.'s in psychology—academic market a little tight these days, no jobs there—rap on what it's all about, and where is Murphy? On the golf course, and since there is no golf course at Esalen that means the president of the ashram is far away, teeing off with John Brodie, the quarterback, because golf is a kind of meditation too—

—it is? And tennis? And bowling? Hunting? Swimming? Hey, this is going to be easier than sitting and staring at the wall, hi-tot-tsu, hu-tot-tsu, mi-it-tsu—how can I attain the mortgage if the taxes go up?

I should have known Murphy would bring East to West through sports, his imperatives are all from sports. "We *have* to go to Pebble Beach tomorrow." "Why do we have to go to Pebble Beach tomorrow, Mr. Bones?" "*Nicklaus* is playing, we have to follow Nicklaus around the course."

Who am I talking to, that Good Ol' Boy my junior-year-roommate, or the great ashram leader? Murphy is in awe of Nicklaus not because of the money he wins or how far he hits the ball or any of that; Nicklaus has the *greatest powers of concentration* in golf. "I've followed him around the course lots," Murphy says. "Nicklaus *plays in a trance.* He and the club and the ball are all the same thing, and there isn't anything else. He can lock right in, real one-pointedness. I think he can influence the flight of the ball after it's hit, even."

Murphy has been into this in his book, *Golf and the Kingdom,* which is a mystic book about golf, or a golf book about mysticism, same thing.

"What Nicklaus needs now is a challenger, somebody to keep his concentration on the absolute razor's edge, the way he was to Arnold Palmer."

So Murphy cancels all his appointments to walk behind Nicklaus, where he can pick up the right vibes. And vibes there are, let me tell you, "energy streamers" that the golf ball rides toward the hole. When the golfer can visualize and execute his shot in a moment of high clarity, the ball rides the energy streamer right up to the green.

John Brodie, ex-Stanford star, seventeen-year quarterback for the 49ers, most valuable player NFL 1970, second most all-time yards gained passing, and so on, is not one to dispute the energy streamers.

"I would have to say that such things seem to exist." Brodie's white teeth flash into a perfect smile. "It's happened to me dozens of times. An intention carries a force, a thought connected with an energy that can stretch itself out in a pass play or a golf shot or a base hit or a thirty-foot jump shot in basketball. I've seen it happen too many times to deny it."

Murphy: "Can we develop this? Practice it? Can you learn to develop clarity and strengthen your intentions?"

Brodie: "Yes."

Brodie is six three, two fifteen, big shoulders, moves gracefully, and as far as I know does not know a Zen master from a rubber duck, but he is about to sound like one:

"The player can't be worrying about the past or the future or the crowd or some other extraneous event. He must be able to respond in the here and now, I believe we all have this naturally, maybe we lose it as we grow up. Sometimes in the heat of the game a player's perception and coordination improve dramatically. At times, I experience a kind of clarity that I've never seen described in any football story, sometimes time seems to slow way down, as if everyone were moving in slow motion. It seems as if I have all the time in the world to watch the receivers run their patterns, and yet I know the defensive line is coming at me just as fast as ever, and yet the whole thing seems like a movie or a dance in slow motion. It's beautiful."

Stoned John Brodie. The defensive line is coming at him in slow motion, like a ballet, the crowd is screaming for twelve hundred pounds of linemen to gobble him up and spit out his white, bleached bones, and he is dancing along, the ball in one very large but somehow dainty hand, in this altered state, stoned on all the vibrations of the moment, seventeen years is a long time to have those tackles coming at you but Brodie stays with it because it's so beautiful—

—Murphy's Esalen has gathered a lot of jocks and coaches together in San Francisco for a sports seminar, Murphy suspects these moments in sport are all unarticulated but similar to the awareness of the Zen master staring at the guy in the sword fight—

—the NBC man nudges me at the seminar. "I heard Brodie was getting a little wiggy," he whispers.

Clot, I think, you do not know Zen from a rubber duck.

Brodie is telling how he has four chances on every play to communicate a pattern to Gene Washington, his wide receiver. First, the play itself, in the huddle. Brodie comes up to the line, the defense shifts, he has a second chance, an audible, a shouted signal. Somebody moves in the enemy backfield, he has a third chance, a quick hand signal. And fourth—"Sometimes I let the ball fly before Gene has made his final move, *without* a pass route exactly; it's sort of intuition and communication, Gene and I are good friends, of course, then you don't know what the cornerbacks and safety men will do, that's part of the fun, you don't know where those guys are going to be a second before something happens, you have to be ready for the sudden glimmer—"

"The pass pattern is from your collective unconscious," Murphy suggests.

Brodie doesn't know about that. "I know the *feeling*," he says. "You can get into another order of reality when you're playing that doesn't fit the grids and coordinates most people lay across life."

I am getting a little worried for Brodie. I am adding to my list of altered states: you can take a chemical, you can run balam balam balam through your head, you can just sit, and you can stand with a football in your hand and twelve hundred pounds of linemen coming at you while you look for your receivers. They all work.

But will the fans understand? The telepathic pass pattern, won't the fans say, *yuhh bum, yuh goddam yogi* if he misses? And then he will end up a well-paid TV commentator, that was a real fine play, just a super play, let's take another look at it from the end zone camera.

"If I were an effect of the fans it would affect me, but I am not an effect." Scientology talk, Big John could only lift his arm to *here* and then Scientology rearranged his perception and he could lift it to *here*.

I asked Murphy why Esalen was getting involved in sports. The Esalen track team, for God's sake, here is Esalen on the frontier supposedly and what are they doing? Sending their own track team to AAU events for seniors. That has to be where they lose all the psychiatrists who don't hate them already. Thank you, Dr. Freud, but could you give us your times in the 220 and 440?

"Isn't this exciting?" Murphy says. "Sport anticipates what the Divine Essence is. Sport is a Western yoga. The Dance of Shiva. Pure play, the delight in the moment, the Now. We need a more balanced and evolutionary culture. We already have physical mobility, why shouldn't we have psychic mobility, the ability to move physically into different states?"

Sure enough, the athletes are beginning to talk to each other about funny spaces which they have trouble describing. "There isn't any language." It's all a bit ambiguous, but it seems they are talking about sports equivalents of the "peak experience" described by Abe Maslow, the late psychologist who hung out at Esalen. Moments of exhilaration and clarity and awareness, the click that tells you the shot is good before you know the shot is good.

We don't have long hours of meditation like they did in the exotic East, and we don't have martial arts, kung fu and judo, but when you're preparing for the Olympics and swimming six hours a day, thousands of miles a year, you get yourself to something of the same state, only you have no roshi or guru to tell you what's happening while your times are getting faster.

The California track coach tells how he does it. First he gets all these sprinters out there, every one of them can travel ten yards in less than a second, a hundred yards splitting somewhere between the ninth and tenth second, all of them straining at the leash. Now he has them run the middle part of the sprint, a running start, then forty or fifty yards that "count," then they keep on another thirty or forty. "Okay," he says, "now do it with four-fifths effort." Really? Cut the effort back? *The times get faster.* "Okay, now run at four-fifths speed and relax your jaw." The sprinters don't believe it, they think the timer's thumb has slipped on the stop watch, four-fifths is faster than five-fifths.

Funny spaces. We're all sitting around the room, coaches, athletes, some of the athletes feel a bit strange, they wouldn't want anybody to hear them talking this way, so it helps to have a big quarterback like Brodie saying it's a ballet, the linemen coming at you in slow motion.

A gentleman gets up who is a well-known diver, deep diver, not fancy diver. He has set up a "surfing and diving ashram." No breathing in and out and looking at the wall, you put your scuba gear on, *then* you can count your breaths. "I had a diver who was skeptical, and then one day, in just thirty feet of water, something happened, and he said that suddenly he felt absolutely at one with the ocean, and *he could hear grains of sand on the bottom.* He spent almost an hour listening to the grains of sand, and his life had been changed ever since."

Nitrogen narcosis, I suggested. Not in thirty feet of water, everybody said angrily.

What is the click that tells you the shot is good before you know it's good? Maybe that isn't so mysterious. Maybe it's right-brained information that usually gets suppressed by the left brain, but sometimes it gets through before it stops to be translated into words.

And that total concentration, some psychologists say we crave it almost instinctively, damping down and focusing, and then opening up with a new state of concentration, that's why people take on activities that demand *total attention,* mountain climbing and tobogganing and skiing and car racing, where the penalties for non-concentration are so great that even the language-using mind shuts up for a minute because it understands that at least for a few minutes it better get out of the way. (The language-using mind gets to come back and write the whole thing up for the Sierra

Club journal, how time slows down, and the climber is suddenly aware of all the crystals in the rocks—)

We all may crave that sort of focusing, but a lot of us pay our dues to the feeling by watching the crazies toboggan down the mountain on TV, while we have a beer can in hand.

Zen and the Cross-court Backhand

I signed up for "yoga tennis." Yoga tennis surfaced at Esalen, and then I pursued it other places. *Sports Illustrated* wanted to know about it, and secretly I hoped to fix my serve while exploring this new frontier. I had one yoga tennis teacher who wore a blue jogging suit and a Sikh beard and a turban; he was a former business-forms salesman who talked a lot about *ki*, energy. And another there was a yoga tennis instructor who hoped to have "a tennis ashram."

But Tim Gallwey did not wear a beard or a turban. Gallwey had been the captain of the Harvard tennis team, and he had been brooding about tennis while following the Guru Maharaj Ji. He was very articulate, and eventually I took him to see my publisher, and Gallwey wrote *The Inner Game of Tennis*.

"We learn tennis element by element," Gallwey said, standing on a tennis court at the California junior college where Esalen was having a sports seminar. "If we learned it as totality, we could learn it in one-hundredth the time. Our biggest problem is Ego, is trying too hard. We know how to play perfect tennis. Perfect tennis is in us all. Everyone knows how to ride a bicycle, and just before we really ride for the first time, we know we know. The problem with Ego is that it has to achieve; we are not sure who we are until by achieving we become. So we hit the ball out and the Ego says, 'Ugh, out.' Then it starts to give commands, 'Do it right.' We shouldn't have a judgment. The ball goes *there,* not out. Ninety percent of the bad things students do are intentional corrections of something else they are doing. We have to let the body experiment and by-pass the mind. The mind acts like a sergeant with the body a private. How can anybody play as a duality?"

I recognized the sergeant's voice right away; in my mind, it says, "Move your feet, dummy," and "Watch the ball." What to do about the sergeant?

"You have to check the mind, to preoccupy it, stop it from fretting. Look at the ball. Look at the *seams* on the ball, watch the pattern, get preoccupied so the mind can't judge. In between points put your mind on your breathing. In, out. In, out. A quiet mind is the secret of yoga tennis. Most people think concentration is fierce effort. Watch your facial muscles after you hit the ball. Are they tensed or relaxed? Concentration is effortless effort, is *not trying.* The body is sophisticated; its computer commands hundreds of muscles instantly; it is wise about itself; the Ego isn't. Higher consciousness is not a mystical term. You see more when all of your energy runs in the same direction. Concentration produces joy, so we look for things that will quiet the mind."

I could see that parking the mind would be essential. I sat next to Jascha Heifetz once at a dinner party and asked him what he thought about when he was giving a concert. He said if the concert was, say, on a Saturday night he thought about the smoked salmon and the marvelous bagel he was going to have on Sunday morning. If he was thinking about the bagel, then who was thinking about the concerto? His hands.

Don't you have to know the right form before you park the mind?

The body seeks out the right form if the mind doesn't get in the way, Gallwey said. No teenager could do a monkey or a locomotive or whatever teenage dance is now rampant from a set of instructions, but he can do it in one night by observing.

Ah, observing. You didn't say observing.

"You have to talk to the body in its native language," said the tennis guru. "Its native language is not English, it is sight and feel, mostly sight. The stream of instructions most students get are verbal and have to be translated by the body before they are understood. If you are taking a tennis lesson, let the pro show you, don't let him tell you. If you want the ball to go to a cross-court corner, get an image of where you want the ball to go and let the body take it over. Say: 'Body, cross-court corner, please.'"

"Let the serve serve itself," Gallwey said. "When I first used this technique my serve got hot. Then I thought, wow, I've mastered the serve and immediately it got cold because it was me, not the serve, serving itself."

This imagining the ball into the corner, was this the power of positive thinking, Norman Vincent Peale?

"Oh, no. Positive thinking is negative thinking in disguise. If you double-fault six times in a row your positive thinking will flip to negative. So I try not to pay compliments because the compliments can always be withheld on the next shot. What we are talking about is *no thinking*."

It seemed a marvelously Rousseauistic philosophy. Man is born with a perfect tennis game and he is everywhere in chains. Rousseau was influenced by the sunny Polynesians brought to Europe by the eighteenth-century sailors; what if they had sailed a little further over, and brought back fierce and aggressive Melanesians? You don't need a tennis pro with negative instuctions, you need a movie of each shot and a ball machine to drill with. It was hard for me to see the difference between the instructions. "Be aware of your racket head," from the tennis guru, and "Follow through, where is your racket head?" from the ordinary pro.

"The distinction is, the pro says, good shot, bad shot," Gallwey said. "I just want to focus awareness, not make a judgment."

It occurred to me that yoga tennis was a misnomer. Hatha yoga has breathing and movement, but what the "yoga tennis" pros had come up with was a version of the Japanese and Chinese martial arts. *Zen in the Art of Archery* would be closer. The student was a middle-aged German philosophy professor in Japan, Eugen Herrigel, and he suffered through the same agonies as a yoga tennis student. He tried to tell his right hand to release the bowstring properly with his sergeant mind. The Zen master never coached him at all. The master said, "The right shot at the right moment does not come because you do not let go of yourself . . . the right art is purposeless, aimless! What stands in your way is that you have a much too willful will. You think that what you do not do yourself does not happen." The breathing exercises were to detach the student from the world, to increase a concentration that would be comparable to "the jolt that a man who has stayed up all night gives himself when he knows that his life depends on all his senses being alert." Nothing more is required of the student than that he copy the teacher: "The teacher does not harass and the pupil does not overtax himself."

One day the Zen student of archery Herr Professor Doktor Herrigel loosed a shot and the master bowed and said, "Just then It shot," and the Herr Professor Doktor gave a whoop of delight and the Zen master got so mad he wouldn't talk to him, because this wasn't the student's achievement and there he was thinking he had done it and taking the credit.

There are some pros playing, said my Zen tennis teachers, who are well into these forms of concentration without articulating them, just as Jack Nicklaus may never have gone hi-tot-tsu hu-tot-tsu mi-it-tsu. Billie Jean King, it is said, meditates upon a tennis ball. Ken Rosewall gets mentioned all the time, a perfectly balanced, classical game. And Stan Smith —if you asked Stan Smith what he was thinking about during one of those booming serves he would say the bagel he had for breakfast. (Nobody would be foolish enough to ask Jimmy Connors.) A grooved game means you can play without your head.

I told some friends about watching the patterns on the ball. One of them said later: "I tried that. It worked, it really worked. But I got so much into watching the patterns on the ball that I didn't get to play tennis, it was like a lot of work, I'd rather be lousy and not watch the patterns on the ball."

There was no immediate impact on my game, but then, the Zen archery student got restless in his fourth year of instruction, when he still had met with no success. Depressed, he said to the master that he hadn't managed yet to get one single arrow off right —four years, and not one single arrow off right—or It had not appeared to loose the arrow—and his stay in Japan was limited and four years he'd been at it.

The master got cross with him. "The way to the goal is not to be measured!" he said. "Of what importance are weeks, months, years?"

Zen has gotten to be a good word now, the true thing, the thing itself. We have *Zen and the Art of Running,* and *Zen and the Art of Seeing,* and an autobiography, *Zen and the Art of Motorcycle Maintenance.* We still have to go through *Zen and Turning Your Spares into Strikes,* and *Zen Your Way to Higher Earnings;* the Zen books are getting shorter and more flowery, with any luck they will soon be mostly soupy photographs and we can be done with it.

I went back to my tennis guru. My requirements were simple: I wanted a serve, that's all, with the power of a rocket, accurate to within six inches, one that would zing into the corner of the service court and spin away with such a dizzying kick that the opponent would retire nauseated.

We went out to the court with a basket of balls. I hit a couple. The Zen master didn't say anything. Some went in, some went out. The Zen master didn't say anything. I hit some more.

"Okay," he said. "Breathe in with your racket back, and out when it moves."

That was easy.

"Okay, now, where should the ball go over the net? And where should it land?"

I pointed.

"Okay, ask your body to send it there, and get out of the way."

"Please, body, send it there."

A miss.

"It's not listening."

"Slow it down. Visualize the whole shot before you hit it. Listen to the sound the ball makes against the string."

It's amazing, but if you really visualize, and you really listen to the sound, you can't go racheta racheta with your mind, which is very uncomfortable, mutiny in the enlisted men's quarters.

We set up an empty tennis ball can in the corner of the service court. I know, those fierce kids in California and Florida who are out hitting three hundred sixty days a year, who hit five hundred serves a day for practice, can knock over the empty can a couple of times a day, but weekend players can't even get the ball in the court.

"Slow it down more. More. Please, body, send the ball—"

"Slower, body, send the ball—"

"Slower. Slower. Make time stand still. No time."

"Please, body, send the ball—"

Zank! The empty tennis ball can went up into the air and bounced metallically.

"Who did that?" I said.

The tennis guru said nothing. He handed me another ball. It went into the corner of the service court, on roughly the same spot. So did the next one.

I began to giggle wildly. I danced around a little, the scarecrow had a brain, the cowardly lion had courage, I had a serve. "I did it! I did it!" I said.

Immediately it went away.

The next five balls went into the net.

"I shouldn't have said that," I said. "That sonofabitch is sure sensitive."

"Please, body, send the ball—"

"Please, body, send the ball—"

"Visualize. Don't use words. Don't think. Use images. In between shots, count your breath."

Now the afternoon began to take on a very eerie quality indeed, an underwater, slow-motion quality. Who-o-o-ck went the ball to its accustomed place in the service court; I had to consciously fight the exhilaration. It went away. My breathing sounded like the breathing in scuba gear. The ball was going into the service court, into the corner, but I wasn't feeling anything, no joy, no sorrow, and this was so uncomfortable. I came up for air. I felt greed.

"It's going in, but it isn't going in very hard," I said. "I want power, more power."

"Power comes from the snap of the wrist. Ask your wrist to snap at the top of the arc, and don't try. Use images: please, wrist, snap at the top."

The serve began to pick up speed.

"I don't know what this is," I said, "but it isn't tennis and it isn't me."

I didn't feel at all well. The next afternoon I went out alone at a tennis club. A guy came up and asked me if I wanted to hit some. We rallied. He was very strong. He asked me if I wanted to play. I thought: he doesn't even know my name, I can lose six-love, six-love, and no one will ever know. I put on my mental scuba gear. I wasn't very nice to play with, because you can't say "Oh, nice shot" when you are breathing into your scuba mask. I watched the pattern on the ball, the serve went in, and far, far away I could hear my opponent talking to himself: "Oh, watch the ball, stupid! Don't hit it out! Don't double-fault! Move your feet, idiot!" He began to hit the ball harder and harder. Some of his hard shots were winners, but more of them began to go out. He began to get better at the end. Six-love, six-two.

"I don't know what was the matter with me today," said my opponent.

I was afraid to say anything, but I shouldn't have been afraid—the serve packed its bags and went away as soon as I got back to playing with people I knew. Sometimes it would reappear for a flash, like a tiny acid rerun. Once, on the court, I shouted, sounding like a madman: "I know you're in there, you bastid, come on out!" Please, body, send it there, please, body—and nothing. Nothing. It is on Its vacation. If I wanted It, It wouldn't come, and if I didn't want It, it might, but then who cared? And gradually it began to seem like there was tennis and Something Else, very difficult to do both at the same time even if Something Else has one hell of a serve.

And this was a bit spooky: It was living in there with me; It could bring the music back on with a thumb twitch, without telling me; It could make the biofeedback machine switch from beep beep to boop boop without letting me know; It wasn't taking any orders from me, and, in fact, It would go away if I even pretended to notice, sensitive bastid, It had a much better serve than I did but wouldn't play with any of my friends, It could take over but only if I would go do some idiot child-task like breath-counting; why does It only like me if I play idiot? It was actually a bit frightening, was It.

The Sweet Music of the Strings

"The siddhi is a by-product of the process, not the process," said Torben. "That's what the yogis say."

Siddhis are powers, odd powers, spooky things yogis can do, or people can do, that are sort of impossible: materialize objects, read minds, knock over empty tennis ball cans at the corner of the court.

"But what does that mean?"

"We-l-l, it doesn't mean anything, does it? It's what the yogis say."

Somehow, I was always asking Torben what does that mean? and Torben would say, it doesn't mean anything, does it? which would make me feel as though the question had been the wrong question.

Torben Ulrich is described as a Danish touring pro, a member of a Danish family that always played the Davis Cup for Denmark—that's not who Torben is. I don't know who Torben is, I get a feeling —very hard to stuff into words—well—

Torben walked into the seminar, the one where the guy was talking about listening to the grains of sand on the bottom of the ocean, and I thought who is *that* because here is this character with the Old Testament beard and lines around the eyes and all the tennis pros stir and ruffle a bit, Torben is also described as a blithe spirit and not like anybody else, that is, I suppose, because he has this ponytail down to his waist tied with a blue ribbon and he is out playing Newcombe and Laver and Smith and—

I wish I could capture that Danish lilt, Torben can bend "no" over three syllables, nooo-ooo oo-ooooo—

Torben wasn't part of the weekend, but he belonged. He stopped by with Jeff Borowiak, former NCAA singles and doubles champion, ex-UCLA captain, top-twenty ranking, haircut like a tall Renaissance prince, Torben is in his mid-forties, these young players pick him up as a guru sometimes—

Torben said: "The egoless game goes further than the ego game. 'I would like to become a better tennis player's really has nothing to do with winning. The Western world is so oriented to winning that the temptation of winning is there almost always. The tennis court, seen as a mandala—"

A mandala, you already know is an object of meditation, a geometric figure, a representation of the cosmos—*the tennis court is a mandala?*

"What does that mean?" I said for the first of a hundred times. "What does that mean, the tennis court is a mandala?"

"It doesn't mean anything," said the soft lilting voice. "It is a mandala if you choose to see it as a mandala, a confined space made an object of activity. If we are centered around the court as an object, the court is a mandala."

"You mean if you're in it or if you look at it?"

Wrong question again.

"Noo-oooo-oooo," Torben said, it doesn't mean anything because you can see the court as anything you like. No-ooo-ooo, I don't think it has much meaning. But if you take it very far, sooner or later you have to see the court as a mandala, sooner or later."

"But what does that mean?" I said, for the third of a hundred times.

Borowiak had gone to Denmark to hang out with Torben. They got up at four in the afternoon—Torben likes to get up at four in the afternoon, and everybody in Denmark likes Torben—one wonders about Mrs. Torben's schedule, after all they have a kid who gets up and goes to school and plays soccer—and every other day they would jog a little, twelve miles or so, through forests that Torben named Forest #1, Forest #2, Forest #3, running through the snow, two-foot drifts sometimes, and then to the saunas and whirlpools of the public baths, and then they would come home and play tapes, Torben is an accomplished musician and a jazz critic for a Copenhagen paper, music with strange instruments like the Indian veena, hours of ragas, or Tibetan monks singing—and have dark bread and cheese, Torben eats a lot of cheese—then they'd play their flutes along with the records, Borowiak's father was a musician, Borowiak had years of music, Torben can play all the reeds—and then, from three to six in the morning, they would play indoor tennis—that's three to six in the morning, must be easy to get on the courts then—and then talk—

"Torben would delve into long discussions on such things as light producing waves in the air creating noises that the ear is not sensitive enough to decipher, certain lights give off sour notes. Or he might wander into his feelings about the longer muscles, he'd demonstrate with diagrams and pencils with rubber hands."

Torben tries these things out—say, twenty-five minutes to open a door—so he can make a map of his muscles, his fingers go onto the doorknob and slowly, slowly, twenty-five minutes later—

—it blew Borowiak's mind. "An explosion of horizons," he said. "There are few people in sports who have this quality, this sense of unification—

Torben was in the Eastern U.S. to play a couple of tournaments and then Forest Hills—it wasn't easy. I would call up—

"Can we get together today?"

"Hey, hey. We might get together today. Would that be a good idea? Maybe we won't. I wonder if we will."

"Sure we will. We just make up our minds to do it, that's all. We say, we'll meet each other at such-and-such a time, at such-and-such a place—

"Y-e-es, ye-e-es, that would be nice, if we could both be at the same place, then we could get together, we could say ten o'clock, or four o'clock, or nine o'clock, or no time at all—"

"Noon?" A little early for Torben, but he has a match that afternoon—

"Noon," said Torben, testing the word, "noon, no-o-o-o-oon, nooo-ooo-ooo-ooon. A very nice quality noon."

Torben practically never made a date, so I would go out to where he was playing, or where he was staying, and appear—"Hey, hey," Torben would say, without surprise. One time in Torben's room, the books were *Asian Journey,* Thomas Merton, a book on acupuncture, and *Buddhist Wisdom.* Another time it was the Tibetan *Book of the Dead.*

Torben Story #21:

Torben has made it to the semifinals of the National Indoor, playing Ismail El Shafei, the Egyptian. Torben beat El Shafei's *father* in the 1948 Davis Cup.

The reporters gather in the press trailer, Torben enters, his hair down past his shoulders, really an Old Testament prophet now, in a gown, his tone lilting and saintly:

"How old are you, really, Torben? Forty-one? Forty-four?"

"How old is old?" says Torben. "What is age? Am I forty-one or twenty-one or sixty-one? Who knows?"

"Do you think you will win tomorrow?"

"No, noo-oooo-ooo, I will not win. What is winning?"

Torben Story #36:

"Torben, you are playing Pancho Gonzalez tomorrow, how do you feel about his fast serve?"

"What is speed?" says Torben. "Is speed fast or slow? Speed is relative to observation. A big serve can come in slow motion."

"Pancho is very hot right now. Will you have trouble with his serve?"

"Pancho's serve is a thing of beauty. How can a thing of beauty be trouble?"

Torben Story #51:

"Torben, you are playing at an age when most players are teaching or running something else, how long will you play? What are your plans when you stop?"

"I could play or I could stop. That assumes a structure to the future. I hate getting involved in schedules and specifics. If we don't eat, we will get hungry. Then we will eat."

"How do you stay so young?"

"Young? How young you are depends on when you died last. If you die every minute, you can last a long time. If you don't establish a past . . . then when you lie down to sleep and journey into night, you can wake up as a new person or whatever you are in the morning. But you're not dragging the day before you along so that you're staggering under this bag of yesterdays: scores, bad shots, rankings. I don't always succeed."

Torben story #62: (the classic)

Torben is at Forest Hills in the fourth round, leading the great Australian, John Newcombe, two sets to none. On a vital point a butterfly flutters into his face and forces a weak volley. Newcombe goes on to win in five sets.

"Did the butterfly bother you on the crucial point?" Torben quotes the ancient *Tao,* Chuang-tzu:

"Was I then a man dreaming I was a butterfly, or am I now a butterfly dreaming I am a man?"

"They sure ask about your age a lot," I said. I really wanted to know, myself, why Torben continued to tour the world. In the hotel lobby, the players—they seemed like such kids—would stop him—are you going to play in the Australian Open, Torben? Will you be in India this year? Why did Torben keep it up, all these hotel rooms, all these plane flights, Buenos Aires and Melbourne and London and Calcutta, when he could be running through the snow to the sauna in Denmark, or whatever?

"Well, we will have to change the idea of aging," Torben said. "A fifty-year-old musician is not out of it, why should an athlete be, if we learn not to burn up our bodies?"

We went to dinner with Tomas Koch, a left-handed Brazilian pro who also wears his long hair in a ponytail. Koch wanted to know if Torben would come and play in a tournament in Brazil. Tomas seemed a little down.

Tomas pushed the glass of water in a circle, in the restaurant, an Indian place which Vijay Amritraj, the lanky Indian, had found.

"Torben, tell me the part again about how there is no opponent."

"No opponent, only the ball."

"No opponent, only the ball."

"The ball moves to you and the ball moves away from you, no opponent. Even when you think you watch the ball, you don't watch it all the time, you see like, in a movie, only the fourth frame and the fifteenth frame and the twenty-sixth frame—when the play goes well, it is a better performance than each actor."

"Is that the click that tells you?" Tomas said.

I kept thinking I had missed a line.

"Are we talking about playing in some sort of altered state?" I asked.

"Oh, Western athletes only get into this for a few seconds, in a crude way," Torben said.

"The grass," Tomas said.

"Very bald and spotty," I volunteered. "I understand they're going to phase it out."

"The grass in Calcutta opens like a flower, you can put your face on it, so many groundskeepers for each blade, the grass in Wimbledon is very lush, such professionals, and each place has a sound," Torben said.

Now I will collapse several conversations, because I stopped asking Torben direct questions, you can't really have much of a conversation with Torben anyway, I was just there, *each place has a sound,* "All the movement can only be best if it is in harmony with the tonic, the keynote sound of the chord. So I don't think, this is music and this is tennis because everything is, traveling, tennis, music, theater, dance, if I am on a plane then this is part of the music, the sound of the engines and the pilot's voice, some tournaments it is hard to find the sound, in the Indoor the air conditioning and the crowd did not make the right sound together—"

"They talk about the home court advantage in basketball," I said, "the vibrations are part of that."

Torben stopped and was staring far away—

"They asked me, you know, to endorse a steel racket, a French company, but I tried it and I couldn't make it work because I couldn't find the sound, the sound of the ball against the racket has to be—"

Torben's voice trailed off, and it was some minutes before he spoke again.

"In music I try to let the sound take over and consume my concentration, and the same in tennis."

In the humid, ninety-degree atmosphere at Forest Hills, a Czech called Vladimir Zednik, all shoulders, looking like a draft choice for the Chicago Bears, overpowered Torben. Overpowered may not be right, because Torben was never out of it, full of deft touches and spins and surprising bursts of power. He did not seem at all upset.

"I could not find my song today," he said.

Laver was playing well.

"Rod is over his trouble," Torben said. "He is so goal-oriented, remember, after the Grand Slam, he won everything in the world that year and then he couldn't play well because he had lost the reason for playing. Poor Rod."

"Poor Rod is right up there," I said. "I don't feel a bit sorry for him."

"The goal is to be free of a goal," Torben said. "Who is that who is playing? Who is that who is making the stroke? Who is that who is making the next stroke? Until they all disappear. If you succeed at tennis then you hang up the racket because you are beyond all that, everything like that."

I had a glimmer of what Torben was talking about, but it did not make me feel at all secure. It would be playing; It would be gliding into Its perfect shots, and I would be out counting daisies somewhere. But maybe this is just the savage irony of I, fighting a potential threat, or an illusory threat.

"Once," Torben said, "Louis Armstrong was in Sweden."

Crinkly lines in the weathered, tanned Torben face, spaces between the big front teeth—

"And," Torben said, "he was going to come to Denmark. And we went to meet him in Göteborg, and we took our instruments, and we played on the ferry with Louis Armstrong all the way across, like the ferry was a Mississippi riverboat with those great jazz musicians, and the *sound* went out over the water and over the freighters and over the ferryboats, and the *sound* came back again, and that was a *wonderful* day."

Torben lost to Pancho Gonzalez in the finals of the seniors'; somebody is always winning and somebody is always losing. And my curiosity—why? why?—had long since dissolved, for obviously if you are alive you are out amidst these textures and these sounds, the sweet music of the strings, and if the music is there then you are the music while the music lasts.

V. Vibes

Ambiguities and Vibes

On the Road from the City of Skepticism, I had to pass through the Valley of Ambiguity.

Here are all these devices aimed directly at shutting up the left-brained, language-using mind. I was being given a hard time by my own left-brained, language-using mind just because it liked language so much. Maybe it is easy for people who aren't word people, dancers or sculptors or mimes, but my left brain, for heaven's sake, will get so fascinated by a single word it will track its origins all the way through Middle English to Indo-European. And read! It will read anything, the label on a ketchup bottle, Reg. U.S. Dept. Agriculture, Article 4 of the Warsaw Convention on the back of the airline ticket about lost luggage, anything. So that was a fight.

On the other hand, my mind was clearly a drunken monkey full of obsolete football scores and rusted bicycles, and therefore certainly not to be trusted, in spite of its verbal facility. And the verbal mind itself was getting very distrustful of everything *it* read in this field, because it was very obvious that the writers who wrote the articles were governed by drunken monkeys, and so were the editors who assigned them. The editors of the Establishment press were continuously reviewing the Alchemist; they would say to the writer, go see this latest guru and tell us why the Dupes are falling for it this time.

(Only in children's stories do the Dupes come out well. Remember that the Wizard of Oz—twenty-fourth descendant of the Alchemist—was a fraud, but he did give the scarecrow a diploma and after that the scarecrow had a brain, and the cowardly lion got a medal for courage and after that he was brave, and the tin woodman got a heart that went ticktock. But then placebos work, we know that.)

Clearly there was something going on that you missed if you simply went to see what the Dupes were falling for.

But the Dupes were really falling for a lot of non-sense, too, by even the most charitable standards. Sweet children were leaving school and home and—three drops of vinegar in the nostril and cry hum!—following the newest Oriental preacher and expecting the world to change next Tuesday. The counter-cultural press erred the other side of putting down the preacher and the Dupes. Everything not rational was true, Saturn was coming into the sixth house of Venus, and sunspots were about to cave in the economy.

So I was ready to believe, or to experience and not judge, but I wanted all my teachers to be perfect. Chogyam Trungpa the Tibetan lama is smart as a whip and he is giving a lecture—a very good lecture too, and he sips from his water glass and I know damn well that is vodka in the water glass. How come he isn't getting high on what he's teaching? I am going to these private sessions with this noted Indian religious leader and he is snuffling. Snuffling? Hay fever? Allergy? A cold? I want to give him some antihistamine. What is the problem, Sire, I ask, and he says, it must be the smog. But I'm breathing the same smog, and I'm not snuffling, hay fever and asthma have some degree of psychogenic causes, could I give him a placebo? If he does all this yoga, how come he's tense?

And I have the same problem with the psychologists. Will Schutz is a great encounter leader and a nice guy, especially once you get to know him, and he wrote a book called *Joy* and he has JOY on his California license plates and when you meet him he is dour as a Scotch accountant. Stanley Keleman writes these books and says, "The body never lies," and his own body the last time I saw it weighed two hundred and fifty pounds and was barely capable of a deep breath, much less a push-up. But I guess it didn't lie.

And then there was the incident of the Senoi. I was

in a class and some of my classmates were into Senoi dream theory. The Senoi are an aboriginal people in Malaysia. They use dreams as a part of community life and they try to influence their dreams and get messages from dreams. If you dream of falling, you tell the dream at breakfast and everybody says, wonderful, where did you fall to and what did you discover? If you didn't discover, go back and dream the dream again and see what you come up with.

An anthropologist called Kilton Stewart wrote about the Senoi, and it's his Senoi chapter in Tart's *Altered States of Consciousness*. The Senoi, Stewart said, are the most adjusted people on earth, no war, no crime, their psychological achievements are better than ours in nuclear physics. Wow! Senoi seminars sprout up in colleges, and Senoi communities, too, nice young California people telling their dreams, and having their children tell their dreams, and I have a problem.

I have a problem because many years ago the U.S. Army put me on a study team in Southeast Asia, and the Senoi were one of my tribes. I dig up the notes. Sure enough, the Senoi, dream culture. But Kilton Stewart has somehow left out that thunderstorms terrify the Senoi, the women peel off their clothes, screeching like banshees, and offer themselves to the thunderstorm, and when you die, if you're a Senoi, your soul goes into the left armpit of a gigantic old woman called Sankal, who lives on an island in a lake at the bottom of a pit. And in present-day Malaysia, the Senoi children are riding the school bus to the government school where they don't get to tell their dreams, and the adults are hanging out trying to cadge tips from the tourists by getting their pictures taken. And the anthropologist who found the Senoi, these peaceable people, who in fact introduced Kilton Stewart to them, Dr. Noone from Cambridge, well, poor Dr. Noone got blowpiped by a poisoned dart from his best Senoi buddy. Southeast Asian version of the Saturday Night Special, a little fracas over a lady.

I really want the Senoi to be this marvelous dream culture, and I don't want my California classmates to be mad at me, but it influences my enthusiasm for Senoi dream culture to recall how you had to hire a shaman to get your soul back out of Sankal's armpit. Now my classmates are mad, they think I am a narc or something. What do I do with my Army notes?

And then there is the Guru Maharaj Ji, the teenage guru. Some of my nice friends are following the Guru Maharaj Ji. Off we go to a *satsang,* a spiritual discourse, delivered by a mahatma, one empowered to spread the Knowledge, a shaved-head, berobed Indian with a singsong delivery. It is a pep talk for the big rally in Houston, the Millennium.

"A man comes back next life as what he meditates upon this time," says the Mahatma. "A man who meditates upon God becomes God. A man who meditates upon wealth is clutching the earth like a snake, a snake loves the earth, and wealth is like the earth, so a man who spends his time thinking upon wealth comes back as a snake. So do not be attached to wealth. Use wealth for the benefit of humanity, bring money for the Millennium even if it is only ten dollars or twenty dollars"— It sounded like Marjoe, the kid preacher— "You've got five dollars, ten dollars under the coffee can in the kitchen, oh, bring it here, bring it here for *Je*sus."

Rennie Davis, the Sixties activist, tells us how the Millennium is going to awaken consciousness that will allow us to plug into the Ground of Being and usher in a thousand years of peace, but it's going to take some money, "so each one of us has to go out and hit our parents—a hundred dollars, fifty dollars."

Hit our parents? Hit our parents? Rennie lost me.

The Guru Maharaj Ji was a setup for the Alchemist-baiting press. He had a Rolls-Royce and all those Hondas and Shri Hans Productions for films and records, and Divine Travel Services, and *Divine Times* (THE LORD IN LONDON! HOLY FAMILY NOW IN ENGLAND!) and vegetarian restaurants—De Tocqueville wrote: "Strange sects endeavor [in America] to strike out extraordinary paths of eternal happiness . . . religious insanity is very common."

"It's natural for the kids to turn to the Second Coming of Santa Claus," said Paul Krassner, the editor of *The Realist,* in Houston.

"He's no Santa Claus, he's the Lord," said Rennie Davis.

"This is the Knowledge you can't get in College," sang Bhole Ji, the Guru Maharaj Ji's brother, who leads the Divine rock band.

"When I got the Knowledge," said Rennie, "I saw this incredible light in the middle of my forehead, a diamond was spinning and getting larger, then the divine music, a heavy roar for a while, then dinnnnnnng, every fiber of my being began to vibrate . . . an incredible wave of bliss shot through me, my mind began to play this incredible rock and roll . . ."

"This is like being with the Nixon CREEP people," said the editor of *The Realist*.

Rennie Davis said Guru Maharaj Ji is "the Lord, the universe, the power of creation itself," and the Guru's followers speak of him with Buddha and Jesus. Not everybody agrees. Agehananda Bharati, the Indian-born chairman of Syracuse University's anthropology department, who has written on Indian religions, says he is "a typical Asian phony."

Along the lines of shaking the techniques out of the disciplines, I wanted to know about the Knowledge. Usually I go on the trips myself, but I had been on enough of them by the time I ran into the Guru Maharaj Ji's crowd. The rite of the Knowledge is secret and those who describe it risk demotion in future incarnations to all sorts of base things, but there have been enough defectors now to give something of a description:

The mahatma is sitting against the middle of a wall, with a very bright light shining on him. First he satsangs you for about two hours about the retribution you're going to suffer if you ever reveal the secret of the Knowledge-giving. Fire and brimstone, suffering and gnashing of teeth, eternal damnation. Then he starts giving Knowledge. First he does your eyes. He presses his knuckles very hard upon your eyeballs and keeps them there until you see the *light*. Then he plugs up your ears with his fingers in a certain way until you hear the *music*. Then he tips your head back in a certain way for the meditative position, and that nectar you taste, that's your snot. Then he tells you the secret word to meditate on, and that's kind of a breath sound that's supposed to represent the divine energy of the world, ah-ha, ah-ha.

The guru's followers weren't happy with that particular account, needless to say. But they knew I was trying to find a Western vocabulary for various phenomena, so we talked about the white light.

"The pressure on the eyeball could certainly get the retinal cells to fire," I said. "That would give you a white light. Lots of things can give you a white light, neurochemical transmitters, hallucinogens—"

"It's not knuckles on the eyeballs, it's *thumbs* on the eyeballs, gently," said a devotee.

"That would stop the saccades, or small involuntary movements of the eye," I said. "Very good for quieting."

"But what about the pineal gland?" asked a pleasant, wide-eyed girl. Every Eastern trip gets to the pineal gland at some point. The pineal body is in the middle of the brain, above the pons, developing from the diencephalon. Its functions, says the textbook, are obscure, as if it were the vestige of something we have evolved away from.

"Descartes said it was the seat of the soul, and it appears in a lot of esoteric disciplines as the Third Eye," I said. "And this was considered so much esoteric baloney, but in 1965 some neurophysiologists found that the nerve to the pineal is a branch of the sympathetic nerves receiving impulses from a branch of nerves that transmit impulses from the eye to the brain."

I was reading from my pineal paragraphs.

"Thus the pineal gland responds by a very indirect route to light in the environment. Though not organized as an eye, it can function as a light receptor."

"Oh my God, there *is* a Third Eye," said the pleasant girl.

The Third Eye stuff got me when I first found the pineal papers. A secret eye in the middle of the brain! What would you see with it?

"Remember, we don't see with our eyes," I said, the anatomy professor, "we see *with the help of our eyes.* What we think of as seeing is a brain function."

I went back to the text.

"The light receptive qualities cause changes in the secretion of the hormone melatonin, which causes the concentration of melanin in pigment cells. In small vertebrates and mammals, seasonal light changes can influence sexual behavior."

"Far out!" said another devotee.

My neurophysiology text didn't have the celestial music or the nectar, but I had scored a lot of points with the Third Eye. We were all agreed on the effects of mantrams.

"Even though you know this," said the devotees, "you don't have the Knowledge. Why don't you get the Knowledge?"

"How long would it take?"

"Oh, if you're really ready, as little as half an hour. Maybe ten minutes. Some people have done it that fast."

The guru's followers were well-scrubbed and smiling and sincere. I did not get the Knowledge.

Almost a year later, some of the devotees told me the Millennium had been a bit disappointing. "We were all so worked up, we really thought flying saucers might land. Rennie Davis said there might be beings on other planets who wanted the Knowledge."

Flying saucers or not, the devotees I met were still there a year later, still in service. They stayed in service even after the guru's mother fired him, saying he had become too Western. Like Eleanor of Aquitaine, she attempted to favor another of her sons, but many of the American followers stuck to the teenage guru. The Guru Maharaj Ji adopted a lower profile.

There remains the unfortunate incident of the blackjacking, not necessarily only as a comment on the people of Divine Light. I wouldn't even bring it up but it shows the *certainty* that seems to come from the evangelical nature of religious enthusiasms.

A reporter for an underground newspaper in Detroit threw a pie in Guru Maharaj Ji's face. "I always wanted to throw a pie in God's face," he said. A week later he was visited by two men, an older Indian and a young American. The Indian zapped the young reporter with a blackjack, causing six skull lacerations, and necessitating a plastic plate in the cerebrum. There is a felony warrant out in Detroit for the two men; the blackjack-wielding Indian turns out to be Mahatma Fakiranand. Was Mahatma Fakiranand stripped of his mahatmadom? No, he was sent to give Knowledge in Europe. "There are no hard and fast rules for being holy," said a Divine Light official. "In India there have been gurus who have led their followers into full-scale wars."

Not just in India. I think of the archbishop leading his troops in the Albigensian Crusade, crying, "Kill them! Kill every man, woman and child! God will reveal who are the true Catholics!" Closer to home, I met a young man who had just defected from the service of the Reverend Sun Myung Moon, a Korean who received a visitation from Jesus Christ on a hillside in 1936, and began preaching his own brand of gospel. The Reverend Sun Myung Moon began collecting not only his own followers from city to city, but hecklers, Jesus freaks who had some dispute in theology with the Korean. At one dinner, the Reverend passed out billy clubs to some of his followers, to aid in the theological dispute with his fellow Christians. Not that this is new. There is a famous letter from Cotton Mather to the commander of the brig *Porpoise,* suggesting that he "waylay the ship *Welcome* near the Cape of Cod, carrying that scamp William Penn and his heretic Quakers and sell the whole lot as slaves to Barbados, thus performing a service to the Lord." And keep the money.

It is said, in the intellectual sections of the counterculture, that our society has been too linear and rational and unfeeling, and in the less intellectual sections *stoned* is good, the uptight Establishment does not know stoned. In 1934 the Nazis in Germany held a tremendous night rally at Nuremberg. The stadium was ringed with antiaircraft searchlights, giving the effect, said the British ambassador, of "a cathedral of ice." Drums beat a hypnotic rhythm; drums and music have been used in many cultures to alter consciousness. Observers said the master orator, Chancellor Hitler, played the crowd like an orchestra, a frenzy of energy. In short, *everybody at Nuremberg was stoned*. A couple of years later they went out to impose the benefits of their certainty on as much of the world as they could reach.

It may be true, we have been goal-oriented, linear, mechanical, unfeeling; but stoned also does not work out well sometimes for the unstoned.

So I had ambiguities. Occasionally my schedule would compound the ambiguities. Nine A.M., Tibetan chanting. Eleven A.M., classwork on smiling to a count of six, or flaring one nostril to a count of six. Stuff to drive the left brain crazy, show the drunken monkey it doesn't run you. One P.M., catch the shuttle plane to attend three P.M. portfolio meeting, bring left brain back in a hurry, read *Wall St. Journal* and briefs on the plane. Make notes for meeting. Seven P.M. catch shuttle plane back, turn left brain off with breathing meditation; breathe in to a count of six, hold one, breathe out to a count of six, visualize breath.

It helps to reassure the language-using mind that it can come back even after it's turned off. Maybe get some help from the rest of the body, skin talk, say. Jung anticipated biofeedback monitoring the skin, wired up his patients while he tried word associations. Subsequent experiments showed that skins could remember, and mirror, and know things before the language-mind translated them.

And this brings us to Vibes. The TM people and the Harvard Medical School people said, meditation can relax you by dropping the level of activity. The incremental idea says, if you turn down the noise in your mind, you can hear what else is going on. Skin talk, stomach talk, heart talk. It's almost the opposite of some kinds of psychiatry, where the waking self is the sober rational one writing out checks to the psychiatrist, and the hidden self is considered an unruly child. "Emotional parasites thriving in the human body," wrote Barbara Brown, a biofeedback researcher, "can be traced . . . to a socially created barrier between the conscious and subconscious worlds. The entire body is reacting one way, crying out signals to a consciousness that is listening only to the consciousness of another society-evolved human product."

Vibes doesn't necessarily mean vibes the way the kids mean it, because that covers their own perceptions, which can be just as red-six-of-spades as those of people who don't use the word vibes. This idea is that your skin or gut is perceiving—perception isn't only through the eyes—things important to your survival. Not that this is so radical, it's in the language, I have a gut feeling, he gets under my skin, she is certainly a pain in the ass.

I have two personal Vibe stories from the money world. After my first six months of chanting and sheer movement and so on in esoteric psychology, I went to the giant glass slab in downtown New York to see my partners. I was limited, meaning I had left my money with them, and they were general, meaning they were doing something with it, and with their own. We sat in the small paneled private dining room. In the other dining room, the bigger one, same floor, the dancer bees were humming with indications of pension-fund clover and the air was heavy with electrical money excitement. I could feel the rhythms of the place like a narcotic in the blood, the same giddiness and rush.

In our dining room, that narcotic excitement was being translated into vigorous buttering of the rolls. The gross national product was going to be this, the interest rates were going to be that, there was thirty billion of cash in the mutual and pension funds, the market was going to turn around—and I noticed something.

There were four of us there and I was not smoking and *there were four lit cigarettes*.

"—the market is as low as it was in fifty-five, it is at the bottom end of its swing," said Leon—

"—as low as it was in fifty-one, I am adjusting for the Korean upsurge in commodity prices—" said Chuck, and I am sitting there starting to see how people can smoke four cigarettes at the same time.

"Leon is smoking two cigarettes," I announced after a while. "One rests on the ashtray while he puffs on the other one, and then he switches them, and sometimes one of you also switches the cigarette you're puffing on with Leon's reserve cigarette in the ashtray, and nobody notices."

Even after I said it, nobody noticed. Leon stubbed out one of the cigarettes and called the waiter, he thought I was complaining about being left out of the smoking.

"Give our guest a cigar," he said to the waiter.

Then we went to the offices and looked at the green-and-white computer sheets that had the portfolios, and something was wrong, the brasses and the flutes and the tympani weren't all together, even though there was high excitement and an estimate for each stock and a Beta rating from the computer, the portfolio had scabs and everybody was picking at them.

"I don't like it," I said.

"What? What? What should we do?"

I said—it was hard to say, because I was trying to translate these vibes—that there was too much activity, everybody was working too hard, pushing and pulling and tugging at the portfolio, and thinking up sixty-seven different reasons for everything, as well as what somebody heard somebody say in the Fed, and what the guy said who came in from the Coast.

"So what should we do?"

I said everybody who ran a portfolio should stand on his head ten minutes a day—I was improvising—and one day a week, Thursday, say, they should not come to work and not work at home and walk barefoot in the grass and think about something else, biology or physics or music, what does the music say, how corn grows—or geraniums, anything—and then on Friday morning first thing before they talk to anybody they should see whether the portfolio looked the same as Wednesday night.

They listened respectfully but I wasn't translating the vibes well enough, so they slapped me on the back and I left, and here is what I thought when I left:

I have been in this group that sits chanting Ra-a-a-m a couple of hours a day, and practices smiling to a count of six, and has a vocabulary so arcane none of them understands it, and they think a Great Cosmic Wave is coming. Plainly, *they are crazy.* And I have just spent the day with people that smoke two cigarettes at a time and make three phone calls at a time, and the portfolios reflect this entropy, and *they are crazy, too.*

Aha, everybody is crazy, there is only thee and me, and thee has been acting a bit queer recently.

The vibes, as it turned out, should have been paid attention. One of the gentlemen smoking two cigarettes had a heart attack within a year. And the portfolios had heart attacks, too, from going down so fast.

But I learn slowly. I opened the mailbox a year later, and here was another portfolio from another group, and when I opened the envelope I got an incredible rash on the skin. Just from reading a list of names and numbers. By now I was more respectful of Vibes, so I tried translating verbally. The message said: *Risk. Flee.*

I called up, and I translated *risk, flee* into boring everyday terms: say, you fellas seem to have a big percentage bunched up in just two situations and not much liquidity or flexibility.

And the managers said, you don't understand, you're out of touch, we have all the facts, here are the facts, blah blah blah.

I had a conflict between my skin, which was continuing to flash *risk, flee,* and the ol' left brain, which said: "These guys are probably right, they're there every day, they get all the information, you're out of touch, they wouldn't be there if they didn't know what they were doing."

So I had to take the responsibility for the Vibes,

and I didn't. The conceptual mind has years of practice against some momentary skin flush, and the skin flush is dumb and emotional, so it loses.

That portfolio went into a spin, too. The skin flush was smarter.

It might not have been. Skin flushes and heart bumps are only signals on our own survival, they do not necessarily keep an accurate score on some game taking place in society, what they have is a personal component that says, *hey, listen.*

"Listen" is not even the right word, it simply transfers to the ear what we mean when we say, perceive more than you see. Or hear. If you perceive, you're smarter than you think you are. But perceive isn't a very dramatic word.

Exercises Old and New

We have been looking at techniques from a variety of uncommon disciplines. Most of the techniques are a bit left-handed. Right-brained, non-linear, nonverbal. That makes them easy to read about—they seem almost idiotically simple—and not hard to do, but hard to keep doing. They're hard to keep doing because we are pitched at a more restless level; they require internal quiet and balance, and there's always something more interesting to do, certainly something more exciting, than exercises like these. Some authorities say that our culture became so lacking in imagination, intuition, mystery, and altered states that it left the opening for Eastern religions and "fundamental" Christian sects to expand.

But these techniques do not always come dressed

exotically. Doctors and management consultants commend the therapeutic effects of moving attention from work to something that isn't treated like work and which mobilizes the body differently. The cardiac specialists who wrote *Type A Behavior and Your Heart* wanted their patients to read Proust. No hardworking, compulsively competitive businessman could possibly read the entire *Remembrance of Things Past,* the pace of Proust and all that detail would drive him nuts—or slow him down, and that's the idea. Peter Drucker, the authority on management policies and techniques, warns the rising executive in *Management* against preoccupation with the job and its goals and office politics. What else should the rising executive do? Well, maybe play in a string quartet, said Pete Drucker. Music is indeed right-brained, and would have a mobilization different from sales projections. Furthermore, the playing in the string quartet should be *important,* important enough to demand concentration and attention. But the ranks of American business are noticeably bereft of fingers used to the viola da gamba. Not many cellists, either.

Here are two contemporary exercises gestalt psychologists will recognize immediately, which are so easy to read about it's hard to believe they could work. Their etiology is uncertain, but they are obvious cousins to the meditation techniques. The first is called Create a Space. It runs something like this:

Create a Space

Think of a time when you were absolutely, totally relaxed. Maybe you were in bed on a Sunday morning with nothing to do and rain on the roof. Maybe you were at a beach, or in a meadow on a summer day. Review all your most relaxed scenes, and pick the one that seems to make you go ah-h-h-h when you remember it. Now try to get back to that feeling, imagine all the details of how that total relaxation felt. The details are important: how did your eyes feel, how did your hands feel, how did your head feel.

When you can put yourself into that space, bring

the space with you. Have the space three feet on each side of you wherever you go. And then, when you're sure of the space, imagine a stressful situation. Now take yourself, and your space, three feet on each side of you, into the imagined stressful situation and let all the details play out.

Create a Space is used in some courses we will come to a bit later. I had a classmate who was a prison psychologist, and he had been teaching Create a Space to his clients, the prisoners. I don't know how he did that, but I went to visit him one afternoon when I was in his home state, and we took a tour. I couldn't tell how well it worked—the vibrations of con and counter-con go on at so many levels between prisoners and prison psychologists—but my classmate, who had been working in prison programs for twelve years, said the prisoners had taken to Create a Space more than anything in his tenure, and they wanted to know more. We talked to some of the prisoners. They all seemed to be named Billy Jack and Jim Bob and Bobby Joe. They were not self-conscious about the exercise.

"It takes a while," said Jim Bob, "but I wear my space past this one guard and he don't bother me no more."

The Wise Thing in the Cave

Like Create a Space, this comes from contemporary rather than esoteric disciplines, gestalt psychology and psychosynthesis, but the roots are the same. The point is to use those intuitive and subsurface powers that get drowned by the noise in the mind, or by the automatic actions of the mind. It helps to have a partner take you through the first couple of times, so that you can lie down with your eyes shut and pay attention to all the details.

The Wise Thing in the Cave also creates a space in imagination. The first time I did the exercise we imagined a field, and walked across the field, and noticed the grass, and the flowers, and then there was a cave, and we went into the cave, and there were stalactites and stalagmites and the sound of water running—and on and on for about fifteen minutes.

Great details once inside the cave, the feel underfoot, the sound of the cave, the echoes. If it's done right, it can be as absorbing as, say, a good movie.

And at the end of the cave is a person or an animal or anything you want, who is very wise. Anybody or anything you want. You get to ask the Wise Thing one question, any question. And you see what It says.

When I told this exercise to some friends, they couldn't understand it. Aren't you just making up the answer? What's such a big deal?

But the voice in the owl or the wise old man or whatever archetype appears is not the voice you're used to, if the exercise works. The voice belongs to It from outer space, the one whose thumb twitch turns off the grating sound, who has a big serve if nobody is looking. It's still you—so is the thumb twitch, or the serve—but another part.

"You do not actively imagine anything in the cave," said our instructor. "You let appear whatever wants to appear, and you let it say whatever it wants to say. You have access to all sorts of material within yourself which you usually ignore."

MEDIUM SHOT

Along the cave, the cave walls tannish and moist, SOUND of gurgling water.

VOICE-OVER

The Instructor's Voice: Now, at the end of the cave is a shape, it is the wise symbol you have picked, go a little closer.

MEDIUM SHOT

There's a shape there all right, but it's hard to see what it is—it's—it's a man, it looks like—

VOICE-OVER

The Instructor's Voice: All right, move a little closer, and now I am going to leave you, proceed at your own pace to the end of the cave and ask your question whenever you are ready—

MEDIUM SHOT

—yes, it's a man, sitting there, that face is familiar, but not too familiar, who the hell?

ZOOM, CLOSING IN

—the face is very distinct, who the hell is that, it's an oldish man, a distinguished face—Claude Rains, in *Caesar and Cleopatra?* almost, no, it's— Walter Lippmann, the old columnist, he used to get annual visits from *CBS Reports* and deliver wisdom on the state of the world—

That's who appeared for me, Walter Lippmann. I couldn't think of anything to ask Walter Lippmann.

A voice came out of the character playing me and said, "How do I get out of this cave?"

Walter Lippman was old, wise, and kindly.

"You will have no trouble," Walter Lippman said. "You know the way. Go back the same way you came."

But I didn't. As soon as Walter Lippman said that, I did the equivalent of waking up and looking around the room, people still had their eyes shut talking to their Wise Things, I thought: I blew it, that's really dumb dialogue for Walter Lippmann, I could have asked him anything and all I wanted to know was how the hell to get out of there.

I thought the whole thing was such a flop I hoped the instructor wouldn't call on me, but he did. Other people had owls and grandmothers and religious figures. The class didn't think Walter Lippman was a flop at all. From my question and Walter Lippmann's answer they knew all about me; it was a little frightening how much they knew. The only thing they thought was dumb was how quickly I dismissed Walter Lippmann's pearl of wisdom.

"Our society worships a seventeen-year-old swigging a Pepsi at the beach and does not listen to its grandfathers," said the instructor.

Carl Jung, the great, pioneering Swiss psychiatrist, had just such a wise old man, whom he called Philemon. The Wise Old Man is an archetype anyway, a symbol from the collective unconscious that Jung said was common to everyone in all cultures. Jung had a dialogue with Philemon, the other-Jung, for much of his life, and recorded it, kept a memoir of the talks.

I could hardly wait to get back and see Walter, but the next time into the cave he wasn't there. It was another Walter. Cronkite. My channel seemed to be permanently tuned to CBS. Hardly fair. The image disintegrated before Walter Cronkite could even say good evening.

The Great Central Philippine Headache Cure

I made that name up. First I was in a course which used this attention technique, and then I was reading Kilton Stewart, the anthropologist, who had by then moved from the Senoi in Malaysia to the Central Philippines, and lo and behold, there are the shamans in the Central Philippines curing headaches with this, an obvious cousin to autogenic training, it breathes me, to the meditations that use color, and to Create a Space. You need two people, one to ask the questions.

Close your eyes and look at your headache. Tell me about it. What color is your headache? Where do you see the color? Where is the headache in your head? Do you still feel it's there, or is it moving? How big is your headache? If it were liquid, would it fill a quart jar? A gallon jar? A bathtub? Can you pour the headache into one of those containers. When I say pour, start pouring, and see if it overflows. Pour.

What does your headache make you think of? Look at that. Now look at the color of your headache. Is it the same? Tell me about the color. A dark shade or a light shade? Is the headache still the same size as when we started? Would you say it's as bad as when we started? No? Keep your eyes closed, breathe evenly, and tell me how big your headache is now. Describe the experience of your headache exactly. All of life is experience and this is experience, what is the experience? What color is the headache now? What does it feel like? How big is it?

And so on. I have seen, in one startling demonstration after another, the Great Central Philippine Headache Cure work. Why on earth does it work? Is it a relaxation technique, or some form of hypnosis? Is it because pain is a signal, and this technique says to the signal, thank you, message received, over and out, go home now, in a physiological rather than a verbal way?

The narrator, or question asker, has to be relaxed, attentive and cool, so that the headache victim's mind doesn't tense itself against the visualizations. Some people say the technique works but the headache comes back later. Why it should work at all is fascinating. If you try it for ten minutes without the headache getting smaller, take two aspirin, breathe evenly, watch the black velvet on the inside of your eyelids for three minutes, and go on about your business.

Mantram as a Block

Now we go back to esoteric psychology for the example, but the process is still the focusing of attention, just as in the headache cure. Earlier we had the mantram as a bone for a yapping beagle, a device for a turnoff which, it seems, drops metabolism and lactate. Mantram as a Block comes out of the Oriental martial arts, as far as I know. The Zen master said, if you're in this sword fight you have to be there, unhindered, every molecule vibrating, as if it's your last moment alive, otherwise you might get cut up and it will be your last moment alive. Mantram as a Block lets you get out of your own way, like breath-counting on the tennis court.

We don't have sword fights any more, we have departmental meetings, or dinner parties for the boss, or confrontations between parents and children. I actually found Mantram as a Block in two courses, neither of which called it that. In one, the master said he had learned it from a martial arts master, and the mantram was meaningless syllables with a very intricate hypnotic rhythm, but repeated in different orders and cadences. It took almost a week to learn with class drills, so there's not much point in putting the exact syllables here, you would have to score it like music.

The mantric syllables have no power of magic; you could do the same thing with "The Night Before Christmas" if those words didn't carry a meaning. You need something with a beat and a pattern and a degree of intricacy; if you blow it, start over. You have to focus your mind's eye on the intricacy while you continue with the department chairman or your spouse or your children or your parents. Contrapuntal music is good—try to hear several lines, not just melody. I don't really believe "The Night Before Christmas" would work, but if it did, it might be like this:

CHAIRMAN: Mr. Jones will now tell us why his report is late when everybody else was on time—
JONES: (Twas the night before Christmas, and all through the house)
I don't want to say that it was computer error, but the fact is
(Not a creature was stirring, not even a mouse) that we were ready two weeks ago, and then—

Jones keeps cool, at the risk of saying something about eight tiny reindeer. Better just abstract "The Night Before Christmas" to its rhythms. Or "Hiawatha." If the Chairman calls on you, get the rhythm revved up and running before you talk.

One of the editors of *Psychology Today* told me Mantram as Block had ruined the fights he had with his wife. She had taken the course; he hadn't, so he only knew abstractedly what was going on. "All I know is," he said, "she gets that damn thing running, and I say the same old things, and she says the same old things, but that damn thing is running in her head, I can feel it, it drives me right up the wall."

The block only has to work once or twice to have some permanent value. If you can get it to work twice, you will have your mind cued: just as the relax-mantram cues *relax,* this cues *centered and ready and calm,* centered and ready and calm. I have used Mantram as a Block in traffic jams outside the airport, with flat tires that weren't supposed to happen, and in verbal scraps. It doesn't disperse the traffic jam or repair the tire or end the fight, but it helps your nerve center of gravity down from your shoulders to your navel, and if your center of gravity is lower you don't tip over so easily.

Fair Witness

This is a yoga exercise which sounds the easiest of all and is the hardest. You create a witness who walks around behind you and notices every single thing—it is, in fact, you—*and does not judge*. It reflects. I Am a Camera.

There she is reaching for a cigarette, not there is that nicotine addict reaching for a cigarette, or whoopee, I need a cigarette, There he is, going to the refrigerator, he is opening the door, his hand is around the beer can, he is taking it out—not, I need one, no I already had a couple, the hell with it, I pay for them, I drink them, and so on.

This is an exercise in mindfulness or awareness, and most people can't do it for three minutes. I can't. People start to play scenes for their Fair Witness, as if it were a judge, or they treat the Fair Witness as a biographer, which is another form of judge, or they get tired of the point of view of the Fair Witness, and go back to their own, or shuttle back and forth.

By plucking these exercises out of their courses, I am guilty of all sort of things, not the least of which is spiritual materialism and reductionism. They are meant as illustration, not as how-to, but if they work, they work.

We have seen now the confusion caused by noise in the mind, the healing effect of quieting the mind, the way the body can send messages that might be true but to which nobody is usually listening, the protecting or integrating of the whole organism by preoccupying the mind, the power of recreating a calm feeling in a stressful time, and the power of imaging.

Eastern psychologies treat all of this, though not in a coherent way to the Western mind, and some Western syntheses also use them.

But you don't have to go to a mountaintop in the Himalayas.

The wisdom that follows is from Satchel Paige, a great black pitcher, denied the opportunity to compete in major leagues for much of his life but certainly one of the great athletes in American history. It is doubtful whether Satch knew the Upanishads, the Bhagavad-Gita, the Vedas, Roberto Assagioli's psychosynthesis, or gestalt psychology. He didn't have to.

Satchel Paige's Rules for Right Living

Avoid fried foods which angry up the blood.

If your stomach disputes you, lie down and pacify it with cooling thoughts.

Keep the juice flowing by jangling around gently as you move.

Go very lightly on the vices such as carrying on in society—the social ramble ain't restful.

Avoid running at all times.

Don't look back. Somethin' might be gaining on you.

See what ol' Satch knew. *Avoid foods that angry up the blood;* diets are common to many disciplines, and when you become sensitive your instincts lead you right, and the food is part of you. *If your stomach disputes you, lie down and pacify it with cooling thoughts.* Psychosynthesis, gestalt therapy, progressive relaxation, autogenic training, meditations, power of mind and the autonomic nervous system. *Keep the juice flowing by jangling around gently as you move.* T'ai chi, the concepts of subtle energy, *chi* or *ki,* centeredness. *Go lightly on the vices . . . the social ramble ain't restful.* Do not become attached, do not identify with what you do, turn down the noise in your mind. *Avoid running at all times.* Where are you going so fast, and what do you get when you get there? *Don't look back, somethin' might be gain-*

ing on you. Stay present; clear the karma, something *is* gaining on you, and on everybody, from day one.

I wish ol' Satch would talk more, he could be a guru with a big following. And as refreshing as another gentleman of my acquaintance, Swami Hal.

Swami Hal and the Yogi Mafia

"If you're going to talk about yogis, you better learn about the yogi Mafia," a friend said.

"The yogi *Mafia?* There is one?"

"We have a swami friend, Hal, who will tell you about it."

But it was no easy task to get to see Hal. For one thing, his ashram was deep in the woods of the Northwest, and not well serviced by public transportation. For another, introductions or no, he did not seem eager to see me. As I bumped along in my rented car in the pine woods, peering amidst the cabins that looked like something left from the CCC, a giant, bearded, berobed figure appeared with the following salutation:

"What the hell do you want?"

I told him I wanted to know about the yogi Mafia.

"Get the hell out of here."

Hal had a gravelly whiskey voice, and a Falstaffian figure. He was an American who had gone to India to become a swami and now ran this little ashram. Hal had a very abrasive manner, but I began to feel, after the first half-hour, that he also had a peculiar honesty. His is one of the few names I've changed. Hal said if I didn't, he would stuff my tape recorder down my throat, and I believed him. He lived in the woods with a few followers and some juvenile delinquents who had been farmed out to him by despairing civil authorities. I asked him what the young incipient hoods did.

"They meditate," Hal said. "Nobody makes them meditate. They do it. And they work on the farm."

"Because it's a religious principle?"

"BECAUSE I'LL KICK THEIR ASSES IF THEY DON'T AND THEY KNOW I CAN DO IT," Hal boomed. "Nobody makes them come here, they pick it, the word goes out, this is a straight place, no liquor, no dope, nobody hassling them, and the word is also out, NOBODY MESSES WITH THE SWAMI. We got alumni who come back and visit. ALUMNI!" Hal boomed. I could see that nobody who didn't weigh two hundred and sixty pounds should mess with the swami. I asked Hal how he got to be a swami but he wouldn't tell me any details.

"What the hell do you care? I went to India, I took my vows, I'm a renunciate, that's what a swami is, and that's what I am. I don't ask anybody for anything, and I'm not proselytizing! Proselytizing! Eastern religions don't seek converts! You want knowledge, you have to stand outside the monastery for a month in the rain! Then they say, okay, you're sincere, you can work in the kitchen for a year! Now look what we got! Instant samadhi! We got Eastern religions in this country out looking for converts, just like the Fundamentalists! Christians proselytize, okay. Moslems, they just tell you, there is no God but Allah, believe it or we'll kill you. That's how Islam spread. The sword! They rode out and held a sword to everybody's throat, and said, this country's gonna be Moslem, right? And everybody who didn't say, yassuh boss, was dead, so they had unanimous acceptance! But what is this, hustling the Eastern religions? What's going on the past ten years in this country?"

"What is going on?" I asked.

"I go to hear Baba Ram Dass," said the swami. "I like Richard. He's a screwed-up guy, but he doesn't rip off the kids. He's working on his sex problems, he's so enthusiastic about his guru, but all right, he's sincere. And outside the hall where Baba Ram Dass, Richard, is speaking, every freak in the world is standing, passing out pamphlets! The Jesus freaks hit me with the Gospels of John. All right, I know the Gospels of John, but I'll take one thank you. Six freaks are dancing in orange robes singing Hare Krishna, banging their tambourines. Two more cults hand me pamphlets. Now mind you, I'm in my swami robes, sandals, no leather, MY SWAMI ROBES and this freak comes up and starts hassling me about Krishna consciousness. That's too much. I say, GET OUT OF MY WAY YOU ASSHOLE I'M BEYOND KRISHNA CONSCIOUSNESS CAN'T YOU SEE I'M A SWAMI? I'M AN INCARNA-TION OF GOD YOU STUPID YOUNG PUP! These kids are all so ignorant of everybody else's trips they're trying to sell me—ME, A SWAMI—on their trip."

"Why are so many kids into all this stuff?"

"I know one answer," Hal said. "Their parents are killing themselves with materialism. Okay, you didn't have to drive through the Oregon woods to hear that. Another reason is, they take materialism for granted, times have been so good they can afford to try these trips. In a Depression everybody is hustling jobs and nobody is trying out Hare Krishna. And there's another reason. They like to hassle their parents. Look, Ma, I'm a Jesus freak, nya nya nya! And the old lady sticks her head in the gas oven."

"Kids really do it to annoy their parents?"

"They don't think of it that way, they do it because it shows independence, but they like to see their parents in a flap. You don't see many thirty-five-year-old freaks because by that time the parents are either dead or have stopped giving a damn. That's only one reason. A lot of kids want to break away, to try another way of life, so they pick something that separates them from their parents but not by so much that their parents want to blow their brains out."

"Like?"

"Like, in India there's a high proportion of Jewish kids. The kid comes back, he's in sandals, he meditates, all right, he's strange, but he's quiet and he's not a Jesus freak screaming into a microphone in some Texas stadium, he's almost acceptable. Like Richard, he lands at the airport, his father sees him in his robes, he says, quick get in the car before anybody sees you, but now his father, the railroad president, is quite proud of him because Richard is very *successful* at this Indian gig. The Protestant kids go to the Jesus freaks, stomping and hollering, a lot of them go to things that are like that, Guru Maharaj Ji or Scientology, secret orders, that bit, and the Catholic kids cause their parents the pain when they first leave the church, they can go in any direction at all that doesn't seem Catholic, with a hierarchy and bossy nuns, but they like things that have mystery and ritual. Now you can see with all these kids roaming around THIS HAS BECOME QUITE A BUSINESS."

"And that's why the yogi Mafia?"

"It's not a real Mafia, more like a gentlemen's agreement."

"But you have meetings?"

"Not formally, but sure, there are conventions and gatherings and whatnot. When I was inducted into the holy order of the Mafia one of them walked over to me and said, we have to stop hassling each other, it's our bread and butter, he slapped my hand. Our bread and butter! That's a good old American term! For an Indian religious leader!"

"How does it work?"

"Well, if I want to get going and, say, Satchadinada is strong in New York, I don't butt into his territory. I go somewhere where the territory is more open. Except Los Angeles, all rules are off for Los Angeles, the place is so freaky that the agreements are suspended for Los Angeles. Those must be some meetings, when the brethren gather, smoking their hash pipes and talking good hard numbers, I wish I was the travel agent for Air India. You gotta realize, some of these movements have sixty, eighty ashrams, and each ashram has fifty or sixty kids, *it's a business.*"

"You sound mad about it."

"Why should I be mad about it? That's not my bag. I don't like these swine who rip off the kids, but otherwise, what the hell do I care? Let everybody take his own trip. A lot of these places, though, are full of sick kids. My God, it's like a chain of clinics."

"Are the kids helped?"

"Some are, some aren't. It depends on the trip, too. A lot of kids are very ignorant."

"Are you saying some of the spiritual leaders are okay and some aren't?"

"Sure."

"Can you tell me which ones?"

"You want to get me assassinated?"

"You're joking."

"I am joking, and you should remember there's just as much ripping off going on under good old Christianity as in more exotic places."

So Hal wouldn't tell me who he thought was okay, and who wasn't, except that I noticed he would refer to some yogi as "that punk" or "that fraud," and when I brought up another name Hal said, "HEY! You leave him alone! He's a real scholar! He's a goddam saint! Gimme that tape recorder!"

He turned it off. I asked Hal if the spiritual quests were part of something permanent.

"It started with drugs," Hal said. "Leary and the LSD. Leary is one of the smartest people I've ever met. They're still using his interpersonal tests in prisons and hospitals. It's a crime they framed him into a fifty-year jail sentence, for what? enough marijuana to make one cigarette? Leary thought psychedelics would change the world. Leary was the Magus, the manipulator. If Leary was the Magus with the white clothes and the rose in his teeth, then Richard had to be the guru. Some pair they were. But he got a power thing, and if you think you're the messiah, somebody is sure as hell going to try nailing you to a cross just to make the myth come out right.

"The drugs did lead the kids to the spiritual quests —not the narcotics, not heroin, but the psychedelics. I think the drugs are fading out. Kids are always going to blast themselves with something to freak out their parents, as long as everybody isn't pulled into one great society, like China, all moving one way, but look how much attitudes have changed in twenty years, attitudes toward sex, and the military, and the government. Some good things are happening. I don't know where it goes, and I doubt if the ruling families will change, but other things do."

I had my usual engineering questions for Hal. Did mantrams really vibrate parts of the body?

"Sure. They clear the mind of thought. Even the Egyptians used Om."

Could you vibrate parts of the body with English?

"Sure, but you'd have to construct it. Sanskrit is a conscious language, built around the vibrations. Look, in English—O-o-o-mmmmooonnnney, M-O-N-E-Y, see what vibrations? Try money! Money! Hawr hawr hawr!"

Hal's booming laugh went echoing through the woods.

"Other cultures have explored the nervous system, and the levels you can get to with it," Hal said. "And you know that, so why are you asking me? Now beat it, and let us get back to work."

I walked back out to the car. I had inched forward about fifty or sixty yards over the ruts when HEY! H-E-Y! went rolling over the car and into the woods. I looked in the rear-view mirror. The sandal-clad, heavily bellied Falstaffian figure was puffing toward the car. I stopped. He caught up, and leaned down to the window. There was sweat in his beard.

"You gonna come back here?"

"I don't know," I said.

"Well, you can if you want to," Hal said.

I didn't know why I would come back, but I was curiously touched.

"Come back sometime and see what my kids have done," he said.

"Okay," I said.

Hal stood up, and slapped the door of the car as if it were the flanks of a horse he wanted to get moving. I put the car back in gear.

"DON'T TAKE ANY WOODEN NICKELS!" he shouted, and I drove away. In the rear-view mirror I could see him standing, legs apart, hands on hip, in the middle of the road, watching.

VI. Packagers

Practices we call out of the ordinary have given some psychologists new fields to study. By bringing the practices into a contemporary vocabulary like that of psychology, we make them lose some of their strangeness, which reduces both attraction and repulsion. Once we have a vocabulary for the exotic, we have made it seem more "real," or at least "real" in the terms that we can handle.

Given the appetites and needs for some of the techniques, it is not surprising, in a business society, that, as Swami Hal says, this has become a business. The gurus et al. don't put it that way, and most of them are teaching something quite traditional and specific.

But in addition to the people passing out something very traditional, there are also people who cut across the fields, synthesizing and packaging, interpreting, considering not only the source but the audience.

Some kids are out following gurus, but there are also people signing up for self-help courses that take a weekend or two, or a couple of nights.

> The mind-cure principles are beginning so to pervade the air that one catches their spirit second hand. One hears of "The Gospel of Relaxation," of the "Don't Worry Movement," of people who repeat to themselves "Youth, health, vigor!" when dressing in the morning. . . .

That is not from yesterday, it is from 1900, William James. *The Varieties of Religious Experience.* So packaging in this country is hardly new. Then, as now, the "mind-cure principles" were activities chiefly of the middle and upper classes, discretionary income diversions. What is interesting is that—though the packagers do not always know it—the ideas and processes they dispense are three to five thousand years old.

Meetings with Remarkable Men

Gurdjieff is dead, and I have no idea whether he thought of himself as a packager. Certainly not the kind of packager who can take ideas, or exotic processes, and sell them in a course. Yet Gurdjieff's ideas filter down into contemporary courses, as we will see; and they are not even Gurdjieff's ideas, they are much older than that. Gurdjieff's processes and exercises are designed to bring people out of their ordinary consciousness, to "wake them up."

Some years ago I had a brief correspondence with a former research biochemist, Robert de Ropp. De Ropp had written a very interesting book called *The Master Game*. Seven years after the brief correspondence, I went to see him in Santa Rosa, California, where he was leading a small Gurdjieff group and getting ready to survive the end of the world.

What people demand from life, De Ropp wrote, is not comfort, wealth or esteem, but games worth playing. People who can't find a game worth playing fall prey to accidie, defined by the Fathers of the Church a long time ago as one of the Deadly Sins, paralysis of the will, generalized boredom, total sloth, now a prelude to what is called "mental illness." Among the broad games that De Ropp listed were the wealth game, the fame game, the glory or victory game, the householder game, the games of art, science and religion. All games played according to rules, trials of wit or strength with definite aims. At the time I had just finished observing that many people in the world of money did not pursue money as the object but rather as a process in a game to be

239

played. This was only one of De Ropp's games, which left me with my ace trumped and the nice correspondence with De Ropp.

The aim of the Master Game is "the attainment of full consciousness or real awakening," wrote De Ropp. Man's ordinary state of consciousness, his so-called waking state, is not the highest level of consciousness of which he is capable. "In fact, this state is so far from real awakening that it could appropriately be called a form of somnambulism, a condition of 'waking sleep.'" Today, De Ropp warned, in this culture, players of the Master Game are regarded as "queer or slightly mad." Further, he warned, teachers and groups involved in the Master Game are difficult to find: "They do not advertise, they operate under disguises. Moreover, there exists an abundance of frauds and fools who pass themselves off as teachers without having any right to do so." So it isn't easy. But "there is in some, not all, men a distinctive hunger for experience in another dimension, for an elevated or expanded state of consciousness." Huxley had said, "The urge to transcend self-conscious selfhood is a principal appetite of the soul." Hence the false track, De Ropp said, of the drug trips.

The idea of a group with a non-advertising Master quietly waking themselves up was very intriguing, I told De Ropp, in the mid-Sixties. I could spare, say, Thursday afternoons from 5:00 to 7:30 for such a venture. De Ropp said it wasn't that easy, you had to devote all your efforts and possibly leave the country to play such a game, and he sent me a little booklet with a picture of this exotic Levantine with black handlebar mustaches called Gurdjieff. I couldn't make head or tail of the little booklet and sent it back, and it was years before I even got to review the Gurdjieff literature.

"Wherever did you get this stuff?" I had asked De Ropp, and that was apparently a question that people also wanted to know of Gurdjieff, for some who have written about it went tracking over Asia Minor and Central Asia to find sources. Gurdjieff himself never gave anybody a straight answer. He was born

George Georgiades in Kars, in eastern Turkey; the name Gurdjieff is the Caucasian form of the Greek name, and Gurdjieff grew up in the swirl of Greeks, Armenians, Yezidis and Assyrians that moved in one direction or another, depending on whether the Russian Army or the Turkish Army was in the valley of Kars.

Gurdjieff's father, said Gurdjieff, could sing the ballads of Gilgamesh that had been sung in the valley of Kars three thousand years before. His aphorisms have the wisdom of peasant aphorisms everywhere in the world:

> If you wish to be rich, make friends with
> the police.
> If you wish to be famous, make friends with
> the reporters.
> If you wish to lose your faith, make friends
> with the priest.
> If you wish to be full, make friends with your
> mother-in-law.
> If you wish to sleep, make friends with your
> wife.

Gurdjieff could speak Armenian, his mother's tongue, and Turkish, which everyone spoke, and in that era a knowledge of Turkish could take you from Albania to Tibet, a range of 6,000 miles. One who follows the Work, said Gurdjieff once, "must be able to make his living with his left foot." That presumes a certain living by the wits. In one account, Gurdjieff worked in the building of a railroad in Greece, and though the plans for the railroad were already drawn, he sold to several towns the right to get the railroad. He seems to have been a healer, and in fact earned half a ship by curing a Greek youth, and he seems to have been enough of a hypnotist that he described one of his tasks as that of freeing people from suggestibility, the mass hypnosis to which they were so prone. He certainly knew carpets and antiques, and when he and a small group of followers were caught, in the Russian Revolution, between the

White and Red armies, Gurdjieff was able to raise money by doing some carpet trading. In another account, while traveling he comes across some Russians who are about to throw away barrels of herring because they have been pickled, and he buys the herring and sells it a couple of days later to people who love pickled herring. That aspect of Gurdjieff does not seem uncommon to the area. An old Lebanese joke has a grandfather asking a four-year-old how much is two and two, and the four-year-old says, are you buying or selling?

Buying and selling was not Gurdjieff's preoccupation. He also studied the origins of Christian liturgy in Cappadocia. As a Czarist Russian agent, he traveled as far as Tibet, and one of his biographers, J. G. Bennett, was the British intelligence officer, fluent in central Asian languages, who kept a dossier on him. And on the travels, Gurdjieff is supposed to have spent time in the centers of the Masters of Wisdom.

The Masters of Wisdom are an old tradition of central Asia. There are, it is said, some people with extra powers, who affect the destiny of mankind from time to time, changing the course of events, averting calamity, injecting new modes of thought into the needs of the changing age. In Tibet, the Masters of Wisdom would be reincarnating Rimpoche Lamas. Gurdjieff's route took him to Samarkand, Bokhara, Tashkent, Afghanistan and Tibet—marvelous names, suitable for the British Victorian adventure stories. Gurdjieff's route is speculation, because he never gave people a straight answer and operated by allusion. And in Samarkand and Tashkent and Balkh, Gurdjieff hung out with some of the teaching schools of Sufism. Sufis are Moslem mystics, and we will come back to them in more detail in a moment. Some schools seem more mystic than Moslem; the Yesevis developed music and exercises for the emotional and physical centers in man that had shamanistic origins. The Mevlevis—there are various spellings—were the whirling dervishes. There is a hierarchy, according to some of this doctrine, which receives revelations of Divine Purpose and transmits them through Transformed Ones to mankind. The Transformed Ones have the gift of transmitting *baraka,* or grace, a word similar to *baruch,* or blessing, in Hebrew.

Gurdjieff and some of his followers eventually went to Berlin, then to Paris, to New York, and back to Paris. What Gurdjieff taught certainly had the Sufi techniques—in New York they put on a demonstration of dervish dancing that left the audience somewhat confused—but almost nothing of Islam.

What did Gurdjieff say? "Man is a machine. He is asleep. He can control nothing; everything controls him." Mechanical man, mechanical desires.

Gurdjieff is not easy to read; he wasn't attuned to writing, and what he does write comes in "legominism," or the transmission of wisdom in a baser form. He has some talented writers around him: Katherine Mansfield died at his Paris mansion, and Kathryn Hulme, who wrote *The Nun's Story,* gave an account of her years with Gurdjieff in *The Undiscovered Country.* So the stories about him have a good deal more charm than those by him. Miss Hulme, for example, decided to give up smoking. Mechanical man; mechanical desires. After a year and a lot of conscious struggle she told Gurdjieff she had licked this particular form of slavery, whereupon he handed her one of his Russian cigarettes. "Anybody can *not* smoke," he said.

In other words, if you're not a slave to smoking, and you're not a slave to not-smoking, *then* you're not a slave any more and you can do whatever you want with your freedom. But being free is harder than being a slave to either smoking or not-smoking, the perils of attachment. Sufi story:

Two men are sitting in a café, and a camel walks past.
"What does that make you think of?" says the first.
"Food," says the other.
"Since when are camels used for food?"
"I haven't eaten today, everything makes me think of food."

Translating from the psychology of perception, we perceive literally what we need to perceive, and tune out what we don't want.

One account of life with Gurdjieff was written by Fritz Peters, who was eleven years old when his aunt took him to live at Gurdjieff's "Institute" outside of Paris. Peters and the other children were bored, so they played pranks, tormenting one old Russian by stealing his false teeth and his reading glasses. The governess in charge of the children brought them up on appropriate charges before Gurdjieff. He rewarded them, peeling off ten francs for each offense. " 'What you not understand is, not everyone can be troublemaker, like you,' said Gurdjieff. 'This important in life, like yeast for bread . . . people live in status-quo, live only by habit, automatically . . . people not understand about learning, think necessary talk all the time, learn through mind, words. Not so. Many things only learn from feeling, even sensation.' " The children shocked the Institute, and Gurdjieff shocked the children—and the governess. Shocks were to be welcomed; they kept one present-tense and unattached.

"Accustom yourself to nothing," Gurdjieff said, but he did his best to accustom himself to roast baby lamb, extraordinary vegetables, exotic candies, and marvelous liqueurs. His activities were financed by donations: "shearing sheep," he called it.

Sometimes it seems as though there was a mountain in central Asia somewhere with the river of these concepts coming down, splitting, and flowing in different directions, east to China and the Tao, south to India, west and southwest to Asia Minor and the Middle East. The Zen archer has his student start with breathing, to eliminate the "I" and become the same as the arrow and the target. Chuang-tzu tells of Prince Hui's wonderful cook, who is so in harmony with the Tao, the cosmos, that when he wields his meat cleaver the stroke he makes is the very essence of the motion to be made with the meat cleaver. An ordinary cook changes his chopper once a month because he hacks, a good cook once a year because he cuts, but Prince Hui's cook's chopper is as fresh as if from the whetstone after nineteen years, and from the precision and single-mindedness of the chopping Prince Hui learned how to live.

"Do one thing at a time," said Gurdjieff, and he had his followers work at handicrafts, cobbling and tailoring, but it is doubtful from the accounts whether any of them ever learned to repair a shoe. Gurdjieff taught that men were three-centered, the three centers being roughly the head, the heart and the "moving center" below the navel, the *hara* or center of gravity in Zen. To educate the "moving center" and draw energy away from the "noise machine" in the head, there were rhythmic activities—sawing wood, spading the garden—and "sacred gymnastics."

Nobody has tested, psychophysiologically, the effect of prosaic rhythmic activities, but we could almost predict the results. In times of great stress, instinctively, Rose Kennedy would go outside and bounce a tennis ball over and over. Digging in the garden has been known to relieve the pressures of commerce, and the circadian rhythms of nature are sought by people on vacations. Jack Nicklaus has probably never heard of Gurdjieff, or Prince Hui and the wonderful cook, but he plays in a trance and has a golf stroke that is the equivalent of the perfectly balanced motion of the wonderful cook's cleaver whistling through the air. Prince Hui's golf pro. It gets less mysterious when you think of mundane examples, and if you think of it as educating the right-brained activities and the muscle hungers and muscle memories that don't get much of a chance in our sedentary world, it gets almost scientific.

Not that Gurdjieff ever gets scientific; science demands communication, and Gurdjieff didn't think people valued what came too easily. If that were all there is to Gurdjieff, then we could enjoy the fables.

But Gurdjieff is also full of astral spirits, and the earth being food for the moon, and the law of octaves, and incredible chemistry involving carbon and hydrogen and oxygen—not the way they are in the chemistry textbook, but as alchemical symbols, I suppose, back to "legominism."

The Alchemist, 1610, faces a complaint from Master Surly that his terms are "a pretty kind of game, somewhat like tricks o' the cards, to cheat a man, with charming." Sir? says the Alchemist.

> *Was not all the knowledge*
> *Of the Egyptians writ in mystic symbols?*
> *Speak not the Scriptures, oft, in parables?*
> *Are not the choicest fables of the poets . . .*
> *Wrapped in perplexing allegories?*

"Two hundred fully conscious people," said Gurdjieff, "could change the whole world." From time to time groups gather to do the Gurdjieff exercises, to educate other parts of the body, to study all the vibrations, to remember themselves. Remembering oneself is one of the prime Gurdjieff exercises, not so far from the instructions of the Khwajagan Sufi masters: be present at every breath, do not let your attention wander, learn not to identify yourself with anything, remember your Friend, i.e., God. (The Khwajagan instructions, possibly from the twelfth century, were written up in Persian in the fifteenth century, and in English in 1958. From some cultures there is a time lag into ours.)

But as the distance from Gurdjieff increases, the spell diminishes. The Gurdjieffians I met turned up in other disciplines, after years of waiting for something to happen, having woven their baskets and done the "stop" exercise so long.

De Ropp's small group lived in a dramatic contemporary house in Santa Rosa, given by an oil-service heir. Posters: mechanical men, mechanical desires. "I spent twelve years with Ouspensky in England," De Ropp said, in clipped British tones. Ouspensky was Gurdjieff's chief pupil, and the author of a number of books about Gurdjieff. Don't go to Gurdjieff, Ouspensky told De Ropp. "Gurdjieff's quite mad." We took a small tour. "We're practically self-sufficient here," said De Ropp. "We grow all our own vegetables, we have our cows, we churn our own butter, we press our own cheese. When it all blows, we'll still be here." When it all blows? When there is no more Pacific Gas & Electric? I was admiring the electric mixer, which served when the butter churn broke, and the splendid ivy-green double-sized refrigerator. "Some of these things will run on methane gas," said De Ropp, "and we're going to get a windmill. Why don't Americans make good windmills? Why should we have to go to Australia or Switzerland?"

De Ropp called his group the Church of the Earth. His chief delight was taking his kayak out into the Pacific and fishing. He wanted to take me kayak-fishing. The fish were going to provide good protein after the collapse, after the energy crisis and the resource crisis and the other crises had finished their work.

"You poor fellow," he said. "The water is already around your ankles, there, in the cities. Like the *Titanic,* just a little brush, hardly felt by anybody, the orchestra keeps playing. Oh, can't you see what will happen to New York? The elevators will stop. The subways will stop. It will be a dead city in twenty or thirty years. And the owl and the bittern will be heard in the streets. The owl and the bittern will be heard in the streets."

De Ropp had been a scientist at Rockefeller University in New York, as well as a research chemist at Lederle.

"I gather you don't like New York," I said, "but must you wish it complete destruction?"

"The owl and the bittern will be heard in the streets," he said firmly. "You better come kayak-fishing with us."

He seemed very cheerful about it and very healthy. "We need more people here with technical skills, carpentry and plumbing," he said.

"So do all the communes," I said. "They're long on English majors and short on carpenters."

"This is just the right place," De Ropp said. "Right climate, not too far from the ocean. Gurdjieff would have found some rich widows, and told them, 'I shall fleece you.' They loved that, rich widows. We should do that, I suppose."

"Carpenters and rich widows," I said. "If I meet any, I'll send them along."

"You don't have too much time," De Ropp said.

A year later, I sent him the windmill catalog from another commune.

But that day, when I got to San Francisco, I told some friends I had been visiting De Ropp.

"Oh, yeah, *The Master Game,* that's a good book," they said. "Is he still doing the Sufi number up there?"

Who's a Sufi?

I am not sure how "Sufi" got to be such a good word on the consciousness circuit. "I have just come back from India," said Baba Ram Dass in one of his lectures, later published, "and next I am going to Chile to study with a Sufi master." Maybe it is the idea of these fully awakened, conscious people, operating from power centers in the high plains of central Asia. Any certainty is better than the uncertainties of life; it is really nice to have a They who are secretly running things. Every once in a while I have a qualm myself. Here is the International Monetary Fund which meets in Basel and tells the Bank of England to shape up, and warns the Bank of Italy that Italy is falling apart, and raps the U.S. Treasury over the knuckles for the Eurodollar overhang, some international leverage there, and who's the new chairman? A Dutch Sufi. Dutch? Sufi? What the hell are they planning in Samarkand?

A Sufi—he said he was a Sufi—came to one of my classes with a set of drums, which he played with his hands. We all formed a circle and danced around, while he chanted: *La illaha il'l Allah.* For two hours. He was one hell of a drummer. Also, when he really got going, his eyeballs rolled up into his head so that only the whites were showing. Very restful, he told me later. As for the rest of us, our palms got very sticky, the movements got more ragged, and finally some people fell down. I suspect that's something of what you get if you go to one of the Sufi weekends advertised amidst the yoga retreats. (Amidst the same ads now are those for Pentecostal churches and Hasidic Jewish retreats. We have chanting and dancing, say the latter, almost wistfully, more to recapture their own than to proselytize, and of course they have chanting and dancing, and have had for hundreds of years.)

Or you can go to weekends where Sufi stories are read aloud from the collections of Idries Shah. You hear them aloud, over and over, so they can sink into a level of consciousness other than the normal linear one. Most of the stories are teaching stories, but unlike parables they are funny, at least the first time. The hero is a wise fool called Mulla Nasrudin, pronounced Nas-ru-DEEN. Nasrudin is down on his hands and knees in the street, and his friend comes along and says what are you doing, and Nasrudin says looking for my house key, and the friend starts to help him, saying where did you drop it, and Nasrudin says by the door, and the friend says, but why don't we look there, then? And Nasrudin says, but there is more light here.

Then you are to think: in your own life, do you look where the light is, or where the key is?

Nasrudin is sprinkling bread crumbs in the street. Why are you doing that? says the straight man. To keep the tigers away, says Nasrudin. But there are no tigers around here, says the straight man. Exactly, says Nasrudin. Effective, isn't it? Do we do that daily, in some way?

In the Hasidic stories of Judaism, there are *rebbes* and beggars. The beggar comes to the door, and the

Hasidic Nasrudin looks around, sees a ring lying on a table, and gives it to the beggar. The *rebbe's* wife screams at him, you dolt (wives are always screaming you dolt, in both Nasrudin and the Hasidic stories)—you dolt, that was a very valuable ring. The householder runs after the beggar and says, hey, friend, that ring is really valuable, don't let the jeweler cheat you when you sell it.

Once I mused, in an article, on the phrase "Sufi master." One was supposed to know a Sufi master by coming into his presence, the baraka would zap you. But how would you know otherwise? "Sufi master," I wrote, "is not like Berkeley Ph.D. You cannot call up and check, because there is no Sufi U." I got a letter signed in flowing Arabic script, but when I went to see the gentleman he turned out to be an American executive, tall, blue-eyed, blond, Scottish-surnamed, not a flowing Arab at all, with an office on Fifth Avenue. He had gotten the Call and gone to Teheran and been initiated, a serious Moslem, fasting, Ramadan, bowing five times a day to Mecca (back to Fifth Avenue, face toward the East River); I asked his secretary if he still bowed to Mecca five times a day when his schedule was crowded and she said yes, he just closes the door. The executive wrote to me because he wanted me to be aware that there was a lot of baloney around, that Idries Shah wasn't a descendant of the Prophet Mohammed, like he said, he was the son of the chauffeur at the British consulate someplace in Pakistan, and true, he had written down some of the Nasrudin stories, those he hadn't made up and so on.

So I began to work on the Sufis. I had lunch with two Middle Eastern diplomats. They wanted to talk about the price of oil. They were both scholarly fellows, so midway through lunch I brought up the Sufis. You have a lot of Sufis in your country, don't you?

Well, er, yes, mystics, aren't they, Hassan? Yes, mystics, rather quaint old fellows, chant a lot.

If was as if they had asked me with great intensity what I knew about the ghost dancers of the Sioux.

And then, gradually, I met serious scholars who gave me serious books; there are Sufis all over the world, and, though it gets to this country only in the Department of Asian and Middle Eastern Studies at the University, quite a bit about Sufism. So you go through *The Sufi Orders in Islam,* and Jalal ud-din-Rumi's Math-nawi-yi Ma nawi, and various books all titled *The Mystics of Islam,* and *The Life and Times of Shaikh Farid-ud-din Ganji-i-Shakar,* and pretty soon you can tell the widespread and moderate Qadiriyah from the Sanusiyah and the Mevlevis and Bektashiyah from the Haddawah, who "do not spoil God's day by work." And something's missing. It's become Islamic History, or Comparative Religion. Out on the consciousness circuit nobody wants to know how Al-Ghazzali pulled a whole synthesis together in the eleventh century, they want to know the Secrets of the Sufi Masters. How to get high. Does that pattern in the carpet really change your consciousness, thus the "flying carpet"? See, if you stare at that special geometry, it will pop the bounds of that left-brained pattern you impose upon the world, and if you don't, it's just a carpet. The sober, left-brained books Rumpelstiltskin away the mystery, and the techniques become "autohypnotic states, hal, plural ahwal, through certain practices of concentration or frenzied dancing and chanting of certain formulas." That fixes it, just a little autohypnosis, from concentration and frenzied dancing. Black Elk doesn't make it rain, Black Elk does his thing and it rains anyway; we have a lousy weatherman and that's why he was predicting continued fair and hot.

A couple of scholars had furtive looks about them, as if dabbling in this stuff was messing with djinn. You remember the djinn, when Aladdin rubbed his lamp, another symbol you see of sleeping powers, and you have to consider quite seriously before you dive into these depths of mind, because when the djinn gets out of the lamp—I liked that uneasiness. I missed the mystery coming out of the power centers over the mountains on the high plains of central Asia. Somebody somewhere ought to know how to get to superconsciousness.

Thanks for the books, gentlemen, I read the ones in English, I have to give the ones in Turkish and Persian back to you as regretfully I am not equipped, and by the way, have you ever tried some of this stuff? Well, er, furtive look, one shouldn't speak too lightly of these things.

There is, of course, a Sufi story to cover this feeling. (It also appears in Russian as the bishop and the pious staretzki.) A scholarly Sufi is walking along the edge of the lake, pondering moral and scholastic problems, and he hears a dervish call coming from an island in the middle of the lake. The scholarly Sufi listens for a while and keeps walking, and it bugs him because the recitation is all wrong, the pronunciation is wrong, and finally he hires a boat and rows out to the island; and there is a dervish sitting in a hut, chanting this chant all wrong. And the scholarly Sufi says, friend, I know you'll appreciate this. And the scholar recites the correct way. I have rowed out here because you're doing it all wrong, this is the way it goes. The island dervish thanks him, and the scholarly one starts rowing to shore, and he hears splish splish splish and turns around, and the second dervish is running across the *surface* of the water to catch up, and says, "Say, friend, could you give me the right way again, I didn't quite get it."

Next Week, Satori 24

Of all the gurus that there are, surely we must have had the only Oscar.

Oscar Ichazo was the "sufi master" that Baba Ram Dass said he was going to Chile to study with. Baba Ram Dass didn't go, but several dozen Americans did. They knew of Oscar from Claudio Naranjo, a Chilean psychiatrist, co-author of *The Psychology of Medita-*

tion, who led groups at Esalen. Oscar had developed a training that could take people to new levels of consciousness, a super package. The Americans spent ten months in Chile, and then forty-two of them decided that the experience was so important they would form a teaching house in New York, to start the spreading of the word. Why New York? The energy of New York excited Oscar: "New York," he said, "has more people prepared for reality than the world has previously seen in one culture." The teaching group took a full-page ad in *The New York Times* headlined THE MOSQUITO THAT BITES THE IRON BULL, and mentioning such exercises as "protoanalysis," and "psychocatalyzers" leading to "the awareness of the tiger," "Permanent 24." A very mysterious ad indeed. Oscar's program was called Arica, after the town in Chile where he had been teaching.

Arica had a drumbeater other than Claudio Naranjo, and that was John Lilly. Lilly had perhaps more academic credentials than anyone on the consciousness circuit. He was an M.D., a psychiatrist, a research neurophysiologist, and after a lot of work on the brain and sensory deprivation he worked with government and foundation aid on communicating with dolphins in a special lab in the Virgin Islands. The dolphin work had brought him a certain degree of fame. Lilly was very enthusiastic about Arica at that point, both in interviews and in a book he wrote called *The Center of the Cyclone.* "Successful heads of corporations," Lilly said in his interview in *Psychology Today,* "already operate at Satori 24. They are joyfully locked into their work. But they have never had maps which suggested to them the possibility of achieving more blissful levels of consciousness."

If I had to translate that Satori 24, I would say it was Jack Nicklaus' golf stroke, or Prince Hui's cook's meat-cleaver stroke, in everything, all the time. The number came from Gurdjieff's levels of vibrations, and as translated by Oscar and John Lilly, the normal state is 96, or ego with a vengeance, getting along, but with pain, guilt, fear, and sometimes alcohol. Forty-eight is neutral, getting and receiving information, 24 is professionalism that can be done without the verbalizing mind. From there down it gets more mystic: 12 is "blissful state, making the Christ, the green qutub, realization of baraka, cosmic energy, heightened bodily awareness"; 6 is "point source of consciousness, energy, light, and love"; 3 is "classical satori, fusion with universal mind." Lilly had, Lilly said, been through all those levels.

(To Gurdjieff's levels of vibrations, Oscar added six more, ranging from 192 to 6,000, all quite disagreeable. Society is in 6,000 most of the time.)

The course was for three months, six days a week, fourteen hours a day, and it cost $3,000. That program certainly did assume an affluent society. It seemed about as far out as you could go, and the very intensity attracted me. Why not start far out, and work one's way back, in the explorations of mind?

"You seem to have created," wrote one of Oscar's interviewers, "the nearest thing we now have to a university for altered states of consciousness." But unlike university, we did not know, at any time, the name of the course we were taking. We would simply show up and do what the trainers told us, rather like falling out into the company street in the Army, awright you guys, first platoon, get in the truck. The Army simile would occur to me again and again—first the lack of a verbal framework, then the physical qualities of the experience, and finally some of the qualities of shared experience.

Among the trainees were a handful of psychologists and psychiatrists, another handful of writers and critics, and a number of Esalenites. But the bulk of the class of sixty were either students and/or women who, through divorce or otherwise, had reached a point of some confusion in their lives. We didn't live together, though many of the trainees shared apartments.

The lack of verbal framework was quite deliberate. If we had started with that, it was said, then we would have experienced the experience through the construct we had already set up verbally.

So: we went on a high-protein diet. No white sugar, no alcohol, low carbohydrates and no animals that are scavengers, e.g., no pork or ham, no crab. We did weeks of largely physical activity: an hour-and-a-half gym, most of whose movements were adapted from hatha yoga. "You do not do the exercises, they will do you." Not surprisingly, the trainees began to lose weight and look better. We did hours of chanting. We did breathing exercises to the *Bolero*. Sit on the floor, open your arms gradually, breathe in all through the ascending phrase, out in the descending phrase. That's hard to do at first. "The *Bolero* is Sufi music," said the trainers. "Different phrases vibrate parts of the body."

We did a lot of dance and movement exercises. That is when I thought, American men get short-changed, because most of their physical activity is competitive and in sudden, tensed bursts of movement. The men are supposed to play football and basketball and golf and tennis and bowling, but it is okay for the women to take a dance class. If you look at the men's sports, you see that it is the warm-ups that have the rhythms and the centering, not the games themselves (the lazy pitches in the bull pen, the ball being tossed around the infield.)

We had some talented musicians drumming for these classes in movement, and videotapes to watch ourselves. We had imagination exercises to sensitize parts of the body—feel your feet gold, your calves gold, your knees gold—that I later found in the Christian mystics. Each of these body parts was supposed to have a mind function, the nose senses possibilities, the hands and feet, goals, and so on. Thought, the trainers reported, does not only belong to the brain. The head must cease its tyrannical control. Consciousness is to be homogenized into the whole organism. If your wires are crossed, say, between your needs (mouth and stomach) and your goals, you make goals of your needs, like sex and hunger.

And we began to do group work that had overtones of encounter. We were given nine types of ego, a kind of personality that we had adapted vis-à-vis the world. The Indolents are lazy and manipulate people, the Plans always live in the future and never quite get around to what they're going to do, and the Go's believe that work is everything and they are their work and they work three times as hard as they have to, very thorough and Germanic. The staff had already assigned each of us into a group, with the help of a questionnaire, but in the guessing game many people guessed correctly.

My group turned out to be Go. "I'm so glad we're Go's," said a matron in my group. "I certainly wouldn't have wanted to be anything else. Now, let's get organized."

"But we have to *give up* this fixation," said another woman. "We work so hard because of our *lacks*."

The antidote to the fixation was a posture, or asana, for meditation. In our case, it was holy law, or: the universe will run without you.

(Later, when it came to administration, the Go's quickly took over much of the work, and the Indolents somehow manipulated them. The Plans lay on the floor planning, and the Stinges hid in the corner. Everybody seemed very relieved to be playing his role in the open, and nobody was in a hurry to give up the role he was used to, even though that prevented him from being "free."

There is nothing particularly radical about a personality grid, and the "Pygmalion effect" says that if you try an experiment in a classroom and tell the class that brown-eyed children are smart and blue-eyed children are dumb, by the end of the semester they start testing that way.)

All of this, so far, without Oscar. He appeared one evening—in his socks, like everybody else, all shoes left always at the door—looking not at all like a guru but like, well, a Latin-American, smallish, balding, mustached, sport-shirted. He spoke with a heavy Spanish accent.

Oscar's talks—we saw a lot of him from that point —always had something of the air of a Presidential press conference because there were always twenty microphones in front of him. Everybody with a tape recorder wanted his own cassette. Oscar surprised us. This training, he said, was not for self-improvement, it was for humanity, because the planet faced a great crisis, a great cosmic wave, in the next ten years. The crisis was related to the wounding of the earth with pollution, depleting resources, and wars. Humanity had to come to consciousness, or face extinction.

Further: the training we were being given would never be given again. Its purpose was to train *teachers;* it would go on another two months beyond the original three, but that wouldn't cost anything, and in fact those who needed money would be paid. (I spent thirty minutes on the Finance Committee, possibly the shortest, time I have ever been in any job. I was used to post-Renaissance bookkeeping: if you don't have the money in the bank, you don't pay everybody a lot, you set up reserves. One stalwart said, "I can't be in *satori* on less than $1,000 a month," and so everybody was paid $1,000 a month until the money ran out.)

The physical and experiential sectors of the training declined in favor of hours of theory, the traps for each ego type, the asanas for each ego type, and finally a theory of what Oscar called "trialectrics," everything is process. Oscar liked making up compound words: kinerhythm was moving the rock with the mantram, psychocalisthenics was the adopted hatha yoga gym, psychocatalyzers were the virtues we were to seek, "cutting the diamond" and the Ark were group exercises. Group work, Oscar said, enabled us to progress much faster than individuals in Oriental disciplines.

Arica, said Oscar, would have to become a tribe. Eventually all humanity would have to become a tribe. With the tribe taking care of needs, the individual ego trip could be given up.

The tribal community took care of some needs so well that most of the couples split up. We went through exercises to rid ourselves of the karma, or consequences of past actions, of money, sex, and power. Some of those who had money and had freed themselves of its karmic powers made contributions that supported the group, like the good tribal members they were. "Karma cleaning" was basically confession and desensitization. A sure cure for prurience is to listen to people telling the sexual story of their lives incident by incident. We would gather in small groups, sit in a circle on the floor, and recite. After three or four days the groups would change, and the stories began to sound more and more ordinary. Some people could tell such a story in two hours, and some took all day.

"Let's see, that was the year I was fourteen," said the pleasant blonde, "and then when I was fifteen I left this convent school and went to the high school. I guess I smoked a little dope and when my parents were away I moved in with my old man—"

—it took a minute to grasp that her old man was not her father, but what Grandmother would call her beau—

"—and we didn't get along so I got another old man, and toward the end of that summer I got into a very bad space with my mother because I told her I might be knocked up, and I wasn't sure which of my old men, oh, and there was Charlie, he was black, that got my mother very uptight because my mother is, you know, country club, and my father was working all the time, and then one night—"

I remember rousing myself from my torpor on the floor to think of these California rich conservative parents, poor bastards pacing the living room, where did we fail? She had riding lessons and ballet lessons and tennis lessons and the best parochial schools and we loved her, where did we go wrong?

"—and then in my junior year in high school, I balled this guy, George, he was—"

—let's see, we ought to be in college by lunchtime, we could be through by three-thirty with any luck because she's only twenty-two, by ten o'clock tonight we could get Harry from thirteen to college, that would bring us to Louise tomorrow morning—next week, money—

—yet there is an effect. Why, said the women to the men, look at all the energy you have put into this feeling that you had to perform, like a contest. And the effect of stony silence on recitations that people thought were quite dramatic reduced the drama. We had spent all that energy for sex, money and power, and here it sounded like an oral reading of the *Congressional Record*.

But even in the fusing tribal activities, all was not love. For one thing, there was an A group and a B group, A being higher level, faster progress, B holding up the caravan, yet, Alice in Wonderland, there were no rational criteria for who was in A and who was in B ever articulated, a vibrational level, more, and people moved from B to A and A to B, or were told they had moved, and when they got to A they were a little cool to the B's who were holding up progress.

I have the feeling there was a lesson in all this, that A's and B's are quite arbitrary, and that Oscar was yanking everybody around to show there is no day-to-day tenure in life. But some people got to stay in A all the time. And then there was always the threat that people could be fired from the school. No reason, no appeal, they would simply be gone in the night, one less body in the company street the next morning. As the training went on, and the trainees had to decide not to go back to school, or to their jobs, this threat became more serious.

As long as the course was simply a course, this wasn't too much of a problem, but many were swept up in the Mission to save Humanity. "This school," said Oscar, "is the most important thing going on in the planet at this time. Arica is going to reconcile mysticism and the modern world. We are talking about a different psychological order of man, with a different psychological structure. Totally balanced, instincts in harmony."

Underlying the mission were quasi-religious overtones, though not distinctly from any one creed. "Essence" in Arica, as in Gurdjieff, as in who knows what before, is the natural state of man, divine unity, but —like the Fall—he loses it, falling prey to the Ego and its fears for survival, its traps and its passions. "There is no peace short of being within the divine consciousness," said Oscar. "The Western secular attempt to live without knowledge of the sacred unity of all things is a failure." Is this a new religion? Oscar was asked. A new church? Oh no, Oscar said. The disciplines are old: Buddhist, Tao, Islamic, Christian, but we don't ask for belief or faith, we just say, try these things and see what happens.

So being fired from the school was not only being dropped along the wayside on the road to Satori 24, it was being dropped from the mission that would save the world. ("Two hundred fully conscious people," Gurdjieff had said, "can change the world.") But alas, where there is a Utopian vision there is frequently a Grand Inquisitor. We have to live in an imperfect society. The Perfect Society has Secret Police, to make sure everything stays perfect.

There was a word in Arica, *chich,* from Oscar's Spanish, *chicherero,* chatter, the trivial talk of the mind. That's what we had to lose. And certain authors and composers and people were more *chich*-y than others—Beethoven had a lot of *chich,* said Oscar. And one night, after a drop to B by an unusual number of people, a committee announced there was too much *chich* in people's minds, and that the committee was proposing that it come to people's apartments and weed out their books and records, taking away the *chich*-y ones, just out of tribal spirit and group love, and then the group's conscousness could be pure again and we could make rapid progress.

And that was too much. Here was Arica barely two years old, and about to have an Index, just like the Roman Church! "Well, Oscar *was* trained as a Jesuit," whispered one mutineer. "I don't want to live in Dublin," I said. "Church censorship. Half the good movies never get there." Somebody else sarcastically suggested a great book-burning on the steps of the Public Library, and the committee beat a humiliated retreat.

That was an important moment. As much as everybody wanted to live in Satori 24, they wanted to live even more in the U.S. Constitution. I went home and read the Constitution, which nobody does after they leave school, except lawyers. The Constitution seemed bigger than the *B-Minor Mass.* It is a fantastic document. All the transactions going on between the gentlemen who wrote it produced a state of extremely high energy, they were stoned just doing the job. In fact, they wrote it in Satori 24.

"Where did you get all this stuff?" I asked Oscar. Some things I had heard were murky with legend. Oscar was from a wealthy family in Bolivia and during World War II they put up some Japanese on the estancia who had to leave the coastline in Peru and Chile, and among the Japanese was a Samurai master who, for room and board, taught Oscar and his brother martial arts—

Oscar was ripe for all this because, if he was not an epileptic, he had attacks which certainly seem like epilepsy, starting at six and a half. "I would experience a lot of pain, my heart would pound, fear I was going to die, then . . . I would die, after a while I would return to my body and discover I was alive. I was terrified, I became very lonely . . ."

Oscar was going to a Jesuit school, and he hoped Communion and prayer would help; it led instead to his disillusion with the Church. And he did learn the martial arts from the wandering Japanese, and his family owned some land so he sought out the Indian shamans, and they introduced him to psychedelic drugs, and then there was hypnotism and yoga and William James and reading in anatomy and physiology, still trying to find out about his condition, and when he was nineteen he left the University at La Paz and became the coffee boy in a Gurdjieff group in Buenos Aires. "About two-thirds of the group were Orientals, strong on Zen and Sufism," said Oscar, "and the cabala."

Eventually Oscar became a full-fledged group member, and then he went to the Orient, "to Hong Kong and India and Tibet, and studied Buddhism and Confucianism and alchemy and the *I Ching*." Some of Oscar's stories sound like early *Terry and the Pirates*.

FADE IN: *Terry and the Pirates* music, beaded curtains parting, a gong. Oscar is studying the *I Ching* in Kowloon. Through one *I Ching* master, Oscar meets another, this one also in the martial arts, the second one throws the *I Ching* to see what future portends and then stares at Oscar, the hexagrams haven't come up before like this, Oscar is the one who is to be taught, he is to go to his hotel and get his things and move in with the very old master, who is maybe ninety-six. "I couldn't believe it," Oscar said. "His skin was like a baby's. I could never catch him, in any exercise. He told me, you have to live like you are living your last second. This idea of awareness is very old. He taught me to go inside sleep without sleeping, not so far out, animals do it, we did it ourselves in the jungle, you are sleeping but you are awake. I learned psychoalchemy from the martial arts."

I was trying to have a hard-nosed interview with Oscar. (*Psychology Today* thought they had a scout in the interior and they hadn't seen a smoke signal in six months.) Where did you get the money for these travels? From my uncle. When you would stop in all these exotic places, how did you know where to go? I had people to look up, from the group in Buenos Aires, and from other people along the way. Now, you stopped with Sufis, who spoke Arabic and Farsi, or Persian, and then other groups spoke Hindi, and Chinese—how did you talk to them? In English. In *English,* Oscar? (Oscar's sentences in English were frequently preceded by the phrase, "Now here come another thing.") Well, language wasn't important. Oscar had an impatience with word culture. Words words words words words. Words were used too much as a screen. "We are in transition to the planetary culture, psychology is the most important thing in the next culture."

Plainly, Oscar's psychology had little to do with rats. "Psychology is the knowledge of the interior of the human psyche. Western psychology is discovering what we already did. A culture starts when man rediscovers Void, what the game is. In the Occident, that isn't part of the culture."

In one respect, Oscar was right. Things had certainly gotten planetary. Here is a counter-tradition, swirling from the Hermetic in Egypt, the Gnostic in Greece, a dash of Zoroastrianism from Persia, the Masters of Wisdom in Central Asia teaching Gurdjieff, a Gurdjieff group appearing in Buenos Aires, where a mustached Bolivian takes it to Arica in Chile, to which come Americans from California, and it ends up on West 57th Street in Manhattan, an escalator goes up from the street through a purple paper tunnel and there in this ex-computer facility are representations of tarot cards on the wall, and the Sanskrit tonic sound, Om, in Sanskrit ॐ. Far out, as my old classmates said so frequently.

But no one ever put it that way. Oscar got his indications by Direct Revelation. That's traditional, too. "I spent forty days in the desert in Cardova . . . I was in a space without connection, my consciousness went inside the enneagram, I returned from the experience and each enneagram was complete, but it was very hard to put into words. Of course, this was my psychic projection." A student from the West pointed out it was within a century and a half since Joseph Smith had gotten a Direct Revelation, and look at the Mormons today, he said.

At that time, all the students who had ever studied with Oscar were gathered for this crash course, pilgrims who had gone to Chile, the ten-month course, the five-month course—was there anybody, I asked, who had reached the state of total clarity and awareness, the one called "Permanent 24" in that ad in *The New York Times*?

"No, nobody," said Oscar. "Not really. Not yet. Permanent 24 takes much more work."

As for me, I went from A to B to C, the last being a group of secondary citizens who were doing some work on the outside, and hence not committed to the Work totally. The C team was kept insulated so as not to drag down the group level. More people were fired from the school. I had to go to Chicago, and the phone in my hotel room rang and said the Work will begin again tomorrow morning, fly back, and I suddenly had to pick between Studs Terkel's radio show and flying back. I didn't fly back. (In Chester Barnard's *Functions of the Executive,* an absolute classic from many years ago, it says that the decision not to decide is a decision.) Also, on my own I had found an appropriate Sufi saying. "Trust in Allah," it said, "but tie your camel first." But I didn't want to miss anything. I really didn't. I took a make-up when I got back, and limped through graduation.

Oscar was true to what he said in one respect: the big course was never given again. Everybody who took it was now expected to go out and teach. And most of them did. They spread around the country, Los Angeles, Atlanta, Boston, Denver, groups of five and ten. They rented houses, put ads in the paper, and started teaching. What they taught was little mini-courses, some for an evening, some for a lunch hour, the longest for forty days. Arica bought rock commercials on the radio and it received a burst of publicity, but it never took off like Transcendental Meditation, or even like the Guru Maharaj Ji. The package was class, not mass.

I knew about the new courses only by hearsay, as I had been dropped unceremoniously even from the mailing list and the newsletter, for what sin I cannot imagine, except perhaps lack of evangelism. (Even the most interesting of esoteric courses have distressing overtones of evangelism.) But then Arica calmed down, the newsletter began to arrive again, and after an absence of about two and a half years I went back to sit in a beginner's course. The spooky talk had all been cleaned up. The chanting was just like breathing, "Ah-h-h" (inhale), "Tu-u-u" (exhale). The meditation was a *kasina,* not called so, staring at a symbol on the wall until its colors began to swirl psychedelically. The "karma cleaning" or confession was done with a deck of cards, each of which had a statement for which we were supposed to supply an example, e.g., "A time I felt ashamed, socially," "A time I felt spiritually confused." Everybody warmed to that. Each participant faced the room and said, "I want to change!" and the whole group would cheer and holler and stomp. It was the most applause some of them had ever had and it was hard to get them to sit down. Oscar had not lost his talent for inventing polychromatic and multitonal experiences. And still to come was the Hypergnostic Awareness —still in the future—Oscar had not lost his talent for naming processes, either. Our old moving meditation, "From Thee we come, to Thee we go," had developed a thumping country-and-western beat that had everybody clapping and stamping and hollering—

—clapping and stamping and hollering? Good heavens! Mid-Manhattan Pentecostalism! The Pentecostalists lost members when they went, upwardly mobile, into the white-collar middle class and got embarrassed by the glossolalia, speaking in tongues, and coming forward for Jesus, and repenting, and now the upper middle class found its bluejean-clad youth clapping and stomping in a package from Samarkand, via Buenos Aires, with music scored for the new age. One Arica song with a contemporary beat was, "My Dear Mind, You Don't Exist." What fun!

I sat in on a seminar in Behavior and Change at a major university, taught by a friend. A graduate student was reporting on his experience at Arica. He counted himself an Arican, but he confused the seminar with those vibrational levels—"See, 6,000 is where society is, 784 is a very depressed state, and 192 is practically suicidal"—and then he began to tell of Oscar's background, how Oscar had learned these mysteries in Hong Kong and Afghanistan and Tibet—the legend was well on its way—and had studied with this very old master—Good heavens, it was my very own hickory-flavored Terry and the Pirates stories from *Psychology Today!*

And I visited headquarters. The furniture looked like Proctor & Gamble's ad agency. Films, I was told, were replacing lectures, there were audio-visual teaching aids, management consultants, cash flow charts on the walls. The staff was going to publish the "psychocalisthenics" just like the Royal Canadian Air Force exercises, and Oscar was writing his autobiography. You could take an Arica course on a sunny beach in Florida during the winter, or on a wilderness trip in the summer, or on a raft floating down the Colorado river, and you could charge it all on Master Charge. (The days of the A group and the B group and looking for the *chich* in people's books were so long ago, I was told, they were regarded with some nostalgia, like hip flasks).

Long before the Road to Satori 24 became eligible for Master Charge, I met a Chilean economist who had been in a simultaneous training group in Chile. It was like a reunion meeting of the Thunderbolt Pilots Association.

"They told me you were in it," I said.

"They told me *you* were in it," he said. "Are you a Go?

I felt I could admit such a failing to an old Thunderbolt pilot, even though Go's are deceitful.

"So am I. I was Director of the Budget in Chile at twenty-six, and Minister of the Interior in my thirties," he said, "so of course I am hung up on work. Terrible."

"But don't you feel the rest of them didn't quite value work enough?"

"Yes, no question. See, we are both still hung up. But they don't get enough work done, in fact they never start till ten-thirty in the morning. The bunch that runs it must be rather crazy, but I thought it remarkable how these differing people—truckdrivers, academics, lawyers—would all come up with the same thing about my persona, how I came across."

"I like the physical stuff best," I said, "and it bothered me that the people who got fired were more interesting than those who stayed."

"Ah," said my friend. "Those who left were still in Ego, there was no room. One mountain, one tiger. One mountain, one tiger."

"Did you ever know anybody who made it out of Ego, into Satori 24?"

"No, never. But we always had such expectation. After all, the diet, the physical stuff—you began to feel differently, lighter—"

"—maybe you would know something with your liver, or your feet, any day—"

"—exactly, you *are* feeling different, and they say, next week, a new exercise! Very powerful! This tremendous sense of *expectation,* next week, the group energy rises and consciousness is transformed, next week, next week—"

"Satori 24!"

"Next week, Satori 24! It sounds good, even as we sit here!"

We sat for a moment.

"It's too bad there isn't one more week," I said, "even though I know what I know, and I don't think anything would be different."

"One more week? Next week?" My Chilean friend burst into laughter. "All right! Maybe it's next week! I'll go if you'll go!"

The High Value of Nothing

Arica had its people doing moving exercises and breathing exercises; EST had them sitting still on folding auditorium chairs for fifteen hours at a stretch. EST stands for Erhard Seminars Training, Erhard being Werner Erhard, the founder. Oscar Ichazo had come from the mystery schools: Werner Erhard came from Sales Motivation and Dale Carnegie. Oscar used Sanskrit mantrams and Sufi geometric symbols, and Werner used plain English, more or less. Werner's package had no chanting, no movement—in fact, not much theory—just two hundred fifty people sitting on chairs, an instructor with a microphone, and portable floor mikes in case anybody wanted to talk back. Oscar's course is never over, Werner's is two weekends, $250 now, though I suppose Werner's isn't over after the two weekends, either. (After the two weekends you can take one-night-a-week seminars in Sex, Money, Power, What's So, and Be Here Now.)

Yet, oddly, many of the antecedents of these packages are complementary, and not indigenous to the elementary schools in this country. Midway through Arica, playing the game of where-does-this-come-from,

I was reading Ouspensky and the Tibetan *Book of the Dead* and the *Sufi Orders of Islam,* and after EST I had to go back to semantics, the semanticists and philosophers, Korzybski and Ludwig Wittgenstein, because EST is at least partially a linguistic pop.

Werner did not care much about the antecedents. He went straight to Motivation and Development from high school in a Philadelphia suburb, where he was called Jack Rosenberg. He took the courses, and in a short time was teaching them. His rather unusual *nom de commerce* was put together from Ludwig Erhard and Werner von Braun. Werner, as he is now called, is good-looking, aggressive and forceful—the salesmen taking his courses must have charged out of the room, confident they were the best salesmen and they were going to sell enough to win the prize trip to Hawaii.

"I could show people how to get what they wanted," Werner said, "and I could act like I was okay, I could produce symbols, but when the people get what they wanted it wasn't what they wanted because they weren't *experiencing* it."

"Experience" is the keynote word in Werner's vocabulary. "Language is terrible, psychology is terrible, how come there's no statement on what experience is, how come I, with no background, have to make one up," Werner said. In a dim way I knew what he meant—Werner has to strain sometimes for what he means, but his forcefulness and enthusiasm do not diminish.

"No," I said, "if there were a statement on what experience is, then people would know the statement and not the experience, they would have one more statement but they wouldn't have experienced the experience."

"Gee, that's right," Werner said. I was talking like a good EST graduate. "Let's see," Werner said, "maybe we can do it with money. Money is the symbol of security, right? It's not the *experience* of security. Some people want the experience of security so they pile up money, but they still don't have the experience of security, they can act *as if* they are experiencing security, they can buy things that *go with* security, but they haven't experienced *out* the barrier between them and feeling secure. Now, if they experience out the barrier between them and feeling secure, they may or may not have more money or less money, but they will have the feeling of security."

"Experiencing out the barrier would be something like a Freudian analyst getting his patient to be aware of unconscious factors he wasn't aware of?"

"Sure. I don't know. Partly. I never know exactly where I get these things."

Werner must have been one of the unlikeliest pilgrims on the consciousness circuit. He did Scientology —itself a mishmash of Freud and Eastern ideas— and yoga and Zen—"I was lucky enough to be stunned by Zen"—and Subud—"that latihan in Subud is like Bedlam"—and encounter and attack therapy and sensitivity, and Dale Carnegie—

"I guess I was looking for Truth, but I was also using each technique in my business. I was lucky, because Business only cares about results. In a university, I would have been crossing departmental lines and getting everybody mad, in a seminary I would have been burned as a witch, but business only cares about results. So if it worked I used it, and if it didn't work I dropped it, and if it worked I used it some more. See, Business couldn't care less. I would say, 'I've added something, I'm going to try some Zen with this group,' and they would say, 'Sure, Werner, just don't get any on the floor, and have our men back to their Division Chief by four-thirty.' Of course, I had to translate from religion or therapy into business, but I had the advantage of not knowing anything, you see, I just said, how can I use it? I'm a mechanic, I know how things work. I could out-Carnegie Carnegie and out-Peale Peale. But those guys just buried the problem."

And then? Werner had mentioned a particular incident that changed everything, ken-sho, sudden flash.

"I was sitting in my wife's Mustang on a hill in San Francisco and I realized, what is, is, and what was, was. Now that sounds absolutely stupid. And what isn't, isn't. It was stunning. See, an archbishop is an archbishop and very important, but an archbishop in Zen, the name, translated, means 'trash can,' that's Zen telling you the way it is. How can you tell people what is, is? It doesn't mean anything. It's nothing. You can't define nothing because that's a definition, but what's valuable in my training is nothing. Nothing is the element of transubstantiation."

"And that was the beginning of EST? So EST means 'it is,' as well."

"Right. EST is—well, a not completely thought-out unified theory—"

"But you started teaching it—"

"Yes. No—you can't teach it, that's what's wrong with teaching, nobody knows what learning is—you can't teach, all you can do is to create a condition that allows experience, but to the degree that it's *believed,* it fails."

I didn't know whether Werner had read Carl Rogers or picked that up out of the air.

"Because then it's belief and not experience?"

"Sure, experience is what's there before the form and structure are applied. See, all we want to do— the transformation is to change the notion of who you are. So that you can see, who is it that thinks, who is it that feels, and if you de-identify not only from things but experiences, from your own experiences, when you reach a critical mass of de-identification, things make sense. The Bible makes sense. Other things make sense."

It's a bit dizzying, all this rap about nothing and experience. It's dizzying like turning over the sentence "This very sentence is false," which is one of the early paradoxes in semantics, because if the very sentence *is* false then it's true, but how can it be true if it's false? "There are only two things in the world," Werner said once, "nothing and semantics."

The metalinguist Benjamin Whorf wrote on how our conceptions molded our perceptions, how difficult it was to perceive what we had no word for. The semanticist Alfred Korzybski, in *Science and Sanity,* wrote, "Every language, having a structure, by the very nature of the language, reflects in its own structure that of the world as assumed by those who evolved language. In other words, we read unconsciously into the world the structure of the language we use." The heaviness we give to nouns in English helps to make our world a world of *things,* more object than process. The structure of the language, in fact, helps us to think that semantics is only words, and therefore not very important, certainly not as important as machine tools or jumbo jets.

The Zen master said, rivers are rivers and mountains are mountains, and we say, of course, how quaint. Then a psychiatrist comes along with some Zen training and a difficult patient, neurotic we would say because of her illegitimate birth. The psychiatrist says, "Who were you before you were an illegitimate child?" The patient bursts into tears, and says, "I am I! Oh, I am I!" That enables us to shrug and say, well, it does some good, in the odd case.

The Vienna-born philosopher Ludwig Wittgenstein has some statements that get to sound very Zen-like, though Wittgenstein never sat counting to three in his life, and in fact went through the heaviest of exercises. *Tractatus Logico-Philosophicus* is one tome, and *Philosophical Investigations* is another, either would do as something to chew on if you are sitting on the runway at O'Hare with the air conditioning off for five hours sometime. Wittgenstein was one of the most influential contemporary philosophers, a Cambridge professor, and in the *Tractatus* he says: "The sense of the world must be outside the world. In the world everything is as it is and happens as it does happen." Wittgenstein, in philosophy, arrived at a position in which the subject-predicate analysis of propositions is abandoned, and to get students to follow he would devise linguistic pops. "The method," wrote one commentator, "consisted in constructing or calling attention to examples of linguistic behavior in such a way as to shock the mind into noticing something which had not been noticed and thereby to free it from what might be called the bind of conception."

"Werner," I said, "you don't by any chance know Ludwig Wittgenstein's *Philosophical Investigations?*"

"No," Werner said firmly. "Look, the general semantics people come to my seminar and say, it's general semantics. The Zen people come and say, it's Zen. But see, all the techniques are bullshit. Understanding it is something you do if you don't get it, you know that. See, enlightenment has no value. You can't be right with it, you can't sit on it, you can't sell it, you can't use it to survive with, and to the degree you value it, it isn't enlightenment."

Werner went to India. Not seeking enlightenment?

"No. I went for a couple of reasons. First of all, in my business, people should go to India."

"You mean credentials, like the Harvard Business School or the Stanford Graduate—"

"Sure." Werner's candor was always disarming. "And second, I wanted to hang out with some of the Indian saints. Because just hanging out opens a space for you."

"Opens a space" is another keystone in Werner's vocabulary. I had asked Werner, in some correspondence, why he had gone to India, correspondence between our several conversations. MY PURPOSE IN GOING (Werner's letters come in capital letters, but that may be the machines he likes) WAS TO MEET AND SHARE WITH SOME OF THAT COUNTRY'S SPIRITUAL LEADERS. MOST OF THE TIME WAS SPENT WITH SWAMI MUKTANANDA AND SATYA SAI BABA, BOTH OF WHOM I THOROUGHLY ENJOYED AND REALIZED BENEFIT FROM.

What benefit?

"Just being around opens a space. See, masters don't give you rules. A master just tells you what is."

That's one of Werner's aphorisms: This is it. There are no hidden meanings. All that mystical stuff is just what's so. A master is someone who found out. Werner's aphorisms are printed in a handy little booklet no bigger than the sayings of Chairman Mao: Life is a rip-off when you expect to get what you want. Life works when you choose what you got. Actually what you got is what you chose. To move on, choose it.

"Take responsibility for" is another keystone phrase. There's no gray area. Once you say you'll take responsibility for, you *will,* in EST. If you say you're coming to the midweek lecture and you don't turn up, someone will call your house and ask for you to look at the barrier between you and taking responsibility for, because if you experience out the barrier, you'll take responsibility for."

Werner has no good words for the Ego, either. Another stream of aphorisms: The purpose of the mind is survival. Ego starts when a being stops considering itself a being and starts being its own point of view. It thinks survival is maintaining that point of view. An ego, therefore, is a point of view attempting to cause its own survival. So its purpose is domination of everything and everybody. An Ego will sacrifice its own body just to be right.

It makes more sense if you let the totality sink in, and don't analyze each component.

The EST course has a little swatch of guided meditation, and variations of Create a Space and the Great Central Philippine Headache cure, and dollops of Scientology theory, and some acting exercises, and some fantasy, pieces borrowed from other courses, especially Dale Carnegie, but what is most characteristic is the rap, so I have tried to give a sampling of the rap:

"See, the whole idea of making it is bullshit. Life is a game, to have a game something has to be more important than something else; if what already is, is more important than what isn't, the game is over, so life is a game in which what isn't is more important than what is, let the good times roll. Life is a game, but living isn't a game, living is what is, experiencing right where you are. Nothing mystical about it."

I said: why couldn't some dropout simply stay in bed all the time, if what is, is?

If he does, then he didn't get it, Werner said, because that's not why people stay in bed all the time, it's unexperienced experience that keeps them there, anxiety or fear, and if they experience out the anxiety, then they either get out of bed or don't get out of bed, but they don't stay in bed because they heard somewhere that what is, is.

"Who's on first, What's on second, and I Don't Know is on third," I said. "I wish Ludwig Wittgenstein could have taken this course. Do you know what the two things were I heard about the course before I took it? That you don't let them eat and you don't let them go to the bathroom."

"People are so strung up in their games that they're crazy," Werner said.

Anybody, said the instructor, one of Werner's verbal Marines, could have their money back in the next ten minutes and leave, but after that everybody who stayed had to agree that they would do what they were told for the rest of the weekend: we had to check our watches at the door, we could only eat if there was a food break, and sure enough, only go to the bathroom if there was a break for that, and we would sit on these chairs as long as necessary, maybe till one or two in the morning, it then being nine A.M. A couple of people left. The portable floor microphones were passed around anytime anyone wanted to talk, to share what they were feeling—but the first hours were slow, and mostly attack: "You people are *turkeys!* A turkey is an animal so dumb it lifts up its head to drink the rain and drowns! Because you don't *experience*, you haven't ever experienced, and you take all your non-experiences and classify them and keep them in a silver box, if you got laid the first time you put that in a box and the next time you opened the box to see if that experience was like the experience in the box—"

A hand goes up, a dignified, pleasant lady with gray hair—"I think you could make your point without all this vile language, it doesn't add to the communication—"

"Fern, honey," says the instructor, "these are only *words,* you don't want to let words run you, Fern, why do you grant the words the power to make you an effect, Fern, there is no difference between fuck and spaghetti!"

Fern gasped with the brutality of "fuck," belted out by Werner's Marine.

"And by the time this course is through, you will be able to go to Mamma Leone's and order a plate of fuck! Or sing this whole bunch a dirty song!"

Fern said if the doors weren't locked and if she hadn't made an agreement, she would leave.

The next morning Fern signaled for a microphone, got up, said she had been thinking about things overnight, and she was going to sing a song—the only dirty one she knew, she said: "Two Irishmen, two Irishmen, were sittin in a ditch," sang Fern to a standing ovation. "I've never done a thing like that in my life," Fern giggled, when the applause died.

"You people," said Werner's verbal Marine, the first day, "don't even know who you are, you have yamayamayama going in your head, all your actions are strung together on your racket, your game, whatever manner it is you found you can survive with, you're interested, you're indifferent, you're ingratiating, some of you are so hip your act is I Don't Have an Act—"

Sure enough, from time to time a hand would go wandering up—when were we going to get a break, I didn't have any breakfast, when are we—

"What is all this?" roared the instructor. "You people are *tubes!* In one end and out the other, you let that run your lives! Who runs your life? You or your body?"

Mechanical man, mechanical desires—

"I wish the people in the courses wouldn't get so hung up on that," Werner said later to me, "but people really *are* tubes. At least we make them look at their tube-ness. At least if you don't let them pee, *you begin to get their attention.* If I could talk to teachers, I would tell them that. See, the truth puts people to sleep. It goes right to the unconscious in them, and most people are unconscious, for the truth to get to the truth that is in people, it has to get through the unconsciousness. So if you can make them uncomfortable in their unconsciousness, enough just make people aware they *are* unconscious, then you have a better chance of letting some truth strike the truth in them—"

"All right, tubes, we will have a thirty-minute break," said the sergeant, along about five o'clock. "Thirty minutes doesn't mean thirty-one minutes. The doors will be locked in thirty minutes."

Nobody had peed on the floor. The hunger pangs had come and gone. But at midnight a lady in front of me kept taking a pack of Viceroys out of her purse, and extracting a cigarette—there is no smoking in EST at any time—and tapping it on the back of her hand, and then putting it back into the pack, and putting the pack back in her purse. Then she wept quietly. I had never seen anybody weep for a cigarette, but I guess you can weep for whatever you're really attached to. However, it is okay to weep. "The doors are locked, we have tigers outside them to scare people away, so in here you can let go."

"Enlightenment," belted the instructor, chalk in hand, before the blackboard, "is the knowledge that you are a machine. YOU ARE A MACHINE!"

A hand went up, a microphone got passed— another resistant, another declaration of independence: "I am Milton Drexler"—Milton had a mustache, Milton is perhaps an accountant, a C.P.A., and this disturbs him, dehumanizes him—"and I AM NOT A MACHINE."

"Don't get me wrong," said the instructor. "Your voice says you have been attacked, your face says you are defending: *I didn't say a Milton Drexler Machine was bad.*"

"We attack their beliefs," Werner said. "Because as long as they look out through beliefs, that's all they see, so maybe you get a belief crumbled for a few minutes."

Sometimes the class would turn on the instructor —this is stupid, this is a rip-off, you don't make any sense, whaddya mean, reasonableness is of a very low order, and I Don't Know is a form of certainty?

"Thank you," says the instructor, "I acknowledge I hear you." But he doesn't react. Can't we make the bastard react?

"You are the worst, coldest bastard I have ever met, you have a lot of problems you ought to look at yourself, and this is all a rip-off."

"Thank you, I acknowledge that I understood you."

"Oh, you could say, what's that thing from aikido —give the other guy the space," said Werner. "You know."

"The guy comes at you," I said, reciting from my aikido class, "but, see, he doesn't want you, he wants the space you're in, so you move out of that space and let him have it, and then he's off balance, and should he happen to want to fall down you push him down."

"Something like that," Werner said. "But that isn't it, either, you can't make a rule like give the other guy the space."

"Because then you have the rule and not the experience, and rules are bullshit."

"You're getting it."

"Don't say that. I don't want to get it, because it might create a problem."

I could say we played Create a Space, and did our acting exercises, and went through more semantics, but that wouldn't communicate the boredom or the Enlightenment. I don't feel so bad about my inability to communicate because sometimes Werner can't do it, either. John Denver, the country-and-western star, went through EST, and one night he was a TV talk show host, and had Werner on, and they asked him what was EST and what did it do, and he said it was a series of techniques to Open Spaces for people, which sometimes increased their aliveness. Werner said this with his usual Dale Carnegie crisp firmness, and John Denver beamed, and everybody went: wha?

EST does not advertise, but it does tell its graduates that they can get their friends to share their own aliveness and well-being by bringing them to a Guest Seminar, from which they can sign up for the Full Seminar, $200. However, graduates are abjured from explaining the course, as "UNDERSTANDING IS THE BOOBY PRIZE AND THINKING THAT YOU KNOW IS AN ACTUAL BARRIER TO EXPERIENCING," as Werner wrote, in a general communication to all graduates. If you do *not* bring a guest, you are asked to look at the barrier between you and bringing a guest. Graduates are also asked to "assist," which means working for free at EST offices from time to time. "Assisting" helps to promote the experience.

EST may have borrowed from Zen, but it was not to be corrupted by selling the answers to the koans. Werner, in fact, wrote a letter warning graduates that they deprived future trainees of the experience if they told them the answers to the koans, the koans having been translated from the traditional to the American, from the puzzles of the Sixth Patriarch to vanilla and chocolate.

What was curious to me was that a high proportion of the EST seminars I attended were filled with verbal people enthusiastic about this course that told them that understanding was the booby prize and thinking was a barrier and everything was so much bullshit. They loved that. You knew they were verbal people because they would signal for the portable microphone and express themselves very well. They would come to the EST seminar, having "looked at" some part of their life—we quickly got used to the Games People Play—and they would tell this role they had discovered like it had never been seen before, and everybody else in the audience who had played that particular game would strike a note of resonance. The games were a real tribute to Eric Berne—See What You Made Me Do, and You're Doing It Wrong, and It's Not My Fault, played between bosses and employees, and parents and children, and husbands and wives. The recognition of the games changed people's points of view.

Some swore it changed their lives. At any seminar, the attendees were encouraged to tell how EST helped them that week. Every self-help course from Dale Carnegie on does that, and the Dale Carnegie course is sixty-five years old, and that one works, too.

EST is spreading all over the place, Los Angeles, New York, Hawaii, Aspen, and "graduates" can attend seminars anywhere for a nominal fee. EST's ability to spread is only limited by the availability of trainers. The "training," the two weekends sitting in a chair, demands of the "trainer" that he be up on a podium before the audience from nine A.M. to midnight, armed with only a pitcher of water, a glass and a microphone, two days in a row, in control and responding. That takes talent, as well as training. Good instructors aren't so easy to come by, because they have to play off the audiences, handle attacks and deliver them, read voices and faces. In my post-graduate seminar, the seminarians would call up and try to find out who the preacher of the evening was, because there was a dramatic fall-off in quality between Broadway and the road show, between the stars and the understudies. The further from the initial training, the thinner the talent. Some of the seminar leaders were young trainees who could not manage their audience, even though they were repeating the rote formulas. The first string had considerable poise, stage presence—the stuff needs a good actor—theater, at its most perfect, also provides catharsis, exhilaration, moments of illumination—theater—actors—

actor! Jock MacGowan, famous in his Beckett roles, on the stage in the old tramp's raincoat, transferring marbles, counting them, from one pocket to another, and then counting them, and then transferring them back again, sixteen in this pocket and seven in this, it's excruciating, this scene from *Molloy,* because he keeps talking and he isn't saying anything; dialogue, like action, is a game to pass the time, as Hamm says in *Endgame.* Or: the two old tramps wait by a tree on a hopelessly acrophobic set, on a road, for Godot, who doesn't come, "nothing happens, nobody comes, nobody goes, it's awful." And each statement by one of the characters is hedged, and qualified, in rustling, murmuring voices until it falls away and falls away and doesn't mean anything. Doesn't mean anything, but—the language-using, stimulus-hungry, left-balanced brain fidgets, *this is boring, this doesn't make any sense,* who the hell is Godot and what happens if he gets here, Theater of the Absurd! Yet something does creep through, around the language or despite it, or because of it, because Beckett is a Joycean master, the first critics denounced *Waiting for Godot,* "a farrago of pointless chit-chat," but the convicts of San Quentin sat transfixed, "Godot is the outside," and now it's almost too late, Godot has been marked *literary classic,* so when the viewer's interior voice starts up, *this is boring, this doesn't make sense,* it gets a slap on the wrist from the second interior voice, *shut up, they say it's a classic.* And what creeps through is that self-canceling definition, the unarticulated experience.

> For to know nothing is nothing, not to want to know anything likewise, but to be beyond knowing anything, that is when peace enters in, to the soul of the incurious seeker,

it says in Beckett's *Molloy,* and in his own voice, in his essay on Proust, says Beckett:

> Life is habit. Or rather life is a succession of habits, since the individual is a succession of individuals . . . habit is the generic term for the countless treaties concluded between the countless subjects that constitute the individual and their countless correlative objects. The periods of transition . . . represent [the moment when] boredom of living is replaced by the suffering of being.

And this "recognition of illusoriness," says the theater critic Martin Esslin, "and prefabricated meaning . . . far from ending in despair . . . is the starting point of a new point in consciousness . . ."

At the end of each of the first two acts of *Godot*, the same lines occur:

> Well, shall we go?
> Yes, let's go.
> *(They do not move.)*

They do not move. In the end, these fellows all disappear up their own tails. Beckett's play *Breath* is eight seconds long, and consists of a breath. Like the artists who hang up a blank canvas, or a sign on the museum door that says THIS MUSEUM IS CLOSED FOR TWO WEEKS, and that's the art. It must be pretty close to the end of the line, crossover time into something else, but it doesn't get us to the something else.

Nothing! In 1924, the Western Electric Company conducted an experiment at its Hawthorne plant to improve production. The women in the experiment did the same work they did before, but experimenters fooled with the lights and the pace. One work break, three work breaks. Hot snacks, no snacks. No matter *what* they did, production improved. Yet nothing had been added. The "Hawthorne effect," it was called, because, though nothing had been added, the point of view of the women working had changed, they were not just women working in a plant, they were part of an experiment, *they were aware of what they were doing,* and so nothing became something.

Goodness, from work theory in sociology to Dale Carnegie to the existentialism loosely—very loosely— underlying the Theater of the Absurd—

"Beckett," I said.

"Who?" Werner said.

"Beckett, Samuel Beckett."

"Nope, don't know him. A lot of people say the same thing. I just stand there where they want to hear it."

Well, if Werner doesn't know Beckett and Wittgenstein and Whorf, then what the hell *was* all that stuff? It sure takes up a lot of linear space here on the page.

"Nothing" did work for EST. Some of its graduates left exhilarated; it was hard to tell which of the derived and distilled exercises produced the exhilaration. Maybe it was the whole package. Or maybe it was the reverse spin: for years, much of our liberal society has told people that whatever is, isn't their fault. Their parents were mean, or indifferent, or overloving. Their teachers were hopelessly stereotyped, their jobs just weren't designed for humanity, the President—any President—is a bum. And here was a message that people created their own experiences and were responsible for themselves! Wow!

Forty thousand people graduated from EST. The waiting list for trainings grew to several months. Werner piloted the company plane, a Cessna 414, around the country. He was so busy he barely had time to train the trainers, much less give the trainings. EST had Facilitators and Communicators, and free programs for schools and prisons, and a summer camp EST training for teenagers. Werner moved up to Chairman; the new Chief Executive Officer was Don Cox, a former Harvard Business School professor, more recently Vice-president for Planning of Coca-Cola. The San Francisco *Chronicle* ran a front-page series on this hometown product. Its tone was irreverent. EST replied in the hurt tones the oil companies used when they defended themselves against making too much money. Making money? Certainly not: EST designed itself to break even. It really did. The *Chronicle* did not understand that money can only produce money, but enthusiasm can produce enthusiasm. It sounded for the moment as if the old Zen equation, archbishop = trash can, had slipped away. Werner sent all his graduates a valentine: I Love You. We knew he did; we knew those phone calls pursuing us when we did not come to Meeting was because: They Care!

EST got itself an absolutely blue-ribbon Advisory Board, educators and psychiatrists who had taken the training. When it encountered the media, it assembled its media graduates and its Advisory Board for a symposium, and abstracted the lessons with astonishing rapidity. EST alumni were a literate bunch; 40 percent of them had some graduate school.

In San Francisco, the EST organization headquarters had all the élan of a growth company on the steep part of the curve. Sometimes it did seem as though we belonged to a United Air Lines that didn't have any planes, only stewardesses and reservations clerks. Every EST graduate became a first name to the staff phoning. EST must have a big phone bill, for its big extended family. When you phoned back, you got a cheerful first-name greeting. "Hi, this is Nancy," said the voice on the phone. "How may I assist you?" Sloppy old conversations were broken into Communications and Acknowledgments. The charts at headquarters show that at the present growth rate, the one million mark would be crossed in—

Plainly, something would happen to EST. It would get too big too fast and have computer trouble. Parkinson's Law would replace the koans of the Sixth Patriarch of Zen. What would happen to EST? It would disappear, I mused. Not because angry parents descended upon it, not because people tire of arcana, as happens in other movements. It would disappear right into United Air Lines, or the Telephone Company. No telling which will be the survivor. A very American ending.

"I guess EST will keep growing because the demand is more than the supply," Werner said. "But don't get me wrong, I don't think the world needs EST, I don't think the world needs anything, the world already is, and that's perfect."

"If nobody needs it, why do you do it."

"I do it because I do it, because that's what I do."

I bet Satchel Paige said something about fish swimming and birds flying, but nobody wrote it down.

From the EST leaflet:

There is no note-taking; there is no written material to study. There is no discipline to follow and no system to use. When the training is over just the result is left.

Registering the Packagers

Are the packages effective? There are many testimonials from happy alumni and some from disgruntled alumni, but there are more alumni all the time. (A multiple alumnus like myself is absolutely inundated by computer-directed mail, because you go onto the mailing list once you "graduate.")

There are no long-range studies to determine effectiveness, any more than there are really long-range studies that determine whether the ladies and gentlemen who switch their deodorants and their toothpastes immediately register success with the opposite sex.

To be properly registered in the paradigm, the effectiveness would need other quantitative measures: aliveness and Satori 24 and so on, which is difficult with either quantitative or verbal language. The meditation people did *quantify* relaxation, and as time goes by they will have longitudinal studies, and all the courses have elements of meditation. So we're on our way.

The demand is more than the supply, Werner said. That means that they don't have to be sold, they are bought. People tell other people. They don't have to tell other people unless something works. Of course, people operate from what one leading psychologist called "cognitive dissonance"; they justify what they have already chosen a little bit, and they weed out conflicts so that they have a totally consistent picture, and they really believe it themselves. Even so, it is a demand-pull field. Sex, Money, Power, What's So—what's so, alone, is what everybody wants to know. If the demand is more than the supply and the old paradigm's rules still go, the supply will rise until an equilibrium is reached.

The packages here may be superseded or they may grow. They are schools unlike our others.

We have been paying some fleeting attention to language and semantics, because we are coming to the end of the paradigm in these accounts, and at the edge, language becomes even more important than from safely in the middle.

I wished, in fantasy, not only for Ludwig Wittgenstein as a traveling companion to the edge of the paradigm, but for Benjamin Whorf. Wittgenstein was the heir to an Austrian steel fortune. He trained as an engineer, got intrigued by philosophy at Cambridge in 1912 and then by Bertrand Russell and mathematics. His *Tractatus,* through the Vienna Circle, helped to create a movement in Philosophy called logical positivism. But Wittgenstein dropped it, gave his fortune away, and went to teach in an elementary school in a mountain village in Austria. Later he came back to a professorship in Cambridge, but he didn't like being a professor . . .

. . . and Benjamin Whorf turned down opportunities to become one. He was, of all things, a fire inspection engineer; a Massachusetts Yankee, a chemical engineer from MIT, B.S., '18, who spent his working life rising in the Hartford Fire Insurance Company through fire prevention technology, at which he was expert. His avocation was languages—Indian languages, Hopi, Shawnee, Choctaw, even Aztec—and he wrote his papers and continued in the insurance business, a couple of blocks away from where the poet, Wallace Stevens, was also becoming a vice-president in the insurance business, some Hartford they had in those days if they could have put it all together, Whorf giving his chalk talks at the Children's Museum . . .

And why is Whorf so intriguing here at the margins of psychology? It may be because of his suggestion that you have been tricked by your language into a certain way of perceiving reality, and that possibly an awareness of the trickery gives you an insight. (The Whorfian thesis is sometimes called Sapir-Whorf, for the contributions of Edward Sapir, an authority not only on Indian languages but the science of language.) The Hopis could create a consistent universe without our meanings for time, energy, space and matter, Whorf wrote. Each language performs an artificial chopping up of the continuous flow of existence in a different way. Children repattern every day, Mississippi is not Mrs. Sippy, the equator is not a menagerie lion but an imaginary line. "A change in language can transform our appreciation of the Cosmos"—"The lower personal mind, caught in a vaster world inscrutable to its methods, uses its strange gift of language to weave the web of Maya or illusion, to make a provisional analysis of reality and then regard it as final . . . Western culture has gone farthest here, farthest in determined thoroughness of provisional analysis, and farthest in determination to regard it as final. The commitment to illusion has been sealed in western Indo-European language, and the road out of illusion for the West lies through a wider understanding of language than western Indo-European can give."

Did the TM people read Benjamin Whorf? Maybe they did, but bogged down in Choctaw tenses, or in the learned comparisons of Bergsonian time and Hopi time, or Newtonian space and matter coming from language, not intuition. If they'd kept going, they would have found something familiar—the mantram, "repatterning states in the nervous system and glands, [assisting] the consciousness into the noumenal pattern world." The noumenon is the thing itself, rather than the phenomenon as which it appears.

Wittgenstein the influential philosopher, Korzybski the Polish-American count, Whorf the Yankee engineer—we could use them in the material ahead, for much of it relates to experience and language. How do we communicate experience if the language is inadequate? Which is really real, the language or the experience?

Let's first, using blunt old English, see where we have come from.

We perceive the world from a certain point. The sociologist Talcott Parsons called the total system of language and perception a "gloss." We lump together isolated perceptions into a totality—we have to be taught this—and what we are taught is what everybody agrees on. The world is an agreement. We have seen from little flicks of semanticists and metalinguists and philosophers what language can do: English, for example, has two genders, masculine and feminine, which these word-people would say leads us to either-or, binary views. You're not losing a daughter, you're gaining a son. Instead of "gloss" I've used "paradigm," which has an element of time, all the glosses day after day, and assumptions of causality and predictability. Our paradigm is largely thing-oriented, materialistic and rational—verbal and intellectual.

Along come some experimental psychologists who tell us that we perceive our own paradigm and that's it. We discard what we perceive outside of it, so we don't even know it's there. (We *still* don't know what's there, because just saying well, we're in a paradigm all right, doesn't show us what's beyond.) Because of the nature of our paradigm, what can be described, it is agreed, is more real than what can't be described. And what can be *measured,* with numbers, is even more real than what can be described verbally, in our paradigm.

Physiologically, say some other experimental psychologists, this leads our culture to be more left-brained than right-brained, the left hemisphere of the brain controlling analysis and speech, and the right, music and movement.

Even though all these assumptions may be true, there is great plasticity, or capacity for change, in the human organism. The optimistic view is that people can certainly grow and use parts of themselves they haven't used.

Meditation, which used to belong exclusively to religion, was a loose end in our paradigm. Now the loose end is being folded in, because meditation has been *measured* and its effects have been given a hypothesis and some level of predictability. Medical researchers have found that, possibly, meditation is an aid to the parasympathetic system, which helps to cool the agitation of the sympathetic system, in which many of us live much of the time. What the measurers did was to bring the language describing meditation from just beyond the paradigm to just within it, and now it wouldn't be surprising to see the borders of the paradigm extended.

Biofeedback has brought a high degree of measurement to the conscious control of the autonomic nervous system—even to the firing of a single neuron. This work was also done by experimental psychologists. The autonomic nervous system was supposed to be beyond conscious control, and now it has crossed the filmsy line, a change in sub-paradigm, with effects in medicine and psychology.

Both meditation and biofeedback have helped to change the view of our ordinary, waking consciousness. The view is not new—it had been espoused by nineteenth-century psychologists such as William James, and in other cultures and other languages, but it is not the track we have been on recently, and certainly not scientifically, insofar as "scientifically" means accurately measured, and with a covering hypothesis and elements of predictability. We can now consider elements beyond this ordinary consciousness, and its limitations as an instrument.

Other cultures have given us traditions we can explore now as psychologies. They are not necessarily coherent alternatives, and frequently they come in bizarre—to us—language, and they do not have our symmetry. But they have elements that can move the edges of our paradigm. By the process of articulation, translation, description and measurement, we may be able to relate to them, though we do run the risk of missing their true natures in the process of applying our traditional analytic mode.

Now we are going to consider some explorers who are right out of the paradigm—they have gone through the holes in it, like Alice down the rabbit hole, and come back to tell us, but so far there is no way to work in what they have said, so it stays just beyond the edge of the paradigm, orbiting discreetly.

From within the paradigm, what some of the explorers have to say sounds, well, wiggy. Bizarre. It

would help to have as first-round choices, Whorf,
Wittgenstein and Korzybski—they even sound like
first-round draft choices—but they are all of them
gone. Maybe we could get Noam Chomsky.

VII. The Far Side of Paradigm

The Senior Astronaut: You Gotta Know the Territory

Baba Ram Dass: Pilgrim, Preacher

Carlos: I Met a Man upon a Stair

Parapsych

The Phoneless Message from Cousin Josie

Uri: Instructions from the Saucer

Randi: A Prestidigitation of Magicians

The Last Paradigm?

"Bosh, Dr. Jung." "You Are Mistaken, Dr. Freud."

What Cell Goes There?

The Mind, the Quantum and the Universe

Primum Vivere

The Senior Astronaut: You Gotta Know the Territory

Even though years had gone by, as an astronaut of inner space I was still a weekend warrior, and John Cunningham Lilly was a real no-foolin' space traveler. First of all, there were all those qualifications—Cal Tech, a medical degree from the University of Pennsylvania, training as a psychoanalyst, research in biophysics, neurophysiology, neuroanatomy—you couldn't design a better program for an Astronaut of Inner Space.

"I have spent much time in rather unusual, unordinary states, spaces, universes, dimensions, realities," Lilly wrote in an autobiography that was to become a cult book. "I speak as one who has been to the highest states of consciousness or of Satori-Samadhi, and as one who has returned to report to those interested. Some who went to these highest levels stayed there. Some came back and taught. Some came back to stay, too awed or frightened or guilty to reach, report, or ever return there . . . it is my firm belief that the experience of highest states of consciousness is necessary for the survival of the human species."

"The old theories," wrote the doctor and neurophysiologist who certainly knew them, "about the action of the brain, of the mind, and of the spirit do not seem to be adequate." And he laid down his axiom: "In the province of the mind, what is believed to be true is true or becomes true, within limits to be found experientially and experimentally. These limits are

293

further beliefs to be transcended. In the province of the mind, there are no limits."

In the Fifties, Lilly worked in Washington at the National Institute of Neurological Diseases and Blindness, mapping electrical activity in the cerebral cortex, and working with the brains of laboratory animals. Then, at the National Institutes of Health, he began to study sensory deprivation. Some neurophysiologists had postulated that if you cut off all stimulation from the brain, it would go to sleep. Lilly built a sensory-deprivation tank. The temperature of the water was 93°, experimentally determined as the temperature at which there is no sensation of hot or cold, in which tactile sensations disappear if you don't move. The water solution was buoyant, to remove the pull of gravity. No sound. No light. Lilly climbed in, and began his trip from the natural to the esoteric sciences.

Cut off from stimulation, the brain, Lilly found, did not go to sleep. Observing his own brain, Lilly found "dreamlike states, trancelike states, mystical states." He was joined, for example, by another person in the tank. And "at other times I apparently tuned in on networks of communication that are normally below our levels of awareness, networks of civilization way beyond ours."

Wiggy. Schizy. Lilly knew exactly what people would say, and he had nothing but contempt for the comments.

"I think the attempt to define all mystical, transcendental and ecstatic experiences which do not fit in with the categories of consensus reality as psychotic is conceptually limiting and comes from a timidity which is not seemly for the honest, open-minded explorer." We have, Lilly said, a built-in survival program, full of fears, and we have to fight through the survival program to find what's beyond. In other words, you're so scared and so determined to perceive the world in a comfortable way that you never get beyond the fear. Lilly had, he said, worked with schizophrenic and psychotic patients. In the tank he was examining *belief structures,* our belief structures imposed limits on what we perceived and experienced; what were the principles governing the human mind?

In the tank, "I began to experience a super-self level, a network of inter-related essences, yours, mine, everybody's, all hooked together. The Universal Mind . . . though it was only later in reading that I found the states I was getting into resembled those attained by other techniques."

A decade later, when LSD was still legal, he dosed himself with it and climbed into an even better tank. There were the Two Guides, now quite famous in the literature, who had appeared each time he had a brush with death, previously when he had been in a coma through a faulty injection, and when he was five and had TB—"Every time I have a job to do, these characters show up and tell me what the job is."

The Two Guides were from universes Lilly didn't necessarily believe existed when he started, but "I defined them as existing" in order to remove the barriers. And out went Lilly, three hundred micrograms of LSD and floating in a sensory deprivation tank, to outer space: high-intensity light . . . "as they approached their presences became more and more powerful, and I noticed more and more of them coming into me. Their thinking, their feeling, their knowledge was pouring into me. They stopped just as it was becoming almost intolerable to have them any closer."

The first time Lilly wrote of the Two Guides, he protested, "It is very hard to put this experience into words, because there were no words exchanged. Pure thought and feeling was being transmitted and received by me and by these two entities—I am a single point of consciousness, of feeling, I have no body, I feel their presence, I see their presence, without eyes, without a body. They tell me I can stay in this place, that I have left my body, but that I can return to it if I wish . . ."

The body, Lilly decided, can take care of itself when one leaves it, and "one can return if things get too tough out there." He continued to experiment with LSD doses and the tank, talking of "earthside time" as different from tank time. It took tremendous energy to control all the fears. With subsequent trips he was able to let go of some of the fears, and use the energy that had been holding the fears to explore further—you must go *beyond* the limiting belief, Lilly said, there are no final, true beliefs, compulsion is being trapped in a known psychic reality, a dead-end space.

On subsequent trips the Two Guides began to sound like the tape in *Mission Impossible*. Lilly had managed to get to these spaces without fear, said the Guides, now "your next assignment, if you wish it, is to achieve this through your own efforts plus the help of others . . . there are several others on your planet capable of teaching you and also learning from you. There are levels beyond where you are now and where we exist to which you can go with the proper work."

Lilly had, at the end of the Sixties, become so fascinated by the personal exploration of inner space that he did not view his dolphin experiments as proper. He had a laboratory in the Virgin Islands, and a staff, and grants, and scientific papers to do, but he began to see the dolphins not as scientific objects but as real entities, and being real, in some sort of prison. He turned the dolphins loose, and went to study with Oscar in Chile. And to write the account of these explorations of all his trips. "You become a point of consciousness, love, energy, warmth, cognition." That was the good trip. There were also the bad trips—demons, absolute blind frantic terror and panic.

The acid crowd had a new guru, and an M.D. neurophysiologist psychiatrist dolphin expert at that. They recognized both the ecstasies and the terrors. When Lilly left Arica, he began to give his own seminars. They were not the usual raps; scientific vocabulary cantered through the sentences, micrograms and dendrites and millivolts. The wandering Lamb Chops did not dig him too long, they said he was "cold." He put people down who asked dumb questions, and verbally rapped people over the knuckles like an old nun when they hadn't done their homework. One of our keys to opening consciousness in our seminar was a book called *The Laws of Form*, which properly you would have to classify as mathematics, Boolean algebra. All things are: true, false, as if true, as if false, and meaningless. Lilly was eventually to add five more categories to this description of existence, of which #8 was love. I sent *The Laws of Form* to some friends, renowned mathematicians at the Institute for Advanced Study. They said it was a nice exercise in Boolean algebra, but what was all this about changing consciousness?

That's the problem with vocabulary. Does the phrase "change consciousness" imply a great expectation or a small one? Perhaps learning mathematics changes your consciousness. Wouldn't learning Chinese, too? Maybe the renowned mathematicians had already had their consciousness subtly changed—they could, after all, speak to each other in Boolean algebra and numerous other disciplines, chalk in hand at the blackboard. Lilly also used chalk in hand at the blackboard.

And what of the Two Guides, and the outer space, and the points of light? Sometimes Lilly later denied the experiences except as in his imagination, and at other times "I felt they had a very secure reality. The two guides warned me that I would go through such phases of skepticism, of doubt . . . during the experiences, I knew this was the truth. At other times I was not sure." And later he said, "The two guides may be aspects of my own functioning at the superself level, they may be helpful constructs or concepts, they may be representatives of a hidden esoteric school, I don't know."

No one who had ever been on a similar trip, altered state however arrived at, doubted the Two Guides as feelings and experience. But were they really "real"? A large number of people—upwards of a million—had experimented with hallucinogens, a much smaller number, alone. Very few people had been in a sensory deprivation tank, and no one had ever plopped into the tank with pure, legal Sandoz LSD. "If you want to be an expert," Lilly said to me once, "invent the territory."

I had my own problems with Lilly's accounts.

They read, first of all, as though dictated while jogging. And the Two Guides seemed very much like the angels a small Catholic boy in St. Paul, Minnesota, would have seen—and as a matter of fact did see, but a horrified nun put him down and said only saints saw visions. Norman Mailer once said we should send a poet among the astronauts to the moon; I began to feel we should have a poet on the labyrinthine, murky explorations of inner space. I had such problems with the language. On one Lilly trip, "I was listening to Beethoven's Ninth Symphony. I literally left my body and went to Heaven" . . . wait, wait, literally? Sure, what one believes to be true either is true or becomes true within limits to be found experientially—true, false, as if true, as if false, meaningless. . . love. Well, the *experience* was there, everybody has the same experience of the certainty within the experience, and of course the metaphor is only a metaphor, but . . . first team! Korzybski! Wittgenstein! Whorf! Off the bench and in there and dig in! We may have to punt.

Lilly bought a place in the Santa Monica mountains and turned it into a tank farm. That was his seminar now. The Samadhi Tank Company began to make them to Lilly's specs. A professor friend of mine, a classmate in a course, acquired a Samadhi Tank and used it in a psych course, the students in pairs, safety man outside the tank in case somebody should freak out and beat on the sides, subject inside, then switch and everybody write a term paper.

I was not put off by the maintenance man who said, "Wouldn't catch me in one of those things," or by signing releases, I undertake all exercises, experiments, and use of the tank at my own sole risk, and neither . . . nor shall be liable for claims, demands, injuries, damages, action or causes of actions whatsoever to my person arising out of or connected with use by me of the tank . . .

I took off all my clothes. Usually we have a safety man, said my professor friend, I have work to do and you don't need one. I'll be back in an hour and a half. It won't seem like an hour and a half, it may seem longer, but I won't forget. Oh yes, some people think there isn't enough air and they're choking and so on, that's just a panic excuse, the air system is fine, so I won't accept that from you.

The lid came down. It seemed quite heavy. Thump thump thump THUMP. What the hell is that? Oh, it's my pulse. Why is it going so fast? Just because that lid seemed so heavy. Is the water really buoyant? Yep, you really have to work to sink, and then you can't stay down. Certainly is black in here. Yessir, eyes wide open and can't see a single thing, weird. Thump . . . thump . . . thump, that's better. *Quiet* in here. *Very* quiet. Certainly is dark. Yep. Wonder how much time has gone by. Thirty seconds? That leaves eighty-nine minutes and thirty seconds, if the sonofabitch doesn't forget I'm in here. No, he wouldn't forget. What if he gets hit by a truck? He wouldn't get hit by a truck either. Now what's *that* little sound?

There was nobody in the tank but me, and the little sounds were all me. Thump thump thump, and little gurgles in the stomach and intestines, and something in the ear, amazing how many little sounds there are that normally you don't hear because the outside world is making so much noise . . . so what. The sergeant-voice arrived, slightly breathless from the tennis court. You dummy, you're not supposed just to lie there, you're supposed to Have an Experience. Lilly got all the way to Arcturus III, for Chrissakes.

Well, here I am in the tank, where the hell are the Two Guides?

I let everything go. I had been holding my head up, unconsciously. It didn't drop as far into the salt water as I thought. Nothing to do. Probably eighty-six minutes to go . . . I couldn't stop thinking about Lilly. Dammit, that was *his* trip, I don't know any angels, that's not my metaphor anyway.

Thump, thump, gurgle, gurgle. Let's do a meditation. What color is your left foot? Where *is* your left foot? Left . . . there it is.

Hey, let's go, said the sergeant-voice. You dummy,

you're using up your tank time with the same old ratcheta ratcheta. Go somewhere! Inner space! Outer space! But stop that!

. . Certainly is *black* in here. Wherever you go normally, you're never in complete blackness, there's always *some* light . . .

I had a momentary vision of some bicycle riders at twilight, a country road. Ah, Altered State of Consciousness. Let go, let go, let go, let's go . . .

. . . and so on.

The building with the tank room was new. The main hallway connecting the several college buildings was several stories high, quite striking architecturally, with kiosks for various college notices. Big posters with bold colors broke up the spaces. Outside, a sunny day, the leaves of the shade trees making nice patterns on the grass. A bit of a breeze. Some people on the college tennis courts, in the distance. I couldn't remember whether my car was in parking lot 3 or parking lot 4, they looked almost exactly alike. I had to walk down one line of cars before I saw it. I got into my car. The speedometer said 15279. I had a fleeting worry—what if I have a flat tire? Then I thought: that's a bit silly, why should I worry about a flat tire, I don't normally. Now, where are the keys, the car keys, I had them—in my right-hand pocket, of my pants, my pants, my pants are on the chair, the chair in the tank room, the tank room? THE TANK ROOM? EEEEEEEEEEEEEEeeeeeeekkkkkkkkkk I'm still back in the tank! Zoooooooooooooooooop!

THUMP THUMP THUMP THUMP thump thump thump . . . thump . . . thump. Whew! Eyes, that's right, my eyes are open but I'm not seeing anything because tank, this is a tank, this is, let's see, Friday afternoon, see, water, salty, thump . . . thump . . . thump car, what was that, 15279 . . . body, am I here? I'm here.

Where the hell are the Two Guides?

Ah-h-h-h, shut up about the Two Guides. Where are the bicycle riders on the country road?

Where's the bottom of this tank?

Let's go back, let's go . . .

I heard footsteps. The lid opened, a silhouetted figure in dim light up there.

"Hi, how you doin?"

"Not ready yet."

"That's an hour and a half. Blink your eyes. In a minute, I'm going to turn the light on in this room."

I said the last hour had certainly gone by quickly. I climbed out. My professor friend was grinning.

"Why are you grinning?" I said.

"Why are *you* grinning? You're giggling. You look very rested."

I said I felt somewhat rested. My fingers and toes were quite wrinkled. I got dressed.

"This course has turned out well," my friend said. He described the reading list for the course. Some of the papers written by the students had been quite interesting. "Some of the kids logged a lot of time, three, four hours at a stretch."

"No bad experiences?"

"Not one. The administration was worried, but the course turned out extremely well."

I told him how Lilly's trip got in my way. "The damn Two Guides," I said. "Of course, he had been on lots more trips. And with pure Sandoz LSD. I'm not sure I'd go back in there with three hundred micrograms of LSD. That's guts ball."

I took a couple of psychological tests. We chatted. "You look much more serene than when you got here," said my friend. Well, they always say that, the people that run the resort, when you're leaving.

Bold posters in the corridor. The sun was still out, the shade trees making nice patterns on the sunny grass. Some people on the college tennis courts, in the distance. The car was in lot 4. I got in. My keys were in my right-hand pocket, and my pants were on. The speedometer said 15279.

Lilly, the senior astronaut, seemed to be able to move effortlessly, almost dizzily, among vibrational levels: here he is doing an exercise in Chile with another man, involving a lot of spooky staring:

"I went automatically into Satori #6 yet holding in #12 and #24. The part of me in #6 took a look around and saw that part of him was peaking into #6 but that he didn't know it. I came back down and reported this to him . . .'he' was in 48, he became extremely angry, going into 96 immediately . . ."

It always seemed to me that there were verbal definitions of subtle feelings, but no parameters, one man's #6 is another man's #12, I was wishing for road signs: WELCOME TO VIBRATIONAL LEVEL #12. PLEASE DIM LIGHTS. DO NOT LITTER.

In Chile, Lilly went into the desert as part of the program. Alone in the desert in a little hut, five days and nights, "I started to cry, lonely at first, for me. I went with the grief. It changed to grief-joy combined and it was for all humans—later [Oscar] called this a special region, making the Christ, the green qutub." (The last word is Arabic, meaning special powers, or one with special powers.)

That's the senior astronaut. When the National Guard goes camping—first of all, we didn't do it in the desert, because there wasn't a desert handy. The instructions were to find a small room with plain walls, remove the pictures, hang a blanket over the window, remove all furniture except a sleeping bag or cot, no reading material, not a word, nothing to listen to, one candle, bring the food for three days, cold food, obviously, nothing to prepare, put the food and water on the floor in the corner, the room should be one where you can be alone undisturbed for three days, the room should be next to a bathroom or handy to one but use the bathroom only in extreme necessity—

—camping in the city. I took: one barbecued chicken, tomatoes, carrots, grapefruit, hard-boiled eggs, cans of tuna, and at the last minute, half a bag of Granola, the cereal, utensils, and a can opener.

Three days, three nights. Very instructive sidelight, not intended as the main part of the exercise: if the exterior stimulation is reduced like that, and you ask yourself whether it's your stomach or your head that's hungry, you really only eat when you're hungry. I emerged with the chicken and the tuna intact. All I had eaten for three days was the grapefruit, the vegetables, and part of the cereal thrown in impromptu at the last moment.

But there was to be no free time. All to be taken up with exercises. Even the more experienced National Guardsmen giggled nervously when handed the programs they were to do alone: first day, jnana yoga. (All yoga is not breathing and twisting. That's hatha. Jnana is with the head, the imagination. Two hours: inhale cold, exhale warm. That's it. That's the warm-up. Inhale warm, exhale cold. Then, four hours: imagine a flower, inhale the flower, exhale the flower. Okay, but *four hours?* Four hours: blow a note on your $1.98 G. Schirmer recorder, chant the note, draw the petals of a lotus in the air, blow the note, chant the note, draw the petals in the air—

—not much there for the left side of the old brain to do. In my case, it arrived with the following message: you know what you're doing? You're sitting in the middle of a blank room, a ganzfeld in perception, and you look like a nut there with your goddam recorder and your imaginary flower; in fact, you *are* a nut and this a crazy, help, help! Inhale the *universe?* Wha?

Midway through the second day, the over-voice had begun to dim. Fading away: you know what this is like? This is like being stuck in the airport hotel in Toledo in a blizzard with no lights and no food and no planes taking off and the radiators are stuck and the phones are out, so big deal, next time you're stuck for three days in the airport hotel in Toledo you'll know some exercises to do—

Flower exercise. The old enneagram, or symbol, from the Masters of Wisdom:

At each point where the interior lines touch the circle, there is a flower of a specific color. So you go from red flower at point one to green flower at point two, and so on, nine points, and back to red flower. Four hours.

Then a rather curious phenomenon began. The mechanism began to run by itself. That is, I did not direct it to go red flower, green flower, but it did anyway. Furthermore, I could just sit there and watch, because I wouldn't know what *shade* of red

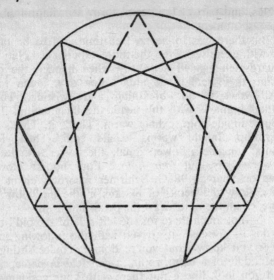

or green was going to turn up. Oh, that's a pretty green. Say, that's a very deep purple, deeper than the last time around.

The mechanism got to the left lower point, the yellow flower, and nothing appeared. Then the yellow flower appeared, just a syncopated beat late. Red flower, green flower, I just sat there staring, childlike and dazzled, Oooh, that's a pretty one, and the flowers appeared *before* the words I could use to describe them. Faster than words! Wow! And when we got to the yellow point, a large *carrot* appeared.

You're no flower, get out of there, I said.

The carrot changed, cartoon-like, back to a flower. I thought that was very funny. Red flower, green flower, purple flower, and this time the yellow flower appeared upside down. The sonofabitch was a real prankster. I laughed right out loud. In fact, I began to feel very good. So I sat there, laughing, not controlling, this flower charade running through its routine, and left-sided, I thought, now isn't this interesting, you're stoned but you're not stoned, you're not stoned because you can still think all these things clearly, this is Tuesday afternoon and you haven't had anything to make you stoned, Granola doesn't do that, and yet there's no question that a very funny flower routine is being run in here.

It got darker after a while, and I found I could make a white spot appear on the black, shadowy wall and move it around by moving my head, that was pretty funny, and the old verbal brain, pretty well beaten back, would appear occasionally with some dry psychological professorial comment: it is well known that language does not appear until the age of umpteen months and that it is cumbersome, images do, physiologically, travel faster than words, but we do admit that the preverbal or nonverbal state is very interesting, More Research Is Needed.

That's not all I saw, but it will do for a start.

Then there were the sounds. Birds. A cardinal, then a robin, then a jay, then something I couldn't identify but something like a song sparrow, then a meadowlark, but more like a Western meadowlark, wasn't he pretty far from home? It wasn't too strange to hear birds, your hearing becomes more focused without distracting sounds, we were only a block from the park, but then I noticed: always in the same order, these birds, first the cardinal, then the robin and the others. It must be a mockingbird, the order is all rigidly the same. In fact, that's quite a compulsive mockingbird out there, he never even mixes them up. The bird sounds ceased when it got dark, and they came back the next day: cardinal, robin, jay—

At the end of the third evening, an instructor came to get me, and perform some closing ceremonies. I wanted to know about my carrot in the lower left-hand corner. I had decided it was an Achievement. I simply wanted to know what satori it came from: #24 didn't seem quite good enough, more like #12, but no sign of a green qutub. No answers on that. "You look peaceful," said the instructor. I decided the whole exercise was so nice I would do it again sometime, but I never did.

Retreats, of course, are very old. The people who thought of them were quite smart.

The bird sounds, as it turns out, were irrelevant but a funny footnote. It took two days after the end of the exercise to care about the headlines, or get riled or stirred up, which shows you can have a vacation with nothing but Granola, carrots, water, a blank room, some exercises, and your own head. Then I was walking down the street near the apartment and wait—what's that—a cardinal, a robin, a jay—the same damn birds, in the same order, what the hell? And now I'm walking down the street, the buses are roaring up Madison Avenue, taxis are honking, and I am, believe me, alert: I am looking for a compulsive mockingbird in mid-Manhattan. I walk a little further, and the sound is—coming from—a flower shop, a flower shop, and I go into the flower shop—the bird sounds are louder, very loud—in fact, they're somewhere amidst all these plants and ferns and greenery, up there, behind the ferns, a loudspeaker, bird sounds from the speaker—

"Uh, excuse me, I hear birds in here, that loudspeaker, you have a bird record on?"

The proprietor, a small man with a mustache in a gray vest, smiles. "You like birds?"

"Sure, sure, I used to know all about them as a kid—"

"It's a tape. From the Audubon. The bird society. It makes it more—peaceful, in here, you know, like a woods."

"It's very nice. I just thought I would stop in and tell you how much I liked it."

The proprietor beamed. "That tape plays over and over. It's not like music, you get tired of certain music, but bird sounds blend right into the plants. It's funny, I had that tape three—no four years now, all the time, and in all that time you're the first person who ever noticed."

There is a traditional way to view these phenomena from well within the paradigm. A generation ago, the distinguished McGill University psychologist Donald Hebb, together with his associates, did a number of experiments on the effects of sensory deprivation. The volunteers were paid to stay in an environment where there wasn't any stimulation at all. Their vision was restricted by translucent plastic visors, their hearing was impeded by an earphone-like pillow, and so on. They were to stay in their cubicles as long as they could.

Hebb's experiment was sponsored by Canada's Defense Research Board. That board was seeking information on two problems among others: the first reports of "brainwashing" were beginning to come back from the Korean war, and radar operators spent long hours watching for Russians coming over the North Pole. Hebb, as a leading psychologist, was interested in motivation, but basically the interest of the experimenters was directed to the effects of monotony and the lack of stimulation. As an example, why did radar operators sometimes fail to see the blips after long hours at the screen? Long-distance truck-drivers had accidents sometimes, according to studies in France and at Harvard, because the drivers began to see "red spiders on the windshield, and non-existent animals running across the road."

Hebb's volunteers were not explorers or medita-tors, and they did not enjoy the experience. They were planning to do some work in their cubicles, think over problems, write speeches, etc. But they couldn't concentrate. Their minds began to drift. With that set and setting, and with the attitudes they brought in, they began to think the experimenters were against them. Their left hemispheres fought the experience. Also, it could be noted that the depriva-tion apparatus was physically uncomfortable: cotton gloves, cardboard cuffs, translucent visors.

"The subjects reported something else to which we at first paid no particular attention, but which was to emerge as the most striking result of the experi-ments," said the report. "Many of them, after long isolation, began to see 'images.' Several subjects seemed to be 'having dreams' *while they were awake*. Not until one of the experimenters himself went through the isolation experience for a long pe-riod did we realize the power and the strangeness of the phenomenon."

The subjects got light-headed, and then irritable. What did they see? "Rows of little yellow men with black caps on and their mouths open. Eyeglasses marching down a street. These scenes were frequently distorted, and were described as being like animated movie cartoons. The hallucinations were not confined to vision. Occasionally a subject heard people in the scene 'talking.' One . . . heard a choir singing 'in full stereophonic sound.' One . . . had a feeling of being hit in the arm by pellets fired from a minature rocket ship he saw. Some subjects reported that they felt as if another body were lying beside them in the cubicle; in one case the two bodies overlapped, partly occupying the same space."

Now this is very useful for the long-distance truckdrivers. Any truckdriver who sees a twenty-foot rabbit hopping across the road should pull up, he has been staring at the image of his headlights on the road, and the white line on the road, and he has put himself right into blank out in ganzfeld, he has stopped registering what is out there and is creating other images.

And the experiments also give us a Rumpelstiltskin for the results. Hallucinations. That takes care of that. (Maybe not true hallucinations. I didn't think the carrot was *really* there in midair, and the gentleman fired upon by the miniature rocket ship didn't think it was a real rocket ship, but hallucinations enough to classify, Rumpelstiltskin.)

From the popularized results of the first sensory deprivation experiments grew some lurid spy stuff. One night my wife was watching *Hawaii Five-O*. The Sinister Foreign Power was picking up our agents and dropping them into a sensory deprivation tank, whereupon they would crack immediately. Only the superhero was able to withstand a couple of hours. I looked up from my reading.

"They have the wrong bunch of agents," I said. "All the kids in Shelby's course have logged more time than that. They fight to get into the tank. You have to sign up three weeks ahead of time."

"Shhh," my wife said.

The hero's own iron brain was about to crack

when the good guys from Hawaii Five-O burst into the room and fished him out. He recovered enough, I think, to slug a couple of the baddies in the donnybrook before the commercial, but don't hold me to the details.

Now here was something strange. In Shelby's course, the kids were elbowing each other to get into a tank. But Hebb's associate Woodbury Heron had called his report "The Pathology of Boredom," in *Scientific American,* and that article had been reprinted many times. Pathology is the study of disease. "A changing sensory environment seems essential for human beings," Heron had written. "Without it, the brain ceases to function in an adequate way." Sensory deprivation was equated with boredom, and boredom with disease, as in the pathology of boredom. And that's how it got to *Hawaii Five-O,* though there may have been some intermediate stages.

Clearly, expectation and attitude were important factors in determining the experience. "In modern society," John Lilly had written, "most people have been programmed to avoid solitude, isolation, and confinement. Television sets in homes are anti-isolation and anti-solitude devices . . . thus, there is a negative attitude toward solitude, isolation, and confinement in most persons. This attitude has been reinforced by those doing research on so-called sensory deprivation . . . the psychiatrists who came into the field . . . made judgments about the phenomena . . . without careful experiment analysis. . . . Negative expectations generated negative results."

(He could have said, yogis go up to the Himalayas and spend two years in a cave, and when they come down sometimes they start a whole new movement and head straight for the Johnny Carson show, where they talk volubly, but that wouldn't have been his style.) Lilly, of course, knew all the sensory deprivation literature. He never used it in his seminars; I suppose he was too irritated by it.

But not all the sensory deprivation research suggested plots for *Hawaii Five-O.* There were literally hundreds of experiments, some with positive results.

But they did not surface above the general din produced by 224 technical psychology journals.

In 1975, however, one of the sensory deprivation researchers, Peter Suedfeld of the University of British Columbia, rounded up the research, rather pointedly, as "The Benefits of Boredom." For some subjects had stayed in a dark, soundproof room for as long as three weeks! The visions, the hallucinations, were due "largely to spontaneous neural firing in the retina," and the "auditory and olfactory perceptions are affected by residual stimuli from the subject's body."

Simple tasks such as memorization were actually performed better by the volunteers emerging from the dark room, though complex tasks were not. Sensitivity to sounds and colors increased. But perhaps most interesting, time spent in a quiet, dark room, even just twenty-four hours, made it easier to change bad habits. Some smokers quit smoking. "In sensory deprivation," said the report, "heavy smokers are not stressed by the absence of cigarettes." Further: sensory deprivation had been used in treating drug addiction, hypertension, snake phobia, and stuttering.

(The sensory deprivation literature, so-called, refers mostly to a quiet, dark room. Lilly's tank called HHDE or hydro-hypodynamic environment in the jargon is too stressful for most subjects because of its strangeness.)

Time goes by! The world turns! Sensory deprivation is good for you! (Somebody is probably getting ready to merchandise a Magic Closet right now.) But whether you find the experience useful or even tolerable, depends on whether you think you can come out whenever you want. Much as I liked the quieting feelings produced by both the ganzfeld room and the tank, I have not been back to either, and if someone had said, "Marine, you die," before dropping me into a tank, I would have found it very stressful.

Buddhist psychology had already recorded the little yellow men with black caps and the stereophonic choirs that arrive with time spent quietly and alone. If you are into meditation, the *makyo* arrive, phenomena. That shows your journey has begun. Everybody gets *makyo*. Don't get interested in them, they will hold up your progress. Don't fight them, just notice them without judging, they will go away. You want to get your mind to one-pointedness, and the *makyo* are just a little test on the road of the pilgrim.

A woman of my acquaintance, getting a doctorate in Oriental religions, spent several weeks meditating in a cell at a Buddhist retreat in India. After a number of days, she began to hear voices.

"First of all," she said, "I could really hear the voices, they weren't voices like when you *imagine* voices. I could hear them. And the voices weren't noble and profound, I am no Joan of Arc, nobody told me to go out and lead France. The horror, the absolute horror, was that the voices were all everyday trivia: move to the back of the bus, please. Put on your rubbers, it's going to rain. Why haven't you written lately? Please fill out both sides of the form, please fill out both sides of the form, please fill out both sides of the form. Did you want the ground chuck or the ground round? How much is this? That price is too high, they called again, you didn't return the call.

"I sat there with my knees under my chin, my hands over my ears, but *I couldn't turn them off*. It was awful, horror, sheer horror, yet it was what goes on all the time, this trivia is existence. Finally I fell asleep, exhausted, the voices were gone.

"At the end of the next day I had an interview with the priest who was supervising. I told him about the voices. He said, 'Oh, good, good, this garbage has to come to the surface every once in a while to be cleaned out.'

"When I left there I felt so light I could walk on treetops. It was exhilarating."

"And now?" I asked her.

"Now there are ups and downs. The voices came back. But I like to get my garbage cleaned out once or twice a year."

Lilly, the senior astronaut, was not particularly interested in the way of the pilgrim. "I prefer understanding rather than devotion," he said. "I prefer fellow seekers rather than charismatic disciples. I am a scientific observer."

The scientific crowd, I ventured, didn't think all of this was so scientific.

"They're hung up in the pre-quantum mechanics world. Where is the observer? They think · the observer is here, the reality is there. Ask them: is mathematics science? Where did the math come from? Where does each advance in math come from? It comes from the inner mind, it can't be explained as a natural science."

So Lilly went on exploring. Into the tank, at least every other day.

"Sometimes I go into these spaces and get instructions and They say, you'll forget these instructions until it's important to use them, but that's the kind of thing you don't like to talk about because somebody might pop you in a strange corner."

"Just tell me one more time," I said, "what's the difference between you and a schizophrenic who also goes to strange spaces?"

Lilly fixed me with a cold blue eye.

"I can come back. Schizophrenics wander into spaces by accident, some of them like it, some of them hate it, but it makes their relationship with other people precarious, and they can't control it. When I climb out of the tank, I'm back. You know the emphasis we put on consensus is the main enemy of investigation in these regions. Safety first, status quo. I have it myself. The fear that the universe is not what you assume it to be is very basic, especially when you know damn well it isn't what you assume it to be. So you struggle with teaching enough people to appreciate that what you think the universe is, isn't true, enough unsure so they don't panic, but so they're not content—then you'll have a first-class investigation."

I pressed on about the spaces. Had I read, Lilly said, *Stranger in a Strange Land?* Or *The Starmaker?* Science fiction. The first has become a cult book, but I am not a science fiction fan. Lilly sometimes seemed an example of Kuhn's criticism of scientific education, very specific in its area but with little experience of the rest of the tradition, maybe that was the problem with the language: did he notice the gap between experience and expression?

"Oh, all the time. I call it coming back through the screen of words."

And the spaces—the tank was a comfortable enough experience, no?

"It can be terrifying, not the tank, but the spaces. I'm uneasy when I get there. It turns your realities around, and when I'm allowed in, most of the time I want to get out. I don't emphasize the terrifying spaces because there are too many people afraid of simple spaces."

From time to time I would check in with the senior astronaut. Sometimes he was grumpy about all this tank time.

"They can get somebody else to go on these trips," he said. "I got out of the tank the other day and I looked in the mirror and I said, you're a retired hero, you've had enough."

Then he found a new drug, entirely legal, that permitted a cold-eyed exploration of inner spaces without panic, a dissociative drug. I won't even tell the name, lest it start a run on both the drug and the FDA.

"You told me six months ago," I said, after he described the new drug, "that you were a retired hero, and now here you go again."

"Almost retired," Lilly said. "This is very interesting."

I had gotten a bit fond of this remote and complex man. Sometimes—rarely—he had touches of humor.

"One of these days," I said, "the battery in your survival program is going to run down. There will be just one last faint message—*don't go on this trip.* When you get that one, cancel the trip, otherwise you'll be off with the Two Guides and that will be the last voyage."

"Survival programs always say don't go," Lilly said. "The territory's still there."

Baba Ram Dass: Pilgrim, Preacher

"I prefer understanding rather than devotion," Lilly had said. The way of the pilgrim was, anyway, already brilliantly represented in the person of Richard Alpert, Baba Ram Dass. I first heard the story on a tape cassette, that was how it spread, people would go hear him and tape it and copy the tape and mail one to their friends, and they would copy the tape and mail it again, an old story with a new technology. Then I heard it in person, several times, and even now, I can turn on the warm cadences in my ear—

"I had an apartment in Cambridge that was filled with antiques and I gave very charming dinner parties. I had a Mercedes-Benz sedan and a Triumph 500 cc motorcycle and a Cessna 172 airplane and an MG sports car and a sailboat and a bicycle. I vacationed in the Caribbean where I did scuba-diving. I was living the way a successful bachelor professor is supposed to live in the American world of 'he who makes it.' "

Thus it begins. It has within it the same sense of expectation that "once upon a time" carries. We know there is going to be a story, and in fact the story is worth attention here not only for its charm but because it became a metaphor, an archetype, bigger than itself.

"I was blessed by everything that Western society could offer: affluence, and love, education, the fruits of advanced technology, including drugs, the best drugs. All that was part of my preparation to now know something else."

The Harvard psychology professor, the ex-sidekick

of Tim Leary, the son of the president of the New Haven Railroad, kicked out for the drug experiments, years more of drug experiments, LSD, hashish, cocaine, who knows what—this gentleman is now sitting amidst banks of flowers facing an audience, most of them in jeans and boots, or the girls in the long granny dresses and sandals, and this gentleman is now balding, with a graying beard and long hair in the back, and the one-stringed instruments have ceased their sound and he just sits there and smiles. And after the longest time, he says, "Well, here we are." And his voice is so warm and he is so relaxed and he smiles and gradually everybody starts to smile, "Here we are," he says again, and here we are, not just in this room but all together on the surface of the planet—"Here we are, and we'll just talk a little, I'll talk some, and then we can get up and walk around and maybe have some cider, and you can talk, or ask questions, and we'll all just hang out for a while."

Ah-h-h-h. And we settle back, because we are going to have Buddha's Four Noble Truths, in this relaxed, funny way. Maybe with some of St. John or St. Theresa, some nice passages read to us. Or some of the cabala. And the Four Noble Truths come out so relaxed, life is suffering because you don't get what you want, or if you get what you want you might lose it, so the cause of the suffering is attachment, or desire. The fourth truth is Buddha's eightfold path for giving up attachment, which comes out to "work on yourself," not in the old Ben Franklin-Horatio Alger way, because that's in the service of the ego, but to where there's still some little bit of divine spark even though there's no body, no feeling, no thoughts, no behavior: "a complete perceptual reorganization of who I am, formless, unlimited, beyond space and time, I am light, love, consciousness, energy. It's a hard one. I'm still working on it."

The audience is rapt because it is not some odd Indian preaching at them, but this colloquial charmer who still has the language of psychology and the metaphors of his generation. So he can say "perceptual reorganization" and we're comfortable. And to explain the name Ram Dass, Servant of God, we have to have the story of Ram, but that's comfortable too, not quite the way it comes out in Hindi, probably:

"So Ram is going through the jungle and he meets these naked ascetics. And they say, 'Hey, Ram, you're God and we're really being bugged by these demons; we can't meditate. Would you mind giving us a mantra because they really make a lot of noise, you know, it's like cats making love on the back fence.' So Ram goes to see his guru, to get the mantra to help the ascetics, and the guru says, 'Come on, baby, what do you mean? I mean, you're God, if you're God, you're the mantra and the demons and the whole business'—oh, I forgot, we're in an incarnation and we have to play this out so here goes—"

Or there are the chakras, physical localizations of psychic energy in the Hindu system, expressed in terms of places, people get hung up in them, the first is survival, that's Africa, the jungle, and the second is the Riviera, sensual gratification, sex, that's the one Freud got hung up in, and the third is power, Washington, Moscow, Peking, London, that's where Adler hung out, and the fourth is the heart chakra, that's Jung's territory, still three more chakras to go—

If you go to the right places, they have Ram Dass's picture on the wall, even outdoors among some of the street vendors of Telegraph Avenue in Berkeley.

And there is always this ability to speak the language: Ram Dass comes back from India and now he is in these funny Indian clothes and so he goes to speak to the psychiatric Grand Rounds, he knows what they are thinking, here is poor Dr. Alpert, used to be at Harvard, took all those drugs, a very interesting case, schizophrenic, because Alpert is sitting *on* the end of the conference table cross-legged working his beads, but when he speaks, he speaks of himself as the case, hallucinations, dissociative experiences, he tells the whole journey in psychodynamic terms, the mandala is "a heuristic device for cognitive centering," and now what the hell are the Grand Rounds to do, but be charmed, and get the message?

In 1967, after all the drugs and all the psychoanalysis, Richard Alpert went to India—I have to summarize the story, he tells it much better himself if you want to hear it—and came into the presence of the Maharishi, a funny old man sitting on a blanket, who knew everything in Alpert's head. (Do not confuse this maharishi, Neem Karoli Baba, with the TM Maharishi or the Guru Maharaj Ji.) He knew what he was thinking, all the time. Alpert's mind raced—CIA? Underground?—and then "like a computer with an insoluble problem, my mind gave up. It burned out its circuitry." A wrenching in the chest, an outpouring of tears, "all I could say was I felt like I was home. The journey was over."

Six months of cold baths at four A.M. and exercise and breathing and communicating only by writing on a slate, and then he came back to the U.S. as Baba Ram Dass. His father the railroad president was much relieved, he called him Rum Dum but it was better than the drug trip, his elder brother the stockbroker called him Rammed Ass, but he began to move around, college campuses mostly, staying only a few days at each place, no set schedule, a sort of Johnny Appleseed of the consciousness story. If there was anything you were hiding, or harboring, that was holding you back, any pain that was difficult to share, you could tell him —he would sit, facing you, running his own mantram through his mind—free, no catches. The crowds began to grow.

Another trip to India: his guru detached him from the Johnny Appleseed role by sending all the wandering American college kids after him, as if to overwhelm him. "I'm good at describing things, but I have no conceptual understanding of what happened, Marishi kept changing roles, a nice old man, an old fool, a wizard, divine. Each label crashed immediately. He took me through fierce trips about anger, jealousy, sex, greed, attachment to the body. I said, 'I don't want to be enlightened, I just want to be pure enough to do whatever work I'm supposed to do.' He gave me a mango, hit me on the head, and said, 'You will be.' "

Another college auditorium, another group, flowers, stringed instruments:

"I didn't want to end up on this path. I wanted something more esoteric, more exquisite, secrets, special powers, to be able to do things to people, I'll go into Mao's mind and Brezhnev's mind, we'll have peace—just have a little shtick to go with it, but all I know is what my guru told me, love everyone, serve everyone, remember God. I have no sense of social responsibility. I do this just to work on myself, no scrapbook, I don't have any model of why I am doing this, I'm not collecting anything, I don't have a goal, the game is just to stay in totally free fall. Ultimately the laws of the universe are not rationally knowable because they are not within the logical rational system, since that is a subsystem, and there's a metasystem of which that's all part, which includes paradox and opposites.

"It sounds very Mickey Mouse to the Western, sophisticated mind to say love everyone, serve everyone, remember God, I know that. I see part of my role as that of a gnostic intermediary, to bring metaphors from one system into another, without attachment, that is, I'm doing it because I'm doing it because I'm doing it. I can't write the script. This is very difficult for our Western culture, where you usually have a model of what you're going to do and you're collecting this for that and you're living in time. See, when Christ said, 'Had ye but faith, ye could move mountains,' he was speaking literal truth, but were you able to move mountains, you wouldn't be you any more, you would be the Being who created the mountain in the first place. At some level as real as this physical plane, there is only one of us, and at another plane there aren't any of us."

There were parts that were difficult for the audiences: reincarnation, the three-year-old child who dies but then maybe its work was done, maybe next time—and it's scarcely arguable, Ram Dass would simply say, "A lot of things are not in the Western model." Like the miracle stories: Maharishi reading Ram Dass's mind. Or: a barber is shaving Maharishi in midmorning, and Marharishi says how are things going, and the barber says, I have a son in Madras and I haven't heard from him in a year. Two days later the barber's son arrives to see his father and says, the craziest thing happened to me, in the middle of the morning two days ago a nutty old man shaving lather over half his face walked in, said, "Here, go see your father, he wants to see you," gave me the bus fare, and disappeared. Or: Ram Dass goes to see Swami Muktananda, who gives him a mantram and shows him a meditation room and—sort of like a dream— Ram Dass is on the astral plane and flying in the room and then tilts a bit and gets frightened and says what am I doing down there lying on my back and zoooop back into his body, and when he emerges from the meditation room, Swami Muktananda says, "Enjoy flying?"

How did he know that?

I asked Swami Muktananda. It was a couple of years later, and Swami Muktananda was in the United States, and his followers set up an ashram in an old school, and he sat, cross-legged, in his socks. With his beard and his beret and his sunglasses, he looked like a stoned jazz musician. But he didn't wear the sunglasses and the beret to receive people. We had been through an "intensive," one day, chanting and discourses, and now we could all approach and ask questions. People would come up, bump their heads on the floor, and ask their question. I was too uptight to bump my head on the floor. People's questions were: should they quit their job, should they leave their spouse, how should they meditate, could they have a mantram, please?

I asked: "You remember when Baba Ram Dass was in your meditation room in India and you were outside of it and he went flying around outside his body and when he came out you said, 'enjoy flying'?"

Muktananda frowned while the translator translated, and midway through he smiled.

"I don't know how I knew, but I remember when he did it," Muktananda said. "Come to my ashram, we'll have you flying in no time."

"I don't want to fly, I just want to know how you knew he was flying," I said.

Muktananda spoke rapidly in Hindi. Then he got up, and grinned. He looked suddenly very, very familiar. Like a long-lost uncle or something. It was bizarre. Then he came up to me, put his arm around my head, and trotted around the room with me in this semi-wrestling hold. Then he scratched my back. It felt good. It would be nice to have a guru around the house, I remember thinking.

I was still trying to collect my perceptions—how did he get to look so familiar so fast—when the translator spoke again.

"Baba really wants to see you again," he said. (Baba was what they call the Swami.) "Really. And he says, do not get hung up in flying, that is not what it's about, it just happens sometimes."

"I don't want to fly," I said. "But if I do, and he knows about it, will he tell me how he knows?"

Ram Dass tells this story: his VW Microbus breaks down one day in India, full of Western kids following him, and everybody gets out to push but a couple of girls. Ram Dass is mad, why shouldn't they push, too, they're young and healthy, Ram Dass gets back and walks into the ashram, and Maharishi says, "Oho, Ram Dass is mad because the girls wouldn't help push the VW."

The rational mind immediately scrambles for plausible explanations: in other cultures there are all sorts of ways information gets transmitted, tom-toms, the way twigs are bent, who knows what, we accept that, even though we can't read broken twigs and tom-toms ourselves, so Maharishi got the word somehow about the VW, or about what Ram Dass was thinking, maybe he's very good at perception, in the tom-tom, broken-twig sense, a flicker from a face tells him something. Does that do it? Not quite.

A psychology professor I know had a visit with Maharishi. "People would come in, and he would make a lot of probes: you have a brother in Bombay, and the guy would say, no, Maharishi, my brother is in Delhi. Sometimes he'd guess right, and sometimes he'd guess wrong. He did have some uncanny perceptions. But all the time, I felt it was a game with him, of no importance, something he used to put people on because the word was around that he had all these strange powers."

"I know I'm pushing you hard," Ram Dass, Dr. Alpert, told a group of psychologists and psychiatrists, "but I'm just trying to give you a feeling. The game is much more interesting than we thought it was. You begin to see this entire physical plane as a training school. The minute you stop treating all of the experiences that every single being has had which don't fit in with your conceptual model of who you are and how it works as hallucinations or irrationality or psychosis or deviance, you understand it as, really, information—all of us are judging all the time, we run these things through rationally, but there are other ways of knowing."

"Who *is* this guy?" I said, to Ram Dass, of Maharishi, sounding like Butch Cassidy squinting at his pursuers.

"I don't know." Ram Dass smiled. He tapped his head. "There's nobody home."

Ram Dass had become an archetype, a metaphor himself. Kids followed him to India, around India. The Indians were a bit bewildered. "The young Americans," they said, "dance and sing kirtan all day." Kirtan are religious chants and songs. "But they're so young. Don't they know the stages? First you're a student, then you go into a profession or a business, then you become a householder, then your household grows up and doesn't need you any more, and *then* you go do kirtan all day."

At home, Ram Dass always had an audience, even with little advance notice. But the audience, like all of us, was fixed in time: now it was no longer kids, it was the kids turning thirty or even thirty-five, in other words the same group, and one day my friend the psychology professor asked his class—and this in psychology, not engineering—how many people had heard of Baba Ram Dass and only one hand went up. "It was stunning," he said, "five years ago it would have been every hand."

But that isn't the end of the story.

Some of the young journeyers to the East, rooted in the Sixties—Ram Dass's audience, Ram Dass's followers—came home and got Ph.D.'s in the psychology of meditation or in Oriental languages or something else related. And they went back to the East on postdoctoral fellowships and began to study the Eastern teachings with the tools of the paradigm, and to chart the more exotic areas of consciousness. It is interesting to read their papers, and see them translate the Eastern metaphors into the language of psychology: "hell" in the Therevadan scriptures meaning anxiety, "the hungry ghosts" meaning cravings or deficiencies, and "the frightened ghosts" meaning irrational fears. Then they found the Eastern stuff went on, and there wasn't anything to translate it with, or into. In other words, the Eastern psychologies extended on into areas not covered by ours. "The gross stuff, the heavy stuff where you can use the EEG and the EKG and so on, is all in the early stages," said one.

By pruning away at the distractions, says one paper, one could arrive at a stage with: a brilliant white light, rapturous feelings, goose flesh, the feeling of levitating, tranquillity of mind and body, devotional feelings, energy, happiness, quick and clear perception, equanimity. That stage is called Pseudo-Nirvana.

"*Pseudo*-Nirvana?" I said. "It sure sounds like the real thing."

"That's only halfway there," said my friends. They were not only into the *Visuddhimagga,* the summary of Buddha's discourses leading to purification, but, being scholars, they were into all the commentaries on the *Visuddhimagga*.

"What comes after Pseudo-Nirvana?" I asked.

"Then there are some of the darker sides of the mind, pain, dread, and so on."

"I might stop at Pseudo-Nirvana. What's beyond pain, dread, and so on?"

"Cessation of pain, dread, and finally, the cessation of everything, total consciousness, consciousness with no object. Beyond time and space."

I am so little advanced that Pseudo-Nirvana still sounded better.

And even drawing on the feelings of my most altered states, I couldn't grasp consciousness without an object. And beyond time and space, I find myself imagining, like science fiction, but there's always an observer, and a "real" time and a "real" space to come back to, and if there really isn't any observer and any time and any space, I start to get a headache and have to stop and think my hands warm.

"The supernormal powers that Western parapsychology is looking for are in the *Visuddhimagga*," said another young friend. "Telekinesis—moving objects with the mind, super-hearing, knowing the minds of others, knowing the past and future, materializing things. It describes these technically, in detail, but only as a caution that they crop up in advanced mastery, are hard to maintain, easy to break, and they're a hindrance on the path. They're a great danger to people who are still in ego and not ready for them, and masters are forbidden to display them to the laity."

"We're going to have a problem," said one scholar, "because there just aren't very many people in what we call this fifth state." The first four being waking, dreaming, sleeping, meditation. "They are hard to find and harder to deal with, and then when you do start to deal with them, the Western techniques of objectifying and cross-validating don't seem to work unless you're in some state yourself that approaches that of the one you're trying to study."

Watching my own mind, I found it saying, well, isn't that interesting, this quaint old document the *Visuddhimagga* is full of parapsychology, but then probably so are the stories of the Andean Indians and the Tibetan stories, Milarepa and Marpa, and the Bible has walking on water and isn't this all interesting Cultural Anthropology and Comparative Religion, and then a second voice would say, you're Rumpelstiltskin-ing it, if you name it and classify it, it will go away.

"There's even another problem," said the first scholar. "If you really get into this, you can lose your point of view, and then writing a paper for some academic journal seems very unimportant."

Poor Reggie has gone native, the regimental commander says of his wandering surgeon—

"Do me a favor," I said. "Just before you decide never to write about it, drop me a post card."

But I know the post card, if there ever is one, will not be like Stanley finding Livingstone.

Carlos: I Met a Man Upon a Star

Carlos Castaneda was an anthropology student the day he met Don Juan, the Yaqui sorcerer, and Carlos became the sorcerer's apprentice. Carlos became to nonordinary reality what Dickens was to the Industrial Revolution. Carlos' first book was full of acknowledgments to professors, and it was copyrighted by the Regents of the University of California: "Space does not conform to Euclidean geometry, time does form a continuous unidirectional flow, causation does not conform to Aristotelian logic, man is not differentiated from non-man or life from death," nonordinary all right, from the moment Carlos first met Don Juan outside the bus station in—was it Yuma? The book didn't say. The first book was really only noticed by the counter-culture Californians, my goodness, there was Mescalito, the spirit of the mushrooms, and the hundred-foot gnat; everybody who had ever been stoned had found another commentator.

But Carlos went on, four Don Juan books, best sellers worldwide, and Don Juan became as well known as Charlie Brown and the other Don Juan and Oliver Twist, and the more famous Don Juan got, the more obscure Carlos got. You couldn't find him: no photographs, no address—"erasing personal history." "The art of a hunter is to become inaccessible," Don Juan told Carlos. "To be inaccessible means that you touch the world around you sparingly. To be unavailable means that you deliberately avoid exhausting yourself and others. To worry is to become accessible."

Sometimes I crossed Carlos's trail, but he was inaccessible—a hunter, a warrior. When I read the books, and reread them, Don Juan sounded wise— wise as, say, a yogi or a Zen master. "What makes us unhappy is to want," said Don Juan, just like the Zen master. "To be poor or wanting is only a thought." Sometimes Don Juan also sounded like an existentialist, Albert Camus in *L'Étranger,* perhaps: "If nothing really matters, how can I go on living?" Don Juan is setting this up: "For me, there is no victory and no defeat or emptiness. Everything is filled to the brim and everything is equal . . ."

Carlos learned his "power spot," and the art of "not sitting," sound shamanistic practices. The parodists leapt into action: one found a mystical ski instructor whose "power spot" was in the bar on a stool; what he was doing was "not skiing."

Yet what Carlos was learning and what Don Juan said were by no means inconsistent with all the other visions of non-ordinary reality, funny as they sounded to the parodists. Carlos knew the UCLA anthropology library very well, and his ambition was to have a Ph.D. in anthropology, which, indeed, he did finally get for one of his books, *Journey to Ixtlan.* And now he would really like to lecture in anthropology, he set the whole field on its ear, except these freaky kids descend upon him, not listening to the anthropology jargon, but trying to see if he has mystical feet, or can disappear—

Some people bothered themselves. Was Don Juan made up? Was it a put-on? Carlos said: I could scarcely make up somebody like Don Juan. No one has ever met Don Juan, though Mexican students have scoured the State of Sonora. Carlos certainly met *somebody*, said Carlos' friends, because he is very changed, he was very shook up by Don Juan even if Don Juan doesn't turn out to talk exactly like Carlos says he does.

Unlike the students scouring the Mexican hills, I didn't want to meet Don Juan because I don't speak Yaqui or Spanish. Anyway Carlos' books stood by themselves, a dazzling performance. It was Carlos' rare interviews that interested me.

Carlos had learned the sorcerer's tricks, the terror and wonder of being alive. He had talked to a coyote and the coyote talked back. ("Coyotes are tricksters," Don Juan warned. "Snakes make better friends.") That sounds strange in cold print, though not so much to the people who had met Mescalito.

But Carlos did not live in Mexico with Don Juan, he lived in Westwood, in Los Angeles. What lessons had he brought back?

He could stop his internal dialogue, even in Los Angeles—in fact, using Los Angeles. "You can use the buzzing of the freeway to teach yourself to listen to the outside world. When we stop the world, the world we stop is the one we usually maintain by our continual inner dialogue. Once you can stop the internal babble you stop maintaining your old world. The descriptions collapse. That is when personality change begins. When you concentrate on sounds, you realize it is difficult for the brain to categorize all the sounds, and in a short while you stop trying. This is unlike visual perception which keeps us forming categories, and thinking. It is so restful when you can turn off the talking, categorizing and judging."

Carlos disrupted his routines. "It is a challenge to live with no routines in a routinary world." (Gurdjieff and the Zen master would nod.) Carlos certainly did live without routines. When he turned in a book, he would not make an appointment with his editor in New York. He would simply appear. "I think he must come in from the stairs, the fire exit, because he never passes a secretary," said Michael, his editor. If you made a date with him, he would smile, say "wonderful," and then not show up. If you did not have a date with him, he might show up and be very funny, absolutely delightful. I missed two encounters with Carlos, one on each coast. I said to Michael, the next time Carlos comes in from the stairs, will you let me know? Certainly, said Michael. But he didn't.

"Once," Carlos said, "I read a bit of the linguistic philosophy of Ludwig Wittgenstein to Don Juan and he laughed and said: 'Your friend Wittgenstein tied the noose too tight around his neck so he can't go anywhere.'"

Very good description of Wittgenstein. Wittgenstein? It would be fun to talk to Carlos. That must have been a good evening. Carlos and this wrinkled old Mexican wizard are out on the ramada of Don Juan's house, maybe smoking Mescalito's mix, or ingesting something else, or maybe Carlos is in the stage beyond that, and they are discussing reality and nonreality. Carlos is reading him Wittgenstein as evening falls. Certainly beats the port and the sherry in the crusty common rooms of Oxford.

I called Michael once, but he was out. The secretary I had been nice to said, "*He*'s here." I didn't have to ask who *he* was. I was close by. I walked to the building, pressed the elevator button, and got in. I was wondering, when he calls United or American does he give his own name? What does he read on the plane? Anthropology, maybe, he does like to lecture about phenomenology and membership and socialization.

I had an odd impulse, I got out of the elevator immediately, found the EXIT sign, and started up the stairs. A secretary passed with an armload of paper work, saving elevator time by walking one flight. Another flight—and then, down the stairs came a small, dark man, maybe five five, one forty, with a rather humorous face. Carlos? Hard to know, there are so few pictures of him. I decided it was.

I turned around and began trotting down the stairs side by side with the gentleman.

"I was just on my way to Michael's office," I said.

The gentleman nodded and did not break his pace.

"I just wanted to say," I said. I stopped. That certainly sounded feeble. "A terrific contribution. Communicates experience, not just reading about it."

The gentleman nodded and continued down the stairs.

We were going downstairs at a rapid rate, and it was obvious that this interview would not last too long.

"Wittgenstein," I said.

Now I had his interest.

"When you and Don Juan were sitting at his house reading Wittgenstein, was it the *Tractatus* or *Philosophical Investigations?*"

The gentleman grinned. "Did I say we read it? I just told him the ideas one evening. I didn't have the book along."

"Which book?"

"Either book."

We were almost to the lobby. In Carlos' last book, Don Juan teaches him the most difficult feat of all, to make a double of yourself. Another person, your duplicate. That was how Don Gennaro could be two hundred miles away and also right there, at the same time. It occurred to me that perhaps this was not Carlos. Half humorously, I said: "This may seem a silly question, but are you Carlos or Carlos' double?"

"I'm Carlos' double," said the gentleman. He laughed.

I did not want to intrude. I could have kept up with him in the lobby crowd if I had really tried, but I didn't.

Parapsych

The Phoneless Message from Cousin Josie

Well, what about this: can people really wake up at night and know that something has happened to some member of their family somewhere else? Or get some glimpse into the future? Or cause objects to fall off the shelf?

The status of parapsychology—the word loosely used to cover such events—can only be described as peculiar.

On the one hand: public interest is avid. Not only has there been a revival of interest in witches and demons, but anyone who claims some sort of extraordinary powers can usually get a public hearing on all the TV talk shows. Might even be able to get a TV show of his own going.

Such interest is probably the descendant of similar fascination with magic and with seances and wobbly ouija boards and talking to the dead.

But also: there is some growing respectability to the study of parapsychology, insofar as a hundred or so educational institutions now have a course in it, or have it as part of another course, and the study itself was finally voted into the American Association for the Advancement of Science in 1969, and a former astronaut, Edgar Mitchell, decided to devote himself to it.

I talked to Mitchell in his office in Palo Alto: Apollo

14 pictures in the background, phones ringing, crisp manner, the moon trip was a "peak experience"— Mitchell had learned the vocabulary of humanistic psychology—maybe even a mystical experience, seeing the earth sit out there like a big blue ball made Mitchell think of all the insanity on the planet, and a need for a radical change in the culture: "I knew we have untapped intuitive and psychic forces which we must utilize if we are to disregard these forces." So Mitchell formed a foundation, the Institute of Noetic Sciences, to "fuse the two modalities of organizing the universe, the objective, pragmatic modality of Western science and the subjective, intuitive approach of the great spiritual doctrines."

And, on that one hand, while parapsychology made it into the science societies and young assistant professors of psychology began to teach it to earnest and curious students and Edgar Mitchell sponsored Uri Geller—

On the other hand, the scientific establishment is still scornful enough that to work in the area labels you as slightly tetched in the head, a poor Reggie due to be sent home, and almost nobody is doing any real work at all in the area. I mean nobody. It was stunning to find out that, while *The Exorcist* could gross $70 million, and while mind readers and nail benders could reach 60 million people a night on television, there weren't twenty-five people in the country, there weren't forty in the Western world, working on parapsychology full-time.

Obviously, parapsychology is beyond the current paradigm. To extend the borders of the paradigm, or at least to look at it the same way we ordinarily look at the universe, we would have to do the following: be able to control some parapsychological events, be able to repeat them, have a hypothesis that would encompass these odd events, a theory with some predictive power, and then further experiments and events would come along and confirm the previous events and, the structure of scientific revolutions, pretty soon the borders of the paradigm would be modified and extended or, if the revolution were big enough, the old paradigm would go right into the museum and the new paradigm would tell us how to explain the world to ourselves.

The handful of serious researchers are working that way, setting up experiments that would hopefully be repeatable, but they have almost no funds. The total funding of parapsychology is less than the cost of a commercial break on a talk show where people are discussing the marvels of telepathy and psychokinesis.

So: if you woke with a start dreaming that cousin Josie was in an auto accident, and she was, just at that time, or if some flash hit you, unreasonably, about some future event which then turned out to happen, or if things fall off the shelf around you, that might be statistical chance or the powers might be real but you are way out there in the blue without a paradigm to sit in.

We've already seen that some things are possible—even repeatable—that previously weren't. Biofeedback showed that the autonomic nervous system could be consciously controlled, and very precisely, without the use of the left-brained, language-using part of the mind. Further: language shapes the way we see the world, and not all cultures have our view of time and space. (The Greeks call anyone who is exactly on time "the Englishman," you don't come for dinner at eight, you come over, and eventually dinner happens.) Maybe our language, our set, and our expectations are excluding us from what's there.

We also know that our perceptions are not only culturally conditioned, but not totally trustworthy. A single word repeated will begin to dissolve into other words. A flashing strobe light on a blank wall will make patterns begin to seem to appear on the wall. A red six of spades will be called a six of hearts.

Out of all there is to be perceived, we know we perceive very little. Here's a chart from physiological psychology, showing how much of the spectrum we can perceive:

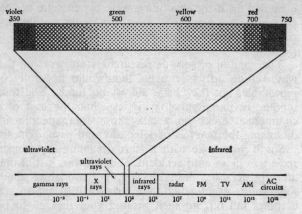

Our brains and nervous systems, it seems, act as a filter. In perception studies there is a famous paper, retitled "What the Frog's Eye Tells the Frog's Brain." Some scientists at MIT wired up frogs—brains, eyeballs and all—to see what the frog actually saw. Frogs do not see what we see; no leaves rustling in the wind, no beautiful sunsets. The frog's eye tells the frog's brain of overhead light interference—could be the shadow of a predator and that something small nearby is flying by, which could possibly be eaten. In other words, the frog's universe is screened down to the minimum needed for survival.

(Add somewhat irrelevant information from perception which might come in handy someday: elephants turn right more easily than left, if you are ever chased by an elephant, and the cobra sways back and forth to get a fix on you, and if you sway in exactly the same arc presumably he can't quite see you.)

The frog's eye/frog's brain experiment supported a more elegantly stated philosophy, coming from the French philosopher Henri Bergson and the English philosopher C. D. Broad, which says that, like the frog, we screen down. "Each person," said Broad, "is at each moment capable of remembering all that has ever happened to him and of perceiving everything that is happening in the universe. The function of the brain and nervous system is to protect us from being overwhelmed and confused by this mass of largely useless and irrelevant knowledge, by shutting out most of what we should otherwise perceive or remember at any moment, and leaving only that very small and special selection which is likely to be practically useful." Aldous Huxley wrote that screening down—his metaphor was a reducing valve—left only "a measly trickle." To express the measly trickle, we had symbols and languages, which did give us the benefits of accumulated experience. "Most people," wrote Huxley, "know only what comes through the reducing valve and is consecrated as genuinely real by the local language." The reducing valve, said Huxley, could be bypassed to some extent by "spiritual exercises," drugs, and "innate gift." "Our narrowed, individual minds regard [the measly trickle] as a complete, or at least sufficient, picture of reality," but even by by-passing the reducing valve, we only get a glimpse of the Mind at Large.

Huxley and Broad, in fact, anticipated the world-renowned neurophysiologists Moruzzi in Italy and Eccles in Australia and the U.S. "There is now evidence," wrote Eccles, "that at any one time we are only conscious of an extremely small fraction of the immense sensory input that is pouring into our brains. In fact, by far the greater part of the activity in the brain, and even in the cerebral cortex, does not reach consciousness at all. However, we have the ability to direct our attention apparently at will to one or another element in the input from our sense organs."

Parapsychology attempts to measure the stuff outside the filter.

Some years ago, a botanist-turned-psychologist, J. B. Rhine, got a grant from the Rockefeller Foundation to work, in his lab in Durham, North Carolina, on people's ability to sense what card is about to be turned up. (Durham has been the center of research in parapsychology ever since.) Rhine's experiments said that some of his subjects guessed the right cards far beyond the range of probability.

There was some controversy about both the method and the statistics, but the experiments were repeated with better controls. At one point, there was even an argument by mathematicians: perhaps the laws of probability were wrong, and needed some tuning up.

The handful of serious parapsychologists, knowing the suspicion that greets any experiments which have no paradigm to support them, set up quite careful controls. Helmut Schmidt, a former physicist working in Durham, tested the ability of subjects to guess which of four lamps would light up, the lighting up of the lamps being random, and the source of that randomness being the emission of elementary particles from radioactive materials. No hands, no chance for cuing or human error. Some of the subject, said Schmidt, made predictive guesses with the probability against chance being 10 million to 1.

At Maimonides Medical Center in New York, Dr. Montague Ullman designed an exponent to cut down on the distraction by all the other noise; such as we don't perceive the signals of telepathy. Ullman tried two undistracted states for his experiments, sleep and blank out in ganzfeld.

In the sleep experiments, a "sender," or a volunteer, a student, a research assistant, a doctoral candidate, would concentrate on a particular picture or print. When the sleeper's psychophysiology showed that he was dreaming—the right EEG reading, and rapid eye movements—he would be woken and would dictate his dreams into a tape recorder. In the morning he would be asked to rate various prints and pictures according to the way they most matched the dream material; various double-blind procedures would be set up to protect the experiment.

I offered myself as a subject for the blank out in ganzfeld. Over the eyes went the split ping-pong balls. Over the ears went the earphones to produce the "white noise." I sat in an easy chair. The "sender" went into an electromagnetically shielded soundproof room. You can't see anything but a diffused white light with those ping-pong balls over your eyes. You get some instructions on the earphones and then off you go, dictating into a small microphone around your neck, free association, anything you see or think.

If your eyes are open but can see only a diffused light, you still get images. I got some geometric shapes, some V's, some interlocked circles flowing by. I dictated continuously, there go some more forms . . . looks like birds flying . . . geese, maybe . . . shrinking circles, imploding.

But by this time, after two years of full-time research and a dozen years of guinea-pigging, my language-using, classifying mind arrived quickly, sounding, as usual, professorial and knowing—

—yep, here we are with geometric shapes again, now that might be from some ocular pressure, as in Barber's paper on the hallucinogens, or that might be from the phosphenes on the eyelids, isn't that interesting.

There goes a shape, I dictated, looks like . . . Mickey Mouse . . . Mickey Mouse's ears, floating by. There are . . . Mickey Mouse's ears again . . . south-southeast, five knots . . .

After a little less than an hour, the ping-pong balls were untaped and the earphones taken off, and I went to look at the pictures the "sender" had been sending. One looked terribly familiar. It was a Disney character, Pinocchio. I reached out for it. Wait, said the interior voice in my ear. Is that close to Mickey Mouse? Mickey Mouse's ears? It really looks the most familiar, but cartoon images are common in sensory deprivation experiences, Mickey Mouse isn't Pinocchio, Pinocchio looks familiar because almost all Disney characters look familiar, especially if you once saw the movie, that black crow in the second picture, we had a black crow shape, didn't we? Looks certainly like one of those black shapes, pick the black crow.

The "sender" had been sending Pinocchio. First hunch right.

Another writer, Francine Gray, saw, once they taped on the split ping-pong balls, images of Arabs in robes, long-gowned ministers, Orthodox priests, and immediately picked, once her experiment was over, a slide of Arabs in long white robes. That was a "direct hit"; my scores were only five out of ten. Her reaction to her "direct hit" was one of anxiety: "a serious headache, blurred vision, perspiration, dizziness, trouble sleeping." "When my view of reality is undermined by something as anomalous as a psychic event, I am in a world of chaos in which no place seems safe," she said. "I realized that this was one of the reasons why parapsychology has tended to remain such an ill-funded, fragile, suspect field of science. We are increasingly titillated by Edgar Cayce, pop ESP courses at the local Y, showman spoon-benders on TV and the whole surge of paperback occultism; but the experience of having our latent psychic capacities confirmed in a laboratory leads to a deep and primitive anxiety from which we tend to withdraw very quickly."

The Maimonides experiments were one of only two ever to be funded by the National Institutes of Mental Health, but they, too, ran out of money. There was money available from rich widows who wanted to talk to their dead husbands, but little for experiments. Somehow the experiments were boring, except to people interested in parapsychology. The "direct hits" seemed open to other interpretations, and the statistics were, well, statistics.

I have an innate bias about statistics anyway, which comes from watching very learned economists miss the gross national product by $150 billion. There's always one more equation. But that's my problem; if the chances of a hit are one in 10 million, the only defects can be in the definition of a hit, and in the probability statistics, but even if the chances aren't one in 10 million, they're certainly better than fifty-fifty.

Parapsychology wasn't helped, in its fragile state, when one of its most promising experimenters was found to have tampered with the machine that produced random impulses for shocking rats on a grid. And, ultimately, the whole Uri Geller adventure may have been a setback.

Uri: Instructions from the Saucer

Uri Geller, a handsome, six-foot three-inch former Israeli paratrooper, left a trail of broken forks and bent nails across the television talk shows, all done with some mysterious powers. His credibility came, at least in part, from the fact that he had been tested at the Stanford Research Institute, a think tank in Menlo Park, California, that was once associated with Stanford University, and now works on the things that think tanks largely supported by the government work on—Russian missile capabilities, and so on. His credibility was further enhanced because it was Captain Mitchell who brought him to both Stanford Research and the TV shows.

I asked Mitchell what the reaction was of NASA to his current project.

"NASA has an engineering mentality," he said, "so they're slightly embarrassed by it. It doesn't fit the paradigm of engineering. They come in from time to time, because all the astronauts had some sort of experience like mine, seeing the earth as a tiny insignificant globe in a vast cosmos, knowing there is some sort of direction where science says there isn't, and that knowing isn't intellectual. Not all the astronauts had reactions like mine—as soon as the heavy tasks were over, on the way home, I had this alternating pathos and ecstasy, hard to describe—but all of them had something, only it surfaced through whatever belief structure they had."

Captain Mitchell had a Ph.D. in engineering; if the so-called "Geller effects" turned out to be true, what was that going to do to engineering and physics?

"Oh, it will expand it, like Einstein did to Newtonian physics. I see it as bimodal, rather than as opposing points of view."

And why was he leading Uri to TV?

"The networks say it sells, and it helps to get the point of view across. I don't think Geller has any idea of why his things work, there just seems to be some sort of channel open that normally gets blocked."

That was the way Geller was regarded at Stanford Research, too, as a kind of *naif,* a prima donna, very difficult to deal with, but who had a channel open that normally gets blocked. The rest of us all have corks in our channels. The scientists who were testing Geller were no rat-runners, they were laser physicists. In the unwritten hierarchy of science, laser physics gets more points than rat-running. Physicists Hal Puthoff and Russell Targ had some funny stories about other people with ESP.

"When people heard we were working on ESP," said Hal, "we got all kinds of visitors. A wife brought in her husband, this truckdriver. He was in despair, they were about to lock him up. He claimed he could hear voices, the neighbors, talking about him. Turned out he *did* hear the neighbors talking about him. He could also see things in other rooms. We tested him on some standard stuff, symbols in envelopes in another room. He tested brilliantly. The doctors put him on Thorazine and he stopped hearing and seeing things and went back to work, the abilities only came back if he stopped the Thorazine."

"We had a four-year-old kid," said Russell, "who would get dressed up because, he said, Aunt Pearl was coming, and the mother would say Aunt Pearl is in Cincinnati, and then Aunt Pearl would walk in unexpectedly. The mother wanted the kid turned off, it was a bother."

"ESP hasn't been trained out of kids," Hal said. "We agree on the physical universe and we don't agree on the power of thought, so we're trapped in the physical universe. But this stuff is growing. By the end of the century, everybody will be in some subculture that brings in the subjective."

Geller's public appearances were generally concerned with making metal objects bend: forks, spoons, big nails. I was surprised to find that he had never done this at Stanford Research—the impression from television, from the coupling of his metal-bending performance with the words "Stanford Research" and "scientists," was that he had been locked up in a Faraday cage, shielded from all contact and interference. There, by some mysterious power, he melted forks.

"We were all set up with rings to bend," Hal said, "but it's never happened."

"Why not?"

"Well, a lab situation is different from a public performance, where he can get people's energies working, he's used to having people watch, controlling them, being relaxed."

What had he done in the lab, if he hadn't bent any metal? Well, he'd generated a magnetic field, and affected the roll of dice, carefully controlled, and made numerous telepathic hits.

How did he do that?

"He says he visualizes a TV screen, and then he reports what comes in on the screen. He thinks the flying saucer people give him the right answers. The other day, a flying saucer was one of the images we had in another room. He kept saying, I'm not getting it, I'm not getting it, and he kept seeing the image of a flying saucer, he was supposed to draw whatever image came through, and finally the flying saucer people whirled by again and said, 'It's *us* this time, dummy, draw *us!*' He drew a flying saucer."

"He was exhibiting ESP, though, before he began to talk about the flying saucer people. Then somebody suggested that to him, and he used it as an explanation. Psychics don't know where their powers come from, or why, and they're afraid they'll go away, so they make up these things, and sometimes they cheat."

A magazine article had suggested that Geller cheated.

"He cheats, he cheats a lot, and also he's real," said one of the physicists.

We were at SRI—security guards, escorts, badges, not because of this research but because of the stuff in other parts of the buildings. Geller was happy with his day at the lab. He had scored a lot of telepathic hits.

"I am feeling good today. The vibrations are very good."

Did he, I wanted to know, use any alcohol or drugs? No, never. Was there anything he could affect besides metal? No, just metal. When he wanted to get a metal ring to break, how did he break it?

"I just concentrate and say, 'Break!' and it breaks."

Geller's demeanor was boyish and enthusiastic.

"I don't know how I do it, I don't know why it happens, I am some sort of a channel."

Right then, he was more interested in cars and girls than in academic discussion of the paranormal. I found I was more interested in the physicists than in Geller. I noted the contents of a bookcase in one of the offices: three full shelves of books on quantum mechanics, light, lasers, masers, all standard physics stuff, and then the anomalies—Jung, *Witchcraft and Magic*.

I spent some time with the physicists.

"When Uri comes to dinner," said one of the wives, "I have to be sure to put the good silver away. He melts forks unconsciously, he can't help it." She showed me a fork Uri had been eating with. It certainly looked melted and twisted.

"Things happen around Uri," said one of the physicists who was not on the project. "We were walking to the parking lot one day, and a large rock fell at our feet out of a clear blue sky."*

"We have all kinds of crazy things on videotape, watches falling out of the ceiling, poltergeists."

"You know," said Hal, "Mitchell left his camera on the moon. It was really a bit embarrassing, they mentioned it on all the subsequent moonshots. So Uri was going to try to bring it back. All kinds of Mitchell stuff began to materialize around him. He dug his spoon into ice cream one day and found a tiepin Mitchell had been missing for two years. Gradually, Mitchell's jewelry box in Texas began to fill up with everything he'd lost, cuff links, tieclasps, stuff gone for years."

"But no camera."

"No, the camera's still up there."

"Do you have any way of explaining this?"

"Modern physics isn't capable of explaining it. On the other hand, equations in physics permit many things that are just ignored, for the time being. Advanced potential models correspond to precognition, some of the waves would start in the future to arrive now. The equations permit it, but the physics textbooks discard the part that runs from the future to the present. Superconductivity has lots of unused equations.

* In the eighteenth century, the French Academy passed a special resolution saying it would reject all further reports of rocks falling out of the sky.

In wave functions, there are particles slower than light, and protons and neutrinos as fast as light, and the equations permit tachyons, which would be faster than light."

"But nobody's found a tachyon."

"Not yet."

"So the right equations might be lying dormant somewhere."

"Sure. We don't know how things happen; every year the laws get violated, and then we say, well, that was good until now."

"But aren't equations just another language, with their own constraints? There's always an equal sign in the middle."

"I think," Hal said, "what we're going to end up with is that thought is senior to physics."

"Sir James Jean did say," I said, "that the universe was looking more like a big thought than a big machine."

"It may be that what we think is real, the physical universe, is an interference pattern in the thought world, the basic ether or tachyon seed or what have you."

The boys were losing me.

"I'm convinced," Hal said, "there are Superintelligences."

"Well, who is it when they appear?"

"Oh, spirits, gods, archangels, large thoughts—"

"There was an ex-Jesuit priest in one of my courses," I said, "who meditated about five hours a day, and could leave his body, and always contacted the same archangel."

"Did he get any good data?" Russell said.

"I asked him," I said, "and he said, no, they mostly went to the beach."

"MacGowan's paper said there were ten *billion* inhabitable planets in this galaxy alone. Some of them are bound to be more advanced than us. Now what would you do if you found Earth? Anthropologists know you don't just lay one culture on another, you'd shock the more primitive one and destroy it. So, maybe they see us as a Skinner box, or like a wild game preserve—"

"Wait, wait—who's They?"

"They—they're probably part robot and part organic, we already know how to make artificial hearts and kidneys, and computers that simulate brains, it wouldn't be hard to see a more advanced being partly mechanical, partly organic, and of course with mechanical evolution time would be much less of a problem."

"So what would the Superintelligences be doing?"

"Oh, monitoring, not hitting us right off, maybe giving us little hints that they're there—some astronomers have noticed signals coming back thirty seconds later, as if they were bounced right back—"

I wanted to know more about the earth as a wild game preserve. I was charmed by the idea that maybe we were considered a national park by the gentlemen from Krypton.

"It's also possible," said one of the SRI physicists not on the ESP project, "that the earth is a prison planet."

"The earth is a prison planet?"

"That this backwash is where entities are sent who are out of harmony."

I looked around. I was having a violent attack of ambiguity. On the one hand, the gentlemen sitting with me at a Chinese restaurant on the peninsula south of San Francisco had Ph.D.'s in physics and established reputations in physics. On the other hand, I wished that some of them hadn't been into Scientology and their subjects into it too, and some of them into Eastern stuff. Why couldn't they be 4-H Club straight, ordinary physicists? Were they kidding? No, they weren't kidding, they knew how it sounded—it was just a hypothesis, mind you—but it was obviously something they'd talked about among themselves before.

"This all sounds like *2001*, science fiction," I said.

"Whatever is real may come up more strange than *2001*," they said.

Part of me was saying, let's get out of here, they are all crazy, Ph.D.'s or no, wiggy people have Ph.D.'s, and another part was totally fascinated. I began to feel a little dizzy. It must have been the monosodium glutamate in the Chinese food.

Randi: A Prestidigitation of Magicians

I went to see Uri whenever he performed publicly and I was around; by this time I knew a lot of people in the audience. Uri was to try to guess a color we were all thinking. He turned away, and a woman wrote "blue" on the blackboard, and then erased it. "Okay, I'm going to take a chance. The color I get is blue." The audience applauded wildly. Uri cut off the applause. He pointed to one corner of the audience. "Who over here," he said, "was sending yellow?" A young man, somewhat sheepishly, raised his hand. "Please don't do that," Uri said, "it confuses me." The man apologized.

Volunteers came forward with rings and pins and keys. Uri would try to bend them, or break them. He said objects of emotional attachment would be of the most value. He couldn't guarantee success, he was tired, from trying to focus his mental powers before senior physicists. We should all be "with" him, send him our own psychic energies. He tried bending rings by putting them in the hands of volunteers and then passing his hands over theirs. It didn't work. We were watching on a television monitor. The audience got a bit restive.

"It's not working," Uri said. "It's not going to work." Plainly, it was not going to come. I knew how he felt; It had that tennis serve that wouldn't come if you wanted it. "Wait—" Uri said. "There? Isn't one broken? No?" No. "Wait—there! There! Didn't it break?" One of the rings, indeed, had broken, though it was hard to tell, on the television monitor.

For hubris, there is nemesis, for matter, there is antimatter, and for Uri Geller, there was James Randi, a bearded, roguish, saucy magician I ran into on the streets of New York. Randi's fame had taken an upward turn from being an anti-Geller.

"He's a magician," Randi said. "It was careless of

them not to know. Physicists are easier to fool than anybody."

"All that metal bending—"

Randi reached for my keys, and began to stroke one of them.

"He couldn't perform on the Carson show because I got to Carson, and we didn't let him bump the table with all the little canisters on them," Randi said. "Then he went on the Griffin show, and Griffin said, ladies and gentlemen, here's a man who failed before thirty-five million people, and that's good enough for me, and the audience cheered."

My office key was beginning to bend.

"Cut that out," I said. The office key continued to bend.

"Bend it back, I don't have another one," I said. Randi reversed it and the office key began to bend the other way.

"We had a bunch of magicians at his last performance. We were laughing. I've videotaped all his shows so I can analyze his tricks."

The office key was bending too much the other way.

"Can't you get the damn thing like it was at first?" I said. "It won't open the door that way."

Randi handed the key back. We were sitting in a restaurant. Absent-mindedly, Randi held a spoon, which began to bend.

"He's very good, though, very, very good," Randi said. "He's one of the best I've ever seen."

"Could I learn to bend a spoon like that?"

"Sure," said Randi, and he showed me.

All of Randi's processes involve what psychologists call cognitive dissonance. You're used to seeing things a certain way, so you continue to see them, and if you have a spoon in the hands, you can make your hands appear to hold the spoon in a way other than they really are, while you give it some pressure.

"Now, watches, Geller starts stopped watches. That's easy. Would you like to move your own watch ahead an hour by mental powers? Let's see—what time have you got? Hold your watch face down in the palm of your hand—that's right—now keeping a circle going on the watch-back with your finger—that's good, that's good—"

Randi began to imitate Geller. He frowned, as if in fierce concentration. "It's not going to work, no, please, you must be with me, somebody is sending me bad vibrations, please everybody send me good vibrations, I don't think I can do it today, I was up all night with the Nobel prize winners, wait, wait, maybe it's going to work—"

The imitation was almost cruel; Randi really had the cadences down.

"Now, look at your watch. I think we have moved it an hour ahead by sheer mental powers."

The watch was an hour ahead. I was mystified. How the hell did that happen? Randi wouldn't show me. He must have gotten a thumbnail on the watch stem at some point, probably when he said, let's see, what time is it, but I sure didn't see it.

"And the telepathy?"

"Some telepathy involves a little pencil point in the thumbnail, and some a quick look at the blackboard when everybody's distracted, and some involves handling the envelopes."

"Is there anything Geller can do that you can't?"

"Yes. I told you, he's very very good—but I'm working on it."

Again I felt a curious ambiguity. If Geller was just a magician, I was disappointed not to have a box seat when the paradigm changed. But there was also a little feeling of relief, that maybe the world was still the way we thought—

—yet the scientist who got a Nobel prize for his work in measuring and clocking impulses in the nervous system, Sir John Eccles, wrote, "I think telepathy is still a tenable belief, but if it exists at all, it provides an extremely imperfect and inefficient way of transferring information from the neural activity of one brain. . . ."

A book came out about Geller. It said that Geller got his instructions from an orbiting computer called Spectra, from the planet Hoova. People began to lose interest.

I had a long talk with a friend of Randi's, Ray Hyman, who teaches a course called Pseudo Psychologies at the University of Oregon.

"They have me billed as a skeptic," Hyman said. "All I want is to get the kids to ask the right questions. Most people are so ignorant of the roles of perception and memory that they don't know what's rare and what's ordinary. The kids have been so oriented to think that the Establishment is lying about everything that they think anything the Establishment excludes must be considered, in this case the scientific establishment. It takes patience to know the phenomena. Young generations are very experience-oriented, and they would rather have the clarity of some experience than something empirically tested, they're almost antiscientific. Sometimes there is a causal explanation. Forty years ago the parapsychologists said bats had ESP, and the antiparapsychologists said they were crazy. Now we know the bats have a sophisticated sonar system, but before radar there was no way to explain it. Two hundred years ago, when the scientific establishment rejected Mesmer's animal magnetism, it also rejected the powers of suggestion which animal magnetism explained. There may be something important going on, and maybe the statistical model doesn't apply. But I don't see very much clearheaded work."

Some psychologists—as opposed to physicists—at Stanford Research Institute tested Geller, and reported to a psychology newsletter, without much fanfare, that they had come up with nothing. The vibes must have been bad. Wherever Geller went, a gaggle of magicians followed, eager to claim him as one of their own.

"Unlike magicians, it doesn't always work for me," said Uri. "That proves I'm real."

"Parapsychology experiments in general, and the Geller experiments in particular, have been set up without adequate controls and with many unconscious biases," said Martin Gardner, a *Scientific American* columnist and amateur magician, "and with no knowledge of magic."

Wherever Geller went, people either wanted to believe very badly or wanted to disbelieve very badly. I found myself sliding into indifference. For I know that I am very easily fooled. Show me a red six of spades and I will call it the six of hearts. Play a tape of a single word over and over and I will hear other words. Sometimes I even see carrots in midair in a ganzfeld room.

And I wasn't really interested in learning magic. I would like to be able to move the hands of your watch ahead an hour, but not enough to spend more than ten minutes learning it, and I know it's in the big magic book you can send away for, or learn from somebody else once you're in the magician's union.

These phenomena, say the ESP fans, are fragile, the people who are "sensitives" don't know where the stuff comes from, and they are frequently erratic and emotional people who sometimes even cheat because they don't know what turns it off and on.

And the hard-nosed stick-to-the-paradigm people say: no experiment yet has turned up any real psychic phenomena that can't be otherwise explained. To convince the hard-nosed, you would have to have a "sensitive" on one coast, another on the other coast, both monitored for any gismos and tiny walkie-talkies, and then one of them would send Watson-come-here-I-want-you and the other would not only get it, but would send back What-hath-God-wrought. Then the physicists would dump over a bin of unused equations and pick some pretty ones that matched up what had just happened.

Ingo, it seemed, could go anyplace, right while sitting there drinking coffee and smoking a cigar.

Ingo was described as a "sensitive" and a "talented psychic."

It made a certain amount of sense that some people should be more sensitive than others. Some people have absolute pitch, they can sing you a middle G with exactly the right amplitude, and some people are tone-deaf. What Ingo could do is called "remote viewing." You give the psychic or sensitive a place, described by the coordinates, latitude thus and longitude thus, and zooop off he goes, and then describes it—it's an island shaped like this in the Indian Ocean, nobody's ever heard of it, he draws a map that's almost it, not quite, but you can see the resemblance. I didn't see Ingo do this, but I was at a seminar where it was reported having been done in the lab, and later I asked Ingo how he did it. Ingo was amused by the whole procedure. Ingo is a former clerk who is now an artist. He began by studying astrology so he could get along with people. I thought, when I first talked to him, that he was from the South, he sounds like the bachelor gentlemen you meet from the South, but he is from Utah.

"I just get the description, and then I let it happen," Ingo said.

"Does it take any time?"

"No, no time at all. It's not the same dimension."

"Did anything in particular equip you to do this sort of travel?"

"Well, your mind says it's not possible, and if you think it isn't possible, then it isn't possible. So you have to clear out your mind of its disbeliefs and open it to any sort of experience, and that takes hours and hours of work, clearing out the unconscious."

Scientology again, all those hours of "auditing," recitation, what's the last time you remember this, what's the time before that, on back into previous lives. Ingo had been heavily into Scientology, like one of the physicists testing him.

I asked Ingo when he first noticed he had some talent in this area. Ingo said his chinchilla could read his mind; when the time came to put him in his cage, his chinchilla disappeared. And then he could read his chinchilla's mind. Something like that.

Ingo was getting impatient with the lab work. "I *may* just dematerialize *every*thing," Ingo said.

Ingo, said the SRI physicists, had been to the back side of the moon before the astronauts, and described it just like they found it. Ingo had been to Jupiter, they were going to check that one out with the Pioneer fly-by.

"What did Ingo see when he went to Jupiter?"

"Oh, gases and clouds and things."

Ingo had been to Mercury, too. He noticed a magnetic field that surprised the scientists.

"NASA is very excited about Ingo's trips," said one of his fans, not a scientist.

I decided to check this with NASA, about six different officials and a lot of phone calls. NASA disclaimed any excitement over Ingo's trips. In fact, they disclaimed the knowledge of Ingo's trips.

"You wouldn't expect them to admit it, would you?" said Ingo's fans. "Not only is it secret, it might affect their funding." The files did show that a NASA official, a couple of years ago, said both NASA and the Soviet Academy of Sciences were studying "energy transfer" and "psycho-physiological information transfer," which sounds like telepathy and astral travel to those that translate that way.

NASA called back.

"We did sponsor an experiment in this area," said the NASA man, "to see whether unusual man-machine learning existed, whether a subject could determine how a randomly lit machine was going to light, determined by a computer."

The idea that it was a machine determined by a computer was important to the NASA man.

"I just wanted to see if Ingo's trip to Jupiter matched yours," I said.

"Oh, Lord," said the NASA man. "We only sponsored this thing with the random computer machine, I don't know anything about these ESP space trips, all our space trips use standard rocketry and telemetry. Those guys at SRI tried to tell us about this 'remote viewing,' but that's not part of the contract. There seems to be some controversy about the results."

The NASA official was getting more and more uncomfortable.

"I suppose we have to be open," he said, "but I have a hard time with this stuff."

"Did you know Ingo went to Mercury?"

"No, I didn't know, I don't want to know, and please don't tell me. We didn't sponsor that. All our probes use regular old rockets."

There was a certain air of put-on about Ingo, which his friends said he adopted for protection.

"Ninety-five percent of all so-called psychics are frauds," Ingo said. "You can't believe what some people will believe."

I wanted to know about the other 5 percent. Ingo shrugged. He said he didn't want to be a laboratory subject any more, he wanted to make some money. He had some premonitions about the economy, and he wanted to know how to capitalize on it. His premonitions were that a terrible depression was just around the corner, which was not an unusual opinion at that time, and that gold would go to $2,000 an ounce. That one was easy; if gold is $150 or $170 and chaos will take it to $2,000, it's a buy.

Then an opportunity did come up for Ingo to make some money. He went dowsing for oil. In dowsing for water, you carry a forked stick, and when it turns down, you start digging. Ingo didn't carry a forked stick in dowsing for oil. He just walked around over the territory that had been mapped.

"There are so many substrata already mapped, but nobody's sure," he said, "so if I just increase the percentages a bit, that's well worth it. But the places you have to go are just awful, very muddy, Louisiana and Texas and Tennessee, and there are a lot of bugs."

To go oil dowsing, Ingo went physically, getting his shoes muddy. The man who hired him was William Keeler, the former chairman of Phillips Petroleum.

Ingo was always pleasant, but also reluctant to talk about his abilities. People would misunderstand too readily. (He is, however, writing several books.)

Perhaps he is right to be reluctant. I started to think: if Ingo can go anyplace on earth with just a latitude and a longitude, if he can go to Jupiter and Mercury and other galaxies just by having his mind clear, think what he could do with an address and a zip code. Why, he could come right to my house, uninvited—not that he isn't pleasant, mind you—and not even have to ring the doorbell. The only people who have come to my house without walking in a door or a window are Santa Claus and the Tooth Fairy, who leaves a quarter under your pillow if you leave him-or-her a tooth, and in a sense both of them were invited, and neither has been around for a while.

So Ingo is well advised to be cautious. A Swedish lady sued Uri Geller; his vibrations, she said, bent the metal coil she used as a birth-control device, and she got pregnant.

I know the appeal of telepathy and clairvoyance and psychokinesis; it is a harmonic of one of our myths, the toddler from the planet Krypton who grows up to be Superman, and the success of that story itself shows how well it resonates with some unconscious theme. People who are titillated by the popular occult assume that somehow the telepathy works *for* you, like a super-shortwave radio, telling you something you need to know. But what if the bad guys had the radio station, and you couldn't turn it off?

Our models for what is possible come largely from nineteenth-century physics. Parapsychology isn't possible in that physics, and if it is, it comes off as some sort of Jules Verne fiction, telepathy like mental radio and psychokinesis like a mental laser, and Jules Verne is fiction.

Two years after my first trip to Stanford Research, I was back there again. Uri and Ingo had come and gone. The magazines and newspapers that dote on psychic phenomena continued to report bent spoons and flying saucers. The editors of the Establishment press had sent the reporters to find What the Dupes Are Falling for Now, printed that story, and gone on to other things. Hal Puthoff and Russell Targ had published a paper in *Nature,* a British science journal so august its editor is addressed in the third person. The journal noted editorially that no spoons bent under laboratory conditions, repeated a criticism of the way the experiment had been set up, and then praised the effort. Science, it said, has to be open, at least this is a start. *The New York Times* wrote an editorial saying the same thing. Stanford Research, with millions in government contracts, continued to back its two oddball physicists at some risk.

I still wasn't that interested in psychic phenomena. As a real skeptic, I did a ten-minute "remote viewing" exercise. Puthoff went off into some far corner of one of the buildings and I was to describe where he was. I was sitting with my eyes shut. I had difficulty separating imagination and remote viewing. The first item that floated into vision was a metallic object, chrome-plated, hinged, attached to a vertical surface, like a door. I described it—you can hear this on the tape—as looking like a stapler, except that one part was curved. Then I went on: tan metal cabinet, large room, safety poster. After ten minutes we shut off the tape recorder and went to where Puthoff sat. I had never been in that part of the building. Tan metal cabinet, table, safety poster. So what, I said, all the offices of Stanford Research have that equipment. I had, after all, been to Stanford half a dozen times.

It was the chrome-plated stapler that jarred me. It turned out to be the handle on the door of a small refrigerator in the middle of the lab. No other lab rooms I had seen had a refrigerator, or a handle like that.

"Not bad," Hal said.

I felt like I had just seen the clock on the wall of the fourth-grade classroom. But I was still rationalizing it, and I was more interested in the possible rationale than some blip like that on a personal screen. So I was interested in the papers of Dr. Evan Harris Walker, a physicist at the U.S. Army Ballistic Research Laboratories, Aberdeen Proving Ground, Maryland 21005. It's a measurement problem in quantum mechanics, said Dr. Walker. Quantum mechanics "is entirely at odds with our common sense conception of the physical world, but this is the correct picture of reality."

It certainly is at odds. Common sense would tell you you can't have two things in the same place at the same time, but quantum mechanics permits it. And: a textbook example, you are in a car on a roller coaster, but the roller coaster has been built wrong and there isn't enough energy to get you over the next hill. Can you get there? Sure, if the next dip is lower, it's called "tunneling." It must work, the products are right at our fingertips. The telephone company's computer that direct-dials and bills the calls contains descendants of the tunnel diode.

Just in case you are into physics, Dr. Walker's rationale uses the state vector, ψ, of the Schrödinger equation. The observer can bias the probabilities, so the observer has to be quantified. It gets harder from there: "Hidden variables interconnect events in different locations in space and time but those variables do not have any functional dependence on the space-time separation of the events." This extension of the Copenhagen interpretation of quantum theory is based on "consciousness as a quantum mechanical event."

I read parts of Dr. Walker's papers to some particle physicists. "Hidden variables can explain lots of things," they said. They weren't turned on.

Dr. Walker gave a talk on physics to a TM group, and met the Maharishi. "As one might expect," he reported, "the Maharishi is an esthetic mystic who burns quantities of musk-flavored incense and speaks about the beauty of how the sap rises in the flower." Two weeks later, a TM functionary called up to get a copy of the talk. "When I hung up the phone," reported Dr. Walker, "the office suddenly was filled with the strong odor of musk incense. Of course, I was not perturbed too much by this since I am aware of the psychological factors that can cause one to reexperience characteristics of past events. As I was rationalizing on this point, my office mate, Dr. Serge Zaroodny, entered and instantly asked, 'What is that odor? Who has been burning incense?' The whole affair struck me as amusing and certainly odd."

The paper in *Nature* helped the atmosphere in the scientific community—for one thing, it cleaned up the magic tricks—but it did not raise any money. The number of serious researchers was headed in the direction of zero, and the old paradigm stood like a fortress with only tiny cracks.

The Last Paradigm?

There are some who believe we are evolving, as Teilhard de Chardin said, in some mysterious way, toward total consciousness, the noösphere, or toward a Hegelian synthesis. There are some who believe we are evolving toward hell in a hand basket, using up all the world's resources at an accelerating rate, running out of energy and the ability to control our destiny. The two views aren't necessarily at odds, though those on the hilltop waiting for the world to end tomorrow morning run the risk of looking sheepish if they have to come back down to town and buy bread at the bakery. We do know the world is changing at an accelerating rate.

It is very hard to extrapolate another paradigm because we use the one we have. Is the current paradigm the last paradigm? Maybe it is, but that was what the cardinals thought who tried Galileo and found him guilty and silenced him.

"Bosh, Dr. Jung." "You Are Mistaken, Dr. Freud."

Here on the far side of the paradigm, the air is a bit thin and inclines us to dizziness. We keep looking in the guidebook to see where we are: if we have come this far, and this is Tuesday, then this must be Belgium. We see things through the belief structures we already have.

If we are rational and skeptical, then we will be wary of the Alchemist and all his cohorts. No shortage of Alchemists these days. No experiments have been carefully enough controlled and proved. There are still some unknowns, but they will become known by the same methods that have made so many unknowns known.

If we are not so rational and skeptical, or had an aunt who could do weird things, then we forgive the eccentric psychics the way we forgive a prima donna for her antics, she still has that voice. That the Establishment frowns is all the more reason to believe; the Establishment filters out what it wants to believe anyway, just like the rest of us.

This division is not new. Carl Jung, the pioneer of psychiatry, said he refused "to commit the fashionable stupidity of regarding everything I cannot explain as a fraud." He experimented with all sorts of things, and in one famous incident, a heavy walnut table, an old heirloom, split during a seance, and soon afterwards a bread knife in a drawer snapped into four pieces "like a pistol shot."

In 1909 Jung went to see Freud, his senior and the acknowledged parent of psychiatry. They were talking about something you can't see, can't hear, and that has, in the terms of physics, no weight, no mass, no velocity—the unconscious. The skeptics considered it bordering on alchemy. And during one conversation, Jung felt a curious sensation in his diaphragm. "At that moment there was such a loud report in the bookcase, which stood right next to us, that we both started up in alarm, fearing the thing was going to topple over us. I said to Freud: 'There, that is an example of a so-called catalytic exteriorization phenomenon.' "

Freud wasn't having any. "That is sheer bosh," he said to Jung.

"It is not," said Jung.

(Nice dialogue between the giants.)

" 'You are mistaken, Herr Professor,' " says Jung, in his own account. " 'And to prove my point I now predict that in a moment there will be another loud report!' Sure enough, no sooner had I said the word than the same detonation went off in the bookcase. To this day I do not know what gave me this certainty. But I knew beyond all doubt the report would come again. Freud only stared aghast at me. I do not know what was in his mind, or what his look meant. In any case, this incident aroused his mistrust of me, and I had the feeling that I had done something against him."

Freud was, indeed, much more cautious. He wrote on parapsychology, but never published the papers; they appeared after his death.

The sober old American Society for Psychical Research, distressed by the boom in psychic interest that somehow did not extend to any serious research, did a survey of bookstores. In some anguish, it reported that 97 percent of what was on the shelves in this area was "occult" and more properly placed in fiction; only 3 percent was genuine psychical research. The rest is This Way to the Egress. Use Healing Rays to Repair the Body! Attract All the Money You Need! Influence the Thoughts of Others! Transform Your Surroundings! Predict Future Events!

I have little trouble with any of these exhortations. Influence the thoughts of others: you dolt, you really don't have it together, do you, and watch where you're stepping. Transform your surroundings: paint, soap, brush, mop. Attract all the money you need: but do you need what you think you need? what is need? what is you? Use healing rays to repair the body: they aren't rays, but the body always heals itself, the physician only sets it up, the medicine only helps. Predict future events: that's easy, the hard part is making the event match the prediction. Shakespeare, *Henry IV*:

GLENDOWER: I can call spirits from the
  vasty deep.
HOTSPUR: Why, so can I, or so can
  any man;
        But will they come when you do call
for them?

What Cell Goes There?

The spirits of the vasty deep are still at large, and there are mysteries that seem like ESP which fall into other sciences. Consider:

We had at our house some Baltimore orioles, the gentleman a handsome orange-and-black fellow with an abnormal space in the leading edge of one wing, where he had run into a twig while dodging a hawk or coming home late after finding some fermenting juniper berries, nothing more serious than a dented fender. Orioles have a distinctive nest which hangs like a purse on the very end of a branch, quite a piece of engineering. One day, the summer's work done, the orioles were packing up to depart. The questioners in the following sequence are children who might now be embarrassed by the purity of their questions, but happily it was recorded on a tape cassette.

"Where are the orioles going?"

We looked it up in the bird book. The orioles were going to Central America, or perhaps Venezuela, for the winter. We looked up Venezuela in the Atlas. Venezuela! All the way down there? Across the sea? How do they know how to get there?

"They go with the other orioles."

"How do the other orioles know how to get there?"

"There's always some oriole who's been there before."

"How did the first oriole know how to get there?"

"He didn't really know it was Venezuela, he was just following the bug supply south."

"How do the orioles know when to go?"

"They notice the bugs are scarcer."

"But there are still plenty of bugs around."

We looked that up. True, the bugs were still around. The birds had light-sensitive cells that told them the days are getting shorter, and they know they better get going.

In the spring, the moppet brigade announced that the orioles were back. (One was heard to ask, while standing under the hanging nest, "Did you have a good time in Venezuela?") Sure enough, same gentleman with the dented fender.

"How did the orioles come back from Venezuela?"

"They came with the other orioles."

"But how did they find this *house?* They never went before, and they never came back before, and there aren't any other orioles around, and it's very far, and even if they followed the bugs north, how did they know which state to go to, and how did they find this house?"

Now the reference material was getting more complex. *Scientific American,* we reported, had discussed planetarium experiments where it appeared that perhaps birds navigated by the position of the stars. The senior moppet was extremely dissatisfied.

"A Pan American *pi*lot," he said, "would have to have special training to go to Venezuela, and he would have known about stars from school, and he would have a radio and special signals, and the stars wouldn't help find something as small as a house in the middle of a *state.*"

"That would be very precise navigation," I said, "but they have good eyesight."

"Besides, the stars are in different places in the spring than when the orioles left, so if they were following stars they would get mixed up but here they are."

Two more candidates for the occult, disillusioned with rational science.

How does a large, droopy-eyed dog, called a bloodhound not from an affinity to the red stuff but because of a long and blooded lineage, take a sniff of a thumb print on a glass slide, walk twenty miles into the middle of a woods two weeks later, ignoring all other smells, and go whoof?

How does the salmon know where to go back to? Well, he tracks the water. Wire him up, as some scientists did, and expose him to different batches of water, and he will ignore them all, but try some hometown water and he will light up the machine. Those are some receptors in the olfactory cells. The vibration of some molecule, or the geometry of the molecule, communicates. But how do the receptor cells know, and how do they communicate?

Or termites. A couple of termites, wandering around, are ineffectual. But as the termites gather, as they reach a critical mass, they form columns, work crews, disposal units, engineering cadres, committees, and throw up crystalline and vaulted chambers, termite cathedrals. How do they know that the nth termite has created the critical mass? How does the column know when to turn, and how does it have the engineering knowledge to build a vault? Pheromones, maybe, hormonal secretions that carry some molecular message to somebody else who can read the pheromones in that molecular language. But how does that communication work?

In the past few years, there has been an exciting explosion in molecular biology. The molecular biologists didn't even have an old crowd defending the paradigm to throw over, because there wasn't anything there before. So: how does one cell know how to make a whole whale? Or, in people: how does the gene instruct the cells that are going to make, say, a liver? What creates that particular shape and biochemical function? There's no command from within the cell, the patterning signal has to be an interaction between cells. The cells produce signals and the other cells pick up the chemical messages. What are these messages that go from cell to cell?

You are sitting there reading, and all the while, just under earshot, there is this absolute racket going on, cell to cell, right there in yourself, except that the boop boop and beep beep do not sound that way, they are rather pieces of chemistry traded.

And if, subliminally, we could pick that up, what

else could we pick up? Doctor, lawyer, merchant, chief? Do you love me? Really?

The physiologists and neurophysiologists tell us there is a vast world out there, beeping and honking and scratching and belching, and we perceive only a small part of it, like the frog whose eyes only see dinner going by or the predator's shadow. And part of that cacophony we do perceive, but we don't know we perceive it—it's probably too far down on the survival scale. Are the vibes real or do we project them? Sometimes, we know, we project them, but sometimes, well, did you ever leave a room and say something funny about that man, or that woman? Schizophrenics, postulates one scientist, may have problems because their signals are flawed, the receptors gummed up; schizophrenics have an unfamiliar odor in their sweat, it is said, attributed to an acid called trans-3-methyl-2-hexanoic. Could we perceive it? We perceive smaller concentrations of other combinations.

Maybe Sherlock Holmes was able to translate strange esters for himself, like the catfish that can tell the boss catfish was in these waters only a few minutes ago.

I called up a psychiatrist friend who works at a classy mental institution. Could you really smell degrees of craziness in people? Sure.

"What does trans-3-methyl-2-hexanoic acid smell like?"

"Oh, it's a rather ripe, rich smell, almost fruity."

Hot on the trail of vibes: could I learn it? Sure, why not, I had learned, ancient Chevalier de Tastevin, to sniff the differences in Burgundies, the strength of the Cortons and the mellowness of the Musignys.

So there I am, under my friend's sponsorship, making the rounds, Doctor Smith, here just for the day, in a borrowed white coat.

"And how are you today?" says my friend, to two patients.

One of the patients smiles and the other one doesn't respond. Doctor Smith is going sniff sniff sniff. Hurried smile: sniff sniff sniff. Too damn much antiseptic in here, or something with an alcohol base.

Mrs. Green is showing Doctor Smith around.

"And this is our day room, where we have supervised activities, arts and crafts."

Sure enough, one guy is making a pair of moccasins, two ladies are weaving something or other, strands are being pulled into baskets.

Sniff sniff sniff, goes Doctor Smith.

Three rather aged ladies and a young man are playing cards. Doctor Smith kibitzes: sniff sniff sniff.

Doctor Smith is getting distressed: "You let them *smoke?*" he asks Mrs. Green.

"Yes," says Mrs. Green. "Are you one of those doctors who really objects to smoking?"

"Yes," says Doctor Smith firmly, for all he is smelling is Marlboros and Viceroys and antiseptic.

"E Wing is a bit tense today," Mrs. Green says.

"Let's go to E Wing," says Doctor Smith. Sniff sniff sniff.

E Wing is indeed tense. Some people scream. Sniff sniff sniff.

Doctor Smith thanks his hosts, come nightfall, for an interesting day. He doesn't think he's found trans-3-methyl-2-hexanoic acid, sniff sniff sniff.

"You really should take care of that cold, Doctor," says Mrs. Green.

Later, Doctor Smith did get a sniff of trans-3-methyl-2-hexanoic acid. Another psychiatrist collected the sweat from rubber bed sheets. Ripe, all right.

Two Georgia researchers came up with a discovery: women in fertile periods produced a pheromone in a vaginal secretion. Vibes, maybe that's why all the fellas are clustered around. Good heavens, Madison Avenue just finished selling strawberry-flavored douches. Now what? Now, I suppose, we will need a douche to follow the strawberry douche, called *Naturel*. Watch your TV commercials for further developments. "*Naturel*, fortified with extra pheromones."

With all that cacophony going on, couldn't there be just one little message from Cousin Josie about Herbie? A focusing of enough energy to bend a nail or float a ping-pong ball into midair? A few molecular strands from tomorrow?

Maybe. But not from our paradigm. We could certainly train ourselves within our sensibilities—people who speak inflected languages have more accurate pitch than we do, and wine tasters can sniff more clues than they have language for.

If you tell me that people perceive all sorts of things they're not aware of, the geometry of passing molecules, an odd cosmic ray here and there, I experience no discomfort. I might even get a little ambitious: How to Tune In on Passing Molecules You've Already Registered. There's more out there than we perceive, and we perceive more than we know.

I know that bodies heal themselves, and sometimes they can get a psychic push or trigger, whether from a sugar pill, a physician, or a healer. But tell me that some people can heal others long-distance, thousands of miles, when the healee doesn't even know he's being healed, and I start to scramble for more ordinary explanations. I know there is lots of territory unexplored and unexplained, but trips to the moon should be on gossamer wings or big rockets, and that goes double for Mercury, Jupiter, and the rest of the universe.

The rules of our paradigm are: what you observe must relate to what we know, and be simply stated, and have a theory and a little bit of elegance, and you have to be able to do it again, or tell why it would work again.

That doesn't mean it will turn out to be true. The astronomy of Ptolemy could predict eclipses, and it had theory, and predictability, but it turned out to be not true. "Phlogiston" helped to explain eighteenth-century chemistry, and "ether," nineteenth-century physics.

Jung had a theory about the bookcases that kept going off like firecrackers—synchronicity, not causality—but since he didn't get to explode a bookcase on cue—causality—it doesn't count as true. What is true is left-brained: you can take it apart and put it together and it will do what you predict.

"It is highly probable," writes a young and respected neurobiologist, "that in due course it will be possible to explain the 'mystic experience' in terms of neurobiology; it is highly improbable that neurobiology will ever be explained in terms of the 'mystic experience.' " The second half of that sentence is bound to be true. Historically, mystics have been very uninterested in explaining the experience in terms of neurobiology. Mostly, they tell stories, or don't say anything at all. What about the first half of the sentence? Is the mystic experience going to turn out to be the right series of nucleotides? But then what? At the edges of paradigms, the temptation to Rumpelstiltskin is very great: name it and it will go away.

The orioles settle down for the winter in Venezuela; the bobolinks go all the way to Argentina. And the position of the stars, as a young friend of mine pointed out, changes from hemisphere to hemisphere and season to season.

The Mind, the Quantum and the Universe

The reason physics got to be king of the hill, said the French geneticist François Jacob, was that physics was the first to have its own language, and that language was mathematics. The molecular biologists are making great strides, unlocking enigmas, solving puzzles, getting neurobiology ready to take over mysticism. The neurobiologists do not think about it much, but their language, with all the inherent assumptions we have learned about language, is based on physics. And the language of physics is less certain than the conclusions of neurobiology.

For example: you remember the Impulse, going tra la la la la la down the axon and stumbling into a Cleft. All physics; the Impulse is a quantifiable charge of electricity, and what happens to the Impulse depends on the constituents of the cells and the positive charges on the sodium and potassium, and the minuses on the chloride and protein, and you measure in millivolts. That sort of physics—and its related chemistry—is elementary, and will probably serve for a long time.

But down the road it turns out that solid old physics is only valid for the medium-sized world we live in, pounds and inches, volts and seconds. Very small or very tall, it begins to make no sense at all. Not common sense, anyway, but we are all respectful, because the next equation may disperse us all.

What follows is not really going to be about physics —it is old stuff anyway to physicists. What follows is about language and meaning and how we see the world, so don't try to sort it out and certainly don't remember it.

First there were crystals, and then smaller than crystals were molecules, and then smaller than molecules were atoms. The atom was like a little solar system, a sun in the middle, the nucleus, and the electrons whirling around it, like planets.

There is a lot of space in a solar system. So there came the parable of Eddington's desk, Eddington being a great English physicist. Looked at normally, Eddington's desk was a nice antique, and looked at atomically, there was almost nothing there, only empty space with a few incredibly tiny specks, the electrons whirling around their nuclei, vast, vast spaces separating them.

(Thus one lecturer on the Void was able to say that we are 99½ percent Void already, so there is only a little way to go, but the last part is the hardest.) From a survival point of view, of course, if Eddington's desk falls on you it hurts like hell, and dropped from high enough it will dispatch you better than $E=mc^2$.

And these subatomic bits were already being troublesome, because they acted sometimes as if they were waves, and sometimes as if they were particles.

And then it turned out that we weren't done by having a nucleus, like a little sun, because there were smaller pieces than the nucleus, first one, then two, then four—omega minuses and neutrinos—and now we are up to several hundred of the little pests, still hunting for the quark, the most elementary particle, and no guarantee that a quark won't turn out to have cousins and ghostly relatives and Son of Quark.

Quarks! The name was borrowed by Dr. Murray Gell-Mann from Joyce, *Finnegans Wake,* "Three quarks for Muster Mark?" Quark is Dr. Gell-Mann's second gift of poetry to physics, for it was he, in the 1950's, who described a quantum number as "strange," so that we could have "strangeness" as a quality of particles. Science must simplify, and the three basic quarks, "things postulated which clarify the world unseen," mathematically underlie all particles, the three quarks being up, down and sideways—but wait, what goes there? Very exciting, a fourth elementary particle, a "charmed quark," whose "charm" is a mathematical concept. With ultra-powerful nuclear accelerators, we may be getting there, the trial of discovery, the basic units of all matter—

"—but we hope we don't see a quark because that might stir up more problems," said my particle adviser. "In fact, we hope we don't even see a quark *track*. Quarks should stay where they are, mathematical." And indeed, no one ever sees any of the mites, nor even the particles in which the quarks may be eternally confined, all they see are tiny tracks in the snow, or, more accurately, bubbles in a bubble chamber, and then from the angles and curves they can figure out who just went by or didn't go by at some unimaginable speed.

Of the particles known today, half are particles and half are antiparticles, the antiparticle having the same mass but with an opposite charge and opposite spin. Antiparticles are rare and not very long-lived. When antiparticles meet their mirror-image they annihilate each other immediately. It is possible that other galaxies are made up of antiparticles, which has led to the speculation that their time would flow backwards to ours. (It also led one physicist to write a poem about such a place, where Dr. Edward Anti-Teller lived, and kept macassars on his chairs.)

Nor is the behavior of the mites anything for Aristotelian logic. For example, if you shoot a particle at another particle at high speed, they break apart into pieces, but *each* of the pieces is as big as the original.

On Wednesday afternoons sometimes, Dr. Richard Feynman of Cal Tech drives up to Malibu and plops into one of John Lilly's tanks. Feynman got the Nobel prize for the backwards-in-time work; a positron traveling forward in time behaves just like an electron moving momentarily backwards in time. The Two Guides from Malibu Meet the Time Machine, the Connecticut Yankee Stops Off on the Way to King Arthur's Court.

Cutest of all the particles, everybody agrees, is the neutrino. Neutrinos are very hard to detect because they have no mass, no electric charge, no magnetic field. They come charging out of the sun and go right through everything as if everything weren't there. Nothing can stop a neutrino except another neutrino, which does happen sometimes, enabling people to record the splat. Neutrinos coming from the sun could tell us things, so the physicists constructed a big vat of cleaning fluid deep in an old Homestake lead mine in South Dakota, deep enough so that other particles from space couldn't find it, and waited for some neutrino on his way through the earth to get asphyxiated. Wrote John Updike:

> Neutrinos, they are very small.
>   They have no charge and have no mass
> And do not interact at all.
> The earth is just a silly ball
>   To them, through which they simply pass
> Like dustmaids down a drafty hall
>   Or photons through a sheet of glass—
>
>   And, scorning barriers of class
> Infiltrate you and me! Like tall
> And painless guillotines, they fall
>   Down through our heads into the grass . . .

One can see why the proponents of ESP—the 3 percent on the bookstore shelves—like to make analogies with subatomic physics. A gang of positrons, or anti-electrons coming back from the future, might bear a message. Or, if neutrinos are accepted ghosts, what about ghosts that do not yet have an equation?

It can be dizzying to think of negative mass and antimatter and particles that aren't there except they are, and mites that go backwards in time for less than an eye blink. On the scale of the very grand, it gets worse. If you took all the space out of Eddington's desk and collapsed it down to its protons, its gravity would increase tremendously and would pull everything into it. A collapsing star becomes a mass so dense that if it became a neutron star ten miles in diameter, a tablespoon of sand would weigh 40,000 billion tons. A bigger star would squeeze itself into matter so dense that it would simply *disappear*, a "black hole," and in the act of its collapse, time isn't time and space isn't space. To a very theoretical astronaut who happened to be in a black hole, it would seem like one second, but in outside time billions of years would have gone by. Where do the items go that disappear into a black hole? Some astrophysicists postulate that the black hole is a tunnel into another universe.

Our own universe expands, reaches a maximum dimension, and contracts. "When the universe finally collapses," writes Professor John Wheeler of Princeton, "the classical general relativity of Einstein offers no way to go beyond the point. If you try to solve the problem on a computer, the computer stops. Smoke comes out. But according to the quantum principle, the dynamics should continue. We can well expect that when the universe collapses, there's a certain probability that it will start a new cycle. Another universe will leave its own track in superspace."

Superspace?

"The stage on which the space of the universe moves is certainly not space itself. Nobody can be a stage for himself; he has to have a larger arena in which to move. The arena in which space does its changing is not even the spacetime of Einstein, for spacetime is the history of space changing with time. The area must be a larger object: superspace. Superspace is not endowed with three or four dimensions—it's endowed with an *infinite* number of dimensions. Any single point in superspace represents an entire, three-dimensional world; nearby points represent slightly different three-dimensional worlds."

I get it. No, I don't get it. Yes, I get it, sort of, if I don't try. Wheeler and his colleagues were looking for the equation behind the universe: what started it? What is beyond the end of time? Would the law of physics still hold without the universe?

Superspace. Black holes where one second is ten billion years. Tunnels to another universe. Infinite dimensions. It would seem, at first glance, that solving Jung's exploding bookcases, or getting messages from Aunt Josie, ought to be a cinch.

Wheeler, a gentle, scholarly man who worked with Einstein and Niels Bohr and other atomic giants, gave a speech on the five hundredth birthday of Copernicus. Look how far we have come, it said, from Copernicus. Darwin and Freud and the double helix of life, everybody had his own list of the remaining mysteries, but his list had three.

Wheeler's three mysteries were: "the mind, the quantum, and the universe." I wrote a note. Plainly, he had been working on the universe. I had been scratching at the mind. "I will meet you," I said, "at the quantum."

"That's some list: the mind, the quantum, and the universe," I said.

"All three," Wheeler said, "threaten the clean separation between observer and observed that used to be the essence of science."

"What's a quantum?" I said. "I thought it was a kind of jump."

"I meant the quantum principle," he said. "It might be better called the Merlin principle. Merlin the magician, pursued, changed first to a fox, then a rabbit, then to a bird on one's shoulder. The Merlin principle keeps changing before us, putting on a new form every decade."

In the 1920's, a young German theoretical physicist, Werner Heisenberg, was working on some of the contradictions in physics. It was an exciting time in physics, and the pioneer group of physicists, if you read their essays and autobiographies, had an enormous amount of fun. Heisenberg visited periodically with Niels Bohr in Denmark. They had long philosophical conversations, and Heisenberg's hay fever was better in Denmark. And without going into the details of the problems, Heisenberg wrote out some pages of non-commutative algebra that were to have a great impact. In physics, the Principle of Uncertainty carries his name; his work got him a Nobel prize at thirty-one. Heisenberg's Uncertainty Principle says that you can't know both the position and the velocity of an electron, all you can have is a statistical probability. The implications went beyond physics: they affected the basic point of view from which we look at things. And that shift is this: the observer is part of the process. That did not begin with Heisenberg, but his name is on the principle.

"In the world of quantum," Wheeler said, "the observer and the observed turn out to have a tight and totally unexpected linkage. The quantum principle demolishes the view we once had that the universe sits safely 'out there,' that we can observe what goes on or in it from behind a foot-thick slab of plate glass without ourselves being involved in what goes on. We have learned that to observe even so minuscule an object as an electron we have to shatter that slab of glass. We have to insert a measuring device. We can put in a device to measure position or a device to measure momentum, but the installation of one prevents the insertion of the other. We ourselves have to decide which it is that we will do. Whichever it is, it has an unpredictable effect on the future of that electron. To that degree the future of the universe is changed. We changed it. We have to cross out the old word 'observer' and replace it by the new word 'participator.' In some strange sense, the quantum principle tells us that we are dealing with a participatory universe."

Here are some possibly clumsy analogies:

An anthropologist goes to visit a primitive tribe. He brings pills for the drinking water, a Polaroid camera, a movie camera, insect repellent, and a rifle. Is the tribe he observes the same tribe that would have been there with no anthropologist to watch? Will the tribe really spend the same time learning to run down an animal, or will it start saving up for a rifle? And if we accept that the tribe won't be the same, how do we know what it was like before, without an anthropologist to tell us?

Or: we have a national election. The polls close in the East, and the computer projections announce the winners on TV. The people in the West still have two hours of voting time. Do they still vote? Would the score have been exactly the same?

The observation of the process has become part of the process.

"We go down and down," Wheeler said, "from crystal to molecule, from molecule to atom. from atom to nucleus, from nucleus to particle, and there is still something beyond both geometry and particle. In the end we have to come back to mind. How can consciousness understand consciousness? There's a paradox. Niels Bohr said we only made progress from paradoxes."

What is really real? That was a starting point for this trip, and the circle—consistent with the laws of conservation—begins to close on itself. It is even a bit chilling to remember that "really" and "real" come from the Latin *res,* thing, and so we are asking how much thingness is a thing, *which has already limited the answer.*

Wheeler's shelves have Pierce and Parmenides and Paracelsus and William James; the European physicists had not only James but Kant and Plato. They begin to sound more like mystics than physicists. Eugene Wigner, another Nobel prizewinner (sorry to keep listing Nobel prizes, it is to show these are serious people), wrote an essay called "Two Kinds of Reality," the first being "my own consciousness" and the second, everything else; "the universal or impersonal reality as a concept is a reality of the second type," useful for communicating, but only possibly valid. Everything but the first type is a construct.

The critics of the quantum physicists, fifty years ago, used to call it "atomysticism." The atom had been the building block of our universe, and Heisenberg wrote: "An atom is not a *thing*. When we get down to the atomic level, the objective world in space and time no longer exists, and the mathematical symbols of theoretical physics refer merely to possibilities, not facts." Now there is a good exercise for wooziness: an atom is not a thing, it is only a possibility, and we are all made up of atoms.

Any good theoretical physicist learns to let go of that wooziness, and in the process, he also learns to sound like a mystic. "When a student of physics makes his first acquaintance with the theory of atomic structure and of quanta," wrote J. Robert Oppenheimer, "he must come to the rather deep and subtle notion which has turned out to be the clue to unraveling that whole domain of physical experience. This is the notion of complementarity, which recognizes that various ways of talking about experience may each have validity, and may each be necessary for the adequate description of the physical world, and yet may stand in mutually exclusive relationship to each other, so that in a situation to which one applies, there may be no consistent possibility of applying the other."

So physicists talk about two realities. Oppenheimer called them "the way of time and history, and the way of eternity and timelessness." Heisenberg called them "the objective world, pursuing its regular course in space and time, [and] a subject, mystically experiencing the unity of the world and no longer confronted by an object or by any objective world." Wigner called the two ways scientific knowledge and natural knowledge:

Scientific knowledge leans on, and is impossible without, the type of knowledge we acquired in babyhood. Furthermore, this original knowledge was probably not at all acquired by us in the active sense; most of it must have been given to us in the same mysterious way, and probably as part of, our consciousness. As to content and usefulness, scientific knowledge is an infinitesimal fraction of the natural knowledge.

"One may say," wrote Heisenberg, "that the human ability to understand may be in a certain sense unlimited. But the existing scientific concepts cover always only a very limited part of reality, and the other part that has not yet been understood is infinite. Whenever we proceed from the known into the unknown we may hope to understand, but we may have to learn at the same time, a new meaning of the word 'understanding.'" The understanding, Heisenberg wrote in another essay, "is recognized even before it is rationally understood in detail." It is, at one place, "the unfolding of abstract structures," the "shuddering before the beautiful of which Plato speaks."

Thin air out here. The mystics have to go through all that meditation, and the physicists have to go through all that math and quantum theory, and in one sense the processes are similar because they require a letting go of daily common sense, and the ability to let the universe be some other way. They arrive at, if not the same place, one that sounds at least recognizable: Einstein's Unified Field Theory was supposed to supplant the surface complexity of nature with a profound simplicity: "Thus all man's perceptions of the world and all his abstract intuitions of reality would merge finally into one, and the deep underlying unity of the universe would be laid bare." Heisenberg saw the "faith in the central order" not only in the unfolding Platonic abstractions but in Bach.

"When is a man in mere understanding?" Meister Eckhart the mystic asked, rhetorically. "When he sees one thing separate from another. And when is a man above mere understanding? That I can tell you: when a man sees All in all."

If we seem to be spending a lot of time on time, it is because time is such a clear element in the paradigm, to show us the limitations of our paradigm. We think of time as being linear, it starts and it moves forward, whether we're there to perceive it or not. But if black holes turn out to be real, and time speeds up incredibly in a black hole, then our regular notion of time moving forward, ticktock, is just something we made up. And time moving backward would not just be the Time Machine, and the Connecticut Yankee, but an example of how we made up the original notion.

I traded some papers with the physicists. I gave them *Four Quartets*. They liked that. Next year if you take Physics 111, you may get this:

> Time present and time past
> Are both perhaps present in time future,
> And time future contained in time past.
> If all time is eternally present
> All time is unredeemable.
> What might have been is an abstraction
> Remaining a perpetual possibility
> Only in a world of speculation.
> What might have been and what has been
> Point to one end, which is always present.
> The end of all our exploring
> Will be to arrive where we started
> And know the place for the first time.

"All these mystics," I said, "keep talking about the unity of everything, and the physicists, when they stop writing equations and start writing words, say they are looking for the equation behind One."

I was talking to still another physicist, another Nobel prize-winner, pictures on his walls of Einstein and Heisenberg and Dirac and de Broglie, hotshot pioneers of this century. Niels Bohr on a motorcycle. Somebody else in ski clothes. A lot of conversation seems to have gone on in boats and on mountaintops.

"Yes, if they stop to think about it," said my physicist. "And sometimes, after a burst of physics, they stop to think about it. Otherwise, not more than anybody else, you worry about grants and meetings and research assistants, but if you get away and sit in a boat on a lake and think where we have come from in fifty years, and where we might be going, maybe the tools of physics give you an extra moment."

"I don't think the public has quite caught up to the quantum," I said, "they're either in materialism or superstition or both. I get uncomfortable myself if I think we're only here as a probability."

"Yes," said my friend, and shot a wrist watch out from one gray, European-suited sleeve. I said I was relieved to see he wore a watch, since my head was full of either physics or Eliot's *Four Quartets,* four poems about time and reality, the intersection of time and timeless. And then there were the little pests that went backwards in time—

"A bookkeeping device," said my friend. "A way of looking at things."

"Like, on the books, the building has been depreciated but it's still standing and still being used."

"I don't know those things," he said. After a generation here, he still has a faint Middle European accent.

"I get very confused about time," I said.

"There is nothing to be confused about," he said. *"Physicists define time to make motion look simple."*

I felt myself slipping a bit. "Is there a real time?"

"Time is real and also time is not real."

I had fallen right into my own quantum example, I was out there with the rest of the public. Some koan, Zen is easier.

"We have satellites in space that are picking up signals from pulsars, spinning stars a universe away, a galaxy away, the signals are regular but the stars may no longer be there. The Clifford-Einstein equations led us to think the building material of the universe is curved space—"

The building material is curved space?

He had glanced at his watch again. "Einstein said, time is what you read from a clock, and my watch says lunchtime. Should we go? *Primum vivere, deinde philosophari.*"

They must learn that in the gymnasia. Somebody threw my high school Latin book out, years ago. I translate that as live first, philosophize later, or maybe, no philosophy on an empty stomach. It seems as profound as anything else.

Primum Vivere

One day Henry David Thoreau had had enough of Walden Pond, and the little cabin he had built there. "I left the woods," he wrote, "for as good a reason as I went there. Perhaps it seemed to me that I had several more lives to live, and could not spare any more time for that one. It is remarkable how easily and insensibly we fall into a particular route, and make a beaten track for ourselves." Emerson was going to Europe, and needed a house-sitter, and Thoreau packed up and went to Emerson's house.

And one day the road into the woods from the Middle of the Journey led out again for me. Perhaps my tape recorder is still on a tree in there. When I went in, I was following a thirst, a kind of curiosity, a sense of excitement, and the experiences were fresh. I had no particular goal or intention. But in time there was an invisible line, after which the experiences were modified by language. Perhaps I would need this language to tell about the woods—and that little impulse made the experience less pure, for the left-brained language would arrive too soon with its own peculiar modes. Then the language would blanket the experience. By calling in the Observer, I was not sure the Participant was the same; the Uncertainty Principle hovered like a large black bird.

I knew that the world is not the way they tell you it is, but what else it is would have to wait. I hoped to get box seats to the Trial of Galileo, to be present when someone sent What Hath God Wrought by telepathy, or to see the first Photograph of a Quark, caught surprised and blinking in its nest. Apocalyptic cries everywhere, population and energy seemed less urgent, for all was process. Paradigms exist in time; what now would time bring?

There were some after-effects. I had followed my courses religiously, and now I had to get all new clothes. For a year I had had no alcohol, and little refined sugar, and all that awareness—reaching, reaching, tasting, tasting—produced a fuller stomach with less food. I didn't think I was fat or even bulky when I began; we never know how we look—"a stocky, blue-jawed figure," a Newsweek article had said of me. Stocky? Blue-jawed? Really? Burly, as a Canadian paper said? No more. A regular gazelle. I became a scale addict, for effortlessly, without tension, my weight was dropping, one pound, two pounds a week, past my Army weight, past my college weight, and it finally leveled off at the weight last registered when I was a skinny seventeen. So I had to get new clothes. (I kept some of the old ones, superstitiously.)

It had not been so hard to give up alcohol in the cause of pursuing awareness. It was more difficult giving up ice cream. An ice-cream chain called Baskin-Robbins moved relentlessly closer to where some of my courses met—curse them, temptation in the way, I lingered outside the window like an executive outside a porn movie at lunch hour. Creme Caramel! Burgundy Cherry! Pralines and Cream!

And Key Lime Pie! That was too much. One day I looked guiltily over my shoulder and ducked in, a single-scoop Key Lime Pie cone, and I was a sinner fallen from pure awareness. I got a rush from an ice-cream cone, a buzz in the head, a high, and a terrible down a couple of hours later as the body system used the sugar from the ice-cream cone and kept right on going into the reserves.

I was not going to make it to Satori #3 this trip. One day in late spring, more than a year after I began the experiential exercises, I went down into my own cellar with a corkscrew. There slept, row on row, all the noble wines I had collected for years, each in its own bassinet of orange tile drainpipe. The tile helped to keep the temperature constant. If I were to give up some of the clarity of experiences in order to record the experiences, I might as well do it here, and record my own fall from grace. On top of all the slumbering vintages was my wine book, in which I had, years ago, recorded the inventory and the taste of each wine, and how well the wines went with various foods. But what to choose? Should we make it a really big ceremony, and drink the last of the Montrachet? Or a mellow, deep Musigny, Comte Georges de Vogue? There was one Musigny 1919, a gift, probably long gone by now inside its bottle, and then 1959, 1961, 1964, 1966—or wait, here are three Lafites out of a case, 1961, 1966—no, too ceremonial. Something more everyday, let's see, Beychevelle, Montrose, Calon-Segur. I pulled a 1962 Calon-Segur and opened it.

Now began a stereo track in which the channels did not match. Channel A clicked on with the first sniff, the first taste, and said:

"This is a pleasant wine, nice bouquet, ready to drink, much less tannin than the 1961—"

Channel B as usual had no words and I had to translate, which took a moment, because involuntarily I sat down heavily. I had taken three swallows and it felt like I had fallen thirty feet. With some difficulty I wrote on page 76 of the wine book:

"Dim memory says this wine matches pleasant. But I can't focus my eyes and I can't stand up. My stomach feels bile green. Muscles heavy. Breathing uneven. Uncertain spasms in throat and stomach. Awful. I feel drugged. *Drugged.*"

And, of course, I was; alcohol is a drug even when it comes from a slumbering Calon-Segur 1962. Can we remember the body's reaction to its first cigarette? I had to sit for a while. Then I left the bottle and went upstairs and ran through the Great Central Philippine Headache Cure.

Within months, the spaces of Channel A and Channel B began to shift. When I was in the midst of all the breathing and chanting and meditating and group work, the headlines in newspapers all seemed much the same, but feelings and emotions and something beyond, which we have no language for, seemed clear. Now, in a more traditional mode of visiting laboratories and talking to brain people, the headlines resumed their sharp distinctions, and the feelings became more blurred and vague. It became easy to skip meditations. I could drink a glass of wine without getting dizzy and nauseated. Sometimes, for some minor distress, it was easier to take an aspirin than lie down and pacify it with cooling thoughts.

Pretty soon, I could read the *Wall Street Journal* without hearing messages from my skin, and I was listening to the words people uttered, and not the timbre of their voices as they talked. I knew I was losing something, but I was on the way back.

There remains the story of the Crazy Indian. That was how I thought of him. I went to a broadcast studio one day, and they said, your Indian friend is in the control room. And I said, I don't have an Indian friend. (I didn't even know whether by Indian they meant Black Elk or Krishna Dass.) I was just starting to read in this area and there is this Indian waving happily in the control room, nobody I knew. When the broadcast was over, I said, I don't believe we've met, and the Indian grinned happily and said, but we know you at the ashram, your money book. "The stock doesn't know you own it!" sang the Indian. "It is going up as long as it is going up! That is what Sri Aurobindo would have written if he wrote in American, and that is what you wrote. So I have brought you a present."

And he gave me a very handsome edition of the works of Sri Aurobindo. I did not want to say, who the hell is Sri Aurobindo, so I said, thank you very much.

But that was not the end of it. I could not lose the Crazy Indian. If I turned right, he turned right. If I jumped into a cab, so did he.

I figured this was a caper of old Suchabanana, so I called Murphy—on my credit card—the Crazy Indian standing outside the phone booth grinning—but Murphy denied any knowledge.

"That was Murphy," I said when I came out of the phone booth. The Crazy Indian did not know Murphy. "Murphy wants to know if he can be the golf coach at the ashram."

The Crazy Indian said certainly, they had a wonderful sports program at the ashram.

If it wasn't Suchabanana, and I wasn't getting paranoid, then maybe old Carl Jung was right that there are no coincidences.

The Crazy Indian did a little bob and said, "Namaste." So we walked down the street and I said, how long are you here for, and the Crazy Indian said he had to leave Saturday morning when his visa expired, and he showed me the visa in his passport. He had only been in the country a week.

"You didn't come here just to hand me that book," I said.

"No," he said, "I came to see two people. You were one. Namaste."

"What is namaste?" I said.

"Oh, that means, I salute the light within you."

"I have a light?"

"Everybody has a light," he said, with an expansive gesture to the hurrying mob outside Pennsylvania Station. The individuals in the mob hurried on, faces down, grim. I began to feel a little rerun of Altered State #6; if time is not time, if owning the earth is a game we play, if there are vibrations we are too dense to feel, well, maybe everybody has a light.

The Crazy Indian ducked away for a moment and came back with some flowers and handed them to me. I was embarrassed. What the hell was I supposed to do with flowers?

"Namaste," I said. "Namaste," I said to the passing crowd.

"Namaste," said the Crazy Indian.

I shook hands firmly and told him I had to leave now—he was about to get on the train with me—and I got on the train and walked through it and every few feet I would stop and give somebody a flower and smile and say, "Namaste." Some of them pulled their newspapers closer around them, but by the end of the train I had given all the flowers away.

Namaste.

Notes and Bibliography

Notes

I. This Side of Paradigm

MYSTERY: TIME, SPACE, INFINITY,
STATISTICAL ABERRATION

5   H. Selye, *The Stress of Life.*

5   "fight or flight": the phrase of Dr. Walter Cannon,
a famous Harvard physiologist. Cannon, *The Wisdom
of the Body.*

7   "a Nigerian princeling": R. Prince in *American Journal
of Psychiatry.* Also see Prince in A. Kiev, ed., *Magic,
Faith and Healing.* This whole theme is done delight-
fully by E. F. Torrey in *The Mind Game.*

THREE STORIES IN WHICH SOMETHING IS GOING ON
WHICH IS VERY HARD TO PHOTOGRAPH

9   Alsop's train story appeared in his *Newsweek* column
(March 11, 1974).

PLACEBOS AND RUMPELSTILTSKIN

Until quite recently, there hasn't been much under
"placebo" in the technical literature, as A. K. Shapiro
reported in his history and overview in *Behavioral
Science* (reprinted in N. E. Miller et al., eds., *Biofeedback and Self-Control*). That essay and Miller's section
in A. M. Freedman et al., eds., *Comprehensive Textbook of Psychiatry,* are the source of some of what
follows. Shapiro has a later paper in A. E. Bergin
and S. L. Garfield, eds., *Handbook of Psychotherapy*

383

and Behavior Change: Empirical Analysis. A group at Johns Hopkins Medical School has a relevant batch of papers: see J. D. Frank; D. Rosenthal and J. D. Frank. Frank has an interesting book, *Persuasion and Healing.*

17   Colored pills: A. A. Baker in Shapiro.

17   Percentages of effectiveness: F. J. Evans in *Psychology Today.*

17   Placebo injections: F. J. Evans in *Psychology Today.*

17   "the vibes give it away": P. E. Feldman in Shapiro; also, N. Miller.

17   As for the actor in the white coat on TV telling you you'll be better by morning, or a scene on TV of people recovering quickly after some TV-advertised medication, please note the manuscript of Dr. Ranieri Gerbi of Pisa in 1794. For toothache, Dr. Gerbi prescribed that a certain species of worm be crushed between thumb and forefinger, and then the fingers held to the pained spot. An independent commission reported that 431 of 629 toothaches stopped immediately! That percentage is right up there with The Leading Pain Reliever, and independent commissions are still reporting similar statistics.

17   Blood pressure, medication and placebos: R. F. Grenfell et al., *Southern Medical Journal,* in Shapiro.

17   Asthma sufferers: Luparello et al. in *Psychosomatic Medicine* (reprinted in N. E. Miller, *Biofeedback and Self-Control*).

17   Stomach pill: R. A. Sternbach in *Psychophysiology.*

18   Witch doctors and psychiatrists: P. Torrey, *The Mind Game.*

PARADIGMS

20   *The Structure of Scientific Revolutions:* Kuhn's paradigm is itself a paradigm, and not without its critics. The more it gets to be an academic buzz-word, the less comfortable I feel with it. But it's probably better than "disciplinary matrix," which is proposed as its successor. No thumbnail reference to the history of science should leave out Karl Popper and Michael Polanyi, especially the latter.

Page

23   "a science about the level . . .": E. Berne, unpublished
     speech, "Away from a Theory of the Impact of Inter-
     personal Interaction on Nonverbal Participation," Golden
     Gate Group Psychotherapy Association, June 20, 1970.
     A very funny and very acute speech.

23   "an unconscious tendency . . .": See also T. Roszak,
     The Making of a Counter Culture and *Where the Waste-
     land Ends* for a general discussion.

23   The parallel between the selectivity of the paradigm
     and that of perception is made loosely in R. Ornstein,
     The Psychology of Consciousness.

24   "A team of Stanford psychologists . . ." Not only
     Stanford psychologists, of course. I started with a file
     called "Stanford Cats," and then "Harvard Med. Cats,"
     and finally ended with "Experience Shapes Perception."
     The Stanford cats are in H. Hirsch in *Science;* also in
     Hirsch and D. N. Spinelli in *Experimental Brain Re-
     search* and Spinelli et al. in *Experimental Brain Research*.
     The Harvard cats are in T. N. Wiesel and D. H. Hubel
     in *Journal of Neurophysiology*. Other Wiesel-Hubel
     papers are fascinating on how the cells of the visual
     cortex encode the visual world, but they don't belong
     here under paradigms. Spinelli has a relevant article
     with Karl Pribram in *Journal of Electroencephalography
     and Clinical Neurophysiology*, 22:143–49 (1967). An
     additional article is in C. Blakemore and J. F. Cooper
     in *Nature*.
        My language about "stripes" is a bit loose. The
     patterns were computer-directed dots, and the change
     in the patterns changed the distribution of the cells in
     the cats' cortexes. But not only does the point remain,
     it's quite significant. This work on perception and ex-
     perience, and the interaction of the organism and the
     environment, didn't begin here and certainly isn't limited
     to the cats here. It's fascinating, and though I some-
     times get overenthusiastic about items from physiological
     psychology where the techniques are beyond me, I wish
     I had the space to do more without getting away from
     the story. I appreciate the direction in reading from
     Richard F. Thompson.

THE ASTRONAUTS OF INNER SPACE

25   Wilder Penfield: "Speech, Perception and the Uncom-
     mitted Cortex" in J. Eccles, *Brain and Conscious Ex-
     perience*. See also Penfield, *Speech and Brain Mech-
     anisms*.

Page

32   "A Harvard Divinity School student . . .": Also a psychologist, Walter Pahnke, now deceased. Pahnke's thesis is unpublished, but see his "Contribution of the Psychology of Religion to the Therapeutic Use of the Psychedelic Substances" in H. Abramson, ed., *The Use of LSD in Psychotherapy and Alcoholism,* and "Drugs and Mysticism" in B. Aaronson and H. Osmond, eds., *Psychedelics: Uses and Implications of Hallucinogenic Drugs.* W. Pahnke and W. Richards, "Implications of Experimental Mysticism," in C. Tart, ed., *Altered States of Consciousness.* The account is from Richard Alpert.

A Very Short History of Some American
Drugs Familiar to Everybody

33   Aspirin usage may actually be much higher. See *New York Times,* 26 (March 27, 1975).

34   Xanthines: L. S. Goodman and A. Gilman, *The Pharmacological Basis of Therapeutics.*

34   "xanthine addict": E. M. Brecher et al., eds., *Licit & Illicit Drugs.* While this is dated, the effects of caffeine continue to be debated in the journals. See *British Medical Journal* (February 8, 1975) and J. F. Graden in *American Journal of Psychiatry.*

36   "'hard drugs'": Summarized from E. M. Brecher et al., eds., *Licit & Illicit Drugs.*

The World's First Acid Trip

Humphrey Osmond spent a number of evenings at my house. His help is gratefully acknowledged. So is that of Jean Houston, R. E. L. Master and Frank Berger, the latter for some tutoring in pharmacology.

37   "'I lay down . . .'": Hofmann's account, in a foreign journal, is partially excerpted in L. S. Goodman and A. Gilman, eds., *The Pharmaceutical Basis of Therapeutics,* and in R. E. Masters and L. Houston, *The Varieties of Psychedelic Experience.*

39   "LSD subject": L. S. Goodman and A. Gilman, eds., *The Pharmacological Basis of Therapeutics.*

39   "An American authority . . .": E. M. Brecher et al., eds., *Licit & Illicit Drugs.*

Page

40 "a review of the literature": E. M. Brecher et al., eds., *Licit & Illicit Drugs*, p. 357. Also see N. Dishotsky et al. in *Science*.

40 "One hospital team . . .": Marlboro Day Hospital, in E. M. Brecher et al., eds., *Licit & Illicit Drugs*, p. 361.

AND A SHORT CHRONICLE OF THE MADNESS

41 "A team of researchers . . .": F. N. Cheek et al. in *Science*.

41 "many people who believe . . .": C. Tart, ed., *Altered States of Consciousness*, pp. 386–87.

41 Mushrooms: Andrew Weil, private communication.

43 Liddy, Owsley, et al.: M. J. Warth in *Village Voice*.

43 Huxley's letter to Osmond: G. Smith, ed., *The Letters of Aldous Huxley*, p. 945.

There is a fairly extensive bibliography on psychedelics in C. Tart, ed., *Altered State of Consciousness*. The dangers are broken out into a section called "Dangers," and there are sections under "General," "Therapeutics," "Legal Aspects," "Pharmacology and Botany," "Sociology and Anthropology," and so on. A good source on dangers is S. Cohen in *JAMA* and other journals. See also the bibliography in T. X. Barber, *LSD, Marihuana, Yoga, and Hypnosis*.

WHAT DID WE LEARN?

49 "neuronal pathways": J. Eccles, *The Neurophysiological Basis of Mind: The Principles of Neurophysiology*. Much easier is Eccles, "The Physiology of Imagination," in T. J. Teyler, ed., *Altered States of Awareness*. Also see K. Pribram, "The Neurophysiology of Remembering," in R. Thompson, ed., *Physiological Psychology*.

Physiological Psychology, Altered States of Awareness, Perception: Mechanisms and Models, Frontiers of Psychological Research and *The Nature and Nurture of Behavior* are all collections in the series *Readings from Scientific American*. They are abstract, college text-level writing but the illustrations and presentation make them reasonably clear.

50 The computer metaphor rages through the sleep literature, too; e.g., E. L. Hartmann, *The Functions of Sleep*,

Page

p. 15: "Greenberg and Leiderman (1966) believe that D-sleep may involve rewinding recent memories onto long-term storage tapes." To be accurate, the metaphor would have to be dynamic, and the computer as equipment is static, but it does get an idea across. Loosely.

50 "dark woods": I know at least three journals which will still publish papers on The Meaning of the Forest. It's interesting to go on and read J. Campbell, *The Mythic Image* and *The Hero with a Thousand Faces*. *The Mythic Image* is beautiful and costs $45.00; *Hero with a Thousand Faces* is a paperback, $4.

52 Houston's "phylogenetic" speculations: R. E. Masters and J. Houston, *The Varieties of Psychedelic Experience*.

53 "V-shaped shadow": L. Thomas, *The Lives of a Cell*, p. 90, after N. Tinberger, *The Study of Instinct*. Further reading on genes: T. Dobzhansky, *Mankind Evolving*; R. Dubos, *So Human an Animal*; S. Luria, *Life . . . the Unfinished Experiment*. All paperbacks. A. Lehninger, *Biochemistry*, is clear but much harder, and $20.

53 Grof's research and theories are discussed in *Journal of Transpersonal Psychology*, 1 (1973), and in a three-part paper presented to the 2nd Interdisciplinary Conference on the Voluntary Control of Internal States, Council Grove, Kansas (1970).

54 "Two sociologists . . .": New York *Times Magazine*, 24 (January 26, 1975).

54 "A Hasidic rabbi . . .": R. Metzner, ed., *The Ecstatic Adventure*, pp. 96–124.

56 " 'our normal waking consciousness' ": W. James, *The Varieties of Religious Experience*. There are several different editions available; this is New American Library, p. 298.

II. Hemispheres

LEFT SIDE, RIGHT SIDE, WHY RALPH NADER CAN'T DANCE

60 It is a bit flip to call Sperry "the captain of left-right research," since every source leads back to him. Sperry's "Brain Bisection and Mechanisms of Consciousness" is in J. C. Eccles, ed., *Brain and Conscious Experience*. Sperry's classic article on hemispheres, "The Great Cerebral Commissure" in *Scientific American*, is re-

printed in S. Coopersmith, ed., *Frontiers of Psychological Research*. "The Eye and the Brain" is repeated in two of the *Scientific American* readers (they do overlap sometimes). Sperry's one-time student, now professor, Michael Gazzaniga has "The Split Brain in Man" in *Physiological Psychology*, again the *Scientific American* reader, and a more technical book, *The Bisected Brain*. Sperry's "A Modified View of Consciousness" is in *Psychological Review*. The patients whom Sperry and Gazzaniga wrote about were sometimes those of Joseph Bogen, the Los Angeles neurosurgeon who wrote a very interesting series, "The Other Side of the Brain," in *Bulletin of the Los Angeles Neurological Society*. One of the Bogen articles and Gazzaniga's "Split Brain" are in R. Ornstein, ed., *The Nature of Human Consciousness*. The patient whose hands battled is in Gazzaniga. "It couldn't even double the number four" is in the discussion following Sperry's "Brain Bisection" paper in Eccles, as above.

I also used sections 1, 4, 5, 6, 10 and 15 of S. J. Dimond and J. G. Beaumont, *Hemisphere Function in the Human Brain*, and Dimond's *The Double Brain*. Without specific citations as background, I have used some of *The Neurosciences: Third Study Program*, edited by Schmitt and Worden. These books are expensive and technical; *Third Neurosciences* is also heavy (nonportable).

Robert Ornstein of the Langley Porter Neuropsychiatric Institute suggested readings, sent copies of journal articles in his files and read sections of the book in manuscript, for which I am thankful.

On the Left Hand (Right Brain), America's Leading Ashram

73   M. Murphy, *Golf in the Kingdom*.

76   " 'Somatosensory deprivation' . . .": J. Prescott in *Intellectual Digest*, 6–10 (March 1974). Certainly a far-out thesis, but then . . .

The Grandma and Grandpa of Gravity

Besides Sam Keen's account of Rolfing in *Psychology Today*, see *Bulletin of Structural Integration*.

Biofeedback: Who's at Home Here?

Virtually the only wheel in town is Aldine Publishing, which collects the annual *Biofeedback and Self-Control*.

While these collections are editorially the best of what went on, as a publishing job it is terrible: photographed journal articles, horrendously priced. Pp. 59–80 of my 1971 *Biofeedback* are missing. Just plain missing. Where is my copy of *Cardiovascular Psychophysiology,* ordered eighteen months ago? I marked up somebody else's. The new annual costs $18.50.

97 "a hundred minus seven . . .": Old stuff from way before biofeedback. E. D. Adrian and B. H. C. Matthews said that arithmetic would reduce alpha, and that was in 1934! In *Brain,* 57:355 (1934). And H. H. Jasper said opening your eyes would reduce alpha, but closing them would bring it back again, and that was published in 1941! In *Epilepsy and Cerebral Localization,* edited by W. Penfield and T. C. Erickson.

97 "A psychologist . . .": Ralph Hefferline of Columbia.

I used as a checklist *Relaxation and Related States: A Bibliography of Psychological and Physiological Research* by Richard J. Davidson and Gary E. Schwartz of the Harvard Psychology Department. Other than Aldine and above, I should cite G. E. Schwartz in *American Scientist* and D. Mostofsky, ed., *Behavior Control and Modification of Physiological Activity.*

Gary Schwartz suggested reading, supplied journal articles from his files and read the manuscript, for which I am thankful.

RESPECTABILITY, CONFIRMATION AND THE MYSTERY OF THE REBELLING RATS

Miller has a summary in A. M. Freedman et al., eds., *Comprehensive Textbook of Psychiatry.* His earlier writings are in N. E. Miller, *Selected Papers;* two more generalized articles are in *Science.* Dworkin has a summary in the first chapter of his *An Effort to Replicate Visceral Learning in the Curarized Rat.* Some of this history is counted in a small, carefully written book, *Visceral Learning,* by G. Jonas, basically a profile of Miller.

104 The difficulties with the curarized rats are described by Miller and Dworkin in P. A. Obrist et al., eds., *Cardiovascular Psychophysiology.*

104 T. Weiss and B. Engel in *Psychosomatic Medicine;* Engel and Bleecker, in *Cardiovascular Psychophysiology.*

Page

105   "two of the biofeedback pioneers": J. Stoyva and T. Budzynski, in the 1972 Aldine *Biofeedback* annual. Also, Budzynski et al. in *Behavior Therapy and Experimental Psychiatry*. Stoyva and Budzyinsky have other entries on biofeedback and tension headaches.

105   "Still another psychologist . . .": M. S. Sterman in L. Birk, *Seminars in Psychiatry*.

106   The material on the Greens is directly from them and from interviews with Elmer Green. Green et al., Menninger Foundation papers. Also J. D. Sargent et al. in *Psychosomatic Medicine* and Green et al. in J. Rose, ed., *Progress of Cybernetics*. The Greens wrote a summary in *Science Year, 1974*. Articles by the Greens and Walters are in several collections, and the Greens have been written up in the popular press, references not included here.

The enthusiasm for biofeedback was far from universal. See D. A. Paskewitz and M. T. Orne in *Science*. And one of the biofeedback researchers who read this chapter said the comparison to James Lind's two sailors sucking on limes was "unnecessarily generous; James Lind's experiments were better controlled than most biofeedback experiments."

WIRING UP THE YOGIS

The most widely collected report on the yogis is B. K. Anand et al. in *Journal of Electroencephalography and Clinical Neurophysiology*. The electroencephalographic study of the Zen masters in *Folio Psychiatria and Neurologia Japonica*, 20 (1966). Other yoga and Zen entries are under H. V. A. Rao et al. in *Journal of the All-India Institute of Mental Health* and M. A. Wenger and B. K. Bagchi in *Behavioral Science*.

113   "big hitters": The Greens' account of Swami Rama is also in *Science Year, 1974*. The account by the Greens of Jack Schwarz is "A Demonstration of Voluntary Control of Bleeding and Pain" in Menninger Foundation papers.

115   "And the perception of pain varies . . .": See R. A. Sternbach, *Principles of Psychophysiology*. "cheerful Gurkha recruits" in the autobiography of John Masters, *Bugles and a Tiger,* and *The Road Past Mandalay*.

Page

115   Melzack has a college-level exposition in R. F. Thompson, ed., *Physiological Psychology*, reprinted from *Scientific American*.

116   "demystify the yogic tricks": T. X. Barber, *LSD, Marihuana, Yoga, and Hypnosis*. The insensitivity to pain relates to a similar discussion of hypnosis and pain in Barber's *Hypnotism, Imagination and Human Potentialities*. See "Hypnotism and Surgical Pain," pp. 79–98. Barber is a prolific writer, and it isn't possible to list all the references; most of them concern hypnosis, but they have some relevance here. Look in the abstracts under Barber, T. X., and Calverly, D. S., and under Barber's associates, Spanos, N. P., and Chaves, J. F.

    T. X. Barber suggested readings, sent articles from his files and discussed a number of points not directly cited, but having a bearing on the whole manuscript, for which I am thankful.

III. Meditations

From William James to the mid-1960's, the literature on meditation is spotty at best. A physician and psychiatrist, Arthur Deikman, wrote two bridging essays: "Deautomatization and the Mystic Experience" in *Psychiatry*, which contains much of the historical material used by Benson et al. in *Psychiatry* (though for some reason it isn't cited), and "Bimodal Consciousness" in *Archives of General Psychiatry*. "Deautomatization" is reprinted in both R. Ornstein, ed., *The Nature of Human Consciousness*, and C. Tart, ed., *Altered States of Consciousness*. "Bimodal" is reprinted in Ornstein. I took a seminar of Deikman's, which provided the background in particular for pp. 165–68.

    TM material from TM. TM has considerably more material than has been referenced here.

122   "not as part of religion": And this section doesn't deal with meditation as part of religion. Further, the psychologies of the religious practices in this section are known generally to the professionals but not to the adherents. Nor does this section deal with meditation as therapy, though there is a growing literature on that subject. See the excellent overview by D. Goleman in *American Journal of Psychotherapy*. Also: E. Gellhorn in *Perspectives in Biology and Medicine* and Gellhorn and W. F. Kiely in *Journal of Nervous and Mental Disease*, 154:399 (1972).

Relaxation techniques using forms of meditation, but not called meditation in W. Luthe, *Autogenic Training,* and Luthe, ed., *Autogenic Therapy. IV. Research and Theory.* Also, Jacobson, *Progressive Relaxation.* And see J. Fagan and I. L. Shepherd, eds., *Gestalt Therapy Now,* especially Naranjo, and R. Assagioli, *Psychosynthesis.*

You Deserve a Break Today

128   Use of this mantram by unauthorized personnel is strictly forbidden.

131   "lactate concentrations": Not to get sidetracked on lactates, but this doesn't seem quite as significant as it first did. Lactate as a concomitant of anxiety was dramatized by Ferris Pitts, Jr., in an article with the striking title "The Biochemistry of Anxiety," in *Scientific American.* But recently it has been widely criticized. See N. Levitt in C. D. Spielberger, ed., *Anxiety: Current Trends in Theory and Research.* The other results from meditation have been duplicated extensively.

132   "hypnosis has no particular physiology": See T. X. Barber, and others.

134   Benson's *Lancet* article: I suppose the importance, to Benson, was that this was the first use of in, out, "one," with quantified results, instead of a mantram with quantified results. Jacobson had similar relaxation techniques forty years ago. A parallel to Benson's article is by J. F. Beary and Benson in *Psychosomatic Medicine.*

134   "beta spikes were appearing": See J. P. Banquet in *Journal of Electroencephalography and Clinical Neurophysiology.*

134   "TM reduced the symptoms of asthma": A. F. Wilson and R. Honsberger in *Clinical Research,* 2, 2 (1937).

135   " 'creativity and intelligence' ": G. Schwartz in *Psychology Today.*

138   Tart's reaction to TM: See C. Tart in *Journal of Transpersonal Psychology.*

142   "nitrogen nitrogen": Needless to say, these elements have been arranged for their poetry, not their biochemistry.

NOISE

143 "My favorite biology watcher": Lewis Thomas.

144 "health is something you . . . have to buy": L. Thomas, "Your Very Good Health," *The Lives of a Cell*, pp. 81–86. I wish everybody would read this, Congress, the drug companies, consumers, Blue Cross . . .

146 "*harmonics* of alpha as well as alpha": My counselors say TM is ahead of itself here. Wallace is referring to J. P. Banquet in *Journal of Electroencephalography and Clinical Neurophysiology*.

151 W. Hess, *Functional Organization of the Diencephalon*.

151 "The tendency of Christians . . .": T. Merton, *Mystics and Zen Masters*, pp. 205–09.

152 Difference between mantram and prayer: Swami Satchidananda, *Integral Yoga—Hatha*.

ECUMENICAL RELAXATION TECHNIQUES

152 "Choose whichever one . . .": I. Progoff, *The Cloud of Unknowing*.

153 "Sit down alone . . ."; R. French, *The Way of the Pilgrim*.

157 D. Goleman, unpublished doctoral dissertation, Harvard University, 1973, summarized in Goleman in *American Journal of Psychotherapy*.

WHY FRANNY FAINTED

162 J. Krishnamurti, *Commentaries on Living: Third Series*, quoted in J. E. Coleman, *The Quiet Mind*.

165 "A group of psychologists . . .": Hebb, Heron and Pritchard at McGill. "tiny projectors on contact lenses" described by Pritchard in R. L. Held and W. Richards, eds., *Perception: Mechanisms and Models*.

165 " 'ganzfeld' "; " 'blank out' ": W. Cohen in *American Journal of Psychology* and T. C. Cadwallander in *American Psychologist*. Ornstein, in *The Psychology of Consciousness*, makes the point about onepointedness or Void and "blank out."

Page

166 "eye movements became stereotyped": C. Furst in *Perception and Psychophysics*.

166 "red six of spades": And other cards, other colors. See J. Bruner in *Psychological Review*. And many other Bruner references in reception and categorization.

171 "When written up . . .": P. Kapleau, *The Three Pillars of Zen*.

172 "American psychotherapist in Japan": J. Huber, *Through an Eastern Window*. This account is reprinted in *Asian Psychology*, edited by Gardner and Lois Murphy.

174 " 'afterglow from this state' ": D. Goleman in *American Journal of Psychotherapy*.

174 Shaker furniture: It's interesting to consider this Shaker hymn in the light of this discussion of Zen psychology:
> Tis a gift to be simple
> Tis a gift to be free
> Tis a gift to come down
> Where you ought to be . . .
> And when we find ourselves in the place just right
> We'll be in the valley of love and delight.

IV. "Sport Is a Western Yoga"

QUARTERBACKING IN AN ALTERED STATE

185 Murphy and Brodie were, at one time, going to write a book together, and they had several public dialogues which I taped. *Intellectual Digest* published a Murphy-Brodie interview in January 1973 which had Brodie's statement about time slowing down, and a very odd pass to Gene Washington not discussed in the text here.

187 " 'There isn't any language' ": But the scholars will be eager to supply their own. M. Csikzentmihalyi in *Journal of Humanistic Psychology* calls a "Flow" state one where "action and awareness are sustained . . . in concentration," "limited stimulus field . . . awareness devoid of concern with outcome," "self-forgetfulness," "skills adequate to meet . . . the demand," "clarity." "Flow" is "an optimal fit between one's capability and the demands of the moment."

The only danger in this is that it leads to the quantification of "Flow." Think what football announcers could do with the statistics.

ZEN AND THE CROSS-COURT BACKHAND

In very different form, I wrote an account of Esalen sports and "yoga tennis" in *Sports Illustrated.*

THE SWEET MUSIC OF THE STRINGS

The Torben stories go round and round in sports magazines; I think Torben enjoys staging them just to see what sort of event the moment will produce. In any case, they inspire lyrical sportswriting, as done by Mark Kram in *Sports Illustrated* and Robert Bradford in *Tennis.* Bradford wrote up Borowiak several years after Torben, and Borowiak's Copenhagen trip is in his Borowiak story.

203   "you are the music"; T. S. Eliot was into the Dharma.

V. Vibes

AMBIGUITIES AND VIBES

207   "The editors of the Establishment press . . .": The press reviews the Alchemist continuously, that is, the "story" is what is up on the storyboard as a "story," and not the "story" itself. For example, on July 4, 1973, there was a large gathering of counter-cultural folk in Central Park in Manhattan. They sat and chanted and formed circles and drew curious passers-by, no story there. But then came a skywriting plane that wrote "OM" in the sky over New York. A clear blue sky and "OM." I was curious. Who hired the plane? Was this the first time anybody skywrote "OM" over a Western city? What was the reaction of sky-gawkers on seeing "OM" instead of "Pepsi-Cola"? What did the skywriter intend? Did "OM" cost less than "Pepsi-Cola"? Then the skywriting plane flew off, and this time when it came back it wrote "OM" in *Sanskrit,* ॐ. Now my curiosity was really up. Certainly this was the first case of Sanskrit skywriting—and right over hundreds of thousands of sky-gawkers! Who on earth was doing this? What was the pilot's reaction upon being given a Sanskrit mantram to skywrite? Right under the "OM," in both English and Sanskrit, was, of course, the headquarters of the New York *Times.* I opened the *Times* —all the news that's fit to print—on July 5. No skywriter. No "OM." Instead, several columns on the break-

Page

up of a hippie festival in Grand Junction, Colorado. As for the TV news, it went to the beach, and never turned its camera upward.

209   "poor Dr. Noone got blowpiped": The story of the search for Dr. Noone is told by his brother, Richard Noone, in *The Rape of the Dream People.*

210   "'the Second Coming of Santa Claus'": F. Gray in *New York Review.*

211   "The mahatma is sitting . . .": F. Gray in *New York Review.* Another account is in *Newsweek,* 157–58 (November 19, 1973).

212   Pineal gland: G. E. W. Wolstenholme and J. Knight, eds., *The Pineal Gland.*

214   "The Indian zapped . . .": F. Gray in *New York Review.*

216   B. Brown, *New Mind, New Body.*

Packagers

MEETINGS WITH REMARKABLE MEN

241   The aphorisms are in G. I. Gurdjieff, *Meetings with Remarkable Men.*

WHO'S A SUFI?

249   The Nasrudin stories are now in a series of paperbacks, done by Idries Shah. *The Dermis Probe, Tales of the Dervishes, Wisdom of the Idiots* and *The Pleasantries of the Incredible Mulla Nasrudin* are Dutton paperbacks, and Shah's *The Sufis* is an Anchor paperback.

249   Some of the Hasidic stories are in M. Buber's *Tales of the Hasidim.*

250   "Idries Shah wasn't a descendant . . .": I have absolutely no information on who is and is not a descendant of the Prophet. There is a similar attack on Shah in *Encounter* by a professor of Persian at the University of Edinburgh, L. P. Elwell-Sutton, who says that Shah has transcribed some Nasrudin stories, that his scholarship is sloppy, that his father was "an unsuccessful medical student turned traveler and publicist" and that the descendants of the Prophet number in the millions.

VI. The Far Side of Paradigm

THE SENIOR ASTRONAUT: YOU GOTTA KNOW
THE TERRITORY

Lilly's books are *The Center of the Cyclone* and *Programming and Metaprogramming in the Human Biocomputer*. His original paper is in *Psychiatric Research Reports*. See also S. Keen's interview with Lilly in *Psychology Today*. Lilly's remarks on the false objectivity of psychologists—"the behavioral view has something to offer . . . but it is incomplete"—are in "Solitude, Isolation and Confinement," Lilly's contribution to a small book with a big title, *The Psychodynamic Implications of Physiological Studies on Sensory Deprivation*, edited by L. Madow and L. Snow.

W. Heron's 1957 article in *Scientific American* is reprinted in S. Coopersmith, ed., *Frontiers of Psychological Research*. An unsigned review of the research to that date is in *Lancet*, 2:1072 (1959).

P. Solomon et al., eds., *Sensory Deprivation*, summarizes a conference which Lilly felt was the Establishment view.

Two chapters of *Isolation: Clinical and Experimental Approaches* by C. A. Brownfield are relevant.

A number of articles are in the collection edited by J. P. Zubek, *Sensory Deprivation: Fifteen Years of Research*.

Peter Suedfeld's article "The Benefits of Boredom" is in *American Scientist*. The first Suedfeld article on cutting down smoking is in *Journal of Applied Social Psychology*, 3:30–38 (1973). The others are referenced in "The Benefits of Boredom."

BABA RAM DASS: PILGRIM, PREACHER

While Ram Dass hasn't written as Ram Dass, his fans have taped his talks and made the edited versions into two books that are quite unique: *Be Here Now* and *The Only Dance There Is*. Not only are they unique, they are fun.

314   "I was blessed . . .'": *Be Here Now*. The other quotations are from *The Only Dance There Is*, tapes of talks made at the Menninger Foundation and the Spring Grove Hospital. And my own tapes.

CARLOS: I MET A MAN UPON A STAR

324   "Space does not conform . . .'" is in the preface by Walter Goldschmidt to *The Teachings of Don Juan: A Yaqui Way of Knowledge*, the first of the Don Juan books. The three that followed are *A Separate Reality*, *Journey to Ixtlan* and *Tales of Power*.

325   The Castaneda statements are from his interview in *Psychology Today* (December 1971).

328   "to make a double of yourself": Note this from G. Reed, *The Psychology of Anomalous Experience*, p. 53: "Shamans and witches cultivate and control their spirit doubles. The shaman double may be dispatched to round up the erring spirit of a patient, or *to bring back news of events in New York . . .*" (my italics)

PARAPSYCH

332   "perception studies": H. K. Hartline at the University of Pennsylvania won a Nobel prize for mapping the

receptive fields of cells. David Hubel and Torsten Wiesel at the Harvard Medical School have already been cited under "Harvard cats." The earlier frog's eye/ frog's brain work was done by Jerome Lettvin and his associates at MIT. See also R. L. Held and W. Richards, eds., *Perception: Mechanisms and Models*, R. F. Thompson's *Physiological Psychology* and *Introduction to Physiological Psychology*. Also P. M. Milner, *Physiological Psychology*.

332   "frog's eye/frog's brain experiment": That wasn't its purpose, of course, but it does seem to be consistent. See H. R. Maturana et al. in *Journal of General Physiology*. The popular version is under J. Y. Lettvin et al. in *Proceedings of the Institute of Radio Engineers*.

333   Eccles' statement is on p. 56 of the paperback edition of *Facing Reality*. See also the summary discussion in his *Brain and Conscious Experience*.

335   "Another writer . . .": New York *Times Magazine* (August 11, 1974).

346   "Some psychologists . . . tested Geller": According to Martin Gardner, *Scientific American* columnist.

351   Targ and Puthoff's *Nature* article: *Nature* also published a critique. Puthoff and Targ continued their physics-parapsychology speculations in "Physics, Entropy and Psychokinesis," SRI paper.

352   E. H. Walker, Rhine Swanton Symposium, AAAS. Not many quantum physicists are into ESP.

"BOSH, DR. JUNG"

355   "one famous incident": C. G. Jung, *Memories, Dreams, Reflections*, A. Jaffe, ed., pp. 155–56.

356   Ninety-seven percent "occult"; 3 percent research: R. A. White and L. A. Dale, *Parapsychology*.

359   Wired-up salmon: T. J. Hara in *Science*. The fish language is in J. H. Todd in *Scientific American*. Some of this derives from pp. 104ff. in *Life . . . the Unfinished Experiment* by S. Luria. But you can read L. Thomas, *The Lives of a Cell*, and get it all with such pleasure.

Page

THE MIND, THE QUANTUM AND THE UNIVERSE

363   Not only François Jacob, of course, but most recently. See "Language and Reality in Modern Physics" in *Physics and Philosophy*, W. Heisenberg, and "Discussions About Language" in *Physics and Beyond*, Heisenberg.

363   "the language of physics is less certain": S. Rose says, "The biologist, although confident of the extensions to the edifice he is creating, all the time has to build in doubt as to whether his physical foundations may not be in quagmire." *The Conscious Brain*, pp. 292–93.

365   "half are particles and half are anti-particles": This didn't quite pass my particle advisers, who wrote, "Certain particles are their own anti-particles. Better to say: many particles come in two forms, particles and anti-particles, the anti-particle having the same mass as the particle. As to their life, particles and anti-particles of a given species are equally stable . . . our world is made up largely of the particles proton, neutron, electron. When one of the corresponding antiparticles is created, it will sooner or later run into one of its counterparts and both will disappear in the annihilation."

    That's in case you want your particles straight. My point was just to create some perspective in time and space. Thanks to: John Wheeler, Tom Stix, Sam Treiman, the Joseph Henry Laboratories, Princeton University.

366   Neutrinos: A very good summary of subatomic physics is in A. Koestler, *The Roots of Coincidence*. Updike's "Cosmic Gall," from *Telephone Poles and Other Poems*, is also there, though I liked some different lines.

367   Wheeler's "superspace" is in *University: A Princeton Quarterly* (Summer 1972), "the mind, the quantum, and the universe" is in J. Wheeler, *Smithsonian and National Academy of Science*. Also Wheeler, "From Relativity to Mutability," in *The Physicist's Conception of Nature*, J. Mehra, ed.

368   " 'What's a quantum?' " Said Ernest Schrödinger, Nobel prizewinning quantum pioneer, "If all this damn'd quantum jumping were really here to stay, I should be sorry I ever got involved." W. Heisenberg, *Physics and Beyond*, p. 75.

Page

370 "real" and *res:* W. Heisenberg, *Physics and Philosophy.*

371 " 'complementarity' ": J. R. Oppenheimer, "Physics in the Contemporary World," in M. Gardner, ed., *Great Essays in Science,* p. 189.

371 " 'eternity and timelessness' ": Oppenheimer, *Science and the Common Understanding,* p. 69. " 'the objective world' ": W. Heisenberg, *"Across the Frontiers,* p. 227. " 'Scientific knowledge . . .' ": E. Wigner, "Two Kinds of Reality," *Symmetries and Reflections: Scientific Essays,* pp. 197–98.

372 " 'the human ability to understand' ": W. Heisenberg, "Role of Modern Physics in Human Thinking," *Physics and Philosophy,* pp. 201–02. "The understanding . . .": Heisenberg, "The Meaning of Beauty in the Exact Sciences," *Across the Frontiers,* pp. 177–78. Also see "Natural Law and the Structure of Matter" and "Wolfgang Pauli's Philosophical Outlook" in the same book. " 'faith in the central order' ": "Elementary Particles and Platonic Philosophy," *Physics and Beyond,* p. 247. And "First Encounter with the Atomic Concept," same volume.

See also, in Wigner, the whole section "Epistemology and Quantum Mechanics."

372 Einstein's Unified Field Theory; " 'all his abstract intuitions of reality' ": L. Barnett, *The Universe and Dr. Einstein,* p. 72.

Einstein wrote this bit of doggerel:
A thought that sometimes makes me hazy:
Am I—or are the others—crazy?
(in A. Koestler, *Act of Creation,* p. 134)

ACKNOWLEDGMENTS

Three people believed this was a book when I thought of it as only an investigation, a sabbatical. Their support contributed to converting their belief into fact. They are: T. George Harris, Lynn Nesbit and James Silberman.

Bibliography

Best-Written Book in the Bibliography
The Lives of a Cell, by Lewis Thomas

Don't be put off by such words as "prokaryocytes," "symbionts," "rhizobial" and "mitochondria," just to take samples from the fourth paragraph. You dont have to know them to get it.

Worst-Written Book in the Bibliography
Being and Time, by Martin Heidegger

Enormous Room for Improvement Dept.
All the books titled *Elements of Neurophysiology*
and all the books titled *The Mystics of Islam*

Most Surprising Essayist
Werner Heisenberg, *Physics and Philosophy*
and *Physics and Beyond*

Most Far-Out Autobiography
Memories, Dreams, Reflections, by C. G. Jung,
edited by Aniela Jaffe

Best Drug Book
Licit & Illicit Drugs,
edited by E. M. Brecher et al.

Best Textbook for Bedside Reading
The Pharmaceutical Basis of Therapeutics,
edited by Louis S. Goodman and Alfred Gilman

You can look up all the pills prescribed for you, and if you can find the generic name, you can save money on prescriptions. Paragraphs in each section are very technical. You might need a chemistry translation, or Lehninger's *Biochemistry*—a classic textbook, but an expensive one.

Best Collections
The Nature of Human Consciousness,
edited by Robert E. Ornstein

Not only the best collection for this book, but the introductions are equally good.

Physiological Psychology,
edited by Richard F. Thompson

Scientific American reader: nice graphics, somewhat abstract writing, and not all easy.

Best Brain Book
The Conscious Brain, by Steven Rose

Most Provocative
The Politics of Experience, by R. D. Laing

Periodicals *

Abrahams, V. C., et al., "Active Muscle Vasodilatation Produced by Stimulation of the Brain Stem: Its Significance in the Defense Reaction." *Journal of Physiology,* 154:491 (1960).

Alsop, Stewart, Column. *Newsweek* (March 11, 1974).

Anand, B. K., Chhina, G. S., and Singh, B. H., "Some Aspects of Electroencephalographic Studies in Yogis." *Journal of Electroencephalography and Clinical Neurophysiology,* 13:452–56 (1961).

——— et al., "Studies on Shri Remananda Yogi During His Stay in an Airtight Box." *Indian Journal of Medical Research,* 49:82–89 (1961).

Bagchi, B. K., and Wenger, M. A., "Electrophysical Correlations of Some Yoga Exercises." *Journal of Electroencephalography and Clinical Neurophysiology, Suppl.,* 7:132–49 (1957).

Baker, A. A., and Thorpe, J. G., "Placebo Response." *AMA Archives of Neurology and Psychiatry,* 78:57 (1957).

Banquet, J. P., "EEG and Meditation." *Journal of Electroencephalography and Clinical Neurophysiology,* 33:449–55 (1972).

———, "Spectral Analysis of EEG and Meditation." *Journal of Electroencephalography and Clinical Neurophysiology,* 35:143–51 (1973).

* This section lists articles in journals, magazines and newspapers, in relation to the notes.

Barber, T. X., "Physiological Effects of Hypnosis." *Psychological Bulletin*, 58:390–419 (1961).

Baynton, Barbara, Interview with James Prescott: "Touching." *Intellectual Digest*, 6–10 (March 1974).

Beary, J. F., and Benson, Herbert, "A Simple Psychophysiologic Technique Which Elicits the Hypometabolic Changes of the Relaxation Response." *Psychosomatic Medicine*, 36, 2:115–20 (March–April, 1974).

Benson, Herbert, Beary, John F., and Canol, Mark P., "The Relaxation Response." *Psychiatry*, 37 (February 1974).

———, Rosner, B. A., and Marzetta, B. R., "Decreased Systolic Blood Pressure in Hypertensive Subjects Who Practiced Meditation." *Journal of Clinical Investigation*, 52:82 (1973).

———, Rosner, B. A., Marzetta, B. R., and Klemchuk, H. M., "Decreased Blood-pressure in Pharmacologically Treated Hypertensive Patients Who Regularly Elicited the Relaxation Response." *Lancet* (February 23, 1974).

Blakemore, C., and Cooper, J. F., "Development of the Brain Depends on Visual Environment." *Nature*, 228:447–78 (1970).

Bogen, J. E. "The Other Side of the Brain." *Bulletin of L.A. Neurological Society*, I., 34:73–105(a); II., 34:135–62 (1969).

——— and Bogen, C. A., "III. The Other Side of the Brain." *Bulletin of L.A. Neurological Society*, 34:181–20 (1969).

——— and Gordon, H. W., "Musical Tests for Functional Lateralization with Intracarotid Amobarbital." *Nature*, 230, 5295:524-25 (April 23, 1971).

———, DeZine, R., Tenhouten, W. D., and Marsh, J. F., "The Other Side of the Brain, IV. The A/P Ration. *Bulletin of L.A. Neurological Society*, 37:49–61 (1972).

———, Gordon, H. W., and Sperry, R. W., "Absence of Deconnexion Syndrome in Two Patients with Partial Section of the Neocommissures." *Brain*, 94:327–36 (1971).

Bois, J. Samuel, "General Semantics and Zen." *ETC: A Review of General Semantics*, XVIII, 1 (April 1961).

Bradford, Robert H., "Torben the First: Free Spirit on the Tour." *Tennis* (September 1971).

Brain, W. Russell, "III. The Physiological Basis of Consciousness." *Brain*, LXXXI:426–55 (1958).

Bruner, Jerome. "On Perceptual Readiness." *Phychological Review*, 64:123–52 (1957).

Bruno, L. J. J., Hefferline, R. F., and Suslowitz, P. D., "Cross-modality Matching of Muscular Tension to Loudness." *Perception and Psychophysics* (1971).

Cadwallander, T. C., "Cessation of Visual Experience Under Prolonged Visual Stimulation." *American Psychologist* (abstract), 13:410 (1958).

Campbell, Colin, "Transcendence Is as American as Ralph Waldo Emerson." *Psychology Today,* 7, 11 (April 1974).

Cannon, Walter B., "The Emergency Function of the Adrenal Medulla in Pain and the Major Emotions." *American Journal of Physiology,* 33:356 (1941).

Cheek, F., Newell, S., and Joffe, M., "Deception in the Illegal Drug Market." *Science,* 176:1276 (1970).

Cohen, W., "Spatial and Textural Characteristics of the Ganzfeld." *American Journal of Psychology,* 70:403–10 (1957).

Czikzentmihalyi, M., "Play and Intrinsic Rewards." *Journal of Humanistic Psychology* (in press).

Deikman, Arthur, "Deautomatization and the Mystic Experience." *Psychiatry,* 29, 4:324–28 (1966).

————, "Bimodal Consciousness." *Archives of General Psychiatry,* 25:481–89 (December 1971).

DiCara, L. V., and Miller, N. E., "Heart-rate Learning in the Non-curarized State, Transfer to the Curarized State, and Subsequent Retraining in the Non-curarized State." *Physiological Behavior,* 4:621–24(b) (1959).

———— and Miller, N. E., "Changes in Heart Rate Instrumentally Learned by Curarized Rats as Avoidance Responses." *Journal of Comparative and Physiological Psychology,* 65:8–12(a) (1968).

Dishotsky, N., Loughman, W., Mogar, R., and Lipscomb, W., "LSD and Genetic Damage." *Science,* 172:431–40 (1971).

Elwell-Sutton, L. P., "Sufism and Pseudo-Sufism." *Encounter,* XLIV, 5 (May 1975).

Engel, B. T., and Hansen, S. P., "Operant Conditioning of Heart Rate Slowing." *Psychophysiology,* 3:176–87 (1966).

Erikson, Erik H., "Stress." *Psychology Today,* 3, 4 (September 1969).

Evans, Frederick J., "Placebo Response: Relationship to Suggestibility and Hypnotizability." *Proceedings of the 77th Annual Convention, American Psychological Association,* 889–90 (1969).

————, "The Power of a Sugar Pill." *Psychology Today,* 7, 11 (April 1974).

Feldenkrais, M., "The Importance of Being Upright." *CIBA-GEIGY Journal,* 1.

————, "Mind and Body." Two lectures delivered at Copenhagen Congress of Functional Movement and Relaxation, Systematics.

Feldman, P. E., "The Personal Element of Psychiatric Research." *American Journal of Psychiatry,* 113:52 (1956).

Furst, C., "Automizing of Visual Attention." *Perception and Psychophysics,* 10, 2 (1971).

Galin, David E., and Ornstein, R. E. "Lateral Specialization of Cognitive Modes: An EEG Study." *Psychophysiology*, 9, 4 (1972).

Gazzaniga, M. S., Bogen, J. E., and Sperry, R. W., "Observations on Visual Perception after the Disconnection of the Cerebral Hemispheres in Man." *Brain*, 88:221–36 (1965).

Gellhorn, E., "The Neurophysiological Basis of Anxiety." *Perspectives in Biology and Medicine*, 8:488 (1965).

Coleman, Daniel, "Meditation and Consciousness: An Asian Approach to Mental Health." *American Journal of Psychotherapy* (in press).

Gorton, Bernard E., "Physiology of Hypnosis." *Psychiatric Quarterly*, 23:317–43, 457–85 (1949).

Graden, J. F., "Anxiety or Caffeinism: A Diagnostic Dilemma." *American Journal of Psychiatry*, 131, 10 (October 1974).

Gray, Francine, "Blissing Out in Houston." *New York Review*, 36–43 (December 13, 1973).

———, "*Parapsychology and Beyond*." New York *Times Magazine*, 13ff. (August 11, 1974).

Green, E., and Green, A., "The Ins and Outs of Mind-body Energy." *Science Year, 1974*, Field Enterprises, Chicago, Illinois.

———, Green, A. M., and Walters, E. D., Sargent, J. D., and Meyer, R. G., Various papers on biofeedback. Especially papers dated September 7, 1971; April 5, 1973; March 9, 1972. The Menninger Foundation, Topeka, Kansas.

Gutmann, Mary C., and Benson, Herbert, "Interaction of Environmental Factors and Systemic Arterial Blood Pressure: A Review." *Medicine*, 50, 6 (1971).

Hara, T. J., et al. "Electroencephalographic Studies of the Homing Salmon." *Science*, 149 (1966).

Hirsch, H. V. B., and Spinelli, D. N., "Visual Experience Modifies Distribution of Horizontally and Vertically Oriented Receptive Fields in Cats." *Science*, 168:869–71 (1970).

——— and Spinelli, D. N., "Modification of the Distribution of Receptive Field Orientation in Cats by Selective Visual Exposure During Development." *Experimental Brain Research*, 13:509–27 (1971).

Hofmann, A., "Psychotomimetic Drugs. *Acta Physiol. Pharmac. Neerl.*, 8:240–58 (1959).

Kahn, Robert L., "Stress." *Psychology Today*, 3, 4 (September 1969).

Kasamatsu, Akira, and Hirai, Tomio, "An Electroencephalographic Study on the Zen Meditation (Zazen) Folio." *Psychiat. Neurol. Japonica*, 20:315–36 (1966).

Keen, Sam, "From Dolphins to LSD—A Conversation with John Lilly." *Psychology Today* (December 1971).

———"The Sorcerer's Apprentice" (interview with Carlos Castaneda). *Psychology Today* (December 1972).

————, "We Have No Desire to Strengthen the Ego or Make It Happy" (conversation with Oscar Ichazo). *Psychology Today* (July 1973).

Kinsbourne, M., and Cook, J., "Generalized and Lateralized Effects of Concurrent Verbalization on a Unimanual Skill." *Quarterly Journal of Experimental Psychology*, 23:341–345 (1971).

Klein, Sheldon, "Zen Buddhism and General Semantics." *A Review of General Semantics*, XIV, 2 (Winter 1956–57).

Koenig, Peter, "Placebo Effect in Patent Medicine." *Psychology Today*, 7, 11 (April 1974).

Kondo, Akihisa, "Zen in Psychotherapy: The Virtue of Sitting." *Chicago Review*, 12, 2 (1958).

Kram, Mark, "The Not So Melancholy Dane." *Sports Illustrated* (April 7, 1969).

Lester, James T., "Stress." *Psychology Today*, 3, 4 (September 1969).

Lettvin, J. Y., Maturana, H. R., McCulloch, W. S., and Pitts, W. H., "What the Frog's Eye Tells the Frog's Brain." *Proceedings of the Institute of Radio Engineers*, 47:1940–51 (1959).

Levy, J. "Possible Basis for the Evolution of Lateral Specialization of the Human Brain." *Nature*, 224:614–15 (1969).

————, Trevarthen, C., and Sperry, R. W., "Perception on Bilateral Chimeric Figures Following Hemispheric Deconnexion." *Brain*, 95:61–78 (1972).

Levy-Agresi, J., and Sperry, R. W., "Differential Perceptual Capacities in Major and Minor Hemispheres." *Proceedings of National Academy of Sciences*, 61:1151 (1968).

Lilly, John C. "Mental Effects of Reduction of Ordinary Levels of Physical Stimuli on Intact Healthy Persons." *Psychiatric Research Reports*, 5:1–9 (1956).

Luparello, T., Leist, N., Lourie, C. R., and Sweet, I., "The Interaction of Psychologic Stimuli and Pharmacologic Agents on Airway Reactivity in Asthmatic Subjects." *Psychosomatic Medicine*, 32:509–21 (1970).

Luria, A. R., "The Functional Organization of the Brain." *Scientific American*, 222:66–79 (1970).

McGlashan, Thomas H., Evans, Fredrick J., and Orne, Martin T., "The Nature of Hypnotic Analgesia and Placebo Response to Experimental Pain." *Psychosomatic Medicine*, 31, 3:227–46 (1969).

McQuade, Walter, "What Stress Can Do to You"; "Doing Something About Stress." *Fortune* (January 1972; May 1973).

Maturana, H. R., Lettvin, J. Y., McCulloch, W. S., and Pitts, W. H., "Anatomy and Physiology of Vision in the Frog." *Journal of General Physiology*, 43/2:129–75 (1960).

Melzak, R., "Why Acupuncture Works." *Psychology Today*, 7, 1:28–37 (June 1973).

——— and Wall, P., "Pain Mechanisms: A New Theory." *Science*, 150:971–79 (1965).

Miller, N. E., "Extending the Domain of Learning." *Science*, 162:671(a) (1966).

———, "From the Brain to Behavior." Invited lecture at XIIth Inter-American Congress of Psychology, Montevideo, Uruguay (March 30–April 6, 1969).

———, "Learning of Visceral and Glandular Responses." *Science*, 163:434–45 (1969).

——— and DiCara, L. V., "Instrumental Learning of Heart Rate Changes in Curarized Rats: Shaping and Specificity to Discriminative Stimulus." *Journal of Comparative and Physiological Psychology*, 65:1–7 (1968).

Olds, J., "Pleasure Centers in the Brain." *Scientific American*, 195:105–16 (1956).

Orme-Johnson, W., "Autonomic Stability and Transcendental Meditation." *Psychosomatic Medicine*, 35, 4:341–49 (July–August 1973).

Otis, Leon S., "If Well Integrated But Anxious, Try." *Psychology Today*, 7, 11 (April 1974).

Paskewitz, David A., and Orne, Martin T., "Visual Effects on Alpha Feedback Training." Science, 181 (July 27, 1973).

Pitts, Ferris N., "The Biochemistry of Anxiety." *Scientific American*, 220:12, 69–75 (February 1969).

Pribram, K. H., "The Neurophysiology of Remembering." *Scientific American*, 220:73–86 (1969).

Prince, R. H., "The Use of Rauwolfia for the Treatment of Psychoses by Nigerian Native Doctors." *American Journal of Psychiatry*, CXVII:147–49 (1960).

Puthoff, Harold, and Targ, Russell, "Physics, Entropy and Psychokinesis." Stanford Research Institute paper presented at Conference on Quantum Physics and Parapsychology, Geneva, Switzerland (August 26–27, 1974).

Radloff, Roland, and Helmreich, Robert, "Stress." *Psychology Today*, 3, 4 (September 1969).

Rao, H. V. A., Krisnaswamy, N. Narasimhaiya, R. L. Hoenis, J., and Govindaswamy, M. V., "Some Experiments on 'Yogis' in Controlled States." *Journal of All-India Institute of Mental Health* 1:49–106 (1958).

Rorvik, David M., "Jack Schwarz Feels No Pain." *Esquire*, 209 (December 1972).

Sargent, J. D., Green, E. E., and Walters, E. D., "Preliminary Reports on the Use of Autogenic Feedback Training in the Treatment of Migraine and Tension Headaches." *Psychosomatic Medicine* (1972).

Schwartz, G. E., "TM Relaxes Some People and Makes Them Feel Better." *Psychology Today*, 7, 11 (April 1974).

————, "Biofeedback: Self-Regulation and the Patterning of Physiological Processes." *American Scientist* (May 1975).

Selye, Hans, "Stress." *Psychology Today*, 3, 4:24 (September 1969).

Shapiro, A. K., "The Placebo Effect in the History of Medical Treatment: Implications for Psychiatry." *American Journal of Psychiatry*. CXVI:298–304 (1959).

————, "A Contribution to the History of the Placebo Effect." *Behavioral Science*, 5:109–35 (1960).

Smith, Adam, "Alumni Notes—Altered States. U." *Psychology Today* (July 1973).

————, "Trying the Dance of Shiva." *Sports Illustrated* (August 13, 1973).

Sperry, R. W., "Neurology and the Mind-brain Problem." *American Scientists*, 40:291–312 (1952).

————, "Cerebral Organization and Behavior." Science, 133:1749 (1961).

————, "The Great Cerebral Commissure." *Scientific American*, 210:42 (1964).

————, "A Modified View of Consciousness." *Psychological Review*, 76:532–36 (1969).

————, "Memory Impairment Following Commissurotomy in Man." *Brain*, 97:263–72 (1974).

Spinelli, D. N., Hirsch, H. V. B., Phelps, R. W., and Metzler, J., "Visual Experience as a Determinant of the Response Characteristics of Cortical Receptive Fields in Cats." *Experimental Brain Research* 15:289–304 (1972).

Sternbach, R. A., "The Effects of Instructional Sets on Automatic Responsivity," *Psychophysiology*, I:67–72 (1964).

Suedfeld, P., "The Benefits of Boredom." *American Scientist*, 63:60 (1975).

Targ, Russell, and Puthoff, Harold, "Information Transmission Under Conditions of Sensory Shielding." *Nature*, 252, 5476:602–07 (October 18, 1974).

Tart, Charles, "A Psychologist's Experience with Transcendental Meditation." *Journal of Transpersonal Psychology*, 2 (1971).

Todd, J. H., "The Chemical Language of Fishes." *Scientific American*, 224 (5):98–108 (1971).

Walker, Evan Harris, "The Compleat Quantum Mechanical Anthropologist." Rhine Swanton Symposium, 73rd Annual American Anthropological Association Meeting, Mexico City (November 19–24, 1974).

Wallace, Robert K., "Physiological Effects of Transcendental Meditation." *Science*, 167:1751–54 (1970).

———— and Benson, Herbert, "The Physiology of Meditation." *Scientific American*, 226:85–90 (1972).

————, Benson, Herbert, and Wilson, Archie F., "A Wakeful

Hypometabolic State." *American Journal of Physiology,* 221:795–99 (1971).

Warth, Mary Jo., "The Story of the Acid Profiteers." *The Village Voice,* 5 (August 22, 1974).

Watts, Alan W., "Beat Zen, Square Zen, and Zen." *Chicago Review,* 12, 2 (1958).

Weiss, T., and Engel, B. T., "Operant Condititoning of Heart Rate in Patients with Premature Ventricular Contractions." *Psychosomatic Medicine,* 33:301–21 (1971).

Wenger, M. A., and Bagchi, B. K., "Studies of Autonomic Functions in Practitioners of Yoga in India." *Behavioral Science,* 6:312–23 (1961).

Whatmore, George B., and Kohli, Daniel P., "Dysponesis: A Neurophysiologic Factor in Functional Disorders." *Behavioral Science,* 13, 2 (March 1968).

Wheeler, J., "The Universe as Home for Man," *Smithsonian and National Academy of Science* (April 25, 1973).

Wienpahl, Paul, "Zen and the Work of Wittgenstein." *Chicago Review,* 12, 2 (1958).

Wiesel, T. N., and Hubel, D. H., "Comparison of the Effects of Unilateral and Bilateral Eye Closure on Cortical Unit Responses in Kittens." *Journal of Neurophysiology,* 28:1029–40 (1965).

Books *

Aaronson, B., and Osmond, H., eds., *Psychedelics: The Uses and Implications of Hallucinogenic Drugs,* Cambridge, Schenkman, 1971.

Abramson, H., ed., *The Uses of LSD in Psychotherapy and Alcoholism.* Indianapolis, Bobbs-Merrill, 1966.

Adam, G., *Interoception and Behavior.* Budapest, Akadémiai Kiadó, 1967.

Allen, J. P. B., and van Buren, P., eds., *Chomsky: Selected Readings.* Oxford University Press, 1971.

Assagioli, Roberto, *Psychosynthesis.* New York, Viking Compass, 1971.

Bailly, J. A., *Rapport des Commissaires par le Roi de l'Examen du Magnetisme Animal.* Paris, Imprimie Royal, 1784.

Barber, T. X., *Hypnosis: A Scientific Approach.* New York, Van Nostrand, Reinhold, 1969.

---

* These volumes back up the note references. Sometimes only a single chapter is relevant. Many of the books are technical, and the technical books are overrepresented.

————, *LSD, Marihuana, Yoga and Hypnosis.* Chicago, Aldine, 1970.

———— et al., eds., *Biofeedback and Self-Control 1970.* Chicago, Aldine, 1971.

————, Spanos, N. P., and Chaves, J. F., *Hypnotism, Imagination and Human Potentialities.* New York, Pergamon Press, 1974.

Barnett, Lincoln, *The Universe and Dr. Einstein.* New York, Morrow, 1957.

Beckett, Samuel, *Molloy.* New York, Grove Press, 1955.

————, *Waiting for Godot.* New York, Grove Press, 1954.

————, *Proust.* New York, Grove Press, n.d.

Bennett, J. G., *Gurdjieff: Making of a New World.* New York, Harper & Row, 1973.

Bergin, A. E., and Garfield, S. L., eds., *Handbook of Psychotherapy and Behavior Change: Empirical Analysis.* New York, Wiley, 1971.

Birk, L., *Seminars in Psychiatry.* New York, Grune & Stratton, 1973.

Bonica, John J., ed., *Pain.* New York, Raven Press, 1973.

Brain, W. Russell, *Mind, Perception, and Science.* Oxford, Blackwell, 1951.

Brecher, E. M., et al., eds., *Licit & Illict Drugs,* Boston, Little, Brown, 1972.

Brown, Barbara, *New Mind, New Body.* New York, Harper & Row, 1974.

Brownfield, C. A. *Isolation: Clinical and Experimental Approaches.* New York, Random House, 1965.

Bruner, Jerome. *On Knowing: Essays for the Left Hand,* Harvard University Press, 1962.

Buber, Martin, *Tales of the Hasidim: Early Masters.* New York, Schocken Books, 1973. (paper)

————, *Tales of the Hasidim: Later Masters.* New York, Schocken Books, 1974. (paper)

Campbell, Joseph, *The Hero with a Thousand Faces,* Bollingen/Princeton, 1968.

————, *The Mythic Image.* Bollingen/Princeton, 1975.

Cannon, W. B., *The Wisdom of the Body.* New York, Norton, 1939.

Castaneda, Carlos, *The Teachings of Don Juan: A Yaqui Way of Knowledge.* University of California Press, 1968.

————, *A Separate Reality.* New York, Simon & Schuster, 1971.

————, *Journey to Ixtlan.* New York, Simon & Schuster, 1972.

————, *Tales of Power.* New York, Simon & Schuster, 1974.

Chomsky, Noam, *Syntactic Structures.* The Hague, Mouton, 1957.

————, *Language and Mind.* New York, Harcourt, Brace & World, 1968.

————, *Aspects of the Theory of Syntax*. Cambridge, MIT Press, 1969.

Cohen, S. A., *The Beyond Within*. New York, Atheneum, 1967.

Coleman, J. E., *The Quiet Mind*. London, Rider & Co., 1971.

Conant, James, *On Understanding Science*. New York, New American Library, 1951.

Coopersmith, Stanley, ed., *Frontiers of Psychological Research*. San Francisco, W. H. Freeman, 1966.

DeBold, R. C., and Leaf, R. C., eds., *LSD, Man and Society*. Wesleyan University Press, 1967.

de Hartmann, T., *Our Life with Mr. Gurdjieff*. New York, Penguin Books, 1972.

Delgado, José M. R., *Physical Control of the Mind*. New York, Harper & Row, 1969.

De Ropp, Robert S., *Drugs and the Mind*. New York, Grove Press-Evergreen, 1957.

————, *The Master Game*. New York, Dell/Delta, 1968.

————, *The Church of the Earth*. New York, Delacorte, 1974.

Dimond, Stuart J., *The Double Brain*. Edinburgh, Churchill Livingstone, 1972.

———— and Beaumont, J. Graham, *Hemisphere Function in the Human Brain*. New York, Wiley, 1974.

Dobzhansky, T., *Mankind Evolving: The Evolution of the Human Species*. Yale University Press, 1962.

Dubos, R., *So Human an Animal*. New York, Scribner's, 1968.

Dworkin, Barry, *An Effort to Replicate Visceral Learning in the Curarized Rat*. New York, Rockefeller University Press, 1973.

Eccles, J. C., ed., *Brain and Conscious Experience*. New York, Springer-Verlag, 1966.

————, *Facing Reality*. New York, Springer-Verlag, 1970.

Esslin, Martin, *The Theatre of the Absurd*. Garden City, N.Y., Anchor Books, 1969.

Fagan, Joen, and Shepherd, Irma L., *Gestalt Therapy Now*. Cupertino, Calif., Science & Behavior Books, 1970.

Feldenkrais, M. *Awareness Through Movement*. New York, Harper & Row, 1972.

————, *Body and Mature Behavior*. New York, International Universities Press, 1949, 1973.

Frank, J. D., *Persuasion and Healing: A Comparative Study of Psychotherapy*. Baltimore, Johns Hopkins Press, 1961.

Freedman, A. M., Kaplan, H. I., and Sadock, B. J., eds., *Comprehensive Textbook of Psychiatry*, 2nd. ed. Baltimore, Williams & Wilkins, 1974.

Freedman, Meyer, and Rosenman, Ray, *Type A Behavior and Your Heart*. New York, Knopf, 1974.

French, Reginald, *The Way of the Pilgrim*. New York, Seabury Press, 1968.

Gardner, M., ed., *Great Essays in Science*. New York, Washington Square Press, 1963.

Gazzaniga, M. S., *The Bisected Brain*. New York, Appleton-Century-Crofts, 1970.

Globus, G. G., Maxwell, G., and Savodnik, I., *Mind and Brain: Philosophical and Scientific Approaches to the "World Knot."* New York, Plenum Press. 1974.

Goodman, Louis S., and Gilman, Alfred, *The Pharmacological Basis of Therapeutics*, 4th ed. New York, Macmillan, 1970.

Gurdjieff, G. I., *Meetings with Remarkable Men*. New York, Dutton, 1963. (paper, 1969)

Hartmann, Ernest L., *The Functions of Sleep*. Yale University Press, 1973.

Heisenberg, Werner, *Physics and Philosophy*. New York, Harper Torchbook, 1962.

———, *Physics and Beyond*. New York, Harper Torchbook, 1971.

———, *Across the Frontiers*. New York, Harper Torchbook, 1974.

Held, Richard L., and Richards, Whitman, *Perception: Mechanisms and Models*. San Francisco, W. H. Freeman, 1972.

Herrigel, Eugen, *Zen in the Art of Archery*. New York, Vintage, 1971.

Hess, Walter R., *The Functional Organization of the Diencephelon*. New York, Grune & Stratton, 1957.

Hirai, Tomio, *The Psychophysiology of Zen*. Tokyo, Igaku Shoin, 1974.

Hoffer, A., and Osmund, H., *The Hallucinogens*. New York, Academic Press, 1967.

Huber, Jack, *Through an Eastern Window*. Boston, Houghton Mifflin, 1967.

Hulme, Kathryn, *Undiscovered Country*. Boston, Atlantic, Little Brown, 1966. (paper)

Huxley, Aldous, *The Doors of Perception*. New York, Harper Colophon, 1963.

Jacobson, Edmund, *Progressive Relaxation*. University of Chicago Press, 1938.

James, W., *Varieties of Religious Experience*. New York, New American Library.

Jonas, Gerald, *Visceral Learning*. New York, Viking, 1973.

Jung, C. G., *Memories, Dreams, Reflections*, Aniela Jaffe, ed. New York, Vintage Books, 1961.

Kamiya, J., et al., eds., *Biofeedback and Self-Control: A Reader*. Chicago, Aldine, 1971.

Kapleau, Philip, *The Three Pillars of Zen*. Boston, Beacon, 1967.

Koestler Arthur, *Act of Creation*. New York, Dell, 1966.

———, *The Roots of Coincidence*. New York, Random House, 1972.

Kiev, A., ed., *Magic, Faith and Healing.* New York, Free Press, 1964.

Krishna, Gopi, *The Biological Basis of Religion and Genius.* New York, Harper & Row, 1971.

Krishnamurti, J., *Commentaries on Living: Third Series.* London, Victor Gollancz, 1962.

Kuhn, Thomas, *The Structure of Scientific Revolutions.* Phoenix Books, University of Chicago Press, 1967.

Laing, R. D., *The Politics of Experience.* New York, Ballantine, 1967.

Lefort, Rafael (pseud.), *The Teachers of Gurdjieff.* New York, Weiser, 1973.

Lehninger, A. L., *Biochemistry: The Molecular Basis of Cell Structure and Function.* New York, Worth, 1970.

Lewin, L., *Phantastica, Narcotic and Stimulating Drugs.* London, Routledge & Kegan Paul, 1931.

Lilly, John, *The Center of the Cyclone.* New York, Julian Press, 1972.

——, *Programming and Metaprogramming in the Human Biocomputer,* rev. New York, Julian Press, 1972.

Lindzey, G., Hall, C., and Thompson, R. F., *Psychology.* New York, Worth. 1975.

Luria, S. E., *Life . . . the Unfinished Experiment.* New York, Scribner's, 1973.

Luthe, W., ed., *Autogenic Therapy,* Vols. 1–5. New York, Grune & Stratton, 1967.

McGuigan, F. J., and Schoonover, R. A., eds., *The Psychophysiology of Thinking: Studies of Covert Processes.* New York, Academic Press, 1973.

Madow, Leo, and Snow, Laurence, *The Psychodynamic Implications of Physiological Studies on Sensory Deprivation.* Springfield, C. C. Thomas, 1970.

Maslow, Abraham, *Religions, Values, and Peak Experiences.* New York, Viking, 1970.

——, *The Farther Reaches of Human Nature.* New York, Viking, 1971.

Masters, John, *Bugles and a Tiger.* New York, Ballantine, 1969.

Masters, R. E., and Houston, Jean, *The Varieties of Psychedelic Experience.* New York, Dell/Delta, 1966.

Mehra, Jagdish, ed., *The Physicist's Conception of Nature.* Boston, D. Reidel, 1973.

Merton, Thomas, *Mystics and Zen Masters.* New York, Dell/Delta, 1967.

——, *Zen and the Birds of Appetite.* New York, New Directions, 1968.

Metzner, Ralph, ed., *The Ecstatic Adventure.* New York, Macmillan, 1968.

Miller, N. E., *Selected Papers.* Chicago, Aldine, 1971.

———— and Dworkin, B., *Biofeedback: Areas of Research and Application.* New York. Academic Press (in press).

———— et al., eds., *Biofeedback and Self-Control, 1973*, Chicago, Aldine, 1974.

Milner, P. M., *Physiological Psychology.* New York, Holt, Rinehart & Winston, 1970.

Moss, Thelma, *The Probability of the Impossible.* New York, Hawthorn Books, 1975.

Mostofsky, D., ed., *Behavior Control and Modification of Physiological Activity.* New York, Appleton-Century-Crofts (in press).

Mountcastle, V. B., ed., *Interhemispheric Relations and Cerebral Dominance.* Baltimore, Johns Hopkins Press, 1962.

Murphy, Gardner, and Murphy, Lois, eds., *Asian Psychology.* New York, Basic Books, 1968.

Murphy, Michael, *Golf in the Kingdom.* New York, Viking, 1972.

Naranjo, Claudio, and Ornstein, Robert, *On the Psychology of Meditation.* New York, Viking/Esalen, 1971.

Noone, Richard, *The Rape of the Dream People.* London, Hutchinson, 1972.

Obrist, P. A., et al., eds., *Cardiovascular Psychophysiology.* Chicago, Aldine, 1974.

Oppenheimer, J. Robert, *Science and the Common Understanding.* New York, Simon & Schuster, 1964.

Ornstein, Robert E., *On the Experience of Time.* Baltimore, Penguin, 1969.

————, *The Psychology of Consciousness.* San Francisco, W. H. Freeman, 1972.

————, ed., *The Nature of Human Consciousness.* San Francisco, W. H. Freeman, 1973.

Ouspensky, P. D., *In Search of the Miraculous.* New York, Harcourt, Brace, 1949.

Penfield, W., *The Excitable Cortex in Conscious Man.* Springfield, C. C. Thomas, 1958.

———— and Erickson, T. C., eds., *Epilepsy and Cerebral Localization.* Springfield, C. C. Thomas, 1941.

———— and Roberts, L., *Speech and Brain Mechanisms.* Princeton University Press, 1959.

Peters, Fritz, *Boyhood with Gurdjieff.* Baltimore, Penguin Books, 1972.

Pines, Maya, *The Brain Changers.* New York, Harcourt Brace, 1973.

Pribram, K. H., ed., *Mood, States and Mind.* Baltimore, Penguin, 1969.

————, *Languages of the Brain: Experimental Paradoxes and Principles in Neuropsychology.* Englewood Cliffs, N.J., Prentice-Hall, 1971.

Progoff, Ira, *The Cloud of Unknowing*. New York, Julian Press, 1969.

Rahula, Walpola, *What the Buddha Taught*. New York, Evergreen-Grove, 1974.

Ram Dass, *Be Here Now*. New Mexico, Lama Foundation, 1971.

———, *The Only Dance There Is*. New York, Doubleday/Anchor, 1974.

Reed, Graham, *The Psychology of Anomalous Experience*. New York, Houghton Mifflin Sentry Books, 1972.

Reps, Paul, ed., *Zen Flesh, Zen Bones*. New York, Doubleday/Anchor, n.d.

Rose, J., ed., *Progress of Cybernetics: Proceedings of the International Congress of the Cybernetics, London, 1969*. London, Gordon & Breach, 1970.

Rose, Steven, *The Conscious Brain*. New York, Knopf, 1973.

Roszak, T., *The Making of a Counter Culture*. New York, Doubleday, 1969.

———, *Where the Wasteland Ends: Politics and Transcendence in Post-Industrial Society*. New York, Doubleday, 1972.

Salinger, J. D., *Franny and Zooey*. New York, Bantam Books, 1972.

Satchidananda, Swami, *Integral Yoga—Hatha*. New York, Holt, Rinehart & Winston, 1970.

Schmitt, F. O., and Worden, F. G., eds., *The Neurosciences: Third Study Program*. Cambridge, MIT Press, 1973.

Scholem, Gershom, *Jewish Mysticism*, 7th ed. New York, Schocken Books, 1973.

Selye, Hans, *The Stress of Life*. New York, McGraw-Hill Paperback, 1956.

Shah, Idries, *The Pleasantries of the Incredible Mulla Nasrudin*. New York, Dutton Paperback, 1971.

———, *Wisdom of the Idiots*. New York, Dutton Paperback, 1971.

———, *The Dermis Probe*. New York, Dutton Paperback, 1971.

———, *The Sufis*. New York, Anchor Edition, 1971.

———, *Caravan of Dreams*. Baltimore, Penguin, 1972.

Shapiro, D., et al., eds., *Biofeedback and Self-Control, 1972*. Chicago, Aldine, 1973.

Sherrington, Charles, *Man on His Nature*. Cambridge University Press, 1940.

Smith, Grover, ed., *The Letters of Aldous Huxley*. New York, Harper & Row, 1969.

Smith, W. L., ed., *Drugs, Development and Cerebral Function*, Ch. 1. Springfield, C. C. Thomas, 1971.

——— and Kinsbourne, M., eds., *Hemisphere Disconnection and Cerebral Function*. Springfield, C. C. Thomas, 1972.

Solomon, Philip, et al., eds., *Sensory Deprivation: A Sympo-*

sium Held at Harvard Medical School. Harvard University Press, 1961.

Spielberger, C. D., ed., *Anxiety: Current Trends in Theory and Research.* New York, Academic Press, 1972.

Stephen, *Monday Night Class.* Seattle, The Book Publishing Company, n.d.

Sternbach, Richard A., *Principles of Psychophysiology.* New York, Academic Press, 1966.

Stewart, Kilton, *Pygmies and Dream Giants.* New York, Norton, 1954.

Stoyva, J., et al., eds., *Biofeedback and Self-Control, 1971.* Chicago, Aldine, 1972.

Tart, C., ed., *Altered States of Consciousness: A Book of Readings.* New York, Wiley, 1969.

Teeven, R. C. et al., *Readings for Introductory Psychology,* New York, Harcourt Brace, 1972.

Teyler, T. J., ed., *Altered States of Awareness: Readings from Scientific American.* San Francisco, W. H. Freeman, 1972.

Thomas, Lewis, *The Lives of a Cell.* New York, Viking, 1974.

Thompson, Richard F., *Physiological Psychology.* San Francisco, W. H. Freeman, 1972.

——, *Introduction to Physiological Psychology.* New York, Harper & Row, 1975.

Tinbergen, N., *The Study of Instinct.* Folcroft, Pa., Folcroft, 1951.

Torrey, E. Fuller, *The Mind Game.* New York, Bantam, 1973.

——, *The Death of Psychiatry.* Radnor, Pa., Chilton, 1974.

Trimingham, J. Spencer, *The Sufi Orders in Islam.* Oxford University Press, 1971.

Trungpa, Chogyam, *Cutting Through Spiritual Materialism.* Berkeley, Calif., Shambala Publications, 1973.

——, *Meditation in Action.* Berkeley, Calif., Shambala Publications, 1969.

——, *Born in Tibet.* New York, Harcourt Brace, 1968.

Updike, John, *Telephone Poles and Other Poems.* New York, 1963.

Von Bonin, G., *Some Papers on the Cerebral Cortex.* Springfield, C. C. Thomas, 1960.

Weil, Andrew, *The Natural Mind.* Boston, Houghton Mifflin, 1972.

White, Rhea A., and Dale, Lewis A., *Parapsychology: Sources of Information.* Scarecrow Press, The American Society for Psychical Research, Metuchen, N.J., 1973.

Widroe, Harvey, ed., *Human Behavior and Brain Function.* Springfield, C. C. Thomas, 1973.

Wigner, Eugene, *Symmetries and Reflections: Scientific Essays.* Cambridge, MIT Press, 1970.

Wilhelm, Richard, trans. C. F. Baynes, trans. *The I Ching or Book of Changes,* Princeton/Bollingen, 1967.

Wolstenholme, G. E. W., and Knight, Julie, eds., *The Pineal Gland*. Edinburgh, London, Churchill Livingstone, 1971.

Yates, Frances, *Giordano Bruno: The Hermetic Tradition*. New York, Vintage, 1969.

Zaehner, R. C., *Zen, Drugs and Mysticism*. New York, Vintage, 1972.

Zubek, J. P., *Sensory Deprivation: Fifteen Years of Research*. New York, Appleton-Century-Crofts, 1969.

No author or editor: *Psychology Today* (textbook). Del Mar, Calif.: CRM Books, 1970.

Learn to live with somebody... yourself.

to your health

Contents

—⌐回⌐—

Contents

CONTENTS

Preface

OUR GOAL IN WRITING *"They Say / I Say"* has been to offer
students a user-friendly model of writing that will help them
put into practice the important principle that writing is a social
activity. Proceeding from the premise that effective writers
enter conversations of other writers and speakers, this book
encourages students to engage with those around them—
including those who disagree with them—instead of just
expressing their ideas "logically." Our own experience teaching first-year writing students has led us to believe that to be
persuasive, arguments need not only supporting evidence but
also motivation and exigency, and that the surest way to
achieve this motivation and exigency is to generate one's own
arguments as a response to those of others—to something "they
say." And to help students write their way into the often daunt-
ing conversations of academia and the wider public sphere, the
book provides templates to help them make sophisticated
rhetorical moves that they might otherwise not think of
attempting.

That *"They Say"* is now being taught at hundreds of colleges
and universities suggests that there is a need for such a book,
and that there is a widespread desire for explicit instruction
that helps writers negotiate the basic moves necessary to "enter

the conversation." Instructors at schools across the country have told us how much this book helps their students learn how to write academic discourse, and some students have written to us saying that it's helped them to "crack the code," as one student put it.

At the same time, many instructors have told us that they wish the book included more readings—to provide examples of the moves taught in this book, and also to spark discussion and writing. Hence this new version, which adds more than thirty readings on four compelling and controversial issues. The readings provide a glimpse into some important conversations of our day—and will, we hope, provoke students to respond and thus to join in those conversations.

HIGHLIGHTS

Thirty-one readings that will provoke students to think— and write. Taken from a wide range of sources, including the *New York Times*, *Slate*, the *National Review*, *Al Jazeera*, bestselling trade books, and more, these readings represent a range of perspectives on four contemporary issues:

- Is Fast Food the New Tobacco? (Chapter 13)
- Are *24*, *Family Guy*, and *Grand Theft Auto* Actually Good For You? (Chapter 14)
- Is Economic Mobility Just a Dream? (Chapter 15)
- Is America Over? (Chapter 16)

The readings function as sources for students' own writing, and the study questions that follow each reading focus students' attention on how each author uses the key moves and invite them to respond with their own views.

A chapter on reading (Chapter 12) encourages students to think of reading as an act of entering conversations. Instead of teaching students merely to identify the author's argument, this chapter shows them how to read with an eye for what arguments the author is responding to—in other words, to think carefully about why the writer is making the argument in the first place, and thus to recognize (and ultimately become a part of) the larger conversation that gives meaning to reading the text.

Two books in one, with the rhetoric up front and the readings in the back. The two parts are linked by cross-references in the margins, leading from the rhetoric to specific examples in the readings and from the readings to the corresponding writing instruction. Teachers can therefore begin with either the rhetoric or the readings, and the links will facilitate movement between one section and the other.

We hope that this new version of *"They Say / I Say"* will spark students' interest in some of the most pressing conversations of our day, and provide them with some of the tools they need to engage in those conversations with dexterity and confidence.

Gerald Graff
Cathy Birkenstein
Russel Durst

PREFACE TO "THEY SAY / I SAY"

EXPERIENCED WRITING INSTRUCTORS have long recognized that writing well means entering into conversation with others. Academic writing in particular calls upon writers not simply to express their own ideas, but to do so as a response to what others have said. The mission statement for the first-year writing program at our own university, for example, describes its goal as helping students "enter a conversation about ideas." A similar statement by another program holds that "intellectual writing is almost always composed in response to others' texts." These statements echo the ideas of rhetorical theorists like Kenneth Burke, Mikhail Bakhtin, and Wayne Booth as well as recent composition scholars like David Bartholomae, Patricia Bizzell, Peter Elbow, Joseph Harris, Andrea Lunsford, Elaine Maimon, Gary Olson, Tilly Warnock, Mike Rose, and others who argue that writing well means engaging the voices of others and letting them in turn engage us.

Yet despite this growing consensus that writing is a social, conversational act, helping student writers actually "enter a conversation about ideas" remains a formidable challenge. This book aims to meet that challenge. Its goal is to demystify academic writing by isolating its basic moves, explaining them clearly, and representing them in the form of templates. In this way, we hope to help students become active participants in the important conversations of the academic world and the wider public sphere.

HIGHLIGHTS

- *Shows that writing well means entering a conversation*, first summarizing others ("they say") to set up one's own argument ("I say").
- *Demystifies academic writing*, showing students "the moves that matter" in language they can readily apply.
- *Provides user-friendly templates* to help writers make those moves in their own writing.

HOW THIS BOOK CAME TO BE

The original idea for this book grew out of our shared interest in democratizing academic culture. First, it grew out of arguments that Gerald Graff has been making throughout his career that schools and colleges need to invite students into the conversations and debates that surround them. More specifically, it is a practical, hands-on companion to his recent book, *Clueless in Academe: How Schooling Obscures the Life of the Mind*, in which he looks at such conversations from the perspective of those who find them mysterious and proposes ways in which such mystification can be overcome. Second, this book grew out of writing templates that Cathy Birkenstein developed in the 1990s, for use in writing and literature courses she was teaching. Many students, she found, could readily grasp what it meant to summarize an author, to support a thesis with evidence, to entertain a counterargument, or to identify a textual contradiction, but they often had trouble putting these concepts into practice in their own writing. When Cathy sketched out templates on the board, however, giving her students some of the language and patterns that these sophisticated moves require, their writing—and even their quality of thought—significantly improved.

This book began, then, when we put our ideas together and realized that these templates might have the potential to open up and clarify academic conversation. We proceeded from the premise that all writers rely on certain stock formulas that they themselves didn't invent—and that many of these formulas are so commonly used that they can be represented in model templates that students can use to structure and even generate what they want to say.

As we developed a working draft of this book, we began using it in first-year writing courses that we teach at UIC. In classroom exercises and writing assignments, we found that students who otherwise struggled to organize their thoughts, or even to think of something to say, did much better when we provided them with templates like the following.

▸ In discussions of _____, a controversial issue is whether _____. While some argue that _____, others contend that _____.

▸ This is not to say that _____.

One virtue of such templates, we found, is that they focus writers' attention not just on what is being said, but on the *forms* that structure what is being said. In other words, they help students focus on the rhetorical patterns that are key to academic success but often pass under the classroom radar.

THE CENTRALITY OF "THEY SAY / I SAY"

The central rhetorical move that we focus on in this book is the "they say / I say" template that gives our book its title. In our view, this template represents the deep, underlying structure, the internal DNA as it were, of all effective argument. Effective persuasive writers do more than make well-supported claims ("I say"); they also map those claims relative to the claims of others ("they say").

Here, for example, the "they say / I say" pattern structures a passage from a recent essay by the media and technology critic Steven Johnson.

> For decades, we've worked under the assumption that mass culture follows a path declining steadily toward lowest-common-denominator standards, presumably because the "masses" want dumb, simple pleasures and big media companies try to give the masses what they want. But . . . the exact opposite is happening: the culture is getting more cognitively demanding, not less.
>
> STEVEN JOHNSON, "Watching TV Makes You Smarter"

In generating his own argument from something "they say," Johnson suggests *why* he needs to say what he is saying: to correct a popular misconception.

Even when writers do not explicitly identify the views they are responding to, as Johnson does, an implicit "they say" can often be discerned, as in the following passage by Zora Neale Hurston.

> I remember the day I became colored.
>
> ZORA NEALE HURSTON, "How It Feels to Be Colored Me"

In order to grasp Hurston's point here, we need to be able to reconstruct the implicit view she is responding to: that racial identity is an innate quality we are simply born with. On the contrary, Hurston suggests, our race is imposed on us by society—something we "become" by virtue of how we are treated.

As these examples suggest, the "they say / I say" model can improve not just student writing, but student reading comprehension as well. Since reading and writing are deeply reciprocal activities, students who learn to make the rhetorical moves represented by the templates in this book figure to become more adept at identifying these same moves in the texts they read. And if we are right that effective arguments are always in dialogue with other arguments, then it follows that in order to understand the types of challenging texts assigned in college, students need to identify the views to which those texts are responding.

Working with the "they say / I say" model can also help with invention, finding something to say. In our experience, students best discover what they want to say not by thinking about a subject in an isolation booth, but by reading texts, listening closely to what other writers say, and looking for an opening in which they can enter the conversation. In other words, listening closely to others and summarizing what they have to say can help writers generate their own ideas.

THE USEFULNESS OF TEMPLATES

Our templates themselves have a generative quality, prompting students to make moves in their writing that they might not otherwise make or even know they should make. The templates in this book can be particularly helpful for students who are unsure about what to say, or who have trouble finding enough to say, often because they see their own beliefs as so self-evident that they need not be argued for. Students like this are often helped, we've found, when we give them a simple template like the following one for entertaining a counterargument (or planting a naysayer, as we call it in Chapter 6).

▸ Of course some object that _____. Although I concede that _____, I still maintain that _____.

What this particular template helps students do is make the seemingly counterintuitive move of questioning their own beliefs, of looking at them from the perspective of those who disagree. In so doing, templates can bring out aspects of students' thoughts that, as they themselves sometimes remark, they didn't even realize were there.

Other templates in this book will help students make a whole host of sophisticated moves that they might not otherwise make: summarizing what someone else says, framing a quotation in one's own words, indicating the view that the writer is responding to, marking the shift from a source's view to the writer's own view, offering evidence for that view, entertaining and answering counterarguments and explaining what is at stake in the first place. In showing students how to make such moves, templates do more than organize students' ideas; they help bring those ideas into existence.

OKAY, BUT *TEMPLATES?*

We are aware, of course, that some instructors may have reservations about templates. Some, for instance, may object that such formulaic devices represent a return to prescriptive forms of instruction that encourage passive learning or lead students to put their writing on automatic pilot.

This is an understandable reaction, we think, to kinds of rote instruction that have indeed encouraged passivity and drained writing of its creativity and dynamic relation to the social world. The trouble is that many students will never learn on their own to make the key intellectual moves that our templates represent. While seasoned writers pick up these moves unconsciously through their reading, many students do not. Consequently, we believe, students need to see these moves represented in the explicit ways that templates provide.

The aim of the templates, then, is not to stifle critical thinking but to be direct with students about the key rhetorical moves that comprise it. Admittedly, no teaching tool can guarantee that students will engage in hard, rigorous thought. Our templates do, however, provide concrete prompts that can stimulate and shape such thought: What do "they say" about my topic? What would a naysayer say about my argument? What is my evidence? Do I need to qualify my point? Who cares?

In fact, templates have a long and rich history. Public orators from ancient Greece and Rome through the European Renaissance studied rhetorical *topoi* or "commonplaces," model passages and formulas that represented the different strategies available to public speakers. In many respects, our templates echo this classical rhetorical tradition of imitating established models.

In our own day, the journal *Nature* offers aspiring contributors a templatelike guideline on the opening page of each manuscript: "Two or three sentences explaining what the main result [of their study] reveals in direct comparison with what was thought to be the case previously, or how the main result adds to previous knowledge."

In the field of education, a form designed by the education

theorist Howard Gardner asks postdoctoral fellowship applicants to complete the following template: "Most scholars in the field believe _____ . As a result of my study, _____ ." That these two examples are geared toward postdoctoral fellows and advanced researchers shows that it is not only struggling undergraduates who can use help making these key rhetorical moves, but experienced academics as well.

Templates have even been used in the teaching of personal narrative. The literary scholar Jane Tompkins devised the following template to help student writers make the often difficult move from telling a story to explaining what it means: "X tells a story about _____ to make the point that _____ . My own experience with _____ yields a point that is similar/different/both similar and different. What I take away from my own experience with _____ is _____ . As a result, I conclude _____ ." We especially like this template because it suggests that "they say / I say" argument need not be mechanical, impersonal, or dry, and that telling a story and making an argument are more compatible activities than many think.

HOW THIS BOOK IS ORGANIZED

Because of its centrality, we have allowed the "they say / I say" format to dictate the structure of this book. So while Part 1 addresses the art of listening to others, Part 2 addresses how to offer one's own response. Part 1 opens with a chapter on "Starting with What Others Are Saying" that explains why it is generally advisable to begin a text by citing others rather than plunging directly into one's own views. Subsequent chapters take up the arts of summarizing and quoting what these others have to say. Part 2 begins with a chapter on different ways of responding, followed by chapters on marking the shift between what "they say" and what "I say," on introducing and answering objections, and on answering the all-important questions "so what?" and "who cares?" Part 3 offers strategies for "Tying It All Together," beginning with a chapter on connection and coherence; followed by a chapter on style, arguing that academic discourse is often perfectly compatible with the informal language that students use outside of school; and concluding with a chapter on the art of metacommentary, showing students how to guide the way readers understand their text. At the end of the book we include an appendix suggesting how the "they say / I say" model can improve classroom discussions, three model essays that we refer to in various chapters, and finally an Index of Templates.

WHAT THIS BOOK DOESN'T DO

There are some things that this book does not try to do. We do not, for instance, cover logical principles of argument such as syllogisms, warrants, logical fallacies, or the differences between inductive and deductive reasoning. Although such concepts can be useful, we believe most of us learn the ins and outs of argumentative writing not by studying logical principles in the abstract, but by plunging into actual discussions and debates, trying out different modes of response, and in this way getting a sense of what works to persuade different audiences and what doesn't. In our view, people learn more about arguing from hearing someone say, "You miss my point. What I'm saying is not _____, but _____," or, "I agree with you that _____, and would even add that _____," than they do from studying the differences between inductive and deductive reasoning. Such formulas give students an immediate sense of what it feels like to enter a public conversation in a way that studying abstract warrants and logical fallacies does not.

We also do not cover the various modes of writing like description, definition, narrative, and comparison/contrast. Nor do we cover the different conventions of writing in the disciplines. It is our belief, that the "they say / I say" pattern cuts across different disciplines and genres of writing, including creative writing. Although students must eventually master the specific writing conventions of their majors, we believe that there is no major or discipline that does not require writers to frame their own claims as a response to what others before them have said. Indeed, students who master the elemental moves prompted by the templates in this book should actually become *better* able to appreciate the differences between disciplines and genres.

ENGAGING THE VOICE OF THE OTHER

A major virtue of the "they say / I say"' model is that it returns writing to its social, conversational base. Although writing does require some degree of solitude, the "they say / I say" model shows students that they can best develop their arguments not just by looking inward, but also by looking outward, listening carefully to other views, and engaging the voice of the other. As a result, this approach to writing has an ethical dimension: it asks students not simply to keep proving and reasserting what they already believe, but to stretch what they believe by putting it up against the beliefs of our increasingly diverse, global society, to engage in the reciprocal exchange that characterizes true democracy.

Gerald Graff
Cathy Birkenstein

INTRODUCTION

Entering the Conversation

---◱---

THINK ABOUT AN activity that you do particularly well: cooking, playing the piano, shooting a basketball, even something as basic as driving a car. If you reflect on this activity, you'll realize that once you mastered it you no longer had to give much conscious thought to the various moves that go into doing it. Performing this activity, in other words, depends on your having learned a series of complicated moves—moves that may seem mysterious or difficult to those who haven't yet learned them.

The same applies to writing. Often without consciously realizing it, accomplished writers routinely rely on a stock of established moves that are crucial for communicating sophisticated ideas. What makes writers masters of their trade is not only their ability to express interesting thoughts, but their mastery of an inventory of basic moves that they probably picked up by reading a wide range of other accomplished writers. Less experienced writers, by contrast, are often unfamiliar with these basic moves, and unsure how to make them in their own writing. This book is intended as a short, user-friendly guide to the basic moves of academic writing.

One of our key premises is that these basic moves are so common that they can be represented in *templates* that you can use right away to structure and even generate your own writ-

1

ing. Perhaps the most distinctive feature of this book is its presentation of many such templates, designed to help you successfully enter not only the world of academic thinking and writing, but also the wider worlds of civic discourse and work.

Rather than focus solely on abstract principles of writing, then, this book offers model templates that help you to put those principles directly into practice. Working with these templates can give you an immediate sense of how to engage in the kinds of critical thinking you are required to do at the college level and in the vocational and public spheres beyond.

Some of these templates represent simple but crucial moves like those used to summarize some widely held belief.

▸ Many Americans assume that _____ .

Others are more complicated.

▸ On the one hand, _____ . On the other hand, _____ .

▸ Author X contradicts herself. At the same time that she argues _____ , she also implies _____ .

▸ I agree that _____ .

▸ This is not to say that _____ .

It is true, of course, that critical thinking and writing go deeper than any set of linguistic formulas, requiring that you question assumptions, develop strong claims, offer supporting reasons and evidence, consider opposing arguments, and so on. But these deeper habits of thought cannot be put into practice unless you have a language for expressing them in clear, organized ways.

STATE YOUR OWN IDEAS AS A
RESPONSE TO OTHERS

The single most important template that we focus on in this book is the "they say _____ , I say _____ " formula that gives our book its title. If there is any one point that we hope you will take away from this book, it is the importance not only of expressing your ideas ("I say"), but of presenting those ideas as a *response to some other person or group* ("they say"). For us, the underlying structure of effective academic writing—and of responsible public discourse—resides not just in stating our own ideas, but in listening closely to others around us, summarizing their views in a way that they will recognize, and responding with our own ideas in kind. Broadly speaking, academic writing is argumentative writing, and we believe that to argue well you need to do more than assert your own ideas. You need to enter a conversation, using what others say (or might say) as a launching pad or sounding board for your own ideas. For this reason, one of the main pieces of advice in this book is to write the voices of others into your text.

In our view, then, the best academic writing has one underlying feature: it is deeply engaged in some way with other people's views. Too often, however, academic writing is taught as a process of saying "true" or "smart" things in a vacuum, as if it were possible to argue effectively without being in conversation *with* someone else. If you have been taught to write a traditional five-paragraph essay, for example, you have learned how to develop a thesis and support it with evidence. This is good advice as far as it goes, but it leaves out the important fact that in the real world we don't make arguments without being provoked. We make arguments because someone has said or done something (or perhaps *not* said or done something) and we need to respond: "I can't see why you like the Lakers so much"; "I agree: it was a great film"; "That argument is contradictory." If it weren't for other people and our need to challenge, agree with, or otherwise respond to them, there would be no reason to argue at all.

To make an impact as a writer, you need to do more than make statements that are logical, well supported, and consistent. You must also find a way of entering a conversation with others' views—with something "they say." In fact, if your own argument doesn't identify the "they say" that you're responding to, then it probably won't make sense. As Figure 1 suggests, *what* you are saying may be clear to your audience, but *why* you are saying it won't be. For it is what others are saying and thinking that motivates our writing and gives it a reason for being. It follows, then, as Figure 2 suggests, that your own argument—the "I say" moment of your text—should always be a response to the arguments of others.

Many writers make explicit "they say/I say" moves in their writing. One famous example is Martin Luther King Jr.'s "Let-

FIGURE 1

FIGURE 2

ter from Birmingham Jail," which consists almost entirely of King's eloquent responses to a public statement by eight clergy-men deploring the civil rights protests he was leading. The letter—which was written in 1963, while King was in prison for leading a demonstration in Birmingham—is structured almost entirely around a framework of summary and response, in which King summarizes and then answers their criticisms. In one typical passage, King writes as follows.

> You deplore the demonstrations taking place in Birmingham. But your statement, I am sorry to say, fails to express a similar concern for the conditions that brought about the demonstrations.
>
> MARTIN LUTHER KING JR., "Letter from Birmingham Jail"

King goes on to agree with his critics that "It is unfortunate that demonstrations are taking place in Birmingham," yet he hastens to add that "it is even more unfortunate that the city's white power structure left the Negro community with no alternative." King's letter is so thoroughly conversational, in fact, that it could be rewritten in the form of a dialogue or play.

King's critics:
King's response:
Critics:
Response:

Clearly, King would not have written his famous letter were it not for his critics, whose views he treats not as objections to his already-formed arguments, but as the motivating source of those arguments, their central reason for being. He quotes not only what his critics have said ("Some have asked: 'Why didn't you give the new city administration time to act?'"), but also things they *might* have said ("One may well ask: 'How can you advocate breaking some laws and obeying others?'")—all to set the stage for what he himself wants to say.

A similar "they say/I say" exchange opens an essay about American patriotism by the social critic Katha Pollitt, who uses her own daughter's comment to represent the national fervor of post-9/11 patriotism that Pollitt goes on to oppose.

My daughter, who goes to Stuyvesant High School only blocks from the former World Trade Center, thinks we should fly the American flag out our window. Definitely not, I say: The flag stands for jingoism and vengeance and war.

KATHA POLLITT, "Put Out No Flags"

As Pollitt's example shows, the "they" you respond to in crafting an argument need not be a famous author, or even someone known to your audience. It can be a family member like Pollitt's daughter, or a friend or classmate who has made a provocative claim. It can even be something an individual or a group might say—or a side of yourself, something you once believed but no longer do, or something you partly believe but also doubt. The important thing is that the "they" (or "you" or "she") represent some wider group—in Pollitt's case, those who patriotically believe in flying the flag.

While King and Pollitt both identify the views they are responding to, in some cases those views, rather than being explicitly named, are left to the reader to infer. See, for instance, if you can identify the implied or unnamed "they say" that the following claim is responding to.

> I like to think I have a certain advantage as a teacher of literature because when I was growing up I disliked and feared books.
>
> GERALD GRAFF, "Disliking Books at an Early Age"

In case you haven't figured it out already, the phantom "they say" here is anyone who thinks that in order to be a good teacher of literature, one must have grown up liking and enjoying books.

As you can see from these examples, many writers use the "they say/I say" format to disagree with others, to challenge standard ways of thinking, and thus to stir up controversy. This point may come as a shock to you if you have always had the impression that in order to succeed academically you need to play it safe and avoid controversy in your writing, making statements that nobody can possibly disagree with. Though this view of writing may appear logical, it is actually a recipe for flat, lifeless writing, and for writing that fails to answer what we call the "so what?" and "who cares?" questions. "William Shakespeare wrote many famous plays and sonnets" may be a perfectly true statement, but precisely because nobody is likely to disagree with it, it goes without saying and thus would seem pointless if said.

Ways of Responding

Just because much argumentative writing is driven by disagreement, it does not follow that *agreement* is ruled out. Although argumentation is often associated with conflict and opposition, the type of conversational "they say/I say" argument that we focus on in this book can be just as useful when you agree as when you disagree.

▸ She argues _____, and I agree because _____.

▸ Her argument that _____ is supported by new research showing that _____.

Nor do you always have to choose between either simply agreeing *or* disagreeing, since the "they say/I say" format also works to both agree and disagree at the same time.

▸ He claims that _____, and I have mixed feelings about it. On the one hand, I agree that _____. On the other hand, I still insist that _____.

This last option—agreeing and disagreeing simultaneously—is one we especially recommend, since it allows you to avoid a simple yes or no response and present a more complicated argument, while containing that complication within a clear "on the one hand/on the other hand" framework.

While the templates we offer in this book can be used to structure your writing at the sentence level, they can also be expanded as needed to almost any length, as the following elaborated "they say/I say" template demonstrates.

▸ In recent discussions of _____, a controversial issue has been whether _____. On the one hand, some argue that _____. From this perspective, _____. On the other hand, however, others argue that _____. In the words of one of this view's main proponents, "_____." According to this view, _____. In sum, then, the issue is whether _____ or _____.

▸ My own view is that _____. Though I concede that _____, I still maintain that _____. For example, _____. Although some might object that _____, I reply that _____. The issue is important because _____.

If you go back over this template, you will see that it helps you make a host of challenging moves (each of which is taken up in forthcoming chapters in this book). First, the template helps you open your text by identifying an issue in some ongoing conversation or debate ("In recent discussions of _____, a controversial issue has been"), then to map some of the voices in this controversy (by using the "on the one hand/on the other hand" structure). The template also helps you to introduce a quotation ("In the words of"), to explain the quotation in your own words ("According to this view"), and—in a new paragraph—to state your own argument ("My own view is that"), to qualify your argument ("Though I concede that"), and then to support your argument with evidence ("For example"). In addition, the template helps you make one of the most crucial moves in argumentative writing, what we call "planting a naysayer in your text," in which you summarize and then answer a likely objection to your own central claim ("Although it might be objected that _____, I reply _____"). Finally, this template helps you shift between general, over-arching claims ("In sum, then") and smaller-scale, supporting claims ("For example").

Again, none of us is born knowing these moves, especially when it comes to academic writing. Hence the need for this book.

Do Templates Stifle Creativity?

If you are like some of our students, your initial response to templates may be skepticism. At first, many of our students complain that using templates will take away their originality and creativity and make them all sound the same. "They'll turn us into writing robots," one of our students insisted. Another agreed, adding, "Hey, I'm a jazz musician. And we don't play by set forms. We create our own." "I'm in college now," another student asserted; "this is third-grade level stuff."

In our view, however, the templates in this book, far from being "third-grade level stuff," represent the stock in trade of sophisticated thinking and writing, and they often require a great deal of practice and instruction to use successfully. As for the belief that pre-established forms undermine creativity, we think it rests on a very limited vision of what creativity is all about. In our view, the above template and the others in this book will actually help your writing become *more* original and creative, not less. After all, even the most creative forms of expression depend on established patterns and structures. Most songwriters, for instance, rely on a time-honored verse-chorus-verse pattern, and few people would call Shakespeare uncreative because he didn't invent the sonnet or dramatic forms that he used to such dazzling effect. Even the most avant-garde, cutting-edge artists (like improvisational jazz musicians) need to master the basic forms that their work improvises on, departs from, and goes beyond, or else their work will come across as uneducated child's play. Ultimately, then, creativity and originality lie not in the avoidance of established forms, but in the imaginative use of them.

Furthermore, these templates do not dictate the *content* of what you say, which can be as original as you can make it, but only suggest a way of formatting *how* you say it. In addition, once you begin to feel comfortable with the templates in this book, you will be able to improvise creatively on them and invent new ones to fit new situations and purposes. In other words, the templates offered here are learning tools to get you started, not structures set in stone. Once you get used to using them, you can even dispense with them altogether, for the rhetorical moves they model will be at your fingertips in an unconscious, instinctive way.

But if you still need proof that writing templates do not stifle creativity, consider the following opening to an essay on the fast-food industry on p. 153.

> If ever there were a newspaper headline custom-made for Jay Leno's monologue, this was it. Kids taking on McDonald's this week, suing the company for making them fat. Isn't that like middle-aged men suing Porsche for making them get speeding tickets? Whatever happened to personal responsibility?
>
> I tend to sympathize with these portly fast-food patrons, though. Maybe that's because I used to be one of them.
>
> DAVID ZINCZENKO, "Don't Blame the Eater"

11

Although Zinczenko relies on a version of the "they say/I say" formula, his writing is anything but dry, robotic, or uncreative. While Zinczenko does not explicitly use the words "they say" and "I say," the template still gives the passage its underlying structure: "*They say* that kids suing fast-food companies for making them fat is a joke; but *I say* such lawsuits are justified."

PUTTING IN YOUR OAR

Though the immediate goal of this book is to help you become a better writer, at a deeper level it invites you to become a certain type of person: a critical, intellectual thinker who, instead of sitting passively on the sidelines, can participate in the debates and conversations of your world in an active and empowered way. Ultimately, this book invites you to become a critical thinker who can enter the types of conversations described eloquently by the philosopher Kenneth Burke in the following widely cited passage. Likening the world of intellectual exchange to a never-ending conversation at a party, Burke writes:

> You come late. When you arrive, others have long preceded you, and they are engaged in a heated discussion, a discussion too heated for them to pause and tell you exactly what it is about. . . . You listen for a while, until you decide that you have caught the tenor of the argument; then you put in your oar. Someone answers; you answer him; another comes to your defense; another aligns himself against you. . . . The hour grows late, you must depart. And you do depart, with the discussion still vigorously in progress.
>
> KENNETH BURKE, *The Philosophy of Literary Form*

What we like about this passage is its suggestion that stating an argument and "putting in your oar" can only be done in conversation with others; that we all enter the dynamic world of ideas not as isolated individuals, but as social beings deeply connected to others who have a stake in what we say.

This ability to enter complex, many-sided conversations has taken on a special urgency in today's diverse, post-9/11 world, where the future for all of us may depend on our ability to put ourselves in the shoes of those who think very differently from us. The central piece of advice in this book—that we listen carefully to others, including those who disagree with us, and then engage with them thoughtfully and respectfully—can help us see beyond our own pet beliefs, which may not be shared by everyone. The mere act of crafting a sentence that begins "Of course, someone might object that _____" may not seem like a way to change the world; but it does have the potential to jog us out of our comfort zones, to get us thinking critically about our own beliefs, and perhaps even to change our minds.

Exercises

1. Read the following paragraph from an essay by Emily Poe, a student at Furman University. Disregarding for the moment what Poe says, focus your attention on the phrases Poe uses to structure what she says (italicized here). Find a paragraph or two in some other text that makes similar moves, and underline the words the writer uses to structure what he or she says. Essays, newspaper editorials, and textbooks might be good places to look.

The term "vegetarian" tends to be synonymous with "tree-hugger" in many people's minds. *They see* vegetarianism as a cult that brainwashes its followers into eliminating an essential part of their daily diets for an abstract goal of "animal welfare." *However,* few vegetarians choose their lifestyle just to follow the crowd. *On the contrary*, many of these supposedly brainwashed people are actually independent thinkers, concerned citizens, and compassionate human beings. *For the truth is* that there are many very good reasons for giving up meat. Perhaps the best reasons are to improve the environment, to encourage humane treatment of livestock, or to enhance one's own health. *In this essay, then*, closely examining a vegetarian diet as compared to a meat-eater's diet will show that vegetarianism is clearly the better option for sustaining the Earth and all its inhabitants.

2. Write a short essay in which you first summarize our rationale for the templates in this book and then articulate your own position in response. If you want, you can use the template below to organize your paragraphs, expanding and modifying it as necessary to fit what you want to say. If you choose not to use the template, explain why you believe your own writing method is preferable.

   ▶ In the Introduction to *"They Say/I Say": The Moves That Matter in Academic Writing,* Gerald Graff and Cathy Birkenstein provide templates designed to _____ . Specifically, Graff and Birkenstein argue that the types of writing templates they offer _____ . As the authors themselves put it, " _____ ." Although some people believe _____ , Graff and Birkenstein insist that _____ . In sum, then, their view is that _____ .

   I agree/disagree/have mixed feelings. In my view, the types of templates that the authors recommend _____ . For instance, _____ . In addition, _____ . Some might object, of course, on the grounds that _____ . Yet I would argue that _____ . Overall, then, I believe _____ —an important point to make given _____ .

1

"THEY SAY"

ONE

"THEY SAY"

Starting with What Others Are Saying

————⌐回⌐————

NOT LONG AGO we attended a talk at an academic conference where the speaker's central claim seemed to be that a certain sociologist—call him Dr. X—had done very good work in
a number of areas of the discipline. The speaker proceeded to
illustrate his thesis by referring extensively and in great detail
to various books and articles by Dr. X and by quoting long passages from them. The speaker was obviously both learned and
impassioned, but as we listened to his talk we found ourselves
somewhat puzzled: the argument—that Dr. X's work was very
important—was clear enough, but why did the speaker need to
make it in the first place? Did anyone dispute it? Were there
commentators in the field who had argued against X's work or
challenged its value? Was the speaker's interpretation of what
X had done somehow novel or revolutionary? Since he gave no
hint of an answer to any of these questions, we could only wonder why he was going on and on about X. It was only after the
speaker finished and took questions from the audience that we
got a clue: in response to one questioner, he referred to several
critics who had vigorously questioned Dr. X's ideas and convinced many sociologists that Dr. X's work was unsound.

This little story illustrates an important lesson: that to give writing the most important thing of all—namely, a point—a writer needs to indicate clearly not only his or her thesis, but also what larger conversation that thesis is responding to. Because our speaker failed to mention what others had said about Dr. X's work, he left his audience unsure about why he felt the need to say what he was saying. Perhaps the point was clear to other sociologists in the audience who were more familiar with the debates over Dr. X's work than we were. But even they, we bet, would have understood the speaker's point better if he'd sketched in some of the larger conversation his own claims were a part of and reminded the audience about what "they say."

This story also illustrates an important lesson about the *order* in which things are said: to keep an audience engaged, a writer needs to explain what he or she is responding to—either before offering that response or, at least, very early in the discussion. Delaying this explanation for more than one or two paragraphs in a very short essay, three or four pages in a longer one, or more than ten or so pages in a book-length text reverses the natural order in which readers process material—and in which writers think and develop ideas. After all, it seems very unlikely that our conference speaker first developed his defense of Dr. X and only later came across Dr. X's critics. As someone knowledgeable in his field, the speaker surely encountered the criticisms first and only then was compelled to respond and, as he saw it, set the record straight.

See how an essay about Wal-Mart opens by quoting its critics,
p. 342, ¶1.

Therefore, when it comes to constructing an argument (whether orally or in writing), we offer you the following advice: remember that you are entering a conversation and therefore need to start with "what others are saying," as the title of this chapter recommends, and then introduce your own ideas as a response. Specifically, we suggest that you summarize what "they say" as soon as you can in your text, and remind readers of it at strategic points as your text unfolds. Though it's true that not all texts follow this practice, we think it's important for all writers to master it before they depart from it.

This is not to say that you must start with a detailed list of everyone who has written on your subject before you offer your own ideas. Had our conference speaker gone to the opposite extreme and spent most of his talk summarizing Dr. X's critics with no hint of what he himself had to say, the audience probably would have had the same frustrated "why-is-he-going-on-like this?" reaction. What we suggest, then, is that as soon as possible you state your own position and the one it's responding to *together*, and that you think of the two as a unit. It is generally best to summarize the ideas you're responding to briefly, at the start of your text, and to delay detailed elaboration until later. The point is to give your readers a quick preview of what is motivating your argument, not to drown them in details this early.

Starting with a summary of others' views may seem to contradict the common advice (which you may have heard from many instructors) that writers lead with their own thesis or claim. Although we agree that you shouldn't keep readers in suspense too long about your central argument, we also believe that you need to present that claim as part of some larger conversation—and that it's important to indicate something about the arguments of others that you are supporting, opposing, amending, complicating, or qualifying. One added benefit of summarizing others' views as soon as you can: those others do some of the work of framing and clarifying the issue you're writing about.

Consider, for example, how George Orwell starts his famous essay "Politics and the English Language" with what others are saying.

> Most people who bother with the matter at all would admit that the English language is in a bad way, but it is generally assumed that we cannot by conscious action do anything about it. Our civilization is decadent and our language—so the argument runs—must inevitably share in the general collapse. . . .
>
> [But] the process is reversible. Modern English . . . is full of bad habits . . . which can be avoided if one is willing to take the necessary trouble.
>
> GEORGE ORWELL, "Politics and the English Language"

Orwell is basically saying, "Most people assume that we cannot do anything about the bad state of the English language. But I say we can."

Of course, there are many other powerful ways to begin. Instead of opening with someone else's views, you could start with an illustrative quotation, a revealing fact or statistic, or—as we do in this chapter—a relevant anecdote. If you choose one of these formats, however, be sure that it in some way illustrates the view you're addressing or leads you to that view directly, with a minimum of steps.

In opening this chapter, for example, we devote the first paragraph to an anecdote about the conference speaker and then move quickly at the start of the second paragraph to the anecdote's "important lesson" regarding what speakers should and shouldn't do. In the following opening, from a 2004 opinion piece in the *New York Times Book Review*, Christina Nehring also moves quickly from an anecdote illustrating something she dislikes to her own claim—that book lovers think too highly of themselves.

> "I'm a reader!" announced the yellow button. "How about you?" I looked at its bearer, a strapping young guy stalking my town's Festival of Books. "I'll bet you're a reader," he volunteered, as though we were two geniuses well met. "No," I replied. "Absolutely not," I wanted to yell, and fling my Barnes & Noble bag at his feet. Instead, I mumbled something apologetic and melted into the crowd.
>
> There's a new piety in the air: the self congratulation of book lovers.
>
> CHRISTINA NEHRING, "Books Make You a Boring Person"

Nehring's anecdote is really a kind of "they say": book lovers keep telling themselves how great they are.

TEMPLATES FOR INTRODUCING WHAT "THEY SAY"

There are lots of conventional moves for introducing what others are saying. Here are some standard templates that we would have recommended to our conference speaker.

- ▸ A number of sociologists have recently suggested that X's work has several fundamental problems.

- ▸ It has become common today to dismiss X's contribution to the field of sociology.

- ▸ In their recent work, Y and Z have offered harsh critiques of Dr. X for _____ .

TEMPLATES FOR INTRODUCING "STANDARD VIEWS"

The following templates can help you make what we call the "standard view" move, in which you introduce a view that has become so widely accepted that by now it is essentially the conventional way of thinking about a topic.

▸ Americans today tend to believe that _____ .

▸ Conventional wisdom has it that _____ .

▸ Common sense seems to dictate that _____ .

▸ The standard way of thinking about topic X has it that _____ .

▸ It is often said that _____ .

▸ My whole life I have heard it said that _____ .

▸ You would think that _____ .

▸ Many people assume that _____ .

These templates are popular because they provide a quick and efficient way to perform one of the most common moves that writers make: challenging widely accepted beliefs, placing them on the examining table and analyzing their strengths and weaknesses.

TEMPLATES FOR MAKING WHAT "THEY SAY" SOMETHING *YOU* SAY

Another way to introduce the views you're responding to is to present them as your own.

▸ I've always believed that _____.

▸ When I was a child, I used to think that _____.

▸ Although I should know better by now, I cannot help thinking that _____.

▸ At the same time that I believe _____, I also believe _____.

TEMPLATES FOR INTRODUCING
SOMETHING IMPLIED OR ASSUMED

Another sophisticated move a writer can make is to summarize a point that is not directly stated in what "they say" but is implied or assumed.

▸ Although none of them have ever said so directly, my teachers have often given me the impression that _____.

▸ One implication of X's treatment of _____ is that _____.

▸ Although X does not say so directly, she apparently assumes that _____.

▸ While they rarely admit as much, _____ often take for granted that _____.

These are templates that can really help you to think critically—to look beyond what others say explicitly and to consider their unstated assumptions, as well as the implications of what they say or assume.

Templates for Introducing
an Ongoing Debate

Sometimes you'll want to open by summarizing a debate that presents two or more views. This kind of opening demon-

See the headline on p. 270, which summarizes a debate about technology.

strates your awareness that there are many ways to look at your subject, the clear mark of someone who knows the subject and therefore is likely to be a reliable, trustworthy guide. Furthermore, opening with a summary of a debate can help you to frame and explore the issue you are writing about before declar-

ing your own view. In this way, you can use the writing process itself to help you discover where you stand instead of having to take a position before you are ready to do so.

Here is a basic template for opening with a debate.

> ▶ In discussions of X, one controversial issue has been _____. On the one hand, _____ argues _____. On the other hand, _____ contends _____. Others even maintain _____. My own view is _____.

The cognitive scientist Mark Aronoff uses this kind of template in an essay on the workings of the human brain.

> Theories of how the mind/brain works have been dominated for centuries by two opposing views. One, rationalism, sees the human mind as coming into this world more or less fully formed—preprogrammed, in modern terms. The other, empiricism, sees the mind of the newborn as largely unstructured, a blank slate.
>
> MARK ARONOFF, "Washington Slept Here"

Another way to open with a debate involves starting with a proposition many people agree with in order to highlight the point(s) on which they ultimately disagree.

▸ When it comes to the topic of _____, most of us will readily agree that _____. Where this agreement usually ends, however, is on the question of _____. Whereas some are convinced that _____, others maintain that _____.

The political writer Thomas Frank uses a variation on this sophisticated move.

> That we are a nation divided is an almost universal lament of this bitter election year. However, the exact property that divides us— elemental though it is said to be—remains a matter of some controversy.
>
> THOMAS FRANK, "American Psyche"

While templates like these help you introduce what others are saying at the start of your text, Chapters 2 and 3 explore the arts of summarizing and quoting in more detail.

KEEP WHAT "THEY SAY" IN VIEW

We can't urge you too strongly to keep in mind what "they say" as you move through the rest of your text. After summarizing the ideas you are responding to at the outset, it's very important to continue to keep those ideas in view. Readers won't be able to follow your unfolding response, much less any complications you may offer, unless you keep reminding them what claims you are responding to.

In other words, even when presenting your own claims, you should keep returning to the motivating "they say." The longer and more complicated your text, the greater the chance that readers will forget what ideas originally motivated it—no matter how clearly you lay them out at the outset. At strategic moments throughout your text, we recommend that you include what we call "return sentences." Here is an example.

▶ In conclusion, then, as I suggested earlier, defenders of _____ can't have it both ways. Their assertion that _____ is contradicted by their claim that _____.

We ourselves use such return sentences at every opportunity in this book to remind you of the view of writing that our book challenges—that good writing means making true or smart or logical statements about a given subject with little or no reference to what others say about it.

By reminding readers of the ideas you're responding to, return sentences ensure that your text maintains a sense of mission and urgency from start to finish. In short, they help ensure that your argument is a genuine response to others' views rather than just a set of observations about a given subject. The difference is huge. To be responsive to others and the conversation you're entering, you need not only to start with what others are saying, but also to continue keeping it in the reader's view.

Exercises

1. The following claims all provide an "I say." See if you can supply a plausible "they say" for each one. It may help to

use one of the Templates for Introducing What "They Say" (p. 21).

    a. Our experiments suggest that there are dangerous levels of Chemical X in the Ohio groundwater.

    b. My own view is that this novel has certain flaws.

    c. Football is so boring.

    d. Male students often dominate class discussions.

    e. In my view the film is really about the problems of romantic relationships.

    f. I'm afraid that templates like the ones in this book will stifle my creativity.

2. Below is a template that we derived from the opening of David Zinczenko's "Don't Blame the Eater" (p. 153). Use the template to structure a passage on a topic of your own choosing. Your first step here should be to find an idea that you support that others not only disagree with, but also actually find laughable (or, as Zinczenko puts it, worthy of a Jay Leno monologue). You might write about one of the topics listed in the previous exercise (the environment, sports, gender relations, the meaning of a book or movie) or any other topic that interests you.

    ▸ If ever there was an idea custom-made for a Jay Leno monologue, this was it: _____. Isn't that like _____? Whatever happened to _____?

        I happen to sympathize with _____, though, perhaps because _____.

TWO

"Her Point Is"

The Art of Summarizing

——◦——

IF IT IS TRUE, as we claim in this book, that to argue persuasively you need to be in dialogue with others, then summarizing others' arguments is central to your arsenal of basic
moves. Because writers who make strong claims need to map
their claims relative to those of other people, it is important to
know how to summarize effectively what those other people
say. (We're using the word "summarizing" here to refer to any
information from others that you present in your own words,
including that which you paraphrase.)

Many writers shy away from summarizing—perhaps because
they don't want to take the trouble to go back to the text in
question and wrestle with what it says, or because they fear that
devoting too much time to other people's ideas will take away
from their own. When assigned to write a response to an article, such writers might offer their own views on the article's *topic*
while hardly mentioning what the article itself argues or says.
At the opposite extreme are those who do nothing *but* summarize. Lacking confidence, perhaps, in their own ideas, these writers so overload their texts with summaries of others' ideas that
their own voice gets lost. And since these summaries are not

animated by the writers' own interests, they often read like mere lists of things that X thinks or Y says—with no clear focus.

As a general rule, a good summary requires balancing what the original author is saying with the writer's own focus. Generally speaking, a summary must at once be true to what the original author says while at the same time emphasizing those aspects of what the author says that interest you, the writer. Striking this delicate balance can be tricky, since it means facing two ways at once: both outward (toward the author being summarized) and inward (toward yourself). Ultimately, it means being respectful of others while simultaneously structuring how you summarize them in light of your own text's central claim.

See how Barack Obama summarizes part of the U.S. Constitution in a speech about race, p. 361, ¶4.

ON THE ONE HAND, PUT YOURSELF IN *THEIR* SHOES

To write a really good summary, you must be able to suspend your own beliefs for a time and put yourself in the shoes of someone else. This means playing what the writing theorist Peter Elbow calls the "believing game," in which you try to inhabit the worldview of those whose conversation you are joining—and whom you are perhaps even disagreeing with—and try to see their argument from their perspective. This ability to temporarily suspend one's own convictions is a hallmark of good actors, who must convincingly "become" characters who in real life they may actually detest. As a writer, when you play the believing game really well, readers should not be able to tell whether you agree or disagree with the ideas you are summarizing.

If, as a writer, you cannot or will not suspend your own beliefs in this way, you are likely to produce summaries that are so obviously biased that they undermine your credibility with readers. Consider the following summary.

> In his article "Don't Blame the Eater," David Zinczenko accuses the fast-food companies of an evil conspiracy to make people fat. I disagree because these companies have to make money.

If you review what Zinczenko actually says (pp. 153–55), you should immediately see that this summary amounts to an unfair distortion. While Zinczenko does argue that the practices of the fast-food industry have the *effect* of making people fat, he never goes so far as to suggest that the fast-food industry conspires to do so with deliberately evil intent.

Another tell-tale sign of this writer's failure to give Zinczenko a fair hearing is the hasty way he abandons the summary after only one sentence and rushes on to his own response. So eager is this writer to disagree that he not only caricatures what Zinczenko says but also gives the article a hasty, superficial reading. Granted, there are many writing situations in which, because of matters of proportion, a one- or two-sentence summary is precisely what you want. Indeed, as writing professor Karen Lunsford (whose own research focuses on argument theory) points out, it is standard in the natural and social sciences to summarize the work of others quickly, in one pithy sentence or phrase, as in the following example.

> Several studies (Crackle, 1992; Pop, 2001; Snap, 1987) suggest that these policies are harmless; moreover, other studies (Dick, 2002; Harry, 2003; Tom, 1987) argue that they even have benefits.

But if your assignment is to respond in writing to a single author like Zinczenko, then you will need to tell your readers enough about his or her argument so they can assess its merits on their own, independent of you.

When a writer fails to play the believing game, he or she often falls prey to what we call "the closest cliché syndrome," in which what gets summarized is not the view the author in question has actually expressed, but a familiar cliché that the writer *mistakes* for the author's view (sometimes because the writer believes it and mistakenly assumes the author must too). So, for example, Martin Luther King Jr.'s passionate defense of civil disobedience in "Letter from Birmingham Jail" gets summarized not as the defense of political protest that it actually is, but as a plea for everyone to "just get along." Similarly, Zinczenko's critique of the fast-food industry might get summarized as a call for over-weight people to take responsibility for their weight.

Whenever you enter into a conversation with others in your writing, then, it is extremely important that you go back to what those others have said, that you study it very closely, and that you not collapse it to something you already have heard or know. Writers who fail to do this end up essentially con-versing with themselves—with imaginary others who are really only the products of their own biases and preconceptions.

On the Other Hand, Know Where *You* Are Going

Even as writing an effective summary requires you to tem-porarily adopt the worldviews of others, it does not mean ignor-ing your own views altogether. Paradoxically, at the same time that summarizing another text requires you to represent fairly what it says, it also requires that your own response exert a quiet influence. A good summary, in other words, has a focus or spin that allows the summary to fit with your own overall agenda while still being true to the text you are summarizing.

If you read the essay by David Zinczenko (pp. 153–55), you should be able to see that an essay on the fast-food industry in general will call for a very different summary than will an essay on parenting, corporate regulation, or warning labels. If you want to include all three, fine; but in that case you'll need to subordinate these three issues to one of Zinczenko's general claims and then make sure this general claim directly sets up your own argument.

For example, suppose you want to argue that it is parents, not fast-food companies, who are to blame for children's obesity. To set up this argument, you will probably want to compose a summary that highlights what Zinczenko says about the fast-food industry and parents. Consider this sample.

In his article "Don't Blame the Eater," David Zinczenko argues that today's fast-food chains fill the nutritional void in children's lives left by their overtaxed working parents. With many parents working long hours and unable to supervise what their children eat, Zinczenko claims, children today regularly turn to low-cost, calorie-laden foods that the fast-food chains are all too eager to supply. When he himself was a young boy, for instance, and his single mother was away at work, he ate at Taco Bell, McDonald's, and other chains on a regular basis, and ended up overweight. Zinczenko's hope is that with the new spate of lawsuits against the food industry, other children with working parents will have healthier choices available to them, and that they will not, like him, become obese.

In my view, however, it is the parents, and not the food chains, who are responsible for their children's obesity. While it is true that many of today's parents work long hours, there are still several things that parents can do to guarantee that their children eat healthy foods.

This summary succeeds not only because it provides one big claim under which several of Zinczenko's points neatly fit ("today's fast-food chains fill the nutritional void in children's lives left by their overtaxed working parents"), but also because this big claim points toward the second paragraph: the writer's own thesis about parental responsibility. A less astute, less focused summary would merely include Zinczenko's indictment of the fast-food industry and ignore what he says about parents.

This advice—to summarize each author in terms of the specific issue your own argument focuses on—may seem painfully obvious. But writers who aren't attuned to these issues often summarize a given author on one issue even though their text actually focuses on another. To avoid this problem, you need to make sure that your "they say" and "I say" are well matched. In fact, aligning what they say with what you say is a good thing to work on when revising what you've written.

Often writers who summarize without regard to their own interests fall prey to what might be called "list summaries," summaries that simply inventory the original author's various points but fail to focus those points around any larger overall claim. If you've ever heard a talk in which the points were connected only by words like "and then," "also," and "in addition," you know how such lists can put listeners to sleep—as shown in Figure 3. A typical list summary sounds like this.

> The author says many different things about his subject. *First* he says.
> . . . *Then* he makes the point that. . . . *In addition* he says. . . .
> *And then* he writes. . . . *Also* he shows that. . . . *And then* he says. . . .

It may be boring list summaries like this that give summaries in general a bad name and even prompt some instructors to discourage their students from summarizing at all.

THE EFFECT OF A TYPICAL LIST SUMMARY

FIGURE 3

In conclusion, writing a good summary means not just representing an author's view accurately, but doing so in a way that fits your own composition's larger agenda. On the one hand, it means playing Peter Elbow's believing game and doing justice to the source; if the summary ignores or misrepresents the source, its bias and unfairness will show. On the other hand, even as it does justice to the source, a summary has to have a slant or spin that prepares the way for your own claims. Once a summary enters your text, you should think of it as joint property—reflecting both the source you are summarizing and you yourself.

SUMMARIZING SATIRICALLY

Thus far in this chapter we have argued that, as a general rule, good summaries require a balance between what someone else has said and your own interests as a writer. Now, however, we want to address one exception to this rule: the satiric summary, in which a writer deliberately gives his or her own spin to someone else's argument in order to reveal a glaring shortcoming in it. Despite our previous comments that well-crafted summaries generally strike a balance between heeding what someone else has said and your own, independent interests, the satiric mode can at times be a very effective form of critique because it lets the summarized argument condemn itself without overt editorializing by you, the writer. If you've ever watched *The Daily Show*, you'll recall that it basically summarizes silly things political leaders have said or done, letting their words or actions undermine themselves.

Consider another example. In late September 2001, President Bush in a speech to Congress urged the nation's "continued participation and confidence in the American economy" as a means of recovering from the terrorist attacks of 9/11. The journalist Allan Sloan made fun of this proposal simply by summarizing it, observing that the president had equated "patriotism with shopping. Maxing out your credit cards at the mall wasn't self indulgence, it was a way to get back at Osama bin Laden." Sloan's summary leaves no doubt where he stands—he considers Bush's proposal ridiculous, or at least too simple.

USE SIGNAL VERBS THAT FIT THE ACTION

In introducing summaries, try to avoid bland formulas like "he talks about," "she says," or "they believe." Though language like this is sometimes serviceable enough, it often fails to capture accurately what the person has said. In some cases, "he says" may even drain the passion out of the ideas you're summarizing.

We suspect that the habit of ignoring the action in what we summarize stems from the mistaken belief we mentioned earlier that writing is about playing it safe and not making waves, a matter of piling up truths and bits of knowledge rather than a dynamic process of doing things to and with other people. People who wouldn't hesitate to *say* "X totally misrepresented" something when chatting with friends will in their writing often opt for far tamer and even less accurate phrases like "X said."

But the authors you summarize at the college level never simply "say" or "discuss" things; they "urge," "emphasize," and "insist on" them. David Zinczenko, for example, doesn't just *say* that fast-food companies contribute to obesity; he *complains* or *protests* that they do; he *challenges, chastises,* and *indicts* those companies. The Declaration of Independence doesn't just *talk about* the treatment of the colonies by the British; it *protests against* it. To do justice to the authors you cite, we recommend that when summarizing—or even when introducing a quotation—you use vivid and precise signal verbs as often as possible. Though "he says" or "she believes" will sometimes be the most appropriate language for the occasion, your text will often be more accurate and lively if you tailor your verbs to suit the precise actions you're describing.

TEMPLATES FOR INTRODUCING
SUMMARIES AND QUOTATIONS

▸ She demonstrates that _____.

▸ In fact, they celebrate the fact that _____.

▸ _____, he admits.

VERBS FOR INTRODUCING
SUMMARIES AND QUOTATIONS

VERBS FOR MAKING A CLAIM

argue	insist
assert	observe
believe	remind us
claim	report
emphasize	suggest

VERBS FOR EXPRESSING AGREEMENT

acknowledge	endorse
admire	extol
agree	praise
celebrate the fact that	reaffirm
corroborate	support
do not deny	verify

VERBS FOR QUESTIONING OR DISAGREEING

complain	disavow
complicate	question
contend	refute
contradict	reject
deny	renounce
deplore the tendency to	repudiate

VERBS FOR MAKING RECOMMENDATIONS

advocate	implore
call for	plead
demand	recommend
encourage	urge
exhort	warn

Exercises

1. To get a feel for Peter Elbow's "believing game," write a summary of some belief that you strongly disagree with. Then write a summary of the position that you actually hold on this topic. Give both summaries to a classmate or two, and see if they can tell which position you endorse. If you've succeeded, they won't be able to tell.

2. Write two different summaries of David Zinczenko's "Don't Blame the Eater" (pp. 153–55). Write the first one for an essay arguing that, contrary to what Zinczenko claims, there *are* inexpensive and convenient alternatives to fast-food restaurants. Write the second for an essay that agrees with Zinczenko in blaming fast-food companies for youthful obesity, but questions his view that bringing lawsuits against those companies is a legitimate response to the problem. Compare your two summaries: though they are of the same article, they should look very different.

THREE

"As He Himself Puts It"

The Art of Quoting

—⌐—

A KEY PREMISE of this book is that to launch an effective argument you need to write the arguments of others into your text. One of the best ways to do this is by not only summarizing what "they say," as suggested in Chapter 2, but by quoting their exact words. Quoting someone else's words gives a tremendous amount of credibility to your summary and helps ensure that it is fair and accurate. In a sense, then, quotations function as a kind of evidence, saying to readers: "Look, I'm not just making this up. She makes this claim and here it is in her exact words."

Yet many writers make a host of mistakes when it comes to quoting, not the least of which is the failure to quote enough in the first place, if at all. Some writers quote too little— perhaps because they don't want to bother going back to the original text and looking up the author's exact words, or because they think they can reconstruct the author's ideas from memory. At the opposite extreme are writers who so overquote that they end up with texts that are short on commentary of their own—maybe because they lack confidence in their ability to comment on the quotations, or because they don't fully understand them and therefore have trouble explaining what they mean.

But the main problem with quotation arises when writers assume that quotations speak for themselves. Because the meaning of a quotation is obvious to *them*, many writers assume that this meaning will also be obvious to their readers, when often it is not. Writers who make this mistake think that their job is done when they've chosen a quotation and inserted it into their text. They draft an essay, slap in a few quotations, and whammo, they're done.

Such writers fail to see that quoting means more than simply enclosing what "they say" in quotation marks. In a way, quotations are orphans: words that have been taken from their original contexts and that need to be integrated into their new textual surroundings. This chapter offers two key ways to produce this sort of integration: (1) by choosing quotations wisely, with an eye to how well they support a particular part of your text, and (2) by surrounding every major quotation with a frame explaining whose words they are, what the quotation means, and how the quotation relates to your text. The point we want to emphasize is that quoting what "they say" must always be connected with what *you* say.

See how one author connects what "they say" to what she wants to say, pp. 236–37, ¶1–4.

Quote Relevant Passages

Before you can select appropriate quotations, you need to have a sense of what you want to do with them—that is, how they will support your text at the particular point where you insert them. Be careful not to select quotations just for the sake of demonstrating that you've read the author's work; you need to make sure they are relevant to your work.

However, finding relevant quotations is not always easy. In fact, sometimes quotations that were initially relevant to your overall argument, or to a key point in it, become less so as your text changes during the process of writing and revising. Given the evolving and messy nature of writing, you may sometimes think that you've found the perfect quotation to support your argument, only to discover later on, as your text develops, that your focus has changed and the quotation no longer works. It can be somewhat misleading, then, to speak of finding your thesis and finding relevant quotations as two separate steps, one coming after the other. When you're deeply engaged in the writing and revising process, there is usually a great deal of back-and-forth between your argument and any quotations you select.

FRAME EVERY QUOTATION

Finding relevant quotations is only part of your job; you also need to present them in a way that makes their relevance and meaning clear to your readers. Since quotations do not speak for themselves, you need to build a frame around them in which you do that speaking for them.

Quotations that are inserted into a text without such a frame are sometimes called "dangling" quotations for the way they're left dangling without any explanation. One graduate teaching assistant we work with, Steve Benton, calls these "hit-and-run" quotations, likening them to car accidents in which the driver speeds away and avoids taking responsibility for the dent in your fender or the smashed taillights as in Figure 4.

On the following page is a typical hit-and-run quotation by a writer responding to an essay by the feminist philosopher Susan Bordo.

DON'T BE A HIT-AND-RUN QUOTER.

FIGURE 4

Susan Bordo writes about women and dieting. "Fiji is just one example. Until television was introduced in 1995, the islands had no reported cases of eating disorders. In 1998, three years after programs from the United States and Britain began broadcasting there, 62 percent of the girls surveyed reported dieting."

I think Bordo is right. Another point Bordo makes is that. . . .

This writer fails to introduce the quotation adequately or explain why he finds it worth quoting. Besides neglecting to say who Bordo is or even that the quoted words are hers, the writer does not explain how her words connect with anything he is saying. He simply drops the quotation in his haste to zoom on to another point.

To adequately frame a quotation, you need to insert it into what we like to call a "quotation sandwich," with the statement introducing it serving as the top slice of bread and the explanation following it serving as the bottom slice. The introductory or lead-in claims should explain who is speaking and set up what the quotation says; the follow-up statements should explain why you consider the quotation to be important and what you take it to say.

TEMPLATES FOR INTRODUCING QUOTATIONS

▸ X states, "_____."

▸ As the prominent philosopher X puts it, "_____."

▸ According to X, "_____."

▸ X himself writes, "_____."

▸ In her book, _____, X maintains that "_____."

▸ Writing in the journal *Commentary*, X complains that "_____."

▸ In X's view, "_____."

▸ X agrees when she writes, "_____."

▸ X disagrees when he writes, "_____."

▸ X complicates matters further when she writes, "_____."

When adding such introductory phrases, be sure to use language that accurately reflects the spirit of the quoted passage. It is quite serviceable to write "Bordo states" or "asserts" in introducing the quotation about Fiji. But given the fact that Bordo is clearly alarmed by the effect of the extension of the media's reach to Fiji, it is far more accurate to use language that reflects her alarm: "Bordo is alarmed that" or "is disturbed by" or "complains." (See Chapter 2 for a list of verbs for introducing what others say.)

Note the verbs Alan Dowd uses, pp. 404–05, ¶1–5.

TEMPLATES FOR EXPLAINING QUOTATIONS

▸ Basically, X is saying _____.

▸ In other words, X believes _____.

▸ In making this comment, X argues that _____.

▸ X is insisting that _____.

▸ X's point is that _____.

▸ The essence of X's argument is that _____.

We suggest getting in the habit of following every major quotation with explanatory sentences structured by templates like these. Consider, for example, how the passage on Bordo might be revised using some of these moves.

The feminist philosopher Susan Bordo deplores the hold that the Western obsession with dieting has on women. Her basic argument is that increasing numbers of women across the globe are being led to see themselves as fat and in need of a diet. Citing the island of Fiji as a case in point, Bordo notes that "until television was introduced in 1995, the islands had no reported cases of eating disorders. In 1998, three years after programs from the United States and Britain began broadcasting there, 62 percent of the girls surveyed reported dieting" (149–50). Bordo's point is that the West's obsession with dieting is spreading even to remote places across the globe. Ultimately, Bordo complains, the culture of dieting will find you, regardless of where you live.

Bordo's observations ring true to me because a friend of mine from a remote area in China speaks of the cult of dieting among young women there. . . .

This framing of the quotation not only helps to better integrate Bordo's words into the writer's text, but also serves to demonstrate the writer's interpretation of what Bordo is saying. While "the feminist philosopher" and "Bordo notes" provide basic information that readers need to know, the sentences that follow the quotation build a bridge between Bordo's words and those of the writer. Just as important, these sentences explain what Bordo is saying in the writer's own words—and thereby make clear that the quotation is being used purposefully to set up the writer's own argument and has not been stuck in just for padding or merely to have a citation.

BLEND THE AUTHOR'S WORDS WITH YOUR OWN

The above framing material works well because it accurately represents Bordo's words while at the same time giving those words the writer's own spin. Instead of simply repeating Bordo word for word, the follow-up sentences echo just enough of her text while still moving the discussion in the writer's own direction.

Notice how the passage refers several times to the key concept of dieting, and how it echoes Bordo's references to "television" and to U.S. and British "broadcasting" by referring to "culture," which is further specified as that of "the West."

Despite some repetition, this passage avoids merely restating what Bordo says. Her reference to 62 percent of Fijian girls dieting is no longer an inert statistic (as it was in the flawed passage presented earlier), but a quantitative example of how "the West's obsession with dieting is spreading . . . across the globe." In effect, the framing creates a kind of hybrid text, a mix of Bordo's words and those of the writer.

But is it possible to overexplain a quotation? And how do you know when you've explained a quotation thoroughly enough? After all, not all quotations require the same amount of explanatory framing, and there are no hard-and-fast rules for knowing how much explanation any quotation needs. As a general rule, the most explanatory framing is needed for quotations that may be hard for readers to process: quotations that are long and complex, that are filled with details or jargon, or that contain hidden complexities.

And yet, though the particular situation usually dictates when and how much to explain a quotation, we will still offer one piece of advice: when in doubt, go for it. It is better to risk being overly explicit about what you take a quotation to mean than to leave the quotation dangling and your readers in doubt. Indeed, we encourage you to provide such explanatory framing even when writing to an audience that you know to be familiar with the author being quoted and able to interpret your quotations on their own. Even in such cases readers need to see how *you* interpret the quotation, since words—especially those of controversial figures—can be interpreted in various ways and used to support different, sometimes opposing, agendas. Your readers need to see what you make of the material you've quoted, if only to be sure that your reading of the material and theirs is on the same page.

HOW *NOT* TO INTRODUCE QUOTATIONS

We want to conclude this chapter by surveying some ways *not* to introduce quotations. Although some writers do so, you should not introduce quotations by saying something like "X asserts an idea that" or "A quote by X says." Introductory phrases like these are both redundant and misleading. In the first example, you could write either "X asserts that" or "X's idea is that," rather than redundantly combining the two. The second example misleads readers, since it is the writer who is doing the quoting, not X (as "a quote by X" implies).

The templates in this book will help you avoid such mistakes. And once you have mastered such templates you probably won't even have to think about them—and will be free to focus on the important, challenging ideas that the templates frame.

Exercises

1. Find a text that quotes someone's exact words as evidence of something that "they say." How has the writer integrated the quotation into his or her own text? How has he or she introduced it, and what if anything has the writer said to explain it and tie it to his or her own text? Based on what you've read in this chapter, are there any changes you would suggest?

2. Look at an essay or a report that you have written for one of your classes. Have you quoted any sources? If so, how have you integrated the quotation into your own text? How have you introduced it? Explained what it means? Indicated how it relates to *your* text? If you haven't done all these things, revise your text to do so, perhaps using the Templates for Introducing Quotations (p. 43) and Explaining Quotations (p. 44). If you've not written anything with quotations, try revising some academic text you've written to do so.

2

"I Say"

"SAY!"

FOUR

"Yes / No / Okay, But"

Three Ways to Respond

—◻—

THE FIRST THREE chapters discuss the "they say" stage of writing, in which you devote your attention to the views of some other person or group. In this chapter we move to the "I say" stage, in which you offer your own argument as a response to what "they" have said.

There are a great many ways to respond, but this chapter concentrates on the three most common and recognizable ways: agreeing, disagreeing, or some combination of both. Although each way of responding is open to endless variation, we focus on these three because readers come to any text needing fairly quickly to learn where the writer stands, and they do this by placing the writer on a mental map of familiar options: the writer agrees with those he or she is responding to, disagrees with them, or presents some combination of both agreeing and disagreeing.

When writers take too long to declare their position relative to views they've summarized or quoted, readers get frustrated, wondering, "Is this guy agreeing or disagreeing? Is he *for* what this other person has said, against it, or what?" For this reason, this chapter's advice applies to reading as well as to writing. Especially with difficult texts, you not only need to find the position the writer is responding to—the "they say"—but you also need to determine whether the writer is agreeing with it, challenging it, or both.

Perhaps you'll worry that fitting your own response into one of these three categories will force you to oversimplify your argument or lessen its complexity, subtlety, or originality. In fact, however, the more complex and subtle your argument is, and the more it departs from the conventional ways people think, the more your readers will need to be able to place it on their mental map in order to process the complex details you present. That is, the complexity, subtlety, and originality of your response are more likely to stand out and be noticed if readers have a baseline sense of where you stand relative to any ideas you've cited. As you move through this chapter, we hope you'll agree that the forms of agreeing, disagreeing, and both agreeing and disagreeing that we discuss, far from being simplistic or one-dimensional, are able to accommodate a high degree of creative, complex thought.

It is always a good tactic to begin your response not by launching directly into a mass of details, but by stating clearly whether you agree, disagree, or both, using a direct, no-nonsense move such as: "I agree," "I disagree," or "I am of two minds. I agree that _____, but I cannot agree that _____." Once you have offered one of these straightforward statements (or one of the many variations discussed below), readers will have a strong grasp of your position and then be able to appreciate whatever complexity you offer as your response unfolds.

Still, you may object that these three basic ways of responding don't cover all the options—that they ignore interpretive or analytical responses, for example. In other words, you might think that when you interpret a literary work you don't necessarily agree or disagree with anything, but simply explain the work's meaning, style, or structure. Many essays about literature and the arts, it might be said, take this form—they interpret a work's meaning, thus rendering matters of agreeing or disagreeing irrelevant.

We would argue, however, that the best interpretations do in fact agree, disagree, or both—that instead of being offered solo, the best interpretations take strong stands relative to other interpretations. In fact, there would be no reason to offer an interpretation of a work of literature or art unless you were responding to the interpretations or possible interpretations of others. Even when you point out features or qualities of an artistic work that others have not noticed, you are implicitly disagreeing with what those interpreters have said by pointing out that they missed or overlooked something that, in your view, is important. In any effective interpretation, then, you need to not only state what you yourself take the work of art to mean, but to do so relative to the interpretations of other readers—be they professional scholars, teachers, classmates, or even hypothetical readers (as in, "Although some readers might think that this poem is about _____ , it is in fact about _____ ").

DISAGREE—AND EXPLAIN WHY

Disagreeing may seem like one of the simpler moves a writer can make, but in fact it poses hidden challenges. You need to do more than simply assert that you disagree with a particular view; you also have to offer persuasive reasons *why* you disagree. After all, disagreeing means more than adding "not" to what someone else has said, more than just saying, "Although they say women's rights are improving, I say women's rights are not improving." Such a response merely contradicts the view it responds to and fails to add anything interesting or new. To make an argument, you need to give reasons why you disagree:

See pp. 207–09 for several reasons why many "obese" people are not fat.

because another's argument fails to take relevant factors into account; because it is based on faulty or incomplete evidence; because it rests on questionable assumptions; or because it uses flawed logic, is contradictory, or overlooks what you take to be the real issue.

To move the conversation forward (and, indeed, to justify your very act of writing), you need to demonstrate that you yourself have something to contribute.

You can even disagree by making what we call the "duh" move, in which you disagree not with the position itself but with the assumption that it is a new or stunning revelation. Here is an example of such a move, used to open a 2003 essay on the state of American schools.

> According to a recent report by some researchers at Stanford University, high school students with college aspirations "often lack crucial information on applying to college and on succeeding academically once they get there."
>
> Well, duh. . . . It shouldn't take a Stanford research team to tell us that when it comes to "succeeding academically," many students don't have a clue.
>
> GERALD GRAFF, "Trickle-Down Obfuscation"

Like all of the other moves discussed in this book, the "duh" move can be tailored to meet the needs of almost any writing situation. If you find the expression "duh" too brash to use with your intended audience, you can always dispense with the term itself and write something like "It is true that . . . ; but we already knew that."

TEMPLATES FOR DISAGREEING, WITH REASONS

▶ I think X is mistaken because she overlooks _____.

▶ X's claim that _____ rests upon the questionable assumption that _____.

▶ I disagree with X's view that _____ because, as recent research has shown, _____.

▶ X contradicts herself/can't have it both ways. On the one hand, she argues _____. But on the other hand, she also says _____.

▶ By focusing on _____, X overlooks the deeper problem of _____.

▶ X claims _____, but we don't need him to tell us that. Anyone familiar with _____ has long known that _____.

You can also disagree by making what we call the "twist it" move, in which you agree with the evidence that someone else has presented, but show through a twist of logic that this evidence actually supports your own position. For example:

> X argues for stricter gun control legislation, saying that the crime rate is on the rise and that we need to restrict the circulation of guns. I agree that the crime rate is on the rise, but that's precisely why I oppose stricter gun control legislation. We need to own guns to protect ourselves against criminals.

In this example of the "twist it" move, the second speaker agrees with the first speaker's claim that the crime rate is on the rise, but then argues that this increasing crime rate is in fact a valid reason for *opposing* gun control legislation.

At times you might be reluctant to express disagreement, for any number of reasons—not wanting to be unpleasant, to hurt someone's feelings, or to make yourself vulnerable to being disagreed with in return. One of these reasons may in fact explain why the conference speaker we describe at the start of Chapter 1 avoided mentioning the disagreement he had with other scholars until he was provoked to do so in the discussion that followed his talk.

As much as we understand this reluctance and have felt it ourselves, we nevertheless believe it is better to state our disagreements in frank yet considerate ways than to deny them. After all, suppressing disagreements doesn't make them go away; it only pushes them underground, where they can fester in private unchecked. Nevertheless, there is no reason why disagreements need to take the form of personal put-downs. Furthermore, there is usually no reason to take issue with *every* aspect of someone else's views. You can single out for criticism only those aspects of what someone else has said that are troubling, and then agree with the rest—although that situation, as we will see, leads to the somewhat more complicated terrain of both agreeing and disagreeing at the same time, taken up later in this chapter.

Agree—but with a Difference

Like disagreeing, agreeing is less simple than it may appear. Just as you need to avoid simply contradicting views you disagree with, you also need to do more than simply echo views you agree with. Even as you're agreeing, it's important to bring something new and fresh to the table, adding something that makes you a valuable participant in the conversation.

There are many moves that enable you to contribute something of your own to a conversation even as you agree with what someone else has said. You may point out some unnoticed evidence or line of reasoning that supports X's claims that X herself hadn't mentioned. You may cite some corroborating personal experience, or a situation not mentioned by X that her views help readers understand. If X's views are particularly challenging or esoteric, what you bring to the table could be an accessible translation—an explanation for readers not already in the know. In other words, your text can usefully contribute to the conversation simply by pointing out unnoticed implications or explaining something that needs to be better understood.

Whatever mode of agreement you choose, the important thing is to open up some difference between your position and the one you're agreeing with rather than simply parroting what it says.

TEMPLATES FOR AGREEING

- I agree that _____ because my experience _____ confirms it.

- X is surely right about _____ because, as she may not be aware, recent studies have shown that _____.

- X's theory of _____ is extremely useful because it sheds insight on the difficult problem of _____.

- I agree that _____, a point that needs emphasizing since so many people believe _____.

- Those unfamiliar with this school of thought may be interested to know that it basically boils down to _____.

Some writers avoid the practice of agreeing almost as much as others avoid disagreeing. In a culture like America's that prizes originality, independence, and competitive individualism, writers sometimes don't like to admit that anyone else has made the same point, seemingly beating them to the punch. In our view, however, as long as you can support a view taken by someone else without merely restating what he or she has said, there is no reason to worry about being "unoriginal." Indeed, there is good reason to rejoice when you agree with others since those others can lend credibility to your argument. While you don't want to present yourself as a mere copycat of someone else's views, you also need to avoid sounding like a lone voice in the wilderness.

But do be aware that whenever you agree with one person's view, you are most likely disagreeing with someone else's. It is hard to align yourself with one position without at least implicitly positioning yourself against others. The feminist psychologist Carol Gilligan does just that in an essay in which she agrees with scientists who argue that the human brain is "hard-wired" for cooperation, but in so doing aligns herself against anyone who believes that the brain is wired for selfishness and competition.

> These findings join a growing convergence of evidence across the human sciences leading to a revolutionary shift in consciousness. . . . If cooperation, typically associated with altruism and self-sacrifice, sets off the same signals of delight as pleasures commonly associated with hedonism and self-indulgence; if the opposition between selfish and selfless, self vs. relationship biologically makes no sense, then a new paradigm is necessary to reframe the very terms of the conversation.
>
> CAROL GILLIGAN, "Sisterhood Is Pleasurable: A Quiet Revolution in Psychology"

In agreeing with some scientists that "the opposition between selfish and selfless . . . makes no sense," Gilligan implicitly disagrees with anyone who thinks the opposition *does* make sense. Basically, what Gilligan says could be boiled down to a template.

▸ I agree that _____, a point that needs emphasizing since so many people believe _____.

▸ If group X is right that _____, as I think they are, then we need to reassess the popular assumption that _____.

What such templates allow you to do, then, is to agree with one view while challenging another—a move that leads into the domain of agreeing and disagreeing simultaneously.

AGREE AND DISAGREE SIMULTANEOUSLY

This last option is often our favorite way of responding. One thing we particularly like about agreeing and disagreeing simultaneously is that it helps us get beyond the kind of "is too"/"is not" exchanges that often characterize the disputes of young children and the more polarized shouting matches of talk radio and TV.

TEMPLATES FOR AGREEING AND DISAGREEING SIMULTANEOUSLY

"Yes and no." "Yes, but . . . " "Although I agree up to a point, I still insist . . . " These are just some of the ways you can make your argument complicated and nuanced while maintaining a clear, reader-friendly framework. The parallel structure—"yes and no"; "on the one hand I agree, on the other I disagree"—

Dana Stevens says "yes, but" to an argument that TV makes us smarter, pp. 231–34.

enables readers to place your argument on that map of positions we spoke of earlier while still keeping your argument sufficiently complex.

Another aspect we like about this option is that it can be tipped subtly toward agreement or disagreement, depending on where you lay your stress. If you want to stress the disagreement end of the spectrum, you would use a template like the one below.

▶ Although I agree with X up to a point, I cannot accept his overall conclusion that _____ .

Conversely, if you want to stress your agreement more than your disagreement, you would use a template like this one.

▶ Although I disagree with much that X says, I fully endorse his final conclusion that _____ .

The first template above might be called a "yes, but . . . " move, the second a "no, but . . . " move. Other versions include the following.

▶ Though I concede that _____ , I still insist that _____ .

▶ X is right that _____ , but she seems on more dubious ground when she claims that _____ .

▶ While X is probably wrong when she claims that _____ , she is right that _____ .

▶ Whereas X provides ample evidence that _____ , Y and Z's research on _____ and _____ convinces me that _____ instead.

Another classic way to agree and disagree at the same time is to make what we call an "I'm of two minds" or a "mixed feelings" move.

▸ I'm of two minds about X's claim that _____. On the one hand, I agree that _____. On the other hand, I'm not sure if _____.

▸ My feelings on the issue are mixed. I do support X's position that _____, but I find Y's argument about _____ and Z's research on _____ to be equally persuasive.

This move can be especially useful if you are responding to new or particularly challenging work and are as yet unsure where you stand. It also lends itself well to the kind of speculative investigation in which you weigh a position's pros and cons rather than come out decisively either for or against. But again, as we suggest earlier, whether you are agreeing, disagreeing, or both agreeing and disagreeing, you need to be as clear as possible, and making a frank statement that you are ambivalent is one way to be clear.

Nevertheless, many writers are as reluctant to express ambivalence as they are to disagree or agree. Some may worry that by expressing ambivalence they will come across as evasive, wishy-washy, or unsure of themselves. Or they may think that their ambivalence will end up confusing readers who require clear-cut statements. In fact, however, expressing ambivalent feelings can serve to demonstrate deep sophistication as a writer. There is nothing wrong with forthrightly declaring that you have mixed feelings, especially after you've considered various options. Indeed, although you never want to be merely evasive, leaving your ambivalence thoughtfully unresolved can demonstrate your integrity as a writer, showing that you are not easily satisfied with viewing complex subjects in simple yes-or-no terms.

Exercises

1. Read the following passage by Jean Anyon, an education professor at Rutgers University, Newark. As you'll see, she summarizes the arguments of several other authors before moving on to tell us what she thinks. Does she agree with those she summarizes, disagree, or some combination of both? How do you know?

Scholars in political economy and the sociology of knowledge have recently argued that public schools in complex industrial societies like our own make available different types of educational experience and curriculum knowledge to students in different social classes. Bowles and Gintis, for example, have argued that students in different social-class backgrounds are rewarded for classroom behaviors that correspond to personality traits allegedly rewarded in the different occupational strata—the working classes for docility and obedience, the managerial classes for initiative and personal assertiveness. Basil Bernstein, Pierre Bourdieu, and Michael W. Apple, focusing on school knowledge, have argued that knowledge and skills leading to social power and regard (medical, legal, managerial) are made available to the advantaged social groups but are withheld from the working classes, to whom a more "practical" curriculum is offered (manual skills, clerical knowledge). While there has been considerable argumentation of these points regarding education in England, France, and North America, there has been little or no attempt to investigate these ideas empirically in elementary or secondary schools and classrooms in this country.

This article offers tentative empirical support (and qualification) of the above arguments by providing illustrative examples of differences in student *work* in classrooms in contrasting social-class communities. . . .

JEAN ANYON, "Social Class and the Hidden Curriculum of Work"

2. Read one of the essays at the back of this book, underlining places where the author agrees with others, disagrees, or both. Then write an essay of your own, responding in some way to the essay. You'll want to summarize and/or quote some of the author's ideas and make clear whether you're agreeing, disagreeing, or both agreeing and disagreeing with what he or she says. Remember that there are templates in this book that can help you get started; see Chapters 1–3 for templates that will help you represent other people's ideas, and Chapter 4 for templates that will get you started with your response.

FIVE

"AND YET"

Distinguishing What You Say
from What They Say

—▣—

IF GOOD ACADEMIC writing involves putting yourself into dialogue with others, it is extremely important that readers be able to tell at every point when you are expressing your own view and when you are stating someone else's. This chapter takes up the problem of moving from what *they* say to what *you* say without confusing readers about who is saying what.

DETERMINE WHO IS SAYING WHAT
IN THE TEXTS YOU READ

Before examining how to signal who is saying what in your own writing, let's look at how to recognize such signals when they appear in the texts you read—an especially important skill when it comes to the challenging works assigned in school. Frequently, when students have trouble understanding difficult texts, it is not just because the texts contain unfamiliar ideas or words, but because they rely on subtle clues to let readers know when a particular view should be attributed to the writer or to someone else. Especially with texts that present a true dialogue of perspectives, readers need to be alert to the often subtle markers that indicate whose voice the writer is speaking in.

Consider how the social critic and educator Gregory Mantsios uses these "voice markers," as they might be called, to distinguish the different perspectives in his essay on America's class inequalities.

> "We are all middle-class," or so it would seem. Our national consciousness, as shaped in large part by the media and our political leadership, provides us with a picture of ourselves as a nation of prosperity and opportunity with an ever expanding middle-class life-style. As a result, our class differences are muted and our collective character is homogenized.
>
> Yet class divisions are real and arguably the most significant factor in determining both our very being in the world and the nature of the society we live in.
>
> GREGORY MANTSIOS, "Rewards and Opportunities:
> The Politics and Economics of Class in the U.S."

Although Mantsios makes it look easy, he is actually making several sophisticated rhetorical moves here that help him distinguish the common view he opposes from his own position.

In the opening sentence, for instance, the phrase "or so it would seem" shows that Mantsios does not necessarily agree with the view he is describing, since writers normally don't present views they themselves hold as ones that only "seem" to be true. Mantsios also places this opening view in quotation marks to signal that it is not his own. He then further distances himself from the belief being summarized in the opening paragraph by attributing it to "our national consciousness, as shaped in large part by the media and our political leadership," and then attributing to this "consciousness" a negative, undesirable "result": one in which "our class differences" get "muted" and "our collective character" gets "homogenized," stripped of its diversity and distinctness. Hence, even before Mantsios has declared his own position, readers can get a pretty solid sense of where he probably stands.

Furthermore, the second paragraph opens with the word "yet," indicating that Mantsios is now shifting to his own view (as opposed to the view he has thus far been referring to). Even the parallelism he sets up between the first and second paragraphs—between the first paragraph's claim that class differences do not exist and the second paragraph's claim that they do—helps throw into sharp relief the differences between the two voices. Finally, Mantsios's use of a direct, authoritative, declarative tone in the second paragraph also suggests a switch in voice. Although he does not use the words "I say" or "I argue," he clearly identifies the view he holds by presenting it not as one that merely *seems* to be true or that *others tell us* is true, but as a view that *is* true or, as Mantsios puts it, "real."

These voice markers are an aspect of reading comprehension that is frequently overlooked. Readers who are unfamiliar with them often take an author's summaries of what someone else believes to be an expression of what the author himself or herself believes. Thus when we teach Mantsios's essay, some students invariably come away thinking that the statement "we are all middle-class" is Mantsios's own position rather than the perspective he is opposing, failing to see that in writing these words Mantsios acts as a kind of ventriloquist, mimicking what others say rather than directly expressing what he himself is thinking.

To see how important such voice markers are, consider what the Mantsios passage looks like if we remove them.

> We are all middle-class. . . . We are a nation of prosperity and opportunity with an ever expanding middle-class life-style. . . .
>
> Class divisions are real and arguably the most significant factor in determining both our very being in the world and the nature of the society we live in.

In contrast to the careful delineation between voices in Mantsios's original text, this unmarked version leaves it hard to tell where his voice begins and the voices of others end. With the markers removed, readers would probably not be able to tell that "We are all middle-class" represents a view the author opposes, and that "Class divisions are real" represents what the author himself believes. Indeed, without the markers, readers might well miss the fact that the second paragraph's claim that "Class divisions are real" contradicts the first paragraph's claim that "We are all middle-class."

See how Bruce Bartlett begins with a view he then tries to refute, p. 312, ¶2.

TEMPLATES FOR SIGNALING WHO IS SAYING WHAT IN YOUR OWN WRITING

To avoid confusion in your own writing, make sure that at every point your readers can clearly tell who is saying what. To do this, you can use as voice-identifying devices many of the templates presented in previous chapters.

▸ X argues _____ .

▸ According to both X and Y, _____ .

▸ Politicians, X argues, should _____.

▸ Most athletes will tell you that _____.

▸ My own view, however, is that _____.

▸ I agree, as X may not realize, that _____.

When stating your own position, as in the last two templates above, you can generally limit the voice markers to your opening and closing claims, since readers will automatically assume that any declarative statements you make between these statements, unless marked otherwise, are your own.

Notice that the last template above uses the first-person "I," as do many of the templates in this book, thus contradicting the common advice about avoiding the first person in academic writing. Although you may have been told that the "I" word encourages self-indulgent opinions rather than well-grounded arguments, we believe that texts using "I" can be just as well supported—or, conversely, just as self-indulgent—as those that don't. For us, well-supported arguments are grounded in persuasive reasons and evidence, not in their use of any particular pronouns.

Furthermore, if you consistently avoid the first person in your writing, you may have trouble making the key move addressed in this chapter: differentiating your views from those of others, or even offering your own views in the first place. But don't just take our word for it. See for yourself how freely the first person is used by the writers quoted in this book, and also by the writers in all your assigned courses.

Nevertheless, certain occasions may warrant avoiding the first person and writing, for example, that "She is correct" or

"It is a fact that she is correct," instead of "I think that she is correct." And since it can be monotonous to read an unvarying series of "I" statements—"I believe . . . I think . . . I argue"—it is a good idea to mix first-person assertions with ones like the following.

▸ X is right that _____.

▸ The evidence shows that _____.

▸ X's assertion that _____ does not fit the facts.

▸ Anyone familiar with _____ should agree that _____.

One might even follow Mantsios's lead, as in the following template.

▸ But _____ are real, and are arguably the most significant factor in _____.

ANOTHER TRICK FOR IDENTIFYING WHO IS SPEAKING

To alert readers about whose perspective you are describing at any given moment, you don't always have to use overt voice markers like "X argues" followed by a summary of the argument. Instead, you can alert readers about whose voice you're speaking in by *embedding* a reference to X's argument in your own sentences. Hence, instead of writing:

Liberals believe that cultural differences need to be respected. I have a problem with this view, however.

you might write:

> I have a problem with *what liberals call cultural differences.*

> There is a major problem with the liberal doctrine about *so-called cultural differences.*

You can also embed references to something you yourself have previously said. So instead of writing two cumbersome sentences like:

> Earlier in this chapter we coined the term "voice markers." We would argue that such markers are extremely important for reading comprehension.

you might write:

> We would argue that "voice markers," as we identified them earlier, are extremely important for reading comprehension.

Embedded references like these allow you to economize your train of thought and refer to other perspectives without any major interruption.

TEMPLATES FOR EMBEDDING VOICE MARKERS

▸ X overlooks what I consider an important point about _____ .

▸ My own view is that what X insists is a _____ is in fact a _____ .

▸ I wholeheartedly endorse what X calls _____ .

▸ These conclusions, which X discusses in _____, add weight to the argument that _____.

When writers fail to use voice-marking devices like these, their summaries of others' views tend to become confused with their own ideas—and vice versa. When readers cannot tell if you are summarizing your own views or endorsing a certain phrase or label, they have to stop and think: "Wait. I thought the author disagreed with this claim. Has she actually been asserting this view all along?" or "Hmmm, I thought she would have objected to this kind of phrase. Is she actually endorsing it?" Getting in the habit of using voice markers will keep you from confusing your readers and help alert you to similar markers in the challenging texts you read.

Exercises

1. To see how one writer signals when she is asserting her own views and when she is summarizing those of someone else, read the following passage by the social historian Julie Charlip. As you do so, identify those spots where Charlip refers to the views of others and the signal phrases she uses to distinguish her views from theirs.

   Marx and Engels wrote: "Society as a whole is more and more splitting up into two great hostile camps, into two great classes directly facing each other—the bourgeoisie and the proletariat" (10). If only that were true, things might be more simple. But in late twentieth-century America, it seems that society is splitting more and more into a plethora of class factions—the working class, the working poor, lower-middle class, upper-middle class, lower uppers, and upper uppers. I find myself not knowing what class I'm from.

In my days as a newspaper reporter, I once asked a sociology professor what he thought about the reported shrinking of the middle class. Oh, it's not the middle class that's disappearing, he said, but the working class. His definition: if you earn thirty thousand dollars a year working in an assembly plant, come home from work, open a beer and watch the game, you are working class; if you earn twenty thousand dollars a year as a school teacher, come home from work to a glass of white wine and PBS, you are middle class.

How do we define class? Is it an issue of values, lifestyle, taste? Is it the kind of work you do, your relationship to the means of production? Is it a matter of how much money you earn? Are we allowed to choose? In this land of supposed classlessness, where we don't have the tradition of English society to keep us in our places, how do we know where we really belong? The average American will tell you he or she is "middle class." I'm sure that's what my father would tell you. But I always felt that we were in some no man's land, suspended between classes, sharing similarities with some and recognizing sharp, exclusionary differences from others. What class do I come from? What class am I in now? As an historian, I seek the answers to these questions in the specificity of my past.

JULIE CHARLIP, "A Real Class Act: Searching
for Identity in the Classless Society"

2. Study a piece of your own writing to see how many perspectives you account for, and how well you distinguish your own voice from those you are summarizing. Consider the following questions:

a. How many perspectives do you engage?
b. What other perspectives might you include?

   c. How do you distinguish your views from the other views you summarize?

   d. Do you use clear voice-signaling phrases?

   e. What options are available to you for clarifying who is saying what?

   f. Which of these options are best suited for this particular text?

If you find that you do *not* include multiple views, or clearly distinguish between your views and others', revise your text to do so.

SIX

"SKEPTICS MAY OBJECT"

Planting a Naysayer in Your Text

———□———

THE WRITER JANE TOMPKINS describes a pattern that repeats itself whenever she writes a book or an article. For the first couple of weeks when she sits down to write, things go relatively well. But then in the middle of the night, several weeks into the writing process, she'll wake up in a cold sweat, suddenly realizing that she has overlooked some major criticism that readers will surely make against her ideas. Her first thought, invariably, is that she will have to give up on the project, or that she will have to throw out what she's written thus far and start over. Then she realizes that "this moment of doubt and panic is where my text really begins." She then revises what she's written in a way that incorporates the criticisms she's anticipated, and her text becomes stronger and more interesting as a result.

This little story contains an important lesson for all writers, experienced and inexperienced alike. It suggests that even though most of us are upset at the idea of someone criticizing our work, such criticisms can actually work to our advantage. Although it's naturally tempting to ignore objections to our ideas, doing so may in fact be a big mistake, since everyone's writing actually improves when we not only listen to these objections but give them an explicit hearing in our writing. Indeed, no single device more quickly improves a piece of writing than the practice of planting a naysayer in the text—saying, for example, that "although some readers may object" to something in your argument, you "would reply that _____."

ANTICIPATE OBJECTIONS

But wait, you say. Isn't the advice to incorporate critical views a recipe for destroying your credibility and undermining your argument? Here you are, trying to say something that will hold up, and we want you to tell readers all the negative things someone might say against you?

Exactly. We *are* urging you to tell readers what others might say against you, but our point is that doing so will actually *enhance* your credibility, not undermine it. For as we argue throughout this book, writing well does not mean piling up uncontroversial truths in a vacuum; it means engaging others in a dialogue or debate—not only by opening your text with a summary of what others have to say, as we suggest in Chapter 1, but also by imagining what others might say against your argument as it unfolds. Once you see writing as an act of entering a conversation, you should also see how opposing arguments can work for you rather than against you.

Paradoxically, the more you give voice to your critics' objections, the more you can disarm those critics, especially if you go on to answer them in convincing ways. When you entertain a counter-argument, you make a kind of preemptive strike, identifying problems with your argument before others can point them out for you. Furthermore, by entertaining counter-arguments, you show respect for your readers, treating them not as gullible dupes but as independent, critical thinkers who are aware that yours is not the only view in town. In addition, by imagining what others might say against your claims, you come across as a generous, broad-minded person who is secure enough to open himself or herself to debate—like the writer in Figure 5.

Conversely, if you don't entertain counter-arguments, you may very likely come across as closed-minded, as if you think your claims are beyond dispute. You might also leave important questions hanging and concerns about your arguments unaddressed. Finally, if you fail to plant a naysayer in your text, you may find that you have very little to say. Many of our own students have said that entertaining counter-arguments makes it easier to generate enough text to meet their assignment's page-length requirements.

Planting a naysayer in your own text is a relatively simple move, as you can see by looking at the following passage from a book by the feminist writer Kim Chernin. Having spent some thirty pages complaining about the pressure on American women to lose weight and be thin, Chernin inserts a whole chapter entitled "The Skeptic," opening it as follows.

> At this point I would like to raise certain objections that have been inspired by the skeptic in me. She feels that I have been ignoring some of the most common assumptions we all make about our bodies and these she wishes to see addressed. For example: "You know perfectly well," she says to me, "that you feel better when you lose weight. You buy new clothes. You look at yourself more eagerly in the mirror. When someone invites you to a party you don't stop and ask yourself whether you want to go. You feel sexier. Admit it. You like yourself better."
>
> KIM CHERNIN, *The Obsession:*
> *Reflections on the Tyranny of Slenderness*

FIGURE 5

In the remainder of the chapter, Chernin answers this skeptic. Though Chernin's inner skeptic challenges her book's central claim (that the pressure to diet seriously harms women's lives), she responds not by repressing its voice but by embracing it and writing it into her text. Note too that instead of dispatching this naysaying voice quickly, as many of us would be tempted to do, Chernin stays with it and gives it a full paragraph's worth of space. By borrowing some of Chernin's language, we can come up with templates for entertaining virtually any objection.

TEMPLATES FOR ENTERTAINING OBJECTIONS

▸ At this point I would like to raise some objections that have been inspired by the skeptic in me. She feels that I have been ignoring _____ . "_____," she says to me, "_____."

▸ Yet some readers may challenge my view that _____ . After all, many believe that _____ . Indeed, my own argument that _____ seems to ignore _____ and _____ .

▸ Of course, many will probably disagree with this assertion that _____ .

Note that the objections in the above templates are attributed not to any specific person or group, but to "skeptics," "readers," or "many." This kind of nameless, faceless naysayer is perfectly appropriate in many cases. But the ideas that motivate arguments and objections often can—and, where possible, should—be ascribed to a specific ideology or school of thought (for example, liberals, Christian fundamentalists, neopragmatists) rather than to anonymous anybodies. In other words, naysayers can be labeled, and you can add precision and impact to your writing by identifying what they are.

TEMPLATES FOR NAMING YOUR NAYSAYERS

▶ Here many *feminists* would probably object that _____.

▶ But *social Darwinists* would certainly take issue with the argument that _____.

▶ *Biologists*, of course, may want to dispute my claim that _____.

▶ Nevertheless, both *followers and critics of Malcolm X* will probably suggest otherwise and argue that _____.

To be sure, some people dislike such labels and may even resent having them applied to themselves. Some feel that such labels put individuals in boxes, stereotyping them and glossing over what makes each individual unique. And it's true that labels can be used inappropriately, in ways that ignore individuality and promote stereotypes. But since the life of ideas, including many of our most private thoughts, is conducted through groups and types rather than by solitary individuals, intellectual exchange requires labels to give definition and serve as a convenient shorthand. If you categorically reject all labels, you give up an important resource and even mislead readers by presenting yourself and others as having no connection to anyone else. You also miss an opportunity to generalize the importance and relevance of your work to some larger conversation. When you attribute a position you are summarizing to liberalism, say, or historical materialism, your argument is no longer just about your own solitary views, but about the intersection of broad ideas and habits of mind that many readers may already have a stake in.

The way to minimize the problem of stereotyping, then, is not to categorically reject labels but to refine and qualify their use, as the following templates demonstrate.

▸ Although not all *Christians* think alike, some of them will probably dispute my claim that _____ .

▸ *Non-native English speakers* are so diverse in their views that it's hard to generalize about them, but some are likely to object on the grounds that _____ .

Another way to avoid needless stereotyping is to qualify labels carefully, substituting "pro bono lawyers" for "lawyers" in general, for example, or "quantitative sociologists" for all "social scientists," and so on.

TEMPLATES FOR INTRODUCING OBJECTIONS INFORMALLY

Objections can also be introduced in ways that are a bit more informal. For instance, you can frame objections in the form of questions.

▸ But is my proposal realistic? What are the chances of its actually being adopted?

▸ Yet is it always true that _____ ? Is it always the case, as I have been suggesting, that _____ ?

▸ However, does the evidence I've cited prove conclusively that _____ ?

You can also let your naysayer speak directly.

▸ "Impossible," you say. "Your evidence must be skewed."

Moves like this allow you to cut directly to the skeptical voice itself, as the singer-songwriter Joe Jackson does in the following excerpt from a 2003 *New York Times* article complaining about the restrictions on public smoking in New York City bars and restaurants.

> I like a couple of cigarettes or a cigar with a drink, and like many other people, I only smoke in bars or nightclubs. Now I can't go to any of my old haunts. Bartenders who were friends have turned into cops, forcing me outside to shiver in the cold and curse under my breath. . . . It's no fun. Smokers are being demonized and victimized all out of proportion.
>
> "Get over it," say the anti-smokers. "You're the minority." I thought a great city was a place where all kinds of minorities could thrive. . . . "Smoking kills," they say. As an occasional smoker with otherwise healthy habits, I'll take my chances. Health consciousness is important, but so are pleasure and freedom of choice.
>
> JOE JACKSON, "Want to Smoke? Go to Hamburg"

Jackson could have begun his second paragraph, in which he shifts from his own voice to that of his imagined naysayer, as follows: "Of course anti-smokers will object that since we smokers are in the minority, we should get over it and sacrifice for the larger social good." Or "Anti-smokers might ask, however, whether the smoking minority shouldn't submit to the non-smoking majority." We think, however, that Jackson gets the job done very well with the more colloquial form he chooses.

See the essay on "Family Guy," pp. 257–68, which notes—and answers—naysayers throughout.

Borrowing a standard move of playwrights and novelists, Jackson cuts directly to the objectors' view and then to his own retort, then back to the objectors' view and then to his own retort again, thereby creating a kind of dialogue or miniature play within his own text. This move works well for Jackson, but only because (using one of the strategies suggested in Chapter 5) he uses quotation marks to make clear at every point whose voice he is in.

Represent Objections Fairly

Once you've decided to introduce a differing or opposing view into your writing, your work has only just begun, since you still need to represent and explain that view with fairness and generosity. Although it is tempting to give opposing views short shrift, to hurry past them, or even to mock them, doing so is usually counterproductive. When writers make the best case they can for their critics (playing what Peter Elbow calls the "believing game"), they actually bolster their credibility with readers, rather than undermine it.

We recommend, then, that whenever you entertain objections in your writing you stay with them for several sentences or even paragraphs and take them as seriously as possible. We also recommend that you read your summary of opposing views with an outsider's eye: put yourself in the shoes of someone who disagrees with you and ask if such a reader would recognize himself in your summary. Would that reader think you have taken his views seriously, as beliefs that reasonable people might hold? Or would he detect a mocking tone, or an oversimplification of his views?

There will always be certain objections, to be sure, that you believe do not deserve to be represented, just as there will be objections that seem so unworthy of respect that they inspire ridicule. Remember, however, that if you do choose to mock a view that you oppose, you are likely to alienate those readers who don't already agree with you—likely the very readers you want to reach. Also be aware that in mocking another's view you may contribute to a hostile argument culture in which someone could ridicule you in return.

ANSWER OBJECTIONS

Finally, besides summarizing objections fairly in your writing, you need to answer those objections persuasively. After all, when you write objections into a text, you always take the risk that readers will find those objections more convincing than the argument you yourself are advancing. In the editorial quoted above, for example, Joe Jackson takes the risk that non-smokers will identify more with the anti-smoking view he summarizes than with the pro-smoking position he endorses. Another case in point is presented in *The Autobiography of Benjamin Franklin* (1868), where at one point Franklin recounts how he was converted to Deism (a religion that exalts reason over spirituality) by reading *anti*-Deist books. When he encountered the views of Deists being negatively summarized by authors who opposed them, Franklin ended up finding the Deist position more persuasive. To avoid having this kind if unintentional reverse effect on readers, you need to do your best to make sure that any counter-argument you address is not more convincing than your own claims. It is good to address objections in your writing, but only if you are able to overcome them.

One surefire way to *fail* to overcome an objection is to dismiss it out of hand—saying, for example, "That's just wrong." The difference between such a response (which offers no supporting reasons whatsoever) and the types of nuanced responses we're promoting in this book is the difference between bullying your readers and genuinely persuading them.

Often the best way to overcome an objection is not to try to refute it completely, but to agree with certain parts while challenging only those you dispute. In other words, in answering counter-arguments, it is often best to say "yes, but" or "yes and no," as we suggest in Chapter 4, treating the counter-view as an opportunity to revise and refine your own position. Rather than building your argument into an impenetrable fortress, it is often best to make concessions while still standing your ground, as Kim Chernin does in the following response to the counter-argument quoted above. While in the voice of the "skeptic," Chernin writes: "Admit it. You like yourself better when you've lost weight." In response, Chernin replies as follows.

> Can I deny these things? No woman who has managed to lose weight would wish to argue with this. Most people feel better about themselves when they become slender. And yet, upon reflection, it seems to me that there is something precarious about this well-being. After all, 98 percent of people who lose weight gain it back. Indeed, 90 percent of those who have dieted "successfully" gain back more than they ever lost. Then, of course, we can no longer bear to look at ourselves in the mirror.

In this way, Chernin shows how you can use a counter-view to improve and refine your overall argument by making a concession. Even as she concedes that losing weight feels good in the short run, she argues that in the long run the weight always returns, making the dieter far more miserable.

TEMPLATES FOR MAKING CONCESSIONS WHILE STILL STANDING YOUR GROUND

▸ Although I grant that _____, I still maintain that _____.

▸ Proponents of X are right to argue that _____. But they exaggerate when they claim that _____.

▸ While it is true that _____, it does not necessarily follow that _____.

▸ On the one hand, I agree with X that _____. But on the other hand, I still insist that _____.

Templates like these show that answering naysayers' objections does not have to be an all-or-nothing affair in which you either definitively refute your critics or they definitively refute you. Often the most productive engagements among differing views end with a combined vision that incorporates elements of each one.

But what if you've tried out all the possible answers you can think of to an objection you've anticipated and you *still* have a nagging feeling that the objection is more convincing than your argument itself? In that case, the best remedy is to go back and make some fundamental revisions to your argument, changing its very substance. Although finding out late in the game that you aren't fully convinced by your own argument can be painful, it can actually make your final text more intellectually honest, challenging, and serious. After all, the goal of writing is not to keep proving that whatever you initially said is right, but to stretch the limits of your thinking. So if planting a strong naysayer in your text forces you to change your mind, that's not a bad thing. Indeed, some would argue that that is what the academic world is all about.

Exercises

1. Read the following passage by the cultural critic Eric Schlosser. As you'll see, he's not planted any naysayers in this text. Do it for him. Insert a brief paragraph stating an objection to his argument and then responding to the objection as he might.

The United States must declare an end to the war on drugs. This war has filled the nation's prisons with poor drug addicts and small-time drug dealers. It has created a multibillion-dollar black market, enriched organized crime groups and promoted the corruption of government officials throughout the world. And it has not stemmed the widespread use of illegal drugs. By any rational measure, this war has been a total failure.

We must develop public policies on substance abuse that are guided not by moral righteousness or political expediency but by common sense. The United States should immediately decriminalize the cultivation and possession of small amounts of marijuana for personal use. Marijuana should no longer be classified as a Schedule I narcotic, and those who seek to use marijuana as medicine should no longer face criminal sanctions. We must shift our entire approach to drug abuse from the criminal justice system to the public health system. Congress should appoint an independent commission to study the harm-reduction policies that have been adopted in Switzerland, Spain, Portugal, and the Netherlands. The commission should recommend policies for the United States based on one important criterion: what works.

In a nation where pharmaceutical companies advertise powerful antidepressants on billboards and where alcohol companies run amusing beer ads during the Super Bowl, the idea of a "drug-free society" is absurd. Like the rest of American society, our drug policy would greatly benefit from less punishment and more compassion.

ERIC SCHLOSSER, "A People's Democratic Platform"

2. Look over something you've written that makes an argument. Check to see if you've anticipated and responded to any objections. If not, revise your text to do so. If so, have you anticipated all the likely objections? Who if anyone have you attributed the objections to? Have you represented them fairly? Have you answered the objections well enough, or do you think you now need to qualify your own argument? Did you use any of the language found in this chapter's templates? Does the introduction of a naysayer strengthen your argument—why, or why not?

SEVEN

"SO WHAT? WHO CARES?"

Saying Why It Matters

—⟨⟩—

BASEBALL IS THE national pastime. Bernini was the best sculptor of the baroque period. Evolution is central to the teaching of biology. So what? Who cares? Why does any of this matter?

How many times have you had reason to ask—or answer—these questions? Regardless of how interesting a topic may be to you as a writer, readers always need to know what is at stake in a text and why they should care. All too often, however, these questions are left unanswered—mainly because writers and speakers assume that audiences will know or will figure out the answers on their own. As a result, students come away from lectures feeling like outsiders to what they've just heard, and their own instructors come away from academic conferences feeling alienated by many of the presentations. The problem is not necessarily that these talks lack a clear, well-focused thesis, or that the thesis is inadequately supported with evidence. Instead, the problem is that the speakers don't address the crucial question of why their arguments matter.

That this crucial question is so often left unaddressed is unfortunate since the speakers generally *could* offer interesting, engaging answers. When pressed, for instance, most academics will tell you that their lectures and articles matter because they address some belief that needs to be corrected or updated—and because their arguments have important, real-world consequences. Yet many academics fail to explicitly identify these reasons and consequences in what they say and write. Rather than assume that audiences will know why their claims matter, all writers need to answer the "so what?" and "who cares?" questions up front. Not everyone can claim to have a cure for cancer or a solution to end poverty. But writers who cannot show that others *should* care and *do* care about their claims will ultimately lose their audiences' interest.

This chapter focuses on various moves that you can make to answer the "who cares?" and "so what?" questions in your own writing. In one sense, the two questions get at the same thing: the relevance or importance of what you are saying. Yet they get at this significance in different ways. Whereas "who cares?" literally asks you to identify a person or group who cares about your claims, "so what?" asks about the real-world applications and consequences of those claims—what difference it would make if they were accepted. We'll look first at ways of making clear who cares.

"WHO CARES?"

To see how one writer answers the "who cares?" question, consider the following passage from the science writer Denise Grady. Writing in the *New York Times*, she explains some of the latest research into fat cells.

> Scientists used to think body fat and the cells it was made of were pretty much inert, just an oily storage compartment. But within the past decade research has shown that fat cells act like chemi-

cal factories and that body fat is potent stuff: a highly active tissue that secretes hormones and other substances with profound and sometimes harmful effects. . . .

In recent years, biologists have begun calling fat an "endocrine organ," comparing it to glands like the thyroid and pituitary, which also release hormones straight into the bloodstream.

DENISE GRADY, "The Secret Life of a Potent Cell"

Notice how Grady's writing reflects the central advice we give in this book, offering a clear claim and also framing that claim as a response to what someone else has said. In so doing, Grady immediately identifies at least one group with a stake in the new research that sees fat as "active," "potent stuff": namely, the scientific community, which formerly believed that body fat is inert. By referring to these scientists, Grady implicitly acknowledges that her text is part of a larger conversation and shows who besides herself has an interest in what she says.

Consider, however, how the passage would read had Grady left out what "scientists used to think" and simply explained the new findings in isolation.

Within the past few decades research has shown that fat cells act like chemical factories and that body fat is potent stuff: a highly active tissue that secretes hormones and other substances. In recent years, biologists have begun calling fat an "endocrine organ," comparing it to glands like the thyroid and pituitary, which also release hormones straight into the bloodstream.

Though this statement is clear and easy to follow, it lacks any indication that anyone needs to hear it. Okay, one nods while reading this passage, fat is an active, potent thing. Sounds plausible enough; no reason to think it's not true. But does anyone really care? Who, if anyone, is interested?

TEMPLATES FOR INDICATING WHO CARES

To address "who cares?" questions in your own writing, we suggest using templates like the following, the first of which mimics Grady's style in the *New York Times*.

▸ _____ used to think _____. But recently [or within the past few decades] _____ suggests that _____.

▸ This interpretation challenges the work of those critics who have long assumed that _____.

▸ These findings challenge the work of earlier researchers, who tended to assume that _____.

▸ Recent studies like these shed new light on _____, which previous studies had not addressed.

Grady might have been more explicit by writing the "who cares?" question directly into her text, as in the following template.

▸ But who really cares? Who besides me and a handful of recent researchers has a stake in these claims? At the very least, the researchers who assumed that fat _____ should care.

To gain greater authority as a writer, it helps to name specific people or groups who have a stake in your claims and to go into some detail about their views.

▸ Researchers have long assumed that _____. For instance, one eminent scholar of cell biology, _____, assumed in _____, her seminal work on cell structures and functions, that fat cells _____. As _____ herself put it, "_____" (200–).

Another leading scientist, _____, argued that fat cells
"_____" (200–). Ultimately, when it came to the nature of fat,
the basic assumption was that _____.

But a new body of research shows that fat cells are far more
complex and that _____.

In other cases, you might refer to certain people or groups who
should care about your claims.

▸ If sports enthusiasts stopped to think about it, many of them
   might simply assume that the most successful athletes
   _____. However, new research shows _____.

▸ These findings challenge dieters' common assumption that
   _____.

▸ At first glance, teenagers might say _____. But on closer
   inspection _____.

Such templates help you to generate interest in your subject by
identifying populations of readers who are likely to have a stake
in it.

"So What?"

Although answering the "who cares?" question is crucial, in
many cases it is not enough, especially if you are writing for
general readers who don't necessarily have a strong investment
in your subject (as Grady is in the *New York Times*). In the case
of Grady's argument about fat cells, such readers may still wonder why it matters that some researchers think fat cells are
active and others think they're inert. Or, to move to a differ-

ent field of study, *so what* if some scholars disagree about Huck Finn's relationship with the runaway slave Jim? Why should anyone besides a few specialists in the field care about such disputes? What, if anything, hinges on them?

The best way to answer such questions about the larger consequences of your claims is to appeal to something that your audience already figures to care about. Whereas the "who cares?" question asks you to identify an interested person or group, the "so what?" question asks you to link your argument to some larger matter that readers already deem important. Thus in analyzing *Huckleberry Finn*, a writer could argue that seemingly narrow disputes about the hero's relationship with Jim actually shed light on what Twain's canonical, widely read novel says about racism in America.

Let's see how Grady invokes such broad, general concerns in her article on fat cells. Her first move is to link researchers' interest in fat cells to a general concern with obesity and health.

> Researchers trying to decipher the biology of fat cells hope to find new ways to help people get rid of excess fat or, at least, prevent obesity from destroying their health. In an increasingly obese world, their efforts have taken on added importance.

Further showing why readers should care, Grady's next move is to demonstrate the even broader relevance and urgency of her subject matter.

> Internationally, more than a billion people are overweight. Obesity and two illnesses linked to it, heart disease and high blood pressure, are on the World Health Organization's list of the top 10 global health risks. In the United States, 65 percent of adults weigh too much, compared with about 56 percent a decade ago, and government researchers blame obesity for at least 300,000 deaths a year.

What Grady implicitly says here is: "Look, dear reader, you may think that these questions about the nature of fat cells I've been pursuing have little to do with everyday life. In fact, however, these questions are extremely important—particularly in our 'increasingly obese world' in which we need to prevent obesity from destroying our health."

Notice that Grady's phrase "in an increasingly _____ world" can be adapted as a strategic move to address the "so what?" question in other fields as well. For example, a sociologist analyzing back-to-nature movements of the past thirty years might make the following statement.

Tom Friedman says "The World Is Flat." So what? See pp. 438–40, ¶41–46.

> In a world increasingly dominated by cellphones and sophisticated computer technology, these attempts to return to nature and simplify one's life are extremely significant forms of protest.

This type of move can be readily applied to other disciplines because no matter how much these disciplines may differ, the need to justify the importance of one's concerns is common to them all.

TEMPLATES FOR ESTABLISHING WHY YOUR CLAIMS MATTER

▶ X matters/is important because _____.

▶ Although X may seem trivial, it is in fact crucial in terms of today's concern over _____.

▶ Ultimately, what is at stake here is _____.

▸ These findings have important consequences for the broader domain of _____ .

▸ My discussion of X is in fact addressing the larger matter of _____ .

▸ These conclusions/This discovery will have significant applications in _____ as well as in _____ .

Finally, you can also treat the "so what?" question as a related aspect of the "who cares?" question.

▸ Although X may seem of concern to only a small group of _____ , it should in fact concern anyone who cares about _____ .

All these templates help you to hook your readers. By suggesting the real-world applications of your claims, the templates not only demonstrate that others care about your claims but also tell your readers why *they* should care. Again, it bears repeating that simply stating and proving your thesis isn't enough. You also need to frame it in a way that helps readers care about it.

WHAT ABOUT READERS WHO ALREADY KNOW WHY IT MATTERS?

At this point, you might wonder if you need to answer the "who cares?" and "so what?" questions in *everything* you write. Is it really necessary to address these questions if you're proposing something so obviously consequential as, say, a cure for a childhood disease or a program to eliminate illiteracy? Isn't it obvious that everyone cares about such problems? Does it really need to be spelled out? And what about when you're writing for audiences who you already know are interested in your claims and who understand perfectly well why they're important? In other words, do you always need to address the "so what?" and "who cares?" questions?

See how Bob Herbert explains why it matters that the U.S. "has lost its way," p. 403, ¶29.

As a rule, yes—although it's true that you can't keep answering them forever and at a certain point must say enough is enough. Although a determined skeptic can infinitely ask why something matters—"Who cares about dieting?" And then, "Who cares about health?"—you have to stop answering at some point in your text. Nevertheless, we urge you to go as far as possible in answering such questions. If you ignore them or give them short shrift, you run the risk that readers will dismiss your text as irrelevant and unimportant. And though some expert readers might already know why your claims matter, even they need to be reminded. Thus the safest move is to be as explicit as possible in answering the "so what?" question, even for those already in the know.

If you take it for granted that readers will somehow intuit the answers to "so what?" and "who cares?" on their own, you may make your work seem less interesting and exciting than it actually is. Therefore we suggest that whether you are offering a cure for cancer or trying to change the way we read Walt Whitman's poetry, be sure to present what you're saying *as a* cure for cancer or a challenge to how Whitman's poetry is read. When you are careful to explain who cares and why, it's a little like bringing a cheerleading squad into your text. When you step back from the text—a move that we discuss in Chapter 10—and explain why it matters, you are urging your audience to keep reading, pay attention, and care.

Exercises

1. Read several articles and essays to see whether they address the "so what?" and "who cares?" questions. Probably you'll find that some do, some don't. The question to consider then is whether it makes a difference to you as a reader. Are those texts that say why it matters more interesting? More persuasive?

2. Look over something you've written yourself. Do you indicate "so what?" and "who cares?"? If not, revise your text to do so. You might use the following template to get started.

▸ My point here—that _____—should interest those who _____. Beyond this limited audience, however, my point should speak to anyone who cares about the larger issue of _____.

3

TYING IT ALL
TOGETHER

EIGHT

"As a Result"

Connecting the Parts

—⬚—

WE ONCE HAD a student named Bill, whose characteristic sentence pattern went something like this.

> Spot is a good dog. He has fleas.

"Connect your sentences," we urged in the margins of Bill's papers. "What does Spot being good have to do with his fleas? These two statements seem unrelated. Can you connect them in some logical way?" When such comments yielded no results, we tried inking in suggested connections for him.

> Spot is a good dog, *but* he has fleas.
> Spot is a good dog, *even though* he has fleas.

But our message failed to get across, and Bill's disconnected sentence pattern persisted to the end of the semester.

And yet, Bill did focus well on his subjects. When he mentioned Spot the dog in one sentence, we could count on Spot the dog being the topic of the following sentence as well. This was not the case with some of Bill's classmates, who sometimes changed topic from sentence to sentence or even from clause to clause within a single sentence. But because Bill neglected to mark his connections, his writing was as frustrating to read as theirs. In all these cases, we had to struggle to figure out on our own how the sentences and paragraphs connected or failed to connect with each other.

What makes such writers so hard to read, in other words, is that they never gesture back to what they have just said or forward to what they plan to say. "Never look back" might be their motto, almost as if they see writing as a process of thinking of something to say about a topic and writing it down, then thinking of something else to say about the topic and writing that down too, and on and on until they've filled the assigned number of pages and can hand the paper in. Each sentence basically starts a new thought, rather than growing out of or extending the thought of the previous sentence.

When Bill talked about his writing habits, he acknowledged that he never went back and read what he had written. Indeed, he told us that, other than using his computer software to check for spelling errors and make sure that his tenses were all aligned, he never actually reread what he wrote before turning it in. Writing for Bill was just that: something he did while sitting at a computer, and reading, including rereading, was a separate activity generally reserved for an easy chair, book in hand. It had never occurred to Bill that to write a good sentence he had to think about how it connected to those that came before and after it; that he had to think hard about the relationship among the sentences he wrote. Each sentence for Bill existed in a sort of tunnel isolated from every other sentence on the page. He never bothered to fit all the parts of his essay together because he apparently thought of writing as a matter of piling up information or insights rather than building an argument. What we suggest in this chapter, then, is that you converse not only with others in your writing, but with yourself: that you establish clear relations between one statement and the next by connecting those statements together.

This chapter addresses the issue of how to connect all the parts of your writing. The best compositions establish a sense of momentum and direction by making explicit connections among their different parts, so that what is said in one sentence (or paragraph) not only sets up what is to come but is clearly informed by what has already been said. When you write a sentence, you create an expectation in the reader's mind that the next sentence will in some way echo and be an extension of the first, even if—*especially if*—the second one takes your argument in a new direction.

It may help to think of each sentence you write as having arms that reach backward and forward, as Figure 6 suggests. When your sentences reach outward like this, they establish connections that help your writing flow smoothly in a way readers appreciate. Conversely, when writing lacks such connections and moves in fits and starts, readers repeatedly have to go back over the sentences and guess at the connections on their own. To prevent such disconnection and make your writing flow, we advise following a "do it yourself" principle, which means that it is your

FIGURE 6

job as a writer to do the hard work of making the connections rather than, as Bill did, leaving this work to your readers.

This chapter offers several moves you can make to put this principle into action: (1) using transition terms (like "therefore" and "yet"); (2) adding pointing words (like "this" or "such"); (3) using certain key terms and phrases throughout your entire text; and (4) repeating yourself, but with a difference—a move that involves repeating elements in your previous sentence, but with enough variation to move the text forward and without being redundant. All these moves require that you always look back and, in crafting any one sentence, think hard about those that precede it.

Notice how we ourselves have used such connecting devices thus far in this chapter. The second paragraph of this chapter, for example, opens with the transitional "And yet," signaling a change in direction, while the third includes the phrase "in other words," telling you to expect a restatement of a point we've just made. If you look through this book, you should be able to find many sentences that contain some word or phrase that explicitly hooks them back to something said earlier, to something about to be said, or both. And many sentences in *this* chapter repeat key terms related to the idea of connection: "connect," "disconnect," "link," "relate," "forward," and "backward."

USE TRANSITIONS

For readers to follow your train of thought, you need not only to connect your sentences and paragraphs to each other, but also to mark the kind of connection you are making. One of the easiest ways to make this move is to use *transitions* (from the Latin root *trans*, "to cross over"), which help you to cross from one point to another in your text. Transitions are usually placed at or near the start of sentences so they can signal to readers where your text is going: in the same direction it has been moving, or in a new direction. More specifically, transitions tell readers whether your text is echoing a previous sentence or paragraph ("in other words"), adding something to it ("in addition"), offering an example of it ("for example"), generalizing from it ("as a result"), or modifying it ("and yet").

The following is a list of commonly used transition terms, categorized according to their different functions.

ADDITION   also, and, besides, furthermore, in addition, indeed, in fact, moreover, so too

EXAMPLE   after all, as an illustration, for example, for instance, specifically, to take a case in point

ELABORATION   actually, by extension, in short, that is, in other words, to put it another way, to put it bluntly, to put it succinctly, ultimately

COMPARISON   along the same lines, in the same way, likewise, similarly

CONTRAST   although, but, by contrast, conversely, despite the fact that, even though, however, in contrast, nevertheless, nonetheless, on the contrary, on the other hand, regardless, whereas, while yet

CAUSE AND EFFECT   accordingly, as a result, consequently, hence, since, so, then, therefore, thus

CONCESSION   admittedly, although it is true, granted, naturally, of course, to be sure

CONCLUSION   as a result, consequently, hence, in conclusion, in short, in sum, therefore, thus, to sum up, to summarize

Ideally, transitions should operate so unobtrusively in a piece of writing that they recede into the background and readers do not even notice that they are there. It's a bit like what happens when drivers use their turn signals before turning right or left: just as other drivers recognize such signals almost unconsciously, readers should process transition terms with a minimum of thought. But even though such terms should function unobtrusively in your writing, they can be among the most powerful tools in your vocabulary. Think how your heart sinks when someone, immediately after praising you, begins a sentence with "but" or "however." No matter what follows, you know it won't be good.

Notice that some transitions can help you not only to move from one sentence to another, but to combine two or more sentences into one. Combining sentences in this way helps prevent the choppy, staccato effect that arises when too many short sentences are strung together, one after the other. For instance, to combine Bill's two choppy sentences ("Spot is a good dog. He has fleas.") into one, better-flowing sentence, we suggested that he rewrite them as: "Spot is a good dog, *even though* he has fleas."

Transitions like these not only guide readers through the twists and turns of your argument, but also help ensure that you *have* an argument in the first place. In fact, we think of words like "but," "yet," "nevertheless," "besides," and others as argument words, since it's hard to use them without making some kind of argument. The word "therefore," for instance, commits you to making sure that the claims leading up to it lead logically to the conclusion that it introduces. "For example" also assumes an argument, since it requires that the material you are introducing stand as an instance or a proof of some preceding generalization. As a result, the more you use transitions, the more you'll be able not only to connect the parts of your text but also to construct a strong argument in the first place.

While you don't need to memorize these transitions, we do suggest that you draw on them so frequently that using them eventually becomes second nature. To be sure, it is possible to overuse these terms, so take time to read over your drafts carefully and eliminate any transitions that are unnecessary. But following the maxim that one needs to learn the basic moves of argument before one can deliberately depart from them, we advise you not to forgo explicit transition terms until you've first mastered their use. In all our years of teaching, we've read countless essays that suffered from having few or no transitions, but we have yet to receive one in which the transitions were overdone. Seasoned writers often do without explicit transitions, but only because they rely heavily on the other types of connecting devices that we turn to in the rest of this chapter.

Read the essay by "The Economist," pp. 316–20, to see how transitions help make an argument.

Before doing so, however, let us warn you about inserting transitions without really thinking through their meanings—using "therefore," say, when your text's logic actually requires "nevertheless" or "however." So beware. Choosing transition terms should involve a bit of mental sweat, since the whole point of using them is to make your writing *more* reader-friendly, not less. The only thing more frustrating than reading Bill-style passages like "Spot is a good dog. He has fleas" is reading misconnected sentences like "Spot is a good dog. For example, he has fleas."

USE POINTING WORDS

Another move you can make to connect the parts of your argument is to use pointing words—which, as their name implies, point or refer backward to some concept in the previous sentence. The most common of these pointing words include "this,"

"these," "that," "those," "their," and "such" (as in "these pointing words" near the start of this sentence) and simple pronouns
like "his," "he," "her," "she," "it," and "their." Such terms help
you create the flow we spoke of earlier that enables readers to
move effortlessly through your text. In a sense, these terms are
like an invisible hand reaching out of your sentence, grabbing
what's needed in the previous sentences and pulling it along.

Like transitions, however, pointing words need to be used
carefully. It's dangerously easy to insert pointing words into your
text that don't refer to a clearly defined object, thinking that
because the object you have in mind is clear to you it will also
be clear to your readers. For example, consider the use of "this"
in the following passage.

> Alexis de Tocqueville was highly critical of democratic societies,
> which he saw as tending toward mob rule. At the same time,
> he accorded democratic societies grudging respect. *This* is seen in
> Tocqueville's statement that . . .

When "this" is used in such a way it becomes an ambiguous or
free-floating pointer, since readers can't tell if it refers to Tocqueville's critical attitude toward democratic societies, his grudging respect for them, or some combination of both. "This what?"
readers mutter as they go back over such passages and try to
figure them out.

You can fix such problems caused by a free-floating pointer
by making sure there is one and only one possible object in the
vicinity that the pointer could be referring to. It also often helps
to name the object the pointer is referring to at the same time
that you point to it, replacing a bald "this," for instance, with
a more precise phrase like "this ambivalence toward democratic
societies" or "this grudging respect."

REPEAT KEY TERMS AND PHRASES

A third move you can make to connect the parts of your argument is to develop a constellation of key terms and phrases, including their synonyms and antonyms, that you repeat throughout your text. Used well, key terms even provide readers with some sense of your topic. Playing with key terms also is a good way to develop a title and appropriate section headings for your text.

For an example of a move that effectively incorporates key terms, notice how often Martin Luther King Jr. uses the key words "criticism(s)" and "statement" in the opening paragraph to his famous "Letter from Birmingham Jail."

> Dear Fellow Clergymen:
>
> While confined here in the Birmingham city jail, I came across your recent *statement* calling my present activities "unwise and untimely." Seldom do I pause to answer *criticism* of my work and ideas. If I sought to answer all the *criticisms* that cross my desk, my secretaries would have little time for anything other than *such correspondence* in the course of the day, and I would have no time for constructive work. But since I feel that you are men of genuine good will and that your *criticisms* are sincerely set forth, I want to try to answer your *statement* in what I hope will be patient and reasonable terms.
>
> MARTIN LUTHER KING JR., "Letter from Birmingham Jail"

Even though King uses the term "criticism(s)" three times and "statement" twice, the effect is not overly repetitive. In fact, these key terms help bind the paragraph together. And though King does not explicitly use those terms in the remainder of his letter, he keeps the concepts in play by elaborately summarizing each of the specific criticisms laid out against him in the statement he has received and then answering them.

For another example of the effective use of key terms, consider the following passage from *Where the Girls Are: Growing Up Female with the Mass Media,* in which the feminist historian Susan Douglas develops a constellation of sharply contrasting key terms around the concept of cultural schizophrenics: women like herself who, Douglas claims, have mixed feelings about the images of ideal femininity with which they are constantly bombarded by the media.

> In a variety of ways, the mass media helped make us the critical schizophrenics we are today, women who rebel against yet submit to prevailing images about what a desirable, worthwhile woman should be. . . . [T]he mass media has engendered in many women a kind of cultural identity crisis. We are ambivalent toward femininity on the one hand and feminism on the other. Pulled in opposite directions—told we were equal, yet told we were subordinate; told we could change history but told we were trapped by history—we got the bends at an early age, and we've never gotten rid of them.
>
> When I open *Vogue,* for example, I am simultaneously infuriated and seduced. . . . I adore the materialism; I despise the materialism. . . . I want to look beautiful; I think wanting to look beautiful is about the most dumb-ass goal you could have. The magazine stokes my desire; the magazine triggers my bile. And this doesn't only happen when I'm reading *Vogue;* it happens all the time. . . . On the one hand, on the other hand—that's not just me—that's what it means to be a woman in America.
>
> To explain this schizophrenia . . .
>
> <div align="right">SUSAN DOUGLAS, <i>Where the Girls Are:
Growing Up Female with the Mass Media</i></div>

In this passage, Douglas establishes "schizophrenia" as a key concept and then echoes it through synonyms like "identity crisis," "ambivalent," "the bends"—and even demonstrates it through a series of contrasting words and phrases:

> rebel against / submit
> told we were equal / told we were subordinate
> told we could change history / told we were trapped by history
> infuriated / seduced
> I adore / I despise
> I want / I think wanting . . . is about the most dumb-ass goal
> stokes my desire / triggers my bile
> on the one hand / on the other hand

These contrasting phrases help explain Douglas's claim that women are being pulled in two directions at once. In so doing, they bind the passage together into a unified whole that, despite its complexity and sophistication, stays focused over its entire length.

REPEAT YOURSELF—BUT WITH A DIFFERENCE

The last move we offer for connecting the parts of your text involves repeating yourself, but with a difference—which basically means saying the same thing you've just said, but in a slightly different way that avoids sounding monotonous. To effectively connect the parts of your argument and keep it moving forward, be careful not to leap from one idea to a different idea or introduce new ideas cold. Instead, try to build bridges between your ideas by echoing what you've just said while simultaneously moving your text into new territory.

Several of the connecting devices discussed in this chapter are ways of repeating yourself in this special way. Key terms, pointing terms, and even many transitions can be used in a way that not only brings something forward from the previous sentence, but in some way alters it. When Douglas, for instance, uses the key term "ambivalent" to echo her earlier reference to schizophrenia, she is repeating herself with a difference—repeating the same concept, but with a different word that adds new associations. When she uses a pointing term in "this schizophrenia," she is also repeating herself with a difference by explicitly naming the conflicting psychological and emotional responses she had earlier outlined but had not labeled.

In addition, when you use transition phrases like "in other words" and "to put it another way," you repeat yourself with a difference, since these phrases help you restate earlier claims but in a different register. When you open a sentence with "in other words," you are basically telling your readers that in case they didn't fully understand what you meant in the last sentence, you are now coming at it again from a slightly different angle; or that since you're presenting a very important idea, you're not going to skip over it quickly but will explore it further to make sure your readers grasp all its aspects.

We would even go so far as to suggest that after your first sentence, almost every sentence you write should include some form of repetition, but with a difference. Whether you are writing a "furthermore" comment that adds to what you have just said or a "for example" statement that illustrates it, each sentence should echo at least one element of the previous sentence in some discernible way. Even when your text changes direction and requires transitions like "in contrast," "however," or "but," you still need to mark that shift by linking the sentence to the one just before it, as in the following example.

> The girl loved basketball. Nevertheless, she feared her height would put her at a disadvantage.

These sentences work because even though the second sentence changes course and qualifies the first, it still echoes key concepts from the first. Not only does "she" echo "the girl," since both refer to the same person, but "feared" echoes "loved" by establishing the contrast mandated by the term "nevertheless." "Nevertheless," then, is not an excuse for changing subjects radically. It too requires a little repetition to help readers shift gears with you and follow your train of thought.

Repetition, in short, is the central means by which you can move from point A to point B in a text. To introduce one last analogy, think of the way experienced rock climbers move up a steep slope. Instead of jumping or lurching from one handhold to the next, good climbers get a secure handhold on the position they have established before reaching for the next ledge. The same thing applies to writing. To move smoothly from point to point in your argument, you need to firmly ground what you say in what you've already said. In this way, your writing remains focused while simultaneously moving forward.

Exercises

1. Read the following passage from the conclusion to a PhD dissertation focusing on the rags-to-riches stories of the American Industrial Revolution. Underline all the con-

necting devices—transitions, pointing terms, key terms, and repetition. For each one, explain how it helps you to read and understand the argument.

The most remarkable thing to me about the American Dream of rags-to-riches success is the extent to which most people think they understand it. The idea that America is a fair, open society that rewards merit (regardless of one's gender, race, or class background), and that individuals control their own economic fate is so pervasive that, like the air we breathe, it can easily be taken for granted. Even critics who expose the idea of individual responsibility as a lie or myth—as an instance of propaganda that unfairly blames the poor for their poverty and legitimates wealth, and that thwarts collective political action—usually assume that they are dealing with a set, already known entity. My goal in this dissertation, however, has been to defamiliarize this deeply familiar story and show that, in many (though not all) its formulations, the American rags-to-riches story contains unexpected complexities and divisions that, largely because of their unexpectedness, have been widely overlooked.

> CATHY BIRKENSTEIN, *Rereading the American Rags-to-Riches Story: Conflict and Contradiction in the Works of Horatio Alger, Booker T. Washington, and Willa Cather*

2. Read over something you've written with an eye for the devices you've used to connect the parts. Underline all the transitions, pointing terms, key terms, and repetition. Do you see any patterns? Do you rely on certain devices more than others? Are there any passages that are hard to follow—and if so, can you make them easier to read by adding appropriate transitions or trying any of the other devices discussed in this chapter? If there are any devices you don't use at all, try revising your text to try them out.

NINE

"Ain't So / Is Not"

Academic Writing Doesn't Mean Setting Aside Your Own Voice

—◻—

Have you ever gotten the impression that writing well in college means setting aside the kind of language you use in everyday conversation? That to impress your instructors you need to use big words, long sentences, and complex sentence structures? If so, then we're here to tell you that it ain't necessarily so. On the contrary, academic writing can—and in our view *should*—be relaxed, easy to follow, and even a little bit fun. Although we don't want to suggest that you avoid using sophisticated, academic terms in your writing, we encourage you to draw upon the kinds of expressions and turns of phrase that you use every day when conversing with family and friends. In this chapter, we want to show you how you can write effective academic arguments while at the same time holding on to some of your own voice.

This point is important, since you may well become turned off from writing if you think your everyday language practices have to be checked at the classroom door. You may end up feeling like a student we know who, when asked how she felt about the writing she does in college, answered, "I do it because I have to, but it's just not me!"

This is not to suggest that *any* language you use among friends has a place in writing. Nor is it to suggest that you may fall back on colloquial usage as an excuse for not learning more rigorous forms of expression. It is, however, to suggest that relaxed, colloquial language can often enliven academic writing and even enhance its rigor and precision. Such informal language also helps you to connect with readers in a personal as well as an intellectual way. In our view, then, it is a mistake to assume that academic writing and everyday language are completely separate things, and that they can never be used together.

Mix Academic and Colloquial Styles

Many successful writers often blend academic, professional language with popular expressions and sayings. Consider, for instance, the following passage from a scholarly article about the way teachers respond to errors in student writing.

Marking and judging formal and mechanical errors in student papers is one area in which composition studies seems to have a multiple-personality disorder. On the one hand, our mellow, student-centered, process-based selves tend to condemn marking formal errors at all. Doing it represents the Bad Old Days. Ms. Fidditch and Mr. Flutesnoot with sharpened red pencils, spilling innocent blood across the page. Useless detail work. Inhumane, perfectionist standards, making our students feel stupid, wrong, trivial, misunderstood. Joseph Williams has pointed out how arbitrary and context-bound our judgments of formal error are. And certainly our noting of errors on student papers gives no one any great joy; as Peter Elbow says, English is most often associated *either* with grammar or with high literature—"two things designed to make folks feel most out of it."

ROBERT CONNORS AND ANDREA LUNSFORD,
"Frequency of Formal Errors in Current College Writing,
or Ma and Pa Kettle Do Research"

This passage blends writing styles in several ways. First, it places informal, relaxed expressions like "mellow," "the Bad Old Days," and "folks" side-by-side with more formal, academic-sounding phrases like "multiple-personality disorder," "student-centered," "process-based," and "arbitrary and context-bound." Even the title of the piece, "Frequency of Formal Errors in Current College Writing, or Ma and Pa Kettle Do Research," blends formal, academic usage on the left side of the comma with a popular-culture reference to the fictional movie characters Ma and Pa Kettle on the right. Second, to give vivid, concrete form to their discussion of grading disciplinarians, Connors and Lunsford conjure up such imaginary figures as the stuffy, old-fashioned task-masters Ms. Fidditch and Mr. Flutesnoot. Through such imaginative uses of language, Connors and Lunsford inject greater force into what might otherwise have been dry, scholarly prose.

Formal/informal mixings like this can be found in countless other texts. Notice how the food industry critic Eric Schlosser describes some changes in the city of Colorado Springs in his best-selling book on fast foods in the United States.

The loopiness once associated with Los Angeles has come full blown to Colorado Springs—the strange, creative energy that crops up where the future's consciously being made, where people walk the fine line separating a visionary from a total nutcase.

ERIC SCHLOSSER, *Fast Food Nation*

Schlosser could have played it safe and referred not to the "loopiness" but to the "eccentricity" associated with Los Angeles, or to "the fine line separating a visionary from a lunatic" instead of " . . . a total nutcase." His decision, however, to go with the more adventuresome, colorful terms gives a liveliness to his writing that would have been lacking with the more conventional terms.

Another example of writing that blends the informal with the formal comes from an essay on the American novelist Willa Cather by the literary critic Judith Fetterley. Discussing "how very successful Cather has been in controlling how we think about her," Fetterley, building on the work of another scholar, writes as follows.

> As Merrill Skaggs has put it, "She is neurotically controlling and self-conscious about her work, but she knows at all points what she is doing. Above all else, she is self-conscious."
> Without question, Cather was a control freak.
>
> JUDITH FETTERLEY, "Willa Cather and the
Question of Sympathy: The Unofficial Story"

This passage demonstrates not only that specialized, psychological phrases like "neurotically controlling" and "self-conscious" are compatible with everyday, popular expressions like "control freak," but also that translating the one type of language into the other, the specialized into the everyday, can help drive home a point. By translating Skaggs's academic description of Cather as "neurotically controlling and self-conscious" into the succinct claim that "Without question, Cather was a control freak," Fetterley suggests that one need not choose between specialized, academic ways of talking and the everyday language of casual conversation. Indeed, her passage offers a simple recipe for

"Hidden Intellectualism," pp. 297–303, mixes colloquial and academic styles.

blending the specialized and the everyday: first make your point in the language of a professional field, and then make it again in everyday language—a great trick, we think, for underscoring a point.

Although one reason to blend languages like this is to give your writing more punch, another reason is to make a political statement—about the way, for example, society unfairly over-values some varieties of language and devalues others. For instance, in the titles of two of her books, *Talkin and Testifyin: The Language of Black America* and *Black Talk: Words and Phrases from the Hood to the Amen Corner*, the language scholar Geneva Smitherman mixes African American vernacular phrases with more scholarly language in order to suggest, as she explicitly argues in these books, that black English vernacular is as legitimate a variety of language as "standard" English. Here are three typical passages.

> In Black America, the oral tradition has served as a fundamental vehicle for gittin ovuh. That tradition preserves the Afro-American heritage and reflects the collective spirit of the race.
>
> Blacks are quick to ridicule "educated fools," people who done gone to school and read all dem books and still don't know nothin!
>
> . . . it is a socially approved verbal strategy for black rappers to talk about how bad they is.
>
> —GENEVA SMITHERMAN, *Talkin and Testifyin:*
> *The Language of Black America*

In these examples, Smitherman blends the standard written English of phrases like "oral tradition" and "fundamental vehicle" with black oral vernacular like "gittin ovuh," "dem books," and "how bad they is." Indeed, she even blends standard English spelling with that of black English variants like "dem" and "ovuh," thus mimicking what some black English vernacular actually sounds like. Although some scholars might object to these unconventional practices, this is precisely Smitherman's point: that our habitual language practices need to be opened up, and that the number of participants in the academic conversation needs to be expanded.

Along similar lines, the writer and activist Gloria Anzaldúa mixes standard English with Tex-Mex, a hybrid blend of English, Castilian Spanish, a North Mexican dialect, and the Indian language Nahuatl, to make a political point about the suppression of the Spanish language in the United States.

> From this racial, ideological, cultural, and biological cross-pollinization, an "alien" consciousness is presently in the making—a new *mestiza* consciousness, *una conciencia de mujer*.
>
> —Gloria Anzaldúa,
> *Borderlands / La Frontera: The New Mestiza*

Like Smitherman, Anzaldúa gets her point across not only through what she says, but through the way she says it, literally showing that the new hybrid, or *mestiza*, consciousness that she describes is, as she puts it, "presently in the making."

When to Mix Styles?
Consider Your Audience and Purpose

Because there are so many options in writing, you should never feel limited in your choice of words, as if such choices are set in stone. You can always play with your language and improve it. You can always dress it up, dress it down, or some combination of both. In dressing down your language, for example, you can make the claim that somebody "failed to notice" something by saying instead that it "flew under the radar." You can state that somebody was "unaware" of something by saying that he was "out to lunch." You could even recast the title of this book, "*They Say/I Say*," as a teenager might say it: "I'm Like/She Goes."

But how do you know when it is better to play things straight and stick to standard English, and when to be more adventuresome and mix things up? When, in other words, should you write "failed to notice" and when is it okay (or more effective) to write "flew under the radar"? Is it *always* appropriate to mix styles? And when you do so, how do you know when enough is enough?

In all situations, think carefully about your audience and purpose. When you write a letter applying for a job, for instance, or submit a grant proposal, where your words will be weighed by an official screening body, using language that's too colloquial or slangy may well jeopardize your chances of success. On such occasions, it is usually best to err on the safe side, conforming as closely as possible to the conventions of standard written English. In other situations for other audiences, however, there is room to be more creative—in this book, for example. Ultimately, your judgments about the appropriate language for the situation should always take into account your likely audience and your purpose in writing.

Although it may have been in the past, academic writing today is no longer the linguistic equivalent of a black-tie affair. To succeed as a writer in college, then, you need not limit your language to the strictly formal; you need not abandon your own voice at the classroom door. Although academic writing does rely on complex sentence patterns and on specialized, disciplinary vocabularies, it is surprising how often such writing draws on the languages of the street, popular culture, our ethnic communities, and home. It is by blending these languages that "standard" English changes over time and the range of possibilities open to all writers continues to grow.

Exercises

1. Take a paragraph from this book and dress it down, rewriting it in informal colloquial language. Then rewrite the same paragraph again by dressing it up, making it much more formal. Then rewrite the paragraph one more time in a way that blends the two styles. Share your paragraphs with a classmate, and discuss which one you prefer and why.

2. Find something you've written for a course, and study it to see whether you've used any of your own everyday expressions, any words or structures that are not "academic." If by chance you don't find any, see if there's a place or two where shifting into more casual or unexpected language would help you make a point, get your reader's attention, or just add a little liveliness to your text. Be sure to keep your audience and purpose in mind, and use language that will be appropriate to both.

TEN

"In Other Words"

The Art of Metacommentary

—▱—

WHENEVER WE TELL PEOPLE that we are writing a chapter on the art of metacommentary, many of them give us a puzzled look and tell us that they have no idea what "metacommentary" is. "We know what commentary is," they'll sometimes say, "but what does it mean when it's *meta?*" Our answer is that they may not know the term, but they probably practice the art of metacommentary on a daily basis whenever they make a point of explaining something they've said or written: "What I meant to say was _____," "My point was not _____, but _____," or "You're probably not going to like what I'm about to say, but _____." In such cases, people are not offering new points, but telling an audience how to interpret what they have already said or are about to say. In terms of writing, then, metacommentary is a way of commenting on your claims and telling readers how—and how *not*—to think about them.

It may help to think of metacommentary as being like the chorus in a Greek play that stands apart from the drama unfolding on the stage and explains its meaning to the audience—or like a voice-over narrator who comments on and explains the action in a television show or movie. Like a Greek chorus or narrator, metacommentary is a sort of second text that stands alongside your main text and explains what it means. In the main text you say something; in the metatext you help readers interpret and process what you've said.

What we are suggesting, then, is that you think of your text as two texts joined at the hip: a main text in which you make your argument, and another in which you "work" your ideas, distinguishing your views from others they may be confused with, anticipating and answering objections, connecting one point to another, explaining why your claim might be controversial, and so forth—in short, guiding readers in processing and interpreting your main points. Figure 7 demonstrates what we mean.

THE MAIN TEXT SAYS SOMETHING, THE METATEXT
TELLS READERS HOW—AND HOW NOT—TO READ IT.

FIGURE 7

USE METACOMMENTARY TO CLARIFY AND ELABORATE

But why do you need metacommentary to tell readers what you mean and guide them through your text? Can't you just clearly *say* what you mean up front? In fact, no matter how clear and precise your writing is, readers can still fail to understand you in any number of ways. Even the best writers can provoke reactions in readers that they didn't intend, and even good readers can get lost in a complicated argument or fail to see how one point connects with another. Readers may also fail to see what follows from your argument, or they may follow your reasoning and examples yet fail to see the larger conclusion you draw from them. They may fail to see your argument's overall significance, or mistake what you are saying for a related claim that you actually want to distance yourself from. As a result, no matter how clear a writer you are, readers may still need you to help them process what you really mean. Because the written word is prone to so much mischief and can be interpreted in so many different ways, we need metacommentary to keep misinterpretations and other communication misfires at bay.

Another reason to master the art of metacommentary is that it will help you develop your ideas and generate more text. If you have ever had trouble producing the required number of pages for a writing project, metacommentary can help you add both length and depth to your writing. We've seen many students try to produce a five-page paper but then sputter to a halt at two or three pages, complaining they've said everything they can think of about their topic. "I've stated my thesis and presented my reasons and evidence," students have told us. "What else is there to do?" It's almost as if such writers have generated a thesis and don't know what to do with it. When these students learn to use

> Tom Friedman uses a lot of metacommentary—see e.g., pp. 426 and 439, ¶11, 44.

...commentary, however, they get more out of their ideas and write longer, more substantial texts. In sum, metacommentary can help you "work" your ideas, drawing out important implications, explaining the ideas from a different angle, clarifying how one idea supports another, and so forth.

So, even when you may think you've said everything possible in an argument, try inserting the following types of metacommentary.

▸ In other words, _____.

▸ What _____ really means is _____.

▸ My point is _____.

When you begin making these metacommentary moves in your writing, we predict you'll be happily surprised at how they'll help to bring out implications of your ideas that you didn't even realize were there.

Let's look at how the cultural critic Neil Postman uses metacommentary in the following passage describing the shift he sees in American culture as it moves away from print and reading to television and movies.

> *It is my intention in this book to show* that a great . . . shift has taken place in America, with the result that the content of much of our public discourse has become dangerous nonsense. *With this in view, my task in the chapters ahead is* straightforward. *I must, first, demonstrate* how, under the governance of the printing press, discourse in America was different from what it is now—generally coherent, serious and rational; *and then* how, under the governance of television, it has become shriveled and absurd. *But to avoid the possibility that my analysis will be interpreted as* standard-brand academic whimpering, a kind of elitist complaint against "junk" on televi-

sion, *I must first explain that* . . . I appreciate junk as much as the next fellow, *and I know full well that* the printing press has generated enough of it to fill the Grand Canyon to overflowing. Television is not old enough to have matched printing's output of junk.

NEIL POSTMAN, *Amusing Ourselves to Death:*
Public Discourse in the Age of Show Business

To see what we mean by metacommentary, look at the phrases above that we have italicized. With these moves, Postman essentially stands apart from his main ideas to help readers follow and understand what he is arguing.

Previewing what he will argue: *It is my intention in this book to show* . . .

Spelling out how he will make his argument: *With this in view, my task in these chapters* . . . *is.* . . . *I must, first, demonstrate* . . . *and then* . . .

Distinguishing his argument from other arguments it may easily be confused with: *But to avoid the possibility that my analysis will be interpreted as* . . . *I must first explain that* . . .

TITLES AS METACOMMENTARY

Even the title of Postman's book, *Amusing Ourselves to Death: Public Discourse in the Age of Show Business*, functions as a form of metacommentary since, like any title, it stands apart from the text itself and tells readers the book's main point: that, while amusing, show business has created what Postman suggests is a destructive form of public discourse.

Titles, in fact, are one of the most important forms of metacommentary, functioning rather like carnival barkers telling passersby what they can expect if they go inside. Subtitles, too often function as metacommentary on a main title, further explaining or elaborating on it. The subtitle of this book, for example, not only explains that this book is about "the moves that matter in academic writing," but indicates that "they say/ I say" is one of these moves. Thinking of a title as metacommentary can actually help you to develop sharper titles, leading you to write something that gives readers some sense of your argument rather than merely announcing your topic, or that it's an "English Essay"—or having no title at all. Essays that bear no title even send the message that the writer has simply not bothered to reflect on what he or she is saying.

USE OTHER MOVES AS METACOMMENTARY

Many of the other moves covered in this book function as metacommentary: entertaining objections, adding transitions, framing quotations, answering "so what?" and "who cares?" When you entertain objections, you stand outside of your text and imagine what a critic might say; when you add transitions, you essentially explain the relationship between various claims. And when you answer the "so what?" and "who cares?" questions, you look beyond your central argument and explain who cares about it and why.

TEMPLATES FOR INTRODUCING METACOMMENTARY

TO WARD OFF POTENTIAL MISUNDERSTANDINGS

This move differentiates your view from ones it might be mistaken for.

▸ Essentially, I am arguing that _____ .

▸ My point is not that we should _____ , but that we should _____ .

▸ What _____ really means is _____ .

TO ALERT READERS TO AN ELABORATION OF A PREVIOUS IDEA

This move says to readers: "In case you didn't get it the first time, I'll try saying the same thing in a different way."

▸ In other words, _____ .

▸ To put it another way, _____ .

TO PROVIDE READERS WITH A ROADMAP TO YOUR TEXT

This move orients readers, giving them advance notice about where you are going and making it easier for them to process and follow your text.

▸ Chapter 2 explores _____ , while Chapter 3 examines _____ .

▸ Having just argued that _____ , let us now turn our attention to _____ .

TO MOVE FROM A GENERAL CLAIM TO A SPECIFIC EXAMPLE

This move signals that you are not just generalizing, that here's a concrete example that illustrates what you're saying.

▸ For example, _____ .

▸ _____ , for instance, demonstrates _____ .

▸ Consider ＿＿＿＿＿, for example.

▸ To take a case in point, ＿＿＿＿＿.

TO INDICATE THAT A CLAIM IS ESPECIALLY IMPORTANT, OR LESS IMPORTANT

This move shows that what you are about to say is either more or less important than what you just said.

▸ Even more important, ＿＿＿＿＿.

▸ But above all, ＿＿＿＿＿.

▸ Incidentally, ＿＿＿＿＿.

▸ By the way, ＿＿＿＿＿.

TO HELP YOU ANTICIPATE AND RESPOND TO OBJECTION

This move helps you imagine and respond to other viewpoints.

▸ Although some readers may object that ＿＿＿＿＿, I would answer that ＿＿＿＿＿.

TO GUIDE READERS TO YOUR MOST GENERAL POINT

This move shows that you are wrapping things up and tying up various subpoints previously made.

▸ In sum, then, ＿＿＿＿＿.

▸ My conclusion, then, is that ＿＿＿＿＿.

▸ In short, ＿＿＿＿＿.

As we note at the start of this chapter, the forms of meta-commentary that we recommend, like all the other moves we discuss in this book, are deeply connected to moves you make in everyday conversation. Rather than being alien or mysterious, the meta-moves that we discuss in this chapter, like the other "moves that matter in academic writing" that this book focuses on, have deep roots in everyday, colloquial speech. But don't take our word for it. Observe for yourself how writers and speakers use metacommentary—not only in the ways we've mentioned, but in ways that you detect on your own. What you'll notice, we think, is that people don't just make claims, but *work* those claims in various ways, elaborating on them, generalizing from them, and distinguishing them from related claims they might be confused with. The more you become aware of these moves in your reading and everyday life, the more options you'll have to draw on as a writer.

Exercises

1. Complete each of the following metacommentary templates in any way that makes sense.

▸ In making a case for the medical use of marijuana, I am not saying that _____.

▸ But my argument will do more than prove that one particular industrial chemical has certain toxic properties. In this article, I will also _____.

▸ My point about the national obsessions with sports reinforces the belief held by many _____ that _____.

▸ I believe, therefore, that the war is completely justified. But let me
back up and explain how I arrived at this conclusion. _____.
In this way, I came to believe that this war is a big mistake.

2. Read over an essay or article with an eye for metacommentary. Does the writer make any of the moves discussed in
this chapter—and if so, how do they affect the success of
the argument? Then read over an essay that you've already
written to see whether it includes any metacommentary.
Start with your title. Does it give readers a good sense of
what your text is about? Do you provide any kind of roadmap
to where your text will go? Check each of the points you
make—do you use metacommentary to elaborate on them?
Is your text long enough, or would metacommentary help
you to fill it out? Using the templates in this chapter, add
at least two instances of metacommentary.

4

ENTERING THE
CONVERSATION

ELEVEN

ENTERING CLASS DISCUSSIONS

—⌐⌐—

THE CONVERSATIONAL PRINCIPLES discussed in this book apply to speaking as well as to writing, and in particular to speaking in classroom discussions. But speaking in class has some special requirements, as the following guidelines suggest:

FRAME YOUR COMMENTS AS A RESPONSE TO SOMETHING THAT HAS ALREADY BEEN SAID

Since the best group discussions are genuine conversations rather than a series of disconnected monologues, the single most important thing you need to do when joining a class discussion is to link what you are about to say to something that has already been said:

- ▶ I really liked the point Aaron made earlier when he said that _____. I agree because _____.

- ▶ I take your point, Nadia, that _____. Still . . .

- ▶ Though Sheila and Ryan seem to be at odds about _____, they may actually not be all that far apart.

In framing your comments this way, it is usually best to name both the person and the idea you're responding to. If you name the person alone ("I agree with Aziz because _____"), it may not be clear to listeners what part of what Aziz said you are referring to.

To Change the Subject, Indicate Explicitly That You Are Doing So

It is fine to try to change the conversation's direction. There's just one catch: you need to make clear to listeners that this is what you are doing. For example:

▶ So far we have been talking about _____. But isn't the real issue here _____?

▶ I'd like to change the subject to one that hasn't yet been addressed.

If you try to change the subject without indicating that you are doing so, your comment will come across as irrelevant rather than as a thoughtful contribution that moves the conversation forward.

Be Even More Explicit Than You Would Be in Writing

Because listeners in an oral discussion can't go back and reread what you just said, they are more easily overloaded than are readers of a print text. For this reason, in a class discussion you will do well to take some extra steps to help listeners follow your train of thought. (1) When you make a comment, limit yourself to one point and one point only. Although you can elaborate on this point, fleshing it out with examples and evidence, it is important that any elaboration be clearly focused on your one point. If you feel you must make two points, either unite them under one larger umbrella point, or make one point first and save the other for later. Trying to bundle two or more claims into one comment too often results in neither point getting the attention it deserves. (2) Use metacommentary to highlight your key point:

▸ In other words, what I'm trying to get at here is _____.

▸ My point is this: _____.

▸ My point, though, is not _____, but _____.

▸ This distinction is important for several reasons: _____.

TWELVE

READING FOR THE CONVERSATION

—◰—

"**WHAT IS THE AUTHOR'S ARGUMENT?** What is he or she trying to say?" For many years, these were the first questions we would ask our classes in a discussion of an assigned reading. The discussion that resulted was often halting, as our students struggled to get a handle on the argument, but eventually, after some awkward silences, the class would come up with something we could all agree was an accurate summary of the author's main thesis. But even after we'd gotten over that hurdle, the discussion would often still seem forced, and would limp along as we all struggled with the question that naturally arose next: Now that we had determined what the author was saying, what did we ourselves have to say?

For a long time we didn't worry much about these halting discussions, justifying them to ourselves as the predictable result of assigning difficult, challenging readings. Several years ago, however, as we started this book and began thinking about writing as the art of entering conversations, we latched onto the idea of leading with some different questions: "What other argument(s) is the writer responding to?" "Is the writer disagreeing or agreeing with something, and if so what?" "What is motivating the writer's argument?" "What other ideas have you encountered in this class or elsewhere that might be pertinent?" The results were dramatic. The discussions that followed tended to be far livelier and to draw in a greater number of students. We were still asking students to look for the main argument, but we were now asking them to see that argument as a response to some other argument that provoked it, gave it a reason for being, and helped all of us see why we should care about it.

What had happened, we realized, was that by changing the opening question, we changed the way our students approached reading, and maybe academic work in general. Instead of thinking of the argument of a text as an isolated entity, they now thought of that argument as one that responded to and provoked other arguments, much as they were accustomed to doing regularly in their daily lives. Furthermore, since they were now dealing not with *one* argument but at least *two* (the author's argument and the one[s] he or she was responding to), they now had alternative ways of seeing the topic at hand. This meant that, instead of just trying to understand the view presented by the author, they were more able to question that view intelligently and engage in the type of discussion and debate that some would say is the hallmark of a college education. In our discussions, a debate might arise between students who found the author's argument convincing and others who found a counterargument even more convincing. At some point, others might intervene to suggest that the opposing positions were too simple, that both might be right or that a third alternative was possible, while still others might object that the discussion thus far had missed the author's real point and suggest that we all go back to the text and pay closer attention to what it actually said.

We eventually realized that the move from reading for the author's argument in isolation to reading for how the author's argument is in dialogue with the arguments of others helped everyone become active critical readers rather than passive recipients of knowledge. It is true, of course, that all good readers bring a critical eye to what they read, looking for the arguments made and the reasons and evidence offered in support of those arguments. But the most sophisticated readers in college and the world beyond move between agreeing with and pushing back against the texts they are reading and are not shy about adding their own views to the conversation.

On some level, reading for the conversation is more rigorous, sophisticated, and demanding than reading for what one author says. It asks that you determine not only what the author thinks, but how what the author thinks fits with what others think, including ultimately yourself. Yet on another level, reading this way is a lot simpler and more familiar than reading for the thesis in isolation, since it returns writing to the primal, everyday act of communicating with other people about real issues.

Recognizing the Conversation

We suggest, then, that when assigned a reading, you imagine the author not as sitting alone in an empty room hunched over a desk or staring at a screen, but as sitting in a crowded coffee shop talking to others who are making claims that he or she is engaging with. In other words, we suggest that you imagine the authors that you read as participating in an ongoing, multi-sided, passionate conversation in which everyone has staked out a position and is trying to persuade others to agree or at least to take his or her position seriously.

The trick in reading for the conversation is to *figure out what views the author is responding to and what the author's own argu-*

ment is—or, to put it in the terms used in this book, to determine the "they say" and the author's "I say": whether the author is agreeing, disagreeing, or some combination thereof.

Another trick in reading for the conversation is to *figure out whether the author explicitly spells out the position that he or she is responding to* or assumes that you, the reader, already know what that view is or can figure it out for yourself. Sometimes authors remain clear about their position throughout a piece of writing, but sometimes they switch back and forth between their own views and the views of those they are responding to, so it is important that you as reader be alert to any such changes.

Consider, for instance, the opening to the selection by David Zinczenko on p. 153.

> If ever there were a newspaper headline custom made for Jay Leno's monologue, this was it. Kids taking on McDonald's this week, suing the company for making them fat. Isn't that like middle-aged men suing Porsche for making them get speeding tickets? Whatever happened to personal responsibility?
>
> I tend to sympathize with these portly fast-food patrons, though. Maybe that's because I used to be one of them.
>
> —DAVID ZINCZENKO, "Don't Blame the Eater"

Following this opening might be hard for a reader who did not know that authors sometimes summarize views that are not their own without signaling explicitly that they are doing so. Since the two paragraphs flatly contradict one another, the only way that such a reader could make sense of them would be by concluding that, in writing the second paragraph, the author had somehow forgotten what he had said in the first.

**See Chapter 6
for more
discussion
of naysayers.** However, if you know that writers frequently ventriloquize the views of others, often those they disagree with, the passage makes sense. You can see that in the first paragraph Zinczenko is summarizing a view he opposes, and that he switches to his own view in the second. He opens, in effect, with a "naysayer" that expresses scorn for his view even before he has told you what that view is. The dead giveaway that it's Zinczenko's own view in the second paragraph and not the other way around? His use of the first-person pronoun "I."

When the "They Say" Is Unstated

But of course not all writers follow such a clear "they say/I say" format, let alone present it as explicitly or as early in their texts as Zinczenko. Some authors identify the view they are responding to in clear, obvious ways, summarizing it at length, using it to set up their own argument, and sometimes even framing it within the types of explicit moves provided in Chapter 6 for entertaining naysayers. However, some writers never identify the view they are answering, and many who do specify that view do so in such an oblique fashion that it can be hard to tell what the other view is.

What, for instance, is the position that Tamara Draut is responding to in the opening paragraph of "The Growing College Gap," reprinted on pp. 378–82?

"The first in her family to graduate from college." How many times have we heard that phrase, or one like it, used to describe a successful American with a modest background? In today's United States, a four-year degree has become the all-but-official ticket to middle-class security. But if your parents don't have much money or higher education in their own right, the road to college—and beyond—looks increasingly treacherous. Despite a sharp increase in the proportion of high school graduates going on to some form of postsecondary education, socio-economic status continues to exert a powerful influence on college admission and completion; in fact, gaps in enrollment by class and race, after declining in the 1960s and 1970s, are once again as wide as they were thirty years ago, and getting wider, even as college has become far more crucial to lifetime fortunes.

—TAMARA DRAUT, "The Growing College Gap"

You might think that the "they say" here is embedded in the third sentence: They say (or we all think) that a four-year degree is "the all-but-official ticket to middle-class security," and you might assume that Draut will go on to disagree.

If you read the passage this way, however, you would be mistaken. Draut is not questioning whether a college degree has become "the ticket to middle-class security," but whether most Americans can secure that ticket, whether college is within the financial reach of most American families. You may have been thrown off by the "but" following the statement that college has become a prerequisite for middle-class security. However, unlike the "though" in Zinczenko's opening, this "but" does not signal that Draut will be disagreeing with the view she has just summarized, a view that in fact she takes as a given. Again, what she disagrees with is that this ticket to middle-class security is still readily available to the middle and working classes.

Were one to imagine Draut in a room talking with others with strong views on this topic, one would need to picture her challenging not those who think college is a ticket to financial security (something she takes for granted), but those who think the doors of college are open to anyone willing to put forth the effort to walk through them. The view that Draut is challenging, then, is not summarized in her opening. Instead, she assumes that readers are already so familiar with this view that they will recognize it

Draut's example suggests that in *texts where the central "they say" is not immediately identified, you have to construct it yourself based on the clues the text provides.* You have to start by locating the writer's thesis, and then imagine some of the arguments that might be made against it. In Draut's case, it is relatively easy to construct such a counterargument: it is the familiar faith in the American Dream of equal opportunity when it comes to access to college. Figuring out the counterargument not only reveals what motivated Draut as a writer, but helps you respond to her essay as an active, critical reader. Constructing this counterargument can also help you recognize when Draut challenges your own views, and this may lead you to question opinions that you previously took for granted.

When the Argument Is About Something "Nobody Is Talking About"

Not all texts are responding to views that you can readily identify, recognize, and summarize. Writers sometimes build their arguments by responding to a *lack* of discussion. These writers build their case not by playing off views that can be identified (like faith in the American Dream or the idea that we are responsible for our body weight), but by filling a void or gap in the conversation. Much research writing in the sciences and the humanities does this, with the argument being generated not by something previous researchers have said, but by the fact that no one has even raised the issue that the writer is putting forth. In such cases, the writer is responding not to what others are saying, but to something that has *not* been said or discussed—to scientists, for example, who have overlooked an obscure plant that offers insights into global warming; or to literary critics who have been so busy focusing on the lead character in a play that they have overlooked the way the servants' relationships reflect the lead character's dealings with his family.

Reading Particularly Challenging Texts

Sometimes it is difficult to figure out the views that writers are responding to not because these writers do not identify those views but because their language and the concepts they are dealing with are particularly challenging. Consider, for instance, the first two sentences of *Gender Trouble: Feminism and the Subversion of Identity*, a book by the feminist philosopher and literary theorist Judith Butler, thought by many to be a particularly difficult writer.

> Contemporary feminist debates over the meaning of gender lead time and again to a certain sense of trouble, as if the indeterminacy of gender might eventually culminate in the failure of feminism. Perhaps trouble need not carry such a negative valence.
>
> —JUDITH BUTLER, *Gender Trouble: Feminism and the Subversion of Identity*

There are many reasons readers may stumble over this relatively short passage, not the least of which is that Butler does not explicitly indicate where her own view begins and the view she is responding to ends. Unlike Zinczenko, Butler does not use the first-person "I" or a phrase such as "in my own view" to show that the position in the second sentence is her own. Nor does Butler offer a clear transition such as "but" or "however" at the start of the second sentence to indicate, as Zinczenko does with "though," that a change of direction has taken place, that in the second sentence she is questioning the argument she has summarized in the first. And finally, like many academic writers, Butler uses abstract, unfamiliar words that many readers may need to look up, like "gender" (sexual identity, male or female), "indeterminacy" (the quality of being impossible to define or pin down), "culminate" (finally result in), and "negative valence" (a term borrowed from chemistry, roughly denoting "negative significance" or "meaning"). For all these reasons, we can imagine many readers feeling intimidated before they reach the third sentence of Butler's book.

But readers who break down this passage into its essential parts will find that it is actually a lucid piece of writing that conforms to the classic "they say/I say" pattern. Though it can be difficult to spot the clashing arguments in the two sentences, close analysis reveals that the first sentence offers a way of looking at a certain type of "trouble" in the realm of feminist politics that is being challenged in the second.

To understand difficult passages of this kind, you need to translate what they say into your own words—to build a bridge, in effect, between the passage's unfamiliar terms and ones more familiar to you. Building such a bridge should help you connect what you already know to what the author is saying—and will then help you move from reading to writing, providing you with some of the language you will need to summarize the text. One major challenge in translating the author's words into your own, however, is to stay true to what the author is actually saying, avoiding what we call "the closest cliché syndrome," in which one mistakes a commonplace idea that one is already familiar with for the more complex one the author is really referring to (mistaking Butler's critique of the concept of "woman," for instance, for the common idea that women must have equal rights). The work of complex writers like Butler, who frequently challenge conventional thinking, cannot always be collapsed into the types of ideas most of us are familiar with. Therefore, in translating it is important that you don't try to fit such writers into your pre-existing beliefs, but instead allow your own views to be challenged. In building a bridge to the writers you read, it is often necessary to meet those writers more than halfway.

For more on the closest cliché syndrome, see Chapter 2.

So what, then, does Butler's opening say? With Butler's words translated into terms that are easier to understand, the first sentence says that for many feminists today, "the indeterminacy of gender"—the inability to define the essence of sexual identity—spells the end of feminism; that the inability to define femininity, presumably the building block of the feminist movement, means serious "trouble" for feminist politics. In contrast, the second sentence suggests that this same "trouble" need not be thought of in such "negative" terms, that the inability to define femininity, or "gender trouble" as Butler calls it in her book's title, may not be such a bad thing, and may even be something that feminist activists can profit from. In other words, Butler's second sentence suggests that highlighting uncertainties about notions of masculinity and femininity can be a powerful feminist tool.

Pulling all these inferences together, then, the opening sentences can be read as follows: "While many contemporary feminists believe that uncertainty about what it means to be a woman will undermine feminist politics, I, Judith Butler, believe that this uncertainty can actually help strengthen feminist politics." Translating Butler's point into this book's basic move: "They say that if we cannot define 'woman,' feminism is in big trouble. But I say that this type of trouble is precisely what feminism needs." Despite its difficulty, then, we hope you agree that this initially intimidating passage does make sense if you stay with it.

We hope it is clear that critical reading is a two-way street. It is just as much about being open to the way that writers can challenge you, maybe even transform you, as it is about questioning those writers. And if you translate a writer's argument into your own words as you read, you will allow the text to take you outside the ideas that you already hold and to introduce you to new terms and concepts. Even if you end up disagreeing with a Tamara Draut, a Judith Butler, or a David Zinczenko, you first have to show that you have really listened to what he or she is saying, have fully grasped his or her arguments, and can accurately summarize those arguments in your own words. Without such deep, attentive listening, any critique you make will be superficial and decidedly *uncritical*. It will be a critique that says more about you than about the writer or idea you're responding to. Ultimately, then, critical reading does not just mean criticizing the writers you read or imposing your own beliefs on them or being a skeptic—although doubt and critique are certainly integral to both the reading and the writing processes. Nobody would ever deny that. Critical reading also means *listening*—to writers and ideas—and allowing them to change what you think.

READINGS

THIRTEEN

IS FAST FOOD THE NEW TOBACCO?

—◫—

IT IS HARD TO LIVE in the United States today and not have a taste for some kind of fast foods—and, at the same time, to feel one should not eat such foods. Whether one is looking at a chocolate doughnut or a bag of potato chips, it is almost impossible not to be pulled in two directions at once: to want the doughnut or chips, but to fear how they will affect one's weight, looks, and health. The McDonald's billboard on the facing page—in which a giant hamburger proclaiming "You Know You Want Me" seems to be answering a voice proclaiming the opposite—captures this conflict well. It is as if a battle is being waged among fast-food corporations, the diet and beauty industries, and the medical profession over what we eat, and resist eating.

The readings in this chapter address this battle and offer various perspectives on how we should respond to it. *Men's Health* magazine editor David Zinczenko and law professor John H. Banzhaf III (known as "the Ralph Nader of Junk Food") blame the fast-food industry for the growing rate of obesity in the United States and argue that this industry should therefore be regulated by the government and courts. According to these authors, fast food is the new tobacco and should be regulated as such. In contrast, the libertarian commentator Radley Balko argues that what we eat should remain a matter of personal responsibility—that staying trim should depend not on government intervention but on individual willpower, which people can use to take control over their own lives.

Others focus on the effects of advertising and corporate policies. The investigative journalist Eric Schlosser (author of *Fast Food Nation*) focuses on the role of advertising and in particular on the way fast food is marketed to young children, while the Canadian writer and activist Yves Engler blames the alleged obesity crisis in today's youth not just on fast-food corporations but on corporate capitalism more generally.

The feminist activist Susie Orbach switches the terms of the discussion away from fast food per se to look at the matters of compulsive overeating and being overweight, particularly among women, suggesting that they are ways of rebelling against the expectations of a sexist, patriarchal society.

But not everyone agrees that being overweight is a problem; in the final essay in this chapter, the legal scholar Paul Campos challenges the assumption that overeating is a pressing social problem that needs to be fixed. According to Campos, being fat, as his title suggests, is "OK" and people should just relax, instead of going on yet another diet.

So read on for a wide range of opinions on the matters of fast food and the so-called obesity "crisis." You'll likely find plenty to agree with, and just as much to disagree with. But whatever you think, this is a conversation that matters, and the pieces in this chapter will challenge you to respond—to see what others advocate, to think about what you believe and why—and then to add your own voice to the conversation.

Don't Blame the Eater

DAVID ZINCZENKO

—▱—

IF EVER THERE were a newspaper headline custom-made for Jay Leno's monologue, this was it. Kids taking on McDonald's this week, suing the company for making them fat. Isn't that like middle-aged men suing Porsche for making them get speeding tickets? Whatever happened to personal responsibility?

I tend to sympathize with these portly fast-food patrons, though. Maybe that's because I used to be one of them.

I grew up as a typical mid-1980s latchkey kid. My parents were split up, my dad off trying to rebuild his life, my mom working long hours to make the monthly bills. Lunch and dinner, for me, was a daily choice between McDonald's, Taco Bell, Kentucky Fried Chicken or Pizza Hut. Then as now, these were the only available options for an American kid to get an affordable meal. By age 15, I had packed 212 pounds of torpid teenage tallow on my once lanky 5-foot-10 frame.

DAVID ZINCZENKO is the editor-in-chief of *Men's Health* magazine and the author of numerous best-selling books, including *Eat This, Not That*. He has contributed op-ed essays to the *New York Times*, the *Los Angeles Times*, and *USA Today*, and has appeared on *Oprah*, *Ellen*, *20/20*, and *Good Morning America*. This piece was first published on the op-ed page of the *New York Times* on November 23, 2002.

Then I got lucky. I went to college, joined the Navy Reserves and got involved with a health magazine. I learned how to manage my diet. But most of the teenagers who live, as I once did, on a fast-food diet won't turn their lives around: They've crossed under the golden arches to a likely fate of lifetime obesity. And the problem isn't just theirs—it's all of ours.

For tips on saying why it matters, see Chapter 7.

Before 1994, diabetes in children was generally caused ₅ by a genetic disorder—only about 5 percent of childhood cases were obesity-related, or Type 2, diabetes. Today, according to the National Institutes of Health, Type 2 diabetes accounts for at least 30 percent of all new childhood cases of diabetes in this country.

Not surprisingly, money spent to treat diabetes has skyrocketed, too. The Centers for Disease Control and Prevention estimate that diabetes accounted for $2.6 billion in health care costs in 1969. Today's number is an unbelievable $100 billion a year.

Shouldn't we know better than to eat two meals a day in fast-food restaurants? That's one argument. But where, exactly, are consumers—particularly teenagers—supposed to find alternatives? Drive down any thoroughfare in America, and I guarantee you'll see one of our country's more than 13,000 McDonald's restaurants. Now, drive back up the block and try to find someplace to buy a grapefruit.

Complicating the lack of alternatives is the lack of information about what, exactly, we're consuming. There are no calorie information charts on fast-food packaging, the way there are on grocery items. Advertisements don't carry warning labels the way tobacco ads do. Prepared foods aren't covered under Food and Drug Administration labeling laws. Some fast-food purveyors will provide calorie information on request, but even that can be hard to understand.

For example, one company's Web site lists its chicken salad as containing 150 calories; the almonds and noodles that come with it (an additional 190 calories) are listed separately. Add a serving of the 280-calorie dressing, and you've got a healthy lunch alternative that comes in at 620 calories. But that's not all. Read the small print on the back of the dressing packet and you'll realize it actually contains 2.5 servings. If you pour what you've been served, you're suddenly up around 1,040 calories, which is half of the government's recommended daily calorie intake. And that doesn't take into account that 450-calorie super-size Coke.

Make fun if you will of these kids launching lawsuits against 10 the fast-food industry, but don't be surprised if you're the next plaintiff. As with the tobacco industry, it may be only a matter of time before state governments begin to see a direct line between the $1 billion that McDonald's and Burger King spend each year on advertising and their own swelling health care costs.

And I'd say the industry is vulnerable. Fast-food companies are marketing to children a product with proven health hazards and no warning labels. They would do well to protect themselves, and their customers, by providing the nutrition information people need to make informed choices about their products. Without such warnings, we'll see more sick, obese children and more angry, litigious parents. I say, let the deep-fried chips fall where they may.

Joining the Conversation

1. Summarize Zinczenko's arguments (his "I say") against the practices of fast-food companies. How persuasive are these arguments?

2. One important move in all good argumentative writing is to introduce possible objections to the position being argued—what this book calls naysayers. What objections does Zinczenko introduce, and how does he respond? Can you think of other objections that he might have noted?

3. How does the story that Zinczenko tells in paragraphs 3 and 4 about his own experience support or fail to support his argument? How could the same story be used to support an argument opposed to Zinczenko's?

4. So what? Who cares? How does Zinczenko make clear to readers why his topic matters? Or, if he does not, how might he do so?

5. Write an essay responding to Zinczenko, using your own experience and knowledge as part of your argument. You may agree, disagree, or both, but be sure to represent Zinczenko's views near the beginning of your text, both summarizing and quoting from his arguments.

What You Eat Is Your Business

RADLEY BALKO

—▣—

THIS JUNE, *Time* magazine and ABC News will host a three-day summit on obesity. ABC News anchor Peter Jennings, who last December anchored the prime-time special "How to Get Fat Without Really Trying," will host. Judging by the scheduled program, the summit promises to be a pep rally for media, nutrition activists, and policy makers—all agitating for a panoply of government anti-obesity initiatives, including prohibiting junk food in school vending machines, federal funding for new bike trails and sidewalks, more demanding labels on foodstuffs, restrictive food marketing to children,

RADLEY BALKO *is a senior editor at* Reason, *a monthly magazine that claims to stand for "free minds and free markets" and to provide an "alternative to right-wing and left-wing opinion magazines." Balko specializes in investigative writing on civil liberties and criminal justice issues. He is also a columnist for* FoxNews.com *and has contributed to such publications as the* Washington Post *and* Playboy. *At* The Agitator, *his personal weblog, he describes himself as a "small-l" libertarian. This essay was first published on May 23, 2004, on* Cato.org, *a site sponsored by the Cato Institute, a foundation that aims to promote the principles of "limited government, individual liberty, free markets, and peace."*

and prodding the food industry into more "responsible" behavior. In other words, bringing government between you and your waistline.

Politicians have already climbed aboard. President Bush earmarked $200 million in his budget for anti-obesity measures. State legislatures and school boards across the country have begun banning snacks and soda from school campuses and vending machines. Senator Joe Lieberman and Oakland Mayor Jerry Brown, among others, have called for a "fat tax" on high-calorie foods. Congress is now considering menu-labeling legislation, which would force restaurants to send every menu item to the laboratory for nutritional testing.

This is the wrong way to fight obesity. Instead of manipulating or intervening in the array of food options available to American consumers, our government ought to be working to foster a sense of responsibility in and ownership of our own health and well-being. But we're doing just the opposite.

For decades now, America's health care system has been migrating toward socialism. Your well-being, shape, and condition have increasingly been deemed matters of "public health," instead of matters of personal responsibility. Our lawmakers just enacted a huge entitlement that requires some people to pay for other people's medicine. Senator Hillary Clinton just penned a lengthy article in the *New York Times Magazine* calling for yet more federal control of health care. All of the Democratic candidates for president boasted plans to push health care further into the public sector. More and more, states are preventing private health insurers from charging overweight and obese clients higher premiums, which effectively removes any financial incentive for maintaining a healthy lifestyle.

We're becoming less responsible for our own health, and 5 more responsible for everyone else's. Your heart attack drives up the cost of my premiums and office visits. And if the government is paying for my anti-cholesterol medication, what incentive is there for me to put down the cheeseburger?

This collective ownership of private health then paves the way for even more federal restrictions on consumer choice and civil liberties. A society where everyone is responsible for everyone else's well-being is a society more apt to accept government restrictions, for example—on what McDonald's can put on its menu, what Safeway or Kroger can put on grocery shelves, or holding food companies responsible for the bad habits of unhealthy consumers.

A growing army of nutritionist activists and food industry foes are egging the process on. Margo Wootan of the Center for Science in the Public Interest has said, "We've got to move beyond 'personal responsibility.'" The largest organization of trial lawyers now encourages its members to weed jury pools of candidates who show "personal responsibility bias." The title of Jennings's special from last December—"How to Get Fat Without Really Trying"—reveals his intent, which is to relieve viewers of responsibility for their own condition. Indeed, Jennings ended the program with an impassioned plea for government intervention to fight obesity.

For tips on distinguishing what you say from what others say, as Balko does here, see Chapter 5.

The best way to alleviate the obesity "public health" crisis is to remove obesity from the realm of public health. It doesn't belong there anyway. It's difficult to think of anything more private and of less public concern than what we choose to put into our bodies. It only becomes a public matter when we force the public to pay for the consequences of those choices. If policymakers want to fight obesity, they'll halt the creeping socialization of medicine, and move to return individual Americans' ownership of their own health and well-being back to individual Americans.

That means freeing insurance companies to reward healthy lifestyles, and penalize poor ones. It means halting plans to further socialize medicine and health care. Congress should also increase access to medical and health savings accounts, which give consumers the option of rolling money reserved for health care into a retirement account. These accounts introduce accountability into the health care system, and encourage caution with one's health care dollar. When money we spend on health care doesn't belong to our employer or the government, but is money we could devote to our own retirement, we're less likely to run to the doctor at the first sign of a cold.

We'll all make better choices about diet, exercise, and personal health when someone else isn't paying for the consequences of those choices.

Joining the Conversation

1. What does Radley Balko claim in this essay? How do you know? What position is he responding to? Cite examples from the text to support your answer.
2. Reread the last sentence of paragraph 1: "In other words, bringing government between you and your waistline." This is actually a sentence fragment, but it functions as metacommentary, inserted by Balko to make sure that readers see his point. Imagine that this statement were not there, and reread the first three paragraphs. Does it make a difference in how you read this piece?
3. Notice the direct quotations in paragraph 7. How has Balko integrated these quotations into his text—how has he introduced them, and what, if anything, has he said to explain

them and tie them to his own text? Are there any changes you might suggest? How do key terms in the quotations echo one another? (See Chapter 3 for advice on quoting, and pp. 109–11 for help on identifying key terms.)

4. Balko makes his own position about the so-called obesity crisis very clear, but does he consider any of the objections that might be offered to his position? If so, how does he deal with those objections? If not, what objections might he have raised?

5. Write an essay responding to Balko, agreeing, disagreeing, or both agreeing and disagreeing with his position. You might want to cite some of David Zinczenko's arguments (see pp. 153–55)—depending on what stand you take, Zinczenko's ideas could serve as support for what you believe, or as one possible objection.

Lawsuits Against Fast-Food Restaurants Are an Effective Way to Combat Obesity

JOHN H. BANZHAF III

—⌑—

Prepared Statement of John H. Banzhaf III

IN 2001 the U.S. Surgeon General issued a report showing that the United States was suffering from an epidemic of obesity which annually killed about 300,000 Americans and cost us over $100 billion a year.[1] Since that time Congress has done virtually nothing of consequence to deal with this problem, just as for many years it did nothing of consequence to address the problem of smoking.

However, since I first proposed that legal action could be a powerful weapon against the public health problem of obesity, just as I had suggested—and then helped prove—that it could

JOHN H. BANZHAF III is a practitioner of public interest law and a professor at the law school at George Washington University. Banzhaf has been called the "Ralph Nader of Junk Food" for starting a movement to use legal action as a weapon against obesity, a movement that is modeled on his earlier successes fighting tobacco companies. The piece included here is his testimony on the Personal Responsibility in Food Consumption Act at a hearing held by the Congressional Subcommittee on Commercial and Administrative Law on June 19, 2003.

be a powerful weapon against the problem of smoking, the mere threat of legal action has proven to be very effective. For example, numerous articles and reports have noted that the threats of lawsuits have already prompted many food companies to take steps likely to reduce obesity.[2]

Yet some Members, not content to simply shirk Congress's responsibility to do something meaningful and effective about America's second most important and expensive preventable health problem, now support an industry-sponsored[3] bailout and protection bill to end what seems to be one of the few effective tools against this problem. FOR SHAME! If it ain't broke, don't fix it, especially until Congress is prepared to adopt comprehensive legislation to help save taxpayers more than $50 BILLION annually in obesity costs.[4]

This bill is based upon two faulty assumptions. The FIRST is that the problem is caused by a lack of personal responsibility. But virtually everyone agrees that this epidemic rise in obesity and in obesity-related diseases[5] occurred largely within the past 15–20 years, and there is no evidence that there has been a corresponding drop in personal and/or parental responsibility.[6]

The SECOND faulty assumption is that, contrary to virtually every serious study, the fast-food industry—with its misleading advertising,[7] failure to clearly and conspicuously disclose nutritional information (as all other foods do)[8] and/or to provide any warnings of the type common to many other products which present risks which are less serious but even better known[9]—is such an insignificant cause of obesity in all cases (including those regarding children)[10] that it deserves unprecedented absolute immunity from all liability.[11]

Neither proposition can be seriously advanced, much less proven, and the public seemingly is rejecting them and is prepared to hold the industry liable in lawsuits.[12]

The industry and its spokesmen claim that all such lawsuits are frivolous, but industries do not need protection against lawsuits which are truly frivolous,[13] only those lawsuits which judges, juries, and appellate courts are likely to take seriously. In this regard note that the smoker lawsuits, the nonsmoker lawsuits, and the lawsuits by the states against the tobacco industry, all were initially called frivolous.[14] But they have all proven their worth, and helped to make a significant dent in the public health problem of smoking.[15]

For tips on acknowledging and responding to objections, see Chapter 6.

In this bill Congress assumes that it can predetermine that in no set of facts involving food litigation should any company be held liable, even for its fair share of the resulting costs.[16] This is presumptuous as well as preposterous, since the bill covers many situations in which most would agree that there should be liability. It also departs from the 200-year-old tradition of letting courts first decide new cases as they arise, and then stepping in to "correct" the process only if the results prove to be clearly contrary to the public interest.

This is especially egregious here because the bill unreasonably and unnecessarily interferes with the rights of states to have their courts decide these issues, at least initially, and is so broad that it seems to affect matters having no relationship to "interstate commerce" and therefore may be, as the U.S. Supreme Court has recently reminded us, beyond Congress's ability to legislate.

For all of these and other reasons, it is respectfully suggested that it is premature—if not presumptuous and preposterous—for Congress at this time to conclude that the one weapon against the war on obesity which appears to be having an impact should be eliminated; that it can decide without waiting for state court trial and appellate judges to consider the myriad of factual situations, legal arguments, and still-undiscovered evidence which may be presented in these trials that no such plaintiffs should even have their day in court; and that an industry should be given unprecedented immunity from all liability without any showing of harm or even serious danger.

Instead, Congress should consider comprehensive legislation aimed at America's epidemic of obesity, wait to see what the effect of the legislative remedies and of fat litigation may be, and then and only then even consider some form of limited immunity. . . .

Both the author and those involved in the movement to use legal action as a weapon against obesity have frequently stated that legislation is far preferable to litigation. Legislation can accomplish more, be applied fairly across the board, and affect many practices that litigation cannot reach. Here are only a few proposals which Congress may wish to consider before it abdicates its own responsibility to regulate, and simply grants the industry unnecessary blanket immunity:

A. Require that all fast-food restaurants display information about the calories and fat in their menu items at the point of purchase when patrons are considering their choices while standing on line, not buried on a web site or on a hard-to-find pamphlet or back wall. Several state bills to require this have been introduced, and Congressional action would avoid confusion due to lack of uniformity.

B. Require that all fast-food restaurants provide appropriate warnings about the danger of eating fattening fast food too often. PepsiCo has promised to do this, and McDonald's is already doing it in France.

C. Require that all fast-food restaurants provide more nutritious alternative menu choices for people who find it inconvenient to eat elsewhere and who want to avoid the many fattening foods which all too frequently are their only choices.

D. Require that all food items intended for young children—e.g., Mighty Kids Meals, Lunchables, etc.—provide information about fat and calorie content not only in terms of adult nutritional requirements but also in terms of the vastly lower requirements for young children so that parents can knowledgeably exercise the parental responsibility they are urged to.

Should the fast-food restaurants do these things—either voluntarily or as a result of uniform legislation—it would appear that they would largely insulate themselves from potential liability. This is a far better approach than simply granting them unearned immunity.

NOTES

1. See <http://www.surgeongeneral.gov/news/pressreleases/pr—obesity.htm>.

2. See generally <http://banzhaf.net/obesitylinks>.

3. "The National Restaurant Association is leading the effort to build support for this bill [H.R. 339] on Capitol Hill. See if your lawmaker is a cosponsor of H.R. 339 and take action to encourage them to sign on if they haven't already." See <http://www.restaurant.org/government/issues/lawsuits—food.cfm>.

4. Fast-food companies are responsible for more than 65 percent of the rise in American obesity, and for more than $50 billion of the annual health care costs obesity imposes on taxpayers, according to a new study for the National Bureau of Economic Statistics. As the *New York Times* reported: "In analyzing the relationship of weight to incomes, food prices, restaurants, workforce participation and other variables, the economists concluded that the growth of fast food accounted for 68 percent of the rise in American obesity." "Belt-Loosening in the Work Force," *New York Times* 2 Mar. 2003.

5. Although some have tried to argue that the huge increase in obesity was caused merely by a change in the definition of "obesity," there has also been a corresponding very large increase in obesity-related diseases such as Type 2 Diabetes—a fact-based phenomenon which obviously was not caused by a mere change in definitions.

6. If there were some kind of precipitous decline in personal responsibility (or in parental responsibility) during the past 15–20 years, one would also expect to see it manifested in a huge increase in other risky personal behaviors such as the use of illicit drugs, the failure to use seat belts, boating and rafting accidents, accidental gun shot injuries, drunk driving accidents, etc. But this has not occurred. Thus one is asked to believe that this relatively recent epidemic of obesity was caused by a dramatic decline in personal and/or parental responsibility for which there is no evidence, and which does not appear to manifest itself with regard to other risky personal choice behaviors.

7. See, e.g., Judge Sweet's initial opinion in *Pelman v. McDonald's*: <http://banzhaf.net/docs/sweet>.

8. The fast-food industry lobbied vigorously and successfully to be virtually excluded from the statute which requires all foods sold in stores to provide prospective consumers with nutritional information, including the amount of calories, fat, and saturated fat. Thus, as Judge Sweet himself pointed out, potential consumers may well be deceived into believing that chicken dishes have less fat than beef entrees, and many customers are totally unaware of the large amounts of fat which are increasingly being found in dishes which purport to be "healthful." <http://banzhaf.net/ docs/sweet1>.

As the business-oriented *Wall Street Journal* recently noted in "That Veggie Wrap You Just Chowed Down Is More Fattening Than a Ham Sandwich" 14 Jan. 2003: "Here's a fast-food nutrition quiz. Which has the fewest calories: a McDonald's Quarter Pounder with Cheese, Panera's Smoked Ham and Swiss sandwich, or Baja Fresh's grilled chicken salad? Surprisingly, it's a Quarter Pounder. The answer is likely to shock diners who are flocking to trendy new eateries such as Fresh City, Baja Fresh Mexican Grill and Panera Bread, all of which promise fresh, nonfried and health-sounding fare . . . the truth is that these and other wraps, salads and sandwiches being hyped as a healthy alternative to fast food are loaded with calories and fat. . . . While the restaurant chains don't make any specific claims about the healthfulness or calorie content of their menu items, they nonetheless give consumers the impression that they are offering healthier food. . . . But consumers are being fooled. . . . But making the healthy choice can be tough. Most restaurants don't display nutrition information inside the restaurant, and the menu offerings often are deceptive. . . . Nutritionists argue that calorie information should be available at the ordering counter."

9. Courts have held that stepladder manufacturers can be held liable not only for failing to provide warnings about falling off the top step—a danger even clearer and more clearly common knowledge than the danger of eating too much fattening food—but even for failing to provide adequate warnings. Similarly, failure to warn about the danger of electrocution from reaching into the back of the television set, or using an electric hair dryer around ground pipes, or of infants eating lead-based paint, have all been held to create potential liability. Warnings, after all, are not designed only for the best and brightest, but also for those with less education; less wisdom, judgment or maturity; and those who may be momentarily forgetful.

10. It is impossible to argue that young children should be held fully responsible for their own lack of judgment or immaturity. Even the simplest contracts they enter into are void or voidable, and girls under the age of consent (often 18) cannot validly consent to engage in sexual intercourse because we conclusively presume that they cannot understand the consequences of their acts. Yet it appears that most girls of 17 understand the consequences of having sex far better than they understand the consequences of eating out often at fast-food restaurants.

For those who then argue that food companies should escape all liability because children's obesity is caused solely by a lack of parental responsibility, the simple answer is that the law does not blame children for the lack of care of their parents, so long as the harm was reasonably foreseeable by the defendant. For example, when McDonald's gives out tiny action figures with the children's meals, it is very careful to warn in big letters of the choking danger present if the toys are given to infants—even though that danger is clearly common knowledge. McDonald's knows that, if a child choked on a part from the toy and suffered brain damage, McDonald's would be held liable for its fair share of the medical costs—despite the clear negligence of the parents—provided that it could have foreseen that this would happen.

With regard to meals served to children, and even meals like Happy Meals and Mighty Kids Meals intended solely for children, McDonald's provides no warnings whatsoever.

11. Congress wisely denied just such immunity to the tobacco industry, even after several multi-million dollar verdicts. The only other instances of industry immunity—shielding gun makers from lawsuits for "harm caused by the criminal or unlawful misuse" of a firearm, limiting the liability of airlines if armed pilots accidentally shoot a crew member or passenger, and limiting

the nuclear industry's liability in the event of a catastrophic accident—are all clearly distinguishable.

12. One recent survey shows that almost half of the public already blame fast-food companies for contributing to the current epidemic of obesity, and another says that jurors are almost as likely to vote against defendants in fat suits as against defendants in tobacco suits." See <http://banzhaf.net/ obesitymediareleases#Jurors—Support—Fat—Suits>.

13. Frivolous" has been defined as "Unworthy of serious attention; trivial." But these lawsuits and the threat of future suits are being taken very seriously by many major business and general interest publications (including one new publication, Obesity Policy Report, devoted primarily to this topic) <http://www. obesitypolicy.com>. The lawsuits are also being taken very seriously by industry and stock analysts. See generally <http:// banzhaf.net/obesitylinks>.

The industry itself has paid for full-page ads in national magazines attacking the suits, and has written Op-Ed pieces opposing them. But their very concern and attention to these legal actions clearly belies any suggestion that the industry regards them as merely frivolous.

14. Indeed, one of the panelists today, Victor Schwartz, once appeared on television with the author and confidently predicted that no smoker lawsuit against a cigarette maker would even get to trial, much less produce a verdict for the plaintiff.

Even the lawyers who represented smokers in such suits were reluctant to represent NONsmokers in suits against the tobacco industry, believing that such suits had little if any chance of success. But one husband-and-wife team has already won $300 million in the first round of a class action nonsmoker lawsuit, and individual nonsmoking plaintiffs are beginning to win also.

Finally, even anti-tobacco lawyers were so sure that state lawsuits against the industry could not possibly succeed that most refused to take them on, and the few that did were called "crazy." Today, of course, we call them multi-millionaires, since these lawsuits—likewise termed "frivolous" in their day—have now resulted in a settlement of over $240 BILLION dollars.

As one reporter, after talking to many legal experts on all sides of the issue put it: "All the legal experts I talked to agreed on one thing: After tobacco overturned years of legal precedent, you can't say any lawsuit is impossible." "Can We Sue Our Own Fat Asses Off?" <http://salon. com/tech/feature/2002/ 05/24/fastfoodlaw/index.html>.

15. See, e.g., "Where the Public Good Prevailed," *The American Prospect* (04/01).

Many articles and reports have suggested that more progress has been made regarding the problem of smoking than any other major public health problem: e.g., abuse of alcohol, illicit drug use, teenage pregnancies, etc. Clearly this is due in large part to the effective use of a wide variety of different kinds of legal actions—exactly what is being planned now with regard to obesity.

16. It should be noted that plaintiffs in fat suits—like plaintiffs in tobacco suits—do not necessarily contend that they bear no responsibility, and/or that the defendant is solely responsible and should pay all of the costs. Instead, plaintiffs in the fat suits—like plaintiffs in the tobacco suits—simply argue that the defendants' failure to clearly and conspicuously provide necessary information, or to provide appropriate warnings, etc., was at least in some part a cause of the resulting medical problem, and that the defendant therefore should bear its fair share of the costs.

Joining the Conversation

1. We know from the title what John Banzhaf argues in his testimony—"Lawsuits Against Fast-Food Restaurants Are an Effective Way to Combat Obesity." What support does he offer for this claim, and what specific changes would he like the restaurants to make?

2. Why is he making this argument? What other views motivate him to write about these lawsuits?

3. What other perspectives on the lawsuit issue does Banzhaf consider? For example, he notes that fast-food industry representatives have claimed that such lawsuits are frivolous. How does he deal with this objection? Does he refute it? Agree with it? Agree and disagree?

4. How would Radley Balko respond to Banzhaf? Read Balko's essay on pp. 157–60 of this chapter, and imagine what he

would say if he'd been in the room when Banzhaf read his testimony.

5. Imagine you are a member of the Congressional committee listening to Banzhaf's testimony. How would you respond? Write a paragraph or two of what you would say, framing your comments as a response to something specific that Banzhaf said. (See Chapter 11 for templates for responding in this way.)

Obesity: Much of the Responsibility Lies with Corporations

YVES ENGLER

IN EARLY OCTOBER there was a quirky report about U.S. coffin makers increasing the size of their product. What this reveals is anything but funny. Obesity is one of today's biggest health crises—1 in 4 of the world's 4 billion adults are overweight and 300 million are clinically obese. In the United States, where the crisis is most pronounced, nearly a third of the population is obese and two-thirds overweight, with the rates substantially higher among the poor. Since 1990 the U.S. obesity rate has doubled and approximately 127 million adults are now overweight and 60 million are obese. During the same period the number of people who are severely obese has nearly quadrupled to nine million. Child obesity is also increasing rapidly.

Outside the United States, especially in the more advanced capitalist nations, obesity is also skyrocketing. In Canada

YVES ENGLER is a Canadian writer and political activist whose books explore issues of student activism and Canadian foreign policy. He has also published articles in the *Toronto Star*, the *Ottawa Citizen*, and *Ecologist*. This essay first appeared in 2003 in *Z Magazine*, "a radical print and online periodical dedicated to resisting injustice, eliminating repression, and creating liberty."

between 1985 and 2001, the prevalence of obesity more than doubled from 7 percent to 14 percent among women and to 16 percent from 6 percent among men. Like the United States, the rates are substantially higher among the poor. According to a study published in the August edition of the *International Journal of Obesity*, 6.4 percent of children in the wealthiest quarter of the population compared with 12.8 percent of those in the poorest quarter are obese.

The health effects of the obesity epidemic are immense. Researchers claim there are links between obesity and more than 30 medical conditions, including heart disease, diabetes, hypertension, cancers, and possibly Alzheimer's. According to the Centers for Disease and Control Prevention, 1 in 3 U.S. children—nearly 50 percent of black and Latino children—born in 2000 will become diabetic unless people start exercising more and eating less. Some 90,000 U.S. cancer deaths a year are linked to obesity. Worldwide, diet-related afflictions such as heart disease, hypertension, and diabetes account for almost 60 percent of deaths annually.

Even in crude economic terms obesity is costly. The U.S. National Institute of Health estimates that the annual costs of treating obesity-related conditions are at least $120 billion.

Invariably though, within a capitalist system some see profit 5 opportunities in the current obesity epidemic. Companies have long used body image as a mechanism to control women. The diet industry is the main beneficiary of rising obesity—or as the *Economist* recently put it, "the business opportunities in obesity." In North America the diet market runs at $30 billion a year, which is expected to increase by nearly 25 percent in the next 3 years to $37 billion in 2006.

For tips on quoting relevant passages, see p. 40.

Some doctors with a stake in the game push deadly weight-loss drugs such as Ephedra. Those who put their faith in the pharmaceutical industry expect a miracle weight-loss drug to save them. In the meantime, severely obese people can get gastric bypass surgery to reduce their stomach size. This $25,000 (up to $100,000 with overall costs) weight-loss procedure is becoming more popular. More than 100,000 U.S. residents will have the surgery this year, even though 10 to 20 percent of those operated on suffer serious complications, including death. If this doesn't work, a medical company has a plan B. If their company-funded studies are to be believed, a highly successful gastric stimulator has been created that sends the stomach electrical impulses to combat hunger.

According to a survey by the Calorie Control Council, 48 million—or 25 percent—of the U.S. adult population are currently on a diet, and if other studies are correct, over 60 percent of U.S. men and 70 percent of women are trying to shed a few extra pounds. A recently published study found that 9- to 14-year-olds who diet may actually gain weight in the long run—possibly due to metabolic changes, but more likely because they resort to binge eating.

Throughout the advanced capitalist world, and to a lesser extent in the periphery, people's diets have changed drastically over the past 30 years. In the United States, spending on fast food now totals $110 billion annually, having increased 18-fold since 1970. The number of fast-food outlets, often started with government subsidies, has doubled from 1 per 2,000 residents to 1 in 1,000 since 1980. Poor areas often have an even higher exposure to fast-food restaurants and fewer supermarkets, four times less in black neighborhoods than white neighborhoods, where healthier products can be found (even though there is evidence that supermarkets in poorer neighborhoods are more profitable per square foot). Outside the United States, fast-food restaurants are also rapidly expanding. For instance, in 1995

Dunkin Donuts opened 1,000 international stores, which by 2000 had increased to 5,000.

It's not only at fast-food restaurants where unhealthy products are being consumed in greater quantities. U.S. residents on average consume an astounding 848—2.3 per day—8-ounce servings of soft drinks annually. In poorer countries people are also increasingly consuming high-calorie soda pop instead of more nutritious drinks. The Mexican soft drink market, 70 percent controlled by Coca-Cola, totals some 633 eight-ounce servings per person annually.

Portion sizes have also expanded. Compared with 20 years 10 ago U.S. hamburger servings have increased by 112 percent, bagels 195 percent, steaks 224 percent, muffins 333 percent, pasta 480 percent, and chocolate chip cookies 700 percent. It has been shown that people consume about 30 percent more when served larger portions. Fast-food outlets and the rest of the food industry often promote their products based on their larger, somehow more empowering, size. As of 1996, a quarter of the $97 billion spent on fast food came from items promoted on the basis of either extra size or larger portions.

The main reason that people are consuming more, especially unhealthy products, is the food industry's relentless advertising, especially to children. U.S. food companies spend more than $30 billion to sell their products, not counting what they spend lobbying favorable policies and support. In 2001, Coca-Cola and Pepsi together spent $3 billion in advertising.

When targeting young kids, companies use cartoon characters, toys, and other items that have a powerful influence over children. In the early 1970s the U.S. food industry fought off regulation of their advertising practices and instead adopted industry-regulated standards—the Children's Advertising Review Unit. Now 40 percent of McDonald's advertising targets children and, according to a 1998 study, they've been highly successful. Of 10,000 children surveyed, 100 percent of U.S., 98 percent of Japanese, and 93 percent of UK children recognized Ronald McDonald, with many of these kids believing Ronald McDonald knows what's best for their health.

The fast-food and soft drink companies have also been successful at getting their products into cash-strapped schools. They get ad spots on Channel One, which is shown in classes. In Texas, the food giants give $54 million a year to schools to sell their wares in vending machines. Maybe the most disturbing example of school infiltration was in 1998 when Colorado Springs school officials agreed to an exclusive agreement with Coke, based on a tripling of school soft drink sales. Recently Coca-Cola Enterprises became an official sponsor of the PTA and John H. Downs Jr., the company's senior vice president for public affairs and chief lobbyist, got a seat on the PTA's board.

The food interests are also hard at work lobbying governments, both behind the scenes and with front groups such as the Center for Consumer Freedom. Three years ago sugar producers and the soft drink industry won a big victory in getting the USDA to soften its dietary guidelines on sugar. Likewise, they convinced a subservient American Dietetic Association to refrain from labeling any foods as unhealthy since according to them, "all foods can fit into a healthy eating style."

Last September, within a week of the European Commission strengthening regulations on companies promoting the health benefits of foods high in fat and sugars, the Food and Drug Administration weakened its guidelines to allow food packages to advertise possible benefits before they are fully approved. Currently, different sectors of the food industry are hard at work shaping changes to the New Food Pyramid. [15]

Internationally a similar process is at work. This past April the World Health Organization (WHO) and the UN food and agricultural organization backed down (due to pressure from the sugar industry) on guidelines, stating that people should limit daily consumption of free sugars to a maximum of 10 percent of energy intakes to avoid chronic diseases. U.S. sugar producers had indicated that they may lobby the Bush administration and Congress to link U.S. funding—about one-fifth of the WHO budget—to changes in research methods at the UN agency.

The food giants are well represented in other ways. In 1978 Coca-Cola, Pepsi-Cola, Kraft, and other food companies founded the International Life Sciences Institute (ILSI) to lobby WHO. It won a position as an NGO "in official relations" with WHO and a specialized consultative status with the Food and Agricultural Organization in 1991. In 1992 the ILSI congratulated themselves after steering the WHO and FAO away from any curbs on sugar consumption.

The 10 percent or 200-calorie increase in energy consumption by the average U.S. resident over the past 25 years is tied to incessant food advertising, political lobbying, and larger portions. Underlying this rise, however, is an agricultural sector that has increased output by some 500 calories per person during this period—after the Nixon administration altered government subsidies, effectively increasing farmers' incentives to expand their yields.

Obesity is related to a variety of other social factors, some of which have received minimal scrutiny. A yet-to-be-properly-studied link is between obesity and nuclear materials, which emit radioactive iodine, tied to thyroid damage. Thyroid disorders, recently found to occur twice as often as previously believed, are linked to weight gain.

Another contributing factor is the large number of teenagers [20] and children not involved in physical activity. Cutbacks to physical education budgets have not helped. The often-elitist nature of school and community sports dissuades many kids from participating. For this reason and others ranging from pre-scribed gender roles to society's indifference to their specific sporting inclinations (such as skateboarding), many teenagers, especially girls, have negative attitudes towards exercise.

Workplaces and their power struggles also affect obesity. The automation of work reduces the amount of energy workers expend. In and of itself this needn't be problematic since automation should also reduce the number of hours worked and increase time for active leisure; not in the United States, where people are working 200 hours a year more than they did in the early 1970s.

According to Linda Rosenstock, the former Director of the National Institute for Occupational Safety and Health, "It turns out that a quarter to a third of workers have high job stress and are drained and used up at the end of the day." Thus, many working people have less time to take part in activities. In addi-tion, after a long day's work, people often turn to TV watch-ing, which is inversely linked to time spent exercising. Busy parents, especially poor working class people, use TV as a babysitter. In this setting children who are naturally active are hindered from activity.

Often the same automation technology, which is supposed to reduce the workload, results in an increased workload (stress level) for those who retain their jobs. A growing body of evi-dence shows that workers who don't feel in control of their work environment have higher job-stress levels. Scientists believe there is a link between stress and the impulse to eat. Food with lots of sugar, fat, and calories appear literally to calm down the body's response to chronic stress. In addition, research indicates that stress hormones encourage the formation of fat cells, particularly the kind that are the most dangerous to health.

Oddly enough, a historical determinant in work-related stress—repetitive assembly line work—has also contributed to obesity in another way. Urban planning, which is intimately linked to the expansion of capital, plays a central role in obesity. How the suburban landscape became the norm is told, in part, by Colleen Fuller in *Caring for Profit*: "Beginning in the 1920s, General Motors president Alfred Sloan and top company executives masterminded a scheme to create a consumer market for automobiles in the United States. At the time, 9 out of 10 people relied on the trolley networks that crisscrossed cities across the country. GM first purchased and then dismantled the nation's trolley companies, ripping up tracks and setting bonfires composed of railcars. In 30 short years GM succeeded in destroying a mass-transit infrastructure that would cost many billions of dollars to resurrect—more money than municipal governments could raise."

It's not just the auto industry (broadly defined) that has reorganized cities in a way that encourages obesity. Land developers are notorious for buying up cheap agricultural land on the outskirts of cities and pushing for land rezoning and the extension of public amenities to these plots. There is substantially more money to be made from selling houses or commercial space than there is in harvesting vegetables. Similarly, today in many towns Wal-Mart has played no small role in undermining the downtown core, one of the only places where people regularly walked.

The suburban landscape is almost entirely subservient to the car. Sidewalks are nonexistent or disconnected, crosswalks are absent or poorly marked, and the speed and volume of vehicular traffic is overwhelming, which makes walking or biking either impractical or dangerous. So people who might otherwise walk are forced to drive even short distances and kids who could easily walk to school must be chauffeured.

A study released in September showed that in the 25 most sprawling U.S. counties people were on average 6 pounds heavier than in the 25 most compact counties. In the past 20 years the number of trips taken on foot in the United States has dropped by 42 percent. Now, fewer than 10 percent of children walk or bike to school regularly, down from 66 percent 30 years ago.

To combat the obesity epidemic we need tighter limits on fast-food marketing. Junk food companies should be kicked out of schools. Perhaps governments should subsidize fruits and vegetables as well as other healthy products. Increased funding for physical education classes, park spaces, and children's sports would help. Increasing exercise opportunities at work, which a group of large employers, ironically headed by Ford Motors and Pepsi Company, is already working on, could help. Also there could be some form of tax break for exercise as is the case in Finland where some 70 percent of the population exercises for 30 minutes 5 times a week.

Most important, we need a movement that effectively challenges the capitalist entities that push their interests no matter the weight or health effects.

Joining the Conversation

1. Yves Engler blames the capitalist economic system for play-ing a major role in the rise of obesity. How does he suggest that capitalism influences eating habits? How persuasive is his argument?

2. In addition to advertising, how else have large corpora-tions contributed to obesity, according to Engler? What objections might members of those corporations raise to his argument?

3. Paragraph 5 includes a quotation from the *Economist*. Why do you think Engler quotes these words directly rather than simply paraphrasing?

4. Paul Campos, in his essay on pp. 206–09, argues that being overweight is not the serious health risk that Engler and oth-ers claim it to be. Read the Campos piece, and then reread Engler's essay. How do you think Campos might respond to Engler's claims about the ill effects of obesity? Which argu-ment do you find more persuasive, and why?

5. Campos and Engler seem to agree on some things and dis-agree on others. Put yourself in Campos's shoes and write an essay responding to Engler, perhaps using one of the tem-plates for agreeing and disagreeing simultaneously on pp. 59–62 as a starting point.

Your Trusted Friends

ERIC SCHLOSSER

—⊡—

BEFORE ENTERING the Ray A. Kroc Museum, you have to walk through McStore. Both sit on the ground floor of McDonald's corporate headquarters, located at One McDonald's Plaza in Oak Brook, Illinois. The headquarters building has oval windows and a gray concrete façade—a look that must have seemed space-age when the building opened three decades ago. Now it seems stolid and drab, an architectural relic of the Nixon era. It resembles the American embassy compounds that always used to attract antiwar protesters, student demonstrators, flag burners. The eighty-acre campus of Hamburger University, McDonald's managerial training center, is a short drive from headquarters. Shuttle buses constantly go back and forth between the campus and McDonald's Plaza, ferrying clean-cut young men and women in khakis who've come to study for their "Degree in Hamburgerology." The course lasts two weeks

ERIC SCHLOSSER is an investigative journalist who is best known for his 2001 book *Fast Food Nation*, an exposé of the practices of the fast-food industry, from which the piece included here is taken. He has also published a children's book, *Chew on This: Everything You Don't Want to Know About Fast Food* (2006), and he contributes regularly to *Rolling Stone*, *Vanity Fair*, *The Nation*, and other magazines.

and trains a few thousand managers, executives, and franchisees each year. Students from out of town stay at the Hyatt on the McDonald's campus. Most of the classes are devoted to personnel issues, teaching lessons in teamwork and employee motivation, promoting "a common McDonald's language" and "a common McDonald's culture." Three flagpoles stand in front of McDonald's Plaza, the heart of the hamburger empire. One flies the Stars and Stripes, another flies the Illinois state flag, and the third flies a bright red flag with golden arches. . . .

Many of the exhibits at the Ray A. Kroc Museum incorporate neat technological tricks. Dioramas appear and then disappear when certain buttons are pushed. The voices of Kroc's friends and coworkers—one of them identified as a McDonald's "vice president of individuality"—boom from speakers at the appropriate cue. Darkened glass cases are suddenly illuminated from within, revealing their contents. . . . The museum does not have a life-size, Audio-Animatronic version of McDonald's founder telling jokes and anecdotes. But one wouldn't be out of place. An interactive exhibit called "Talk to Ray" shows video clips of Kroc appearing on the *Phil Donohue Show*, being interviewed by Tom Snyder, and chatting with Reverend Robert Schiller at the altar of Orange County's Crystal Cathedral. "Talk to Ray" permits the viewer to ask Kroc as many as thirty-six predetermined questions about various subjects; old videos of Kroc supply the answers. The exhibit wasn't working properly the day of my visit. Ray wouldn't take my questions, and so I just listened to him repeating the same speeches.

The Disneyesque tone of the museum reflects, among other things, many of the similarities between the McDonald's Corporation and the Walt Disney Company. It also reflects the similar paths of the two men who founded these corporate giants. Ray Kroc and Walt Disney were both from Illinois; they were born a year apart. Disney in 1901, Kroc in 1902; they knew each other as young men, serving together in the same World War I ambulance corps; and they both fled the Midwest and settled in southern California, where they played central roles in the creation of new American industries. The film critic Richard Schickel has described Disney's powerful inner need "to order, control, and keep clean any environment he inhabited."[1] The same could easily be said about Ray Kroc, whose obsession with cleanliness and control became one of the hallmarks of his restaurant chain. Kroc cleaned the holes in his mop wringer with a toothbrush.

Kroc and Disney both dropped out of high school and later added the trappings of formal education to their companies. The training school for Disney's theme-park employees was named Disneyland University. More importantly, the two men shared the same vision of America, the same optimistic faith in technology, the same conservative political views. They were charismatic figures who provided an overall corporate vision and grasped the public mood, relying on others to handle the creative and financial details. Walt Disney neither wrote, nor drew the animated classics that bore his name. Ray Kroc's attempts to add new dishes to McDonald's menu—such as Kolacky, a Bohemian pastry, and the Hulaburger, a sandwich featuring grilled pineapple and cheese—were unsuccessful. Both men, however, knew how to find and motivate the right talent. While Disney was much more famous and achieved success sooner, Kroc may have been more influential. His company inspired more imitators, wielded more power over the American economy—and spawned a mascot even more famous than Mickey Mouse.[2]

Despite all their success as businessmen and entrepreneurs, 5 as cultural figures and advocates for a particular brand of Americanism, perhaps the most significant achievement of these two men lay elsewhere. Walt Disney and Ray Kroc were masterful salesmen. They perfected the art of selling things to children. And their success led many others to aim marketing efforts at kids, turning America's youngest consumers into a demographic group that is now avidly studied, analyzed, and targeted by the world's largest corporations. . . .

Better Living

Among other cultural innovations, Walt Disney pioneered the marketing strategy now known as "synergy." During the 1930s, he signed licensing agreements with dozens of firms, granting them the right to use Mickey Mouse on their products and in their ads. In 1938 *Snow White* proved a turning point in film marketing: Disney had signed seventy licensing deals prior to the film's release.[3] Snow White toys, books, clothes, snacks, and records were already for sale when the film opened. Disney later used television to achieve a degree of synergy beyond anything that anyone had previously dared. His first television broadcast, *One Hour in Wonderland* (1950), culminated in a promotion for the upcoming Disney film *Alice in Wonderland*. His first television series, *Disneyland* (1954), provided weekly updates on the construction work at his theme park. ABC, which broadcast the show, owned a large financial stake in the Anaheim venture. Disneyland's other major investor, Western Printing and Lithography, printed Disney books such as *The Walt Disney Story of Our Friend the Atom*. In the guise of televised entertainment, episodes of *Disneyland* were often thinly disguised infomercials, promoting films, books, toys, an amusement park—and, most of all, Disney himself, the living, breathing incarnation of a brand, the man who neatly tied all the other commodities together into one cheerful, friendly, patriotic idea.

Ray Kroc could only dream, during McDonald's tough early years, of having such marketing tools at his disposal. He was forced to rely instead on his wits, his charisma, and his instinct for promotion. Kroc believed completely in whatever he sold and pitched McDonald's franchises with an almost religious fervor. He also knew a few things about publicity, having auditioned talent for a Chicago radio station in the 1920s and performed in nightclubs for years. Kroc hired a publicity firm led by a gag writer and a former MGM road manager to get McDonald's into the news. Children would be the new restaurant chain's target customers. The McDonald brothers had aimed for a family crowd, and now Kroc improved and refined their marketing strategy. He'd picked the right moment. America was in the middle of a baby boom; the number of children had soared in the decade after World War II. Kroc wanted to create a safe, clean, all-American place for kids. The McDonald's franchise agreement required every new restaurant to fly the Stars and Stripes. Kroc understood that how he sold food was just as important as how the food tasted. He liked to tell people that he was really in show business, not the restaurant business. Promoting McDonald's to children was a clever, pragmatic decision. "A child who loves our TV commercials," Kroc explained, "and brings her grandparents to a McDonald's gives us two more customers."[4]

The McDonald's Corporation's first mascot was Speedee, a winking little chef with a hamburger for a head. The character was later renamed Archie McDonald. Speedy was the name of Alka-Seltzer's mascot, and it seemed unwise to imply any connection between the two brands. In 1960, Oscar Goldstein, a McDonald's franchisee in Washington, D.C., decided to sponsor *Bozo's Circus,* a local children's television show. Bozo's appearance at a McDonald's restaurant drew large crowds. When the local NBC station canceled *Bozo's Circus* in 1963, Goldstein hired its star—Willard Scott, later the weatherman on NBC's *Today* show—to invent a new clown who could make restaurant appearances. An ad agency designed the outfit, Scott came up with the name Ronald McDonald, and a star was born.[5] Two years later the McDonald's Corporation introduced Ronald McDonald to the rest of the United States through a major ad campaign. But Willard Scott no longer played the part. He was deemed too overweight; McDonald's wanted someone thinner to sell its hamburgers, shakes, and fries.

The late-1960s expansion of the McDonald's restaurant chain coincided with declining fortunes at the Walt Disney Company. Disney was no longer alive, and his vision of America embodied just about everything that kids of the sixties were rebelling against. Although McDonald's was hardly a promoter of whole foods and psychedelia, it had the great advantage of seeming new—and there was something trippy about Ronald McDonald, his clothes, and his friends. As McDonald's mascot began to rival Mickey Mouse in name recognition, Kroc made plans to create his own Disneyland. He was a highly competitive man who liked, whenever possible, to settle the score. "If they were drowning to death," Kroc once said about his business rivals, "I would put a hose in their mouth."[6] He planned to buy 1,500 acres of land northeast of Los Angeles and build a new amusement park there. The park, tentatively called Western World, would have a cowboy theme.[7] Other McDonald's executives opposed the idea, worried that Western World would divert funds from the restaurant business and lose millions. Kroc offered to option the land with his own money, but finally listened to his close advisers and scrapped the plan. The McDonald's Corporation later considered buying Astro World in Houston. Instead of investing in a large theme park, the company pursued a more decentralized approach. It built small Playlands and McDonaldlands all over the United States.

The fantasy world of McDonaldland borrowed a good deal 10 from Walt Disney's Magic Kingdom. Don Ament, who gave McDonaldland its distinctive look, was a former Disney set designer. Richard and Robert Sherman—who had written and composed, among other things, all the songs in Disney's *Mary Poppins*, Disneyland's "It's a Great, Big, Beautiful Tomorrow" and "It's a Small World, After All"—were enlisted for the first McDonaldland commercials. Ronald McDonald, Mayor McCheese, and the other characters in the ads made McDonald's seem like more than just another place to eat. McDonaldland—with its hamburger patch, apple pie trees, and Filet-O-Fish fountain—had one crucial thing in common with Disneyland. Almost everything in it was for sale. McDonald's soon loomed large in the imagination of toddlers, the intended audience for the ads. The restaurant chain evoked a series of pleasing images in a youngster's mind: bright colors, a playground, a toy, a clown, a drink with a straw, little pieces of food wrapped up like a present. Kroc had succeeded, like his old Red Cross comrade, at selling something intangible to children, along with their fries.

Kid Kustomers

Twenty-five years ago, only a handful of American companies directed their marketing at children—Disney, McDonald's, candy makers, toy makers, manufacturers of breakfast cereal. Today children are being targeted by phone companies, oil companies, and automobile companies, as well as clothing stores and restaurant chains. The explosion in children's advertising occurred during the 1980s. Many working parents, feeling guilty about spending less time with their kids, started spending more money on them. One marketing expert has called the 1980s "the decade of the child consumer."[8] After largely ignoring children for years, Madison Avenue began to scrutinize and pursue them. Major ad agencies now have children's divisions, and a variety of marketing firms focus solely on kids. These groups tend to have sweet-sounding names: Small Talk, Kid Connection, Kid2Kid, the Gepetto Group, Just Kids, Inc. At least three industry publications—*Youth Market*

"How many thousands do you figure *you've* eaten?"

Alert, Selling to Kids, and *Marketing to Kids Report*—cover the latest ad campaigns and market research. The growth in children's advertising has been driven by efforts to increase not just current, but also future, consumption. Hoping that nostalgic childhood memories of a brand will lead to a lifetime of purchases, companies now plan "cradle-to-grave" advertising strategies. They have come to believe what Ray Kroc and Walt Disney realized long ago—a person's "brand loyalty" may begin as early as the age of two.[9] Indeed, market research has found that children often recognize a brand logo before they can recognize their own name.[10] . . .

Before trying to affect children's behavior, advertisers have to learn about their tastes.[11] Today's market researchers not only conduct surveys of children in shopping malls, they also organize focus groups for kids as young as two or three. They analyze children's artwork, hire children to run focus groups, stage slumber parties and then question children into the night. They send cultural anthropologists into homes, stores, fast-food restaurants, and other places where kids like to gather, quietly and surreptitiously observing the behavior of prospective customers. They study the academic literature on child development, seeking insights from the work of theorists such as Erik Erikson and Jean Piaget. They study the fantasy lives of young children, then apply the findings in advertisements and product designs.

Dan S. Acuff—the president of Youth Market System Consulting and the author of *What Kids Buy and Why* (1997)—stresses the importance of dream research. Studies suggest that until the age of six, roughly 80 percent of children's dreams are about animals.[12] Rounded, soft creatures like Barney, Disney's animated characters, and the Teletubbies therefore have an obvious appeal to young children. The Character Lab, a division of Youth Market System Consulting, uses a proprietary technique called Character Appeal Quadrant Analysis to help companies develop new mascots. The technique purports to create imaginary characters who perfectly fit the targeted age group's level of cognitive and neurological development.

Children's clubs have for years been considered an effective means of targeting ads and collecting demographic information; the clubs appeal to a child's fundamental need for status and belonging. Disney's Mickey Mouse Club, formed in 1930, was one of the trailblazers. During the 1980s and 1990s, children's clubs proliferated, as corporations used them to solicit the names, addresses, zip codes, and personal comments of young customers. "Marketing messages sent through a club not only can be personalized," James McNeal advises, "they can be tailored for a certain age or geographical group."[13] A well-designed and well-run children's club can be extremely good for business. According to one Burger King executive, the creation of a Burger King Kids Club in 1991 increased the sales of children's meals as much as 300 percent.[14]

The Internet has become another powerful tool for assembling data about children. In 1998 a federal investigation of Web sites aimed at children found that 89 percent requested personal information from kids; only 1 percent required that children obtain parental approval before supplying the information.[15] A character on the McDonald's Web site told children that Ronald McDonald was "the ultimate authority in everything."[16] The site encouraged kids to send Ronald an e-mail revealing their favorite menu item at McDonald's, their favorite book, their favorite sports team—and their name.[17] Fast-food Web sites no longer ask children to provide personal information without first gaining parental approval; to do so is now a violation of federal law, thanks to the Children's Online Privacy Protection Act, which took effect in April of 2000.

Despite the growing importance of the Internet, television remains the primary medium for children's advertising. The effects of these TV ads have long been a subject of controversy. In 1978, the Federal Trade Commission (FTC) tried to ban all television ads directed at children seven years old or younger. Many studies had found that young children often could not tell the difference between television programming and television advertising. They also could not comprehend the real purpose of commercials and trusted that advertising claims were true. Michael Pertschuk, the head of the FTC, argued that children need to be shielded from advertising that preys upon their immaturity. "They cannot protect themselves," he said, "against adults who exploit their present-mindedness."[18]

The FTC's proposed ban was supported by the American Academy of Pediatrics, the National Congress of Parents and Teachers, the Consumers Union, and the Child Welfare League, among others. But it was attacked by the National Association of Broadcasters, the Toy Manufacturers of America, and the Association of National Advertisers. The industry groups lobbied Congress to prevent any restrictions on children's ads and sued in federal court to block Pertschuk from participating in future FTC meetings on the subject. In April of 1981, three months after the inauguration of President Ronald Reagan, an FTC staff report argued that a ban on ads aimed at children would be impractical, effectively killing the proposal. "We are delighted by the FTC's reasonable recommendation," said the head of the National Association of Broadcasters.[19]

The Saturday-morning children's ads that caused angry debates twenty years ago now seem almost quaint. Far from being banned, TV advertising aimed at kids is now broadcast twenty-four hours a day, closed-captioned and in stereo. Nickelodeon, the Disney Channel, the Cartoon Network, and the other children's cable networks are now responsible for about 80 percent of all television viewing by kids.[20] None of these networks existed before 1979. The typical American child now spends about twenty-one hours a week watching television— roughly one and a half months of TV every year.[21] That does not include the time children spend in front of a screen watching videos, playing video games, or using the computer. Outside of school, the typical American child spends more time watching television than doing any other activity except sleeping.[22] During the course of a year, he or she watches more than thirty thousand TV commercials.[23] Even the nation's youngest children are watching a great deal of television. About one-quarter of American children between the ages of two and five have a TV in their room.[24]

Perfect Synergy

Although the fast-food chains annually spend about $3 billion on television advertising, their marketing efforts directed at children extend far beyond such conventional ads.[25] The McDonald's Corporation now operates more than eight thousand playgrounds at its restaurants in the United States. Burger King has more than two thousand.[26] A manufacturer of "playlands" explains why fast-food operators build these largely plastic structures: "Playlands bring in children, who bring in parents, who bring in money."[27] As American cities and towns spend less money on children's recreation, fast-food restaurants have become gathering spaces for families with young children. Every month about 90 percent of American children between the ages of three and nine visit a McDonald's.[28] The seesaws, slides, and pits full of plastic

When to quote, when to summarize? See Chapters 2 and 3.

balls have proven to be an effective lure. "But when it gets down to brass tacks," a *Brandweek* article on fast-food notes, "the key to attracting kids is toys, toys, toys."[29]

The fast-food industry has forged promotional links with the nation's leading toy manufacturers, giving away simple toys with children's meals and selling more elaborate ones at a discount. The major toy crazes of recent years—including Pokémon cards, Cabbage Patch Kids, and Tamogotchis—have been abetted by fast-food promotions. A successful promotion easily doubles or triples the weekly sales volume of children's meals. The chains often distribute numerous versions of a toy, encouraging repeat visits by small children and adult collectors who hope to obtain complete sets. In 1999 McDonald's distributed eighty different types of Furby. According to a publication called *Tomart's Price Guide to McDonald's Happy Meal Collectibles*, some fast-food giveaways are now worth hundreds of dollars.[30]

Rod Taylor, a *Brandweek* columnist, called McDonald's 1997 Teenie Beanie Baby giveaway one of the most successful promotions in the history of American advertising.[31] At the time McDonald's sold about 10 million Happy Meals in a typical week. Over the course of ten days in April of 1997, by including a Teenie Beanie Baby with each purchase, McDonald's sold about 100 million Happy Meals. Rarely has a marketing effort achieved such an extraordinary rate of sales among its intended consumers. Happy Meals are marketed to children between the ages of three and nine: within ten days about four Teenie Beanie Baby Happy Meals were sold for every American child in that age group. Not all of those Happy Meals were purchased for children. Many adult collectors bought Teenie Beanie Baby Happy Meals, kept the dolls, and threw away the food.

The competition for young customers has led the fast-food chains to form marketing alliances not just with toy companies, but with sports leagues and Hollywood studios. McDonald's has staged promotions with the National Basketball Association and the Olympics. Pizza Hut, Taco Bell, and KFC signed a three-year deal with the NCAA. Wendy's has linked with the National Hockey League. Burger King and Nickelodeon, Denny's and Major League Baseball, McDonald's and the Fox Kids Network have all formed partnerships that mix advertisements for fast food with children's entertainment. Burger King has sold chicken nuggets shaped like Teletubbies. McDonald's now has its own line of children's videos starring Ronald McDonald. *The Wacky Adventures of Ronald McDonald* is being produced by Klasky-Csupo, the company that makes *Rugrats* and *The Simpsons*. The videos feature the McDonaldland characters and sell for $3.49. "We see this as a great opportunity," a McDonald's executive said in a press release, "to create a more meaningful relationship between Ronald and kids."[32]

All of these cross-promotions have strengthened the ties between Hollywood and the fast-food industry. In the past few years, the major studios have started to recruit fast-food executives. Susan Frank, a former director of national marketing for McDonald's, later became a marketing executive at the Fox Kids Network. She now runs a new family-oriented cable network jointly owned by Hallmark Entertainment and the Jim Henson Company, creator of the Muppets. Ken Snelgrove, who for many years worked as a marketer for Burger King and McDonald's, now works at MGM. Brad Ball, a former senior vice president of marketing at McDonald's, is now the head of marketing for Warner Brothers. Not long after being hired, Ball told the *Hollywood Reporter* that there was little difference between selling films and selling hamburgers.[33] John Cywinski, the former head of marketing at Burger King, became the head of marketing for Walt Disney's film division in 1996, then left the job to work for McDonald's. Forty years after Bozo's first promotional appearance at a McDonald's, amid all the marketing deals, giveaways, and executive swaps, America's fast-food culture has become indistinguishable from the popular culture of its children.

In May of 1996, the Walt Disney Company signed a ten-year global marketing agreement with the McDonald's Corporation. By linking with a fast-food company, a Hollywood studio typically gains anywhere from $25 million to $45 million in additional advertising for a film, often doubling its ad budget. These licensing deals are usually negotiated on a per-film basis; the 1996 agreement with Disney gave McDonald's exclusive rights to that studio's output of films and videos. Some industry observers thought Disney benefited more from the deal, gaining a steady source of marketing funds.[34] According to the terms of the agreement, Disney characters could never be depicted sitting in a McDonald's restaurant or eating any of the chain's food. In the early 1980s, the McDonald's Corporation had turned away offers to buy Disney; a decade later, McDonald's executives sounded a bit defensive about having given Disney greater control over how their joint promotions would be run.[35] "A lot of people can't get used to the fact that two big global brands with this kind of credibility can forge this kind of working relationship," a McDonald's executive told a reporter. "It's about their theme parks, their next movie, their characters, their videos. . . . It's bigger than a hamburger. It's about the integration of our two brands, long-term."[36]

The life's work of Walt Disney and Ray Kroc had come full- 25
circle, uniting in perfect synergy. McDonald's began to sell its
hamburgers and french fries at Disney's theme parks. The ethos
of McDonaldland and of Disneyland, never far apart, have
finally become one. Now you can buy a Happy Meal at the
Happiest Place on Earth.

NOTES

1. Richard Schickel, *The Disney Version: The Life, Times, Art, and Commerce of Walt Disney* (New York: Avon, 1968) 24.

2. According to John Love, Ronald McDonald is the most widely recognized commercial character in the United States. John Love, *Behind the Arches* (New York: Bantam, 1986) 222.

3. See Steven Watts, *The Magic Kingdom: Walt Disney and the American Way of Life* (Boston: Houghton, 1977) 161–62.

4. Ray Kroc, *Grinding It Out: The Making of McDonald's* (Washington, DC: H. Regnery, 1977) 114.

5. For the story of Willard Scott and Ronald McDonald, see Love, *Behind the Arches,* 218–22, 244–45.

6. Quoted in Penny Moser, "The McDonald's Mystique," *Fortune* 4 July 1988.

7. For Kroc's amusement park schemes, see Love, *Behind the Arches,* 411–13.

8. James U. McNeal, *Kids As Customers: A Handbook of Marketing to Children* (New York: Lexington, 1992) 6.

9. Cited in "Brand Aware," *Children's Business* June 2000.

10. See "Brand Consciousness," *IFF on Kids: Kid Focus,* no. 3.

11. For a sense of the techniques now being used by marketers, see Tom McGee, "Getting Inside Kids' Heads," *American Demographics* Jan. 1997.

12. Cited in Dan S. Acuff with Robert H. Reiner, *What Kids Buy and Why: The Psychology of Marketing to Kids* (New York: Free P, 1977) 45–46.

13. McNeal, *Kids As Customers,* 175.

14. Cited in Karen Benezra, "Keeping Burger King on a Roll," *Brandweek* 15 Jan. 1996.

15. Cited in "Children's Online Privacy Proposed Rule Issued by FTC," press release, Federal Trade Commission, 20 Apr. 1999.

16. Quoted in "Is Your Kid Caught Up in the Web?" *Consumer Reports* May 1997.

17. See Matthew McAllester, "Life in Cyberspace: What's McDonald's Doing with Kids' E-mail Responses?" *Newsday* 20 July 1997.

18. Quoted in Linda E. Demkovich, "Pulling the Sweet Tooth of Children's TV Advertising," *National Journal* 7 Jan. 1978.

19. Quoted in A. O. Sulzberger, Jr., "FTC Staff Urges End to Child-TV Ad Study," *New York Times* 3 Apr. 1981.

20. Cited in Steve McClellan and Richard Tedesco, "Children's TV Market May Be Played Out," *Broadcasting & Cable* 1 Mar. 1999.

21. Cited in "Policy Statement: Media Education," American Academy of Pediatrics, Aug. 1999.

22. Cited in "Policy Statement: Children, Adolescents, and Television," American Academy of Pediatrics, Oct. 1995.

23. Cited in Mary C. Martin, "Children's Understanding of the Intent of Advertising: A Meta-Analysis," *Journal of Public Policy & Marketing* (Fall 1997).

24. Cited in Lisa Jennings, "Baby, Hand Me the Remote," *Scripps Howard News Service* 13 Oct. 1999.

25. Interview with Lynn Fava, Competitive Media Reporting.

26. Cited in "Fast Food and Playgrounds: A Natural Combination," promotional material, Playlandservices, Inc.

27. Cited in "Fast Food and Playgrounds."

28. Cited in Rod Taylor, "The Beanie Factor," *Brandweek* 16 June 1997.

29. Sam Bradley and Betsey Spethmann, "Subway's Kid Pack: The Ties That Sell," *Brandweek* 10 Oct. 1994.

30. Meredith Williams, *Tomart's Price Guide to McDonald's Happy Meal Collectibles* (Dayton, OH: Tomart, 1995).

31. The story of McDonald's Teenie Beanie Baby promotion can be found in Taylor, "The Beanie Factor."

32. Quoted in "McDonald's Launches Second Animated Video in Series Starring Ronald McDonald," press release, McDonald's Corporation, 21 Jan. 1999.

33. See T. L. Stanley, *Hollywood Reporter* 26 May 1998.

34. See Thomas R. King, "Mickey May Be the Big Winner in Disney-McDonald's Alliance," *Wall Street Journal* 24 May 1996.

35. See Monci Jo Williams, "McDonald's Refuses to Plateau," *Fortune* 12 Nov. 1984.

36. Quoted in James Bates, "You Want First-Run Features with Those Fries?" *Newsday* 11 May 1997.

Joining the Conversation

1. While this piece is largely informational, giving statistics and other data on sales and company policies, Eric Schlosser's position on the practice of marketing to children is clear. What is that position, and how does he let us know what he thinks?

2. Schlosser presents ample evidence that McDonald's and other fast-food chains have grown rich in large part through their effective advertising and promotions. What other reasons can you think of for the enormous success of the fast-food industry? How, if at all, do they relate to those that Schlosser provides?

3. This piece was written for a general audience, in an informal voice and with entertaining details. How would the writing be different if it were written for an academic audience, such as a college writing class?

4. This reading comes from *Fast Food Nation: The Dark Side of the All-American Meal*, Schlosser's book about the U.S. fast-food industry and culture. How do the book's title and subtitle function as metacommentary? How, in other words, do they give readers some sense of Schlosser's argument?

5. What do you think? Should the fast-food industry be allowed to market directly to young children? Write an essay responding to Schlosser. You can agree with his position, disagree, or both agree and disagree, but use his position on fast-food marketing as the one that you respond to (the "they say").

Fat as a Feminist Issue

SUSIE ORBACH

OBESITY AND OVEREATING have joined sex as central issues in the lives of many women today. In the United States, 50 percent of women are estimated to be overweight. Every women's magazine has a diet column. Diet doctors and clinics flourish. The names of diet foods are now part of our general vocabulary. Physical fitness and beauty are every woman's goals. While this preoccupation with fat and food has become so common that we tend to take it for granted, being fat, feeling fat and the compulsion to overeat are, in fact, serious and painful experiences for the women involved.

SUSIE ORBACH is a visiting professor in the sociology department at the London School of Economics. She has published several books on women's health and emotional well-being, including *Hunger Strike: The Anorectic's Struggle as a Metaphor for Our Age* (1986) and *Fat Is a Feminist Issue* (1978), from which this piece is taken. Orbach has worked extensively, as both an author and a therapist, on women's weight issues, and she served as an adviser to Princess Diana when she was suffering from bulimia. She appears frequently on British television and radio and is now a consultant to the British National Health Service.

Being fat isolates and invalidates a woman. Almost inevitably, the explanations offered for fatness point a finger at the failure of women themselves to control their weight, control their appetites and control their impulses. Women suffering from the problem of compulsive eating endure double anguish: feeling out of step with the rest of society, and believing that it is all their own fault. . . .

Here's the "they say." For tips on starting with that move, see Chapter 1.

A feminist perspective to the problem of women's compulsive eating is essential if we are to move on from the ineffective blame-the-victim approach.[1] . . . Feminism insists that those painful personal experiences derive from the social context into which female babies are born, and within which they develop to become adult women. The fact that compulsive eating is overwhelmingly a woman's problem suggests that it has something to do with the experience of being female in our society. Feminism argues that being fat represents an attempt to break free of society's sex stereotypes. Getting fat can thus be understood as a definite and purposeful act; it is a directed, conscious or unconscious, challenge to sex-role stereotyping and culturally defined experience of womanhood.

Fat is a social disease, and fat is a feminist issue. Fat is *not* about lack of self-control or lack of willpower. Fat *is* about protection, sex, nurturance, strength, boundaries, mothering, substance, assertion and rage. It is a response to the inequality of the sexes. Fat expresses experiences of women today in ways that are seldom examined and even more seldom treated. . . . What is it about the social position of women that leads them to respond to it by getting fat?

The current ideological justification for inequality of the sexes has been built on the concept of the innate differences between women and men. Women alone can give birth to and breast-feed their infants and, as a result, a primary dependency relationship develops between mother and child. While this biological capacity is the only known genetic difference between men and women,[2] it is used as the basis on which to divide unequally women and men's labor, power, roles and expectations. The division of labor has become institutionalized. Women's capacity to reproduce and provide nourishment has relegated her to the care and socialization of children.

The relegation of women to the social roles of wife and mother has several significant consequences that contribute to the problem of fat. First, in order to become a wife and mother, a woman has to have a man. Getting a man is presented as an almost unattainable and yet essential goal. To get a man, a woman has to learn to regard herself as an item, a commodity, a sex object. Much of her experience and identity depends on how she and others see her. As John Berger says in *Ways of Seeing:* "Men *act* and women *appear*. Men look at women. Women watch themselves being looked at. This determines not only most relations between men and women, but also the relation of women to themselves."[3]

This emphasis on presentation as the central aspect of a woman's existence makes her extremely self-conscious. It demands that she occupy herself with a self-image that others will find pleasing and attractive—an image that will immediately convey what kind of woman she is. She must observe and evaluate herself, scrutinizing every detail of herself as though she were an outside judge. She attempts to make herself in the image of womanhood presented by billboards, newspapers, magazines and television. The media present women either in a sexual context or within the family, reflecting a woman's two prescribed roles, first as a sex object, and then as a mother. She is brought up to marry by "catching" a man with her good looks and pleasing manner. To do this she must look appealing, earthy, sensual, sexual, virginal, innocent, reliable, daring, mysterious, coquettish and thin. In other words, she offers her self-image on the marriage marketplace. As a married woman, her sexuality will be sanctioned and her economic needs will be looked after. She will have achieved the first step of womanhood.

Since women are taught to see themselves from the outside as candidates for men, they become prey to the huge fashion and diet industries that first set up the ideal images and then exhort women to meet them. The message is loud and clear—the woman's body is not her own. The woman's body is not satisfactory as it is. It must be thin, free of "unwanted hair," deodorized, perfumed and clothed. It must conform to an ideal physical type. Family and school socialization teaches girls to groom themselves properly. Furthermore, the job is never-ending, for the image changes from year to year. In the early 1960s, the only way to feel acceptable was to be skinny and flat chested with long straight hair. The first of these was achieved by near starvation, the second, by binding one's breasts with an ace bandage and the third, by ironing one's hair. Then in the early 1970s, the look was curly hair and full breasts. Just as styles in clothes change seasonally, so women's bodies are expected to change to fit these fashions. Long and skinny one year, petite and demure the next, women are continually manipulated by images of proper womanhood, which are extremely powerful because they are presented as the only reality. To ignore them means to risk being an outcast. Women are urged to conform, to help out the economy by continuous consumption of goods and clothing that are quickly made unwearable by the next season's fashion styles in clothes and body shapes. In the background, a ten billion dollar industry waits to remold bodies to the latest fashion. In this way, women are caught in an attempt to conform to a standard that is *externally* defined and constantly changing. But these models of femininity are experienced by women as unreal, frightening and unattainable. They produce a picture that is far removed from the reality of women's day-to-day lives.

The one constant in these images is that a woman must be thin. For many women, compulsive eating and being fat have become one way to avoid being marketed or seen as the ideal woman: "My fat says 'screw you' to all who want me to be the perfect mom, sweetheart, [and] maid. Take me for who *I* am, not for who I'm supposed to be. If you are really interested in *me*, you can wade through the layers and find out who I am." In this way, fat expresses a rebellion against the powerlessness of the woman, against the pressure to look and act in a certain way and against being evaluated on her ability to create an image of herself.

NOTES

1. William Ryan, *Blame the Victim* (New York, 1971). This book shows how we come to blame the victims of oppression rather than its perpetrators.

2. Dorothy Griffiths and Esther Saraga, "Sex Differences in a Sexist Society," International Conference on Sex-role Stereotyping, British Psychological Society, Cardiff, Wales, July 1977.

3. John Berger et al., *Ways of Seeing* (London, 1972) 47.

Joining the Conversation

1. Susie Orbach begins by citing what others say about obesity as an issue among women in the United States, noting in paragraph 2 that "almost inevitably, the explanations offered for fatness point a finger at the failure of women themselves to control their weight." That's her "they say"; what then does *she* say? Cite lines from her text in your answer.

2. In paragraphs 3 and 4, Orbach describes a feminist perspective on compulsive eating and obesity. Summarize that perspective.

3. Orbach focuses on weight and body image as a woman's issue, but men too face pressures concerning diet and body image. What are some of those pressures?

4. Does Orbach introduce any naysayers, any objections or possible objections to her own position? If so, what are they? If not, what objections might she have considered, and how do you think she would have dealt with them?

5. Orbach says that being overweight is for many women a way of rebelling against social pressures to be thin. What do you think? Write an essay in which you agree, disagree, or both agree and disagree with her position, but be sure to summarize or quote Orbach's views before you offer your own.

Being Fat Is OK

PAUL CAMPOS

—⌑—

ACCORDING to the federal government, I'm fat. Excuse me: "overweight." That's because, even though I run 35 to 40 miles per week, and am in excellent overall health, my height of five feet, eight inches and weight of 165 pounds gives me a Body Mass Index figure that makes me overweight, according to the BMI charts.

The BMI is what the government uses when it tells Americans that 61 percent of us are overweight. Every adult who has a BMI of 25 or higher is in this group. Nearly half of the people in this category have a BMI of 30 or higher, and are thus considered clinically "obese." There's just one problem with these figures: They are based on a remarkably elaborate series

PAUL CAMPOS is a law professor at the University of Colorado, specializing in constitutional law and legal theory, and the author of numerous scholarly articles and books on the American legal system. He also writes a regular column for the *Rocky Mountain News* in which he discusses political, social, and legal issues. He is the author of *The Obesity Myth: Why America's Obsession with Weight Is Hazardous to Your Health* (2004). The essay here was first published in *Jewish World Review* in 2001.

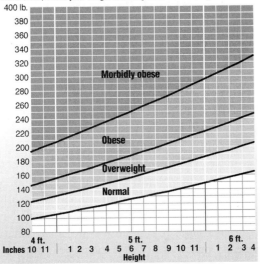

Judging your weight

To find out if you are overweight or obese, according to the Body Mass Index, locate your weight and height on the following chart:

of lies—lies about fat, fitness, and health that, not coincidentally, serve the interests of America's $50 billion-per-year diet industry.

Now "lie" is a harsh word. But it is the only word that accurately reflects the dishonesty of the propaganda war that the diet industry, with the eager cooperation of our government, is carrying out against the American people.

Lie No. 1: We know that fat people are less healthy than thin people because they are fat. Due to the effectiveness of the diet industry's propaganda, most people treat this assertion as being self-evidently true. In fact, there is no solid scientific basis for this claim.

For tips on disagreeing and explaining why, see Chapter 4.

As the editors of no less an authority than the *New England Journal of Medicine* have pointed out, "the data linking overweight and death are limited, fragmentary, and often ambiguous." The most basic axiom of the scientific method is that demonstrating a correlation between A and B isn't the same thing as proving that A causes B, or vice versa. Yet, as the editors emphasize, this fundamental rule of scientific inquiry is violated again and again when the subject is the supposed health risks of fat.

For example, we know that fat people are much more likely to be poor than thin people, and that being fat in America today makes a person fair game for the most brazen forms of discrimination. Both of these generalizations have long been true as regards African Americans—yet no rational person would suggest that poor health among black people is caused by their skin color, rather than by such factors as poverty and discrimination.

Lie No. 2: We know that fat people would be as healthy as thin people if they lost weight. In the words of the editors of the *New England Journal:* "We simply do not know whether a person who loses 20 pounds will acquire the same reduced risk as a person who started out 20 pounds lighter . . . some [studies have] even suggested that weight loss increases mortality."

Lie No. 3: Fat people can choose to be thinner. The failure rate for diets is estimated to be between 90 percent and 98 percent, depending on how failure is defined. Furthermore, it has been proven over and over again that any statistically significant group of dieters will end up weighing more, on average, than a comparable group that never began dieting. Dieting to avoid getting fat makes exactly as much sense as smoking to avoid getting lung cancer.

We don't know the answer to such basic questions as whether being fat causes health problems and whether losing weight is good or bad for you because, in order to answer such questions scientifically, studies would have to be done in which half the subjects would lose weight and keep it off. Here's the biggest irony of the diet racket: The reason no such studies exist is that there is no known way to accomplish this.

As things stand, the American diet industry is a $50 billion- 10 a-year scam that provides its customers with totally ineffective cures for an imaginary disease. Bon appetit!

Joining the Conversation

1. This essay offers a strongly worded response to what Paul Campos calls a "propaganda war." What argument is Campos responding to—the "they say"—and what, according to him, is its motivation?

2. Campos presents and attempts to refute what he calls three "lies." Does he convince you? Why? If not, why not?

3. Campos disputes the idea, which many people seem to believe, that thin people are healthier than fat people. Does he offer any naysayers—that is, arguments that thin people may indeed be healthier? If not, can you present some?

4. This brief essay was written for an online magazine, which may be one reason it is quite short and its language is so casual. How might it be different if it were written for a more academic purpose—for a college writing class, for example?

5. Campos appears to be arguing against the very idea that many Americans are overweight, suggesting that this view is a myth spread by the U.S. diet industry to help it earn greater profits. Write a response to Campos in which you define the issue and present your own perspective.

FOURTEEN

ARE *24*, *FAMILY GUY*, AND *GRAND THEFT AUTO* ACTUALLY GOOD FOR YOU?

IS THERE ANYBODY UNDER FIFTY whose parents haven't worried that he or she was watching too much TV? It almost goes without saying that most people believe that excessive exposure to the popular media—not only to television shows like *American Idol*, but also to Hollywood films, tabloid magazines, Facebook, video games, and the Internet—both dumbs us down and makes us more likely to tolerate acts of violence if not to commit them ourselves. A recent article in the *New Yorker* even suggests that the abuse of prisoners by the American military in Iraq and at Guantánamo was directly influenced by the hit TV series *24*, whose hero often resorts to torture to extract information from villains. George F. Will, in an article in this chapter, goes so far as to speculate that reality shows in which contestants play Russian Roulette with real bullets could become part of our nightly entertainment.

Some of the writers in this chapter, however, argue that such alarmist views of the popular media are seriously overstated.

Steven Johnson, for instance, acknowledges that some TV shows and video games do perhaps "dumb us down," but argues that the more sophisticated ones actually deepen our intelligence and sharpen our ability to follow multiple plot lines and narratives. Amy Goldwasser also challenges the idea that today's popular media are a vast wasteland by asking us to rethink core assumptions many of us hold about email, the Internet, and other forms of online communication. Douglas Rushkoff argues that Bart Simpson offers a model of subversive thinking that can help us view the political establishment more critically, and Antonia Peacocke suggests the same is true of *Family Guy,* even if it sometimes takes things "too far."

These views are countered not only by Will but also by Roz Chast, who shows what instant messaging would have done to Shakespeare's lofty language, and also by Naomi Rockler-Gladen, who argues that today's media are so permeated by petty consumer values that they have blunted our critical capacities. Sherry Turkle looks askance at today's media-saturated culture, but for a slightly different reason—because of the way cell phones, computers, and other portable technologies undermine public spaces and community. Dana Stevens, on the other hand, doesn't really buy any of the above arguments, questioning those who think TV is "good" for us as well as those who think the opposite.

As the final author in this unit, Gerald Graff shifts the focus of the debate slightly, asking us to consider not just *what* media texts we consume but *how* (with what kind of intellectual attention) we consume them and suggesting that it matters less whether we read Marvel comics or *Macbeth,* as long as we approach what we read with a critical eye and question and theorize about it in analytical, intellectual ways.

Watching TV Makes You Smarter

STEVEN JOHNSON

—⌐回⌐—

SCIENTIST A: *Has he asked for anything special?*
SCIENTIST B: *Yes, this morning for breakfast . . . he requested something called "wheat germ, organic honey and tiger's milk."*
SCIENTIST A: *Oh, yes. Those were the charmed substances that some years ago were felt to contain life-preserving properties.*
SCIENTIST B: *You mean there was no deep fat? No steak or cream pies or . . . hot fudge?*
SCIENTIST A: *Those were thought to be unhealthy.*

—From Woody Allen's *Sleeper*

ON JANUARY 24, the Fox network showed an episode of its hit drama *24*, the real-time thriller known for its cliffhanger tension and often-gruesome violence. Over the preceding weeks, a number of public controversies had erupted around *24*, mostly focused on its portrait of Muslim terrorists and its penchant for torture scenes. The episode that was shown on

STEVEN JOHNSON is the author of five books, among them *Mind Wide Open: Your Brain and the Neuroscience of Everyday Life* (2005). The piece included here was first published in the *New York Times Magazine* in 2005; it is an excerpt from a book-length work published the same year, *Everything Bad Is Good for You: How Today's Popular Culture Is Actually Making Us Smarter*.

the twenty-fourth only fanned the flames higher: in one scene, a terrorist enlists a hit man to kill his child for not fully supporting the jihadist cause; in another scene, the secretary of defense authorizes the torture of his son to uncover evidence of a terrorist plot.

But the explicit violence and the post-9/11 terrorist anxiety are not the only elements of 24 that would have been unthinkable on prime-time network television 20 years ago. Alongside the notable change in content lies an equally notable change in form. During its 44 minutes—a real-time hour, minus 16 minutes for commercials—the episode connects the lives of 21 distinct characters, each with a clearly defined "story arc," as the Hollywood jargon has it: a defined personality with motivations and obstacles and specific relationships with other characters. Nine primary narrative threads wind their way through those 44 minutes, each drawing extensively upon events and information revealed in earlier episodes. Draw a map of all those intersecting plots and personalities, and you get structure that—where formal complexity is concerned—more closely resembles *Middlemarch* than a hit TV drama of years past like *Bonanza*.

For decades, we've worked under the assumption that mass culture follows a path declining steadily toward lowest-common-denominator standards, presumably because the "masses" want dumb, simple pleasures and big media companies try to give the masses what they want. But as that 24 episode suggests, the exact opposite is happening: the culture is getting more cognitively demanding, not less. To make sense of an episode of 24, you have to integrate far more information than you would have a few decades ago watching a comparable show. Beneath the violence and the ethnic stereotypes, another trend appears: to keep up with entertainment like 24, you have to pay attention, make

For other ways of representing "standard views," see p. 22.

inferences, track shifting social relationships. This is what I call the Sleeper Curve: the most debased forms of mass diversion—video games and violent television dramas and juvenile sitcoms—turn out to be nutritional after all.

I believe that the Sleeper Curve is the single most important new force altering the mental development of young people today, and I believe it is largely a force for good: enhancing our cognitive faculties, not dumbing them down. And yet you almost never hear this story in popular accounts of today's media. Instead, you hear dire tales of addiction, violence, mindless escapism. It's assumed that shows that promote smoking or gratuitous violence are bad for us, while those that thunder against teen pregnancy or intolerance have a positive role in society. Judged by that morality-play standard, the story of popular culture over the past 50 years—if not 500—is a story of decline: the morals of the stories have grown darker and more ambiguous, and the antiheroes have multiplied.

The usual counterargument here is that what media have 5 lost in moral clarity, they have gained in realism. The real world doesn't come in nicely packaged public-service announcements, and we're better off with entertainment like *The Sopranos* that reflects our fallen state with all its ethical ambiguity. I happen to be sympathetic to that argument, but it's not the one I want to make here. I think there is another way to assess the social virtue of pop culture, one that looks at media as a kind of cognitive workout, not as a series of life lessons. There may indeed be more "negative messages" in the mediasphere today. But that's not the only way to evaluate whether our television shows or video games are having a positive impact. Just as important—if not more important—is the kind of thinking you have to do to make sense of a cultural experience. That is where the Sleeper Curve becomes visible.

Televised Intelligence

Consider the cognitive demands that televised narratives place on their viewers. With many shows that we associate with "quality" entertainment—*The Mary Tyler Moore Show*, *Murphy Brown*, *Frasier*—the intelligence arrives fully formed in the words and actions of the characters on-screen. They say witty things to one another and avoid lapsing into tired sitcom clichés, and we smile along in our living rooms, enjoying the company of these smart people. But assuming we're bright enough to understand the sentences they're saying, there's no intellectual labor involved in enjoying the show as a viewer. You no more challenge your mind by watching these intelligent shows than you challenge your body watching *Monday Night Football*. The intellectual work is happening on-screen, not off.

But another kind of televised intelligence is on the rise. Think of the cognitive benefits conventionally ascribed to reading: attention, patience, retention, the parsing of narrative threads. Over the last half-century, programming on TV has increased the demands it places on precisely these mental faculties. This growing complexity involves three primary elements: multiple threading, flashing arrows and social networks.

According to television lore, the age of multiple threads began with the arrival in 1981 of *Hill Street Blues*, the Steven Bochco police drama invariably praised for its "gritty realism." Watch an episode of *Hill Street Blues* side by side with any major drama from the preceding decades—*Starsky and Hutch*, for instance, or *Dragnet*—and the structural transformation will jump out at you. The earlier shows follow one or two lead characters, adhere to a single dominant plot and reach a decisive conclusion at the end of the episode. Draw an outline of the narrative threads in almost every *Dragnet* episode, and it will be a single line: from the initial crime scene, through the investigation, to the eventual cracking of the case. A typical *Starsky and Hutch* episode offers only the slightest variation on this linear formula: the introduction of a comic subplot that usually appears only at the tail ends of the episode, creating a structure that looks like the graph below. The vertical axis represents the number of individual threads, and the horizontal axis is time.

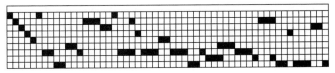

Starsky and Hutch (any episode)

A *Hill Street Blues* episode complicates the picture in a number of profound ways. The narrative weaves together a collection of distinct strands—sometimes as many as 10, though at least half of the threads involve only a few quick scenes scattered through the episode. The number of primary characters—and not just bit parts—swells significantly. And the episode has fuzzy borders: picking up one or two threads from previous episodes at the outset and leaving one or two threads open at the end. Charted graphically, an average episode looks like this graph:

Hill Street Blues (episode 85)

Critics generally cite *Hill Street Blues* as the beginning of 10 "serious drama" native in the television medium—differentiating the series from the single-episode dramatic programs from the 1950s, which were Broadway plays performed in front of a camera. But the *Hill Street* innovations weren't all that original; they'd long played a defining role in popular television, just not during the evening hours. The structure of a *Hill Street* episode—and indeed of all the critically acclaimed dramas that followed, from *thirtysomething* to *Six Feet Under*—is the structure of a soap opera. *Hill Street Blues* might have sparked a new golden age of television drama during its seven-year run, but it did so by using a few crucial tricks that *Guiding Light* and *General Hospital* mastered long before.

Bochco's genius with *Hill Street* was to marry complex narrative structure with complex subject matter. *Dallas* had already shown that the extended, interwoven threads of the soap-opera genre could survive the weeklong interruptions of a prime-time show, but the actual content of *Dallas* was fluff. (The most probing issue it addressed was the question, now folkloric, of who shot J.R.) *All in the Family* and *Rhoda* showed that you could tackle complex social issues, but they did their tackling in the comfort of the sitcom living room. *Hill Street* had richly drawn characters confronting difficult social issues and a narrative structure to match.

Since *Hill Street* appeared, the multi-threaded drama has become the most widespread fictional genre on prime time: *St. Elsewhere, L.A. Law, thirtysomething, Twin Peaks, N.Y.P.D. Blue, E.R., The West Wing, Alias, Lost.* (The only prominent holdouts in drama are shows like *Law and Order* that have essentially updated the venerable *Dragnet* format and thus remained anchored to a single narrative line.) Since the early 1980s, however, there has been a noticeable increase in narrative complexity in these dramas. The most ambitious show on TV to date, *The Sopranos*, routinely follows up to a dozen distinct threads over the course of an episode, with more than 20 recurring characters. An episode from late in the first season looks like this:

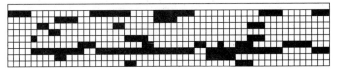

The Sopranos (episode 8)

The total number of active threads equals the multiple plots of *Hill Street*, but here each thread is more substantial. The show doesn't offer a clear distinction between dominant and minor plots; each story line carries its weight in the mix. The episode also displays a chordal mode of storytelling entirely absent from *Hill Street*: a single scene in *The Sopranos* will often connect to three different threads at the same time, layering one plot atop another. And every single thread in this *Sopranos*

Dragnet (any episode)

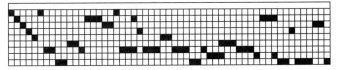

Starsky and Hutch (any episode)

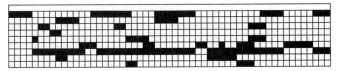

Hill Street Blues (episode 85)

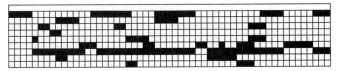

The Sopranos (episode 8)

episode builds on events from previous episodes and continues on through the rest of the season and beyond.

Put those charts together, and you have a portrait of the Sleeper Curve rising over the past 30 years of popular television. In a sense, this is as much a map of cognitive changes in the popular mind as it is a map of on-screen developments, as if the media titans decided to condition our brains to follow ever-larger numbers of simultaneous threads. Before *Hill Street*, the conventional wisdom among television execs was that audiences wouldn't be comfortable following more than three plots in a single episode, and indeed, the *Hill Street* pilot, which was shown in January 1981, brought complaints from viewers that the show was too complicated. Fast-forward two decades, and shows like *The Sopranos* engage their audiences with narratives that make *Hill Street* look like *Three's Company*. Audiences happily embrace that complexity because they've been trained by two decades of multi-threaded dramas.

Multi-threading is the most celebrated structural feature of 15 the modern television drama, and it certainly deserves some of the honor that has been doled out to it. And yet multi-threading is only part of the story.

The Case for Confusion

Shortly after the arrival of the first-generation slasher movies—*Halloween, Friday the 13th*—Paramount released a mock-slasher flick called *Student Bodies*, parodying the genre just as the *Scream* series would do 15 years later. In one scene, the obligatory nubile teenage baby sitter hears a noise outside a suburban house; she opens the door to investigate, finds nothing and then goes back inside. As the door shuts behind her, the camera swoops in on the doorknob, and we see that she has left the door unlocked. The camera pulls back and then swoops down again for emphasis. And then a flashing arrow appears on the screen, with text that helpfully explains: "Unlocked!"

That flashing arrow is parody, of course, but it's merely an exaggerated version of a device popular stories use all the time. When a sci-fi script inserts into some advanced lab a nonscientist who keeps asking the science geeks to explain what they're doing with that particle accelerator, that's a flashing arrow that gives the audience precisely the information it needs in order to make sense of the ensuing plot. ("Whatever you do, don't spill water on it, or you'll set off a massive explosion!") These hints serve as a kind of narrative hand-holding. Implicitly, they say to the audience, "We realize you have no idea what a particle accelerator is, but here's the deal: all you need to know is that it's a big fancy thing that explodes when wet." They focus the mind on relevant details: "Don't worry about whether the baby sitter is going to break up with her boyfriend. Worry about that guy lurking in the bushes." They reduce the amount of analytic work you need to do to make sense of a story. All you have to do is follow the arrows.

By this standard, popular television has never been harder to follow. If narrative threads have experienced a population explosion over the past 20 years, flashing arrows have grown correspondingly scarce. Watching our pinnacle of early '80s TV drama, *Hill Street Blues*, we find there's an informational wholeness to each scene that differs markedly from what you see on shows like *The West Wing* or *The Sopranos* or *Alias* or *E.R.*

Hill Street has ambiguities about future events: will a convicted killer be executed? Will Furillo marry Joyce Davenport? Will Renko find it in himself to bust a favorite singer for cocaine possession? But the present tense of each scene explains itself to the viewer with little ambiguity. There's an open question or a mystery driving each of these stories—how will it all turn out?—but there's no mystery about the immediate activity on the screen. A contemporary drama like *The West Wing*, on the other hand, constantly embeds mysteries into the present-tense events: you see characters performing actions or discussing events about which crucial information has been deliberately withheld. Anyone who has watched more than a handful of *The West Wing* episodes closely will know the feeling: scene after scene refers to some clearly crucial but unexplained piece of information, and after the sixth reference, you'll find yourself wishing you could rewind the tape to figure out what they're talking about, assuming you've missed something. And then you realize that you're supposed to be confused. The open question posed by these sequences is not "How will this turn out in the end?" The question is "What's happening right now?"

The deliberate lack of hand-holding extends down to the microlevel of dialogue as well. Popular entertainment that addresses technical issues—whether they are the intricacies of passing legislation, or of performing a heart bypass, or of operating a particle accelerator—conventionally switches between two modes of information in dialogue: texture and substance. Texture is all the arcane verbiage provided to convince the viewer that they're watching Actual Doctors at Work; substance is the material planted amid the background texture that the viewer needs to make sense of the plot.

Conventionally, narratives demarcate the line between texture and substance by inserting cues that flag or translate the important data. There's an unintentionally comical moment in the 2004 blockbuster *The Day After Tomorrow* in which the beleaguered climatologist (played by Dennis Quaid) announces his theory about the imminent arrival of a new ice age to a gathering of government officials. In his speech, he warns that "we have hit a critical desalinization point!" At this moment, the writer-director Roland Emmerich—a master of brazen arrow-flashing—has an official follow with the obliging remark: "It would explain what's driving this extreme weather." They might as well have had a flashing "Unlocked!" arrow on the screen.

The dialogue on shows like *The West Wing* and *E.R.*, on the other hand, doesn't talk down to its audiences. It rushes by, the words accelerating in sync with the high-speed tracking shots that glide through the corridors and operating rooms. The characters talk faster in these shows, but the truly remarkable thing about the dialogue is not purely a matter of speed; it's the willingness to immerse the audience in information that most viewers won't understand. Here's a typical scene from *E.R.*:

[WEAVER AND WRIGHT push a gurney containing a 16-year-old girl. Her parents, JANNA AND FRANK MIKAMI, follow close behind. CARTER AND LUCY fall in.]

WEAVER: 16-year-old, unconscious, history of biliary atresia.

CARTER: Hepatic coma?

WEAVER: Looks like it.

MR. MIKAMI: She was doing fine until six months ago.

CARTER: What medication is she on?

MRS. MIKAMI: Ampicillin, tobramycin, vitamins a, d and k.

LUCY: Skin's jaundiced.

WEAVER: Same with the sclera. Breath smells sweet.

CARTER: Fetor hepaticus?

WEAVER: Yep.

LUCY: What's that?

WEAVER: Her liver's shut down. Let's dip a urine. [To CARTER] Guys, it's getting a little crowded in here, why don't you deal with the parents? Start lactulose, 30 cc's per NG.

CARTER: We're giving medicine to clean her blood.
WEAVER: Blood in the urine, two-plus.
CARTER: The liver failure is causing her blood not to clot.
MRS. MIKAMI: Oh, God. . . .
CARTER: Is she on the transplant list?
MR. MIKAMI: She's been Status 2a for six months, but they haven't been able to find her a match.
CARTER: Why? What's her blood type?
MR. MIKAMI: AB.
[This hits CARTER like a lightning bolt. LUCY gets it, too. They share a look.]

There are flashing arrows here, of course—"The liver failure is causing her blood not to clot"—but the ratio of medical jargon to layperson translation is remarkably high. From a purely narrative point of view, the decisive line arrives at the very end: "AB." The 16-year-old's blood type connects her to an earlier plot line, involving a cerebral-hemorrhage victim who—after being dramatically revived in one of the opening scenes—ends up brain-dead. Far earlier, before the liver-failure scene above, Carter briefly discusses harvesting the hemorrhage victim's organs for transplants, and another doctor makes a passing reference to his blood type being the rare AB (thus making him an unlikely donor). The twist here revolves around a statistically unlikely event happening at the E.R.—an otherwise perfect liver donor showing up just in time to donate his liver to a recipient with the same rare blood type. But the show reveals this twist with remarkable subtlety. To make sense of that last "AB" line—and the look of disbelief on Carter's and Lucy's faces—you have to recall a passing remark uttered earlier regarding a character who belongs to a completely different thread. Shows like E.R. may have more blood and guts than popular TV had a generation ago, but when it comes to story-telling, they possess a quality that can only be described as sub-tlety and discretion.

Even Bad TV Is Better

Skeptics might argue that I have stacked the deck here by focus-ing on relatively highbrow titles like *The Sopranos* or *The West Wing*, when in fact the most significant change in the last five years of narrative entertainment involves reality TV. Does the contemporary pop cultural landscape look quite as promising if the representative show is *Joe Millionaire* instead of *The West Wing*?

I think it does, but to answer that question properly, you have to avoid the tendency to sentimentalize the past. When people talk about the golden age of television in the early '70s—invoking shows like *The Mary Tyler Moore Show* and *All in the Family*—they forget to mention how awful most television pro-gramming was during much of that decade. If you're going to look at pop-culture trends, you have to compare apples to apples, or in this case, lemons to lemons. The relevant com-parison is not between *Joe Millionaire* and *MASH*; it's between *Joe Millionaire* and *The Newlywed Game*, or between *Survivor* and *The Love Boat*.

What you see when you make these head-to-head compar-isons is that a rising tide of complexity has been lifting pro-gramming at the bottom of the quality spectrum and at the top. *The Sopranos* is several times more demanding of its audiences than *Hill Street* was, and *Joe Millionaire* has made comparable advances over *Battle of the Network Stars*. This is the ultimate test of the Sleeper Curve theory: even the junk has improved.

If early television took its cues from the stage, today's real-ity programming is reliably structured like a video game: a series of competitive tests, growing more challenging over time. Many reality shows borrow a subtler device from gaming culture as well: the rules aren't fully established at the outset. You learn as you play.

On a show like *Survivor* or *The Apprentice*, the participants—and the audience—know the general objective of the series, but each episode involves new challenges that haven't been ordained in advance. The final round of the first season of *The Apprentice*, for instance, threw a monkey wrench into the strategy that governed the play up to that point, when Trump announced that the two remaining apprentices would have to assemble and manage a team of subordinates who had already been fired in earlier episodes of the show. All of a sudden the overarching objective of the game—do anything to avoid being fired—presented a potential conflict to the remaining two contenders: the structure of the final round favored the survivor who had maintained the best relationships with his comrades. Suddenly, it wasn't enough just to have clawed your way to the top; you had to have made friends while clawing. The original *Joe Millionaire* went so far as to undermine the most fundamental convention of all—that the show's creators don't openly lie to the contestants about the prizes—by inducing a construction worker to pose as man of means while 20 women competed for his attention.

Reality programming borrowed another key ingredient from games: the intellectual labor of probing the system's rules for weak spots and opportunities. As each show discloses its conventions, and each participant reveals his or her personality traits and background, the intrigue in watching comes from figuring out how the participants should best navigate the environment that has been created for them. The pleasure in these shows comes not from watching other people being humiliated on national television; it comes from depositing other people in a complex, high-pressure environment where no established strategies exist and watching them find their bearings. That's why the water-cooler conversation about these shows invariably tracks in on the strategy displayed on the previous night's episode: why did Kwame pick Omarosa in that final round? What devious strategy is Richard Hatch concocting now?

When we watch these shows, the part of our brain that monitors the emotional lives of the people around us—the part that tracks subtle shifts in intonation and gesture and facial expression—scrutinizes the action on the screen, looking for clues. We trust certain characters implicitly and vote others off the island in a heartbeat. Traditional narrative shows also trigger emotional connections to the characters, but those connections don't have the same participatory effect, because traditional narratives aren't explicitly about strategy. The phrase "Monday-morning quarterbacking" describes the engaged feeling that spectators have in relation to games as opposed to stories. We absorb stories, but we second-guess games. Reality programming has brought that second-guessing to prime time, only the game in question revolves around social dexterity rather than the physical kind.

The Rewards of Smart Culture

The quickest way to appreciate the Sleeper Curve's cognition 30 training is to sit down and watch a few hours of hit programming from the late '70s on Nick at Nite or the SOAPnet channel or on DVD. The modern viewer who watches a show like *Dallas* today will be bored by the content—not just because the show is less salacious than today's soap operas (which it is by a small margin) but also because the show contains far less information in each scene, despite the fact that its soap-opera structure made it one of the most complicated narratives on television in its prime. With *Dallas*, the modern viewer doesn't have to think to make sense of what's going on, and not having to think is boring. Many recent hit shows—*24*, *Survivor*, *The Sopranos*, *Alias*, *Lost*, *The Simpsons*, *E.R.*—take the opposite approach, layering each scene with a thick network of affiliations. You have to focus to follow the plot, and in focusing you're exercising the parts of your brain that map social networks, that fill in missing information, that connect multiple narrative threads.

Of course, the entertainment industry isn't increasing the cognitive complexity of its products for charitable reasons. The Sleeper Curve exists because there's money to be made by making culture smarter. The economics of television syndication and DVD sales mean that there's a tremendous financial pressure to make programs that can be watched multiple times, revealing new nuances and shadings on the third viewing. Meanwhile, the Web has created a forum for annotation and commentary that allows more complicated shows to prosper, thanks to the fan sites where each episode of shows like *Lost* or *Alias* is dissected with an intensity usually reserved for Talmud scholars. Finally, interactive games have trained a new generation of media consumers to probe complex environments and to think on their feet, and that gamer audience has now come to expect the same challenges from their television shows. In the end, the Sleeper Curve tells us something about the human mind. It may be drawn toward the sensational where content is concerned—sex does sell, after all. But the mind also likes to be challenged; there's real pleasure to be found in solving puzzles, detecting patterns or unpacking a complex narrative system.

In pointing out some of the ways that popular culture has improved our minds, I am not arguing that parents should stop paying attention to the way their children amuse themselves. What I am arguing for is a change in the criteria we use to determine what really is cognitive junk food and what is genuinely nourishing. Instead of a show's violent or tawdry content, instead of wardrobe malfunctions or the F-word, the true test should be whether a given show engages or sedates the mind. Is it a single thread strung together with predictable punch lines every 30 seconds? Or does it map a complex social network? Is your on-screen character running around shooting everything in sight, or is she trying to solve problems and manage resources? If your kids want to watch reality TV, encourage them to watch *Survivor* over *Fear Factor*. If they want to watch a mystery show, encourage *24* over *Law and Order*. If they want to play a violent game, encourage *Grand Theft Auto* over *Quake*. Indeed, it might be just as helpful to have a rating system that used mental labor and not obscenity and violence as its classification scheme for the world of mass culture.

Kids and grown-ups each can learn from their increasingly shared obsessions. Too often we imagine the blurring of kid and grown-up cultures as a series of violations: the 9-year-olds who have to have nipple broaches explained to them thanks to Janet Jackson; the middle-aged guy who can't wait to get home to his Xbox. But this demographic blur has a commendable side that we don't acknowledge enough. The kids are forced to think like grown-ups: analyzing complex social networks, managing resources, tracking subtle narrative intertwinings, recognizing long-term patterns. The grown-ups, in turn, get to learn from the kids: decoding each new technological wave, parsing the interfaces and discovering the intellectual rewards of play. Parents should see this as an opportunity, not a crisis. Smart culture is no longer something you force your kids to ingest, like green vegetables. It's something you share.

Joining the Conversation

1. Steven Johnson makes clear in his opening paragraphs what view he is arguing against. What is that view (his "they say")? How does the dialogue from the Woody Allen movie *Sleeper* relate to that view?

2. Johnson's own argument relates to the intellectual effects of television viewing. Find his thesis statement, locate his supporting discussion, and write a concise summary of the whole argument.

3. Pick an example of popular entertainment that Johnson discusses or another one of comparable quality that you are familiar with, and imagine how someone could use it to make a case *against* Johnson's argument.

4. Compare Johnson's view with that of Dana Stevens, whose essay "Thinking Outside the Idiot Box" follows on p. 231. Which piece do you find more persuasive, and why?

5. Write a response to Johnson using your own experiences and observations as support for what you say. Consider the audience you wish to address, and craft your opening and choice of examples with that audience in mind.

Thinking Outside the Idiot Box

DANA STEVENS

—◻—

Does watching TV make you smarter?
Duh . . . I dunno.

IF WATCHING TV really makes you smarter, as Steven Johnson argued in an article in yesterday's *New York Times Magazine* (an excerpt from his forthcoming book) then I guess I need
to watch a lot more of it, because try as I might, I could make
no sense of Johnson's piece. As far as I can tell, his thesis is
that television shows have slowly grown more and more complicated over the last two decades (this paradigm shift apparently having begun with *Hill Street Blues*, the Gutenberg Bible
of the smart-TV era), so that now, like rats in a behaviorist's
maze, trained viewers can differentiate among up to 12 distinct
plotlines in shows like *The Sopranos*. (The technical term for

DANA STEVENS is *Slate's* movie critic and has also written for the *New
York Times*, *Bookforum*, and the *Atlantic*. Stevens has a Ph.D. in comparative literature from the University of California at Berkeley.
"Thinking Outside the Idiot Box" was first published in *Slate* on March
25, 2005, as a direct response to "Watching TV Makes You Smarter,"
the article by Steven Johnson on pp. 213–30.

this great leap forward in human cognition: "multi-threading.")
In other words, if I understand correctly, watching TV teaches
you to watch more TV—a truth already grasped by the makers
of children's programming like *Teletubbies*, which is essentially
a tutorial instructing toddlers in the basics of vegging out.

As long as Johnson defines intelligence strictly in quantitative cog-sci terms ("attention, patience, retention, the parsing
of narrative threads," etc.), his case may seem solid. Those of
us who grew up in caveman days, fashioning crude stone tools
while watching *Starsky and Hutch,* are indeed now better
positioned than our forebears to follow such complex narrative
fare as *The Sopranos* (though the analogy is faulty in that *The
Sopranos* is clearly one of the high-end, sophisticated shows of
its day, better compared to '70s offerings like *Soap* or *Mary Hartman, Mary Hartman*). But does that make us any smarter?

Not only does Johnson fail to account for the impact of the
16 minutes' worth of commercials that interrupt any given
episode of, say, *24* (a show he singles out as particularly "nutritional"), but he breezily dismisses recent controversies about
the program's representation of Muslim terrorists or its implicit
endorsement of torture, preferring to concentrate on
how the show's formal structure teaches us to "pay attention, make inferences, track shifting social relationships." Wait a minute—isn't a fictional program's
connection to real-life political events like torture and
racial profiling one of the "social relationships" we
should be paying attention *to*? *24* is the perfect example
of a TV show that challenges its audience's cognitive
faculties with intricate plotlines and rapid-fire information
while actively discouraging them from thinking too much about
the vigilante ethic it portrays. It's really good at teaching you
to think . . . about future episodes of *24*.

> A mix of formal and informal styles is appropriate in "Slate." See Chapter 9 on mixing styles in academic writing.

Johnson's claim for television as a tool for brain enhancement seems deeply, hilariously bogus—not unlike the graphically mesmerizing plot diagram he provides of "any episode" of *Starsky and Hutch* as a foil for the far fancier grid representing *The Sopranos*. (No matter how many times I return to that *Starsky and Hutch* diagram, it remains funny—in contrast to, say, the latest episode of *Joey*.) But I don't know that I have a lot more sympathy for the wet-blanket Puritanism of the anti-TV crowd.

Today being the first day of this year's TV Turnoff Week, there are a lot of articles out there about what Lisa Simpson would call the "endumbening" effect of television viewing. [An] interview with Kalle Lasn, a co-founder of TV Turnoff Week who also edits the "culture-jamming" journal *Adbusters*, focuses on the TV-B-Gone, a hand-held remote-control device that can switch off most television sets from between 20 and 50 feet away, restoring calm to public places like airports, bars, or banks. The device seems appealingly subversive, but ultimately, its function as a tool of social control can't help but invoke the very content-based censorship that the PBS crowd so deplores. There's an inescapably patronizing tone in the marketing of the TV-B-Gone, illustrated by Lasn's explanation of why he failed to zap one bank of public screens: "I was at the airport the other day, and there was a big TV set that a number of people were watching, and for some reason I didn't want to switch it off because it was some nature show." SO a football game in a bar is zapworthy, but spacing out to leopards in the Qantas terminal is A-OK? What if the nature show is violent, like the Discovery Channel's *Animal Face-Off*? What if the zapper is not an anti-television liberal, but a right-winger offended by Will and Grace's living arrangement, or Janet Jackson's breast? Who decides?

From the vantage point of someone who watches a hell of a lot of TV (but still far less than the average American), the medium seems neither like a brain-liquefying poison nor a salutary tonic. Certainly for young children, who are fresh meat for the advertising industry, the idea of a week (or an entire childhood) without TV makes a lot of sense. But shouldn't grown men and women be trusted to judge their own dosages, just as they would decide on the number of drinks they can handle at the bar? And shouldn't we choose our favorite shows because we like them, not because they force our otherwise helpless cortexes to "manag[e] resources" and "recognize long-term patterns"? There couldn't be a better time to test Steven Johnson's theory than National TV Turnoff Week—just turn the set off till Sunday and see if you get any dumber. I'd participate in the experiment myself, but in my case, watching television is definitely a smart thing to do—I get paid for it.

Joining the Conversation

1. In her opening paragraph, Dana Stevens summarizes Steven Johnson's thesis statement from "Watching TV Makes You Smarter" (pp. 213–30). How can you tell Stevens is not speaking for herself here, but rather is describing a view that she disagrees with? What metacommentary can you find that signals her intent?

2. What specific criticisms does Stevens make of the Johnson essay? Which one is most persuasive to you, and why?

3. While strongly disagreeing with Johnson's view that television viewing can be intellectually enriching, Stevens insists that she also does not like "the wet-blanket Puritanism of the anti-TV crowd," a position one could argue is repre-

sented in the reading by George F. Will (pp. 293–96). What exactly is Stevens's position?

4. How do you think Steven Johnson might answer Stevens's objections?

5. Write an essay taking your own stand on the intellectual merits of television, considering the arguments of Dana Stevens, Steven Johnson (pp. 213–30), and George F. Will (pp. 293–96), and framing your essay as a response to one of them.

What's the Matter with Kids Today?

AMY GOLDWASSER

**Nothing, actually. Aside from our panic
that the Internet is melting their brains.**

THE OTHER WEEK was only the latest takedown of what has
become a fashionable segment of the population to bash: the
American teenager. A phone (land line!) survey of 1,200
17-year-olds, conducted by the research organization Common
Core and released February 26, found our young people to be
living in "stunning ignorance" of history and literature.

This furthered the report that the National Endowment for
the Arts came out with at the end of 2007, lamenting "the
diminished role of voluntary reading in American life," particularly among 13- to 17-year-olds, and Doris Lessing's condemnation, in her acceptance speech for the Nobel Prize in

AMY GOLDWASSER is a freelance editor for *Vogue, Seventeen,* and the
New Yorker, among other publications, and teaches editing at the
Columbia Publishing Course. She is the editor of *Red: The Next Gen-
eration of American Writers—Teenage Girls—On What Fires Up Their Lives
Today,* a 2007 collection of essays by teenage girls from across the
United States. The piece included here first appeared in *Salon* in 2008.

literature, of "a fragmenting culture" in which "young men and women . . . have read nothing, knowing only some specialty or other, for instance, computers."

Kids today—we're telling you!—don't read, don't write, don't care about anything farther in front of them than their iPods. The Internet, according to 88-year-old Lessing (whose specialty is sturdy typewriters, or perhaps pens), has "seduced a whole generation into its inanities."

Or is it the older generation that the Internet has seduced— into the inanities of leveling charges based on fear, ignorance and old-media, multiple-choice testing? So much so that we can't see that the Internet is only a means of communication, and one that has created a generation, perhaps the first, of writers, activists, storytellers? When the world worked in hard copy, no parent or teacher ever begrudged teenagers who disappeared into their rooms to write letters to friends—or a movie review, or an editorial for the school paper on the first president they'll vote for. Even 15-year-old boys are sharing some part of their feelings with someone out there.

We're talking about 33 million Americans who are fluent 5 in texting, e-mailing, blogging, IM'ing and constantly amending their profiles on social network sites—which, on average, 30 of their friends will visit every day, hanging out and writing for 20 minutes or so each. They're connected, they're collaborative, they're used to writing about themselves. In fact, they choose to write about themselves, on their own time, rather than its being a forced labor when a paper's due in school. Regularly, often late at night, they're generating a body of intimate written work. They appreciate the value of a good story and the power of a speech that moves: Ninety-seven percent of the teenagers in the Common Core survey connected "I have a dream" with its speaker—they can watch Dr. King deliver it on demand—and eight in ten knew what *To Kill a Mockingbird* is about.

This is, of course, the kind of knowledge we should be encouraging. The Internet has turned teenagers into honest documentarians of their own lives—reporters embedded in their homes, their schools, their own heads.

But this is also why it's dangerous, why we can't seem to recognize that it's just a medium. We're afraid. Our kids know things we don't. They drove the presidential debates onto YouTube and very well may determine the outcome of this election. They're texting at the dinner table and responsible for pretty much every enduring consumer cultural phenomenon: iPod, iTunes, iPhone; Harry Potter, *High School Musical*; large hot drinks with gingerbread flavoring. They can sell ads on their social network pages, and they essentially made MySpace worth $580 million and *Juno* an Oscar winner.

Besides, we're tired of having to ask them every time we need to find Season 2 of *Heroes*, calculate a carbon footprint or upload photos to Facebook (now that we're allowed on).

Plus, they're blogging about us.

So we've made the Internet one more thing unknowable 10 about the American teenager, when, really, it's one of the few revelations. We conduct these surveys and overgeneralize—labeling like the mean girls, driven by the same jealousy and insecurity.

Common Core drew its multiple-choice questions for teens from a test administered by the federal government in 1986. Twenty-plus years ago, high school students didn't have the Internet to store their trivia. Now they know that the specific dates and what-was-that-prince's-name will always be there; they can free their brains to go a little deeper into the concepts instead of the copyrights, step back and consider what Scout and Atticus were really fighting for. To criticize teenagers' author-to-book title matching on the spot, over the phone, is similar to cold-calling over-40s and claiming their long-division skills or date of *Jaws* recall is rusty. This is what we all rely on the Internet for.

That's not to say some of the survey findings aren't disturbing. It's crushing to hear that one in four teens could not identify Adolf Hitler's role in world history, for instance. But it's not because teenagers were online that they missed this. Had a parent introduced 20 minutes of researching the Holocaust to one month of their teen's Internet life, or a teacher assigned *The Diary of Anne Frank* (arguably a 13-year-old girl's blog)— if we worked with, rather than against, the way this generation voluntarily takes in information—we might not be able to pick up the phone and expose tragic pockets of ignorance.

The average teen chooses to spend an average of 16.7 hours a week reading and writing online. Yet the NEA report did not consider this to be "voluntary" reading and writing. Its findings also concluded that "literary reading declined significantly in a period of rising Internet use." The corollary is weak—this has as well been a period of rising franchises of frozen yogurt that doesn't taste like frozen yogurt, of global warming, of declining rates of pregnancy and illicit drug use among teenagers, and of girls sweeping the country's most prestigious high school science competition for the first time.

Teenagers today read and write for fun; it's part of their social lives. We need to start celebrating this unprecedented surge, incorporating it as an educational tool instead of meeting it with punishing pop quizzes and suspicion.

We need to start trusting our kids to communicate as they 15 will online—even when that comes with the risk that they'll spill the family secrets or campaign for a candidate who's not ours.

Once we stop regarding the Internet as a villain, stop presenting it as the enemy of history and literature and worldly knowledge, then our teenagers have the potential to become the next great voices of America. One of them, 70 years from now, might even get up there to accept the very award Lessing did—and thank the Internet for making him or her a writer and a thinker.

Joining the Conversation

1. What is the view that Amy Goldwasser argues against, and what evidence does she offer in support of that view?

2. What is your reaction to the quotation from Nobel Prize–winning writer Doris Lessing, in paragraph 2? Why do you think Goldwasser quotes Lessing?

3. What benefits does Goldwasser attribute to young people's Internet use? What support does she provide for her position? Compare and contrast the learning benefits that Goldwasser says the Internet offers with what Steven Johnson says about the benefits of watching TV. How does each author seem to understand thinking and learning as they relate to our interactions with technology?

4. So who cares? Does Goldwasser make clear to her readers why this topic matters? What else could she say to make this point more effectively?

5. In paragraph 16, Goldwasser asserts, "Once we stop regarding the Internet as a villain, stop presenting it as the enemy of history and literature and worldly knowledge, then our teenagers have the potential to become the next great voices of America." Using this statement as a "they say," write your own essay in response to this assertion.

Bart Simpson: Prince of Irreverence

DOUGLAS RUSHKOFF

———◻———

THE SIMPSONS is the closest thing in America to a national media literacy program. By pretending to be a kids' cartoon, the show gets away with murder—that is, the virtual murder of our most coercive media iconography and techniques. What began as entertaining interstitial material for an alternative network variety show has revealed itself, in the twenty-first century, as nothing short of a media revolution.

The marginality of the show's origins may be the very reason *The Simpsons* works so well. The Simpson characters were born to provide *The Tracey Ullman Show* with a way of cutting to commercial breaks. Their very function as a form of media

DOUGLAS RUSHKOFF teaches media theory at New York University. According to his blog, he "focuses on the ways people, cultures, and institutions create, share, and influence each other's values," seeing " 'media' as the landscape where this interaction takes place, and 'literacy' as the ability to participate consciously in it." His books include *Open Source Democracy: How Online Communication Is Changing Offline Politics* (2003) and *Media Virus: Hidden Agendas in Popular Culture* (1996). The essay here was first published in *Leaving Springfield: The Simpsons and the Possibility of Oppositional Culture* (2004).

was to bridge the discontinuity inherent to broadcast television. They existed to pave over the breaks. Rather than dampening the effects of these gaps in the broadcast stream, however, they heightened them. They acknowledge the jagged edges and recombinant forms behind the glossy patina of American television, and by doing so, initiated its deconstruction.

Consider, for a moment, the way we thought of media before this cartoon family satirized us into consciousness. Media used to be a top-down affair. A few rich guys in suits sat in offices at the tops of tall buildings and decided which stories would be in the headlines or on the evening news and how they would be told.

As a result, we came to think of information as something fed to us from above. We counted on the editors of the *New York Times* to deliver "all the news that's fit to print," and Walter Cronkite to tell us "that's the way it was." We had no reason not to trust the editorial decisions of the media managers upon whom we depended to present, accurately, what was going on in the world around us. In fact, most of us did not even realize such decisions were being made at all. The television became America's unquestioned window to the world, as *The Simpsons'* opening sequence—which shows each family member rushing home to gather at the television set—plainly acknowledges.

But we call the stuff on television "programming" for a rea- 5
son. Television programmers are not programming television sets or evening schedules; they are programming the viewers. Whether they are convincing us to buy a product, vote for a candidate, adopt an ideology, or simply confirm a moral platitude, the underlying reason for making television is to hold onto our attention and then sell us a bill of goods. Since the time of the Bible and Aristotle through today's over-determined

three-act action movies, the best tool at the programmer's disposal has been the story. However, thanks to interactive technologies such as the remote control and cynical attitudes such as Bart Simpson's, the story just does not hold together anymore.

For the most part, television stories program their audiences by bringing them into a state of tension. The author creates a character we like and identify with and then puts that character in some sort of jeopardy. As the character moves up the incline plane toward crisis, we follow him vicariously, while taking on his anxiety as our own. Helplessly we follow him into danger, disease, or divorce, and just when we cannot take any more tension without bursting, our hero discovers a way out. He finds a moral, a product, an agenda, or a strategy—the one preferred by the screenwriter or program sponsor, of course— that rescues him from danger and his audience from the awful vicarious anxiety. Then, everyone lives happily ever after. This is what it means to "enter-tain"—literally "to hold within"— and it only works on a captive audience.

In the old days of television, when characters would get into danger, the viewer had little choice but to submit. To change the channel would have required getting up out of the La-Z-Boy chair, walking up to the television set, and turning the dial. Fifty calories of human effort; too much effort for a man of Homer's generation, anyway.

The remote control has changed all that. With an expenditure of, perhaps, .0001 calories, the anxious viewer is liberated from tortuous imprisonment and free to watch another program. Although most well-behaved adult viewers will soldier on through a story, children raised with remotes in their hands have much less reverence for well-crafted story arcs and zap away without a moment's hesitation. Instead of watching one program, they skim through ten at a time. They do not "watch TV," they watch the television itself, guiding their own paths through the entirety of media rather than following the prescribed course of any one programmer. No matter how much we complain about our children's short attention spans or even their Attention Deficit Disorders, their ability to disconnect from programming has released them from the hypnotic spell of even the best television mesmerizers.

The Nintendo-style joystick further empowered children while compounding the programmer's dilemma. In the old days, the television image was unchangeable, gospel truth piped into the home from the top of some glass building. Today, children have the experience of manipulating the image on the screen. This televisual interactivity has fundamentally altered their perception of and reverence for the television image. Just as the remote control allows viewers to deconstruct the television image, the joystick has demystified the pixel itself. The news-reader is just another middle-aged man manipulating his joy-stick. Hierarchy and authority are diminished, and the programmers' weapons neutralized. Sure, they might sit back and watch a program now and again—but they do so volun-tarily, and with full knowledge of their complicity. It is not an involuntary surrender.

A person who is doing rather than receiving is much less 10 easily provoked into a state of tension. The people I call "screenagers," those raised with interactive devices in their media arsenals, are natives in a media space where even the best television producers are immigrants. Like Bart Simpson, they speak the media language better than their parents do and they see through clumsy attempts to program them into submission. They never forget for a moment that they are watching media and they resent those who try to draw them in and sell them something. They will not be part of a "target market," at least not without a fight.

What kind of television, then, appeals to such an audience? Programs that celebrate the screenager's irreverence for the image while providing a new sort of narrative arc for the sponsor-wary audience. It is the ethos and behavior embodied by screenager role model and anti-hero Bart Simpson.

His name intended as an anagram for "brat," Bart embodies youth culture's ironic distance from media and its willingness to disassemble and resplice even the most sacred cultural and ideological constructs. From within the plastic safety of his incarnation as an animated character, Bart can do much more than simply watch and comment on media iconography. Once a media figure has entered his animated world, Bart can interact with it, satirize it, or even become it. Although *The Simpsons* began as a sideshow, these animated tidbits became more popular than the live-action portion of *The Tracey Ullman Show*, and Fox Television decided to give the Simpson family their own series. It is not coincidental that what began as a bridging device between a show and its commercials—a media paste—developed into a self-similar media pastiche.

The Simpsons' creator, comic-strip artist Matt Groening, has long understood how to mask his countercultural agenda: "I find you can get away with all sorts of unusual ideas if you present them with a smile on your face," he said in an early 1990s interview.[1] In fact, the show's mischievous ten-year-old protagonist is really just the screen presence of Groening's inner nature. For his self-portrait in a *Spin* magazine article, Groening simply drew a picture of Bart and then scribbled the likeness of his own glasses and beard over it. Bart functions as Matt Groening's "smile," and the child permits him—and the

The Simpsons

show's young, Harvard-educated writing staff—to get away with a hell of a lot. *The Simpsons* takes place in a town called Springfield, named after the fictional location of *Father Knows Best,* making it clear that the Simpson family is meant as a contemporary answer to the media reality presented to us in the fifties and sixties. *The Simpsons* is the American media family turned on its head, told from the point of view of not the smartest member of the family, but the most ironic. Audiences delight in watching Bart effortlessly outwit his parents, teachers, and local institutions. This show is so irreverent that it provoked an attack from the first president Bush, who pleaded for the American family to be more like the Waltons than the Simpsons. The show's writers quickly responded, letting Bart say during one episode, "Hey, man, we're just like the Waltons. Both families are praying for an end to the Depression." The show shares many of the viral features common in other

Father Knows Best

programs from the nineties. Murphy Brown's office dartboard, for example, was used as a meme slot; in each episode it had a different satirical note pinned to it. *The Simpsons'* writers also create little slots for the most attentive viewers to glean extra memes.[2] The opening credits always begin with Bart writing a different message on his classroom bulletin board and one of at least twenty-one different saxophone solos from his sister, Lisa.[3] Every episode has at least one film reenactment, usually from Hitchcock or Kubrick, to satirize an aspect of the modern cultural experience. In a spoof of modern American child care, writers re-created a scene from *The Birds*, except here, Homer Simpson rescued his baby daughter from a day-care center by passing through a playground of menacingly perched babies.

These media references form the basis for the show's role as a media literacy primer. The joy of traditional television storytelling is simply getting to the ending. The reward is making it through to the character's escape from danger. While most episodes of *The Simpsons* incorporate a dramatic nod to such storytelling convention, the screenagers watching the program could not care less about whether Principal Skinner gets married or if Homer finds his donut. These story arcs are there for the adult viewers only. No, the pleasure of watching *The Simpsons* for its media-literate (read: younger) viewers is the joy of pattern recognition. The show provides a succession of "aha" moments—those moments when we recognize which other forms of media are being parodied. We are rewarded with self-congratulatory laughter whenever we make a connection between the scene we are watching and the movie, commercial, or program on which it is based.

In this sense, *The Simpsons* deconstructs and informs the media soup of which it is a part. Rather than drawing us into the hypnotic spell of the traditional storyteller, the program invites us to make active and conscious comparisons of its own scenes with those of other, less transparent, media forms. By doing so, the show's writers help us in our efforts to develop immunity to their coercive effects.

The show's supervisors through *The Simpsons*' golden years of the mid-1990s, Mike Reiss and Al Jean, were both *Harvard Lampoon* veterans. When I met with them on the Fox lot, they told me how they delighted in animation's ability to serve as a platform for sophisticated social and media satire. "About two-thirds of the writers have been Harvard graduates," explained Jean, "so it's one of the most literate shows in TV."

Does this quotation need to be explained? See pp. 41–45 for tips on doing so.

"We take subjects on the show," added Reiss, who was Jean's classmate, "that we can parody. Homer goes to college or into a game show. We'll take Super Bowl Sunday, and then parody the Bud Bowl, and how merchants capitalize on the event." Having been raised on media themselves, the Diet Coke–drinking, baseball-jacketed pair gravitated toward parodying the media aspects of the subjects they pick. They did not comment on social issues as much as they did the media imagery around a particular social issue.

"These days television in general seems to be feeding on itself. Parodying itself," Jean told me. "Some of the most creative stuff we write comes from just having the Simpsons watch TV." Which they do often. Many episodes are still about what happens on the Simpsons' own television set, allowing the characters to feed off television, which itself is feeding off other television. In this self-reflexive circus, it is Bart who is least likely to be fooled by anything. His father, Homer, represents an earlier generation and can easily be manipulated by television commercials and publicity stunts such as "clear beer." "Homer certainly falls for every trick," admitted Reiss, "even believing the Publishers Clearing House mailing that he is a winner." When Homer acquires an illegal cable television hookup, he became so addicted to the tube that he almost dies ("Homer vs. Lisa and the 8th Commandment"). Lisa, the brilliant member of the family, maintains a faith in the social institutions of her world, works hard to get good grades in school, and even entered and won a *Reader's Digest* essay contest about patriotism.

"But Lisa feels completely alienated by the media around her," Jean warned me. "The writers empathize with her more than any other character. She has a more intellectual reaction to how disquieting her life has become. When Homer believes he may die from a heart attack, he tells the children, 'I have some terrible news.' Lisa answers, 'Oh, we can take anything. We're the MTV generation. We feel neither highs nor lows.' Homer asks what it's like, and she just goes 'Eh.' It was right out there."

Bart's reaction to his cultural alienation, on the other hand, is much more of a lesson in Gen X* strategy. Bart is a ten-year-old media strategist—or at least an unconscious media manipulator—and his exploits reveal the complexity of the current pop media from the inside out. In one episode ("Radio Bart")—the show that earned Reiss and Jean their first Emmy nomination—Homer sees a commercial for a product he feels will make a great birthday gift for Bart: a microphone that can be used to broadcast to a special radio from many feet away (a parody of a toy called Mr. Microphone). At first, Bart is bored with the gift and plays with a labeler he also received instead. Bart has fun renaming things and leaving messages like "property of Bart Simpson" on every object in his home; one such label on a beer in the fridge convinces Homer that the can is off limits. Bart's joy, clearly, is media . . . and subversive disinformation.

Homer plays with the radio instead, trying to get Bart's interest, but the boy knows the toy does not really send messages into the mediaspace; it only broadcasts to one little radio. Bart finally takes interest in the toy when he realizes its subversive value. After playing several smaller-scale pranks, he accidentally drops the radio down a well and gets the idea for his master plan. Co-opting a media event out of real history, when a little girl struggled for life at the bottom of a well as rescuers worked to save her and the world listened via radio, Bart uses his toy radio to fool the world and launch his own media virus.[4]

*Gen X Describes people born between ca. 1965 and 1980.

He creates a little boy named Timmy O'Toole, who cries for help from the bottom of the well. When police and rescuers prove too fat to get into the well to rescue the boy, a tremendous media event develops. News teams set up camp around the well, much in the fashion they gather around any real-world media event such as the OJ Trial* or Waco† standoff. They conduct interviews with the unseen Timmy—an opportunity Bart exploits to make political progress against his mean school principal. In Timmy's voice he tells reporters the story of how he came to fall into the well: he is an orphan, new to the neighborhood, and was rejected for admission to the local school by the principal because his clothes were too shabby. The next day, front-page stories calling for the principal's dismissal appear. Eventually, the virus grows to the point where the real-world pop musician, Sting, and Krusty the Klown, a television personality from within the world of *The Simpsons*, record an aid song and video to raise money for the Timmy O'Toole cause called "We're Sending Our Love Down the Well." The song hits number one on the charts.

So Bart, by unconsciously exploiting a do-it-yourself media toy to launch viruses, feeds back to mainstream culture. He does this both as a character in Springfield, USA, and as a media icon in our datasphere, satirizing the real Sting's charity recordings. The character Bart gets revenge against his principal and enjoys a terrific prank. The icon Bart conducts a lesson in

*OJ Trial   In the mid-1990s, former football star O.J. Simpson was tried and acquitted in the murder of his ex-wife, Nicole Simpson, and her friend Ron Goldman.

†Waco   Refers to the 1993 assault by federal authorities on a compound housing members of an extreme Christian sect, the Branch Davidians, suspected of abusing children in the compound. Seventy-six church members were killed in the assault.

advanced media activism. Most important, it is through Bart that the writers of *The Simpsons* are enabled to voice their own, more self-conscious comments on the media.

Finally, Bart remembers that he has put a label on his radio toy, earmarking it "property of Bart Simpson." He decides he better get the radio out of the well before it, and his own identity, are discovered. In his attempt to get the damning evidence out from the bottom of the well, however, Bart really does fall in. He calls for help, admitting what he has done. Once there is a real child in the well, however, and one who had attempted to play a prank on the media at that, everyone loses interest in the tragedy. The virus is blown. The Sting song plummets on the charts, and the television news crews pack up and leave. It is left to Bart's mom and dad to dig him out by hand. In our current self-fed media, according to the writers of *The Simpsons*, a real event can have much less impact than a constructed virus, especially when its intention is revealed.

No matter how activist the show appears, its creators insist 25 that they have no particular agenda. Reiss insisted he promoted no point of view on any issue. In fact, he claimed to have picked the show's subjects and targets almost randomly: "The show eats up so much material that we're constantly just stoking it like a furnace when we parody a lot of movies and TV. And now so many of our writers are themselves the children of TV writers. There's already a second generation rolling in of people who not only watched TV but watched tons of it. And this is our mass culture. Where everyone used to know the catechism, now they all know episodes of *The Twilight Zone*, our common frame of reference."

Reiss was being deceptively casual. Even if he and the other writers claim to have no particular agenda—which is debatable—they readily admit to serving the media machine as a whole. As writers, they see themselves as "feeding" the show and using other media references as the fodder. It is as if the show is a living thing, consuming media culture, recombining it, and spitting it out as second-generation media, with a spin.

Even Bart is in on the gag. In one episode ("So It's Come to This: A Simpsons Clip Show"), when Homer is in the hospital, the family stands around his sickbed recalling incidents from the past, leading to a satire of the flashback format used by shows to create a new episode out of "greatest hit" scenes from old ones. As the family reminisces together about past events, Bart raises a seeming non sequitur. His mother, Marge, asks him, "Why did you bring that up?" "It was an amusing episode," replies Bart, half looking at the camera, before he quickly adds, "of our . . . lives." Bart knows he is on a television show and knows the kinds of tricks his own writers use to fill up airtime.

Such self-consciousness allows *The Simpsons* to serve as a lesson in modern media discontinuity. Bart skateboards through each episode, demonstrating the necessary ironic detachment needed to move through increasingly disorienting edits. "It's animation," explained Jean, who has since returned to writing for the program. "It's very segmented, so we just lift things in and out. If you watch an old episode of *I Love Lucy*, you'll find it laborious because they take so long to set something up. The thesis of *The Simpsons* is nihilism. There's nothing to believe in anymore once you assume that organized structures and institutions are out to get you."

"Right," chimed in Reiss, finally admitting to an agenda. "The overarching point is that the media's stupid and manipulative, TV is narcotic, and all big institutions are corrupt and evil." These writers make their points both in the plots of the particular episodes and in the cut-and-paste style of the show. By deconstructing and reframing the images in our media, they allow us to see them more objectively, or at least with more ironic distance. They encourage us to question the ways institutional forces are presented to us through the media and urge us to see the fickle nature of our own responses. Figures from the television world are represented as cartoon characters not just to accentuate certain features, but also to allow for total recontextualization of their identities. These are not simple caricatures, but pop cultural samples, juxtaposed in order to illuminate the way they affect us.

As writers and producers, Reiss and Jean served almost as "channels" for the media as received through their own attitudinal filters. While they experience their function as simply to "stoke the furnace," the media images they choose to dissemble are the ones they feel *need* to be exposed and criticized.

Reiss admitted to me, "I feel that in this way *The Simpsons* is the ultimate of what you call a media virus. It sounds a little insidious because I have kids of my own, and the reason we're a hit is because so many kids watch us and make us a huge enterprise. But we're feeding them a lot of ideas and notions that they didn't sign on for. That's not what they're watching for. We all come from this background of comedy that has never been big and popular—it's this Letterman school or *Saturday Night Live*, *Harvard Lampoon*, *National Lampoon*. We used to be there, too."

The Simpsons provided its writers with a durable viral shell for their most irreverent memes: "It's as though we finally found a vehicle for this sensibility, where we can do the kind of humor and the attitudes, yet in a package that more people are willing to embrace. I think if it were a live-action show, it wouldn't be a hit," Reiss concluded quite accurately.

Like a Trojan Horse, *The Simpsons* sneaks into our homes looking like one thing, before releasing something else, far different, into our lives.

Notes

1. *Spin* Jan. 1993: 55.

2. "Memes" are the geneticist Richard Dawkins's term for bits of ideological and conceptual code within cultural systems analogous to the roles of genes in the transmission and evolution of biological information. See Dawkins, "Universal Parasitism and the Co-Evolution of Extended Phenotypes," *Whole Earth Review* 62 (Spring 1989): 90–99.

3. Chad Lehman describes the solos on *The Simpsons Archive* website (April 15, 2002, http://www.snpp.com/guides/sololist.html). The solos are performed by saxophonist Terry Harrington (*The Simpsons Archive*, April 15, 2002, http://www.snpp.com/guides/lisa-4.html#4.1.7]).

4. "Media virus" refers to the central theoretical concept of the book from which this essay is derived. Rushkoff defines media viruses as "media events provoking real social change" by acting like biological viruses, which use the cover and protection of a protein shell to inject rogue DNA into the cells of the host organism. Similarly, media viruses use the "protein shell" of a media event, whether spontaneous or manufactured (examples range from Rodney King* and OJ Simpson to *The Simpsons*) to inject "ideological code" into the media culture. As in a biological host, the media virus starts with a single media event but eventually affects the entire cultural system. See *Media Virus! Hidden Agendas in Popular Culture* (New York: Ballantine Books, 1996), 9.

Joining the Conversation

1. Douglas Rushkoff claims in his opening paragraph that "*The Simpsons* is the closest thing in America to a national media

Rodney King An African American man who was beaten by Los Angeles police after a high-speed chase in 1991. The incident was caught on videotape, sparking public outrage.

literacy program" and describes the show as "nothing short of a media revolution." What features of the cartoon is he referring to in these two slightly different claims? How, according to Rushkoff, do they make the show so influential and different from previous programming?

2. The first sentence of this essay says clearly what Rushkoff wants to argue about *The Simpsons*, but he doesn't spell out what view he is responding to. What unstated view do you think he's arguing against? Write out a sentence or two summarizing the "they say."

3. Rushkoff is writing *about* young people (or, as he puts it, "screenagers") but not necessarily *for* an audience of young people. Who would you say is the audience he is writing for? How do you think this essay might be different—in its language, its tone, and its arguments—if Rushkoff were writing primarily for young viewers of *The Simpsons*?

4. What happens in the long example of the episode where Bart acts as a "media manipulator" and creates a scenario in which a little boy has supposedly fallen down a well? How does this example illustrate Rushkoff's larger argument about the significance of the show?

5. Choose a television show that you and your peers watch regularly, and write an essay in which you give your view of what makes it so popular.

Family Guy and Freud:
Jokes and Their Relation
to the Unconscious

ANTONIA PEACOCKE

—⊡—

WHILE SLOUCHING IN FRONT of the television after a long day, you probably don't think a lot about famous psychologists of the twentieth century. Somehow, these figures don't come up often in prime-time—or even daytime—TV programming. Whether you're watching *Living Lohan* or the *NewsHour*, the likelihood is that you are not thinking of Sigmund Freud, even if you've heard of his book *Jokes and Their Relation to the Unconscious*. I say that you should be.

What made me think of Freud in the first place, actually, was *Family Guy*, the cartoon created by Seth MacFarlane.

ANTONIA PEACOCKE is a student at Harvard University, where she plans to study physics. She was born in London and moved to New York at age 10, on exactly the same day that the fourth Harry Potter book came out. She's always loved writing and worked as a copy editor and columnist for her high school newspaper—and received the Catherine Fairfax MacRae Prize for Excellence in Both English and Mathematics. A National Merit Scholar, she wrote the essay here specifically for this book.

(Seriously—stay with me here.) Any of my friends can tell you that this program holds endless fascination for me; as a matter of fact, my high school rag-sheet "perfect mate" was the baby Stewie Griffin, a character on the show. Embarrassingly enough, I have almost reached the point at which I can perform one-woman versions of several episodes. I know every website that streams the show for free, and I still refuse to return the five *Family Guy* DVDs a friend lent me in 2006. Before I was such a devotee, however, I was adamantly opposed to the program for its particular brand of humor.

It will come as no surprise that I was not alone in this view; many still denounce *Family Guy* as bigoted and crude. *New York Times* journalist Stuart Elliott claimed just this year that "the characters on the Fox television series *Family Guy* . . . purposely offen[d] just about every group of people you could name." Likewise Stephen Dubner, co-author of *Freakonomics*, called *Family Guy* "a cartoon comedy that packs more gags per minute about race, sex, incest, bestiality, etc. than any other show [he] can think of." Comparing its level of offense to that of Don Imus's infamous comments about the Rutgers women's basketball team in the same year, comments that threw the popular CBS radio talk-show host off the air, Dubner said he wondered why Imus couldn't get away with as much as *Family Guy* could.

Dubner did not know about all the trouble *Family Guy* has had. In fact, it must be one of the few television shows in history that has been canceled not just once, but twice. After its premiere in April 1999, the show ran until August 2000, but was besieged by so many complaints, some of them from Mac-Farlane's old high school headmaster, Rev. Richardson W. Schell, that Fox shelved it until July 2001 (Weinraub). Still

Peter and Stewie Griffin

afraid of causing a commotion, though, Fox had the cartoon
censored and irregularly scheduled; as a result, its ratings fell so
low that 2002 saw its second cancellation (Weinraub). But then
it came back with a vengeance—I'll get into that later.

Family Guy has found trouble more recently, too. In 2007 5
comedian Carol Burnett sued Fox for 6 million dollars, claiming that the show's parody of the Charwoman, a character that
she had created for *The Carol Burnett Show*, not only violated
copyright but also besmirched the character's name in revenge
for Burnett's refusal to grant permission to use her theme song
("Carol Burnett Sues over *Family Guy* Parody"). The suit came
after MacFarlane had made the Charwoman into a cleaning
woman for a pornography store in one episode of *Family Guy*.
Burnett lost, but U.S. district judge Dean Pregerson agreed that

he could "fully appreciate how distasteful and offensive the segment [was] to Ms. Burnett" (qtd. in Grossberg).

I must admit, I can see how parts of the show might seem offensive if taken at face value. Look, for example, at the mock fifties instructional video that features in the episode "I Am Peter, Hear Me Roar."

[*The screen becomes black and white. Vapid music plays in the background. The screen reads "*WOMEN IN THE WORKPLACE *ca. 1956," then switches to a shot of an office with various women working on typewriters. A businessman speaks to the camera.*]

BUSINESSMAN: Irrational and emotionally fragile by nature, female coworkers are a peculiar animal. They are very insecure about their appearance. Be sure to tell them how good they look every day, even if they're homely and unkempt. [*He turns to an unattractive female typist.*] You're doing a great job, Muriel, and you're prettier than Mamie van Doren! [*She smiles. He grins at the camera, raising one eyebrow knowingly, and winks.*] And remember, nothing says "Good job!" like a firm open-palm slap on the behind. [*He walks past a woman bent over a file cabinet and demonstrates enthusiastically. She smiles, looking flattered. He grins at the camera again as the music comes to an end.*]

Laughing at something so blatantly sexist could cause anyone a pang of guilt, and before I thought more about the show this seemed to be a huge problem. I agreed with Dubner, and I failed to see how anyone could laugh at such jokes without feeling at least slightly ashamed.

Soon, though, I found myself forced to give *Family Guy* a chance. It was simply everywhere: my brother and many of my friends watched it religiously, and its devoted fans relentlessly proselytized for it. In case you have any doubts about its immense popularity, consider these facts. On Facebook, the universal forum for my generation, there are currently 23 separate *Family Guy* fan groups with a combined membership of 1,669 people (compared with only 6 groups protesting against *Family Guy*, with 105 members total). Users of the well-respected Internet Movie Database rate the show 8.8 out of 10. The box-set DVDs were the best-selling television DVDs of 2003 in the United States (Moloney). Among the public and within the industry, the show receives fantastic acclaim; it has won eight awards, including three primetime Emmys (IMDb). Most importantly, each time it was cancelled fans provided the brute force necessary to get it back on the air. In 2000, online campaigns did the trick; in 2002, devotees demonstrated outside Fox Studios, refused to watch the Fox network, and boycotted any companies that advertised on it (Moloney). Given the show's high profile, both with my friends and family and in the world at large, it would have been more work for me to avoid the Griffin family than to let myself sink into their animated world.

With more exposure, I found myself crafting a more positive view of *Family Guy*. Those who don't often watch the program, as Dubner admits he doesn't, could easily come to think that the cartoon takes pleasure in controversial humor just for its own sake. But those who pay more attention and think about the creators' intentions can see that *Family Guy* intelligently satirizes some aspects of American culture.

Some of this satire is actually quite obvious. Take, for instance, a quip Brian the dog makes about Stewie's literary choices in a fourth-season episode, "PTV." (Never mind that a dog and a baby can both read and hold lengthy conversations.)

[The Griffins are in their car. Brian turns to Stewie, who sits reading in his car seat.]

BRIAN: *East of Eden?* So you, you, you pretty much do whatever Oprah tells you to, huh?

STEWIE: You know, this book's been around for fifty years. It's a classic.

BRIAN: But you just got it last week. And there's a giant Oprah sticker on the front.

STEWIE: Oh—oh—oh, is that what that is? Oh, lemme just peel that right off.

BRIAN: So, uh, what are you gonna read after that one?

STEWIE: Well, she hasn't told us yet—damn!

Brian and Stewie demonstrate insightfully and comically how Americans are willing to follow the instructions of a celebrity blindly—and less willing to admit that they are doing so.

The more off-color jokes, though, those that give *Family Guy* 10 a bad name, attract a different kind of viewer. Such viewers are not "rats in a behaviorist's maze," as *Slate* writer Dana Stevens labels modern American television consumers in her article "Thinking Outside the Idiot Box." They are conscious and critical viewers, akin to the "screenagers" identified by Douglas Rushkoff in an essay entitled "Bart Simpson: Prince of Irreverence" (294). They are not—and this I cannot stress enough, self-serving as it may seem—immoral or easily manipulated people.

Rushkoff's piece analyzes the humor of *The Simpsons*, a show criticized for many of the same reasons as *Family Guy*. "The people I call 'screenagers,'" Rushkoff explains, " . . . speak the media language better than their parents do and they see through clumsy attempts to program them into submission" (294). He claims that gaming technology has made my generation realize that television is programmed for us with certain intentions; since we can control characters in the virtual world, we are more aware that characters on TV are similarly controlled. "Sure, [these 'screenagers'] might sit back and watch a program now and again," Rushkoff explains, "but they do so voluntarily, and with full knowledge of their complicity. It is not an involuntary surrender" (294). In his opinion, our critical eyes and our unwillingness to be programmed by the programmers make for an entirely new relationship with the shows we watch. Thus we enjoy *The Simpsons'* parodies of mass media culture since we are skeptical of it ourselves.

Rushkoff's argument about *The Simpsons* actually applies to *Family Guy* as well, except in one dimension: Rushkoff writes that *The Simpsons'* creators do "not comment on social issues as much as they [do on] the media imagery around a particular social issue" (296). MacFarlane and company seem to do the reverse. Trusting in their viewers' ability to analyze what they are watching, the creators of *Family Guy* point out the weaknesses and defects of U.S. society in a mocking and sometimes intolerant way.

Taken in this light, the "instructional video" quoted above becomes not only funny but also insightful. In its satire, viewers can recognize the sickly sweet and falsely sensitive sexism of the 1950s in observing just how conveniently self-serving the speaker of the video appears. The message of the clip denounces and ridicules sexism rather than condoning it. It is an excerpt that perfectly exemplifies the bold-faced candor of the show, from which it derives a lot of its appeal.

Making such comically outrageous remarks on the air also serves to expose certain prejudiced attitudes as outrageous themselves. Taking these comments at face value would be as foolish as taking Jonathan Swift's "Modest Proposal" seriously. Furthermore, while they put bigoted words into the mouths of their characters, the show's writers cannot be accused of portraying these characters positively. Peter Griffin, the "family guy" of the show's title, probably says and does the most offensive things of all—but as a lazy, overweight, and insensitive failure of a man, he is hardly presented as someone to admire. Nobody in his or her right mind would observe Peter's behavior and deem it worth emulation.

Family Guy has its own responses to accusations of crudity. 15 In the episode "PTV," Peter sets up his own television station broadcasting from home and the Griffin family finds itself confronting the Federal Communications Commission directly. The episode makes many tongue-in-cheek jabs at the FCC, some of which are sung in a rousing musical number, but also sneaks in some of the creator's own opinions. The plot comes to a climax when the FCC begins to censor "real life" in the town of Quahog; officials place black censor bars in front of newly showered Griffins and blow foghorns whenever characters curse. MacFarlane makes an important point: that no amount of television censorship will ever change the harsh nature of reality—and to censor reality is mere folly. Likewise, he puts explicit arguments about censorship into lines spoken by his characters, as when Brian says that "responsibility lies with the parents [and] there are plenty of things that are much worse for children than television."

It must be said too that not all of *Family Guy*'s humor could be construed as offensive. Some of its jokes are more tame and insightful, the kind you might expect from the *New Yorker*. The following light commentary on the usefulness of high school algebra from "When You Wish Upon a Weinstein" could hardly be accused of upsetting anyone—except, perhaps, a few high school math teachers.

[*Shot of Peter on the couch and his son Chris lying at his feet and doing homework.*]

CHRIS: Dad, can you help me with my math? [My teacher] says if I don't learn it, I won't be able to function in the real world.

[*Shot of Chris standing holding a map in a run-down gas station next to an attendant in overalls and a trucker cap reading "*PUMP THIS.*" The attendant speaks with a Southern accent and gestures casually to show the different road configurations.*]

ATTENDANT: Okay, now what you gotta do is go down the road past the old Johnson place, and you're gonna find two roads, one parallel and one perpendicular. Now keep going until you come to a highway that bisects it at a 45-degree angle. [*Crosses his arms.*] Solve for x.

[*Shot of Chris lying on the ground next to the attendant in fetal position, sucking his thumb. His map lies abandoned near him.*]

In fact, *Family Guy* does not aim to hurt, and its creators take certain measures to keep it from hitting too hard. In an interview on *Access Hollywood*, Seth MacFarlane plainly states that there are certain jokes too upsetting to certain groups to go on the air. Similarly, to ensure that the easily misunderstood show doesn't fall into the hands of those too young to understand it, Fox will not license *Family Guy* rights to any products intended for children under the age of fourteen (Elliott).

However, this is not to say that MacFarlane's mission is corrective or noble. It is worth remembering that he wants only to amuse, a goal for which he was criticized by several of his professors at the Rhode Island School of Design (Weinraub).

For this reason, his humor can be dangerous. On the one hand, I don't agree with George Will's reductive and generalized statement in his article "Reality Television: Oxymoron" that "entertainment seeking a mass audience is ratcheting up the violence, sexuality, and degradation, becoming increasingly coarse and trying to be . . . shocking in an unshockable society." I believe *Family Guy* has its intelligent points, and some of its seemingly "coarse" scenes often have hidden merit. I must concede, though, that a few of the show's scenes seem to be doing just what Will claims; sometimes the creators do seem to cross— or, perhaps, eagerly race past—the line of indecency. In one such crude scene, an elderly dog slowly races a paraplegic and Peter, who has just been hit by a car, to get to a severed finger belonging to Peter himself ("Whistle While Your Wife Works"). Nor do I find it particularly funny when Stewie physically abuses Brian in a bloody fight over gambling money ("Patriot Games").

Thus, while *Family Guy* can provide a sort of relief by breaking down taboos, we must still wonder whether or not these taboos exist for a reason. An excess of offensive jokes, especially those that are often misconstrued, can seem to grant tacit permission to think offensively if it's done for comedy—and laughing at others' expense can be cruel, no matter how funny. Jokes all have their origins, and the funniest ones are those that hit home the hardest; if we listen to Freud, these are the ones that let our animalistic and aggressive impulses surface from the unconscious. The distinction between a shamelessly candid but insightful joke and a merely shameless joke is a slight but important one. While I love *Family Guy* as much as any fan, it's important not to lose sight of what's truly unfunny in real life— even as we appreciate what is hilarious in fiction.

The Griffin family watches TV.

Works Cited

"Carol Burnett Sues over *Family Guy* Parody." *Canadian Broadcasting Centre* 16 Mar. 2007. 14 July 2008 <http://www.cbc.ca/arts/tv/story/2007/03/16/burnett-sues.html>.

Dubner, Stephen J. "Why Is *Family Guy* Okay When Imus Wasn't?" Web log post. *Freakonomics: The Hidden Side of Everything* 3 Dec. 2007. 14 July 2008 <http://freakonomics.blogs.nytimes.com/2007/12/03/why-is-family-guy-okay-when-imus-wasnt>.

Elliott, Stuart. "Crude? So What? These Characters Still Find Work in Ads." *New York Times Online* 18 June 2008. 14 July 2008 <http://www.nytimes.com/2008/06/18/business/media/18adco.html>.

Facebook. Search for *Family Guy* under "Groups." 14 July 2008 <http://www.facebook.com>.

Freud, Sigmund. *Jokes and Their Relation to the Unconscious*. 1905. Trans. James Strachey. New York: Norton. 1989.

Grossberg, Josh. "Carol Burnett Can't Stop Stewie." *E! News* 5 June 2007. 14 Jul. 2008 <http://www.eonline.com/news/article/index>.

"I Am Peter, Hear Me Roar." *Family Guy*. Prod. Seth MacFarlane. Twentieth Century Fox. 28 Mar. 2000. 14 July 2008 <http://www.familyguy.com>.

Internet Movie Database. *Family Guy*. Ed. unknown. Last update date unknown. 14 July 2008 <http://www.imdb.com/title/tt0182576>.

MacFarlane, Seth. Interview. *Access Hollywood*. Online posting on YouTube. 8 May 2007. 14 July 2008 <http://www.youtube.com/watch?v=rKURWCicyQU>.

Moloney, Ben Adam. "*Family Guy*—The TV Series." British Broadcasting Corporation. 30 Sept. 2004. 14 Jul. 2008 <http://www.bbc.co.uk/dna/h2g2/A2982369>.

"Patriot Games." *Family Guy*. Prod. Seth MacFarlane. Twentieth Century Fox. 29 Jan. 2006. 22 July 2008 <http://www.familyguy.com>.

"PTV." *Family Guy*. Prod. Seth MacFarlane. Twentieth Century Fox. 6 Nov. 2005. 14 July 2008 <http://www.familyguy.com>.

Rushkoff, Douglas. "Bart Simpson: Prince of Irreverence." *Leaving Springfield: The Simpsons and the Possibility of Oppositional Culture*. Ed. John Alberti. Detroit: Wayne State UP, 2004. 292–301.

Stevens, Dana. "Thinking Outside the Idiot Box." *Slate* 25 Mar. 2005. 14 Jul. 2008 <http://www.slate.com/id/2117395>.

Weinraub, Bernard. "The Young Guy of 'Family Guy': A 30-Year-Old's Cartoon Hit Makes an Unexpected Comeback." *New York Times Online* 7 Jul. 2004. 14 July 2008 <http://query.nytimes.com/gst/fullpage.html>.

"When You Wish Upon a Weinstein." *Family Guy*. Prod. Seth MacFarlane. Twentieth Century Fox. 9 Nov. 2003. 22 July 2008 <http://www.familyguy.com>.

"Whistle While Your Wife Works." *Family Guy*. Prod. Seth MacFarlane. Twentieth Century Fox. 12 Nov. 2006. 14 July 2008 <http://www.familyguy.com>.

Will, George F. "Reality Television: Oxymoron." *Washington Post* 21 June 2001. A25.

Joining the Conversation

1. How would you characterize Antonia Peacocke's argument about the television cartoon *Family Guy*? What does she like about the show? What doesn't she like? What would you say is her overall opinion of *Family Guy*?

2. Find two places in the essay where Peacocke puts forward arguments that she herself disagrees with. Analyze what she says about these arguments. What would you say are her reasons for including these opposing views?

3. While making a serious argument, Peacocke frequently uses humor to make her points. Identify two or three examples where she does so, and explain the role that such humor plays in helping her develop her argument.

4. Peacocke cites a number of authors with selections in this chapter, including Dana Stevens, Douglas Rushkoff, and George Will. How does she weave their ideas in with her own ideas? How fairly does she represent their views?

5. Some might see Peacocke's essay as proof of Gerald Graff's argument in "Hidden Intellectualism" (pp. 297–305) that pop culture can be a subject for serious intellectual analysis. Write an essay on this topic, using Peacocke's essay either to support or to refute Graff's argument.

Can You Hear Me Now?

SHERRY TURKLE

—☐—

Thanks to technology, people have never been more connected—or more alienated.

I HAVE TRAVELED 36 hours to a conference on robotic technology in central Japan. The grand ballroom is WI-FI enabled, and the speaker is using the Web for his presentation. Laptops are open, fingers are flying. But the audience is not listening. Most seem to be doing their e-mail, downloading files, surfing the Web, or looking for a cartoon to illustrate an upcoming presentation. Every once in a while audience members give the speaker some attention, lowering their laptop screens in a kind of digital curtsy.

SHERRY TURKLE is a professor of the social studies of science and technology at MIT and the founder and current director of the MIT Initiative on Technology and Self, a center of research on the evolving connections between people and artifacts. She has written several books, among them *The Second Self: Computers and the Human Spirit* (1984) and *Evocative Objects: Things We Think With* (2007). The piece included here was first published in *Forbes* magazine in 2007.

In the hallway outside the plenary session attendees are on their phones or using laptops and PDAs to check their e-mail. Clusters of people chat with each other, making dinner plans, "networking" in that old sense of the term—the sense that implies sharing a meal. But at this conference it is clear that what people mostly want from public space is to be alone with their personal networks. It is good to come together physically, but it is more important to stay tethered to the people who define one's virtual identity, the identity that counts. I think of how Freud believed in the power of communities to control and subvert us, and a psychoanalytic pun comes to mind: "virtuality and its discontents."

The phrase comes back to me months later as I interview business consultants who seem to have lost touch with their best instincts for how to maintain the bonds that make them most competitive. They are complaining about the BlackBerry revolution. They accept it as inevitable, decry it as corrosive. Consultants used to talk to one another as they waited to give presentations; now they spend that time doing e-mail. Those who once bonded during limousine rides to airports now spend this time on their BlackBerrys. Some say they are making better use of their "downtime," but they argue their point without conviction. This waiting time and going-to-the-airport time was never downtime; it was work time. It was precious time when far-flung global teams solidified relationships and refined ideas.

We live in techno-enthusiastic times, and we are most likely to celebrate our gadgets. Certainly the advertising that sells us our devices has us working from beautiful, remote locations that signal our status. We are connected, tethered, so important that our physical presence is no longer required. There is much talk of new efficiencies; we can work from anywhere and all the time. But tethered life is complex; it is helpful to measure our thrilling new networks against what they may be doing to us as people.

Here I offer five troubles that try my tethered soul.   5

There Is a New State of the Self, Itself

By the 1990s the Internet provided spaces for the projection of self. Through online games known as Multi-User Domains, one was able to create avatars that could be deployed into virtual lives. Although the games often took the forms of medieval quests, players admitted that virtual environments owed their holding power to the opportunities they offered for exploring identity. The plain represented themselves as glamorous; the introverted could try out being bold. People built the dream houses in the virtual that they could not afford in the real. They took online jobs of responsibility. They often had relationships, partners, and even "marriages" of significant emotional importance. They had lots of virtual sex.

These days it is easier for people without technical expertise to blend their real and virtual lives. In the world of Second Life, a virtual world produced by Linden Lab, you can make real money; you can run a real business. Indeed, for many who enjoy online life, it is easier to express intimacy in the virtual world than in rl, that being real life. For those who are lonely yet fearful of intimacy, online life provides environments where one can be a loner yet not alone, have the illusion of companionship without the demands of sustained, intimate friendship.

Since the late 1990s social computing has offered an opportunity to experiment with a virtual second self. Now this metaphor doesn't go far enough. Our new online intimacies create a world in which it makes sense to speak of a new state of the self, itself. "I am on my cell . . . online . . . instant messaging . . . on the Web"—these phrases suggest a new placement of the subject, wired into society through technology.

Are We Losing the Time to Take Our Time?

The self that grows up with multitasking and rapid response measures success by calls made, e-mails answered, and messages responded to. Self-esteem is calibrated by what the technology proposes, by what it makes easy. We live a contradiction: Insisting that our world is increasingly complex, we nevertheless have created a communications culture that has decreased the time available for us to sit and think, uninterrupted. We are primed to receive a quick message to which we are expected to give a rapid response. Children growing up with this may never know another way. Their experience raises a question for us all: Are we leaving enough time to take our time on the things that matter?

We spend hours keeping up with our e-mails. One person 10 tells me, "I look at my watch to see the time. I look at my BlackBerry to get a sense of my life." Think of the BlackBerry user watching the BlackBerry movie of his life as someone watching a movie that takes on a life of its own. People become alienated from their own experience and anxious about watching a version of their lives scrolling along faster than they can handle. They are not able to keep up with the unedited version of their lives, but they are responsible for it. People speak of BlackBerry addiction. Yet in modern life we have been made into self-disciplined souls who mind the rules, the time, our tasks. Always-on/always-on-you technology takes the job of self-monitoring to a new level.

BlackBerry users describe that sense of encroachment of the device on their time. One says, "I don't have enough time alone with my mind"; another, "I artificially make time to think." Such formulations depend on an "I" separate from the technology, a self that can put the technology aside so as to function apart from its demands. But it's in conflict with a growing reality of lives lived in the presence of screens, whether on a laptop, palmtop, cell phone, or BlackBerry. We are learning to see ourselves as cyborgs, at one with our devices. To put it most starkly: To make more time means turning off our devices, disengaging from the always-on culture. But this is not a simple proposition, since our devices have become more closely coupled to our sense of our bodies and increasingly feel like extensions of our minds.

Our tethering devices provide a social and psychological Global Positioning System, a form of navigation for tethered selves. One television producer, accustomed to being linked to the world via her cell and Palm handheld, revealed that for her, the Palm's inner spaces were where her self resides: "When my Palm crashed it was like a death. It was more than I could handle. I felt as though I had lost my mind."

The Tethered Adolescent

Kids get cell phones from their parents. In return they are expected to answer their parents' calls. On the one hand this arrangement gives teenagers new freedoms. On the other they do not have the experience of being alone and having to count on themselves; there is always a parent on speed dial. This provides comfort in a dangerous world, yet there is a price to pay in the development of autonomy. There used to be a moment in the life of an urban child, usually between the ages of 12 and 14, when there was a first time to navigate the city alone. It was a rite of passage that communicated, "You are on your own and responsible. If you feel frightened, you have to experience these feelings." The cell phone tether buffers this moment; with the parents on tap, children think differently about themselves.

Adolescents naturally want to check out ideas and attitudes with peers. But when technology brings us to the point where we're used to sharing thoughts and feelings instantaneously, it can lead to a new dependence. Emotional life can move from "I have a feeling, I want to call a friend," to "I want to feel something, I need to make a call." In either case it comes at the expense of cultivating the ability to be alone and to manage and contain one's emotions.

And what of adolescence as a time of self-reflection? We 15 communicate with instant messages, "check-in" cell calls, and emoticons. All of these are meant to quickly communicate a state. They are not intended to open a dialogue about complexity of feeling. (Technological determinism has its place here: Cell calls get poor reception, are easily dropped, and are optimized for texting.) The culture that grows up around the cell phone is a communications culture, but it is not necessarily a culture of self-reflection—which depends on having an emotion, experiencing it, sometimes electing to share it with another person, thinking about it differently over time. When interchanges are reduced to the shorthand of emoticon emotions, questions such as "Who am I?" and "Who are you?" are reformatted for the small screen and flattened out in the process.

Virtuality and Its Discontents

The virtual life of Facebook or MySpace is titillating, but our fragile planet needs our action in the real. We have to worry that we may be connecting globally but relating parochially.

We have become virtuosos of self-presentation, accustomed to living our lives in public. The idea that "we're all being observed all the time anyway, so who needs privacy?" has become a commonplace. Put another way, people say, "As long as I'm not doing anything wrong, who cares who's watching me?" This state of mind leaves us vulnerable to political abuse. Last June I attended the Webby Awards, an event to recognize the best and most influential Web sites. Thomas Friedman won for his argument that the Web had created a "flat" world of economic and political opportunity, a world in which a high school junior in Brooklyn competes with a peer in Bangalore. MySpace won a special commendation as the year's most pathbreaking site.

The awards took place just as the government wiretapping scandal was dominating the press. When the question of illegal eavesdropping came up, a common reaction among the gathered Weberati was to turn the issue into a nonissue. We heard, "All information is good information" and "Information wants to be free" and "If you have nothing to hide, you have nothing to fear." At a pre-awards cocktail party one Web luminary spoke animatedly about Michel Foucault's* idea of the panopticon, an architectural structure of spokes of a wheel built out from a hub, used as a metaphor for how the modern state disciplines its citizens. When the panopticon serves as a model for a prison, a guard stands at its center. Since each prisoner (citizen) knows that the guard might be looking at him or her at any moment, the question of whether the guard is actually looking—or if there is a guard at all—ceases to matter. The structure itself has created its disciplined citizen. By analogy, said my conversation partner at the cocktail hour, on the Internet someone might always be watching; it doesn't matter if from time to time someone is. Foucault's discussion of the panopticon had been a critical take on disciplinary society. Here it had become a justification for the U.S. government to spy on its citizens. All around me there were nods of assent.

High school and college students give up their privacy on MySpace about everything from musical preferences to sexual hang-ups. They are not likely to be troubled by an anonymous government agency knowing whom they call or what Web sites they frequent. People become gratified by a certain public exposure; it is more validation than violation.

Split Attention

Contemporary professional life is rich in examples of people 20 ignoring those they are meeting with to give priority to online others whom they consider a more relevant audience. Students

*__Michel Foucault__ (1926–84)   French philosopher; author of acclaimed analyses of social institutions.

do e-mail during classes; faculty members do e-mail during meetings; parents do e-mail while talking with their children; people do e-mail as they walk down the street, drive cars, or have dinner with their families. Indeed, people talk on the phone, hold a face-to-face meeting, and do their e-mail at the same time. Once done surreptitiously, the habit of self-splitting in different worlds is becoming normalized. Your dinner partner looks down with a quick glance and you know he his checking his BlackBerry.

"Being put on pause" is how one of my students describes the feeling of walking down the street with a friend who has just taken a call on his cell. "I mean I can't go anywhere; I can't just pull out some work. I've just been stopped in midsentence and am expected to remember, to hold the thread of the conversation until he wants to pick it up again."

Traditional telephones tied us to friends, family, colleagues from school and work and, most recently, to commercial, political, and philanthropic solicitations. Things are no longer so simple. These days our devices link us to humans and to objects that represent them: answering machines, Web sites, and personal pages on social networking sites. Sometimes we engage with avatars who anonymously stand in for others, enabling us to express ourselves in intimate ways to strangers, in part because we and they are able to veil who we really are. Sometimes we engage with synthetic voice-recognition protocols that simulate real people as they try to assist us with technical and administrative issues. We order food, clothes, and airline tickets this way. On the Internet we interact with bots, anthropomorphic programs that converse with us about a variety of matters, from routine to romantic. In online games we are partnered with "nonplayer characters," artificial intelligences that are not linked to human players. The games require that we put our trust in these characters that can save our fictional lives in the game. It is a small jump from trusting nonplayer characters—computer programs, that is—to putting one's trust in a robotic companion.

When my daughter, Rebecca, was 14, we went to the Darwin exhibition at the American Museum of Natural History, which documents his life and thought and somewhat defensively presents the theory of evolution as the central truth that underpins contemporary biology. At the entrance are two Galápagos tortoises. One is hidden from view; the other rests in its cage, utterly still. "They could have used a robot," Rebecca remarks, thinking it a shame to bring the turtle all this way when it's just going to sit there. She is concerned for the imprisoned turtle and unmoved by its authenticity. It is Thanksgiving weekend. The line is long, the crowd frozen in place, and my question, "Do you care that the turtle is alive?" is a welcome diversion. Most of the votes for the robots echo Rebecca's sentiment that, in this setting, aliveness doesn't seem worth the trouble. A 12-year-old girl is adamant: "For what the turtles do, you didn't have to have the live ones." Her father looks at her, uncomprehending: "But the point is that they are real."

When Animal Kingdom opened in Orlando, populated by breathing animals, its first visitors complained they were not as "realistic" as the animatronic creatures in other parts of Disney World. The robotic crocodiles slapped their tails and rolled their eyes; the biological ones, like the Galápagos tortoises, pretty much kept to themselves.

I ask another question of the museumgoers: "If you put in a robot instead of the live turtle, do you think people should be told that the turtle is not alive?" Not really, say several of the children. Data on "aliveness" can be shared on a "need to know" basis, for a purpose. But what are the purposes of living things?

Twenty-five years ago the Japanese realized that demography was working against them and there would never be enough young people to take care of their aging population. Instead of having foreigners take care of their elderly, they decided to build robots and put them in nursing homes. Doctors and nurses like them; so do family members of the elderly, because it is easier to leave your mom playing with a robot than to leave her staring at a wall or a TV. Very often the elderly like them, I think, mostly because they sense there are no other options. Said one woman about Aibo, Sony's household-entertainment robot, "It is better than a real dog. . . . It won't do dangerous things, and it won't betray you. . . . Also, it won't die suddenly and make you feel very sad."

Might such robotic arrangements even benefit the elderly and their children in the short run in a feel-good sense but be bad for us in our lives as moral beings? The answer does not depend on what computers can do today or what they are likely to be able to do in the future. It hangs on the question of what we will be like, what kind of people we are becoming as we develop very intimate relationships with our machines.

Why we should care. See pp. 92–95 for tips on saying why it matters.

Joining the Conversation

1. Sherry Turkle opens her essay by questioning the human costs of technological development: "Thanks to technology, people have never been more connected—or more alienated." Summarize briefly the five points she makes about

how life is diminished by what she sees as an over-reliance on technology.

2. What view is Turkle arguing against? Where in her essay do you find a statement or other indication of that view? What examples can you find throughout the essay where she mentions a point of view that she disagrees with? What is her purpose in mentioning such examples?

3. This piece was written for *Forbes*, a business magazine known as "the capitalist tool" and for its annual list of the richest Americans. If Turkle were writing for an audience of young, technologically proficient people who are comfortable using the gadgetry she describes, how might she have written the essay differently?

4. Turkle argues that children do not learn personal responsibility as quickly as they used to because they are in such constant touch with their parents via cell phone. Does she offer any naysayers to this argument? If not, what counterarguments can you suggest?

5. Do you agree with Turkle? Disagree? Agree *and* disagree? Write an essay setting forth what you think, being careful to frame your argument as a response to what Turkle says.

ROZ CHAST is a staff cartoonist for the *New Yorker*, where this cartoon first appeared in 2002. She is also the author or illustrator of many books, among them *Theories of Everything* (2006).

Joining the Conversation

1. What argument is Roz Chast making with this cartoon? That is, what larger point about young people's use of technology is she trying to make?
2. What assumption or position do you think Chast is responding to?
3. This is a visual text, though it includes words as well as pictures. Imagine you wanted to cite this cartoon in an essay about instant messaging. Write a paragraph about the point Chast makes, quoting from the cartoon for examples. Be sure to introduce any quotations and to follow them up with your own explanation.
4. Rewrite the dialogue between Romeo and Juliet using formal English. How does this change in language affect the way you read the cartoon? What sort of pictures should accompany your revision?
5. Take a passage from another classic literary text and rewrite it as Chast has here, as an instant message. You might try something from *The Odyssey*, *Pride and Prejudice*, *The Great Gatsby*, or any other text you have studied.

Me Against the Media:
From the Trenches of a Media Lit Class

NAOMI ROCKLER-GLADEN

—⌐回⌐—

I STROLL INTO MY Critical Media Studies classroom, drinking an icy bottle of Pepsi and wearing a Nike baseball cap. A few of my students glance up from their cell phones and iPods long enough to notice me.

"Um, nice hat," someone comments.

"Thank you," I say. "Today's class is proudly sponsored by Nike, a strong advocate of education. When it comes to education, Nike says, 'Just do it!'" I take a swig of my Pepsi. "Can you guess who else is sponsoring our class today?" The few students who have actually done the reading chuckle, because they know that today's class is about the pervasiveness of consumerism in schools and in popular culture.

Over the years, I've resorted to lots of gimmicks like these in my quest to teach students about consumerism. I try to make

NAOMI ROCKLER-GLADEN is an author who specializes in topics on education and media literacy. She is the featured writer for the "Campus Life" section of *Suite101.com,* "a go-to online magazine with something to say about everything," and formerly taught media studies at Colorado State University. She wrote the article included here for *Adbusters* magazine in 2007.

my students more aware of how the media naturalize consumerism through advertisements, product placement, and especially through advertiser-friendly programming. You might be surprised to hear that I find this to be the single most difficult topic to teach. I teach about many controversial media issues—ownership, violence, race and gender representation—and students contemplate these topics enthusiastically. But when it comes to consumerism, it's a brick wall. Five minutes into any such discussion, I brace myself for the inevitable chorus of, "Oh, come on. It's just a bunch of ads."

Corporations and advertising executives should rejoice, as 5 this reticence of young people to think critically about the role of consumerism is money in their pockets. Advertisers have always coveted the 18- to 34-year-old group—the legions of the so-called "Age of Acquisition" who have few established brand loyalties and lots of pocket change. Today's Generation Y youth, born roughly between 1977 and 1997, are especially desirable because they are the children of Baby Boomers, and therefore represent a population explosion. Run the term "Generation Y" through a search engine, and you'll find dozens of sites with information about how companies can take advantage of this marketing gold mine. Multinationals are deeply invested in the collective consumer choices of my students. When my students fail to show concern, these corporations become all the more powerful.

What position is she responding to? See Chapter 12 for tips on spotting the "they say."

To demonstrate to my students how media content itself naturalizes consumerism, I used to show my students a clip from the 1991 movie *Father of the Bride*. In this clip, the father is horrified that his daughter wants him to spend about $130,000 on her wedding. He would prefer to have a simple wedding reception at the local Steak Pit, but the whole family rejects this idea. Even the adolescent son understands this is "unacceptable"; he comments, "I don't think you want the word 'pit' on a wedding invitation." When the father complains that his first car cost less than the wedding cake, the wedding coordinator bursts into laughter and says, "Welcome to the '90s." After the daughter agrees to downsize the wedding, her father discovers her, asleep, reading a magazine article with tips on how to throw a budget wedding. Suddenly ashamed of himself, he agrees to fund the extravagant wedding. Dad learns his lesson: consumerism-fueled expectations may be outrageous, but they are necessary, and failure to adhere to these expectations is silly, miserly, and downright unloving.

I quit showing this clip. It didn't work. Oh, they got the point, that media content often promotes the agenda of advertisers. Unfortunately, the clip would inevitably lead to a version of the following:

> A female student raises her hand shyly and says, "I understand why this is bad, but I want a big wedding." A dozen ponytailed heads nod in harmony.

> "I mean, not as big as the one in the movie," someone responds, "but you know, the flowers, the cake, the dress, the ring, all that stuff. I've daydreamed about my wedding since I was a little girl."

> "Me too," the first student says, and frowns. "Does that make me a bad person?"

Therein lies the trouble. The dreams, the memories, the rites of passage of Generation Y—all of these are intricately intertwined with consumerism. By placing wedding consumption under scrutiny, this student feels like she is being attacked personally. To this student, the suggestion there is something wrong with consumerism is akin to suggesting that there is something wrong with her.

While all of us in the postwar Western world have grown up with the association between happiness and consumption, this association is all the more powerful with Generation Y. They have been reared with unlimited advertising and limited models of social consciousness or activism. Let's look at the experiences of my students, a fairly typical U.S. sample of Generation Y. They were born in the 1980s under the Reagan administration, when two important trends in children's television occurred: Reagan, ever the media deregulator, relaxed requirements for educational programming at the same time as he relaxed restrictions on advertising to children. This helped bring forth a new marketing tactic—which Tom Engelhardt has called the "Shortcake Strategy"—in which children's TV shows were created for the exclusive purpose of marketing large collections of children's toys. Some of the happiest, most prized childhood memories of Generation Y are filled with these shows and toys—Strawberry Shortcake, He-Man, the Care Bears. Discussing the politics of this kind of marketing with students is even harder than discussing wedding excess. A student once wrote in my teacher evaluation, "Great class, but please don't go hating on Strawberry Shortcake."

This is the first generation that came of age in the era of rampant advertising in the schools, as well as Channel One, the news program piped into schools complete with advertisements. As a Generation Xer who graduated from high school in 1988, I recall very few ads in school. A relatively short time later, the hallways, lunchrooms, and sports facilities of cash-strapped schools are now frequently sponsored by corporations. When I ask students if this happened in their schools, they supply neverending examples: stadiums dotted by Nike swooshes, lunchrooms filled with Pizza Hut and Chick-Fil-A, a back-to-school party sponsored by Outback Steakhouse, even book covers underwritten by corporations. Then, of course, there's the prom. Eschewed by some of my Gen X counterparts, the prom is back and bigger than ever, teaching future brides and grooms important lessons about gowns, limos, and flowers. Ask a Gen Y member which mall he or she grew up in, and you may well get an answer.

The reality is that many young people don't take con- 10 sumerism seriously because they feel that as individuals, it does not affect them. As media activists like Jean Kilbourne have argued, this illusion that advertising affects "everybody else but me" is nothing new, but I think this is even more the case with Generation Y. Students claim violence in the media doesn't matter because they grew up playing Doom and they didn't turn out violent. Or they claim that unrealistic images of women in the media do matter because they know a lot of girls with eating disorders. Many young people don't seem to have a language for understanding that the media doesn't just affect us on an individual level—the media impacts society politically, economically, and ideologically. A student might dismiss ads in his high school by saying they did not affect him: nonetheless, I argue, the proliferation of ads in high schools have affected culture as a whole.

Again, this individualist way of looking at media effects isn't entirely new, especially in an individualist nation like the United States, where social scientists for years have been obsessed with trying to draw links between individual behavior and the media. But Generation Y is a particularly individualist cohort. The Me Generation is back. Just like in the 1970s, young people are frightened and disgusted with current events and have retreated away from politics, with their iPods, PlayStations, and all the other isolating technology the consumer market can offer. But the '70s were different because the '60s didn't die overnight. Me Generation or not, the language of activism was still spoken in the '70s, and many young people then were involved in movements such as Women's Liberation. To what activist language has Generation Y been exposed? It's three years into their own Vietnam, and they aren't exactly flooding the streets with protesters. Often students tell me that they find politics to be boring and irrelevant to their own experiences.

It's pretty hard to engage a group of young people in a discussion of the political implications of consumerism when they are not engaged in politics much at all. Consumerism is a personal choice, and most of my students cannot see beyond that. They shop at Wal-Mart because it's cheap, and buy coffee at Starbucks because they like the mochas. Sweatshops? Globalization? It's not so much that they don't care about these things (though many don't). Rather, they haven't been taught to think of consumerism as something that extends beyond their own enjoyable trip to the mall, just as they haven't been taught that their personal consumer decisions are political.

To me, perhaps the most frustrating argument students make about consumerism is that it shouldn't be a societal concern because "it's the parents' responsibility." Parents are responsible for refusing to buy their kids $200 basketball shoes, for making sure they eat a healthy lunch in the cafeteria, and for instilling values that, according to my students, will somehow make their children immune to the effects of advertisements. This argument disturbs me, partly because my students seem to show no compassion for kids with parents who are unwilling or unable to be this active in their kids' development. But most of all, this disturbs me because it lets corporations off the hook for the effects they have on society. It doesn't matter how or to whom a company markets their products; it only matters how parents raise their children. Once again, consumerism becomes the business of individual families, not society.

So, what can media activists do? I think the first step is to find ways to appeal to members of this generation on the level of the individual. Young people might not initially care about the plight of a Nike worker in Vietnam or a Wal-Mart worker in Houston. They may, however, be concerned with how credit card companies lure in college students, or how college bookstores jack up prices needlessly, or how car insurance companies charge them exorbitant amounts. When I ask students to give examples of how corporations have screwed them over personally, the room fills up with raised hands. This is a good way to show them that although consumerism has brought them happiness in their lives, it has also brought them problems.

A second activist strategy of reaching Generation Y is to 15 find examples in popular culture. Generation Y is all about pop culture. I've found that my students are amenable to discussions about how advertisers and media producers consciously create media content that "trains" young people to be consumers. Young people need to know that corporations see them as a market to manipulate, and often will respond to this argument, because who wants to be manipulated? The trick is to find popular culture texts they relate to that have a strong pro-consumerism bent. I've had some success in the past with the "Pottery Barn" episode of *Friends*. In this episode, Rachel lies to her roommate Phoebe and tells her their new furniture is antique. Actually, it came from Pottery Barn, but Phoebe hates commercial furniture. Rachel is caught in her lie when the two walk by Pottery Barn and see most of the furniture in the display window. But then Phoebe sees a lamp in the window and decides she must buy it. Phoebe learns her lesson: commercial furniture is good. Another good source of proconsumerism media is reality television, a favorite of students and chock-full of product placement.

A third strategy is simply to get young people to talk to their parents about their experiences growing up and how people "back in the day" felt about corporate power and consumerism. These are the children of Baby Boomers, after all, so even if they haven't been around activism, their parents have. One of my favorite assignments is to get students to interview older family members about popular culture and their past experiences. Students love this assignment.

So, there's hope. When I wear my Nike hat to class, some of the students get it, and inevitably, a student stops by my office at the end of the semester and announces she has stopped going to Starbucks. But this is no easy task, and media activists would be well advised to work hard to relate to Generation Y. The advertisers are certainly paying attention to them, and so should we.

Joining the Conversation

1. Reread the following sentence in paragraph 4: "I try to make my students more aware of how the media naturalize consumerism through advertisements, product placement, and especially through advertiser-friendly programming." What exactly is the author saying here?

2. This piece was written for *Adbusters*, an anti-consumerist magazine published in Canada. How might it be different if

it had been written in a textbook, say for a media studies class? Notice that it is *about* students; how would it be different if it were written *for* an audience of students?

3. Identify and summarize in your own words the counterarguments that Naomi Rockler-Gladen entertains in this article. How fairly does she represent these counterarguments, and how well does she answer them?

4. There's no doubt that Rockler-Gladen cares passionately about this issue, but does she make clear why it matters? If so, where does she do so? If not, how might she have done so?

5. Read Amy Goldwasser's essay on pp. 236–40. Contrast Rockler-Gladen's view that young people are easily manipulated by consumer advertising with Goldwasser's argument that young people today are strong critical thinkers. What do you think? Write an essay taking your own stand on this issue, providing examples from your own experiences and observations. Frame your essay as a response to one or both authors, citing their arguments as appropriate, either as support for what you say or as a naysayer.

Reality Television: Oxymoron

GEORGE F. WILL

—⌐▣⌐—

FRED ALLEN, a mordantly sophisticated radio performer, died just as television was permeating America, in 1956. He warned us: "Imitation is the sincerest form of television." So there will be imitations of *Fear Factor*.

That NBC program, in its first episode last week, attracted nearly 12 million voyeurs to watch simpletons confront their fears, for a fee. In that episode, confronters were covered by a swarm of biting rats. This week the program featured a willingness to eat worms and sit in a tub of them.

Fear Factor is an imitation of an MTV program, *Jackass*, named, perhaps, for its target viewer. But American television is being imitative. ABC's *Nightline* reports that French, Spanish, and Japanese television have similar programming, although none has—yet—matched the Peruvian show that pays poor people to eat maggots and be splattered with frog excrement.

Last spring NBC concocted XFL football, promising more

GEORGE F. WILL is a syndicated columnist for the *Washington Post* and *Newsweek* who writes about politics and other topics. He is also an analyst with ABC News. He won the Pulitzer Prize for distinguished commentary in 1977. The piece included here was first published in the *Washington Post* in June 2001.

violence on the field and more cheerleaders' breasts on the sidelines than the NFL provides. The league drew a big audience for the first telecast, but the ratings began to plunge by the third quarter, and the league died after one season.

Optimists concluded that NBC had underestimated the viewing public. The optimists were, as usual, wrong. NBC understood that it had underestimated only the perversity required to rivet the attention of millions in an era when graphic violence and sexual puerilities are quotidian television. So NBC sank to the challenge of thinking lower. But it had better not rest on its laurels because its competitors in the race to the bottom will not rest, and the bottom is not yet in sight.

The possible permutations of perversity programming—the proper name for what is called, oxymoronically, "reality television"—are as limitless as, apparently, is the supply of despicably greedy or spectacularly stupid people willing to degrade themselves for money. (A philosophical puzzle: Can such people be degraded?) But perhaps the monetary incentive is superfluous, given today's endemic exhibitionism that makes many people feel unrecognized, unauthenticated—or something—unless they are presented, graphically, to an audience.

Celebration of "Choice"

Ours is an age besotted with graphic entertainments. And in an increasingly infantilized society, whose moral philosophy is reducible to a celebration of "choice," adults are decreasingly distinguishable from children in their absorption in entertainments and the kinds of entertainments they are absorbed in—video games, computer games, handheld games, movies on their computers, and so on. This is progress: more sophisticated delivery of stupidity.

An optimistic premise of our society in which "choice" is the ideal that trumps all others, is that competition improves things, burning away the dross and leaving the gold. This often works with commodities like cars but not with mass culture. There competition corrupts.

America, determined to amuse itself into inanition, is becoming increasingly desensitized. So entertainment seeking a mass audience is ratcheting up the violence, sexuality, and degradation, becoming increasingly coarse and trying to be— its largest challenge—shocking in an unshockable society.

The primitive cosmopolitans among us invariably say: Relax. 10 Chaucer's Wife of Bath, the Impressionists, and James Joyce's *Ulysses* have been considered scandalous. As the Supreme Court has said, "One man's vulgarity is another man's lyric."

All right, then: One man's bearbaiting is another's opera. That British pastime involved pitting a chained bear against a pack of dogs, who fought, and usually killed, the bear. The historian Macaulay famously said that the Puritans opposed bearbaiting not because it gave pain to the bears but because it gave pleasure to the spectators. The Puritans were right: Some pleasures are contemptible because they are coarsening. They are not merely private vices; they have public consequences in driving the culture's downward spiral.

Like Heroin Pushers

A mass audience is its own justification to purveyors of perversity television, who say: We are only supplying a market. As though there was a strong spontaneous demand for televised degradation. The argument that the existence of customers justifies the product distinguishes the pur-

See Chapter 6 on acknowledging naysayers.

veyors of *Fear Factor* not at all from heroin pushers, who are not the purveyors' moral inferiors.

How will a "pro-choice" society object to a program—let's call it "Who *Really* Wants to be a Millionaire?"—on which consenting contestants will be offered $1 million to play Russian roulette with a revolver loaded with a real bullet? Imagine the audience for the chance to see violent death in living color in prime time in the comfort of one's living room. That's entertainment.

Joining the Conversation

1. George F. Will describes as a "race to the bottom" the TV shows in which people "degrade themselves for money." What TV shows might fit his definition? Where in his critique is a "they say" that defends such programming?
2. Will uses strong language to convey his negative view not just of television programming but of many other aspects of society. He discusses "today's endemic exhibitionism," for instance, and talks of life "in an increasingly infantilized society." How does he see TV fitting into this larger picture?
3. This piece was syndicated to more than 400 papers, and yet it's written in language that is quite formal, even academic. How does Will's formal style relate to his argument about the "downward spiral" of popular culture today—and to the kind of people he wants his readers to become?
4. Compare Will's views of television viewers today with the views of Steven Johnson (pp. 213–30) or Dana Stevens (pp. 231–34).
5. Write an essay responding to Will, drawing on your own experience as a television viewer and citing the opinions of at least one other author in this chapter.

Hidden Intellectualism

GERALD GRAFF

——◫——

EVERYONE KNOWS SOME young person who is impressively "street smart" but does poorly in school. What a waste, we think, that one who is so intelligent about so many things in life seems unable to apply that intelligence to academic work. What doesn't occur to us, though, is that schools and colleges might be at fault for missing the opportunity to tap into such street smarts and channel them into good academic work.

Nor do we consider one of the major reasons why schools and colleges overlook the intellectual potential of street smarts: the fact that we associate those street smarts with anti-intellectual concerns. We associate the educated life, the life of the mind, too narrowly and exclusively with subjects and texts that we consider inherently weighty and academic. We

GERALD GRAFF, one of the co-authors of this book, is a professor of English and education at the University of Illinois at Chicago. He is the 2008 President of the Modern Language Association, a U.S.-based professional association of scholars and teachers of English and other languages. This essay is adapted from his 2003 book *Clueless in Academe: How Schooling Obscures the Life of the Mind*.

assume that it's possible to wax intellectual about Plato, Shakespeare, the French Revolution, and nuclear fission, but not about cars, dating, fashion, sports, TV, or video games.

The trouble with this assumption is that no necessary connection has ever been established between any text or subject and the educational depth and weight of the discussion it can generate. Real intellectuals turn any subject, See pp. 53–56 for tips on disagreeing, with reasons. however lightweight it may seem, into grist for their mill through the thoughtful questions they bring to it, whereas a dullard will find a way to drain the interest out of the richest subject. That's why a George Orwell writing on the cultural meanings of penny postcards is infinitely more substantial than the cogitations of many professors on Shakespeare or globalization.

Students do need to read models of intellectually challenging writing—and Orwell is a great one—if they are to become intellectuals themselves. But they would be more prone to take on intellectual identities if we encouraged them to do so at first on subjects that interest them rather than ones that interest us.

I offer my own adolescent experience as a case in point. 5 Until I entered college, I hated books and cared only for sports. The only reading I cared to do or could do was sports magazines, on which I became hooked, becoming a regular reader of *Sport* magazine in the late forties, *Sports Illustrated* when it began publishing in 1954, and the annual magazine guides to professional baseball, football, and basketball. I also loved the sports novels for boys of John R. Tunis and Clair Bee and autobiographies of sports stars like Joe DiMaggio's *Lucky to Be a Yankee* and Bob Feller's *Strikeout Story*. In short, I was your typical teenage anti-intellectual—or so I believed for a long time. I have recently come to think, however, that my preference for sports over schoolwork was not anti-intellectualism so much as intellectualism by other means.

In the Chicago neighborhood I grew up in, which had become a melting pot after World War II, our block was solidly middle class, but just a block away—doubtless concentrated there by the real estate companies—were African Americans, Native Americans, and "hillbilly" whites who had recently fled postwar joblessness in the South and Appalachia. Negotiating this class boundary was a tricky matter. On the one hand, it was necessary to maintain the boundary between "clean-cut" boys like me and working-class "hoods," as we called them, which meant that it was good to be openly smart in a bookish sort of way. On the other hand, I was desperate for the approval of the hoods, whom I encountered daily on the playing field and in the neighborhood, and for this purpose it was not at all good to be book-smart. The hoods would turn on you if they sensed you were putting on airs over them: "Who you lookin' at, smart ass?" as a leather-jacketed youth once said to me as he relieved me of my pocket change along with my self-respect.

I grew up torn, then, between the need to prove I was smart and the fear of a beating if I proved it too well; between the need not to jeopardize my respectable future and the need to impress the hoods. As I lived it, the conflict came down to a choice between being physically tough and being verbal. For a boy in my neighborhood and elementary school, only being "tough" earned you complete legitimacy. I still recall endless, complicated debates in this period with my closest pals over who was "the toughest guy in the school." If you were less than negligible as a fighter, as I was, you settled for the next best thing, which was to be inarticulate, carefully hiding telltale marks of literacy like correct grammar and pronunciation.

In one way, then, it would be hard to imagine an adolescence more thoroughly anti-intellectual than mine. Yet in retrospect, I see that it's more complicated, that I and the 1950s themselves were not simply hostile toward intellectualism, but divided and ambivalent. When Marilyn Monroe married the playwright Arthur Miller in 1956 after divorcing the retired baseball star Joe DiMaggio, the symbolic triumph of geek over jock suggested the way the wind was blowing. Even Elvis, according to his biographer Peter Guralnick, turns out to have supported Adlai over Ike in the presidential election of 1956. "I don't dig the intellectual bit," he told reporters. "But I'm telling you, man, he knows the most."

Though I too thought I did not "dig the intellectual bit," I see now that I was unwittingly in training for it. The germs had actually been planted in the seemingly philistine debates about which boys were the toughest. I see now that in the interminable analysis of sports teams, movies, and toughness that my friends and I engaged in—a type of analysis, needless to say, that the real toughs would never have stooped to—I was already betraying an allegiance to the egghead world. I was practicing being an intellectual before I knew that was what I wanted to be.

It was in these discussions with friends about toughness and sports, I think, and in my reading of sports books and magazines, that I began to learn the rudiments of the intellectual life: how to make an argument, weigh different kinds of evidence, move between particulars and generalizations, summarize the views of others, and enter a conversation about ideas. It was in reading and arguing about sports and toughness that I experienced what it felt like to propose a generalization, restate and respond to a counterargument, and perform other intellectualizing operations, including composing the kind of sentences I am writing now.

Only much later did it dawn on me that the sports world was more compelling than school because it was *more intellectual than school,* not less. Sports after all was full of challenging arguments, debates, problems for analysis, and intricate statistics that you could care about, as school conspicuously was not. I believe that street smarts beat out book smarts in our culture not because street smarts are nonintellectual, as we generally suppose, but because they satisfy an intellectual thirst more thoroughly than school culture, which seems pale and unreal.

They also satisfy the thirst for community. When you entered sports debates, you became part of a community that was not limited to your family and friends, but was national and public. Whereas schoolwork isolated you from others, the pennant race or Ted Williams's .400 batting average was something you could talk about with people you had never met. Sports introduced you not only to a culture steeped in argument, but to a public argument culture that transcended the personal. I can't blame my schools for failing to make intellectual culture resemble the Super Bowl, but I do fault them for failing to learn anything from the sports and entertainment worlds about how to organize and represent intellectual culture, how to exploit its gamelike element and turn it into arresting public spectacle that might have competed more successfully for my youthful attention.

For here is another thing that never dawned on me and is still kept hidden from students, with tragic results: that the real intellectual world, the one that existed in the big world beyond school, is organized very much like the world of team sports, with rival texts, rival interpretations and evaluations of texts, rival theories of why they should be read and taught, and elaborate team competitions in which "fans" of writers, intellectual systems, methodologies, and -isms contend against each other.

To be sure, school contained plenty of competition, which became more invidious as one moved up the ladder (and has become even more so today with the advent of high-stakes testing). In this competition, points were scored not by making arguments, but by a show of information or vast reading, by grade-grubbing, or other forms of oneupmanship. School competition, in short, reproduced the less attractive features of sports culture without those that create close bonds and community.

And in distancing themselves from anything as enjoyable 15 and absorbing as sports, my schools missed the opportunity to capitalize on an element of drama and conflict that the intellectual world shares with sports. Consequently, I failed to see the parallels between the sports and academic worlds that could have helped me cross more readily from one argument culture to the other.

Sports is only one of the domains whose potential for literacy training (and not only for males) is seriously underestimated by educators, who see sports as competing with academic development rather than a route to it. But if this argument suggests why it is a good idea to assign readings and topics that are close to students' existing interests, it also suggests the limits of this tactic. For students who get excited about the chance to write about their passion for cars will often write as poorly and unreflectively on that topic as on Shakespeare or Plato. Here is the flip side of what I pointed out before: that there's no necessary relation between the degree of interest a student shows in a text or subject and the quality of thought or expression such a student manifests in writing or talking about it. The challenge, as college professor Ned Laff has put it, "is not simply to exploit students' nonacademic interests, but to get them to see those interests through academic eyes."

To say that students need to see their interests "through academic eyes" is to say that street smarts are not enough. Making students' nonacademic interests an object of academic study is useful, then, for getting students' attention and overcoming their boredom and alienation, but this tactic won't in itself necessarily move them closer to an academically rigorous treatment of those interests. On the other hand, inviting students to write about cars, sports, or clothing fashions does not have to be a pedagogical cop-out as long as students are required to see these interests "through academic eyes," that is, to think and write about cars, sports, and fashions in a reflective, analytical way, one that sees them as microcosms of what is going on in the wider culture.

If I am right, then schools and colleges are missing an opportunity when they do not encourage students to take their nonacademic interests as objects of academic study. It is self-defeating to decline to introduce any text or subject that figures to engage students who will otherwise tune out academic work entirely. If a student cannot get interested in Mill's *On Liberty* but will read *Sports Illustrated* or *Vogue* or the hip-hop magazine Source with absorption, this is a strong argument for assigning the magazines over the classic. It's a good bet that if students get hooked on reading and writing by doing term papers on *Source*, they will eventually get to *On Liberty*. But even if they don't, the magazine reading will make them more literate and reflective than they would be otherwise. So it makes pedagogical sense to develop classroom units on sports, cars, fashions, rap music, and other such topics. Give me the student anytime who writes a sharply argued, sociologically acute analysis of an issue of *Source* over the student who writes a lifeless explication of *Hamlet* or Socrates' *Apology*.

Joining the Conversation

1. Gerald Graff begins his essay with the view that we generally associate "book smarts" with intellectualism and "street smarts" with anti-intellectualism. Graff then provides an extended example from his early life to counter this viewpoint. What do you think of his argument that boyhood conversations about sports provided a solid foundation for his later intellectual life? What support does he provide, and how persuasive is it?

2. Graff argues in paragraph 13 that the intellectual world is much like the world of team sports, with "rival texts . . . , rival theories . . . , and elaborate team competitions." Can you think of any examples from your own experience that support this assertion? In what ways do you think "the real intellectual world" is different from the world of team sports?

3. How does Graff's own language support his argument about pop culture and academic work? How does his writing compare with that of Douglas Rushkoff (pp. 241–55) or George F. Will (pp. 293–96)?

4. So what? Who cares? Graff does not answer these questions explicitly. Do it for him: write a brief paragraph saying why his argument matters, and for whom.

5. Graff argues that schools should encourage students to think critically, read, and write about areas of personal interest such as cars, fashion, or music—as long as they do so in an intellectually serious way. What do you think? Write an essay considering the educational merits of such a proposal, taking Graff's argument as a "they say."

FIFTEEN

IS ECONOMIC MOBILITY JUST A DREAM?

IT IS HARD TO IMAGINE ANYTHING more fundamental to most Americans than the belief that we are the authors of our own fate—that we are in the driver's seat and in control, particularly when it comes to our economic success. We go to school, study, get jobs, and work hard, all with the assumption that doing so will allow us to achieve financial security, climb the economic ladder, outperform our parents, and perhaps even achieve great wealth. This faith in the American Dream, in the United States as a land of opportunity, dates back to a claim made in the eighteenth century by the French writer J. Hector St. John de Crèvecoeur. He thought that what made "the new American" unique, in contrast to the oppressed classes in monarchical societies, was the opportunity to reap "the rewards of [one's] industry" in direct proportion to "the progress of [one's] labour." Take away this faith that we will be justly rewarded for our hard work and it might become hard for many of us to get up in the morning and do our best.

According to several of the writers in this unit, who express a classic *liberal* position, this faith in the American Dream *has* been taken away, having been undermined by a combination of global economic developments and government policies that have perilously widened the gulf between the very rich and the rest of us. Labor activist Holly Sklar and Princeton economist Paul Krugman each highlight how income for the wealthiest Americans has recently increased while middle-class incomes have remained stagnant. They then offer policy recommendations to increase opportunities for all. Tamara Draut, an expert on economic security issues, argues that income inequities have seriously limited opportunities in higher education for middle-class and poorer Americans. Though these liberals question whether the dream of equal opportunity ever delivered for most Americans in the way that de Crèvecoeur suggested, they argue that the last two decades have so shifted the balance of wealth and power to large corporations and the privileged few that even the humble financial security that average Americans dream about is becoming just that: a dream with little chance of realization.

Bruce Bartlett, however, takes a *conservative* position, replying that these alarmist liberal critiques are unwarranted and that the American Dream is as alive and well as ever. According to Bartlett, a former adviser to President Ronald Reagan, evidence suggests that average Americans remain as optimistic as ever about their prospects for achieving material prosperity.

While liberals and conservatives argue over possibilities for upward mobility, others, particularly the *Economist*, the weekly publication read by business, political, and financial decision makers, take a middle-ground position. In an article included in this chapter, the *Economist* argues that, while the rich may be getting richer in the United States and other Americans, for the most part, are not, the potential for large-scale upward mobility still exists and can be realized with a few straightforward shifts in economic policy.

A touchstone case of the economic debate between liberals and conservatives is the controversy surrounding the mega-chain Wal-Mart. Liberal journalist Karen Olsson critiques the retail giant for keeping employees' salaries and benefits low in its quest for high profits, while conservative economist and columnist Sebastian Mallaby argues that Wal-Mart is only doing what it must to survive in a difficult economy, that Americans want and benefit from the store's low prices, and that its salaries and benefits are better than people may think.

Finally, Barack Obama, in a highly acclaimed speech on race and opportunity delivered during his presidential campaign, argues for the importance of ensuring the continued existence of the American Dream for all despite differences in race, class, and education. As you read this chapter, you will find a variety of perspectives on this vital issue, and you will have a chance to make your own contribution to this ongoing discussion.

The Growing Gulf Between the Rich and the Rest of Us

HOLLY SKLAR

——▢——

GUESS WHICH COUNTRY the *CIA World Factbook** describes when it says, "Since 1975, practically all the gains in household income have gone to the top 20 percent of households."

If you guessed the United States, you're right.

The United States has rising levels of poverty and inequality not found in other rich democracies. It also has less mobility out of poverty.

Since 2000, America's billionaire club has gained 76 more members while the typical household has lost income and the poverty count has grown by more than 5 million people.

Poverty and inequality take a daily toll seldom seen on television. "The infant mortality rate in the United States com- 5

HOLLY SKLAR, a policy analyst and syndicated columnist, is the author of *Raise the Floor: Wages and Policies That Work for All of Us* (2001) and is writing a book about revitalizing the American Dream. This essay was published in 2005 on *ZNet*, a site whose name was inspired by the movie *Z*, in which the letter *z* symbolizes the spirit of resistance.

***CIA World Factbook**   Almanac of information about countries of the world published annually by the U.S. Central Intelligence Agency.

pares with that in Malaysia—a country with a quarter the income," says the 2005 Human Development Report. "Infant death rates are higher for [black] children in Washington, D.C., than for children in Kerala, India."

Income and wealth in America are increasingly concentrated at the very top—the realm of the Forbes 400.

You could have banked $1 million a day every day for the last two years and still have far to go to make the new *Forbes* list of the 400 richest Americans.

It took a minimum of $900 million to get on the Forbes 400 this year. That's up $150 million from 2004.

For tips on maintaining an informal tone, as Sklar does, see Chapter 9.

"Surging real estate and oil prices drove up several fortunes and helped pave the way for 33 new members," *Forbes* notes.

Middle-class households, meanwhile, are a medical crisis or outsourced job away from bankruptcy. 10

With 374 billionaires, the Forbes 400 will soon be billionaires only.

Bill Gates remains No. 1 on the Forbes 400 with $51 billion. Low-paid Wal-Mart workers can find Walton family heirs in five of the top 10 spots; another Wal-Mart heir ranks No. 116.

Former Bechtel president Stephen Bechtel Jr. and his son, CEO Riley Bechtel, tie for No. 109 on the Forbes 400 with $2.4 billion apiece. The politically powerful Bechtel has gotten a no-bid contract for hurricane reconstruction despite a pattern of cost overruns and shoddy work from Iraq to Boston's leaky "Big Dig" tunnel/highway project.

The Forbes 400 is a group so small they could have watched this year's Sugar Bowl from the private boxes of the Superdome.

Yet combined Forbes 400 wealth totals more than $1.1 trillion—an amount greater than the gross domestic product of Spain or Canada, the world's eighth- and ninth-largest economies. 15

The number of Americans in poverty is a group so large it would take the combined populations of Louisiana, Mississippi, Alabama, and Texas, plus Arkansas, to match it. That's according to the Census Bureau's latest count of 37 million people below the poverty line.

Millions more Americans can't afford adequate health care, housing, child care, food, transportation, and other basic expenses above the official poverty thresholds, which are set too low. The poverty threshold for a single person under age 65 was just $9,827 in 2004. For a two-adult, two-child family, it was just $19,157.

By contrast, the Economic Policy Institute's Basic Family Budget Calculator says the national median basic needs budget (including taxes and tax credits) for a two-parent, two-child family was $39,984 in 2004. It was $38,136 in New Orleans and $33,636 in Biloxi, Mississippi.

America is becoming a downwardly mobile society instead of an upwardly mobile society. Median household income fell for the fifth year in a row to $44,389 in 2004—down from $46,129 in 1999, adjusting for inflation. The Bush administration is using hurricane "recovery" to camouflage policies that will deepen inequality and poverty. They are bringing windfall profits to companies like Bechtel while suspending regulations that shore up wages for workers.

More tax cuts are in the pipeline for wealthy Americans who 20 can afford the $17,000 watch, $160,000 coat, and $10 million helicopter on the Forbes Cost of Living Extremely Well Index.

More budget cuts are in the pipeline for Medicaid, Food Stamps, and other safety nets for Americans whose wages don't even cover the cost of necessities.

Without a change in course, the gulf between the rich and the rest of America will continue to widen, weakening our economy and our democracy. The American Dream will be history instead of poverty.

1. Holly Sklar begins by asking us to make a guess. How effective is this as an introduction for this essay? Does it make you want to read on? Why or why not? What sort of discussion does it lead you to expect from the rest of the essay?

2. Sklar does not state a "they say" in this piece. Think about the argument she is responding to. Why would she not acknowledge it explicitly?

3. In paragraph 20, Sklar asserts that there are "tax cuts . . . in the pipeline for wealthy Americans who can afford the $17,000 watch, $160,000 coat, and $10 million helicopter," and then in the next paragraph, she refers to "budget cuts . . . in the pipeline for Medicaid, Food Stamps, and other safety nets" for the poor. What conclusions do you draw from this contrast?

4. Sklar concludes this piece ominously: "Without a change in course, the gulf between the rich and the rest of America will continue to widen, weakening our economy and our democracy. The American Dream will be history instead of poverty." Are you convinced? Or can you think of objections that she has not anticipated or answered? What other arguments and/or evidence might she have provided to strengthen her case?

5. This essay was written to be published on a Web site. How would it have been written differently if it were an academic essay? How could Sklar have developed specific points?

The Truth About Wages

BRUCE BARTLETT

—▭—

While average incomes are flat, the rich are not getting richer at the expense of the poor.

THERE HAS BEEN A BIG DEBATE going on among Democrats about why workers aren't outraged by their economic condition and therefore more hostile to Republican economic policies and more sympathetic to Democratic policies.

On the surface, it would appear that workers should be in open revolt. According to the Bureau of Labor Statistics, the average worker is no better off today than he was seven years ago in real terms. In August 2006, his average weekly earnings were $275.49. In August 1999, they were 275.61. (Both statistics are in constant 1982 dollars.)

BRUCE BARTLETT, an economist, was a domestic policy adviser to President Ronald Reagan and a treasury official under President George H. W. Bush. His books include *Reaganomics: Supply-Side Economics in Action* (1982) and *Impostor: How George W. Bush Bankrupted America and Betrayed the Reagan Legacy* (2006). "The Truth About Wages" was first published in 2006 on *NRO*, the Web site of the *National Review*, a biweekly magazine of conservative news, commentary, and opinion.

Census Bureau data confirm this trend. According to recently released data, median annual earnings for men fell to $41,386 in 2005 from $43,158 in 2003 (in 2005 dollars) despite steady economic growth. Male earnings in 2005 were lower than in every year since 1997. Female earnings also fell in 2005 to $31,858 from $32,285 a year earlier, and were lower than in any year since 2000.

Looking at the broadest measure of economic well-being, median household income, we also see flatness. In 2005, the median income—the point at which half of households are above and half are below—was $46,326. This was up from 2002, 2003, and 2004, but below levels registered from 1998 to 2001. Median household income peaked in 1999 at $47,671 (in 2005 dollars) and fell every year thereafter until 2005's small uptick.

There is no simple explanation for worker passivity in the face of income stagnation. One argument is that labor union membership has fallen sharply over the last generation and consequently workers have no organizational mechanism through which to bargain for higher wages or protest wage stagnation politically. In 2005, labor-union membership was down to just 7.8 percent of private-sector workers from 24.2 percent in 1973.

Another possibility is that workers have been so beaten down by layoffs and givebacks in recent years that they are grateful enough just to have jobs, even if their pay stinks. And because of declining health coverage by employers, those lucky enough to have health insurance may feel compelled to hold on to such jobs. If they switch to another job, they may get higher pay, but they might lose their health benefits in the process.

Indeed, the rising cost of health benefits is a key reason for the flatness of average worker wages. From the point of view of employers, total labor costs have risen sharply. But all of the increase has gone into benefits, leaving nothing left over to raise wages. Workers may not like this fact, but they accept its reality.

Says who? See Chapter 6 on acknowledging other views.

According to the Bureau of Labor Statistics, wages and salaries have fallen from 72.6 percent of total compensation in 2000 to 70 percent in June of this year. At the same time, health benefits have risen from 5.9 percent of compensation to 7.7 percent.

Still another explanation is that the changing demographics of the population have eased the transition to an economy with slower wage growth. Many baby boomers have just seen the last of their children finish college and leave home. Suddenly, they have had a huge increase in their discretionary income as the enormous costs of tuition and child care that they have borne for decades have now disappeared. They may not be any better off in terms of their family income, but they feel a lot better off financially.

Finally, despite wage and income stagnation at the macro 10 level, people continue to move out of the working class into the middle and upper classes. According to the Census Bureau, the percentage of all households with an income below $25,000 per year (in 2005 dollars) fell to 27.1 percent last year from 27.6 percent in 2004. In 1995, 28.9 percent fell into this income class. In 1985, the percentage was 30.5 percent and in 1975 it was 33.1 percent.

At the same time, the percentage of households that are considered well-to-do—those with an income above $75,000 (in 2005 dollars)—rose to 28.3 percent last year from 27.9 percent in 2004. In 1995, only 24.4 percent of households had that much income, up from 20.2 percent in 1985 and 14 percent in 1975.

In short, despite all the talk about the rich getting richer at the expense of the poor, the fact is that the percentage of households with low incomes has fallen and the percentage of those with high incomes has risen. This is perhaps the main reason why Democrats have had trouble getting traction on the income issue: There are fewer people in the income class to which they historically have directed their message. The more people there are in the $75,000-plus income category the more people there are who are receptive to the Republican message of low taxes.

Joining the Conversation

1. At the beginning of his second paragraph, Bruce Bartlett asserts that "[o]n the surface, it would appear that workers should be in open revolt." Given that observation, what sort of position would you expect him to take? Why?

2. In paragraphs 5 to 11, Bartlett lists many possible reasons why workers appear to be less upset than Democratic party officials think they should be. What evidence does he provide that workers aren't in fact angry over the fall in their real incomes? Are you convinced? Why or why not?

3. What are some objections to Bartlett's argument? How has he acknowledged and responded to any naysayers?

4. Compare Bartlett's discussion to that of Holly Sklar (on pp. 308–11). How can you explain the different evidence they provide and the apparently contradictory conclusions they reach? Which author do you find more persuasive, and why?

5. Turn Bartlett's argument into a "they say" about the relative satisfaction level of American workers, and respond with your own "I say," either agreeing (but with some difference between your position and his), disagreeing (and explaining why), or agreeing and disagreeing.

Inequality and the American Dream

THE ECONOMIST

———— ▣ ————

**The world's most impressive economic machine
needs a little adjusting**

MORE THAN ANY OTHER COUNTRY, America defines itself
by a collective dream: the dream of economic opportunity and
upward mobility. Its proudest boast is that it offers a chance of
the good life to everybody who is willing to work hard and play
by the rules. This ideal has made the United States the world's
strongest magnet for immigrants; it has also reconciled ordinary Americans to the rough side of a dynamic economy, with
all its inequalities and insecurities. Who cares if the boss earns
300 times more than the average working stiff, if the stiff knows
he can become the boss?

THE ECONOMIST is a London-based weekly publication read by an
international audience of business, political, and financial decision
makers. Its articles focus on world news, politics, business, science,
technology, and the arts. "Inequality and the American Dream" was
published in June 2006. Like almost all pieces in the *Economist*, it
included no author byline.

Look around the world and the supremacy of "the American model" might seem assured. No other rich country has so successfully harnessed the modern juggernauts of technology and globalisation. The hallmarks of American capitalism—a willingness to take risks, a light regulatory touch, and sharp competition—have spawned enormous wealth. "This economy is powerful, productive, and prosperous," George Bush boasted recently, and by many yardsticks he is right. Growth is fast, unemployment is low, and profits are fat. It is hardly surprising that so many other governments are trying to "Americanise" their economies—whether through the European Union's Lisbon Agenda or Japan's Koizumi reforms.

These 2 paragraphs seem to contradict each other. See pp. 140–42 on recognizing the conversation.

Yet many people feel unhappy about the American model—not least in the United States. Only one in four Americans believes the economy is in good shape. While firms' profits have soared, wages for the typical worker have barely budged. The middle class—admittedly a vague term in America—feels squeezed. A college degree is no longer a passport to ever-higher pay. Now politicians are playing on these fears. From the left, populists complain about Mr. Bush's plutocratic friends exporting jobs abroad; from the right, nativists howl about immigrants wrecking the system.

A Global Argument

The debate about the American model echoes far beyond the nation's shores. Europeans have long held that America does not look after its poor—a prejudice reinforced by the ghastly scenes after Hurricane Katrina. The sharp decline in America's image abroad has much to do with foreign policy, but Americanisation has also become synonymous with globalisation. Across the rich world, global competition is forcing economies to become more flexible, often increasing inequality; Japan is one example. The logic of many non-Americans is that if globalisation makes their economy more like America's, and the American model is defective, then free trade and open markets must be bad.

This debate mixes up three arguments—about inequality, meritocracy, and immigration. The word that America should worry about most is the one you hear least—meritocracy.

Begin with inequality. The flip side of America's economic dynamism is that it has become more unequal—but in a more complex way than first appears. America's rich have been pulling away from the rest of the population, as the returns for talent and capital in a global market have increased. Even if American business stopped at the water's edge, Bill Gates and the partners of Goldman Sachs would still be wealthy people; but since software and investment banking are global industries, Mr. Gates is worth $50 billion and the average pay-and-benefits package for Goldman's 22,400 employees is above $500,000.

On the other hand, the current wave of globalisation may not be widening the gap between the poor and the rest. Indeed, the headwinds of the global economy are being felt less by Americans at the bottom than by those in the middle. The jobs threatened by outsourcing—data processing, accounting, and so on—are white-collar jobs; the jobs done by the poor—cleaning and table-waiting, for example—could never be done from Bangalore.

Those at the bottom have different fears, immigration high among them. Their jobs cannot be exported to rival countries perhaps, but rival workers can and are being imported to America. Yet there is surprisingly little evidence that the arrival of low-skilled workers has pulled poor Americans' wages down. And it has certainly provided a far better life for new arrivals than the one they left behind.

A Long Ladder Is Fine, But It Must Have Rungs

To many who would discredit American capitalism, this sort of coldhearted number crunching is beside the point. Any system in which the spoils are distributed so unevenly is morally wrong, they say. This newspaper disagrees. Inequality is not inherently wrong—as long as three conditions are met: first, society as a whole is getting richer; second, there is a safety net for the very poor; and third, everybody, regardless of class, race, creed, or sex, has an opportunity to climb up through the system. A dynamic, fast-growing economy may sometimes look ugly, but it offers far more hope than a stagnant one for everybody in the United States.

This is not to let the American system off the hook when 10 it comes to social mobility. Although the United States is seen as a world of opportunity, the reality may be different. Some studies have shown that it is easier for poorer children to rise through society in many European countries than in America. There is a particular fear about the engine of American meritocracy, its education system. Only 3 percent of students at top colleges come from the poorest quarter of the population. Poor children are trapped in dismal schools, while richer parents spend ever more cash on tutoring their offspring.

What, if anything, needs to be done? A meritocracy works only if it is seen to be fair. There are some unfair ways in which rich Americans have rewarded themselves, from backdated share options to reserved places at universities for the offspring of alumni. And a few of Mr. Bush's fiscal choices are not helping. Why make the tax system less progressive at a time when the most affluent are doing best?

That said, government should not be looking for ways to haul the rich down. Rather, it should help others, especially the extremely poor, to climb up—and that must mean education. Parts of the American system are still magnificent, such as its community colleges. But as countless international league tables show, its schools are not. Education is a political football, tossed about between Republicans who refuse to reform a locally based funding system that starves schools in poor districts, and Democrats who will never dare offend their paymasters in the teachers' unions.

The other challenge is to create a social-welfare system that matches a global business world of fast-changing careers. No country has done this well. But the answer has to be broader than just "trade-adjustment" assistance or tax breaks for hard-hit areas. Health care, for instance, needs reform. America's traditional way of providing it through companies is crumbling. The public pension system, too, needs an overhaul.

These are mightily complicated areas, but the United States has always had a genius for translating the highfalutin talk of the American Dream into practical policies, such as the GI Bill, a scholarship scheme for returning troops after the second world war. The country needs another burst of practical idealism. It is still the model the rest of the world is following.

Joining the Conversation

1. This article begins with a succinct summary of the American Dream. What is your understanding of this concept? What role, if any, has it played or does it play in your own goals and actions?

2. Paragraphs 2 and 3 summarize what others are saying. Paragraph 2 discusses ways in which the American Dream has been a success and is envied and emulated around the world. Paragraph 3 considers the downside of the American model. Why do you think that this article opens with a discussion of two seemingly contradictory perspectives on this issue?

3. Paragraph 5 raises three key issues: inequality, meritocracy, and immigration. What does the article argue about each of these aspects of the U.S. economy?

4. According to this article, paragraph 9 in particular, economic inequality is not inherently wrong, as long as three conditions are met. What are those conditions, and what do you think about this view?

5. This article takes a middle position between that of Sklar (pp. 308–11) and Bartlett (pp. 312–15). What do you think? Write an essay about the American Dream. Open by summarizing the debate, following the guidelines on pp. 24–25, and then give your own view. You'll want to quote or summarize details from Sklar, Bartlett, and the *Economist*, either as support or as naysayers.

Confronting Inequality

PAUL KRUGMAN

—◻—

THE **A**MERICA **I** GREW UP IN was a relatively equal middle-class society. Over the past generation, however, the country has returned to Gilded Age levels of inequality. In this chapter I'll outline policies that can help reverse these changes. I'll begin with the question of values. Why should we care about high and rising inequality?

One reason to care about inequality is the straightforward matter of living standards. The lion's share of economic growth in America over the past thirty years has gone to a small, wealthy minority, to such an extent that it's unclear whether the typical family has benefited at all from technological progress and the rising productivity it brings. The lack of clear economic progress for lower- and middle-income families is in itself an important reason to seek a more equal distribution of income.

PAUL KRUGMAN teaches economics at Princeton and writes an op-ed column in the *New York Times*. He was awarded the Nobel Prize in Economics in 2008. Krugman is the author of many books, among them *The Age of Diminished Expectations* (1989) and *The Great Unraveling: Losing Our Way in the New Century* (2003). "Confronting Inequality" is a chapter from his 2007 book, *The Conscience of a Liberal*.

Beyond that, however, is the damage extreme inequality does to our society and our democracy. Ever since America's founding, our idea of ourselves has been that of a nation without sharp class distinctions—not a leveled society of perfect equality, but one in which the gap between the economic elite and the typical citizen isn't an unbridgeable chasm. That's why Thomas Jefferson wrote, "The small landholders are the most precious part of a state."[1] Translated into modern terms as an assertion that a broad middle class is the most precious part of a state, Jefferson's statement remains as true as ever. High inequality, which has turned us into a nation with a much-weakened middle class, has a corrosive effect on social relations and politics, one that has become ever more apparent as America has moved deeper into a new Gilded Age.

The Costs of Inequality

One of the best arguments I've ever seen for the social costs of inequality came from a movement conservative trying to argue the opposite. In 1997 Irving Kristol, one of the original neoconservative intellectuals, published an article in the *Wall Street Journal* called "Income Inequality Without Class Conflict." Kristol argued that we shouldn't worry about income inequality, because whatever the numbers may say, class distinctions are, in reality, all but gone. Today, he asserted,

> income inequality tends to be swamped by even greater social equality. . . . In all of our major cities, there is not a single restaurant where a CEO can lunch or dine with the absolute assurance that he will not run into his secretary. If you fly first class, who will be your traveling companions? You never know. If you go to

Paris, you will be lost in a crowd of young people flashing their credit cards.[2]

By claiming that income inequality doesn't matter because we have social equality, Kristol was in effect admitting that income inequality *would* be a problem if it led to social inequality. And here's the thing: It does. Kristol's fantasy of a world in which the rich live just like you and me, and nobody feels socially inferior, bears no resemblance to the real America we live in.

See p. 55 on using someone else's evidence to support your position.

Lifestyles of the rich and famous are arguably the least important part of the story, yet it's worth pointing out that Kristol's vision of CEOs rubbing shoulders with the middle class is totally contradicted by the reporting of Robert Frank of the *Wall Street Journal*, whose assigned beat is covering the lives of the wealthy. In his book *Richistan* Frank describes what he learned:

> Today's rich had formed their own virtual country. . . . [T]hey had built a self-contained world unto themselves, complete with their own health-care system (concierge doctors), travel network (Net Jets, destination clubs), separate economy. . . . The rich weren't just getting richer; they were becoming financial foreigners, creating their own country within a country, their own society within a society, and their economy within an economy.[3]

The fact is that vast income inequality inevitably brings vast social inequality in its train. And this social inequality isn't just a matter of envy and insults. It has real, negative consequences for the way people live in this country. It may not matter much that the great majority of Americans can't afford to stay in the eleven-thousand-dollar-a-night hotel suites popping up in luxury hotels around the world.[4] It matters a great deal that mil-

A man and woman, with their two dogs, board a private jet in Aspen, Colorado.

lions of middle-class families buy houses they can't really afford, taking on more mortgage debt than they can safely handle, because they're desperate to send their children to a good school—and intensifying inequality means that the desirable school districts are growing fewer in number, and more expensive to live in.

Elizabeth Warren, a Harvard Law School expert in bankruptcy, and Amelia Warren Tyagi, a business consultant, have studied the rise of bankruptcy in the United States. By 2005, just before a new law making it much harder for individuals to declare bankruptcy took effect, the number of families filing for bankruptcy each year was five times its level in the early 1980s. The proximate reason for this surge in bankruptcies was that families were taking on more debt—and this led to moralistic pronouncements about people spending too much on luxuries

Crowds of passengers get on and off planes at O'Hare International Airport in Chicago.

they can't afford. What Warren and Tyagi found, however, was that middle-class families were actually spending *less* on luxuries than they had in the 1970s. Instead the rise in debt mainly reflected increased spending on housing, largely driven by competition to get into good school districts. Middle-class Americans have been caught up in a rat race, not because they're greedy or foolish but because they're trying to give their children a chance in an increasingly unequal society.[5] And they're right to be worried: A bad start can ruin a child's chances for life.

Americans still tend to say, when asked, that individuals can make their own place in society. According to one survey 61 percent of Americans agree with the statement that "people get rewarded for their effort," compared with 49 percent in Canada and only 23 percent in France.[6] In reality, however,

America has vast inequality of opportunity as well as results. We may believe that anyone can succeed through hard work and determination, but the facts say otherwise.

There are many pieces of evidence showing that Horatio 10 Alger stories are very rare in real life. One of the most striking comes from a study published by the National Center for Education Statistics, which tracked the educational experience of Americans who were eighth graders in 1988. Those eighth graders were sorted both by apparent talent, as measured by a mathematics test, and by the socioeconomic status of their parents, as measured by occupations, incomes, and education.

The key result is shown in Table 1. Not surprisingly, both getting a high test score and having high-status parents increased a student's chance of finishing college. But family status mattered more. Students who scored in the bottom fourth on the exam, but came from families whose status put them in the top fourth—what we used to call RDKs, for "rich dumb kids," when I was a teenager—were more likely to finish college than students who scored in the top fourth but whose parents were in the bottom fourth. What this tells us is that the idea that we have anything close to equality of opportunity is clearly a fantasy. It would be closer to the truth, though not

Table 1. Percentage of 1988 Eighth Graders Finishing College

	Score in Bottom Quartile	Score in Top Quartile
Parents in Bottom Quartile	3	29
Parents in Top Quartile	30	74

Source: National Center for Education Statistics, *The Condition of Education 2003*, 47.

the whole truth, to say that in modern America, class—inherited class—usually trumps talent.

Isn't that true everywhere? Not to the same extent. International comparisons of "intergenerational mobility," the extent to which people can achieve higher status than their parents, are tricky because countries don't collect perfectly comparable data. Nonetheless it's clear that Horatio Alger has moved to someplace in Europe: Mobility is highest in the Scandinavian countries, and most results suggest that mobility is lower in the United States than it is in France, Canada, and maybe even Britain. Not only don't Americans have equal opportunity, opportunity is less equal here than elsewhere in the West.

It's not hard to understand why. Our unique lack of universal health care, all by itself, puts Americans who are unlucky in their parents at a disadvantage: Because American children from low-income families are often uninsured, they're more likely to have health problems that derail their life chances. Poor nutrition, thanks to low income and a lack of social support, can have the same effect. Life disruptions that affect a child's parents can also make upward mobility hard—and the weakness of the U.S. social safety net makes such disruptions more likely and worse if they happen. Then there's the highly uneven quality of U.S. basic education, and so on. What it all comes down to is that although the principle of "equality of opportunity, not equality of results" sounds fine, it's a largely fictitious distinction. A society with highly unequal results is, more or less inevitably, a society with highly unequal opportunity, too. If you truly believe that all Americans are entitled to an equal chance at the starting line, that's an argument for doing something to reduce inequality.

America's high inequality, then, imposes serious costs on our society that go beyond the way it holds down the purchasing power of most families. And there's another way in which inequality damages us: It corrupts our politics. "If there are men in this country big enough to own the government of the United States," said Woodrow Wilson in 1913, in words that would be almost inconceivable from a modern president, "they are going to own it."[7] Well, now there are, and they do. Not completely, of course, but hardly a week goes by without the disclosure of a case in which the influence of money has grotesquely distorted U.S. government policy.

As this book went to press, there was a spectacular exam-ple: The way even some Democrats rallied to the support of hedge fund managers, who receive an unconscionable tax break. Through a quirk in the way the tax laws have been interpreted, these managers—some of whom make more than a billion dollars a year—get to have most of their earnings taxed at the capital gains rate, which is only 15 percent, even as other high earners pay a 35 percent rate. The hedge fund tax loophole costs the government more than $6 billion a year in lost revenue, roughly the cost of providing health care to three million children.[8] Almost $2 billion of the total goes to just twenty-five individuals. Even conservative economists believe that the tax break is unjustified, and should be eliminated.[9]

Yet the tax break has powerful political support—and not just from Republicans. In July 2007 Senator Charles Schumer of New York, the head of the Democratic Senatorial Campaign Committee, let it be known that he would favor eliminating the hedge fund loophole only if other, deeply entrenched tax breaks were eliminated at the same time. As everyone understood, this was a "poison pill," a way of blocking reform without explicitly saying no. And although Schumer denied it, everyone also suspected that his position was driven by the large sums hedge funds contribute to Democratic political campaigns.[10]

The hedge fund loophole is a classic example of how the concentration of income in a few hands corrupts politics. Beyond that is the bigger story of how income inequality has reinforced the rise of movement conservatism, a fundamentally undemocratic force. Rising inequality has to an important extent been caused by the rightward shift of our politics, but the causation also runs the other way. The new wealth of the rich has increased their influence, sustaining the institutions of movement conservatism and pulling the Republican Party even further into the movement's orbit. The ugliness of our politics is in large part a reflection of the inequality of our income distribution.

More broadly still, high levels of inequality strain the bonds that hold us together as a society. There has been a long-term downward trend in the extent to which Americans trust either the government or one another. In the sixties, most Americans agreed with the proposition that "most people can be trusted"; today most disagree.[11] In the sixties, most Americans believed that the government is run "for the benefit of all"; today, most believe that it's run for "a few big interests."[12] And there's convincing evidence that growing inequality is behind our growing cynicism, which is making the United States seem increasingly like a Latin American country. As the political scientists Eric Uslaner and Mitchell Brown point out (and support with extensive data), "In a world of haves and have-nots, those at either end of the economic spectrum have little reason to believe that 'most people can be trusted' . . . social trust rests on a foundation of economic equality."[13] . . .

The Arithmetic of Equalization

Suppose we agree that the United States should become more like other advanced countries, whose tax and benefit systems do much more than ours to reduce inequality. The next question is what that decision might involve.

In part it would involve undoing many of the tax cuts for 20 the wealthy that movement conservatives have pushed through since 1980. Table 2 shows what has happened to three tax rates that strongly affect the top 1 percent of the U.S. population, while having little effect on anyone else. Between 1979 and 2006 the top tax rate on earned income was cut in half; the tax rate on capital gains was cut almost as much; the tax rate on corporate profits fell by more than a quarter. High incomes in America are much less taxed than they used to be. Thus raising taxes on the rich back toward historical levels can pay for part, though only part, of a stronger safety net that limits inequality.

The first step toward restoring progressivity to the tax system is to let the Bush tax cuts for the very well off expire at the end of 2010, as they are now scheduled to. That alone would raise a significant amount of revenue. The nonpartisan Urban-Brookings Joint Tax Policy Center estimates that letting the Bush tax cuts expire for people with incomes over two hundred thousand dollars would be worth about $140 billion a year starting in 2012. That's enough to pay for the subsidies needed to implement universal health care. A tax-cut rollback of this kind, used to finance health care reform, would significantly reduce inequality. It would do so partly by modestly reducing incomes at the top: The Tax Policy Center estimates that allowing the Bush tax cuts to expire for Americans making more than two hundred thousand dollars a year would

TABLE 2. THREE TOP RATES (PERCENTAGE)

	TOP TAX ON EARNED INCOME	TOP TAX ON LONG-TERM CAPITAL GAINS	TOP TAX ON CORPORATE PROFITS
1979	70	28	48
2006	35	15	35

Source: Urban-Brookings Tax Policy Center <http://taxpolicycenter.org/taxfacts/tfdb/tftemplate.cfm>.

reduce the aftertax incomes of the richest 1 percent of Americans by about 4.5 percent compared with what they would be if the Bush tax cuts were made permanent. Meanwhile middle- and lower-income Americans would be assured of health care— one of the key aspects of being truly middle class.[14]

Another relatively easy move from a political point of view would be closing some of the obvious loopholes in the U.S. system. These include the rule described earlier that allows financial wheeler-dealers, such as hedge fund managers, to classify their earnings as capital gains, taxed at a 15 percent rate rather than 35 percent. The major tax loopholes also include rules that let corporations, drug companies in particular, shift recorded profits to low-tax jurisdictions overseas, costing billions more; one recent study estimates that tax avoidance by multinationals costs about $50 billion a year.[15]

Going beyond rolling back the Bush cuts and closing obvious loopholes would be a more difficult political undertaking. Yet there can be rapid shifts in what seems politically realistic. At the end of 2004 it seemed all too possible that Social Security, the centerpiece of the New Deal, would be privatized and effectively phased out. Today Social Security appears safe, and universal health care seems within reach. If universal health care can be achieved, and the New Deal idea that government can be a force for good is reinvigorated, things that now seem off the table might not look so far out.

Both historical and international evidence show that there is room for tax increases at the top that go beyond merely rolling back the Bush cuts. Even before the Bush tax cuts, top tax rates in the United States were low by historical standards—the tax rate on the top bracket was only 39.6 percent during the Clinton years, compared with 70 percent in the seventies and 50 percent even *after* Reagan's 1981 tax cut. Top U.S. tax rates are also low compared with those in European countries. For example, in Britain, the top income tax rate is 40 percent, seemingly equivalent to the top rate of the Clinton years. However, in Britain employers also pay a social insurance tax—the equivalent of the employer share of FICA* here—that applies to all earned income. (Most of the U.S. equivalent is levied only on income up to a maximum of $97,500.) As a result very highly paid British employees face an effective tax rate of almost 48 percent. In France effective top rates are even higher. Also, in Britain capital gains are taxed as ordinary income, so that the effective tax rate on capital gains for people with high income is 40 percent, compared with 15 percent in the United States.[16] Taxing capital gains as ordinary income in the United States would yield significantly more revenue, and also limit the range of tax abuses like the hedge fund loophole.

Also, from the New Deal until the 1970s it was considered 25 normal and appropriate to have "super" tax rates on very-high-income individuals. Only a few people were subject to the 70 percent top bracket in the 70s, let alone the 90 percent-plus top rates of the Eisenhower years. It used to be argued that a

*FICA Federal Insurance Contributions Act, an employment tax that helps fund Social Security and Medicare.

surtax on very high incomes serves no real purpose other than punishing the rich because it wouldn't raise much money, but that's no longer true. Today the top 0.1 percent of Americans, a class with a minimum income of about $1.3 million and an average income of about $3.5 million, receives more than 7 percent of all income—up from just 2.2 percent in 1979.[17] A surtax on that income would yield a significant amount of revenue, which could be used to help a lot of people. All in all, then, the next step after rolling back the Bush tax cuts and implementing universal health care should be a broader effort to restore the progressivity of U.S. taxes, and use the revenue to pay for more benefits that help lower- and middle-income families.

Realistically, however, this would not be enough to pay for social expenditures comparable to those in other advanced countries, not even the relatively modest Canadian level. In addition to imposing higher taxes on the rich, other advanced countries also impose higher taxes on the middle class, through both higher social insurance payments and value-added taxes— in effect, national sales taxes. Social insurance taxes and VATs are not, in themselves, progressive. Their effect in reducing inequality is indirect but large: They pay for benefits, and these benefits are worth more as a percentage of income to people with lower incomes.

As a political matter, persuading the public that middle-income families would be better off paying somewhat higher taxes in return for a stronger social safety net will be a hard sell after decades of antitax, antigovernment propaganda. Much as I would like to see the United States devote another 2 or 3 percent of GDP* to social expenditure beyond health care, it's probably an

---

*GDP   Gross domestic product. One measure of income and output for a country's economy.

endeavor that has to wait until liberals have established a strong track record of successfully using the government to make peoples' lives better and more secure. This is one reason health care reform, which is tremendously important in itself, would have further benefits: It would blaze the trail for a wider progressive agenda. This is also the reason movement conservatives are fiercely determined not to let health care reform succeed.

Reducing Market Inequality

Aftermarket policies can do a great deal to reduce inequality. But that should not be our whole focus. The Great Compression* also involved a sharp reduction in the inequality of market income. This was accomplished in part through wage controls during World War II, an experience we hope won't be repeated. Still, there are several steps we can take.

The first step has already been taken: In 2007 Congress passed the first increase in the minimum wage within a decade. In the 1950s and 1960s the minimum wage averaged about half of the average wage. By 2006, however, the purchasing power of the minimum wage had been so eroded by inflation that in real terms it was at its lowest point since 1955, and was only 31 percent of the average wage. Thanks to the new Democratic majority in Congress, the minimum is scheduled to rise from its current $5.15 an hour to $7.25 by 2009. This won't restore all the erosion, but it's an important first step.

There are two common but somewhat contradictory objec- 30 tions often heard to increasing the minimum wage. On one hand, it's argued that raising the minimum wage will reduce employment and increase unemployment. On the other it's

*See paragraph 40.

argued that raising the minimum will have little or no effect in raising wages. The evidence, however, suggests that a minimum wage increase will in fact have modest positive effects.

On the employment side, a classic study by David Card of Berkeley and Alan Krueger of Princeton, two of America's best labor economists, found no evidence that minimum wage increases in the range the United States has experienced led to job losses.[18] Their work has been furiously attacked both because it seems to contradict Econ 101 and because it was ideologically disturbing to many. Yet it has stood up very well to repeated challenges, and new cases confirming its results keep coming in. For example, the state of Washington has a minimum wage almost three dollars an hour higher than its neighbor Idaho; business experiences near the state line seem to indicate that, if anything, Washington has gained jobs at Idaho's expense. "Small-business owners in Washington," reported the *New York Times*, "say they have prospered far beyond their expectation. . . . Idaho teenagers cross the state line to work in fast-food restaurants in Washington."

All the empirical evidence suggests that minimum wage increases *in the range that is likely to take place* do not lead to significant job losses. True, an increase in the minimum wage to, say, fifteen dollars an hour would probably cause job losses, because it would dramatically raise the cost of employment in some industries. But that's not what's on—or even near— the table.

Meanwhile minimum wage increases can have fairly significant effects on wages at the bottom end of the scale. The Economic Policy Institute estimates that the worst-paid 10 percent of the U.S. labor force, 13 million workers, will gain from the just-enacted minimum wage increase. Of these, 5.6 million are currently being paid less than the new minimum wage, and would see a direct benefit. The rest are workers earning more than the new minimum wage, who would benefit from ripple effects of the higher minimum.

The minimum wage, however, matters mainly to low-paid workers. Any broader effort to reduce market inequality will have to do something about incomes further up the scale. The most important tool in that respect is likely to be an end to the thirty-year tilt of government policy against unions.

The drastic decline in the U.S. union movement was not, 35 as is often claimed, an inevitable result of globalization and increased competition. International comparisons show that the U.S. union decline is unique, even though other countries faced the same global pressures. Again, in 1960 Canada and the United States had essentially equal rates of unionization, 32 and 30 percent of wage and salary workers, respectively. By 1999 U.S. unionization was down to 13 percent, but Canadian unionization was unchanged. The sources of union decline in America lie not in market forces but in the political climate created by movement conservatism, which allowed employers to engage in union-busting activities and punish workers for supporting union organizers. Without that changed political climate, much of the service economy—especially giant retailers like Wal-Mart—would probably by unionized today.

A new political climate could revitalize the union movement—and revitalizing unions should be a key progressive goal. Specific legislation, such as the Employee Free Choice Act, which would reduce the ability of employers to intimidate workers into rejecting a union, is only part of what's needed. It's also crucial to enforce labor laws already on the books. Much if not most of the antiunion activity that led to the sharp decline in American unionization was illegal even under existing law. But employers judged, correctly, that they could get away with it.

The hard-to-answer question is the extent to which a newly empowered U.S. union movement would reduce inequality. International comparisons suggest that it might make quite a lot of difference. The sharpest increases in wage inequality in the Western world have taken place in the United States and in Britain, both of which experienced sharp declines in union membership. (Britain is still far more unionized than America, but it used to have more than 50 percent unionization.) Canada, although its economy is closely linked to that of the United States, appears to have had substantially less increase in wage inequality—and it's likely that the persistence of a strong union movement is an important reason why. Unions raise the wages of their members, who tend to be in the middle of the wage distribution; they also tend to equalize wages among members. Perhaps most important, they act as a countervailing force to management, enforcing social norms that limit very high and very low pay even among people who aren't union members. They also mobilize their members to vote for progressive policies. Would getting the United States back to historical levels of unionization undo a large part of the Great Divergence? We don't know—but it might, and encouraging a union resurgence should be a major goal of progressive policy.

A reinvigorated union movement isn't the only change that could reduce extreme inequalities in pay. A number of other factors discouraged very high paychecks for a generation after World War II. One was a change in the political climate: Very high executive pay used to provoke public scrutiny, congressional hearings, and even presidential intervention. But that all ended in the Reagan years.

Historical experience still suggests that a new progressive majority should not be shy about questioning private-sector pay when it seems outrageous. Moral suasion was effective in the past, and could be so again.

Another Great Compression?

The Great Compression, the abrupt reduction in economic ⁴⁰ inequality that took place in the United States in the 1930s and 1940s, took place at a time of crisis. Today America's state is troubled, but we're not in the midst of a great depression or a world war. Correspondingly, we shouldn't expect changes as drastic or sudden as those that took place seventy years ago. The process of reducing inequality now is likely to be more of a Great Moderation than a Great Compression.

Yet it is possible, both as an economic matter and in terms of practical politics, to reduce inequality and make America a middle-class nation again. And now is the time to get started.

NOTES

1. Thomas Jefferson, letter to James Madison, 28 Oct. 1785 <http://press-pubs.uchicago.edu/founders/documents/v1ch15s32.html>.

2. Irving Kristol, "Income Inequality Without Class Conflict," *Wall Street Journal* 18 Dec. 1997: A22.

3. Robert Frank, *Richistan: A Journey Through the American Wealth Boom and the Lives of the New Rich* (Crown, 2007) 3–4.

4. "Suites for the Sweet," *Newsweek International* July 2–9 <http://www. msnbc.msn.com/id/19388720/site/newsweek>, part of a special report on "Secret Habits of the Super Rich."

5. Elizabeth Warren and Amelia Warren Tyagi, "What's Hurting the Middle Class," *Boston Review* (Sept./Oct. 2005) <http://bostonreview.net/BR30.5/warrentyagi.html>.

6. Tom Hertz, *Understanding Mobility in America* (Center for American Progress, 2006) <http://www.americanprogress.org/issues/2006/04/b1579981.html>.

7. Woodrow Wilson, *The New Freedom* (Doubleday, 1913), Project Gutenberg <http://www.gutenberg.org/files/14811/14811-h/14811-h.htm>.

8. "Tax Breaks for Billionaires," Economic Policy Institute Policy Memorandum no. 120 <http://www.epi.org/content.cfm/pm120>.

9. See, for example, Jessica Holzer, "Conservatives Break with GOP Leaders on a Tax Bill," *The Hill* 18 July 2007 <http://thehill.com/leading-the-news/conservatives-break-with-gop-leaders-on-a-tax-bill-2007-07-18.html>.

10. "In Opposing Tax Plan, Schumer Supports Wall Street Over Party," *New York Times* 30 July 2007: A1.

11. Eric M. Uslaner and Mitchell Brown, "Inequality, Trust, and Civic Engagement," *American Politics Research* 33.6 (2005): 868–94.

12. *The ANES Guide to Public Opinion and Electoral Behavior*, table 5A.2 <http://electionstudies.org/nesguide/toptable/tab5a_2.htm>.

13. Uslaner and Brown, "Inequality, Trust, and Civic Engagement."

14. Tax Policy Center, "Options to Extend the 2001–2006 Tax Cuts, Static Impact on Individual Income and Estate Tax Liability and Revenue ($ billions), 2008–17," Table T07-0126 <http://taxpolicycenter.org/TaxModel/tmdb/Content/PDF/T07-0126.pdf>.

15. Kimberly A. Clausing, "Multinational Firm Tax Avoidance and U.S. Government Revenue" (working paper, Wellesley College, Wellesley, MA, 2007).

16. OECD Tax Database <http://www.oecd.org/ctp/taxdatabase>.

17. Piketty and Saez, 2005 preliminary estimates <http://elsa.berkeley.edu/~saez/TabFig2005prel.xls>.

18. David Card and Alan B. Krueger, "Minimum Wages and Employment: A Case Study of the Fast-Food Industry in New Jersey and Pennsylvania," *American Economic Review* 84.4 (1994): 772–93.

Joining the Conversation

1. Krugman begins by asking the "so what?" question in paragraph 1: "Why should we care about high and rising inequality?" How does he answer this question?

2. What evidence does Krugman provide for the prevalence of economic inequality in U.S. society? How convincing is this evidence to you?

3. Notice how many direct quotations Krugman includes. Why do you think he includes so many? What, if anything, do the quotations contribute that a summary or paraphrase would not?

4. In paragraph 4 Krugman quotes someone whose views he does not agree with, but then uses those views to support his own argument. How do you know he is quoting a view that he disagrees with?

5. Write an essay responding to Krugman, agreeing with him on some points and disagreeing with him on others. Start by summarizing his arguments before moving on to give your own views. See guidelines on pp. 59–62 that will help you to agree and disagree simultaneously.

Up Against Wal-Mart

KAREN OLSSON

—⟨▫⟩—

JENNIFER MCLAUGHLIN IS 22, has a baby, drives a truck, wears wide-leg jeans and spiky plastic chokers, dyes her hair dark red, and works at Wal-Mart. The store in Paris, Texas— Wal-Mart Supercenter #148—is just down the road from the modest apartment complex where McLaughlin lives with her boyfriend and her one-year-old son; five days a week she drives to the store, puts on a blue vest with "How May I Help You?" emblazoned across the back, and clocks in. Some days she works in the Garden Center and some days in the toy department. The pace is frenetic, even by the normally fast-paced standards of retailing; often, it seems, there simply aren't enough people around to get the job done. On a given shift McLaughlin might man a register, hop on a mechanical lift to retrieve something from a high shelf, catch fish from a tank, run over to another

KAREN OLSSON is a writer-at-large for *Texas Monthly* and also writes for *Slate.com*, the *Washington Post*, the *Baffler*, and the *Nation*. She has won awards from the Association of Alternative Newsweeklies for her investigative reporting and feature stories. "Up Against Wal-Mart" appeared in the March/April 2003 issue of *Mother Jones*, a nonprofit magazine with a commitment to social justice that boasts of a tradition of "smart, fearless" investigative reporting.

department to help locate an item, restock the shelves, dust off the bike racks, or field questions about potting soil and lawn mowers. "It's stressful," she says. "They push you to the limit. They just want to see how much they can get away with without having to hire someone else."

Then there's the matter of her pay. After three years with the company, McLaughlin earns only $16,800 a year. "And I'm considered high-paid," she says. "The way they pay you, you cannot make it by yourself without having a second job or someone to help you, unless you've been there for 20 years or you're a manager." Because health insurance on the Wal-Mart plan would deduct up to $85 from her biweekly paycheck of $550, she goes without, and relies on Medicaid to cover her son, Gage.

Complaints about understaffing and low pay are not uncommon among retail workers—but Wal-Mart is no mere

peddler of saucepans and boom boxes. The company is the world's largest retailer, with $220 billion in sales, and the nation's largest private employer, with 3,372 stores and more than 1 million hourly workers. Its annual revenues account for 2 percent of America's entire domestic product. Even as the economy has slowed, the company has continued to metastasize, with plans to add 800,000 more jobs worldwide by 2007.

Give its staggering size and rapid expansion, Wal-Mart increasingly sets the standard for wages and benefits throughout the U.S. economy. "Americans can't live on a Wal-Mart paycheck," says Greg Denier, communications director for the United Food and Commercial Workers International Union (UFCW). "Yet it's the dominant employer, and what they pay will be the future of working America." The average hourly worker at Wal-Mart earns barely $18,000 a year at a company that pocketed $6.6 billion in profits last year. Forty percent of employees opt not to receive coverage under the company's medical plan, which costs up to $2,844 a year, plus a deductible. As Jennifer McLaughlin puts it, "They're on top of the Fortune 500, and I can't get health insurance for my kid." Angered by the disparity between profits and wages, thousands of former and current employees like McLaughlin have started to fight the company on a variety of fronts. Workers in 27 states are suing Wal-Mart for violating wage-and-hour laws; in the first of the cases to go to trial, an Oregon jury found the company guilty in December of systematically forcing employees to work overtime without pay. The retailer also faces a sex-discrimination lawsuit that accuses it of wrongly denying promotions and equal pay to 700,000 women. And across the country, workers have launched a massive drive to organize a union at Wal-Mart, demanding better wages and working conditions. Employees at more than 100 stores in 25 states—including

Supercenter #148 in Paris—are currently trying to unionize the company, and in July the UFCW launched an organizing blitz in the Midwest, hoping to mobilize nearly 120,000 workers in Michigan, Kentucky, Ohio, and Indiana.

Wal-Mart has responded to the union drive by trying to stop workers from organizing—sometimes in violation of federal labor law. In 10 separate cases, the National Labor Relations Board has ruled that Wal-Mart repeatedly broke the law by interrogating workers, confiscating union literature, and firing union supporters. At the first sign of organizing in a store, Wal-Mart dispatches a team of union busters from its headquarters in Bentonville, Arkansas, sometimes setting up surveillance cameras to monitor workers. "In my 35 years in labor relations, I've never seen a company that will go to the lengths that Wal-Mart goes to, to avoid a union," says Martin Levitt, a management consultant who helped the company develop its anti-union tactics before writing a book called *Confessions of a Union Buster*. "They have zero tolerance."

The retaliation can be extreme. In February 2000, the meat-cutting department at a Wal-Mart in Jacksonville, Texas, voted to join the UFCW—the only Wal-Mart in the nation where workers successfully organized a union. Two weeks after the vote, the company announced it was eliminating its meat-cutting departments in all of its stores nationwide. It also fired four workers who voted for the union. "They held a meeting and said there was nothing we could do," recalls Dotty Jones, a former meat cutter in Jacksonville. "No matter which way the election went, they would hold it up in court until we were old and gray."

If you've seen one Wal-Mart, you've seen the Paris store, more or less: a gray cinder-block warehouse of a building, with a red stripe across the front, flags on the roof, WAL-MART spelled in large capitals in the center, and the company credos ("We Sell for Less" and "Everyday Low Prices") to the left and the right. Inside, the cavernous store is bathed in a dim fluorescent light that makes the white walls and linoleum look dingy, and on a Friday shortly before Christmas, the merchandise is everywhere: not only in bins and on shelves, but in boxes waiting to be unloaded, or just stationed in some odd corner, like the pine gun cabinets ($169.87) lined up by the rest rooms. Television monitors advertise thermometers and compact discs. Christmas carols play over the audio system, and yet there's a kind of silence to the place, a suspension of ordinary life, as shoppers in their trances drift through the store and fill carts with tubs of popcorn, a microwave, a chess set, dog biscuits. Here Protestant thrift and consumer wants are reconciled, for the moment anyway, in carts brimming with bargains.

Wal-Mart's success story was scripted by its founder, Sam Walton, whose genius was not so much for innovation as for picking which of his competitors' innovations to copy in his own stores. In 1945, Walton bought a franchise variety store in Newport, Arkansas. The most successful retailers, he noticed, were chains like Sears and A&P, which distributed goods to stores most efficiently, lowered prices to generate a larger volume of sales, and in the process generated a lot of cash to finance further expansion. These, in turn, would serve as basic principles of Walton's business. As he explains in his autobiography, *Sam Walton, Made in America*, he drove long distances to buy ladies' panties at lower prices, recognizing that selling more pairs at four for a dollar would bring greater profits than selling fewer pairs at three for a dollar. The women of northeastern Arkansas were soon awash in underwear, and a discounter was born. Walton opened his first Wal-Mart Discount City in 1962 and gradually expanded out from his Arkansas base. By 1970 Wal-Mart owned 32 outlets; by 1980 there were 276; by 1990, 1,528 in 29 states.

The company grew, in no small part, by dint of its legendary frugality—a habit that started with Sam Walton himself, who drove an old pickup truck and shared hotel rooms on company trips and insisted on keeping the headquarters in Arkansas as plain as possible. Payroll, of course, tends to be a rather larger expense than hotel rooms, and Walton kept that as low as he could, too. He paid his first clerks 50 to 60 cents an hour— substantially below minimum wage at the time—by taking questionable advantage of a small-business exemption to the Fair Labor Standards Act. In 1970, Walton fended off an organizing push by the Retail Clerks Union in two small Missouri towns by hiring a professional union buster, John Tate, to lecture workers on the negative aspects of unions. On Tate's advice, he also took steps to win his workers over, encouraging them to air concerns with managers and implementing a profit-sharing program.

A few years later, Wal-Mart hired a consulting firm named 10 Alpha Associates to develop a "union avoidance program." Martin Levitt, the consultant who worked on the program, says that Wal-Mart does "whatever it takes to wear people down and destroy their spirit." Each manager, he says, is taught to take union organizing personally: "Anyone supporting a union is slapping that supervisor in the face." The company also encouraged employees to believe in the good intentions of "Mr. Sam," who peppered his autobiography with tributes to his "associates": "If you want to take care of the customers you have to make sure you're taking care of the people in the stores."

Yet many Wal-Mart workers allege that the company Walton left behind when he died in 1992 is anything but a benevolent caretaker. "We're underpaid, and I'm worried about my retirement," says an overnight stocker in Minnesota who asked not to be identified. "I imagine I'll be working until I'm 90." Her daughter works as a stocker, too, but after nine years she doesn't make enough to support her children. "She's had to go down to the food bank, and I've sent stuff over for them," her mother says. "They just can't do it." On the job, she adds, workers are forced to scramble to make up for understaffing. "We're short—we have a skimpy crew at night. We've got pallets stacked over our heads, and we can't get caught up with all of it."

A quick look around at the store in Paris makes clear what an employee is up against: thousands of items (90,000 in a typical Wal-Mart) that customers are constantly removing from the shelves and not putting back, or putting back in the wrong place, or dropping on the floor—the store a kind of Augean stable,* with a corps of blue-vested Herculeses trying to keep things clean. (When I mention this to Jennifer McLaughlin, she tells me that's why no one likes to work the 2 a.m. to 11 a.m. shift, because "all it is, is putting stuff back.") To get the job done, according to the dozens of employee lawsuits filed against the company, Wal-Mart routinely forces employees to work overtime without pay. In the Oregon wage-and-hour case, a former personnel manager named Carolyn Thiebes testified that supervisors, pressured by company headquarters to keep payroll low, regularly deleted hours from time records and reprimanded employees who claimed overtime. In 2000, Wal-Mart settled similar lawsuits involving 67,000 workers in New Mexico and Colorado, reportedly paying more than $50 million.

---

*Augean stable   In Greek mythology, a huge stable belonging to King Augeas that Hercules cleaned in a single day as part of his Twelve Labors.

Wal-Mart blames unpaid overtime on individual department managers, insisting that such practices violate company policy. "We rely on our associates," says spokesman Bill Wertz. "It makes no business sense whatsoever to mistreat them." But Russell Lloyd, an attorney representing Wal-Mart employees in Texas, says the company "has a pattern throughout all stores of treating their workers the same way." Corporate headquarters collects reams of data on every store and every employee, he says, and uses sales figures to calculate how many hours of labor it wants to allot to each store. Store managers are then required to schedule fewer hours than the number allotted, and their performance is monitored in daily reports back to Bentonville. To meet the goals, supervisors pressure employees to work extra hours without pay.

"I was asked to work off the clock, sometimes by the store manager, sometimes by the assistant manager," says Liberty Morales Serna, a former employee in Houston. "They would know you'd clocked out already, and they'd say, 'Do me a favor. I don't have anyone coming in—could you stay here?' It would be like four or five hours. They were understaffed, and they expected you to work these hours."

When Judy Danneman, a widow raising three children, went 15 to work as an hourly department manager, in West Palm Beach, Florida, she quickly realized that she would have to climb the management ladder in order to survive—because, as she puts it, "my kids had this bad habit of eating." The only way to do that, she says, was to work off the clock: "Working unpaid overtime equaled saving your job." When she finally became an assistant manager, Danneman knew she had to enforce the same policy: "I knew for my department managers to get their work done, they had to work off the clock. It was an unwritten rule. The majority of them were single mothers raising children, or else married women with children. It was sad, and it was totally demanding and very draining and very stressful."

In fact, more than two-thirds of all Wal-Mart employees are women—yet women make up less than 10 percent of top store managers. Back when she was first lady of Arkansas, Hillary Clinton became the first woman appointed to the Wal-Mart board, and tried to get the company to hire more women managers, but that effort apparently went the way of national health insurance. Wal-Mart today has the same percentage of women in management that the average company had in 1975.

Attorneys representing workers contend that Wal-Mart is too tightly controlled from headquarters in Arkansas to claim ignorance of what's happening in its stores. "In Bentonville they control the air conditioning, the music, and the freezer temperature for each store," says Brad Seligman, a lawyer with the Impact Fund, a nonprofit legal organization in Berkeley. "Most companies divide stores into regions, and then you have a home office of senior management. At Wal-Mart, the regional managers are based in Bentonville; they're on the road Sunday to Wednesday, and then back meeting with management Thursday to Saturday. They're the ones who make the fundamental employee decisions—and the home office knows exactly what they are doing."

The company insists it adequately trains and promotes female managers. But in 2001, a Wal-Mart executive conducted an internal study that showed the company pays female store managers less than men in the same position. "Their focus at Wal-Mart has always relentlessly been on the bottom line and on cost cutting," says Seligman. "Virtually every other consideration is secondary—or third or fourth or fifth."

To protect the bottom line Wal-Mart is as aggressive at fighting off unions as it is at cutting costs. Employees approached by co-workers about joining a union are "scared to even talk," says Ricky Braswell, a "greeter" at the store in Paris. "They're afraid they'll lose their jobs."

In Paris, it was Jennifer McLaughlin's boyfriend, 21-year-old 20 Eric Jackson, who first started talking about a union. Raised by a mother who works in a factory, Jackson always assumed he would find a job after high school rather than go on to college. But the few factory jobs in Paris are highly sought after, so Jackson wound up at Wal-Mart, which employs 350 people out of a local workforce of only 22,000. "People ain't got no other place to go," he says. "There's no other jobs to be had."

Jackson started as an evening cashier earning $5.75 an hour, and it wasn't long before he was regularly asked to perform the duties of a customer service manager, supervising the other cashiers and scheduling their breaks. He asked for a promotion, but three months later he was still doing the extra work for no extra pay. "I took it because I wanted more money, but I never got the raise," Jackson says. "They knew they could do it to me." He fought for the promotion and eventually won, but by then he had already contacted a local union office about organizing the store.

"When Eric first suggested it, I looked at him like he was on crack," says McLaughlin. "I said, 'You can't take down a company like Wal-Mart with a union.'" Nevertheless, Jackson arranged for a UFCW organizer to come to Paris and meet with a small group of workers one June afternoon at the Pizza Inn. But the company soon caught wind of the organizing effort. As one worker left an early meeting of union supporters, he spotted a Wal-Mart manager in the parking lot. From then on, workers seen as pro-union were watched closely by management.

"By the time we had our first meeting, they were holding their first anti-union meeting," says McLaughlin. The response came straight from the company's union-avoidance playbook: Troops from the Bentonville "People Division" were flown in, and employees were required to attend hour-long meetings, where they were shown anti-labor videos and warned about unions. "They tend to treat you like you're simple, and they use real bad scare tactics," says McLaughlin. Those who supported the union, she says, were told, "Some people just don't belong at Wal-Mart."

McLaughlin isn't shy about speaking her mind, and in the meeting she confronted one of the men from the People Division. "Let me tell you, I used to have epilepsy," she told him. "My dad was in a union, and we had health insurance, and I got better. I don't have health insurance. If my child got epilepsy, what would I do? Doesn't a union help you to get company-paid insurance?" The man, she recalls, became flustered. "Jennifer, I don't have an answer about that," he said. "I'll have to get back with you."

The meetings were just beginning. "The videos and group meetings are the surface cosmetics," says Levitt, the former consultant. "Where Wal-Mart beats the union is through a one-on-one process implemented from Bentonville. They carefully instruct management to individually work over each employee who might be a union sympathizer." In Paris, Eric Jackson was called into a back room by five managers and made to watch an anti-union video and participate in a role-playing exercise. "I was supposed to be a manager, and one of them was the associate who came to me with a question about a union," says Jackson. "So I quoted the video. I said, 'We do not believe we need a union at Wal-Mart,' and they were like, 'Good, good!' and then I said, 'We're not anti-union—we're pro-associate,' just like I'm supposed to say."

Before the onslaught by the company, says McLaughlin, she talked to more than 70 workers at the Paris store who were prepared to sign cards calling for a vote on union representation, but that number quickly dwindled. Those who'd signed cards felt they were being watched. "All of a sudden the cameras start going up," says Chris Bills, who works in the receiving area. "Now there's three in receiving. This one manager took up smoking so he could sit with us on our breaks." Other hourly employees learned for the first time that they were actually counted as managers. "They said we were considered management, so we shouldn't get involved with the union stuff," says Dianne Smallwood, a former customer service manager who worked at the store seven years. Employees opposed to the union were given "pro-associate" buttons to wear, while managers amended the dress code to exclude T-shirts with any kind of writing on them, apparently to prevent workers from wearing union shirts.

Wal-Mart declined to let *Mother Jones* interview store managers or representatives from the People Division in Bentonville, but says it sends out people from corporate headquarters "to answer questions associates may have and to make sure that all store personnel are aware of their legal requirements and meet those requirements exactly." But the company has also made clear that keeping its stores union-free is as much a part of Wal-Mart culture as door greeters and blue aprons. "Union representation may work well for others," says Cynthia Illick, a company spokeswoman. "However, it is not a fit for Wal-Mart."

With the company so determined to ward off unions, the prospects of employees in towns like Paris, Texas, winning significant improvements in wages and working conditions seem awfully slim. "It's a long process," Jennifer McLaughlin concedes. "I wish it could be done in the next year, but people come and go, and for every one union card you get signed, two others ones who signed cards have gotten fired or left. It's real frustrating, and a lot of times I don't want to do it no more. But I'm not going to give up until I end up leaving the store."

In the end, the success of the organizing drives may depend on labor's ability to mobilize more than just store employees. "We'll never bring Wal-Mart to the table store by store," says Bernie Hesse, an organizer for UFCW Local 789 in Minneapolis. "I can get all the cards signed I want, and they'll still crush us. They'll close the frigging store, I'm convinced. We've got to do it in conjunction with the community." That means going to small businesses and religious leaders and local officials, he says, and convincing them that it's in their interest to stand up to Wal-Mart. "As a community we've got to say, 'All right, if you want to come here and do business, here's what you've got to do—you've got to pay a living wage, you've got to provide affordable health insurance.'"

See pp. 42–45 on framing quotations to support your argument.

Putting together such a broad initiative can be "like pulling teeth," Hesse says, but the stakes are high. If employees succeed in improving wages and working conditions at the country's largest employer, they could effectively set a new benchmark for service-sector jobs throughout the economy. Some 27 million Americans currently make $8.70 an hour or less—and by the end of the decade, Hesse notes, nearly 2 million people worldwide will work at Wal-Mart.

"These are the jobs our kids are going to have," he says.

Joining the Conversation

1. This article opens with two paragraphs describing the life of one Wal-Mart employee. How does the opening pave the way for the discussion that follows?

2. This selection comes from *Mother Jones*, a magazine that tends to be pro-union. Go through the article and find examples of pro-union and anti-union discussion. How can you tell which examples represent the author's point of view and which represent opposing viewpoints?

3. Karen Olsson provides many facts and much personal testimony to support her argument against Wal-Mart. How well does she consider positions other than her own? What naysayers does she include?

4. Notice how many quotations this article includes. What do the quotations add to the argument? Try rewriting one or two paragraphs that include direct quotations, replacing the quotations with summaries. How does this change affect the argument? What if anything can you conclude about quoting and summarizing?

5. It's clear that the author assumes her audience is sympathetic to her pro-union viewpoint. What if she were arguing on behalf of Wal-Mart employees to an audience of Wal-Mart executives—how would her argument be different? Try revising several paragraphs to reach those executives.

Progressive Wal-Mart. Really.

SEBASTIAN MALLABY

—⊡—

THERE S A COMIC SIDE to the anti-Wal-Mart campaign brewing in Maryland and across the country. Only by summoning up the most naive view of corporate behavior can the critics be shocked—shocked!—by the giant retailer's machinations. Wal-Mart is plotting to contain health costs! But isn't that what every company does in the face of medical inflation? Wal-Mart has a war room to defend its image! Well, yeah, it's up against a hostile campaign featuring billboards, newspaper ads, and a critical documentary movie. Wal-Mart aims to enrich shareholders and put rivals out of business! Hello? What business doesn't do that?

Wal-Mart's critics allege that the retailer is bad for poor Americans. This claim is backward: As Jason Furman of New York University puts it, Wal-Mart is "a progressive success

SEBASTIAN MALLABY is a columnist for the *Washington Post* and the former Washington bureau chief for the *Economist*. He is also a fellow at the Council on Foreign Relations. Mallaby has written *The World's Banker: A Story of Failed States, Financial Crises, and the Wealth and Poverty of Nations* (2004) and is currently writing a book on hedge funds. "Progressive Wal-Mart. Really." appeared in the *Washington Post* on November 28, 2005.

story." Furman advised John "Benedict Arnold" Kerry in the 2004 campaign and has never received any payment from Wal-Mart; he is no corporate apologist. But he points out that Wal-Mart's discounting on food alone boosts the welfare of American shoppers by at least $50 billion a year. The savings are possibly five times that much if you count all of Wal-Mart's products.

These gains are especially important to poor and moderate-income families. The average Wal-Mart customer earns $35,000 a year, compared with $50,000 at Target and $74,000 at Costco. Moreover, Wal-Mart's "everyday low prices" make the biggest difference to the poor, since they spend a higher proportion of income on food and other basics. As a force for poverty relief, Wal-Mart's $200 billion-plus assistance to consumers may rival many federal programs. Those programs are better targeted at the needy, but they are dramatically smaller. Food stamps were worth $33 billion in 2005, and the earned-income tax credit was worth $40 billion.

Set against these savings for consumers, Wal-Mart's alleged suppression of wages appears trivial. Arindrajit Dube of the University of California at Berkeley, a leading Wal-Mart critic, has calculated that the firm has caused a $4.7 billion annual loss of wages for workers in the retail sector. This number is disputed: Wal-Mart's pay and benefits can be made to look good or bad depending on which other firms you compare them to. When Wal-Mart opened a store in Glendale, Arizona, last year, it received 8,000 applications for 525 jobs, suggesting that not everyone believes the pay and benefits are unattractive.

But let's say we accept Dube's calculation that retail work- 5 ers take home $4.7 billion less per year because Wal-Mart has busted unions and generally been ruthless. That loss to workers would still be dwarfed by the $50 billion-plus that Wal-Mart consumers save on food, never mind the much larger sums that they save altogether. Indeed, Furman points out that the wage suppression is so small that even its "victims" may be better off. Retail workers may take home less pay, but their purchasing power probably still grows thanks to Wal-Mart's low prices.

To be fair, the $4.7 billion of wage suppression in the retail sector excludes Wal-Mart's efforts to drive down wages at its suppliers. *Wal-Mart: The High Cost of Low Price,* the new anti-Wal-Mart movie that's circulating among activist groups, has the requisite passage about Chinese workers getting pennies per day, sweating to keep Wal-Mart's shelves stocked with cheap clothing. But no study has shown whether Wal-Mart's tactics actually do suppress wages in China or elsewhere, and suppression seems unlikely in poor countries. The Chinese garment workers are mainly migrants from farms, where earnings are even worse than at Wal-Mart's subcontractors and where the labor is still more grueling.

For tips on acknowledging and answering objections, see Chapter 6.

Wal-Mart's critics also paint the company as a parasite on taxpayers, because 5 percent of its workers are on Medicaid. Actually that's a typical level for large retail firms, and the national average for all firms is 4 percent. Moreover, it's ironic that Wal-Mart's enemies, who are mainly progressives, should even raise this issue. In the 1990s progressives argued loudly for the reform that allowed poor Americans to keep Medicaid benefits even if they had a job. Now that this policy is helping workers at Wal-Mart, progressives shouldn't blame the company. Besides, many progressives favor a national health system. In other words, they attack Wal-Mart for having 5 percent of its workers receive health care courtesy of taxpayers when the policy that they support would increase that share to 100 percent.

Companies like Wal-Mart are not run by saints. They can treat workers and competitors roughly. They may be poor stewards of the environment. When they break the law they must be punished. Wal-Mart is at the center of the globalized, technology-driven economy that's radically increased American inequality, so it's not surprising that it has critics. But globalization and business innovation are nonetheless the engines of progress; and if that sounds too abstract, think of the $200 billion-plus that Wal-Mart consumers gain annually. If critics prevent the firm from opening new branches, they will prevent ordinary families from sharing in those gains. Poor Americans will be chief among the casualties.

Joining the Conversation

1. This article defends the retail giant Wal-Mart against a variety of criticisms. What arguments in particular is Sebastian Mallaby responding to here?
2. How exactly does the author respond to what critics of Wal-Mart say? Does he agree? Disagree? Agree and disagree? Give specific examples from the text.
3. Does Mallaby anticipate any possible objections to his position? How does he do so, and how effective is he in this regard? Can you come up with other objections? How fair would you say he is in representing the objections?
4. Read the article by Karen Olsson on pp. 342–54. How do you think Olsson would respond to Mallaby's argument? How might Mallaby respond to Olsson?
5. Mallaby concludes by saying that "If critics prevent [Wal-Mart] from opening new branches, they will prevent ordinary families from sharing in those gains. Poor Americans will be chief among the casualties." Respond with an essay of your own, using this quotation as your "they say."

A More Perfect Union

BARACK OBAMA

"**W**E THE PEOPLE, in order to form a more perfect union."

Two hundred and twenty-one years ago, in a hall that still stands across the street, a group of men gathered and, with these simple words, launched America's improbable experiment in democracy. Farmers and scholars; statesmen and patriots who had traveled across an ocean to escape tyranny and persecution finally made real their declaration of independence at a Philadelphia convention that lasted through the spring of 1787.

The document they produced was eventually signed but ultimately unfinished. It was stained by this nation's original sin of slavery, a question that divided the colonies and brought the convention to a stalemate until the founders chose to allow the

BARACK OBAMA is the president of the United States. Before entering politics, Obama worked as a community organizer and civil rights attorney and taught law at the University of Chicago. Obama has written two books: a memoir of his youth titled *Dreams from My Father* (1995), and a personal commentary on U.S. politics titled *The Audacity of Hope* (2006). "A More Perfect Union" is a speech Obama delivered in March 2008 responding to controversial statements made by his former pastor. The speech's title comes from the Preamble to the U.S. Constitution.

slave trade to continue for at least twenty more years, and to leave any final resolution to future generations.

Of course, the answer to the slavery question was already embedded within our Constitution—a Constitution that had at its very core the ideal of equal citizenship under the law; a Constitution that promised its people liberty, and justice, and a union that could be and should be perfected over time.

And yet words on a parchment would not be enough to 5 deliver slaves from bondage, or provide men and women of every color and creed their full rights and obligations as citizens of the United States. What would be needed were Americans in successive generations who were willing to do their part—through protests and struggle, on the streets and in the courts, through a civil war and civil disobedience and always at great risk—to narrow that gap between the promise of our ideals and the reality of their time.

This was one of the tasks we set forth at the beginning of this campaign—to continue the long march of those who came before us, a march for a more just, more equal, more free, more caring, and more prosperous America. I chose to run for the presidency at this moment in history because I believe deeply that we cannot solve the challenges of our time unless we solve them together—unless we perfect our union by understanding that we may have different stories, but we hold common hopes; that we may not look the same and we may not have come from the same place, but we all want to move in the same direction—toward a better future for our children and our grandchildren.

This belief comes from my unyielding faith in the decency and generosity of the American people. But it also comes from my own American story.

I am the son of a black man from Kenya and a white woman from Kansas. I was raised with the help of a white grandfather who survived a Depression to serve in Patton's Army during World War II and a white grandmother who worked on a bomber assembly line at Fort Leavenworth while he was overseas. I've gone to some of the best schools in America and lived in one of the world's poorest nations. I am married to a black American who carries within her the blood of slaves and slaveowners—an inheritance we pass on to our two precious daughters. I have brothers, sisters, nieces, nephews, uncles, and cousins, of every race and every hue, scattered across three continents, and for as long as I live, I will never forget that in no other country on Earth is my story even possible.

It's a story that hasn't made me the most conventional candidate. But it is a story that has seared into my genetic makeup the idea that this nation is more than the sum of its parts— that out of many, we are truly one.

Throughout the first year of this campaign, against all predictions to the contrary, we saw how hungry the American people were for this message of unity. Despite the temptation to view my candidacy through a purely racial lens, we won commanding victories in states with some of the whitest populations in the country. In South Carolina, where the Confederate Flag still flies, we built a powerful coalition of African Americans and white Americans.

This is not to say that race has not been an issue in the campaign. At various stages in the campaign, some commentators have deemed me either "too black" or "not black enough." We saw racial tensions bubble to the surface during the week before the South Carolina primary. The press has scoured every exit poll for the latest evidence of racial polarization, not just in terms of white and black, but black and brown as well.

And yet, it has only been in the last couple of weeks that the discussion of race in this campaign has taken a particularly divisive turn.

On one end of the spectrum, we've heard the implication that my candidacy is somehow an exercise in affirmative action; that it's based solely on the desire of wide-eyed liberals to purchase racial reconciliation on the cheap. On the other end, we've heard my former pastor, Reverend Jeremiah Wright, use incendiary language to express views that have the potential not only to widen the racial divide, but views that denigrate both the greatness and the goodness of our nation; that rightly offend white and black alike.

I have already condemned, in unequivocal terms, the statements of Reverend Wright that have caused such controversy. For some, nagging questions remain. Did I know him to be an occasionally fierce critic of American domestic and foreign policy? Of course. Did I ever hear him make remarks that could be considered controversial while I sat in church? Yes. Did I strongly disagree with many of his political views? Absolutely—just as I'm sure many of you have heard remarks from your pastors, priests, or rabbis with which you strongly disagreed.

But the remarks that have caused this recent firestorm weren't 15 simply controversial. They weren't simply a religious leader's efforts to speak out against perceived injustice. Instead, they expressed a profoundly distorted view of this country—a view that sees white racism as endemic, and that elevates what is wrong with America above all that we know is right with America; a view that sees the conflicts in the Middle East as rooted primarily in the actions of stalwart allies like Israel, instead of emanating from the perverse and hateful ideologies of radical Islam.

As such, Reverend Wright's comments were not only wrong but divisive, divisive at a time when we need unity; racially charged

at a time when we need to come together to solve a set of monumental problems—two wars, a terrorist threat, a falling economy,
a chronic health care crisis, and potentially devastating climate
change; problems that are neither black or white or Latino or
Asian, but rather problems that confront us all.

Given my background, my politics, and my professed values
and ideals, there will no doubt be those for whom my statements of condemnation are not enough. Why associate myself
with Reverend Wright in the first place, they may ask? Why
not join another church? And I confess that if all that I knew
of Reverend Wright were the snippets of those sermons that
have run in an endless loop on the television and YouTube, or
if Trinity United Church of Christ conformed to the caricatures being peddled by some commentators, there is no doubt
that I would react in much the same way.

But the truth is, that isn't all that I know of the man. The
man I met more than twenty years ago is a man who helped
introduce me to my Christian faith, a man who spoke to me
about our obligations to love one another; to care for the sick
and lift up the poor. He is a man who served his country as a
U.S. Marine; who has studied and lectured at some of the finest
universities and seminaries in the country; and who for over
thirty years led a church that serves the community by doing
God's work here on Earth—by housing the homeless, minis-
tering to the needy, providing day care services and scholarships and prison ministries, and reaching out to those suffering
from HIV/AIDs.

In my first book, *Dreams from My Father*, I described the
experience of my first service at Trinity:

People began to shout, to rise from their seats and clap and cry
out, a forceful wind carrying the reverend's voice up into the rafters.

. . . And in that single note—hope!—I heard something else; at the foot of that cross, inside the thousands of churches across the city, I imagined the stories of ordinary black people merging with the stories of David and Goliath, Moses and Pharaoh, the Christians in the lion's den, Ezekiel's field of dry bones. Those stories— of survival, and freedom, and hope—became our story, my story; the blood that had spilled was our blood, the tears our tears; until this black church, on this bright day, seemed once more a vessel carrying the story of a people into future generations and into a larger world. Our trials and triumphs became at once unique and universal, black and more than block; in chronicling our journey, the stories and songs gave us a means to reclaim memories that we didn't need to feel shame about . . . memories that all people might study and cherish—and with which we could start to rebuild.

That has been my experience at Trinity. Like other predominantly black churches across the country, Trinity embodies the black community in its entirety—the doctor and the welfare mom, the model student and the former gang-banger. Like other black churches, Trinity's services are full of raucous laughter and sometimes bawdy humor. They are full of dancing, clapping, screaming, and shouting that may seem jarring to the untrained ear. The church contains in full the kindness and cruelty, the fierce intelligence and the shocking ignorance, the struggles and successes, the love and, yes, the bitterness and bias that make up the black experience in America.

And this helps explain, perhaps, my relationship with Reverend Wright. As imperfect as he may be, he has been like family to me. He strengthened my faith, officiated at my wedding, and baptized my children. Not once in my conversations with him have I heard him talk about any ethnic group in derogatory terms, or treat whites with whom he interacted with anything but courtesy and respect. He contains within him the contradictions—the good and the bad—of the community that he has served diligently for so many years.

I can no more disown him than I can disown the black community. I can no more disown him than I can my white grandmother—a woman who helped raise me, a woman who sacrificed again and again for me, a woman who loves me as much as she loves anything in this world, but a woman who once confessed her fear of black men who passed by her on the street, and who on more than one occasion has uttered racial or ethnic stereotypes that made me cringe.

These people are a part of me. And they are a part of America, this country that I love.

Some will see this as an attempt to justify or excuse comments that are simply inexcusable. I can assure you it is not. I suppose the politically safe thing would be to move on from this episode and just hope that it fades into the woodwork. We can dismiss Reverend Wright as a crank or a demagogue, just as some have dismissed Geraldine Ferraro, in the aftermath of her recent statements,* as harboring some deep-seated racial bias.

But race is an issue that I believe this nation cannot afford to ignore right now. We would be making the same mistake that Reverend Wright made in his offending sermons about America—to simplify and stereotype and amplify the negative to the point that it distorts reality.

---

*Ferraro's statements   Geraldine Ferraro, the first woman vice-presidential candidate for a major political party, in 1984, and later a supporter of Hillary Clinton's campaign, commented that, given current prejudices, Barack Obama had an easier time running for president as an African American man than Hillary Clinton had as a woman. Ferraro was asked to resign from Clinton's campaign following these remarks.

The fact is that the comments that have been made and the ₂₅ issues that have surfaced over the last few weeks reflect the complexities of race in this country that we've never really worked through—a part of our union that we have yet to perfect. And if we walk away now, if we simply retreat into our respective corners, we will never be able to come together and solve challenges like health care, or education, or the need to find good jobs for every American.

See Chapter 7 for ways of saying why it matters, as Obama does here.

Understanding this reality requires a reminder of how we arrived at this point. As William Faulkner* once wrote, "The past isn't dead and buried. In fact, it isn't even past." We do not need to recite here the history of racial injustice in this country. But we do need to remind ourselves that so many of the disparities that exist in the African American community today can be directly traced to inequalities passed on from an earlier generation that suffered under the brutal legacy of slavery and Jim Crow.†

Segregated schools were, and are, inferior schools; we still haven't fixed them, fifty years after *Brown v. Board of Education*,‡ and the inferior education they provided, then and now, helps explain the pervasive achievement gap between today's black and white students.

Legalized discrimination—where blacks were prevented, often through violence, from owning property, or loans were

---

*__William Faulkner__ (1897–1962)   Nobel Prize-winning American novelist most of whose work was set in his native Mississippi.

†__Jim Crow__   Refers to laws enforcing segregation between black and white people, primarily in the South, between 1876 and 1965, when the landmark Civil Rights Act was passed by Congress.

‡*__Brown v. Board of Education__*   1954 Supreme Court decision that made separate schools for black and white students unconstitutional.

not granted to African American business owners, or black homeowners could not access FHA mortgages,* or blacks were excluded from unions, or the police force, or fire departments—meant that black families could not amass any meaningful wealth to bequeath to future generations. That history helps explain the wealth and income gap between black and white, and the concentrated pockets of poverty that persists in so many of today's urban and rural communities.

A lack of economic opportunity among black men, and the shame and frustration that came from not being able to provide for one's family, contributed to the erosion of black families—a problem that welfare policies for many years may have worsened. And the lack of basic services in so many urban black neighborhoods—parks for kids to play in, police walking the beat, regular garbage pick-up, and building code enforcement—all helped create a cycle of violence, blight, and neglect that continue to haunt us.

This is the reality in which Reverend Wright and other 30 African Americans of his generation grew up. They came of age in the late fifties and early sixties, a time when segregation was still the law of the land and opportunity was systematically constricted. What's remarkable is not how many failed in the face of discrimination, but rather how many men and women overcame the odds; how many were able to make a way out of no way for those like me who would come after them.

But for all those who scratched and clawed their way to get a piece of the American Dream, there were many who didn't make it—those who were ultimately defeated, in one way or

*FHA mortgages   Loans backed by the Federal Housing Administration that historically have allowed lower-income Americans to buy homes when they otherwise might not be able to.

another, by discrimination. That legacy of defeat was passed on to future generations—those young men and increasingly young women who we see standing on street corners or languishing in our prisons, without hope or prospects for the future. Even for those blacks who did make it, questions of race, and racism, continue to define their worldview in fundamental ways. For the men and women of Reverend Wright's generation, the memories of humiliation and doubt and fear have not gone away; nor has the anger and the bitterness of those years. That anger may not get expressed in public, in front of white co-workers or white friends. But it does find voice in the barbershop or around the kitchen table. At times, that anger is exploited by politicians, to gin up votes along racial lines, or to make up for a politician's own failings.

And occasionally it finds a voice in the church on Sunday morning, in the pulpit and in the pews. The fact that so many people are surprised to hear that anger in some of Reverend Wright's sermons simply reminds us of the old truism that the most segregated hour in American life occurs on Sunday morning. That anger is not always productive; indeed, all too often it distracts attention from solving real problems; it keeps us from squarely facing our own complicity in our condition, and prevents the African American community from forging the alliances it needs to bring about real change. But the anger is real; it is powerful; and to simply wish it away, to condemn it without understanding its roots, only serves to widen the chasm of misunderstanding that exists between the races.

In fact, a similar anger exists within segments of the white community. Most working- and middle-class white Americans don't feel that they have been particularly privileged by their race. Their experience is the immigrant experience—as far as they're concerned, no one's handed them anything, they've built it from scratch. They've worked hard all their lives, many times only to see their jobs shipped overseas or their pension dumped after a lifetime of labor. They are anxious about their futures, and feel their dreams slipping away; in an era of stagnant wages and global competition, opportunity comes to be seen as a zero sum game, in which your dreams come at my expense. So when they are told to bus their children to a school across town; when they hear that an African American is getting an advantage in landing a good job or a spot in a good college because of an injustice that they themselves never committed; when they're told that their fears about crime in urban neighborhoods are somehow prejudiced, resentment builds over time.

Like the anger within the black community, these resentments aren't always expressed in polite company. But they have helped shape the political landscape for at least a generation. Anger over welfare and affirmative action helped forge the Reagan Coalition. Politicians routinely exploited fears of crime for their own electoral ends. Talk show hosts and conservative commentators built entire careers unmasking bogus claims of racism while dismissing legitimate discussions of racial injustice and inequality as mere political correctness or reverse racism.

Just as black anger often proved counterproductive, so have these white resentments distracted attention from the real culprits of the middle-class squeeze—a corporate culture rife with inside dealing, questionable accounting practices, and short-term greed; a Washington dominated by lobbyists and special interests; economic policies that favor the few over the many. And yet, to wish away the resentments of white Americans, to label them as misguided or even racist, without recognizing they are grounded in legitimate concerns—this too widens the racial divide, and blocks the path to understanding.

This is where we are right now. It's a racial stalemate we've been stuck in for years. Contrary to the claims of some of my critics, black and white, I have never been so naïve as to believe that we can get beyond our racial divisions in a single election cycle, or with a single candidacy—particularly a candidacy as imperfect as my own.

See Chapter 6 for tips on answering naysayers.

But I have asserted a firm conviction—a conviction rooted in my faith in God and my faith in the American people—that working together we can move beyond some of our old racial wounds, and that in fact we have no choice if we are to continue on the path of a more perfect union.

For the African American community, that path means embracing the burdens of our past without becoming victims of our past. It means continuing to insist on a full measure of justice in every aspect of American life. But it also means binding our particular grievances—for better health care, and better schools, and better jobs—to the larger aspirations of all Americans—the white woman struggling to break the glass ceiling, the white man who's been laid off, the immigrant trying to feed his family. And it means taking full responsibility for our own lives—by demanding more from our fathers, and spending more time with our children, and reading to them, and teaching them that while they may face challenges and discrimination in their own lives, they must never succumb to despair or cynicism; they must always believe that they can write their own destiny.

Ironically, this quintessentially American—and yes, conservative—notion of self-help found frequent expression in Reverend Wright's sermons. But what my former pastor too often failed to understand is that embarking on a program of self-help also requires a belief that society can change.

The profound mistake of Reverend Wright's sermons is not 40 that he spoke about racism in our society. It's that he spoke as if our society was static; as if no progress has been made; as if this country—a country that has made it possible for one of his own members to run for the highest office in the land and build a coalition of white and black, Latino and Asian, rich and poor, young and old—is still irrevocably bound to a tragic past. But what we know—what we have seen—is that America can change. That is true genius of this nation. What we have already achieved gives us hope—the audacity to hope—for what we can and must achieve tomorrow.

In the white community, the path to a more perfect union means acknowledging that what ails the African American community does not just exist in the minds of black people; that the legacy of discrimination—and current incidents of discrimination, while less overt than in the past—are real and must be addressed. Not just with words, but with deeds—by investing in our schools and our communities; by enforcing our civil rights laws and ensuring fairness in our criminal justice system; by providing this generation with ladders of opportunity that were unavailable for previous generations. It requires all Americans to realize that your dreams do not have to come at the expense of my dreams; that investing in the health, welfare, and education of black and brown and white children will ultimately help all of America prosper.

In the end, then, what is called for is nothing more, and nothing less, than what all the world's great religions demand— that we do unto others as we would have them do unto us. Let us be our brother's keeper, Scripture tells us. Let us be our sister's keeper. Let us find that common stake we all have in one another, and let our politics reflect that spirit as well.

For we have a choice in this country. We can accept a politics that breeds division, and conflict, and cynicism. We can tackle race only as spectacle—as we did in the O.J. trial*—or in the wake of tragedy, as we did in the aftermath of Katrina†— or as fodder for the nightly news. We can play Reverend Wright's sermons on every channel, every day and talk about them from now until the election, and make the only question in this campaign whether or not the American people think that I somehow believe or sympathize with his most offensive words. We can pounce on some gaffe by a Hillary supporter as evidence that she's playing the race card, or we can speculate on whether white men will all flock to John McCain in the general election regardless of his policies.

We can do that.

But if we do, I can tell you that in the next election, we'll 45 be talking about some other distraction. And then another one. And then another one. And nothing will change.

That is one option. Or, at this moment, in this election, we can come together and say, "Not this time." This time we want to talk about the crumbling schools that are stealing the future of black children and white children and Asian children and Hispanic children and Native American children. This time we want to reject the cynicism that tells us that these kids can't learn; that those kids who don't look like us are somebody else's

---

***O.J. trial** In the mid-1990s, former football star O.J. Simpson was tried and acquitted for the murder of his ex-wife, Nicole Simpson, and her friend Ron Goldman.

†**Katrina** Hurricane that devastated New Orleans and much of the north-central Gulf Coast in 2005.

problem. The children of America are not those kids, they are our kids, and we will not let them fall behind in a twenty-first century economy. Not this time.

This time we want to talk about how the lines in the Emergency Room are filled with whites and blacks and Hispanics who do not have health care; who don't have the power on their own to overcome the special interests in Washington, but who can take them on if we do it together.

This time we want to talk about the shuttered mills that once provided a decent life for men and women of every race, and the homes for sale that once belonged to Americans from every religion, every region, every walk of life. This time we want to talk about the fact that the real problem is not that someone who doesn't look like you might take your job; it's that the corporation you work for will ship it overseas for nothing more than a profit.

This time we want to talk about the men and women of every color and creed who serve together, and fight together, and bleed together under the same proud flag. We want to talk about how to bring them home from a war that never should've been authorized and never should've been waged, and we want to talk about how we'll show our patriotism by caring for them, and their families, and giving them the benefits they have earned.

I would not be running for President if I didn't believe with 50 all my heart that this is what the vast majority of Americans want for this country. This union may never be perfect, but generation after generation has shown that it can always be perfected. And today, whenever I find myself feeling doubtful or cynical about this possibility, what gives me the most hope is the next generation—the young people whose attitudes and beliefs and openness to change have already made history in this election.

There is one story in particular that I'd like to leave you with today—a story I told when I had the great honor of speaking on Dr. King's birthday at his home church, Ebenezer Baptist, in Atlanta.

There is a young, twenty-three-year-old white woman named Ashley Baia who organized for our campaign in Florence, South Carolina. She had been working to organize a mostly African American community since the beginning of this campaign, and one day she was at a roundtable discussion where everyone went around telling their story and why they were there.

And Ashley said that when she was nine years old, her mother got cancer. And because she had to miss days of work, she was let go and lost her health care. They had to file for bankruptcy, and that's when Ashley decided that she had to do something to help her mom.

She knew that food was one of their most expensive costs, and so Ashley convinced her mother that what she really liked and really wanted to eat more than anything else was mustard and relish sandwiches. Because that was the cheapest way to eat.

She did this for a year until her mom got better, and she told everyone at the roundtable that the reason she joined our campaign was so that she could help the millions of other children in the country who want and need to help their parents too. 55

Now Ashley might have made a different choice. Perhaps somebody told her along the way that the source of her mother's problems were blacks who were on welfare and too lazy to work, or Hispanics who were coming into the country illegally. But she didn't. She sought out allies in her fight against injustice.

Anyway, Ashley finishes her story and then goes around the room and asks everyone else why they're supporting the campaign. They all have different stories and reasons. Many bring up a specific issue. And finally they come to this elderly black man who's been sitting there quietly the entire time. And Ashley asks him why he's there. And he does not bring up a specific issue. He does not say health care or the economy. He does not say education or the war. He does not say that he was there because of Barack Obama. He simply says to everyone in the room, "I am here because of Ashley."

"I'm here because of Ashley." By itself, that single moment of recognition between that young white girl and that old black man is not enough. It is not enough to give health care to the sick, or jobs to the jobless, or education to our children.

But it is where we start. It is where our union grows stronger. And as so many generations have come to realize over the course of the 221 years since a band of patriots signed that document in Philadelphia, that is where the perfection begins.

Joining the Conversation

1. Barack Obama gave this speech about the role of race in U.S. life during the 2008 presidential primary race in response to criticism and massive media coverage of inflammatory remarks made by his former pastor, Reverend Jeremiah Wright. He begins by quoting from the Preamble of the U.S. Constitution. How does this quotation set the stage for the speech that follows?
2. After discussing the Constitution and his optimistic belief in "a more just, more equal, more free, more caring, and more prosperous America" (paragraph 6), Obama briefly

tells his own life story. What does he gain by explaining his own unusual background? What is his purpose for doing so?

3. Obama discusses at length Reverend Wright, his church, and what he, Obama, gained from entering the world of that church. Reread this discussion (in paragraphs 12 to 21), paying attention to how he begins with what others say about Reverend Wright to frame what he, Obama, says—about Wright, race in America, and more. Summarize Obama's "they say" and "I say."

4. This is a speech about race, and yet we include it in a chapter about economic opportunity. In fact, Obama says in paragraph 25 that the media reactions to Reverend Wright's comments "reflect the complexities of race in this country that we've never really worked through" and that Americans must work through these complexities in order to "solve challenges like health care, or education, or the need to find good jobs for every American." Why, in Obama's view, is it so important that we as Americans engage in a full and frank conversation about all these issues?

5. Some say that this is one of the best campaign speeches ever given in the United States. What do you think? Write an essay or a speech responding to what Obama says here. Start by summarizing or quoting from his speech.

The Growing College Gap

TAMARA DRAUT

—◻—

"THE FIRST IN HER FAMILY to graduate from college." How many times have we heard that phrase, or one like it, used to describe a successful American with a modest background? In today's United States, a four-year degree has become the all-but-official ticket to middle-class security. But if your parents don't have much money or higher education in their own right, the road to college—and beyond—looks increasingly treacherous. Despite a sharp increase in the proportion of high school graduates going on to some form of postsecondary education,

TAMARA DRAUT is the director of the Economic Opportunity Program at Demos, a nonpartisan public policy research and advocacy organization whose Web site says it is dedicated to "a more equitable economy, a vibrant and inclusive deomocracy, an empowered public sector that works for the common good, and responsible U.S. engagement in an interdependent world." Draut's writing has appeared in the *New York Times*, the *Wall Street Journal*, and *Newsweek*, and she is a frequent commentator on ABC's *World News Tonight*, CNN's *Lou Dobbs Tonight*, and *Fox News*. She is the author of *Strapped: Why America's 20- and 30-Somethings Can't Get Ahead* (2006). "The Growing College Gap" appeared in *Inequality Matters: The Growing Economic Divide in America and Its Poisonous Consequences* (2006).

socioeconomic status continues to exert a powerful influence on college admission and completion; in fact, gaps in enrollment by class and race, after declining in the 1960s and 1970s, are once again as wide as they were thirty years ago, and getting wider, even as college has become far more crucial to lifetime fortunes.

Since the seventies, income differences between workers with high school diplomas and those with bachelor's degrees have grown steadily. A young person with some college can now expect to earn, on average, about $1.5 million over the course of a lifetime; an associate-degree holder will make slightly more: $1.6 million. By contrast, a young adult with a bachelor's degree can look forward to average lifetime earnings of $2.1 million—roughly a one-third advantage over those who don't finish college, and a twofold advantage over those who never get past high school. The wage premium goes up further for holders of advanced and professional degrees. A master's degree yields about $2.5 million; a professional degree (the kind associated with lawyers and doctors) is worth about $4.4 million.

Dollars tell only part of the story. Back in the seventies, a professional with a college degree and a blue-collar worker with a high school degree could live in the same community, own similar cars, eat at the same restaurants, and send their kids to a good public school. But as the incomes of high school and college grads have diverged, so too has their quality of life. The college-haves and college-have-nots increasingly live in separate worlds, largely defined by enormous differences in earning power.

About 70 percent of today's high school graduates attend college. But that impressive-sounding figure glides over the increasingly hierarchical structure of American higher education. African American, Latino, and lower-income students are more likely to be enrolled in two-year community-college programs, while wealthier students are battling it out for seats at a handful of elite private institutions. The increasing demand by employers for graduate degrees is perpetuating further class inequality in a spiraling credential craze.

The paradox facing young adults today is meeting the 5 demand for more credentials in a context of declining financial aid support and skyrocketing tuition. The more diplomas you earn, the better your chances of getting into the middle class and staying there. Unfortunately, as the postindustrial transition gained steam and the college-haves took a greater and greater share of the spoils, elected officials began changing the focus of financial aid in ways that would perpetuate inequities in access to higher education. Over the last two decades, this country has steadily retreated from both the spirit and the policies that did so much to open doors of opportunity during the long postwar expansion.

In 1944, Congress passed the GI Bill, which was intended to provide millions of returning veterans with the education, skills, and money to readjust successfully to civilian life. The GI Bill offered grants to help cover the cost of tuition, books, and health insurance. It included a monthly stipend for living expenses. Over its seven years, the legislation cost the government about $91 billion in today's dollars. About 8 million veterans took advantage of its various provisions; 2.3 million attended colleges and universities. By 1960, half the members of Congress had gone to college on the GI Bill.

A generation after the GI Bill, Congress enacted the Higher Education Act of 1965 (HEA), which established the system of college grants and student loans on which today's system is largely based. While the GI Bill had focused on veterans, the

HEA was meant to ensure access to college for all. Upon signing the bill, President Lyndon Johnson summarized its key goals: "The Higher Education Act of 1965 means that a high school senior anywhere in this great land of ours can apply to any college or any university in any of the 50 states and not be turned away because his family is poor."

As a result of this landmark legislation, the number of low-income students in American colleges and universities nearly doubled between 1965 and 1971. In 1972, grant aid was further expanded through the creation of Pell Grants. Throughout the seventies, low-income students continued to close the enrollment gap between them and their wealthier classmates. Unfortunately, progress has stalled since the late 1970s.

During the 1980s, as the haves were quickly pulling away from the have-nots, our nation began a steady and prolonged retreat from the goal of making college affordable. Grant aid declined on a per student basis, loan aid outpaced grant aid, and need-based aid fell out of fashion as more states and institutions started giving away financial aid dollars based on grades or test scores. In the 1990s, President Bill Clinton further exacerbated the shift away from need-based aid at the federal level. The HOPE Scholarship and Lifetime Learning tax credits initiated during the Clinton administration now account for about 8 percent of federal financial aid. Despite claims that the tax credits would help families pay for college, they've done little to stem the tide of student borrowing, which has risen steadily. In addition, the benefits of the HOPE credit overwhelmingly go to middle- and upper-income individuals. And in the new century, states have consistently slashed their support for state and community colleges as a way to deal with their budget deficits—ushering in rapidly rising tuition costs.

The federal aid system has failed to address two major trends 10 in higher education: more students going to college and rising tuition costs. Tuition has more than doubled since 1980 in inflation-adjusted dollars, rising much faster than the average family's income. In the 2003 school year alone, the price rose as much as 24 percent at some state schools. While the federal government is spending more than ever before on student aid, over $70 billion to be exact, funding has not kept pace with enrollments or tuition prices. That means that aid is spread more thinly across a greater number of students.

The anemia of the federal financial aid program becomes clear when we examine the purchasing power of the Pell Grant, our country's primary way of making college affordable for low-income students. In 1976–1977, Pell Grants covered 72 percent of the average price of a four-year college. Today, the average Pell Grant covers 34 percent of the costs at a four-year college. In order for the maximum Pell award to cover the same share of costs at a public four-year institution as it did in 1977, it would have to rise from $3,750 to around $7,000.

It wasn't only federal policy changes that contributed to the affordability crisis hitting families today. Over the last decade, both state governments and colleges themselves have shifted their aid dollars toward merit-based awards, rather than need-based. This shift happened rather quickly and it coincided with rising enrollments and rising tuition costs. Between 1991 and 2001, spending by the states on need-based scholarships for undergraduates increased 7.7 percent annually, while spending on merit programs increased by 18.3 percent annually. The proportion of state grants awarded based on merit, rather than need, rose from 11 percent to 24 percent during this period.

When student aid is focused on merit rather than need, it tends to go to students from families who can already afford college tuition. A merit award typically doesn't change behavior—these students would have gone to college without the scholarship. The same can't be said for need-based aid. The availability of grant aid has a big influence on whether lower-income students will enroll in college at all.

Given the extraordinary shift in financial aid, it's not surprising that college-enrollment gaps between poor and wealthy students are as high as they were three decades ago. The difference in college enrollment rates among white, black, and Hispanic students has actually widened over the last thirty years: in 2000, the enrollment gap between white and black students was 11 percentage points, up from only 5 percentage points in 1972. The enrollment gap between white and Hispanic students was 13 percentage points in 2000, up from a 5 percentage-point gap in 1972.

"I sure hope Social Security is around when I'm 65. I'll need it to finish paying off my college loans."

As grant aid has dwindled and tuitions at public colleges 15 have skyrocketed, students from low- and moderate-income households often find that even after grant and loan aid, they're thousands of dollars short of the money needed to pay for college. According to the Advisory Committee on Student Financial Assistance—a body that was created in 1986 by Congress to advise on student aid—in 2001 alone, unmet need forced 410,000 *college-qualified* students from households with incomes less than $50,000 to enroll in community college instead of going to a four-year college or university. Another 168,000 *college-qualified* students don't enroll in any college at all. Unmet need has forced low- and moderate-income students to abandon the most successful recipe for obtaining a college degree: full-time on-campus study.

As a result of declining federal aid and increased demand for postsecondary education, enrollments at community colleges have soared. Today, community colleges enroll 44 percent of all undergraduates attending colleges. For many young adults, community colleges are their only choice for postsecondary education, either because they're not academically prepared for university-level study or because they're seeking specific skills training. But increasingly, students who can't afford the cost of a four-year college are turning to community colleges. Forty percent of young adults report that they either delayed going to school or went to a less expensive school because of student loans. Nearly six out of ten African American and Hispanic college students, and four out of ten white students, report that they would have chosen a different school if money were not an issue.

The inequity in college choice that is driven by dwindling grant aid and soaring tuition costs means many young people aren't receiving the amount of education they desire or could accomplish. Of all college entrants, half of low-income students attend community colleges, compared to just one in ten high-income students. As the cost of four-year colleges has risen, more students are choosing to start down the bachelor's degree path at a community college. The research is mixed on the success of this strategy. Only about 40 percent of community college students who enroll with the intention of transferring end up doing so, according to one study. Other studies find that bachelor's-seeking students who enroll in community colleges with the intention of transferring to a four-year college are much less likely to earn their degree. One of the main reasons why persistence may be lower at community colleges is that unlike students at four-year colleges, eighteen- to twenty-two-year-olds at community colleges are more likely to work full-time and attend school on a part-time basis. Even among students who enroll in community college specifically to get an associate's degree, many don't complete their schooling. Five years after entering community college, only about one in five students who enrolled with the intention of getting an associate's degree had accomplished that goal. In the struggle between doing classwork and paid work, it is usually the classwork that ends up being dropped.

For the low-income students who are able to attend four-year colleges, the likelihood of them dropping out is much higher. Students from low-income families complete degrees at a much lower rate than their wealthy counterparts: within five years of entering college, 40 percent of students from the top socioeconomic quartile will earn a four-year degree, compared to only 6 percent of students from the lowest quartile.

The inequity in higher education isn't limited to disparities by race and class in who goes to four-year colleges and who goes to community colleges. At the undergraduate level, there is now an enormous quality gap too. Nearly three-quarters of students at the nation's top 146 colleges come from families in the top quarter of the socioeconomic status (SES) scale. Only 3 percent are from the lowest SES quartile, and only 10 percent are culled from the entire bottom half of the SES distribution. These 146 colleges represent the top two tiers in *Barron's Profiles of American Colleges 2005*, constituting the most selective 10 percent of the 1,400 four-year institutions in the nation. There is actually greater underrepresentation on these elite college campuses by class than there is by race, though blacks and Hispanics are still underrepresented. Black and Hispanic students make up only 6 percent of the freshman classes at these selective institutions, even though they make up 15 percent and 13 percent, respectively, of the eighteen-year-old population.

The benefits of attending the nation's best are multiple. 20 Students in selective colleges are more likely to graduate and more likely to get into top-notch graduate schools. There is also a wage premium enjoyed by graduates of top schools, though its magnitude is not as significant as many believe. The same study finds, however, that students from lower SES backgrounds gain more of a wage premium than their higher SES counterparts from attending elite colleges. Why would the gain be greater for students from lower-income backgrounds? It's likely because attending an elite college gives these students access to a social and professional network that they otherwise wouldn't have access to.

The class cleavage that has developed at the country's best colleges has been facilitated by fierce competition among undergraduate colleges to compete for the best students. Over the last decade, middle-class and first-generation students have struggled to afford a decent education from public universities.

But as they've been borrowing and working their way through public colleges, their upper-income counterparts have been engaged in a battle of a whole different nature. They are competing for slots at the nation's most elite schools, fearing that getting into anything less than a name-brand school will result in a life of mediocrity, or complete failure. Fueling this race to the top is a profound sense of the reality that being one of the "winners" today is the only sure way to the good life. As the spoils of our economy are increasingly spread among only a small group of top performers, getting into the winner's circle from the outset is imperative. And there is a burgeoning, profitable industry of tutors and consultants at the ready to help students boost test scores, sharpen essays, and nail an interview.

Run-of-the-mill prep courses from places like Kaplan or Princeton Review cost $800, with individual tutoring available for $1,900 to $4,199, depending on the number of hours. Test preparers are just some among the cadre of professionals for hire to help students get into the best schools. An admissions consultant typically charges about $150 an hour or offers packages that may run from $1,500 to $3,000. These consultants help students find the right college for their abilities and aspirations; they coach them on interviews with admission officers; and they can help add sparkle and shine to a lackluster college essay. There are still other ways to boost a high school résumé and beef up a college application. There are intellectual boot camps that allow high school students to take college courses and get a feel for the campus environment. Getting a sneak peek at the college experience doesn't come cheap; these trial runs cost from $4,000 to $6,000.

There are also special tours that allow students to tour different campuses with a group of other ambitious students. One package includes all the tony East Coast schools—Georgetown,

Columbia, Yale, Harvard, and others—for just over $2,000. With airfare and meals factored in, the total cost could exceed $3,000.

While the news media make it seem as if test preparation and consultants have become ubiquitous, the reality is that the high cost of these services makes them out of reach of the average family. According to the trade association for professional education consultants, only 6 percent of high school graduates get help from professionals. But that's up from 1 percent in 1990. Compare that to the amount of free college guidance offered at public high schools, which is essentially zero. The average high school guidance counselor has a caseload of nearly five hundred students a year.

The vast and growing disparities in who gets into college 25 and completes bachelor's degrees is becoming even more troubling as four years of college are increasingly viewed as only the first rung on the credential ladder. In many ways, a bachelor's degree has become equivalent to what a high school degree used to be: the bare minimum for competing in the economy. As a result, a master's degree is becoming the new bachelor's degree. The growing demand for advanced degrees is being fueled by a credential craze among America's professional class. Occupations that used to require only bachelor's degrees have steadily been upgrading their educational requirements. To get to the management level in any business field now requires an MBA. Even social workers, librarians, and teachers are expected to earn a master's degree. The demand for advanced degrees began growing in the late 1970s as the society transitioned from an industrialized to a knowledge-based economy. And not coincidentally, over the same period the economy was becoming a winner-take-all system in which the rewards were increasingly concentrated at the top among CEOs, shareholders, and top executives. Judith Glazer, a scholar who studies trends in higher education, points to several related factors behind the proliferation of advanced degrees: individuals wanting job advancement and mobility, a demand from employers for more highly trained practitioners, and an eagerness in many professions to enhance their status by upgrading the degree requirement for entry to the occupation. This credential craze stands in stark contrast to the purpose and pursuit of advanced degrees a generation ago. Prior to the mid-1970s, most master's degrees were in nonprofessional fields, stressing theory over practice. The motivation for graduate study wasn't a better job or better money, but pure intellectual pursuit. Not anymore. Today about 85 percent of all master's degrees are practice-oriented, as opposed to theoretical. Business and education are the major dominators in the master's degree craze, with each representing about 25 percent of all advanced degrees.

The demand for graduate degrees is generating more inequality in access to higher education. The number of students earning graduate degrees rose 58 percent between 1986 and 1999, to just under 500,000, but the number of bachelor's degrees rose by only 25 percent, to just over 1.2 million. Just as the rich have gotten richer over the last two decades, the well-educated have gotten supereducated.

Even though graduate enrollments are growing among women and students of color, holders of advanced degrees are still a very select group. Numerous studies have found that among students who wish to pursue an advanced degree, those with high levels of undergraduate debt are less likely to pursue additional study. College students who graduate with debt are more likely to have parents without college degrees, come from low-income backgrounds, or be students of color. The surging demand for advanced degrees by employers has put many first-generation holders of bachelor's degrees at a disadvantage.

The current inequities in access to higher education will become even more acute as the largest generation since the baby boomers begins to age out of high school. The traditional college-age population is projected to grow by 16 percent between 2000 and 2015. This generation will be more ethnically diverse, better prepared for college, and more likely to have financial need for college. By 2015, 43 percent of the college-age population will be nonwhite, with students from low-income families representing an increasing proportion of high school students.

Without major new efforts by the federal and state governments and our nation's colleges to widen access to higher education, a new social inequality will emerge. We'll have a well-educated minority that is mostly white, and a swelling, undereducated majority that is mostly African American and Latino. As the college-age population grows swiftly, our nation's financial aid system will leave millions of college-ready students without the means to fulfill their dreams. The Advisory Committee on Student Financial Assistance projects that if current enrollment trends persist, over the next decade 4.4 million students from households with incomes below $50,000 will not attend a four-year college, and 2 million students will not attend college at all. And those are conservative estimates. Who knows how many scientists, nurses, teachers, and doctors we will lose as a result?

The loss to both individuals and society is just too large to 30 allow such social cleavages to develop.

Who is Draut responding to? See Chapter 11 for help figuring that out.

Joining the Conversation

1. What is the "college gap" that Tamara Draut refers to? What are some of the examples she provides for the existence of this gap?
2. What details does Draut give to support her claim that the college gap is growing?
3. Draut contends that in the 1960s and 1970s there was more government support for low- and middle-income students to attend college. Why, in her view, has this support declined in the years since then?
4. What is Draut's argument, and what position is she arguing against? How do you know? Since Draut's "they say" is not explicit, try constructing one to frame her argument.
5. Draut states that there's been a shift in recent years from need-based aid for low- and middle-income students to merit-based aid, which tends to go to wealthier students. What is your own view? Write an essay responding to Draut, agreeing with her, disagreeing, or agreeing *and* disagreeing. Be sure to summarize or quote from her piece; you can also cite your own personal experience.

SIXTEEN

IS AMERICA OVER?

AT THIS MOMENT, at the pinnacle of its power," writes journalist Bob Herbert in his essay in this chapter, "the United
States is a country that has lost its way." Herbert highlights
America's loss of international moral standing in the wake of
the Iraq war, as well as the national increase in economic
inequality, writing that, at some point after World War II, "we
took a wrong turn," letting "the selfish, the vain, the greedy,
and the incompetent take control of our nation." Taking an
equally dark vision of where the United States is heading, historian and social critic Morris Berman stresses how the Iraq war
has discredited America's global standing, maiming and killing
thousands of innocent people. Hady Amr, a former U.S. government official who now studies America's relationship with
the Muslim world, argues that, though the United States was
once admired internationally, we are now "loathed for our
hypocrisy" throughout the world. Princeton University professor Michael D. Lemonick contends that decades of shrinking
investment and increasing international competition pose serious threats to U.S. dominance in science and technology.
According to these worried writers, without a radical change
of direction, America could soon be "over."

Others, however, are less gloomy and find more reason to be hopeful. Conservative think-tank fellow Alan W. Dowd, for instance, insists that America is still on top, arguing that such pessimistic "declinists," as he refers to them, ignore both "America's muscular economic output" and how U.S. military might is needed to keep that output going. And Thomas L. Friedman, writing about what he calls "globalization 3.0," sees the changes in the world's economy in positive terms, not just for Americans but for our trading partners abroad, if only we all could tune in and appreciate the wonderful technological advances surrounding us. Fareed Zakaria worries less that the United States is slipping but points out how much other nations are gaining in economic and political power—and suggests that Americans need to become more knowledgeable about the rest of the world if we are to maintain our international leadership. The chapter ends on a more optimistic note, with an op-ed piece written by the columnist Roger Cohen shortly after Barack Obama was elected president. "Obama's idea," says Cohen, is that "America can be better than it has been. It can reach beyond post-9/11 anger and fear to embody once more what the world still craves from the American idea: hope."

This chapter thus offers a range of views on the role of the United States in a rapidly changing world, and on what the future could hold. As you read these selections and think about the arguments they make, you will find much to ponder, and, we hope, you will be inspired to join the conversation.

A Fire in the Basement

BOB HERBERT

The eleven-year-old girl looked up at the police officers. "What's that word?" she asked. "Home-a-seed?"

She was told the word was homicide.

"What's that?" she asked.

The interrogation room grew quiet. No one answered.

MOST OF THE STORIES I write are about people in trouble. Sometimes the wounds are self-inflicted, but most often they are the result of other people's bad behavior—sometimes the government's bad behavior. The frightened eleven-year-old who couldn't read the word *homicide* became the youngest person ever charged with capital murder in the United States. She was publicly humiliated and sent off to a juvenile prison in Texas by a coterie of ferociously self-righteous officials who could have stepped right out of the Middle Ages. It turned out that the girl was innocent, but she remained locked up for three years before lawyers and advocates could secure her release.

BOB HERBERT has been an op-ed columnist for the *New York Times* since 1993. His column, dedicated to issues such as race and poverty in the United States, is syndicated in many other newspapers. Herbert has taught journalism at Brooklyn College and the Columbia University Graduate School of Journalism. "A Fire in the Basement" serves as the introduction to his collection of editorials from 1995 to 2004, *Promises Betrayed: Waking Up from the American Dream* (2005).

A reporter making the rounds will spend an inordinate amount of time trespassing in the precincts that were so well understood by the old blues masters, the places ravaged by hypocrisy and double-dealing, hatred and murder, acts of terror and endless war. These are the places where the suffering occurs and that tell us the most about the times in which we live.

I remember listening to a twenty-seven-year-old army sergeant in Dale City, Virginia, as he sat in a wheelchair in his parents' basement on a sunny summer afternoon and described the very weird experience of being blown up by a roadside bomb in Iraq. "Everything went in slow motion for about fifteen seconds," he said. He felt an excruciating sensation of flaming hot metal and a searing, all-encompassing pain. When his life resumed normal speed, everything he once knew about himself and the world had changed. His family life would be different. His days as a splendid athlete were over. His spinal cord had been severed in the blast.

I'm troubled as never before about what's happening in the United States right now. I grew up at a time when the great promise of America probably was at its peak. Optimism ruled in the 1950s and '60s. Jobs were plentiful and standards of living were improving. Access to a decent education was becoming easier. Despite tremendous problems—the war in Vietnam, bitter and sometimes deadly racial struggles, assassinations—there was a sense that the nation was trying to right its wrongs, that it was moving in the right direction, however difficult and dangerous the road might seem.

I don't feel that sense as I travel the country now, meeting 5 and talking with ordinary men and women who are directly affected by the major events of our time. The winds have shifted and are blowing from a more ominous direction. There are too many stories now about anxious and bewildered men and women who are desperate for work but can't find jobs, about middle-class families drowning in debt, about public schools swarming with students but starved of books and supplies, about gays caught in the backlash of disputes over values, about sick people who can't afford lifesaving drugs, about hunger and homelessness and innocents sent off to prison, and about young men and women killed and maimed in George W. Bush's dark venture in Iraq.

It's not that life in America was better in the 1960s. It wasn't. But it seemed to be moving in a better direction. For me, a young person with energy, ambition, and prodigious dreams, that counted for a lot.

The United States today is more powerful and prosperous than ever, but it feels very much like a nation on edge. The electorate is sliced right down the middle, with the two sides glaring at each other, as if from armed camps. The joy and optimism that one would expect to be widespread in the most successful nation in the history of the world are oddly missing. Instead there is a sense of things out of whack, of the center caving, of obligations unmet and promises betrayed. A suburban school district in Oregon ran out of money during a budget meltdown a couple of years ago, so it chopped nearly a month off the school calendar. The schools were closed and the kids were sent home. A high school physics teacher that I interviewed seemed almost in despair. "During the Great Depression we didn't close schools," he said. "We didn't close schools during World War II." He wondered aloud if he wasn't part of the most civically irresponsible generation in a hundred years.

In Tulia, Texas, a dusty panhandle town not far from Amarillo, one of the worse criminal justice atrocities of the last half-century was carried out. Dozens of men and women, more than

10 percent of the town's entire black population, were arrested in a drug sting run amok. A few whites who had relationships with blacks were also arrested. A local newspaper hailed the sweeping of such trash from Tulia's streets. No drugs were found in the sting, and no money or weapons were recovered. There were no witnesses, save the lone rogue cop who fingered the suspects, a twisted individual who referred to black people as "niggers" and scribbled notes about his activities on his arms and legs. Nevertheless, prison terms of 20 years, 60 years, 90 years, 300 years were handed down. Innocent people began copping pleas to escape sentences that approached or exceeded life in prison. A woman named Tonya White avoided incarceration only after she managed to produce records of a bank transaction, showing that she was in Oklahoma when she was supposed to have been selling drugs to the cop in Tulia.

I'll never forget the grief-stricken face of Freddie Brookins Sr., a man in his late forties whose son, Freddie Jr., was caught up in this episode. Brookins Sr. sat in the living room of his modest home and in a soft, cigarette-husky voice explained to me the dilemma his family had faced. Freddie Jr. had been offered a plea bargain and a relatively light prison sentence. But the family knew he was innocent. The father couldn't bear to advise his son to plead guilty to a crime he hadn't committed. So Freddie Jr. went to trial and was promptly convicted and sentenced to 20 years in state prison.

Eventually, because of the pressure of media coverage and 10 lawsuits by the NAACP Legal Defense and Educational Fund, the truth emerged and nearly all of the Tulia defendants were freed. But that took a long time, and would never have happened if the case hadn't been picked up and relentlessly pursued by the press.

It would be one thing if stories like these were rare, if they were bizarre onetime occurrences that we learned a lesson from and prevented from happening again. But the stories I cover are not rare. They're distillations of problems that are widespread, deeply entrenched, and powerfully destructive. In many cases they are the stories of good people who get badly hurt, people whose lives are ruined, or even lost, because of conditions or decisions that should never have been allowed to prevail.

Problems left to fester are the seed corn of calamities. It's not pure coincidence that a nation that tolerates horrendous abuses in its criminal justice system would, in wartime, seek out ways to escape the constraints of the Geneva Conventions, and even to justify torture.

Some years ago I covered a story about an actor in New York who was stunned to find himself arrested, along with several other people, in the lobby of his apartment building. He'd done absolutely nothing wrong. When I asked a deputy police commissioner why the man had been arrested, she said the police were investigating a crime and had decided to grab everyone in the lobby and "sort it out later."

That's exactly the rationale that was used in the sweep of so-called terror suspects who ended up in U.S. custody at Guantánamo Bay in the aftermath of the September 11 attacks. It didn't matter whether the detainees had done anything wrong. The government would sort that out later.

I'm convinced that America itself, like so many of the people 15 I write about, is in serious trouble, a society that has stopped chasing the fundamental tenets of its mythic dream. The nation has grown largely indifferent to abuses of power and social injustice. Flag-waving politicians still give lip service to the great American ideals of freedom, justice, equality, and opportunity, but in an era of preventive war and so-called conservative values, we've all but stopped pursuing them. And that's dangerous. Throughout our history the pursuit of those ideals—however imperfect the effort, however strained, timid, slow, and haphazard—was the only thing that made the United States special.

The war in Iraq, immorally launched and incompetently waged, will not be characterized by history as the noble campaign of a powerful nation striding toward greatness. It will be seen as the tragically foolish act of a nation unwilling to learn the lessons of Vietnam. The abuse of prisoners abroad and the war on civil liberties at home are hardly evidence that the better angels of our nature are in the ascent. The United States was always at its best at those points in history when it chased its cherished ideals like a mariner following the stars. At this moment, at the pinnacle of its power, the United States is a country that has lost its way. "When a nation goes down, or a society perishes," said Carl Sandburg, "one condition may always be found; they forgot where they came from. They lost sight of what had brought them along."

We are sliding backward in other ways. Franklin Roosevelt told us: "The test of our progress is not whether we add more to the abundance of those who have too much; it is whether we provide enough for those who have too little." Square that with the current appalling disparities in wealth and income in the United States and the emergence of a mind-bogglingly irresponsible ruling class whose core mission is indisputably to serve the interests of the very rich. The total wealth of the lucky 1 percent at the top of America's social pyramid is a colossal $2 trillion, more than the wealth of all the Americans in the bottom 90 percent combined.

For tips on blending quoted words with your own, see p. 45.

I saw this in its starkest relief one rainy Tuesday morning during the Christmas shopping season. A group of shivering homeless men, one of them nibbling at the core of an apple, had gathered for shelter on the steps of a Presbyterian church on Fifth Avenue in Manhattan, near Rockefeller Center. Across the street, arrayed like glittering jewels, were some of the most exclusive shops the nation has to offer: Tiffany, Gucci, Fortunoff, Cartier, Versace. Among the items offered for sale were an emerald ring for $1.9 million and a diamond necklace for $10 million. A fountain pen could be had for a mere $102,000. Nearby was a candy emporium where the chocolate was $62 a pound.

Today's disparities rival, and maybe even exceed, the garish inequities of the Gilded Age at the end of the nineteenth century. The barons of twenty-first-century America, otherwise known as CEOs, have salaries 400 to 500 times the income of the workers, our present-day serfs, who labor for them full time.

In Chicago I spent time with a few of that city's 100,000 20 young people, ages sixteen to twenty-four, who are at the very bottom of the economic pyramid. They are out of school, out of work, and, in my view, all but out of hope. In New York there are 200,000 such youngsters, and across the United States a staggering 5.5 million. These kids haunt the streets and the malls and the bowling alleys all day and much of the night. They're part of the American family but there is virtually no effort to find employment for them, or get them into training programs, or back into school. They're not even counted when the official jobless statistics are tallied. They're ignored. So they hustle for money wherever they can, in some cases drifting into drug selling, gang membership, prostitution, or worse. A seventeen-year-old in Chicago named Audrey Roberts told me,

"The stuff you hear about on the news, that's our everyday life. I've seen girls get raped, beaten up. I saw a boy get his head blown away. That happened right in front of me."

Connect the dots. Many of the young American men and women who ended up as the targets of snipers and bombers in Iraq had joined the military precisely because their economic opportunities and social options back home were grim. Again and again they will tell you that they joined the army to get a steady paycheck or an education, any opportunity to get ahead. Official statistics mask the reality of the nation's difficult economic landscape. Nearly 9 million Americans are out of work, and many millions more are underemployed and underpaid. Nearly a third of all American working families live in poverty. According to the Department of Agriculture, more than 12 million families are struggling just to feed themselves. Record levels of household debt and personal bankruptcies are being recorded as cash-strapped families increasingly borrow just to make ends meet.

In 1946, after a long depression and the worst of all wars, Harry Truman looked out at a world that was largely in ruins. He did not wring his hands or shrink faintheartedly from the task at hand. He embarked on the greatest renewal and reconstruction program the world has ever known. Recognizing the crucial importance of American leadership, he led the way to the creation of the United Nations and NATO, and to the Marshall Plan to rebuild Western Europe.

Here at home he built the platform that was used to launch America's great postwar run. We built schools and housing and highways, and over the next few decades developed a standard of living that was the envy of the world. We made big advances in civil rights and women's rights and civil liberties. We committed ourselves to protecting the rights of workers and consumers, and even the criminally accused. We made the environment a priority. .

All along the way there were astonishing strides in medicine and other disciplines, and technological advances that took us to the moon and beyond, and that brought us into a computer age that revolutionized the world.

It was a hell of a few decades.

Now where are we? At some point late in that postwar run, we took a wrong turn. That can-do era sputtered to an end, and we let the selfish, the vain, the greedy, and the incompetent take control of our nation and tell us what we can't do. We can't build first-class schools. We can't provide a reasonable wage for all working men and women. We can't follow through on the promise of Social Security. We can't deliver affordable drugs to the sick and infirm. We can't clean up the slums, or rescue the millions of children trapped in the clutches of poverty. We can't protect the environment.

The nation's leaders have looted the Treasury, mortgaged the future for generations to come, and driven us into a sinkhole in Iraq. And they've done it with impunity. Remember President Bush's "middle-class" tax cuts? "Over the coming decade," says Robert Reich, a former secretary of labor, "the Bush tax cuts will transfer more wealth to the richest one percent of the population than any fiscal policies in history."

If I had one wish for this country it would be for leadership that would arouse the consciousness of the masses to the deceit and injustice all around them. There are still plenty of valiant individuals who head out each day and put up a terrific fight on behalf of the poor and the oppressed and anyone else who might need a boost or a hand—or just a fair shake. But too often they're overmatched by the fat cats and the ideologues who have a stranglehold on the nation's financial resources and political power.

Time is not on our side. We've been attacked from without, but the greater danger to the essence of America is within. There's a fire in the basement of the United States and we're behaving as if we cannot even smell the smoke.

Joining the Conversation

1. Why do you think Bob Herbert titles his essay "A Fire in the Basement"? Exactly what kind of crisis is he referring to? What view about the present condition of the United States is he arguing against?
2. Herbert provides many examples of people suffering, in trouble, or being treated unfairly. What, in his opinion, is the underlying cause of these problems?
3. Reread paragraphs 22 through 25, about the rebuilding of the United States in the decades after World War II. How does this brief discussion of postwar history fit into Herbert's larger argument about the present situation?
4. Can you find any naysayers, or possible objections to Herbert's own argument, anywhere in his text? If not, try to come up with two or three and figure out where you could introduce them appropriately in his essay.
5. Construct an argument of your own that responds to Herbert's charges and to his call for action, agreeing with him, disagreeing, or both agreeing and disagreeing. Whatever stand you take, be sure you consider other positions as well in your text.

The Decline and Fall of Declinism

ALAN W. DOWD

—▣—

**Some people don't want to admit it, but America is
in great shape.**

UNDER THE HEADING "The end of a U.S.-centric world?"
the PostGlobal section of the *Washington Post* website recently
declared that "U.S. influence is in steep decline." It was just
the latest verse in a growing chorus of declinist doomsaying at
home and abroad.

In 2004, Pat Buchanan lamented "the decline and fall of the
greatest industrial republic the world had ever seen." In 2005,
the *Guardian*'s Polly Toynbee concluded that Hurricane Katrina exposed "a hollow superpower." In 2007, Pierre Hassner
of the Paris-based National Foundation for Political Science
declared, "It will not be the New American Century."

ALAN W. DOWD is a contributing editor at the *World Politics Review*,
a foreign policy and national security daily published on the Internet,
and his articles have appeared in the *American Legion Magazine*, the
National Review Online, and *Policy Review*. He was formerly a contributing writer to the American Enterprise Institute, a conservative
think tank. "The Decline and Fall of Declinism" appeared in *The
American* (28 Aug. 2007), a business and economics magazine published by the American Enterprise Institute.

And the dirge goes on.

It's a familiar tune, of course. We heard it in the early 1990s, when economists, political scientists, and pundits were quipping that while the U.S. and Soviet military superpowers waged the Cold War, it was economic superpowers Japan and Germany that won it; in the 1980s, when Paul Kennedy led the chorus by concluding that America was tumbling toward "imperial overstretch"; in the 1970s, when the U.S. slipped into a malaise; and in the 1960s, which began with the United States unable to dislodge a communist dictator 90 miles off its coast and ended with the United States unable to hold back the spread of communism half a world away.

But the declinists were wrong yesterday. And if their record— 5 and America's—are any indication, they are just as wrong today.

See p. 19 for tips on stating your position early in your text.

Any discussion of U.S. power has to begin with its enormous economy. At $13.13 trillion, the U.S. economy represents 20 percent of global output. It's growing faster than Britain's, Australia's, Germany's, Japan's, Canada's, even faster than the vaunted European Union.

In fact, even when Europe cobbles together its 25 economies under the EU banner, it still falls short of U.S. GDP*—and will fall further behind as the century wears on. Gerard Baker of the *Times of London* notes that the U.S. economy will be twice the size of Europe's by 2021.

On the other side of the world, some see China's booming economy as a threat to U.S. economic primacy. However, as Baker observes, the United States is adding "twice as much in absolute terms to global output" as China. The immense gap

*GDP Gross domestic product. One measure of income and output for a country's economy.

in per capita income—$44,244 in the U.S. versus $2,069 in China—adds further perspective to the picture.

America's muscular economic output comes courtesy of the American worker, who is growing ever more productive. Matthew Slaughter of the National Bureau of Economic Research details in the *Wall Street Journal* how, beginning in 1995, U.S. worker productivity began to accelerate. "From 1996 through 2006 it doubled, to an average annual rate of 2.7 percent."

Another recent analysis—surprisingly filed by the *New York* 10 *Times*—notes that this technology-driven "productivity miracle" has not manifested itself in other developed economies. Citing research by John Van Reenen and others at the London School of Economics, the *Times* concludes that when U.S. firms take over foreign firms, the latter enjoy "a tremendous productivity advantage over a non-American alternative. . . . It is as if the invisible hand of the American marketplace were somehow passing along a secret handshake to these firms." As Reenen and his colleagues conclude, it appears that the way "U.S. firms are organized or managed . . . enables better exploitation of IT."*

This should come as no surprise. As Derek Leebaert explains in *The Fifty-Year Wound*, the information technologies that began emerging in the late 1980s "forced decentralization and demanded the sort of adaptivity made for America."

So what do these numbers and comparisons tell us? For starters, as historian Niall Ferguson points out in *Colossus*, they tell us that the U.S. share of global productivity "exceeds the highest share of global output ever achieved by Britain by a factor of more than two."

*IT   Information technology.

They also serve to explain how the United States can withstand not just the human losses and psychological blows of a 9/11 or Katrina, but the sort of economic and financial blows that would have overwhelmed any other country on earth.

Just consider what the U.S. economy has *lost* since 9/11. One estimate posited that by the end of 2003 the U.S. could have lost as much as $500 billion dollars in GDP as a result of 9/11. That's roughly the size of the entire Iranian economy or half the Canadian economy.

As to Katrina, Congress poured $122 billion into the vast disaster area—and that was just in the 12 months immediately following the storm.

None of this was budgeted or foreseen, yet the U.S. economy dusted itself off and soldiered on.

While the declinists routinely remind us that the United States spends more on defense than the next 15 countries combined, they seldom note that the current defense budget accounts for barely 4 percent of GDP—a smaller percentage than the United States spent on defense at any time during the Cold War. In fact, defense outlays consumed as much as 10 percent of GDP in the 1950s, and 6 percent in the 1980s.

The diplomats who roam the corridors of the UN and the corporate chiefs who run the EU's sprawling public-private conglomerates dare not say it aloud, but the American military does the dirty work to keep the global economy going—and growing. "The hidden hand of the market will never work without a hidden fist," as Thomas Friedman observed in 1999.

"Globalization," adds Robert Kaplan, "could not occur without American ships and sailors."

Some argue that globalization is just another word for Americanization, and they may be right.

Dell and HP dominate the global PC market. More than 330 million PCs are running Microsoft software worldwide. Apple iTunes has displaced Sony's music-downloading system—inside Japan. Google was created by a pair of Stanford grad students without any government help at all, yet it so dominates the Web that the EU is pouring some $290 million into birthing an answer.

Ferguson observes that half of the 30,000 McDonald's restaurants are located somewhere other than the United States, and that 70 percent of Coke's thirsty drinkers reside *outside* North America. Starbucks has stores in 39 countries—from Austria to the United Arab Emirates to Australia.

Wal-Mart has 2,700 stores outside the United States, planting the low-price banner in 14 countries. "In the past year," boasts the Wal-Mart corporation, "the company became majority owner of Seiyu in Japan, completed its acquisition of Sonae in Brazil, and expanded into six new markets including Northern Ireland, Costa Rica, El Salvador, Guatemala, Honduras, and Nicaragua." Wal-Mart projects global sales of $344 billion in 2007, positioning the retail juggernaut just outside the top 30 in global rankings—for national GDPs.

The converse, even in this global economy, simply does not hold. Although Americans are notorious for appropriating from other cultures, they are not flocking to British retailers, or buying Afri Cola, or logging on to some Euro-Google, or purchasing French PCs.

But don't take my word for it. As French president Nicolas 25 Sarkozy matter-of-factly puts it, "The United States is the world's leading economic, military, and monetary power. . . . Your economy is flourishing, your intellectual life is rich."

Not bad for a nation in "steep decline."

Joining the Conversation

1. Alan W. Dowd begins his essay with several paragraphs laying out a position that he then goes on to disagree with—naysayers, in other words. Do you find this approach to be an effective way of opening this essay? Why or why not?

2. This essay presents a view that almost completely contradicts that expressed in the previous essay, by Bob Herbert (pp. 394–403). List the evidence that each author presents, and compare the two lists. How might you incorporate ideas from both in an essay of your own? What would your thesis be, and how would you support it?

3. Assess Dowd's use of economic statistics in making his argument. They seem to present an impressive picture of American prosperity, but are there other ways of interpreting the numbers? Is there information he doesn't present that might weaken his case? How in your view does Dowd use the concept of a U.S. "decline"? What other types of decline does he not consider, if any?

4. Why does this argument matter? How well does Dowd convey the importance of his argument and the topic in general? What if anything might be added to make this point more effectively?

5. Write your own essay in response to Dowd. You might want to bring in some of the arguments raised by Herbert (pp. 394–403) or Thomas L. Friedman (pp. 421–40), whether as support for your view or as possible objections.

The Last Superpower

FAREED ZAKARIA

MANY OBSERVERS AND COMMENTATORS have looked at
the vitality of [today's] emerging world and concluded that the
United States has had its day. Andy Grove, the founder of Intel,
puts it bluntly. "America is in danger of following Europe down
the tubes," he says, "and the worst part is that nobody knows
it. They're all in denial, patting themselves on the back as the
Titanic heads straight for the iceberg full speed ahead." Thomas
Friedman describes watching waves of young Indian professionals get to work for the night shift at Infosys in Bangalore.
"Oh, my God, there are so many of them, and they just keep
coming, wave after wave. How in the world can it possibly be
good for my daughters and millions of other Americans that
these Indians can do the same jobs as they can for a fraction

FAREED ZAKARIA is the current editor of *Newsweek International* and
the former managing editor of *Foreign Affairs,* a journal on U.S. foreign policy and international affairs. He is the author of several books,
including *The Future of Freedom* (2003). *Esquire* magazine named him
"one of the 21 most important people of the 21st Century" in 1999.
"The Last Superpower" comes from his book *The Post-American World*
(2008), which argues that the United States is not necessarily in
decline but the rest of the world's powers are on the rise.

of the wages?"[1] "Globalization is striking back," writes Gabor Steingart, an editor at Germany's leading news magazine, *Der Spiegel,* in a bestselling book. As its rivals have prospered, he argues, the United States has lost key industries, its people have stopped saving money, and its government has become increasingly indebted to Asian central banks.[2]

What's puzzling, however, is that these trends have been around for a while—and they have actually helped America's bottom line. Over the past twenty years, as globalization and outsourcing have accelerated dramatically, America's growth rate has averaged just over 3 percent, a full percentage point higher than that of Germany and France. (Japan averaged 2.3 percent over the same period.) Productivity growth, the elixir of modern economics, has been over 2.5 percent for a decade now, again a full percentage point higher than the European average. Even American exports held up, despite a decade-long spike in the value of the dollar that ended recently. In 1980, U.S. exports represented 10 percent of the world total; in 2007, that figure was still almost 9 percent. According to the World Economic Forum, the United States remains the most competitive economy in the world and ranks first in innovation, ninth in technological readiness, second in company spending for research and technology, and second in the quality of its research institutions. China does not come within thirty countries of the United States in any of these, and India breaks the top ten on only one count: market size. In virtually every sector that advanced industrial countries participate in, U.S. firms lead the world in productivity and profits.

The United States' share of the global economy has been remarkably steady through wars, depressions, and a slew of other powers rising. With 5 percent of the world's population, the United States has generated between 20 and 30 percent of world output for 125 years. There will surely be some slippage of America's position over the next few decades. This is not a political statement but a mathematical one. As other countries grow faster, America's relative economic weight will fall. But the decline need not be large-scale, rapid, or consequential, as long as the United States can adapt to new challenges as well as it adapted to those it confronted over the last century. In the next few decades, the rise of the emerging nations is likely to come mostly at the expense of Western Europe and Japan, which are locked in a slow, demographically determined decline.

America will face the most intense economic competition it has ever faced. The American economic and social system knows how to respond and adjust to such pressures. The reforms needed are obvious but because they mean some pain now for long-term gain, the political system cannot make them. The more difficult challenge that the United States faces is international. It will confront a global order quite different from the one it is used to operating in. For now, the United States remains the most powerful player. But every year the balance shifts.

For the roughly two decades since 1989, the power of the 5 United States has defined the international order. All roads have led to Washington, and American ideas about politics, economics, and foreign policy have been the starting points for global action. Washington has been the most powerful outside actor on every continent in the world, dominating the Western Hemisphere, remaining the crucial outside balancer in Europe and East Asia, expanding its role in the Middle East and Central and South Asia, and everywhere remaining the only country that can provide the muscle for any serious global military operation. For every country—from Russia and China to South Africa and India—its most important relationship in the world has been the relationship with the United States.

That influence reached its apogee with Iraq. Despite the reluctance, opposition, or active hostility of much of the world, the United States was able to launch an unprovoked attack on a sovereign country and to enlist dozens of countries and international agencies to assist it during and after the invasion. It is not just the complications of Iraq that have unwound this order. Even had Iraq been a glorious success, the method of its execution would have made utterly clear the unchallenged power of the United States—and it is this exercise of unipolarity* that has provoked a reaction around the world. The unipolar order of the last two decades is waning not because of Iraq but because of the broader diffusion of power across the world.

On some matters, unipolarity seems already to have ended. The European Union now represents the largest trade bloc on the globe, creating bipolarity, and as China and then other emerging giants gain size, the bipolar realm of trade might become tripolar and then multipolar. In every realm except military, similar shifts are underway. In general, however, the notion of a multipolar world, with four or five players of roughly equal weight, does not describe reality today or in the near future. Europe cannot act militarily or even politically as one. Japan and Germany are hamstrung by their past. China and India are still developing. Instead, the international system is more accurately described by Samuel Huntington's term "uni-multipolarity," or what Chinese geopoliticians call "many powers and one superpower." The messy language reflects the messy

---

*__unipolarity__ In world politics, a situation in which one state has most of the political, economic, cultural, and military power.

reality. The United States remains by far the most powerful country but in a world with several other important great powers and with greater assertiveness and activity from all actors. This hybrid international system—more democratic, more dynamic, more open, more connected—is one we are likely to live with for several decades. It is easier to define what it is not than what it is, easier to describe the era it is moving away from than the era it is moving toward—hence *the post-American world*.

The United States occupies the top spot in the emerging system, but it is also the country that is most challenged by the new order. Most other great powers will see their role in the world expand. That process is already underway. China and India are becoming bigger players in their neighborhoods and beyond. Russia has ended its post-Soviet accommodation and is becoming more forceful, even aggressive. Japan, though not a rising power, is now more willing to voice its views and positions to its neighbors. Europe acts on matters of trade and economics with immense strength and purpose. Brazil and Mexico are becoming more vocal on Latin American issues. South Africa has positioned itself as a leader of the African continent. All these countries are taking up more space in the international arena than they did before.

For the United States, the arrow is pointing in the opposite direction. Economics is not a zero-sum game—the rise of other players expands the pie, which is good for all—but geopolitics is a struggle for influence and control. As other countries become more active, America's enormous space for action will inevitably diminish. Can the United States accommodate itself to the rise of other powers, of various political stripes, on several continents? This does not mean becoming resigned to chaos or aggression; far from it. But the only way for the United

States to deter rogue actions will be to create a broad, durable coalition against them. And that will be possible only if Washington can show that it is willing to allow other countries to become stakeholders in the new order. In today's international order, progress means compromise. No country will get its way entirely. These are easy words to write or say but difficult to implement. They mean accepting the growth in power and influence of other countries, the prominence of interests and concerns. This balance—between accommodation and deterrence—is the chief challenge for American foreign policy in the next few decades.

I began by arguing that the new order did not herald American decline, because I believe that America has enormous strengths and that the new world will not throw up a new superpower but rather a diversity of forces that Washington can navigate and even help direct. But still, as the rest of the world rises, in purely economic terms, America will experience relative decline. As others grow faster, its share of the pie will be smaller (though the shift will likely be small for many years). In addition, the new nongovernmental forces that are increasingly active will constrain Washington substantially.

This is a challenge for Washington but also for everyone else. For almost three centuries, the world has been undergirded by the presence of a large liberal hegemon*—first Britain, then the United States. These two superpowers helped create and maintain an open world economy, protecting trade routes and sea lanes, acting as lenders of last resort, holding the reserve currency, investing abroad, and keeping their own markets open. They also tipped the military balance

See Chapter 7 for tips on saying why it matters.

*__hegemon__   A government or state that has so much power over others that it can dictate their policies.

4 1 5

against the great aggressors of their ages, from Napoleon's France, to Germany, to the Soviet Union. For all its abuses of power, the United States has been the creator and sustainer of the current order of open trade and democratic government—an order that has been benign and beneficial for the vast majority of humankind. As things change, and as America's role changes, that order could begin to fracture. The collapse of the dollar—to the point where there was no global reserve currency—would be a problem for the world just as much as for America. And solving common problems in an era of diffusion and decentralization could turn out to be far more difficult without a superpower.

Some Americans have become acutely conscious of the changing world. American business is increasingly aware of the shifts taking place around the world and is responding to them rapidly and unsentimentally. Large U.S.-based multinationals almost uniformly report that their growth now relies on penetrating new foreign markets. With annual revenue growth of 2–3 percent a year in the United States and 10–15 percent a year abroad, they know they have to adapt to a post-American world—or else lose out in it. A similar awareness is visible in America's universities, where more and more students study and travel abroad and interact with foreign students. Younger Americans live comfortably with the knowledge that the latest trends—in finance, architecture, art, technology—might originate in London, Shanghai, Seoul, Tallinn, or Mumbai.

But this outward orientation is not yet common in American society more broadly. The American economy remains internally focused, though this is changing, with trade making up 28 percent of GDP (compared with 38 percent for Germany). Insularity has been one of nature's blessings to America, bordered as it is by two vast oceans and two benign neighbors. America has not been sullied by the machinations and weariness of the Old World and has always been able to imagine a new and different order—whether in Germany, Japan, or even Iraq. But at the same time, this isolation has left Americans quite unaware of the world beyond their borders. Americans speak few languages, know little about foreign cultures, and remain unconvinced that they need to rectify this. Americans rarely benchmark to global standards because they are sure that their way must be the best and most advanced. The result is that they are increasingly suspicious of this emerging global era. There is a growing gap between America's worldly business elite and cosmopolitan class, on the one hand, and the majority of the American people, on the other. Without real efforts to bridge it, this divide could destroy America's competitive edge and its political future.

Popular suspicions are fed and encouraged by an irresponsible national political culture. In Washington, new thinking about a new world is sorely lacking. It is easy enough to criticize the Bush administration of its arrogance and unilateralism, which have handicapped America abroad. But the problem is not confined to Bush, Cheney, Rumsfeld, or the Republicans, even though they have become the party of chest-thumping machismo, proud to be despised abroad. Listen to some Democrats in Washington, and you hear a weaker unilateralism—on trade, labor standards, and various pet human rights issues. On terrorism, both parties continue to speak in language entirely designed for a domestic audience with no concern for the poisonous effect it has everywhere else. American politicians constantly and promiscuously demand, label, sanction, and condemn whole countries for myriad failings. Over the last fifteen years, the United States has placed sanctions on half the world's population. We are the only country in the world to issue annual report cards on every other country's behavior. Washington, D.C., has become a bubble, smug and out of touch with the world outside.

The 2007 Pew Global Attitudes Survey showed a remark- 15 able increase worldwide in positive views about free trade, markets, and democracy. Large majorities in countries from China and Germany to Bangladesh and Nigeria said that growing trade ties between countries were good. Of the forty-seven countries polled, however, the one that came in dead last in terms of support for free trade was the United States. In the five years the survey has been done, no country has seen as great a drop-off as the United States.

Or take a look at the attitudes toward foreign companies. When asked whether they had a positive impact, a surprisingly large number of people in countries like Brazil, Nigeria, India, and Bangladesh said yes. Those countries have typically been suspicious of Western multinationals. (South Asia's unease has some basis; after all, it was initially colonized by a multinational corporation, the British East India Company.) And yet, 73 percent in India, 75 percent in Bangladesh, 70 percent in Brazil, and 82 percent in Nigeria now have positive views of these companies. The figure for America, in contrast, is 45 percent, which places us in the bottom five. We want the world to accept American companies with open arms, but when they come here—that's a different matter. Attitudes on immigration represent an even larger reversal. On an issue where the United States has been the model for the world, the country has regressed toward an angry defensive crouch. Where we once wanted to pioneer every new technology, we now look at innovation fearfully, wondering how it will change things.

The irony is that the rise of the rest is a consequence of American ideas and actions. For sixty years, American politicians and diplomats have traveled around the world pushing countries to open their markets, free up their politics, and embrace trade and technology. We have urged peoples in distant lands to take up the challenge of competing in the global economy, freeing up their currencies, and developing new industries. We counseled them to be unafraid of change and learn the secrets of our success. And it worked: the natives have gotten good at capitalism. But now we are becoming suspicious of the very things we have long celebrated—free markets, trade, immigration, and technological changes. And all this is happening when the tide is going our way. Just as the world is opening up, America is closing down.

Generations from now, when historians write about these times, they might note that, in the early decades of the twenty-first century, the United States succeeded in its great and historic mission—it globalized the world. But along the way, they might write, it forgot to globalize itself.

NOTES

1. Thomas L. Friedman, *The World Is Flat: A Brief History of the Twenty-first Century* (New York: Farrar, 2005) 226. Andy Grove's statement is quoted in Clyde Prestowitz, *Three Billion New Capitalists: The Great Shift of Wealth and Power to the East* (New York: Basic, 2005) 8.

2. Gabor Steingart, *The War for Wealth: Why Globalization Is Bleeding the West of Its Prosperity* (New York: McGraw, 2008).

Joining the Conversation

1. What is Fareed Zakaria's main point in this essay, and what argument(s) is he responding to? Summarize the "I say" and "they say" of his argument.

2. In writing about the short-term future of the United States in paragraph 4, Zakaria asserts that the country "will face the most intense economic competition it has ever faced." Summarize his arguments about the domestic and international challenges that he believes the United States will face.

3. In paragraph 13, Zakaria discusses the effects of the United States' history of isolation from the rest of the world. He writes, "Americans speak few languages, know little about foreign cultures, and remain unconvinced that they need to rectify this. Americans rarely benchmark to global standards because they are sure that their way must be the best and most advanced. The result is that they are increasingly suspicious of this emerging global era." These comments are the reflections of someone who was born and raised abroad but has chosen to live his life in the United States. How would you respond to his characterization of Americans based on your own experiences and observations?

4. What audience do you think Zakaria is attempting to reach in this essay? How do you know? Of what is he trying to persuade the reader, and how effective do you think he is?

5. Zakaria concludes his essay by suggesting that future historians might note that "the United States succeeded in its great and historic mission—it globalized the world. But along the way, they might write, it forgot to globalize itself" (paragraph 18). Write a response to this point in which you agree with it, disagree with it, or both agree and disagree.

The World Is Flat

THOMAS L. FRIEDMAN

—⌐🔲⌐—

NO ONE EVER gave me directions like this on a golf course before: "Aim at either Microsoft or IBM." I was standing on the first tee at the KGA Golf Club in downtown Bangalore, in southern India, when my playing partner pointed at two shiny glass-and-steel buildings off in the distance, just behind the first green. The Goldman Sachs building wasn't done yet; otherwise he could have pointed that out as well and made it a three-some. HP and Texas Instruments had their offices on the back nine, along the tenth hole. That wasn't all. The tee markers were from Epson, the printer company, and one of our caddies was wearing a hat from 3M. Outside, some of the traffic signs were also sponsored by Texas Instruments, and the Pizza Hut billboard on the way over showed a steaming pizza, under the headline "Gigabites of Taste!"

THOMAS L. FRIEDMAN is a columnist with the *New York Times*, writing regular op-ed pieces on foreign affairs. He has been awarded the Pulitzer Prize three times. His books include *From Beirut to Jerusalem* (1989), *The Lexus and the Olive Tree* (1999), and *The World Is Flat: A Brief History of the Twenty-first Century* (2005), from which the piece here was taken.

The golf course at the Karnataka Golf Association in Bangalore, India.

No, this definitely wasn't Kansas. It didn't even seem like India. Was this the New World, the Old World, or the Next World?

I had come to Bangalore, India's Silicon Valley, on my own Columbus-like journey of exploration. Columbus sailed with the *Niña*, the *Pinta*, and the *Santa María* in an effort to discover a shorter, more direct route to India by heading west, across the Atlantic, on what he presumed to be an open sea route to the East Indies—rather than going south and east around Africa, as Portuguese explorers of his day were trying to do. India and the magical Spice Islands of the East were famed at the time for their gold, pearls, gems, and silk—a source of untold riches. Finding this shortcut by sea to India, at a time when the Muslim powers of the day had blocked the overland routes from Europe, was a way for both Columbus and the Spanish monarchy to become wealthy and powerful. When Columbus set sail, he apparently assumed the Earth was round, which was why he was convinced that he could get to India by going west. He miscalculated the distance, though. He thought the Earth was a smaller sphere than it is. He also did not anticipate running into a landmass before he reached the East Indies. Nevertheless, he called the aboriginal peoples he encountered in the new world "Indians." Returning home, though, Columbus was able to tell his patrons, King Ferdinand and Queen Isabella, that although he never did find India, he could confirm that the world was indeed round.

I set out for India by going due east, via Frankfurt. I had Lufthansa business class. I knew exactly which direction I was going thanks to the GPS map displayed on the screen that popped out of the armrest of my airline seat. I landed safely and on schedule. I too encountered people called Indians. I too was searching for the source of India's riches. Columbus was searching for hardware—precious metals, silk, and spices—the source of wealth in his day. I was searching for software, brainpower, complex algorithms, knowledge workers, call centers, transmission protocols, breakthroughs in optical engineering—the sources of wealth in our day. Columbus was happy to make the Indians he met his slaves, a pool of free manual labor.

I just wanted to understand why the Indians I met were taking our work, why they had become such an important pool for the outsourcing of service and information technology work from America and other industrialized countries. Columbus had more than one hundred men on his three ships; I had a small crew from the Discovery Times channel that fit comfortably into two banged-up vans, with Indian drivers who drove barefoot. When I set sail, so to speak, I too assumed that the world was round, but what I encountered in the real India profoundly shook my faith in that notion. Columbus accidentally ran into America but thought he had discovered part of India. I actually found India and thought many of the people I met there were Americans. Some had actually taken American names, and others were doing great imitations of American accents at call centers and American business techniques at software labs.

Columbus reported to his king and queen that the world was round, and he went down in history as the man who first made this discovery. I returned home and shared my discovery only with my wife, and only in a whisper.

"Honey," I confided, "I think the world is flat."

How did I come to this conclusion? I guess you could say it all started in Nandan Nilekani's conference room at Infosys Technologies Limited. Infosys is one of the jewels of the Indian information technology world, and Nilekani, the company's CEO, is one of the most thoughtful and respected captains of Indian industry. I drove with the Discovery Times crew out to the Infosys campus, about forty minutes from the heart of Bangalore, to tour the facility and interview Nilekani. The Infosys campus is reached by a pockmarked road, with sacred cows, horse-drawn carts, and motorized rickshaws all jostling alongside our vans. Once you enter the gates of Infosys, though, you are in a different world. A massive resort-size swimming pool nestles amid boulders and manicured lawns, adjacent to a huge putting green. There are multiple restaurants and a fabulous health club. Glass-and-steel buildings seem to sprout up like weeds each week. In some of those buildings, Infosys employees are writing specific software programs for American or European companies; in others, they are running the back rooms of major American- and European-based multinationals—everything from computer maintenance to specific research projects to answering customer calls routed there from all over the world. Security is tight, cameras monitor the doors, and if you are working for American Express, you cannot get into the building that is managing services and research for General Electric. Young Indian engineers, men and women, walk briskly from building to building, dangling ID badges. One looked like he could do my taxes. Another looked like she could take my computer apart. And a third looked like she designed it!

After sitting for an interview, Nilekani gave our TV crew a tour of Infosys's global conferencing center—ground zero of the Indian outsourcing industry. It was a cavernous wood-paneled room that looked like a tiered classroom from an Ivy League law school. On one end was a massive wall-size screen and overhead there were cameras in the ceiling for teleconferencing. "So this is our conference room, probably the largest screen in Asia—this is forty digital screens [put together]," Nilekani explained proudly, pointing to the biggest flat-screen TV I had ever seen. Infosys, he said, can hold a virtual meeting of the key players from its entire global supply chain for any project at any time on that supersize screen. So their American designers could be on the screen speaking with their Indian software writers and their Asian manufacturers all at once. "We could be sitting here, somebody from New York, London, Boston, San Francisco, all live. And maybe the implementation is in Singapore, so the Singapore person could also be live here. . . . That's globalization," said Nilekani. Above the screen there were eight clocks that pretty well summed up the Infosys work-day: 24/7/365. The clocks were labeled US West, US East, GMT, India, Singapore, Hong Kong, Japan, Australia.

"Outsourcing is just one dimension of a much more funda- 10 mental thing happening today in the world," Nilekani explained. "What happened over the last [few] years is that there was a massive investment in technology, especially in the bubble era, when hundreds of millions of dollars were invested in putting broadband connectivity around the world, undersea cables, all those things." At the same time, he added, computers became cheaper and dispersed all over the world, and there was an explosion of software—e-mail, search engines like Google, and proprietary software that can chop up any piece of work and send one part to Boston, one part to Bangalore, and one part to Beijing, making it easy for anyone to do remote development. When all of these things suddenly came together around 2000, added Nilekani, they "created a platform where intellectual work, intellectual capital, could be delivered from anywhere. It could be disaggregated, delivered, distributed, produced, and put back together again—and this gave a whole new degree of freedom to the way we do work, especially work of an intellectual nature. . . . And what you are seeing in Bangalore today is really the culmination of all these things coming together."

We were sitting on the couch outside of Nilekani's office, waiting for the TV crew to set up its cameras. At one point, summing up the implications of all this, Nilekani uttered a phrase that rang in my ear. He said to me, "Tom, the playing field is being leveled." He meant that countries like India are now able to compete for global knowledge work as never before—and that America had better get ready for this. America was going to be challenged, but, he insisted, the challenge would be good for America because we are always at our best when we are being challenged. As I left the Infosys campus that evening and bounced along the road back to Bangalore, I kept chewing on that phrase: "The playing field is being leveled."

What Nandan is saying, I thought, is that the playing field is being flattened . . . Flattened? Flattened? My God, he's telling me the world is flat!

Here I was in Bangalore—more than five hundred years after Columbus sailed over the horizon, using the rudimentary navigational technologies of his day, and returned safely to prove definitively that the world was round—and one of India's smartest engineers, trained at his country's top technical institute and backed by the most modern technologies of his day, was essentially telling me that the world was *flat*—as flat as that screen on which he can host a meeting of his whole global supply chain. Even more interesting, he was citing this development as a good thing, as a new milestone in human progress and a great opportunity for India and the world—the fact that we had made our world flat!

In the back of that van, I scribbled down four words in my notebook: "The world is flat." As soon as I wrote them, I realized that this was the underlying message of everything that I had seen and heard in Bangalore in two weeks of filming. The global competitive playing field was being leveled. The world was being flattened.

As I came to this realization, I was filled with both excite- 15 ment and dread. The journalist in me was excited at having found a framework to better understand the morning headlines and to explain what was happening in the world today. Clearly, it is now possible for more people than ever to collaborate and compete in real time with more other people on more different kinds of work from more different corners of the planet and on a more equal footing than at any previous time in the history of the world—using computers, e-mail, networks, teleconferencing, and dynamic new software. That is what Nandan was telling me. That was what I discovered on my journey to India and beyond. When you start to think of the world as flat, a lot of things make sense in ways they did not before. But I was also excited personally, because what the flattening of the world means is that we are now connecting all the knowledge centers on the planet together into a single global network, which—if politics and terrorism do not get in the way—could usher in an amazing era of prosperity and innovation.

But contemplating the flat world also left me filled with dread, professional and personal. My personal dread derived from the obvious fact that it's not only the software writers and computer geeks who get empowered to collaborate on work in a flat world. It's also al-Qaeda and other terrorist networks. The playing field is not being leveled only in ways that draw in and superempower a whole new group of innovators. It's being leveled in a way that draws in and superempowers a whole new group of angry, frustrated, and humiliated men and women.

Professionally, the recognition that the world was flat was unnerving because I realized that this flattening had been taking place while I was sleeping, and I had missed it. I wasn't really sleeping, but I was otherwise engaged. Before 9/11, I was focused on tracking globalization and exploring the tension between the "Lexus" forces of economic integration and the "Olive Tree" forces of identity and nationalism—hence my 1999 book, *The Lexus and the Olive Tree*. But after 9/11, the olive tree wars became all-consuming for me. I spent almost all my time traveling in the Arab and Muslim worlds. During those years I lost the trail of globalization.

I found that trail again on my journey to Bangalore in February 2004. Once I did, I realized that something really important had happened while I was fixated on the olive groves of Kabul and Baghdad. Globalization had gone to a whole new level. If you put *The Lexus and the Olive Tree* and this book together, the broad historical argument you end up with is that there have been three great eras of globalization. The first lasted from 1492—when Columbus set sail, opening trade between the Old World and the New World—until around 1800. I would call this era Globalization 1.0. It shrank the world from a size large to a size medium. Globalization 1.0 was about countries and muscles. That is, in Globalization 1.0 the key agent of change, the dynamic force driving the process of global integration was how much brawn—how much muscle, how much horsepower, wind power, or, later, steam power—your country had and how creatively you could deploy it. In this era, countries and governments (often inspired by religion or imperialism or a combination of both) led the way in breaking down walls and knitting the world together, driving global integration. In Globalization 1.0, the primary questions were: Where does my country fit into global competition and opportunities? How can I go global and collaborate with others through my country?

The second great era, Globalization 2.0, lasted roughly from 1800 to 2000, interrupted by the Great Depression and World Wars I and II. This era shrank the world from a size medium to a size small. In Globalization 2.0, the key agent of change, the dynamic force driving global integration, was multinational companies. These multinationals went global for markets and labor, spearheaded first by the expansion of the Dutch and English joint-stock companies and the Industrial Revolution. In the first half of this era, global integration was powered by falling transportation costs, thanks to the steam engine and the railroad, and in the second half by falling telecommunication costs—thanks to the diffusion of the telegraph, telephones, the PC, satellites, fiber-optic cable, and the early version of the World Wide Web. It was during this era that we really saw the birth and maturation of a global economy, in the sense that there was enough movement of goods and information from continent to continent for there to be a global market, with global arbitrage in products and labor. The dynamic forces behind this era of globalization were breakthroughs in hardware—from steamships and railroads in the beginning to telephones and mainframe computers toward the end. And the big questions in this era were: Where does my company fit into the global economy? How does it take advantage of the opportunities? How can I go global and collaborate with others through my company? *The Lexus and the Olive Tree* was primarily about the climax of this era, an era when the walls started falling all around the world, and integration, and the backlash to it, went to a whole new level. But even as the walls fell, there were still a lot of barriers to seamless global integration. Remember, when Bill Clinton was elected president in 1992, virtually no one outside of government and the academy had e-mail, and when I was writing *The Lexus and the Olive Tree* in 1998, the Internet and e-commerce were just taking off.

Well, they took off—along with a lot of other things 20 that came together while I was sleeping. And that is why I argue . . . that around the year 2000 we entered a whole new era: Globalization 3.0. Globalization 3.0 is shrinking the world from a size small to a size tiny and flattening the playing field at the same time. And while the dynamic force in Globalization 1.0 was countries globalizing and the dynamic force in

Globalization 2.0 was companies globalizing, the dynamic force in Globalization 3.0—the thing that gives it its unique character—is the newfound power for *individuals* to collaborate and compete globally. And the lever that is enabling individuals and groups to go global so easily and so seamlessly is not horsepower, and not hardware, but software—all sorts of new applications—in conjunction with the creation of a global fiber-optic network that has made us all next-door neighbors. Individuals must, and can, now ask, Where do *I* fit into the global competition and opportunities of the day, and how can *I*, on my own, collaborate with others globally?

But Globalization 3.0 not only differs from the previous eras in how it is shrinking and flattening the world and in how it is empowering individuals. It is different in that Globalization 1.0 and 2.0 were driven primarily by European and American individuals and businesses. Even though China actually had the biggest economy in the world in the eighteenth century, it was Western countries, companies, and explorers who were doing most of the globalizing and shaping of the system. But going forward, this will be less and less true. Because it is flattening and shrinking the world, Globalization 3.0 is going to be more and more driven not only by individuals but also by a much more diverse—non-Western, non-white—group of individuals. Individuals from every corner of the flat world are being empowered. Globalization 3.0 makes it possible for so many more people to plug and play, and you are going to see every color of the human rainbow take part.

(While this empowerment of individuals to act globally is the most important new feature of Globalization 3.0, companies—large and small—have been newly empowered in this era as well.)

Needless to say, I had only the vaguest appreciation of all this as I left Nandan's office that day in Bangalore. But as I sat contemplating these changes on the balcony of my hotel room that evening, I did know one thing: I wanted to drop every-thing and write a book that would enable me to understand how this flattening process happened and what its implications might be for countries, companies, and individuals. So I picked up the phone and called my wife, Ann, and told her, "I am going to write a book called *The World Is Flat*." She was both amused and curious—well, maybe *more* amused than curious! Eventually, I was able to bring her around, and I hope I will be able to do the same with you, dear reader. Let me start by taking you back to the beginning of my journey to India, and other points east, and share with you some of the encounters that led me to conclude the world was no longer round—but flat.

Jaithirth "Jerry" Rao was one of the first people I met in Ban-galore—and I hadn't been with him for more than a few min-utes at the Leela Palace hotel before he told me that he could handle my tax returns and any other accounting needs I had—from Bangalore. No thanks, I demurred, I already have an accountant in Chicago. Jerry just smiled. He was too polite to say it—that he may already be my accountant, or rather my accountant's accountant, thanks to the explosion in the out-sourcing of tax preparation.

"This is happening as we speak," said Rao, a native of Mum-bai, formerly Bombay, whose Indian firm, MphasiS, has a team of Indian accountants able to do outsourced accounting work from any state in America and the federal government. "We have tied up with several small and medium-sized CPA firms in America."

"You mean like my accountant?" I asked. "Yes, like your accountant," said Rao with a smile. Rao's company has pioneered a work flow software program with a standardized format that makes the outsourcing of tax returns cheap and easy. The whole process starts, Jerry explained, with an accountant in the United States scanning my last year's tax returns, plus my W-2, W-4, 1099, bonuses, and stock statements—everything—into a computer server, which is physically located in California or Texas. "Now your accountant, if he is going to have your taxes done overseas, knows that you would prefer not to have your surname be known or your Social Security number known [to someone outside the country], so he can choose to suppress that information," said Rao. "The accountants in India call up all the raw information directly from the server in America [using a password], and they complete your tax returns, with you remaining anonymous. All the data stays in the U.S. to comply with privacy regulations. . . . We take data protection and privacy very seriously. The accountant in India can see the data on his screen, but he cannot take a download of it or print it out—our program does not allow it. The most he could do would be to try to memorize it, if he had some ill intention. The accountants are not allowed to even take a paper and pen into the room when they are working on the returns."

I was intrigued at just how advanced this form of service outsourcing had become. "We are doing several thousand returns," said Rao. What's more, "Your CPA in America need not even be in their office. They can be sitting on a beach in California and e-mail us and say, 'Jerry, you are really good at doing New York State returns, so you do Tom's returns. And Sonia, you and your team in Delhi do the Washington and Florida returns.' Sonia, by the way, is working out of her house in India, with no overhead [for the company to pay]. 'And these others, they are really complicated, so I will do them myself.'"

In 2003, some 25,000 U.S. tax returns were done in India. In 2004, the number was 100,000. In 2005, it is expected to be 400,000. In a decade, you will assume that your accountant has outsourced the basic preparation of your tax returns—if not more.

"How did you get into this?" I asked Rao.

"My friend Jeroen Tas, a Dutchman, and I were both work- ing in California for Citigroup," Rao explained. "I was his boss and we were coming back from New York one day together on a flight and I said that I was planning to quit and he said, 'So am I.' We both said, 'Why don't we start our own business?' So in 1997–98, we put together a business plan to provide high-end Internet solutions for big companies. . . . Two years ago, though, I went to a technology convention in Las Vegas and was approached by some medium-size [American] accounting firms, and they said they could not afford to set up big tax outsourcing operations to India, but the big guys could, and [the medium guys] wanted to get ahead of them. So we developed a software product called VTR—Virtual Tax Room—to enable these medium-size accounting firms to easily outsource tax returns. . . .

Some of the signs of flattening I encountered back home, though, had nothing to do with economics. On October 3, 2004, I appeared on the CBS News Sunday morning show *Face the Nation*, hosted by veteran CBS correspondent Bob Schieffer. CBS had been in the news a lot in previous weeks because of Dan Rather's *60 Minutes* report about President George W. Bush's Air National Guard service that turned out to be based on bogus documents. After the show that Sunday, Schieffer mentioned that the oddest thing had happened to him the week before. When he walked out of the CBS studio, a young reporter was waiting for him on the sidewalk. This isn't all that unusual, because as with all the Sunday morning shows, the major networks—CBS, NBC, ABC, CNN, and Fox—always send crews to one another's studios to grab exit interviews with the guests. But this young man, Schieffer explained, was not from a major network. He politely introduced himself as a reporter for a Web site called InDC Journal and asked whether he could ask Schieffer a few questions. Schieffer, being a polite fellow, said sure. The young man interviewed him on a device Schieffer did not recognize and then asked if he could take his picture. A picture? Schieffer noticed that the young man had no camera. He didn't need one. He turned his cell phone around and snapped Schieffer's picture.

"So I came in the next morning and looked up this Web site and there was my picture and the interview and there were already three hundred comments about it," said Schieffer, who, though keenly aware of online journalism, was nevertheless taken aback at the incredibly fast, low-cost, and solo manner in which this young man had put him up in lights.

I was intrigued by this story, so I tracked down the young man from InDC Journal. His name is Bill Ardolino, and he is a very thoughtful guy. I conducted my own interview with him online—how else?—and began by asking about what equipment he was using as a one-man network/newspaper.

"I used a minuscule MP3 player/digital recorder (three and a half inches by two inches) to get the recording, and a separate small digital camera phone to snap his picture," said Ardolino. "Not quite as sexy as an all-in-one phone/camera/recorder (which does exist), but a statement on the ubiquity and miniaturization of technology nonetheless. I carry this equipment around D.C. at all times because, hey, you never know. What's perhaps more startling is how well Mr. Schieffer thought on his feet, after being jumped on by some stranger with interview questions. He blew me away."

Ardolino said the MP3 player cost him about $125. It is ₃₅ "primarily designed to play music," he explained, but it also "comes prepackaged as a digital recorder that creates a WAV sound file that can be uploaded back to a computer. . . . Basically, I'd say that the barrier to entry to do journalism that requires portable, ad hoc recording equipment, is [now] about $100–$200 to $300 if you add a camera, $400 to $500 for a pretty nice recorder and a pretty nice camera. [But] $200 is all that you need to get the job done."

What prompted him to become his own news network?

"Being an independent journalist is a hobby that sprang from my frustration about biased, incomplete, selective, and/or incompetent information gathering by the mainstream media," explained Ardolino, who describes himself as a "center-right libertarian." "Independent journalism and its relative, blogging, are expressions of market forces—a need is not being met by current information sources. I started taking pictures and doing interviews of the antiwar rallies in D.C., because the media was grossly misrepresenting the nature of the groups that were organizing the gatherings—unrepentant Marxists, explicit and implicit supporters of terror, etc. I originally chose to use humor as a device, but I've since branched out. Do I have more power, power to get my message out, yes. The Schieffer interview actually brought in about twenty-five thousand visits in twenty-four hours. My peak day since I've started was fifty-five thousand when I helped break 'Rathergate.' . . . I interviewed the first forensics expert in the Dan Rather National Guard story, and he was then specifically picked up by the *Washington Post*, *Chicago Sun-Times*, *Globe*, *NYT*, etc. within forty-eight hours.

"The pace of information gathering and correction in the CBS fake memo story was astounding," he continued. "It wasn't just that CBS News 'stonewalled' after the fact, it was arguably that they couldn't keep up with an army of dedicated fact-checkers. The speed and openness of the medium is something that runs rings around the old process. . . . I'm a twenty-nine-year-old marketing manager [who] always wanted to write for a living but hated the AP style book. As überblogger Glenn Reynolds likes to say, blogs have given the people a chance to stop yelling at their TV and have a say in the process. I think that they serve as sort of a 'fifth estate' that works in conjunction with the mainstream media (often by keeping an eye on them or feeding them raw info) and potentially function as a journalism and commmentary farm system that provides a new means to establish success.

"Like many facets of the topic that you're talking about in your book, there are good and bad aspects of the development. The splintering of media makes for a lot of incoherence or selective-cognition (look at our country's population), but it also decentralizes power and provides a better guarantee that the *complete* trust *is* there . . . somewhere . . . in pieces."

On any given day one can come across any number of sto- 40 ries, like the encounter between Bob Schieffer and Bill Ardolino, that tell you that old hierarchies are being flattened and the playing field is being leveled. As Micah L. Sifry nicely put it in the *Nation* magazine (November 22, 2004): "The era of top-down politics—where campaigns, institutions, and journalism were cloistered communities powered by hard-to-amass capital—is over. Something wilder, more engaging, and infinitely more satisfying to individual participants is arising alongside the old order."

I offer the Schieffer-Ardolino encounter as just one example of how the flattening of the world has happened faster and changed rules, roles, and relationships more quickly than we could have imagined. And, though I know it is a cliché, I have to say it nevertheless: *You ain't seen nothin' yet.* We are entering a phase where we are going to see the digitization, virtualization, and automation of almost everything. The gains in productivity will be staggering for those countries, companies, and individuals who can absorb the new technological tools. And we are entering a phase where more people than ever before in the history of the world are going to have access to these tools—as innovators, as collaborators, and, alas, even as terrorists. You say you want a revolution? Well, the real information revolution is about to begin. I call this new phase Globalization 3.0 because it followed Globalization 2.0, but I think this new era of globalization will prove to be such a difference of degree that it will be seen, in time, as a difference in kind. That is why I introduced the idea that the world has gone from round to flat. Everywhere you turn, hierarchies are being challenged from below or transforming themselves from top-down structures into more horizontal and collaborative ones.

"Globalization is the word we came up with to describe the changing relationships between governments and big businesses," said David Rothkopf, a former senior Department of Commerce official in the Clinton administration and now a private strategic consultant. "But what is going on today is a much broader, much more profound phenomenon." It is not simply about how governments, business, and people communicate, not just about how organizations interact, but is about the emergence of completely new social, political, and business models. "It is about things that impact some of the deepest, most ingrained aspects of society right down to the nature of the social contract," added Rothkopf. "What happens if the political entity in which you are located no longer corresponds to a job that takes place in cyberspace, or no longer really encompasses workers collaborating with other workers in different corners of the globe, or no longer really captures products produced in multiple places simultaneously? Who regulates the work? Who taxes it? Who should benefit from those taxes?"

If I am right about the flattening of the world, it will be remembered as one of those fundamental changes—like the rise of the nation-state or the Industrial Revolution—each of which, in its day, noted Rothkopf, produced changes in the role of individuals, the role and form of governments, the way we innovated, the way we conducted business, the role of women, the way we fought wars, the way we educated ourselves, the way religion responded, the way art was expressed, the way science and research were conducted, not to mention the political labels we assigned to ourselves and to our opponents. "There are certain pivot points or watersheds in history that are greater than others because the changes they produced were so sweeping, multifaceted, and hard to predict at the time," Rothkopf said.

If the prospect of this flattening—and all of the pressures, dislocations, and opportunities accompanying it—causes you unease about the future, you are neither alone nor wrong. Whenever civilization has gone through one of these disruptive, dislocating technological revolutions—like Gutenberg's introduction of the printing press—the whole world has changed in profound ways. But there is something about the flattening of the world that is going to be qualitatively different from other such profound changes: the speed and breadth with which it is taking hold. The introduction of printing happened over a period of decades and for a long time affected only a relatively small part of the planet. Same with the Industrial Revolution. This flattening process is happening at warp speed and directly or indirectly touching a lot more people on the planet at once. The faster and broader this transition to a new era, the more likely is the potential for disruption, as opposed to an orderly transfer of power from the old winners to the new winners.

To put it another way, the experiences of the high-tech companies in the last few decades who failed to navigate the rapid changes brought about in their marketplace by these types of forces may be a warning to all the businesses, institutions, and nation-states that are now facing these inevitable, even predictable, changes but lack the leadership, flexibility, and imagination to adapt—not because they are not smart or aware, but because the speed of change is simply overwhelming them.

45

So what? See Chapter 7 for tips on telling readers why it matters.

And that is why the great challenge for our time will be to absorb these changes in ways that do not overwhelm people but also do not leave them behind. None of this will be easy. But this is our task. It is inevitable and unavoidable.

Joining the Conversation

1. Thomas L. Friedman contrasts his surprising assertion that the world is flat with Christopher Columbus's famous discovery more than 500 years ago that the world was round. What does Friedman mean by his assertion, and how do the examples he provides support his view? Why do you think he places his own journey of discovery in the context of Columbus's?

2. Friedman is extremely impressed with the high level of business development in areas previously thought of as poor and underdeveloped, such as Bangalore, India, and with how such development has created a "level playing field" on which America must now compete with many other countries. This prospect, he says in paragraph 15, filled him "with both excitement and dread." What accounts for these conflicting emotions? How do you, a college student in the United States, respond to the situation that Friedman describes?

3. What does Friedman mean by "a whole new era: Globalization 3.0" (paragraph 20)? What does he see as the implications of this new age for Americans?

4. Throughout this piece, Friedman quotes from many conversations—with business leaders, with his wife, with journalists, and with politicians. The tone of these conversations is often informal and chatty. What do these quotations add to his text that other ways of relating the information might not? Imagine that he'd chosen to summarize these conversations rather than quote directly; how would that strategy have affected his argument?

5. Find and read three reviews of *The World Is Flat: A Brief History of the Twenty-first Century*, from which this selection came. Then, write your own review assessing Friedman's argument. In doing so, you may draw upon material from the other reviews as well as from other readings in this chapter.

The Meaning of 9/11

MORRIS BERMAN

THE AMERICAN INVASION OF IRAQ in the spring of 2003 was about a lot of things, but it certainly wasn't about Iraq. Nor was it intended to be, although the Bush Jr. administration obviously could not say so publicly. As *Rebuilding America's Defenses*, the PNAC* report, clearly states, Saddam Hussein was nothing more than an "immediate justification" for a larger goal, that of having "a substantial American presence in the Gulf." Indeed, on the eve of the 2003 attack, George Bush and Tony Blair, from their odd, symbolic isolation on the Azores, declared that Britain and the United States would invade Iraq even if Hussein left the country(!). But as the report makes clear, American hegemony is hardly to be limited to the Middle East; the neoconservative agenda is about control of the entire world (as well as outer space), and about imposing the

MORRIS BERMAN has taught at the Catholic University and the Tecnológico de Monterrey in Mexico City. His work, which combines cultural history and social criticism, includes *The Twilight of American Culture* (2000) and *Dark Ages America: The Final Phase of Empire* (2006), from which "The Meaning of 9/11" is taken.

*PNAC   The Project for a New American Century, a neoconservative think tank based in Washington, D.C.

American political and economic model on that world. Bush Sr. may not have been particularly astute, but at least he was living in a finite universe. With Bush Jr. we enter a kind of surreal terrain; the Void is now so vast as to be incomprehensible. The framework has become eschatological, building on a post-9/11 vocabulary: "crusade," "infinite justice," and so on. The enemy—"evil"—can never be See pp. 41–45 for tips on framing quotations. defeated by definition; there are no possible criteria for what a victory would consist of. As the renowned Slovenian philosopher Slavoj Žižek put it, "What if the true purpose of the war is to pass to a global emergency state?" In effect, the goal becomes war itself, war without end. . . . But none of this is about Iraq per se; Iraq was merely the target of a convenient, if paranoid, psychological projection. As the British journalist George Monbiot predicted even before the "National Security Strategy" was issued by the White House in September 2002, "If the U.S. were not preparing to attack Iraq, it would be preparing to attack another nation. The U.S. will go to war because it needs a country with which to go to war."[1]

The Lies

The sordid tale of how the neocons and the Bush administration tricked the country into war has been told, *mutatis mutandis*,* many times by a variety of journalists and scholars across the political spectrum, from Hans Blix to Patrick Buchanan, as well as by government insiders whose versions of events echo and corroborate each other's. Particularly comprehensive are the study by Stefan Halper and Jonathan Clarke, *America*

---

*__mutatis mutandis__ Latin for "with the necessary changes having been made."

Alone, and a lengthy article in the May 2004 issue of *Vanity Fair*, "The Path to War." Briefly, the story goes something like this: given the fact that Iraq had been in the neocon crosshairs since 1992, and that the PNAC report blatantly stated that invading the country would require another Pearl Harbor, the inner circle around Bush wasted no time making their move in the wake of 9/11. While the rest of us were in shock and mourning, they began a deliberate, cynical manipulation of the political situation. To implement their plans, they would conflate Iraq with 9/11 and terrorism. Thus by 2:40 P.M. on September 11, Donald Rumsfeld raised the possibility of going after Iraq, and less than a day later told the inner circle that this was preferable to going after Afghanistan inasmuch as the former had "better targets." Also on 9/11, Rumsfeld said to his aides: "Go massive. Sweep it all up. Things related and not." Conflation was definitely the name of the game. Richard Clarke, then head of counterterrorism, and other officials were soon being presumed to find Iraq–Al Qaeda links. As *New York Times* columnist Paul Krugman writes, "The Iraq hawks set out to corrupt the process of intelligence assessment." The fix was in; this was a war they were simply going to have, come hell or high water. "Truth" was not part of the equation.[2]

So on 17 September 2001, the president signed a top secret document for going to war against Afghanistan that also directed the Pentagon to begin planning military operations for a war on Iraq. This plan was known only to the inner circle, and not told to the opponents of military action—such as the State Department, which didn't know about it until it was a fait accompli. No paper trail was kept, no record of meetings. Condoleezza Rice told Bush that he needed to go after all rogue nations' weapons of mass destruction. One official later said the entire program was theological: "It's almost a religion—that it will be the end of society if we don't take action now." Bush subsequently signed a secret intelligence order directing the CIA to undertake a covert program to topple Hussein, which included assassination. In short, the decision to invade Iraq was made almost immediately after 9/11, but kept under wraps for several months.[3]

The next step, then, was to make up a story and sell it to the American people; the State of the Union address of January 2002 would be the opening wedge of this campaign. Bush's speechwriter, David Frum, recounts in his memoir that in December 2001 he was told to come up with a justification for war against Iraq that would go into that address. Thus was born the "axis of evil," a phrase chosen for its theological resonance, according to the neocons, with Bush darkly hinting at the new direction: "I will not wait on events, while dangers gather." In April, Bush told a British reporter, "I made up my mind that Saddam needs to go." After that, administration discussion was all about tactics, and General Tommy Franks, head of the U.S. Central Command, began visiting the White House to brief the president on plans for the war. Next came the West Point speech of 1 June 2002, announcing the new policy of preemptive war; the next month, when Richard Haass, the director of policy planning for the State Department, intended to go to the White House to raise some objections, Rice told him that the decision had been made and he shouldn't waste his breath arguing about it.[4]

The problem, however, was that not enough people wanted 5 war. A Gallup poll of mid-August 2002 showed support for the war at 53 percent, down 8 percentage points from two months before. To make things worse, elite opinion—including that of figures from earlier administrations, such as Brent Scowcroft (Bush Sr.'s national security adviser, who argued that an invasion of Iraq would dilute the war on terrorism and lessen the cooperation of nations needed to fight it), Henry Kissinger, former secretary of state Lawrence Eagleburger, and conservative Republicans in Congress—was heavily against it. All of these men felt that the Bush Jr. administration hadn't made the case for Iraq being an imminent threat. "There is scant evidence," wrote Scowcroft in an op-ed piece in the *Wall Street Journal*, "to tie Saddam to terrorist organizations, and even less to the September 11 attacks."[5]

What to do? One tactic was to keep repeating a lie—namely, that Iraq and Al Qaeda were linked. Thus on 25 September 2002 both Rice and the president publicly insisted on the Iraq–Al Qaeda link; the day after that Rumsfeld declared he had "bulletproof" evidence of ties between Hussein and Al Qaeda; and in a speech given in Cincinnati on October 7, Bush claimed that Iraq was an immediate threat and might strike U.S. territory with the help of terrorist groups using WMD* on any given day. Unfortunately, also on October 7, CIA director George Tenet wrote a letter to Congress that did not support these assertions. CIA analysis in general concluded that Iraq had little reason to provoke the United States; it was simply not its modus operandi. This was also the consensus of the U.S. intelligence community as given in the National Intelligence Estimate on Iraq, which circulated within the administration in October. But the Bush administration had an important lever: after September 11, Tenet was under attack because of the CIA's failure to prevent the events of that day. Indeed, a number of congressional leaders wanted the director to resign. Hence, tactic number two: Bush kept Tenet on, but the president and the inner circle pressured him to endorse key

*WMD Weapons of mass destruction.

elements of the case for war even when this required ignoring CIA findings. And so Tenet caved; he began to make concessions, ambiguous statements about the possibility of Iraq–Al Qaeda contacts, along with his later infamous "slam dunk" remark about Iraq's possessing WMD. When Richard Clarke, along with CIA and FBI experts, wrote a report showing that no such contacts existed, Condoleezza Rice's office sent it back, saying: "Wrong answer. . . . Do it again."[6]

Which brings us to the third tactic, for which the Bush Jr. administration borrowed a leaf from the Bush Sr. administration's book: manufacture a nuclear threat. That was the trump card for war in 1991 (along with phony or distorted atrocity stories), and it worked just as well the second time around. The major "campaign" for this was scheduled for September 2002 as well, to coincide with tactic number one, but Cheney made two speeches in August to prepare the terrain. In a question-and-answer session at the Commonwealth Club in San Francisco on August 7, he told his audience that it was "the judgment of many of us that in the not-too-distant future, [Saddam Hussein] will acquire nuclear weapons"; in a talk to the national convention of the Veterans of Foreign Wars in Nashville on August 26, he declared, "We know that Saddam has resumed his efforts to acquire nuclear weapons." Cheney cited Lieutenant General Hussein Kamel, a son-in-law of Hussein who defected in 1995, as one of his sources for this "knowledge," which illustrates an interesting pattern in the type of disinformation the administration was putting out. Kamel had been head of the Iraqi weapons program—nuclear as well as chemical and biological—for ten years, and he became famous for exposing Iraq's deceptions regarding WMD. But what he also told the U.N. inspectors, and the International Atomic Energy Agency (IAEA), and which was additionally told to the

CIA, was that he personally ordered the destruction of Iraq's WMD, nuclear weapons included, after the Gulf War. Cheney was referring to Kamel's testimony about the earlier deceptions, and conveniently neglected to mention that Kamel had destroyed Iraq's nuclear capability in 1991. It was also the case that Kamel had returned to Iraq and was killed in February 1996, so he could hardly have been a source for what U.S. officials knew in 2002. In any event, *Newsweek* broke the story regarding Kamel's destruction of Iraqi nukes on 24 February 2003; during the four months prior to that, the Kamel story was cited four times by writers on the *New York Times* op-ed page as evidence for Iraq *having* nuclear weapons, and therefore as a reason to go to war. Bush also referred to it in his Cincinnati speech of 7 October 2002; and Colin Powell selectively used the Kamel information in his presentation to the U.N. Security Council on 5 February 2003, again as an argument for Iraqi nuclear capability. Prior to the attack on Iraq, however, and for the most part after it as well, no major newspapers or TV shows picked up on the *Newsweek* story, and the whole thing fell off the proverbial radar screen.[7] . . .

What was pretty clear in the aftermath of all this was that the decision to go to war drove the intelligence, not the reverse. The Bush administration, writes one columnist, disseminated information "that ranged from selective to preposterous"; but the crucial internal message was, If you value your job, you'd better get with the program (members of the Defense Intelligence Agency, or DIA, report being told this explicitly). Quite a few intelligence experts at the CIA and other agencies (most speaking on condition of anonymity) later told reporters that they had been pressed to distort evidence or tailor it to conform to the administration's views—in particular, to state that Iraq had WMD and terrorist links.

As Richard Clarke discovered, if they wrote reports skeptical of these views, they were encouraged to "rethink" it and to "go back and find the right answer." Professionals in the Pentagon and elsewhere who had dissenting views—including a number of senior officers assigned to the Joint Chiefs of Staff—were excluded or marginalized. One former official with the National Security Council told reporters at *The New Republic* that the government's approach "was a classic case of . . . rumor-intelligence plugged into various speeches and accepted as gospel." Most administration officials, according to these reporters, "probably knew they were constructing castles out of sand."[8]

As for the war itself, from the viewpoint of the attackers it was a cakewalk (at least until it was officially over). The battle plan was called "shock and awe," the idea being that America would strike with such speed and overwhelming force (aerial and cruise missile bombardment) that the Iraqi citizenry would be psychologically demoralized, thereby willing to give up without a fight. Indeed, on the eve of battle, American newspapers were reporting that the United States has assembled a force with more firepower than ever seen before in a single battle." There was something surreal, or "mental," about all of this: why would we need to assemble such a force to go at it in this way, especially since the American government really didn't believe the war was about WMD or the evil nature of Saddam Hussein or any genuine threat to the United States? I recall, around this time, listening to an interview on the Diane Rehm show on National Public Radio with one of the military strategists close to the battle plan. The violence involved, as he described it, reminded me of Picasso's *Guernica*,* or the firebombing of

---

*Picasso's *Guernica*   A famous painting of the bombing of a town in Spain during the Spanish Civil War.

Dresden.* As the man told Diane and the listening audience
how the plan worked, his voice became increasingly excited.
Innocent human beings, apparently, were not part of the equation . . . or maybe that *was* the point. This kind of sadism always
has an odd sexual feel to it; I couldn't help thinking how the
politics of empire had finally rotted the American soul. When
a civilization finally hollows itself out, there is nothing much
left for it to do except turn into a case study from a textbook
by Wilhelm Reich,† in which you get off on the cruelty you
can visit on the powerless. Disturbingly, this is a lot of the psychology that hovered over the torture or slaughter in Vietnam,
during the Gulf war, or at Abu Ghraib.‡ And when a powerful nation can pick fights only with the small and the weak, it
is because appearances to the contrary, it is weak itself.[9]

The war began on 19 March 2003 (Washington time) and [10]
"ended" about April 8. According to initial Iraqi estimates,
civilian deaths numbered between 6,100 and 7,800. In fact, the
damage we wreaked on that miserable country proved to be
much worse. A study released by a research team at Johns Hopkins a year and a half later put the civilian death toll at 100,000,
adding that more than half of the deaths caused by the occupation forces were women and children. Subsequent surveys by
the United Nations indicated that 400,000 young children in
Iraq were "wasting"—that is, suffering from acute malnutrition.
As Dr. Richard Horton, the editor of the British medical jour-

*__Dresden__ A German industrial city heavily bombed by the Allies
during World War II.

†__Wilhelm Reich__ A psychoanalyst born in Austria who emigrated to
America in the 1930s and studied character development.

‡__Abu Ghraib__ An American prison camp in Iraq in which Iraqi prisoners were treated extremely harshly.

nal *The Lancet* (which published the Johns Hopkins study), acerbically put it, "Democratic imperialism has led to more deaths, not fewer."[10]

The U.S. government, of course, repeatedly emphasized the "liberatory" aspect of the invasion: after all, Saddam Hussein was widely feared and hated, and there were a great many Iraqis who were quite happy to see him go. Thus much was made of the toppling of the statue of the Iraqi leader in Baghdad on April 9, in front of huge, cheering crowds, an event that seemed to say "It was worth it, after all." Like a great deal associated with this war, this was far more image than substance: it was an American soldier, not an Iraqi citizen, who pulled the statue down, and there *was* no crowd in the town square. U.S. newspapers did not reproduce the full image, but the picture available on the Internet showed three American tanks and a few dozen Iraqis gathered nearby, in a small section of the square. Close-up photos suggest that the active participants were members of the INC,* who rode in on the back of the tanks. As in the case of Bush's postwar arrival on the aircraft carrier USS *Abraham Lincoln,* this was largely PR, a misleading form of symbolism—although it played extremely well back home.[11]

Talk about bringing "democracy" to Iraq was also PR; it also played well to a gullible American public, but the U.S. government's actions render the claims dubious. Thus when the Baghdad Shiite weekly *Al Hawza* began running anti-American articles, Paul Bremer, the temporary military governor of Iraq ("proconsul"), had American soldiers chain and padlock the doors of the newspaper's offices. Bremer also empowered an appointed electoral commission to "eliminate political parties or candidates" it disapproved of. Ayad Allawi,

---

*INC Iraqi National Congress.

President Bush declares "mission accomplished" aboard the USS *Abraham Lincoln* on 1 May 2003.

the interim prime minister chosen to act as our puppet after Ahmad Chalabi suddenly fell from grace, moved (in August 2004) to shut down the Baghdad offices of Al Jazeera* when it refused to adjust its editorial policies to his liking. In addition, he armed himself with the power to declare martial law and reinstated the death penalty. Worst of all, this was a leader

*Al Jazeera   An Arabic TV news network, based in Qatar.

who had no popular mandate. Labeling the whole thing a charade, Scott Ritter makes the obvious point: "Allawi's government," he writes, "hand-picked by the United States from the
ranks of anti-Saddam expatriates, lacks not only a constituency
inside Iraq but also legitimacy in the eyes of many ordinary
Iraqi citizens."[12] This is, at best, a Potemkin democracy.*

One very significant event that took place during the invasion, but which failed to capture much attention in the United
States, was the looting of the archaeological museums in Baghdad. This struck me as being highly symbolic, but having a powerful level of reality to it as well. Indeed, the Nigerian novelist
Ben Okri, writing in *The Guardian*† on 19 April 2003, felt that
those of us in the West were now "at the epicenter of a shift
in the history of the world." American forces moved in to protect the oil fields; the matter of ancient Mesopotamia, of Iraq's
museums and libraries, was of no consequence to them. In fact,
Marines defaced some of the ancient walls at the site of the
Sumerian city of Ur (near modern-day An Nasiriyah), the
famous Ur of the Chaldees excavated by Leonard Woolley in
the 1920s and 1930s, and the legendary birthplace of Abraham.
For the most part, in the days after the fall of the Iraqi government, the U.S. military just stood by while looters picked
these institutions clean. In fact, the Pentagon was repeatedly
warned of this possibility in advance of the war, writes *New
York Times* columnist Frank Rich, but at the highest levels of
the White House, the Pentagon, and Central Command, no
one cared. From presidential press secretary Ari Fleischer to

*Potemkin democracy   A fake democracy. Refers to the fake villages
that may have been built during the Crimean War by Grigori
Potemkin, a Russian minister of state, to fool Catherine the Great in
her tour of the area in 1787.

†*The Guardian*   A British newspaper.

Donald Rumsfeld, they simply trivialized the whole thing. ("Stuff happens!" cried Rumsfeld, and made a joke out of it.) "By protecting Iraq's oil but not its cultural mother lode," writes Rich, "America echoes the values of no one more than Saddam. . . ." Thus U.S. armed forces allowed tablets containing bits of the Gilgamesh epic* to be stolen, but somehow managed to secure the lavish homes of Hussein's elite, "where the cultural gems ranged from videos of old James Bond movies to the collected novels of Danielle Steele." All of this, writes Okri, represents "a signal absence of the true values of civilization."[13]

And this is really the point. After all, if your "values" are those of corporate consumerism, you don't really *have* a civilization. So why worry if manuscripts, books, and cuneiform tablets from Sumer and Babylon are stolen or burned? How many Americans, do you think, can define "cuneiform"† or identify Mesopotamia? Someone like George W. Bush would probably be only too happy to bulldoze these museums and libraries and replace them with shopping malls—the "real freedom" referred to in the 2002 "National Security Strategy." Thus Okri writes, "The end of the world begins not with the barbarians at the gate, but with the barbarians at the highest levels of state."[14] True, but it takes barbarians in the streets cheering the barbarians at the highest levels of state to make a new Dark Age a reality. The American government didn't care about the destruction of our Western heritage because, like the American people, it no longer identifies with it, and couldn't care less about it. Future historians may record this

*Gilgamesh epic   An early work of literature, written on clay tablets as early as 1700 B.C.E. in Mesopotamia, the area between the Tigris and Euphrates Rivers, including much of modern Iraq.

†cuneiform   An early form of writing done on clay tablets.

shift as the real, symbolic significance of the 2003 Iraqi war, although obviously it has been building for decades.

Notes

1. Rebecca Mead, "The Marx Brother," *New Yorker* 5 May 2003: 47; and George Monbiot, "The Logic of Empire," *Guardian Weekly* 15–21 Aug. 2002: 13. The statement by Bush and Blair from the Azores was reported by Michael Gordon in the *New York Times* 18 Mar. 2003. For two particularly insightful discussions of these issues, see Jay Bookman, "The President's Real Goal in Iraq," *Atlanta Journal-Constitution* 29 Sept. 2002, and Anatol Lieven, "The Push for War," *London Review of Books* 24.19 (3 Oct. 2002).

2. David Stout, "White House Launches Counterattack on Critic," *International Herald Tribune* 23 Mar. 2004: 1, 4; Hendrik Hertzberg, "In the Soup," *New Yorker* 10 May 2004: 98–102; and Paul Krugman, "A Pattern of Corruption in U.S. Intelligence," *International Herald Tribune* 16 July 2003: 8. A report posted on CBS.com during September 2002 revealed Rumsfeld's intent to "sweep" everything together.

The comprehensive sources on the run-up to war are Stefan Halper and Jonathan Clarke, *America Alone* (Cambridge: Cambridge UP, 2004), and Bryan Burrough et al., "The Path to War," *Vanity Fair* May 2004: 228–44, 281–94. Other valuable exposés of the 2003 war are James Bamford, *A Pretext for War* (New York: Doubleday, 2004); Joseph Wilson, *The Politics of Truth* (New York: Carroll, 2004); Richard Clarke, *Against All Enemies* (New York: Free, 2004); Bob Woodward, *Plan of Attack* (New York: Simon, 2004); Ron Suskind, *The Price of Loyalty* (New York: Simon, 2004); Patrick Buchanan, *Where the Right Went Wrong* (New York: St. Martin's, 2004); Hans Blix, *Disarming Iraq* (New York: Pantheon, 2004); John Prados, *Hoodwinked* (New York: New, 2004); and James Mann, *Rise of the Vulkans* (New York: Viking, 2004). These monographs were valuable sources for much of what follows.

3. Glenn Kessler, "U.S. Decision on Iraq Has Puzzling Past," *Washington Post* 12 Jan. 2003: A1.

4. Kessler; John B. Judis and Spencer Ackerman, "The Selling of the Iraq War," *New Republic* 30 June 2003 (I used the online version, which incorporated corrections to the print version: ⟨www.tnr.com⟩ posted 19 June 2003);

and Nicholas Lemann, "How It Came to War," *New Yorker* 31 Mar. 2003: 34–40.

5. Judis and Ackerman, "Selling of the Iraq War"; Dilip Hiro, *Iraq: In the Eye of the Storm* (New York: Nation, 2002): 98; and Todd S. Purdum and Patrick E. Tyler, "Republicans Break Ranks over Bush's Iraq Policy," *International Herald Tribune* 17–18 Aug. 2002: 1, 5. The Scowcroft op-ed piece appeared in the *Wall Street Journal* 15 Aug. 2002.

6. Hiro, *Iraq,* 213; Judis and Ackerman, "Selling of the Iraq War"; Michael R. Gordon, "CIA Letter Shows Split over Iraq," *International Herald Tribune* 11 Oct. 2002: 1, 8; Paul Krugman, "The War on Truth Is Not over Yet," *International Herald Tribune* 11 June 2003: 8; Suzanne Goldenberg, "CIA Had Doubts on Iraq Link to al-Qaeda," *Guardian Weekly* 12–18 June 2003: 1; Bill Keller, "Corrupted Intelligence Weakens America," *International Herald Tribune* 14–15 June 2003: 10; Walter Pincus, "Report Cast Doubt on Iraq–Al Qaeda Connection," *Washington Post* 22 June 2003: A1, 19; Seymour M. Hersh, "Selective Intelligence," *New Yorker* 12 May 2003: 44–51; and Burrough et al., "Path to War" 238.

7. Barton Gellman and Walter Pincus, "Depiction of Threat Outgrew Supporting Evidence," *Washington Post* 10 Aug. 2003: A9. The story about *Newsweek* was posted by Fairness and Accuracy in Reporting on 27 Feb. 2003 as "Star Witness on Iraq Said Weapons Were Destroyed," at ⟨www.fair.org/press-releases/kamel.html⟩; see also John Barry, "Exclusive: The Defector's Secrets," *Newsweek* 3 Mar. 2003: 6 (for transcript of Kamel interview, see ⟨http://middleeastreference.org.uk/kamel.html⟩). The Gellman and Pincus article does say that Kamel's testimony was "the reverse of Cheney's description."

8. Keller, "Corrupted Intelligence Weakens America" 10; James Risen and Douglas Jehl, "Expert Said to Tell Legislators He Was Pressed to Distort Some Evidence," *New York Times* 25 June 2003: 11; Burrough et al., "Path to War" 242; Kristof, "Missing in Action"; Philip Gourevitch, "Might and Right," *New Yorker* 16–23 June 2003: 69–70; Judis and Ackerman, "Selling of the Iraq War"; and Halper and Clarke, *America Alone* 224. A 2003 report by the Carnegie Endowment for International Peace also notes the intense pressure put on intelligence experts to conform to administration views (see "How Was the U.S. So Misled?," *International Herald Tribune* 12 Jan. 2004: 8). On the de facto inevitability of the war, and the diplomatic debacle involved, see James P. Rubin, "Stumbling into War," *Foreign Affairs* 82.5 (Sept.–Oct. 2003): 46–66.

9. Newspaper quote is from Joseph Fitchett, "Speed Is Core Element of U.S. Battle Strategy," *International Herald Tribune* 21 Mar. 2003: 1. The stan-

dard text reference on "shock and awe" is Harlan K. Ullman et al., *Shock and Awe* (Washington, D.C.: NDU, 1996) (Ullman was Colin Powell's teacher at the National War College). To see what shock and awe looks like on the human level, the reader might wish to look at the Web site ⟨www.marchforjustice.com/shock&awe.php⟩.

10. Karl Vick, "Children Pay Cost of Iraq's Chaos," *Washington Post* 21 Nov. 2004: A1, 31. On the Johns Hopkins study, see Elisabeth Rosenthal, "Iraqi Toll Is Put at 100,000," *International Herald Tribune* 29 Oct. 2004: 1, 8; and Les Roberts et al., "Mortality Before and After the 2003 Invasion of Iraq: Cluster Sample Survey," *The Lancet* 364.9445 (30 Oct. 2004), posted at ⟨www.thelancet.com⟩ on 29 Oct. 2004. Civilian casualty and mortality figures are also available at ⟨www.iraqbodycount.net⟩.

11. The statue is discussed by Alexander Cockburn in "The Decline and Fall of American Journalism," *Nation* 12 May 2003: 9. The Internet photo I refer to was posted at ⟨www.counterpunch.org/statue.html⟩.

12. "The Wrong Message in Iraq," *International Herald Tribune* 31 Mar. 2004: 8; "Mission Accomplished II?," The *Nation* 19–26 July 2004: 3; "Banning Bad News in Iraq," *International Herald Tribune* 11 Aug. 2004: 6; "Allawi Shows the Face of Iraqi Democracy," *International Herald Tribune* 25–26 Sept. 2004: 6; and Scott Ritter, "Saddam's People Are Winning the War," *International Herald Tribune* 23 July 2004: 7.

13. Ben Okri, "The New Dark Age," The *Guardian*, 19 Apr. 2003; Edmund L. Andrews, "Looters Sack Ancient Sites in Iraq," *International Herald Tribune* 24–25 May 2003: 1, 4; and Frank Rich, "A Damning Jigsaw Puzzle in Baghdad," *International Herald Tribune* 26–27 Apr. 2003: 20. See also Ernest Beck, "What Was Taken and When," *ARTnews* June 2003: 44–48, for a longer discussion of lost treasures. On Marines defacing sites at Ur, see Chalmers Johnson, *The Sorrows of Empire* (New York: Metropolitan/Henry Holt, 2004) 234.

14. Okri, "New Dark Age."

Joining the Conversation

1. What, in Morris Berman's view, is the true meaning of 9/11? What, in his opinion, does the U.S. response to 9/11 say about the American government and people?

2. At times Berman uses strong language to express his opinions; for example, he calls the section about how the Bush administration convinced the United States to enter the Iraq war "The Lies." Find other examples of such charged language. What does such language contribute to the development of Berman's argument that more measured or neutral language might not?

3. In presenting such a negative picture of the Bush administration, does Berman offer any naysayers to his own views? If not, suggest some and decide where in the text they might go.

4. How likely is this piece to convince someone who has a more positive view of the Bush policies and actions? What advice would you give to Berman about how he could better persuade such a reader to take his position seriously?

5. Respond to Berman's argument. Start by summarizing his views, and then agree with them, disagree, or both agree and disagree. Remember: if you agree, you still need to add something new to the conversation; if you disagree or have mixed feelings, you need to explain why.

Kidnapped in Pakistan:
The End of American Ideals?

HADY AMR

—▣—

**Doha, Qatar—You have not read this
in the news before.**

THREE MONTHS AGO, an American citizen was kidnapped
in Northwest Pakistan. He was murdered. His body was just
recently recovered by his bereaved family. I learned about the
kidnapping shortly after it happened, when my dear friend
Ayesha wrote to tell me that her brother, Imran, had been
abducted in Northwest Pakistan, still bravely expecting him to
be recovered.

Ayesha and I had first met in 1999 as co-workers at our office
in Washington, D.C., on 17th and K Street after she had grad-

HADY AMR directs the Brookings Doha Center in Qatar and has worked
at the World Bank, UNICEF, and the U.S. Department of Defense. At
the Brookings Institute, a nonpartisan public policy organization, his
work focuses on political issues of the Arab world, including a 2004
report, "The Need to Communicate: How to Improve U.S. Public Diplo-
macy with the Islamic World." "Kidnapped in Pakistan" first appeared
in 2008, on *Aljazeera.com*, the site of Aljazeera Publishing, an independent media organization based in London.

uated from Georgetown University. We worked together on projects funded by the United States Agency for International Development, the part of our government that gives out overseas development assistance. Since 9/11, the United States has spent more than $10 billion on aid to Pakistan—two-thirds military, one-third economic development—with mediocre results.

Ayesha and I became close friends. Friends because back then there were so few American Muslims working in the policy community in Washington. Friends because we both retained an interest in improving the lives of, and the U.S. relationship with, the people from the vast region of the Middle East and South Asia that our families had emigrated from— hers from Pakistan, mine from Lebanon.

I moved on to work on Al Gore's 2000 presidential campaign. Ayesha went on to Harvard to build more fruitful pastures to earn a master's degree in education and ultimately returned to Pakistan to pursue her dream of working to improve the state of education for the children of Pakistan. One of the pluses, she told me when she decided to move to Pakistan, was to be closer to her brother Imran and her two nephews.

The presence of Ayesha—a highly successful Muslim Amer- 5 ican with a graduate degree in education from Harvard—working on improving Pakistan's education system in one of Pakistan's more conservative areas, could only bolster the image of America as a fair playing field on which American Muslims can succeed.

But her individual contribution to U.S.-Pakistan relations clearly wasn't enough.

While Ayesha and I were corresponding about the kidnapping of her brother, I suggested engaging the U.S. Government and offered, through the relationships I had developed over my years working with Washington's officialdom, to try to help engage the United States at a high level. Despite my persistence, Ayesha, after careful reflection, thought it better to not involve our government.

Why? Because she felt that the chances of negotiating her brother's release with criminals, terrorists—or both—were higher if the U.S. government, loathed on the local scene, was kept out of the picture and if local channels handled the matter.

While the true motives of the kidnapping and his eventual murder remain unclear, what is clear to me is this: Ayesha and her family felt that when push came to shove, the local Pakistani officials had better stature from which to approach the kidnappers than our own government.

What little solace Ayesha and Imran's family can feel at this 10 moment can only, I believe, be found in the fact that evidence now shows that Imran was murdered probably the day after his abduction. They do not have to second-guess themselves about their response.

But I can feel no solace whatsoever. My government has conducted itself in such a manner that in places where we were once admired for our ideals, we are so loathed for our hypocrisy that our own citizens, when their lives are on the line, feel it safer to engage the help of local officials instead of the mighty U.S. government.

Whose fault is this? I can only blame myself, my fellow citizens, and our elected representatives in Washington for conducting ourselves in such a way—voting to go to war in Iraq on flimsy evidence, not reacting more harshly to the Abu Ghraib prison abuses, allowing the perpetual detention of prisoners held mostly without charge in Guantánamo Bay for half a decade now. Our actions are indefensible, our reputation is severely damaged, and our ability to defend our citizens is non-existent.

Who's he arguing with? See Chapter 11 for help figuring it out.

When I was born in April 1967, America was admired across the Muslim world as the shining light on the hill, breathing hope for a positive future. Today, we are loathed and distrusted by huge majorities from the eastern shores of the Atlantic to the western shores of the Pacific, from sea to shining sea.

Something, something at home, has got to change.

Joining the Conversation

1. Hady Amr writes about how the United States is now distrusted "in places where we were once admired for our ideals" (paragraph 11). What exactly is he arguing? What, in other words, is his "I say"?

2. Amr goes into some detail about his relationship with the sister of the kidnapping victim and also about his career and that of his friend. What do you think is the purpose of this background information in the article as a whole?

3. Why did Ayesha, the sister of the kidnapping victim, not involve the U.S. government in trying to free her brother? According to Amr, what does her decision say about attitudes toward the United States across the Muslim world? What does he believe caused these attitudes?

4. Amr clearly states his own position on attitudes in the Muslim world toward the United States. Does he consider any possible arguments that might be raised against his view? If not, what objections might have been raised?

5. Write an essay that begins where Amr's article ends, perhaps by quoting him as saying that "Something . . . has got to change" (paragraph 14). You'll need to develop Amr's position and then respond with your own views.

Are We Losing Our Edge?

MICHAEL D. LEMONICK

—◻—

GABRIEL AEPPLI was born in Switzerland, but when he was one year old, his father came to the United States to pursue a career as a mathematician. Back then, America was a scientific "city on the hill," a place where enormous resources, academic freedom, a tradition of skepticism, and a history of excellence lured everyone from astronomers to zoologists from all over the world, and like Aeppli's father, many of them never had any interest in leaving.

Aeppli, now forty-eight, attended M.I.T., where he got a Ph.D. in electrical engineering, and went on to work at Bell Labs, the legendary research arm of AT&T. Then he moved on to the NEC research laboratory, outside Princeton, N.J., as a senior research scientist. But while industrial labs used to be well-funded

MICHAEL D. LEMONICK is a journalist who specializes in science and medical writing. He was a senior science writer at *Time* magazine for more than twenty years and still contributes to *Time* by writing a blog called *Eye on Science*, where he reports on "what's hot, what's cool, what's controversial, and what's just plain silly in the world of science." He teaches science writing at Princeton University and is the author of five books. "Are We Losing Our Edge?" appeared in *Time* on 5 February 2006.

havens for freewheeling scientific inquiry, says Aeppli, "my career was limited because opportunities to lead were very few." So he left for an academic job in Britain. He now holds a chair in physics at University College London and also directs the London Center for Nanotechnology. "I've been able to start with a clean sheet of paper and create something unique in a world-class city," he says. "We doubt that could be done anywhere else."

Edison Liu is a Hong Kong native who studied in the United States and eventually rose to become director of the division of clinical sciences at the National Cancer Institute. But in 2001 the government of Singapore made him an offer he couldn't refuse: the directorship of the brand-new Genome Institute along with a $25 million starting budget—part of a $288 million integrated network of life-science research centers and biotech start-ups called Biopolis. Says Liu: "I came because I saw that the entire leadership of the country, the fabric of the country was thirsting for biology."

If those were just isolated cases, they would be easy to dismiss. Such stories, though, have become disturbingly common. After more than a half-century of unchallenged superiority in virtually every field of science and technology, from basic research to product development, America is starting to lose ground to other nations. It's still on top for now; the United States continues to lead the world in economic performance, business and government efficiency, and in the strength of its infrastructure. As recently as 2001, the United States, with just 6 percent of the world's population, churned out 41 percent of its Ph.D.s. And its labs regularly achieve technological feats, as last month's rollout of a new, superpowerful Macintosh computer and the launch of a space probe to Pluto make clear.

But by almost any measure—academic prizes, patents [5] granted to U.S. companies, the trade deficit in high-technology products—we're losing ground while countries like China, South Korea, and India are catching up fast. Unless things change, they will overtake us, and the breathtaking burst of discovery that has been driving our economy for the past half-century will be over. In his 2005 best seller, *The World Is Flat*, Thomas Friedman argues that globalization has collapsed the old hierarchy of economic engine-nations into a world where the ambitious everywhere can compete across borders against one another, and he identifies the science problem as a big part of that development. Borrowing a phrase from Shirley Ann Jackson, president of Rensselaer Polytechnic Institute, he calls it America's "quiet crisis."

Some critics have tried to put the blame for the United States' scientific decline on President George W. Bush, citing his hostility to stem-cell research, his downplaying of global warming, his statements in support of "intelligent design" as an alternative to evolution, and his Administration's appointment of nonscientists to scientific panels as well as its alleged quashing of dissenting scientists. Although that record has certainly roiled the scientific community at home, experts in business and academia have been warning for decades that U.S. science was heading for trouble for three simple reasons. The Federal Government, beset by deficits for most of the past three decades, has steadily been cutting back on investment in research and development. Corporations, under increasing pressure from their stockholders for quick profits, have been doing the same and focusing on short-term products. And the quality of education in math and science in elementary and high schools has plummeted, leading to a drop in the number of students majoring in technical fields in college and graduate school. In the past, hungry immigrants looking for America's prestigious Ph.D.s made up for that decline in the U.S.

science and engineering labor force. Now if they come to America for Ph.D.s, students often return with them to gleaming labs in their homelands.

The warnings about those three forces have been largely ignored. In the aftermath of 9/11, for example, the political class complained that nobody had heeded a report issued nine months earlier by former senators Gary Hart and Warren Rudman warning of a major terrorist attack on U.S. soil. The report also said "the inadequacies of our systems of research and education" posed a threat to U.S. national security greater "than any potential conventional war that we might imagine." Nobody paid attention to that part either.

People are paying attention now, though. Responding to an increasingly insistent drumbeat of lobbying over the past few months from industry leaders, scientists, and legislators, Bush announced in his State of the Union address last week the launch of what he called the American Competitiveness Initiative. The plan: double federal funding of research in basic areas like nanotechnology, supercomputing, and alternative energy; make permanent the R&D tax credit;* and train 70,000 additional high school science and math teachers. Aboard Air Force One the next morning, the President told Lamar Alexander, the Tennessee Republican Senator who has been pushing the idea hard for the past year, that he's determined to make it happen. "I want to make sure that everyone knew I was taking this seriously," said Bush.

In contrast to his then dead-end proposal to reform Social Security, so are lawmakers on both sides of the aisle. Last spring Alexander, along with Democratic Senator Jeff Bingaman of

*R&D tax credit A tax refund for companies for doing research and development activities.

New Mexico, wrote to the prestigious National Academies, an umbrella group that includes the National Academy of Sciences and the National Academy of Engineering, and asked for a formal assessment of the United States' eroding superiority in science and technology.

The result, produced in just three months: a 505-page report, [10] co-authored by a team of distinguished scientists, CEOs, Nobel prizewinners, and university presidents—including Texas A&M president Robert Gates, director of the CIA under President George H. W. Bush and a close friend of the Bush family. Titled "Rising Above the Gathering Storm: Energizing and Employing America for a Brighter Economic Future," it outlined in detail just how bad the situation was in nearly every area of research and called for new government funding. At about the same time, the National Association of Manufacturers and the Chamber of Commerce were issuing reports with similar conclusions.

Democrats seized publicly on the issue first. In November, House minority leader Nancy Pelosi announced a series of proposals modeled on those in "Gathering Storm." Tellingly, though, she avoided criticizing the President, going as far as removing some negative language at the last moment. The idea, said a party official, was to get something accomplished, not just score political points. Even so, Pelosi's opening shot made Republicans nervous. "The feeling," says an industry official who was involved in discussions with the White House, "was, 'We cannot let them have this issue.'" Indeed, top Bush aides, including Karl Rove and the Secretaries of Labor, Education, and Commerce, began lobbying internally for some sort of presidential initiative. Bush aides say the indispensable player in moving the package to the presidential podium was Bush's workout partner and close friend former Commerce Secretary

Donald Evans, who made it a crusade after a fellow Texan on the National Academies committee handed him the report. "This is like Sputnik," Evans tells *Time*. "We need to give this the same focus and energy."

By December 6, when Republican Representative Sherwood Boehlert, chairman of the House Science Committee, met with Office of Management and Budget (OMB) director Josh Bolten to press for more money for scientific research, Boehlert found Bolten unexpectedly receptive. Later that day, four Cabinet Secretaries showed up for a meeting on scientific research held at the Commerce Department. Energy Secretary Samuel Bodman surprised Boehlert by staying all day. Although the Congressman has been advocating increased scientific research for years, Boehlert says, "Now it was getting the visibility." Soon Bush himself was pushing the proposals through the OMB, which often rips such initiatives apart.

If all that was at stake was some sort of bragging rights—who has the most Nobels, who gets to look down its national nose at the rest of the world—none of that would have happened because it wouldn't really matter. After all, Americans may have invented the integrated circuit and the Internet and the lightbulb, but people all over the world get to use them. Same goes for the statin drugs that lower cholesterol and the iPod. And we are obviously free to use inventions made elsewhere, such as Velcro and the ballpoint pen.

There's much more to it, though. "Imagine," says Stanford University president John Hennessy, "that the next round of innovations in networking is done in India or China. How many years is it before either Cisco relocates to India or China and grows most of its new jobs there or the next Cisco is actually created there?" That's not so farfetched, says Du Pont CEO Chad Holliday: "If the United States doesn't get its act together, Du Pont is going to go to the countries that do, and so are IBM and Intel. We'd much rather be here, but we have an obligation to our employees and shareholders to bring value where we can."

That means not only that Americans have to be better than 15 the rest of the world at inventing things but also that we have to be better at the basic research that precedes invention. Back in the nineteenth and early twentieth centuries, people like Edison, Morse, and the Wright brothers proved that Americans were pretty good at creating useful technology. But all of it was based on fundamental science done in places like Britain, Germany, and France, where the true intellectual action was.

If not for Hitler, it might still be, but his aggression drove scientists out of Europe, and the desperate need to defeat him galvanized the United States and Britain into pouring money into defense research, creating powerful new technologies— radar, sonar, the atom bomb. United States leaders learned that pure research like atomic and electromagnetic physics, combined with massive government funding, could lead to dramatic breakthroughs in military technology. Because the Soviet Union almost immediately became just as ominous a threat as Nazi Germany had been, Congress created the National Science Foundation in 1950 to fund basic and applied science, mostly at universities, "to promote the progress of science; to advance the national health, prosperity, and welfare; to secure the national defense. . . ." In 1958 it founded NASA in response to renewed fears of Soviet technical competition ignited by the launch of Sputnik the previous year. Also in 1957 and for the same reason, the Department of Defense started the Advanced Research Projects Agency (ARPA). And it established or beefed up national laboratories in New Mexico, California, Illinois, Washington, and New York.

All those organizations focused in varying degrees on applied science—attempts to invent useful new technologies—but all of them put money into pure science as well. So did private corporations, including AT&T, IBM, and Xerox, which hired not just engineers but also mathematicians, physicists, biologists, and even astronomers and gave them free rein. The strategy led to utterly impractical but revolutionary discoveries. The Big Bang theory of the cosmos, to name just one example, got its first experimental proof at AT&T's Bell Labs.

But the strategy paid off in an avalanche of astonishing and profitable technologies as well, from computer chips to fiber-optic cables to lasers to gene splicing and more. According to a 2003 National Academies report, no fewer than nineteen multibillion-dollar industries resulted from fundamental research in information technology alone. Yet, says David Patterson, president of the Association for Computing Machinery, "people have this idea of academic research as this fuzzy, ivory-tower stuff that probably doesn't pay off."

That extraordinary track record also made scientists and engineers into national heroes. They won the war, they got us to the moon, they protected us from polio and dozens of other illnesses, and they gave us a standard of living far higher than that of any other country. Young people were inspired to emulate their egghead heroes, and federal funding made that possible. Energy Secretary Bodman, for example, recalls that he went to graduate school on a National Science Foundation fellowship in 1960. "Without that fellowship," he says, "I can virtually guarantee I wouldn't have done it."

For nearly a half-century, the strategy of putting money into 20 science guaranteed that the United States would lead the world by just about every measure of scientific and technological prowess. So, what changed? American business, for one thing.

Competitive pressure and the need to prop up stock prices forced many companies to abandon research and focus mostly on short-term product development. Freewheeling corporate research labs that didn't contribute visibly to the bottom line— AT&T's Bell Labs, Xerox's Palo Alto Research Center, IBM's Thomas J. Watson Research Center—have been restructured.

Much the same happened to military-funded research. The Defense Advanced Research Projects Agency (DARPA, the successor agency to ARPA) halved its funding of academic information-technology research from 2001 to 2004. "They say that because we're in a war, we need to have a shorter-term focus," laments Patterson. "But during Vietnam," he says, DARPA-funded researchers "laid the technology, the underlying vocabulary, of the Internet. They were doing fundamental, important, long-term research."

Nonmilitary research grants, meanwhile, have been essentially flat for the past fifteen years. The one exception: the National Institutes of Health, whose budget doubled from 1998 to 2003. "Unless there's an emotional appeal, basic research is well beyond the time span of the next election," says Craig Barrett, chairman of Intel. "There is a very emotional attachment to research on cancer or chronic illness. It's much more difficult to say, What will the structure of the transistor look like in the next fifteen years?"

As the size of individual grants shrinks, university researchers have to win more of them to keep research going, which requires enormous amounts of extra paperwork. "It's decreased their quality of life," says Paul Jennings, provost of Caltech and a civil engineer. When students see how much time a professor spends on bureaucratic busywork, says Jennings, they say, "I don't want to do that." It's not just red tape either, says Paul Nurse, president of Rockefeller University and a 2001 Nobel laureate in physiology or medicine. "If we compare what our best undergraduates get paid as a graduate student vs. what they get paid in investment banking, there's no doubt that there's tremendous economic pressure to suck you away from what is perhaps your first academic love." As for teaching science at the precollege level, salaries and working conditions are even more dismal.

Students at élite universities are getting that message loud and clear. Melisa Gao, twenty, is a senior majoring in chemistry at Princeton, but when recruiters from consulting firms and investment banks showed up on campus last fall, she went on several interviews, and she will take a job as a consultant after graduation. She says, "They love the fact that science majors can think analytically, that we're comfortable with numbers." Increasingly, science majors love those companies back. Gao says, "There are no guarantees if you go into science, especially as a woman. You have to worry about getting tenure. Or if you go into industry, it takes you a long time to work your way up the ladder." If you go into finance or consulting instead, "by the time your roommate is out of grad school, you've been promoted, plus you're making a lot more money, while they're stuck in lab."

Even at M.I.T., the United States' premier engineering 25 school, the traditional career path has lost its appeal for some students. Says junior Nicholas Pearce, a chemical-engineering major from Chicago: "It's marketed as—I don't want to say dead end but sort of 'O.K., here's your role, here's your lab, here's what you're going to be working on.' Even if it's a really cool product, you're locked into it." Like Gao, Pearce is leaning toward consulting. "If you're an M.I.T. grad and you're going to get paid $50,000 to work in a cubicle all day—as opposed to $60,000 in a team setting, plus a bonus, plus this, plus that— it seems like a no-brainer."

Another problem has been the tarnished image of science itself. Catchphrases that felt inspiring in the 1950s—"Better living through chemistry," "Atoms for peace"—have a darker connotation today. Du Pont, which invented nylon, became known as well for napalm. Chernobyl and Three Mile Island soured Americans on nuclear power. Shuttle crashes and a defective Hubble telescope made NASA look inept. Substances from DDT to PCBs to ozone-eating chlorofluorocarbons proved more dangerous than anyone realized. Drug disasters like the thalidomide scandal made some people nervous about the unintended consequences of new drug treatments. It's in that context of skepticism toward science that some reasonable questions have been raised lately about genetically modified foods and the scope of human embryonic work.

Even so, the U.S. commitment to science might have remained strong if the Soviet Union hadn't collapsed in the late '80s. "We don't have this shadow of Sputnik or the cold war overhanging us," says Stanford's Hennessy, "and we need a different form of inspiration." In fact, says Robert Birgeneau, a physicist and chancellor of the University of California, Berkeley, it already exists, if only we would recognize it. "We have a different kind of war, an economic war," he says. "The importance of investing in long-term research for winning that war hasn't been understood."

Even so, in fact, but . . . See pp. 104–07 on how transitions help construct arguments.

Not in this country, anyway. But other nations, realizing how successful the U.S. model of scientific research has been, have begun to copy it in earnest. Finland decided back in the 1970s to focus on electronics and a handful of other high-tech industries, and now has the most research scientists per capita in the world. South Korea decided to concentrate on reproductive technology, and although the research of superstar Hwang Woo Suk has been exposed as mostly fraudulent, the country has plenty of other world-class experts in cloning and stem-cell research.

Singapore, meanwhile, with its Biopolis project, is pulling in top biomedical scientists—not just Edison Liu but Americans like geneticist Sydney Brenner and, most recently, husband-and-wife cancer researchers Neal Copeland and Nancy Jenkins, who are leaving the National Cancer Institute after two decades. They turned down competing offers from Stanford and the Memorial Sloan-Kettering Cancer Center because, Copeland says, "what's going on over there is amazing. There's plenty of funding and a lot less bureaucracy." Moreover, says Liu, "In the United States the state government says, Let's do one thing, while the Federal Government is trying to stamp it out." Singapore, by contrast, has a single set of reasonably permissive regulations.

Small, economically developed countries aren't the only ones that have created science-friendly cultures: 54 percent of the staff at the Chinese Academy of Engineering and an astonishing 81 percent of the scientists at the Chinese Academy of Sciences are people who have returned from abroad. Deng Hongkui's story is typical. When he went to the United States in 1989 for postgraduate study in virology, he thought he would go back to China only to visit family and friends. But in 2000 he returned as director of one of Peking University's newest research centers. Deng was promised his own team of students and faculty members and whatever state-of-the-art facilities he needed to pursue his research on stem cells. It clearly wasn't the same country he had left eleven years earlier. "It was more exciting, more dynamic," he says. "Before I never [thought] about doing research there because I needed resources, but it looked to me that resources were available. The whole environment was changing."

Those countries offer more than just funding. They're also determined to reproduce the spirit of wide-open inquiry that has made U.S. science so appealing and successful, says Steven Chu, director of the Lawrence Berkeley National Laboratory in Berkeley, California, and a 1997 Nobelist in physics. Wherever he goes, administrators at foreign universities ask him how to create an American-style learning and thinking environment. "They are catching up quickly," he says.

That is especially true in China, where the government has put its muscle behind an all-out effort to transform homegrown science. "Ten years ago in China, it was virtually all derivative stuff," says Chu. "Students would sit and listen and try to capture every word. Now they're asking lots of questions." During a hundredth-anniversary celebration for Peking University a few years ago, Chu found himself seated next to China's Minister for Education. "She was asking for my autograph," he says, shaking his head. "It was totally topsy-turvy. Can you imagine in the United States the Secretary of Education fawning on a Nobel prizewinner? It just won't happen." In his book Thomas Friedman puts it another way: "In China today, Bill Gates is Britney Spears. In America today, Britney Spears is Britney Spears—and that is our problem."

Indeed, P. Roy Vagelos, a former CEO and chairman of Merck, traveled last fall to China, where he met a number of U.S.-educated Chinese scientists who had returned to work in their homeland. "The new labs are spectacular," he says. "Unbelievable. The equipment leaves nothing to be desired." The government is doling out generous research grants to academic scientists. In all, it invested nearly 110 billion yuan on science in 2004, up from less than 50 billion yuan in 1999. Chinese scientists also get cash awards that can run into thousands of dollars for getting papers published in scholarly journals.

The beefing up of research labs in China and elsewhere is not just luring natives back to their homeland. It is also retaining promising students who might once have gone to the United States to study. That matters because keeping U.S. universities the best in the world depends on luring the very best students. Tougher visa regulations put in place after 9/11 don't help either. Chu has plenty of horror stories. One former student went home to Taiwan for a brief vacation. When he applied for his re-entry visa, he said he was studying atomic physics. Even though that subject had nothing to do with nuclear-weapons work, eighteen months passed before he could return. "These stories get passed around," says Chu. "If you're being courted all around the world, if you could go to graduate school anywhere you wanted, why would you come to the United States?"

In absolute terms, of course, the United States is still the world leader in scientific research. A half-century's worth of momentum is tough to derail. Yet, says Shirley Tilghman, president of Princeton and a molecular biologist, "there's still reason to feel some urgency. The world is not standing still while we take a pause."

For the first time in decades, however, there's hope that the pause may be ending. Given its bipartisan appeal, the Bush Competitiveness Initiative is likely to pass. Funding won't be easy, given the soaring deficit, but the people who dole out the money are enthusiastic. "I am very, very supportive," Representative Frank Wolf, the House Republican in charge of science funding, told *Time*, "and I think the President is going to get what he requested." Sometimes, marvels Alexander, "these things sit for years and then suddenly come together in a big way."

Joining the Conversation

1. What argument does Michael D. Lemonick make about the current state of scientific and technological innovation in the United States? What reasons does he provide to support his argument? What do you consider to be the most persuasive evidence given in support of his argument?

2. Lemonick describes efforts of other nations to compete with U.S. researchers in coming up with new discoveries and products. How do these descriptions function as part of the larger argument? That is, why are conditions in other countries relevant in examining the state of science and technology in the United States?

3. Re-read the quotations from Stanford University president John Hennessy and DuPont CEO Chad Holliday in paragraph 14. How does Lemonick incorporate these quotations into his text? How does he introduce them and explain them? How does his surrounding text frame the quotations in a way that advances his own argument?

4. After providing substantial evidence of how the United States is "losing [its] edge," the article concludes on a more positive note by discussing some promising signs of renewed government commitment to research and development. Why do you think Lemonick chose to end in this somewhat upbeat way?

5. Lemonick worries that there's been a decline in U.S. research competitiveness with other countries, whereas Bob Herbert considers a different kind of decline in the essay that opens this chapter (pp. 394–403). Write an essay stating your own views about where the United States stands today in relation to the rest of the world. Cite examples from Lemonick and Herbert and others in this chapter as appropriate.

Perfecting the Union

ROGER COHEN

———▣———

BEYOND IRAQ, beyond the economy, beyond health care, there was something even more fundamental at stake in this U.S. election won by Barack Obama: the self-respect of the American people.

For almost eight years, Americans have seen words stripped of meaning, lives sacrificed to confront nonexistent Iraqi weapons, and other existences ravaged by serial incompetence on an epic scale.

Against all this, Obama made a simple bet and stuck to it. If you trusted in the fundamental decency, civility and good sense of the American people, even at the end of a season of fear and loss, you could forge a new politics and win the day.

Four years ago, at the Democratic convention, in the speech that lifted him from obscurity, Obama said: "For alongside our

ROGER COHEN is a columnist for the *New York Times* and the *International Herald Tribune*, where his columns focus on international politics. He was born in England to South African parents and spent part of his childhood in apartheid South Africa, only recently becoming a U.S. citizen. This op-ed piece appeared in the *Times* on 5 November 2008, one day after Obama was elected president.

famous individualism, there's another ingredient in the American saga: a belief that we are connected as one people."

He never wavered from that theme. "In this country, we rise 5 or fall as one nation, as one people," he declared in his victory speech to a joyous crowd in Chicago.

In that four-year span, Obama never got angry. Without breaking a sweat, he took down two of the most ruthless political machines on the planet: first the Clintons and then the Republican Party. . . .

Obama's idea, put simply, was that America can be better than it has been. It can reach beyond post-9/11 anger and fear to embody once more what the world still craves from the American idea: hope.

America can mean what it says. It can respect its friends and probe its enemies before it tries to shock and awe them. It can listen. It can rediscover the commonwealth beyond the frenzied individualism that took down Wall Street.

I know, these are mere words, they will not right the deficit or disarm an enemy. But words count. That has been a lesson of the Bush years.

You can't proclaim freedom as you torture. You can't pro- 10 mote democracy as you disappear people. You can't stand for the rule of law and strip prisoners of basic rights. You can't dispense with the transparency and regulation essential to modern capital markets and hope still to be the beacon of free enterprise.

Or rather, you can do all these things but then you find yourself alone.

Obama will reinvest words with meaning. That is the basis of everything. And an American leader able to improvise a grammatical, even a moving, English sentence is no bad thing.

Americans, in the inevitable recession ahead, will have a leader who can summon their better natures rather than speak, as Bush has, to their spite.

I voted in Brooklyn. There was a two-hour line. I got talking to the woman behind me. I told her that as a naturalized American I was voting for the first time. When I emerged from the voting booth the woman said: "Congratulations."

That single word said a lot about citizenship as an idea and a responsibility, rather than a thing of blood or ethnicity or race.

And it occurred to me that Obama's core conviction about the "American saga"—his belief in the connectedness of all American—stemmed from his own unlikely experience of American transformation. 15

A Kenyan father passing briefly through these shores; a chance encounter with a young Kansan woman; a biracial boy handed off here and there but fortunate at least in the accident of Hawaiian birth.

Obama has spoken without cease about his conviction of American possibility born from this experience. He intuited that, after years of the debasement of so many core American ideas, a case for what the preamble to the U.S. Constitution calls "a more perfect union" would resonate.

He was rarely explicit about race, although he spoke of slavery as America's "original sin." He did not need to be. At a time of national soul-searching, what could better symbolize a "more perfect union" and the overcoming of the wounds of that original sin than the election to the White House of an African-American?

And what stronger emblem could be offered to the world of an American renewal startling enough to challenge the assumptions of every state on earth?

The other day I got an email saying simply this: Rosa Parks 20
sat in 1955. Martin Luther King walked in 1963. Barack Obama
ran in 2008. That our children might fly.

Tough days lie ahead. But it's a moment to dream. Americans have earned that right, along with the renewed respect of
the world.

Joining the Conversation

1. What is Roger Cohen's argument? What argument(s) do you
   think he is responding to? Where in his text can you see a
   "they say"?
2. Written in the euphoria following Obama's victory, this is
   a hopeful piece. Does Cohen acknowledge any perspectives
   that are not so optimistic—and if so, what are they, and how
   does he respond? What other perspectives could he have
   considered?
3. Some skeptics objected that Cohen's article was mere cheerleading, offering a naive, overly optimistic view of what
   Obama's presidency would look like and noting that the
   change he promised would be difficult to achieve. Reading
   this piece months or even years after Obama was sworn in,
   how would you now assess the skeptics' position?
4. Based on his piece here, how do you think Cohen would
   respond to the question this chapter poses, whether or not
   America is "over"? Cite examples from his text in your
   response.
5. Is America over? Write an essay responding to this question,
   citing Cohen and other texts from this chapter.

PERMISSIONS
ACKNOWLEDGMENTS

———

Hady Amr: "Kidnapped in Pakistan: End of American Ideals?" Common Ground News Service, 8 Apr. 2008. This article was written for the Common Ground News Service. Reprinted with permission.

Radley Balko: "What You Eat Is Your Business." The Cato Institute, 23 May 2004. Reprinted by permission of the Copyright Clearance Center.

John H. Banzhaf III: "Lawsuits Against Fast-Food Restaurants Are an Effective Way to Combat Obesity." Testimony before the U.S. House Subcommittee on Commercial and Administrative Law, Committee on the Judiciary, Washington, D.C., 19 June 2003.

Bruce Bartlett: "The Truth About Wages." *National Review*, 29 Sept. 2006. Reprinted by permission of the author.

Morris Berman: "The Meaning of 9/11." From *Dark Ages America* by Morris Berman. Copyright © 2006 by Morris Berman. Used by permission of W. W. Norton & Company, Inc.

Paul Campos: "Being Fat Is OK." *Jewish World Review*, 23 Apr. 2001. Reprinted by permission of the author.

Roger Cohen: "Perfecting the Union." *The New York Times*, 5 Nov. 2008.

Alan W. Dowd: "The Decline and Fall of Declinism." *The American*, 28 Aug. 2007. This article was reprinted with permission from *The American* magazine. Copyright 2008, *The American*. www.american.com.

Tamara Draut: "The Growing College Gap." From *Inequality Matters: The Growing Divide in America and Its Poisonous Consequences* (edited by James Lardner and David A. Smith).

The Economist: "Inequality and the American Dream." *The Economist*, 17 July 2006, Vol. 379, Issue 8482. Reprinted by permission of the Copyright Clearance Center.

Yves Engler: "Much of the Responsibility for Obesity Lies With Corporations." *Z Magazine*, Vol. 16, Dec. 2003. Reprinted by permission of Z Communications.

Thomas Friedman: "The World Is Flat." From *The World Is Flat: A Brief History of the Twenty-First Century*. Reprinted by permission of Farrar, Straus, and Giroux, LLC.

Amy Goldwasser: "What's the Matter with Kids Today?" This article first appeared on Salon.com, at www.salon.com. An online version remains in the Salon archives. Reprinted with permission.

Gerald Graff: "Hidden Intellectualism." Adapted from *Clueless in Academe: How Schooling Obscures the Life of the Mind.* Copyright © 2003 Yale University. Reprinted by permission of Yale University Press.

Bob Herbert: "A Fire in the Basement." From *Promises Betrayed*.

Steven Johnson: "Watching TV Makes You Smarter." By Steven Johnson. Originally published in the *New York Times*, 24 Apr. 2005. Reprinted by permission of Paradigm.

Paul Krugman: "Confronting Inequality." From *The Conscience of a Liberal* by Paul Krugman. Copyright © 2007 by Paul Krugman. Used by permission of W. W. Norton & Company.

Michael D. Lemonick: "Are We Losing Our Edge?" *Time.com*, 5 Feb. 2006. Reprinted by permission of Rightslink.

Sebastian Mallaby: "Progressive Wal-Mart. Really." From the *Washington Post*, 28 Nov. 2005. Copyright © 2005 the Washington Post. All rights reserved. Used by permission and protected by the copyright laws of the United States. The printing, copying, redistribution, or retransmission of the material without express written permission is prohibited.

Barack Obama: "A More Perfect Union."

Karen Olsson: "Up Against Wal-Mart." *Mother Jones*, Mar./Apr. 2003. © 2003, Foundation for National Progress. Reprinted by permission of *Mother Jones*.

Susie Orbach: Introduction, pp. 3-9, from *Fat Is a Feminist Issue*. Reprinted by permission of the author.

Antonia Peacocke: "*Family Guy* and Freud: Jokes and Their Relation to the Unconscious." Copyright © 2008 by Antonia Peacocke.

Naomi Rockler-Gladen: "Me Against the Media: From the Trenches of a Media Lit Class." *Adbusters*, 2 Mar. 2007. Reprinted by permission, courtesy www.adbusters.org.

Douglas Rushkoff: "Bart Simpson: Prince of Irreverence." Revised and expanded in *Leaving Springfield: The Simpsons and the Possibility of Oppositional Culture*, edited by John Alberti and published by Wayne State University Press.

Eric Schlosser: "Your Trusted Friends." From *Fast Food Nation: The Dark Side of the All-American Meal* by Eric Schlosser. Reprinted by permission of Houghton Mifflin Harcourt Publishing Company. All rights reserved.

Holly Sklar: "The Growing Gulf Between the Rich and the Rest of Us." *ZNET Daily Commentaries*, 24 Oct. 2005. Reprinted by permission of Z Communications.

Dana Stevens: "Thinking Outside the Idiot Box." By Dana Stevens, movie critic (and former TV critic) for *Slate*. *Slate Magazine*, 25 Apr. 2005. Reprinted with permission of the author.

Sherry Turkle: "Can You Hear Me Now?" *Forbes Magazine*, 5 May 2007. Reprinted by permission of *Forbes Magazine*. © 2008 Forbes Media LLC.

George Will: "Reality Television: Oxymoron." Townhall.com, 21 June 2001. Reprinted by permission of PARS, on behalf of the Washington Post Writers Group.

Fareed Zakaria: "The Last Superpower." From *The Post-American World* by Fareed Zakaria. Copyright © 2008 by Fareed Zakaria. Used by permission of W. W. Norton & Company, Inc.

David Zinczenko: "Don't Blame the Eater." *The New York Times*, 23 Nov. 2002. Reprinted by permission of the author.

IMAGES

150: Courtesy Marilyn Moller; **189:** © The New Yorker Collection 1973, Al Ross, from cartoonbank.com. All rights reserved; **207:** *The Seattle Times* 2003/Newscom; **246:** © 20th Century Fox. All rights reserved; **247:** AP Photo; **259:** © 20th Century Fox Film Corp. All rights reserved. Courtesy Everett Collection; **267:** © 20th Century Fox Film Corp. All rights reserved. Courtesy Everett Collection; **274:** The New Yorker Collection 2000, Sidney Harris, from cartoonbank.com. All rights reserved; **282:** © The New Yorker Collection 2002, Roz Chast, from cartoonbank.com. All rights reserved; **325:** Michael Brands/*The New York Times*/Redux; **326:** AP Photo; **343:** J. D. Pooley/Getty Images/Newscom; **383:** Carol Simpson Production; **422:** Jean Paul Guilloteau/Express-REA/Redux; **452:** AP Photo.

ACKNOWLEDGMENTS

We have our superb editor, Marilyn Moller, to thank for this book. It was Marilyn who first encouraged us to write it, and she has devoted herself tirelessly to helping us at every stage of the process. We never failed to benefit from her incisive suggestions, her unfailing patience, and her cheerful good humor.

Our thanks go as well to John Darger, Norton's Chicago representative, who also offered early encouragement to write *"They Say/I Say,"* and to Marian Johnson, who generously managed the editing of this version. Thanks too go to Katharine Ings, for her astute copyediting; to Maggie Wagner, for the striking design; to Jane Searle, for her superb management of the production process; to Debra Morton Hoyt, for her excellent work on the cover; and to Ana Cooke, for helping with many things large and small.

Thanks to Kirk Boyle, doctoral student in English at the University of Cincinnati, for his invaluable help in tracking down the readings for the book.

We owe special thanks to our colleagues in the English department at the University of Illinois at Chicago: Walter Benn Michaels, our former department head, and Ann Feldman, Director of University Writing Programs, for encouraging us to teach first-year composition courses at UIC in which we could try out ideas and drafts of our manuscript. Mark

Canuel, Lon Kaufman, Tom Moss, Diane Chin, Vainis Aleksa, and Matt Pavesich have also been very supportive of our efforts. We are especially grateful to Ann and Diane for bringing us into their graduate course on the teaching of writing, and to Ann, Tom, Diane, and Matt for inviting us to present our ideas in UIC's Mile 8 workshops for writing instructors. The encouragement, suggestions, and criticisms we received at these sessions have proved invaluable. Our deep gratitude also goes to our research assistant for the past two years, Matt Oakes.

We are also especially grateful to Steve Benton and Nadya Pittendrigh, who taught a section of composition with us using an early draft of this book. Steve made many helpful suggestions, particularly regarding the exercises. We are grateful to Andy Young, a lecturer at UIC who has tested our book in his courses and who gave us extremely helpful feedback. And we thank Vershawn A. Young, whose work on code-meshing influenced our argument in Chapter 9, and Hillel Crandus, whose classroom handout inspired Chapter 11, "Entering Classroom Discussions."

We are grateful to the many colleagues and friends who've let us talk our ideas out with them and given extremely helpful responses. UIC's former dean, Stanley Fish, has been central in this respect, both in personal conversations and in his incisive articles calling for greater focus on form in the teaching of writing. Our conversations with Jane Tompkins have also been integral to this book, as was the composition course that Jane co-taught with Gerald entitled "Can We Talk?" Lenny Davis, too, offered both intellectual insight and emotional support, as did Heather Arnet, Jennifer Ashton, Janet Atwill, Kyra Auslander, Noel Barker, Jim Benton, Jack Brereton, Tim Cantrick, Marsha Cassidy, David Chinitz, Lisa Chinitz, Pat

Chu, Bridget O'Rourke Flisk, Steve Flisk, Gwynne Gertz, Judy Gardiner, Howard Gardner, Ben Hale, Scott Hammerl, Patricia Harkin, Andy Hoberek, John Huntington, Joe Janangelo, Paul Jay, David Jolliffe, Jo Liebermann, Maurice J. Meilleur, Greg Meyerson, Alan Meyers, Anna Minkov, Chris Newfield, Jim Phelan, Paul Psilos, Charles Ross, Evan Seymour, Eileen Seifert, David Shumway, Herb Simons, Jim Sosnoski, David Steiner, Chuck Venegoni, Marla Weeg, Virginia Wexman, Jeffrey Williams, Lynn Woodbury, and the late Wayne Booth, whose friendship we dearly miss.

We are grateful for having had the opportunity to present our ideas to a number of schools: Augustana College, Brandeis University, Bryn Mawr College, Columbia University, Community College of Philadelphia, California State University at Bakersfield, California State University at Northridge, University of California at Riverside, University of Delaware, DePauw University, Drew University, Duke University, Duquesne University, Elmhurst College, Furman University, Gettysburg College, Harper College, Harvard University, Haverford College, Hunter College, Illinois State University, Lawrence University, the Lawrenceville School, University of Maryland at College Park, University of Memphis, University of Missouri at Columbia, New Trier High School, Northern Michigan University, North Carolina A&T University, State University of New York at Stony Brook, University of North Florida, University of Notre Dame, Oregon State University, University of Portland, University of Rochester, St. Ambrose University, St. Andrew's School, St. Charles High School, Southern Connecticut State University, University of South Florida, Swarthmore College, University of Tennessee at Knoxville, University of Texas at Arlington, Tulane University, Union College, University of West Virginia at Morgantown, and the University of Wisconsin at Whitewater.

We particularly thank those who helped arrange these visits and discussed writing issues with us: Jeff Abernathy, Herman Asarnow, John Austin, Greg Barnheisel, Joe Bizup, Chris Breu, John Caldwell, Irene Clark, Dean Philip Cohen, Cathy D'Agostino, Tom Deans, Gaurav Desai, Kathleen Dudden-Rowlands, Lisa Ede, Emory Elliott, Kim Flachmann, Ronald Fortune, George Haggerty, Donald Hall, Elizabeth Hatmaker, Harry Hellenbrand, Nicole Henderson, Doug Hesse, Joe Harris, Van Hillard, Andrew Hoberek, Michael Hustedde, Sara Jameson, T. R. Johnson, David Jones, Ann Kaplan, Linda Kinnahan, Dean Georg Kleine, Albert Labriola, Thomas McFadden, Connie Mick, Margaret Oakes, John O'Connor, Gary Olson, Emily Poe, Dominick Randolph, Monica Rico, Kelly Ritter, Dean Howard Ross, Deborah Rossen-Knill, Mike Shea, Evan Seymour, Erec Smith, Nancy Sommers, Stephen Spector, Timothy Spurgin, Ron Strickland, Trig Thoreson, Judy Trost, Robert Weisbuch, and Lynn Worsham.

For inviting us to present our ideas at their conferences, we are grateful to John Brereton and Richard Wendorf at the Boston Athenaeum; Wendy Katkin of the Reinvention Center of SUNY Stony Brook; Luchen Li of the Michigan English Association; Lisa Lee and Barbara Ransby of the Public Square in Chicago; Don Lazere of the University of Tennessee at Knoxville, chair of a panel at the MLA; Dennis Baron of the University of Illinois at Urbana-Champaign and Alfie Guy of Yale University, chairs of panels at CCCC; George Crandell and Steve Hubbard, co-directors of the Aceta conference at Auburn University; Mary Beth Rose of the Humanities Institute at the University of Illinois at Chicago; Diana Smith of St. Anne's Belfield School and the University of Virginia; Jim

Maddox and Victor Luftig of the Bread Loaf School of English; and Jan Fitzsimmons and Jerry Berberet of the Associated Colleges of Illinois.

A very special thanks goes to those who reviewed the materials for this new edition: Marie Elizabeth Brockman (Central Michigan University); Ronald Clark Brooks (Oklahoma State University); Beth Buyserie (Washington State University); Michael Donnelly (University of Tampa); Karen Gardiner (University of Alabama); Greg Glau (Northern Arizona University); Anita Helle (Oregon State University); Michael Hennessy (Texas State University); Asao Inoue (California State University at Fresno); Sara Jameson (Oregon State University); Joseph Jones (University of Memphis); Amy S. Lerman (Mesa Community College); Marc Lawrence MacDonald (Central Michigan University); Andrew Manno (Raritan Valley Community College); Sylvia Newman (Weber State University); Carole Clark Papper (Hofstra University); Eileen Seifert (DePaul University); Evan Seymour (Community College of Philadelphia); Renee Shea (Bowie State University); Marcy Taylor (Central Michigan University); Rita Treutel (University of Alabama at Birmingham); Margaret Weaver (Missouri State University); Leah Williams (University of New Hampshire); and Tina Žigon (State University of New York at Buffalo).

Thanks also goes to those who reviewed the manuscript for the original version of "*They Say*"; their suggestions contributed enormously to this book: Alan Ainsworth (Houston Community College); Rise Axelrod (University of California, Riverside); Bob Baron (Mesa Community College); David Bartholomae (University of Pittsburgh); Diane Belcher (Georgia State University); Michel De Benedictis (Miami Dade College); Joseph Bizup (Columbia University); Patricia Bizzell (College of the Holy Cross); John Brereton (Harvard University); Richard Bullock (Wright State University); Charles Cooper (University of California, San Diego); Christine Cozzens (Agnes Scott College); Sarah Duerden (Arizona State University); Russel Durst (University of Cincinnati); Joseph Harris (Duke University); Paul Heilker (Virginia Polytechnic Institute); Michael Hennessy (Texas State University); Karen Lunsford (University of California, Santa Barbara); Libby Miles (University of Rhode Island); Mike Rose (University of California, Los Angeles); William H. Smith (Weatherford College); Scott Stevens (Western Washington University); Patricia Sullivan (University of Colorado); Pamela Wright (University of California, San Diego); Daniel Zimmerman (Middlesex Community College).

INDEX OF TEMPLATES

INTRODUCING WHAT "THEY SAY" *(p. 21)*

▸ A number of sociologists have recently suggested that X's work has several fundamental problems.

▸ It has become common today to dismiss X's contribution to the field of sociology.

▸ In their recent work, Y and Z have offered harsh critiques of Dr. X for _____ .

INTRODUCING "STANDARD VIEWS" *(p. 22)*

▸ Americans today tend to believe that _____ .

▸ Conventional wisdom has it that _____ .

▸ Common sense seems to dictate that _____ .

▸ The standard way of thinking about topic X has it that _____ .

▸ It is often said that _____ .

▸ My whole life I have heard it said that _____ .

▸ You would think that _____ .

▸ Many people assume that _____ .

MAKING WHAT "THEY SAY" SOMETHING YOU SAY *(pp. 22–23)*

▶ I've always believed that _____.

▶ When I was a child, I used to think that _____.

▶ Although I should know better by now, I cannot help thinking that _____.

▶ At the same time that I believe _____, I also believe _____.

INTRODUCING SOMETHING IMPLIED OR ASSUMED *(p. 23)*

▶ Although none of them have ever said so directly, my teachers have often given me the impression that _____.

▶ One implication of X's treatment of _____ is that _____.

▶ Although X does not say so directly, she apparently assumes that _____.

▶ While they rarely admit as much, _____ often take for granted that _____.

INTRODUCING AN ONGOING DEBATE *(p. 24)*

▶ In discussions of X, one controversial issue has been _____. On the one hand, _____ argues _____. On the other hand, _____ contends _____. Others even maintain _____. My own view is _____.

▸ When it comes to the topic of _____, most of us will readily agree that _____. Where this agreement usually ends, however, is on the question of _____. Whereas some are convinced that _____, others maintain that _____.

▸ In conclusion, then, as I suggested earlier, defenders of_____ can't have it both ways. Their assertion that _____ is contradicted by their claim that _____.

CAPTURING AUTHORIAL ACTION *(pp. 35–37)*

▸ X acknowledges that _____.

▸ X agrees that _____.

▸ X argues that _____.

▸ X believes that _____.

▸ X denies/does not deny that _____.

▸ X claims that _____.

▸ X complains that _____.

▸ X concedes that _____.

▸ X demonstrates that _____.

▸ X deplores the tendency to _____.

▸ X celebrates the fact that _____.

▸ X emphasizes that _____.

▸ X insists that _____.

- ▶ X observes that _____.

- ▶ X questions whether _____.

- ▶ X refutes the claim that _____.

- ▶ X reminds us that _____.

- ▶ X reports that _____.

- ▶ X suggests that _____.

- ▶ X urges us to _____.

INTRODUCING QUOTATIONS *(p. 43)*

- ▶ X states, "_____."

- ▶ As the prominent philosopher X puts it, "_____."

- ▶ According to X, "_____."

- ▶ X himself writes, "_____."

- ▶ In her book, _____, X maintains that "_____."

- ▶ Writing in the journal *Commentary*, X complains that "_____."

- ▶ In X's view, "_____."

- ▶ X agrees when she writes, "_____."

- ▶ X disagrees when he writes, "_____."

- ▶ X complicates matters further when he writes, "_____."

Index of Templates

EXPLAINING QUOTATIONS *(p. 44)*

▸ Basically, X is saying _____.

▸ In other words, X believes _____.

▸ In making this comment, X argues that _____.

▸ X is insisting that _____.

▸ X's point is that _____.

▸ The essence of X's argument is that _____.

DISAGREEING, WITH REASONS *(p. 55)*

▸ I think X is mistaken because she overlooks _____.

▸ X's claim that _____ rests upon the questionable assumption that _____.

▸ I disagree with X's view that _____ because, as recent research has shown, _____.

▸ X contradicts herself/can't have it both ways. On the one hand, she argues _____. But on the other hand, she also says _____.

▸ By focusing on _____, X overlooks the deeper problem of _____.

▸ X claims _____, but we don't need him to tell us that. Anyone familiar with _____ has long known that _____.

AGREEING—WITH A DIFFERENCE (p. 57)

▸ I agree that _____ because my experience _____ confirms it.

▸ X surely is right about _____ because, as she may not be aware, recent studies have shown that _____.

▸ X's theory of _____ is extremely useful because it sheds insight on the difficult problem of _____.

▸ I agree that _____, a point that needs emphasizing since so many people believe _____.

▸ Those unfamiliar with this school of thought may be interested to know that it basically boils down to _____.

▸ If group X is right that _____, as I think it is, then we need to reassess the popular assumption that _____.

AGREEING AND DISAGREEING SIMULTANEOUSLY (pp. 59–61)

▸ Although I agree with X up to a point, I cannot accept his overall conclusion that _____.

▸ Although I disagree with much that X says, I fully endorse his final conclusion that _____.

▸ Though I concede that _____, I still insist that _____.

▸ Whereas X provides ample evidence that _____, Y and Z's research on _____ and _____ convinces me that _____ instead.

Index of Templates

- X is right that _____, but she seems on more dubious ground when she claims that _____.

- While X is probably wrong when she claims that _____, she is right that _____.

- I'm of two minds about X's claim that _____. On the one hand, I agree that _____. On the other hand, I'm not sure if _____.

- My feelings on the issue are mixed. I do support X's position that _____, but I find Y's argument about _____ and Z's research on _____ to be equally persuasive.

SIGNALING WHO IS SAYING WHAT (p. 67)

- X argues _____.

- According to both X and Y, _____.

- Politicians who _____, X argues, should _____.

- Most athletes will tell you that _____.

- My own view, however, is that _____.

- I agree, as X may not realize, that _____.

- But _____ are real and, arguably, the most significant factor in _____.

- But X is wrong that _____.

- However, it is simply not true that _____.

- Indeed, it is highly likely that _____.

- But the view that _____ does not fit all the facts.

- X is right that _____.

- X is wrong that _____.

- X is both right and wrong that _____.

- Yet a sober analysis of the matter reveals _____.

- Nevertheless, new research shows _____.

- Anyone familiar with _____ should see that _____.

EMBEDDING VOICE MARKERS *(pp. 70–71)*

- X overlooks what I consider an important point about _____.

- My own view is that what X insists is a _____ is in fact a _____.

- I wholeheartedly endorse what X calls _____.

- These conclusions, which X discusses in _____, add weight to the argument that _____.

ENTERTAINING OBJECTIONS *(p. 78)*

- At this point I would like to raise some objections that have been inspired by the skeptic in me. She feels that I have been ignoring _____. "_____," she says to me, "_____."

▶ Yet some readers may challenge the view that _____. After all, many believe _____. Indeed, my own argument that _____ seems to ignore _____ and _____.

▶ Of course, many will probably disagree with this assertion that _____.

NAMING YOUR NAYSAYERS *(p. 79)*

▶ Here many *feminists* would probably object that _____.

▶ But *social Darwinists* would certainly take issue with the argument that _____.

▶ *Biologists*, of course, may want to dispute my claim that _____.

▶ Nevertheless, both *followers and critics of Malcolm X* will probably argue that _____.

▶ Although not all *Christians* think alike, some of them will probably dispute my claim that _____.

▶ *Non-native English speakers* are so diverse in their views that it's hard to generalize about them, but some are likely to object on the grounds that _____.

INTRODUCING OBJECTIONS INFORMALLY *(p. 80)*

▶ But is my proposal realistic? What are the chances of its actually being adopted?

▶ Yet is it always true that _____? Is it always the case, as I have been suggesting, that _____?

▶ However, does the evidence I've cited prove conclusively that _____?

▶ "Impossible," you say. "Your evidence must be skewed."

MAKING CONCESSIONS WHILE STILL STANDING YOUR GROUND *(p. 85)*

▶ Although I grant that _____, I still maintain that _____.

▶ Proponents of X are right to argue that _____. But they exaggerate when they claim that _____.

▶ While it is true that _____, it does not necessarily follow that _____.

▶ On the one hand, I agree with X that _____. But on the other hand, I still insist that _____.

INDICATING WHO CARES *(p. 91)*

▶ _____ used to think _____. But recently [or within the past few decades] _____ suggests that _____.

▶ What this new research does, then, is correct the mistaken impression, held by many earlier researchers, that _____.

▶ These findings challenge the work of earlier researchers, who tended to assume that _____.

▸ Recent studies like these shed new light on _____, which previous studies had not addressed.

▸ Researchers have long assumed that _____. For instance, one eminent scholar of cell biology, _____, assumed in _____, her seminal work on cell structures and functions, that fat cells _____. As _____ herself put it, "_____" (200-). Another leading scientist, _____, argued that fat cells "_____" (200-). Ultimately, when it came to the nature of fat, the basic assumption was that _____.

   But a new body of research shows that fat cells are far more complex and that _____.

▸ If sports enthusiasts stopped to think about it, many of them might simply assume that the most successful athletes _____. However, new research shows _____.

▸ These findings challenge dieters' common assumptions that _____.

▸ At first glance, teenagers appear to _____. But on closer inspection _____.

ESTABLISHING WHY YOUR CLAIMS MATTER *(pp. 94–95)*

▸ X matters/is important because _____.

▸ Although X may seem trivial, it is in fact crucial in terms of today's concern over _____.

▸ Ultimately, what is at stake here is _____.

- ▸ These findings have important consequences for the broader domain of _____.

- ▸ My discussion of X is in fact addressing the larger matter of _____.

- ▸ These conclusions/This discovery will have significant applications in _____ as well as in _____.

- ▸ Although X may seem of concern to only a small group of _____, it should in fact concern anyone who cares about _____.

COMMONLY USED TRANSITIONS

Cause and Effect

accordingly

as a result

consequently

hence

it follows, then

since

so

then

therefore

thus

Conclusion

as a result

consequently

hence

in conclusion, then

in short

in sum, then

it follows, then

so

the upshot of all this is that

therefore

thus

to sum up

to summarize

Comparison

along the same lines

in the same way

likewise

similarly

Index of Templates

Contrast

although	nevertheless
but	nonetheless
by contrast	on the contrary
conversely	on the other hand
despite the fact that	regardless
even though	whereas
however	while
in contrast	yet

Addition

also	in fact
and	indeed
besides	moreover
furthermore	so too
in addition	

Concession

admittedly	of course
although it is true that	naturally
granted	to be sure
I concede that	

Example

after all	for instance
as an illustration	specifically
consider	to take a case in point
for example	

Elaboration

actually	to put it another way
by extension	to put it bluntly
in short	to put it succinctly
that is	ultimately
in other words	

ADDING METACOMMENTARY *(pp. 128–30)*

▶ In other words, _____ .

▶ What _____ really means by this is _____ .

▶ My point is _____ .

▶ Essentially, I am arguing that _____ .

▶ My point is not that we should _____ , but that we should _____ .

▶ What _____ really means is _____ .

▶ In other words, _____ .

▶ To put it another way, _____ .

▶ In sum, then, _____ .

▶ My conclusion, then, is that, _____ .

▶ In short, _____ .

▶ What is more important, _____ .

▶ Incidentally, _____ .

▶ By the way, _____ .

▶ Chapter 2 explores _____ , while Chapter 3 examines _____ .

▶ Having just argued that _____ , let us now turn our attention to _____ .

▶ Although some readers may object that _____ , I would answer that _____ .

Index of Authors and Titles

ABOUT THE AUTHORS

GERALD GRAFF, a Professor of English and Education at the University of Illinois at Chicago and 2008 President of the Modern Language Association of America, has had a major impact on teachers through such books as *Professing Literature: An Institutional History*, *Beyond the Culture Wars: How Teaching the Conflicts Can Revitalize American Education*, and, most recently, *Clueless in Academe: How Schooling Obscures the Life of the Mind*.

CATHY BIRKENSTEIN, who first developed the templates used in this book, is a Lecturer in English at the University of Illinois at Chicago. She received her PhD in American literature and is currently working on a study of Booker T. Washington. Together Gerald and Cathy teach courses in composition and conduct campus workshops on writing. They live with their son, Aaron, in Chicago.

RUSSEL DURST, who edited the readings in this book, is Head of the English Department at the University of Cincinnati, where he teaches courses in composition, writing pedagogy and research, English linguistics, and the Hebrew Bible as literature. A past President of the National Conference on Research in Language and Literacy, he is the author of several books, including *Collision Course: Conflict, Negotiation, and Learning in College Composition*.